AN ANNOTATED BIBLIOGRAPHY OF NINETEENTH-CENTURY GRAMMARS OF ENGLISH

AMSTERDAM STUDIES IN THE THEORY AND HISTORY OF LINGUISTIC SCIENCE

General Editor
E. F. KONRAD KOERNER
(University of Ottawa)

Series V

LIBRARY & INFORMATION SOURCES IN LINGUISTICS

Advisory Editorial Board

Mohammed H. Bakalla (Riyadh); Jivco Boyadjiev (Sofia)
Frank Di Trolio (Gainesville, Fla.); Mark Janse (Gent)
Aleksander Szwedek (Toruń); Joseph L. Subbiondo (Stockton, Calif.)
Matsuji Tajima (Fukuoka, Japan)

Volume 26

Manfred Görlach

An Annotated Bibliography of Nineteenth-Century Grammars of English

AN ANNOTATED BIBLIOGRAPHY OF NINETEENTH-CENTURY GRAMMARS OF ENGLISH

MANFRED GÖRLACH
University of Cologne

With a Foreword by

IAN MICHAEL

JOHN BENJAMINS PUBLISHING COMPANY
AMSTERDAM/PHILADELPHIA

The paper used in this publication meets the minimum requirements of American National Standard for Information Sciences — Permanence of Paper for Printed Library Materials, ANSI Z39.48-1984.

The illustrations inserted at the end of chapters are reproduced from Emil Reicke, *Magister und Scholaren. Illustrierte Geschichte des Unterrichtswesens*. Leipzig: Diederichs, 1901.

Library of Congress Cataloging-in-Publication Data

Görlach, Manfred.
   An annotated bibliography of 19th-century grammars of English / Manfred Görlach : with a foreword by Ian Michael.
      p.   cm. -- (Amsterdam studies in the theory and history of linguistic science. Series V, Library and information sources in linguistics, ISSN 0165-7267; v. 26)
   Includes bibliographical references (p.   ) and indexes.
   1. English language--19th century--Grammar--Bibliography. I. Title. II. Series: Amsterdam studies in the theory and history of linguistic science. Series V, Library and information sources in linguistics : v. 26.
Z2014.G7G67   1998
[PE1098]
016.4282'09'034--dc21   98-36269
ISBN 90 272 3752 2 (Eur.) / 1 55619 256 8 (US) (alk. paper)   CIP

© Copyright 1998 - John Benjamins B.V.
No part of this book may be reproduced in any form, by print, photoprint, microfilm, or any other means, without written permission from the publisher.

John Benjamins Publishing Co. • P.O.Box 75577 • 1070 AN Amsterdam • The Netherlands
John Benjamins North America • P.O.Box 27519 • Philadelphia PA 19118-0519 • USA

Frontispiece. Two scenes of 'comical grammar teaching' surrounded by the authorities Lindley Murray (cf. EL 106), 'Mr Vyse' and Dr Dilworth (cf. EL 4), reproduced from Percival Leigh. 1840. *The comic English grammar* (no. 1073).

Preface

English-speaking people seem to have had, for three centuries, a confused relationship with grammar. They have not, in the schools, thought about in very deeply, but they have thought it important. They have disagreed amongst themselves as to what, in any particular context, the term should cover and on the meaning of its constituents. They admit the conceptual confusion of the parts of speech and even teach it to young children; but they are intolerant of socially determined variations of usage, which they denounce as ungrammatical. Yet they have produced English grammars in quite astonishing quantities - each much like most of the others. Is this vast contradictory output an expression of obstinate individualism? Is it powered by commercial pressures?

Today 'grammar' still carries a more powerful charge than do other linguistic terms. To the journalist, to the writer of indignant letters to the press, grammar seems to represent both a threat and something to be defended: a threat because language is dangerous; it makes innovative and disturbing ideas easy to handle; it spreads them. But grammar represents also an aspect of society which needs to be defended because it is stable and reassuring as correct spelling and received pronunciation.

Defensive and proprietorial attitudes to grammar are, in Britain, educationally harmful. Trivial matters of correctness are made to stand for the whole study of language: a study we have not yet learnt to handle at the school level.

At their best nineteenth-century English grammars treated a broad range of linguistic topics; at their very best they did so in a fresh and experimental spirit. The many grammars which were merely repetitive derived their popularity and many of their limitations from attitudes which are still common today; but these attitudes do not explain the surprising quantity in which the grammars were produced. This apparent over-production is a striking and puzzling phenomenon.

In order to examine the problem we need to know how many grammars were produced, and as much about them as we can record. This is not a trivial or neurotic undertaking: it points to a significant aspect of social history. In this vast project Manfred Görlach has made an heroic and all but complete examination of nineteenth-century English grammars. I may describe his important work in these terms because I have had the privilege of being associated with it, sufficiently to see how skillful it is but not sufficiently to make my praise of it immodest.

Ian Michael

List of Abbreviations

²18..	=	second edition in 18..
Am.	=	American
anon.	=	anonymous/-ly
anr.	=	another
a18..	=	ante
c.	=	cent
c18..	=	circa, about
cf.	=	compare
cm	=	centimetres
corr.	=	corrected
DNB	=	*Dictionary of National Biography*
E	=	etymology
ed.	=	edition
EL	=	*English Linguistics* (reprint series)
enl.	=	enlarged
facs.	=	facsimile
impr.	=	improved
Lit.	=	literature dealing with the individual grammar
n.d.	=	no date
no.	=	number/entry in this bibliography
n.p.	=	no place
NUC	=	*National Union Catalogue*
O	=	orthography
OESP	=	standard sequence of orthography, etymology, syntax and prosody
P	=	prosody
p.c.	=	personal communication
pr.	=	printed
pseud.	=	pseudonym
p18..	=	post
Q/A	=	question and answer (catechism)
ʳ18..	=	reprinted
repr.	=	reprint(ed)
rev.	=	revised
S	=	syntax
ster.	=	stereotyped
UL	=	University Library
vol.	=	volume

Contents

Frontispiece   v
Preface   vi
List of Abbreviations   vii
Contents   viii

Part I:
An annotated bibliography of 19th-century grammars of English (*ABiNGE*)

1. Introduction	1
2. The history of the *ABiNGE* project	2
3. The aims of the bibliography	4
3.1 The definition of the genre	4
3.2 Authors	5
3.3 Titles of works	5
3.4 Places and publishers, pages and sizes	6
3.5 Editions and years	6
3.6 Descriptions of contents and evaluations	6
3.7 Locations	7
3.8 British as against American publications	7
3.9 Studies of authors and individual grammars	7
4. Topics worthy of detailed study	7
5. Reprints	10
A) Most important titles	11
B) Supplementary titles	12
6. Conclusion	13
7. How to read the annotated bibliography	14
8. Sigils indicating locations in libraries	16
9. Other sources	17
10. References	18

Part II:
Alphabetical List of 19th-century English Grammars by British and American Authors   24

Appendix: Titles not included in the main list   357
    0. 18th-century works   357
    1. Books on Anglo-Saxon & language history   364
    2. Treatises on language (incl. educational and philosophical reflexions)   368
    3. Treatments of individual levels (spelling, pronunciation, punctuation, morphology, derivation)   371
    4. Books on logic, rhetoric, elocution, style and composition   376
    5. Advice on good English   378
    6. Bilingual grammars and books meant for foreign learners   379
    7. Dialect   384
    8. Minimal grammars in dictionaries and encyclopedic works   384
    9. Introductions to other studies   385

Indices   386
A: Index of names   386
    A1: Revisions of earlier grammars listed under the editors' names and keys etc. adapted to individual grammars   386
    A2: Second authors (revisers, translators, and pseudonyms)   386
    A3: Mentions of other grammars (mainly as sources)   387
    A4: Judgements quoted from earlier grammarians   389
B: Index of places of publication (publishers for London)   389
    B1: Provincial (outside London / the U.S.)   389
    B2: London (by publishers)   390
    B3: The United States   393
    B4: Colonial   395
    B5: The European Continent   395

An annotated bibliography of 19th-century grammars of English[1] (ABiNGE)

1. Introduction

The beginnings of the writing of grammar books of the vernacular before 1800 have been documented and analysed very fully (cf. Alston, 1967-72 & 1974, Leitner 1986, Leonard 1929, Michael 1970 and 1987, Robins 1986, Sundby *et al.* 1991 and Vorlat 1975); various studies have taught us to understand the development of grammatical description and the teaching of English to 1800, when prescriptive grammarians had left few areas uncharted and unregularized. The explosive increase of grammar books after Lowth's and Priestley's works of the 1760s is especially noteworthy - such numbers point ahead to the 19th century when education became accessible to much wider circles of society in a great number and variety of schools and the teaching of grammar came to be obligatory from 1870/72 with the advent of general education.

Whereas these general trends of the 19th century are well-known to scholars working in different disciplines of social history, and the history of education in particular, it is still true that major sections of the evidence are largely uncollected. This is especially so for school books: there is virtually a gap between the 18th century and the present grammatical tradition (which is partly based on the work of non-natives like Maetzner, Jespersen, Poutsma and Visser).

This gap became obvious to me when I was writing a chapter on contemporary grammar teaching for my book on English in 19th-century England (Görlach 1995, fc.). Although we know that the notable expansion of literacy and the reading public, and their views on correctness and good style, are based on the (largely prescriptive) grammars used in school, there has been only little research on this interrelationship so far - unsurprisingly when we realize that most of the spade work remains to be done. Although we have very useful surveys on 19th-century teaching in the handbooks by Michael (1987) and Howatt (1984), and Michael's work contains a list of over 800 19th-century school books collected in a very informative appendix, there is no comprehensive bibliography of school grammars to date.

---

[1] This account would have been impossible without the expert help of Ian Michael who shared his data and expertise in an unusually generous way, and to whom this book is dedicated. R.C. Alston also greatly helped by making information on the holdings of the British Library, Bodleian and American libraries available. Katja Lenz and Kristina Ritter were of enormous help in sifting the data and putting them on the computer. Special thanks are due to the staffs of the British Library and the Bodleian Library, who supplied me with excessive numbers of books, and my colleagues R.F.S. Hamer, Mervyn Jones and Andrew Watson, who generously provided me with accommodation in Oxford and London.

2. The history of the ABiNGE project

In 1995 I made a serious start to collect data on 19th-century grammars. Working from the catalogue of Cambridge UL, I inspected as many books as possible in the short time I had available. After my return home I asked research students to put the list of 19th-century titles in Michael (1987: 387-604) on to the computer. When I went to London to look at a selection of these books, R.C. Alston kindly provided me with printouts of the relevant entries in the British Library and Bodleian Library plus a list of the holdings of US libraries (online). It took a year to combine all these data, and to add further information collected from the *National Union Catalogue*. Also, I spent many hours in London and Oxford extending the list of grammars and describing a selection of these at least briefly. Ian Michael was kind enough to add all the details he had collected in his files when involved in his earlier research.

The result of these efforts is a list of some 1,930 books[2] of which some 900 have been seen and briefly described by at least one of us (I.M. alone: 228, M.G. alone: 625, both: 48).[3] It became clear quite soon that neither comprehensiveness nor consistency of description nor a proper analysis of the huge masses of data were possible to achieve, and this for various reasons:

1. Each of the libraries one might visit has only a selection of relevant books. Even to compare successive editions of the same work is strictly impossible because one cannot place them side by side. What is more, many editions do not survive so that even basic information like the date of the first edition can often not be provided - not to mention entire books that are not preserved at all, or have not been identified so far.
2. Since these restrictions are impossible to overcome in principle, I decided to use the services of the British Library and the Bodleian as fully as possible, checking all the entries in the catalogues and adding as much information on grammars not correctly catalogued (as was often the case with smaller grammars bound together into larger volumes).

---

[2]Counting individual works is a subjective affair: keys and exercises accompanying grammar books were often published independently and sometimes bound together; Grammar books might be split up into booklets intended for individual grades or combined; new editions and revisions of earlier books might be published under different titles - or the same author and title be listed for books whose size may be variously indicated as of 100, 300 and 500 pages. While these facts are worrying for anyone intent on statistical accounts, they do not mean so much where contents and cultural history are concerned.

[3]Thus, 46.6% of the titles mentioned were inspected; the ratio increases if the fact is taken into account that some 193 titles are known from references only. Also, 747 of the books are available only in American libraries (and of the titles only inferred from references, another 43 are American books).

This procedure means that books held in libraries outside London and Oxford are listed only if information was available in catalogues,[4] and only their titles were noted, but the books were not consulted and described - since I lacked the time and money for extensive travel.

3. Surveys in earlier books (most notably Martin 1821, Hunter 1848, Brown 1851, Lowres 1863 and Skeat 1891) list (and sometimes discuss) many grammar books that cannot be identified with books catalogued in the major libraries; this means that they do not survive, or survive but have not been identified - or were incorrectly quoted in the 19th-century sources (some lists, like those in Hunter 1848 and Lowres 1863 are remarkably unreliable.) However, I have included all these titles in the bibliography on the chance that a copy of these books may be found in due course.

4. Finally, consistency in the descriptions was impossible to achieve even where Ian Michael or Manfred Görlach had inspected a copy of an individual work. The great number of books seen made it normally not feasible to re-order a volume to check a description, and many details were not ascertainable even from the book itself.

5. What would have been desirable but proved completely impossible to achieve at our present state of knowledge was to give a history of grammar-book writing and publishing in the 19th century. I am aware of the fact that some sources are still untapped that might be used for a more comprehensive history — most notably a full analysis of the archives of 19th-century publishers of schoolbooks. However, even the use of these will bring us only somewhat closer to the aim but not right to it - due to the gaps of data which cannot be completely filled by reconstruction (cf. Michael 1997).

A statistical survey of the 1930 works listed is as follows: 193 = 10 % (marked '!') are known only from references, mostly from 19th-century grammars or advertisements (of these 150 are British and 43 American). The total of 1930 is broken up into 790 works (= 40,9%) published in the United States (as far as we can tell from the data listed in the bibliographies etc.); the rest, 1140 (= 59,1%), were published elsewhere - which means Britain in more than 95% of the cases.

Of the 1740 titles which have a library location, 51,7% were inspected by Michael and Görlach; most of the books not yet inspected are available in

---

[4]For Britain, the catalogues of Cambridge UL, Edinburgh UL, Aberdeen and Glasgow UL, Hull, Nottingham and Sheffield UL were searched; for America, the *NUC* data were combined with online information.

the United States only, and were thus not easily accessible.[5]

3. The aims of the bibliography

The present survey is to provide as complete bibliographical information on 19th-century grammar books of English written in English as was possible. The majority of books included (and discussed) is clearly from England and the United States (3.8.). The following problems had an influence on the compilation and should be kept in mind when using the book:

3.1 The definition of the genre[6]

A grammar book in the narrow sense is a book intended for use in schools or for private reference which contains a description of the structure of a language at least on the levels of spelling/pronunciation and syntax (with the treatment of vocabulary, etymology, prosody and style as optional features). The text will often be in form of definitions, rules, notes, and exercises, and may be divided into several volumes (grammar, exercises, key, teacher's handbook etc.) and be graded according to the age of pupils.

The following types of books present problems of classification:

a) books devoted to one topic, such as spellers, handbooks on proper pronunciation, treatises on the proper use of *shall/will*, etc.;
b) books concentrating on lexicology (lists of synonyms, homonyms, etc.);
c) books on style and good writing, letter writers and books on elocution;
d) sections devoted to grammar in books which have more comprehensive aims (encyclopedias, books on good manners, etc.);
e) treatises discussing language in expository (often philosophical) ways; accounts devoted mainly to explanations of the historical development of the English language;
f) polyglot grammars in which English is described only in contrasting function;
g) books originally written in other languages, and for teaching English as a foreign language.

---

[5]It is hoped that the groundwork now laid by the full list of 19th-century grammars will stimulate an American colleague to complete our work; such a project would certainly be a very rewarding topic for a doctoral dissertation.

[6]The problem of genre definition is discussed in Michael (1987:6-13) who suggests ten genres of schoolbooks (and gives statistics for the books he inspected) but who is aware of classificational problems for individual works.

I have tried to exclude as many of these as possible (on inspecting the books, and rarely on the basis of the title alone), but have put these 'rejects' in appendices. It should be noted that these lists originate from my reclassification of what is listed as 'grammars' in catalogues - the titles in the appendices are therefore neither comprehensive nor representative of their genres.

For a statistical analysis, one of the problems is to decide what makes an independent publication. A grammar and the corresponding exercises, keys etc. can be bound together or published in the form of small booklets - these are often advertised as alternatives for the prospective buyer. Finally, there is the problem of dates. Many 18th-century grammar books were reprinted in the 19th century, whether in their original form or in various degrees of revision and updating. Although their permanent influence on grammatical thinking should be documented, I have here excluded all books known to be first published before 1800 - with the partial exception of L. Murray's works. However, a special study would be necessary to document how much 'Murray' is found in books that go under his name, and how much of his text was taken over, often without acknowledgment, into grammars written by others. The best bibliographical survey of Murray's works is still the list published in Alston I (1968; cf. Reibel 1996); various aspects are discussed in the collection edited by Tieken-Boon (1996) - but not the question raised by my remark.

3.2 *Authors*

The names of authors are given in as complete form as possible, together with their life dates if available and their profession/status, especially if mentioned on the title page. There will be cross-references to authors whose books were published anonymously or under pseudonyms. All this does not exclude erroneous attributions of authors quoted under incorrect names nor does it always help to distinguish between authors of the same names. Wherever possible, data on authors are complemented from other sources (such as the *DNB*) - but in many cases we do not know more than the author's name.

3.3 *Titles of works*

Titles are quoted in comparatively full form, since many descriptions of the contents on the title page can serve for a characterization of the work in question (such texts were equivalent to modern blurbs).

I have not attempted to reproduce the various typefaces or different sizes which make many title pages before 1900 look so different from modern ones. Rather, I have italicized the main title and used 'prose' capitalization throughout. The consequence is a certain loss of emphasis, but there is no easy way of reproducing typographic distinctions.

3.4 *Places and publishers, pages and sizes.*

I have again given comparatively full information, but have abbreviated the data where a whole string of publishers was mentioned on the title page. Note that the details provided in catalogues vary a great deal.

Pages and sizes. Pagination is given as in the book described; where roman numbering is continued (rather than Arabic starting afresh with 1) I have noted the fact as e.g. viii+[9]-125 pp. Sizes are given in cms; allowing for the fact that books were often cut down in the binding process, this information can only be a rough approximation but it will still be helpful in identifying a book. Wherever my description comes from catalogues, the data were taken over, whether measurements are in cms or the format is indicated as, say, 8°/octavo, etc.

3.5 *Editions and years*

In the first stage of collecting I aimed at a comprehensive coverage of all editions extant, but later found that the amount of detail was stifling for some books whereas it was very poor for others. Therefore, I reduced the data on richly documented works - the first edition and the last published before 1900 are always provided, but I have been selective in some cases where the full information is easily available from the catalogue of the B.L. and in the *NUC* (and have indicated the number of editions left out in parentheses). All data in this section are necessarily incomplete and possibly quite a few are even misleading since I had to depend on what was indicated in the copies inspected and mentioned in library catalogues. My entries also include modern reprints, esp. facsimiles.

3.6 *Descriptions of contents and evaluations*

Except for a few cases where descriptions were taken over from early grammarians (marked as drawn from Martin, Hunter and Brown in particular), all descriptions are modern, supplied by I.M. and/or M.G.; the absence of such a description indicates, then, that neither of us has seen the book. We concentrated on factual accounts of the contents, but noted sources mentioned in the book, and often quoted from advertisements and self-characterizations. Where we felt competent to do so, we added succinct evaluative remarks; more detailed analyses may prove us wrong or could lead us to modify our statements, but I still think the remarks in their present form will be felt to be helpful, for all their subjective nature. Both authors agreed that the descriptions should be conflated in the final stage of the redaction so that the source of the evaluation is no longer recoverable.

3.7 Locations

British libraries which have the book in question are indicated by sigils among which L(ondon BL), O(xford Bodl.) and C(ambridge UL) are most frequent (see the full list of sigils on p. 16-7). American libraries are combined under $ if the information comes from the online list; by @ if from the *NUC*.

This information is complemented by evidence provided by early grammarians who listed grammar books they used or knew of; the following are most frequently mentioned: Hu(nter 1848), Ma(rtin 1828), etc. (see the list of sigils on p. 17-8). Where early grammar books are known exclusively from such attestations, I have marked the entry by an initial exclamation mark, to indicate that no copy is known to survive and that the entry may in fact be erroneous.

3.8 *British as against American publications*

It is insufficiently explored which and how many of the grammar books were known and used on either side of the Atlantic, and how many were in fact *produced* with the intention of being sold in both areas - the majority of the books were, however, used in the country that produced them. As far as the decision was easy, I have marked by an initial $ books published in America (= the U.S. and very few in Canada), which leaves unmarked all unidentified American publications and those from the rest of the world, mostly Britain: more than 90% of the latter were published in England and Scotland, few in Ireland, and almost none elsewhere (not counting grammars for EFL published in Germany, etc.).

3.9 *Studies of authors and individual grammars*

The initial intention was to provide selective references to modern studies on individual authors (like the ones by Leitner 1991a, Wächtler 1986 and 1991, Walmsley 1991 and Tieken-Boon 1996) but the plan proved to be very difficult to pursue. Although the documentation collected in passing (= **Lit.**) is uneven, it may still contain some useful references; it would certainly be worthwile to complement the list and thus provide a much fuller account of the reception of 19th-century grammars - if a scholar can be found to take on the vast task.

4. *Topics worthy of detailed study*

It is hoped that the annotated bibliography will facilitate the proper study of various individual aspects of 19th-century grammar writing and use - investigations which will in turn improve the bibliography. The following topics are in particular need of comprehensive study (cf. Michael 1987:346-71):

1. Biographical studies of selected authors. How did their careers determine their activities, e.g. as school masters or as professional writers of school books of various kinds?
2. Interdependence of grammars: how far are sources mentioned and also used in the books? Is there name-dropping in the hope of better sales (as when grammar books were claimed to be based on 'Murray')? What is the individual writer's attitude to cribbing? - one remembers Noah Webster's caustic remarks (1828) when he bitterly complained about L. Murray's thefts from his books. Contrast the following quotation which openly justifies the practice:

> In preparing this work, the Author has used the common privilege of elementary writers: so far as it was convenient for his purpose, he has availed himself of the labors of his predecessors. For the omission of authors' names, it is perhaps unnecessary to apologize. "From the alterations," says Murray in the introduction to English Grammar, "which have been frequently made in the sentiments and the language, to suit the connexion, and to adapt them to the particular purposes for which they are introduced; and, in many instances, from the uncertainty to whom the passages originally belonged, the insertion of names could seldom be made with propriety. But if this could have been generally done, a work of this nature would derive no advantage from it, equal to the inconvenience of crowding the pages w[ith] a repetition of names and references." (Putnam 1831:4)

3. The study of grammatical terminology: What terms are used with which idiosyncratic differences? How far do authors stick to the mainstream nomenclature? Do they argue about the adequacy of earlier terms, and justify their own proposals, with proper definitions? Do they suggest English terms for Latin and Latinate ones? How far are terms and aims which are formulated no longer fully intelligible? (such as "purity, clearness, strength, and precision" of expression mentioned by Anon. 1816 and quoted by Michael 1987:348). In particular:
4. What is the status of 'etymology': is the term used in the older sense as inflection/derivation/provenience, or in the modern one restricted to provenience/word history? Is 'etymology' one of the four constituent parts of grammar?
5. Is there a section on 'orthography' and does it include 'pronunciation'- which may in fact predominate in the chapter? Is there an independent treatment of pronunciation, possibly in scientific terms?
6. How many parts of speech are there, how are they defined, and how much does the classification tell us about the grammatical tradition followed? (It is likely that the systems described for the time before 1800 by Michael (1970) - he counted 58 different systems in use, 1987:344) are no longer valid for the 19th century, but the specific method chosen

could help to determine how traditional the approach of an individual writer is, and what he put in the place of the old system).
7. How much attention is given to syntax and how is this defined (contrast the 'classical' system based on concord with 'modern' methods based on sentence analysis); how much room is given to etymological and syntactic parsing?
8. Is there a section on 'prosody'? Does a section on 'style' (composition, proper elocution) exist? How is this justified as a part of grammar?
9. What is the relevance of arguments taken from the history of English? Is a separate section on history included, or do diachronic treatments pervade the classification and line of argument throughout? How far are data from 'philology' and comparative linguistics employed to explain (and justify) English structures?
10. How far can we distinguish between a 'British' and an 'American' tradition? The question becomes relevant (and even virulent) in the 19th century. Whereas the first American grammar of English was published in 1773 and textbooks originating in America were rare until 1790 (Michael 1987:3), their number exploded in the 19th century, and there was a great deal of competition (better known from the related field of the "War of the dictionaries"). How many 'national' features are found? Is there a time lag in the acceptance of new ideas, and how many features remain restricted to one tradition? What does the history of book publishing and selling contribute to our understanding?
11. How far are contents, structures and modes of presentation determined by the uses the grammar book is intended to serve? In particular, what types of schools are mentioned, or what advice given for self-study? Are there references to Sunday schools, Mechanics' Institutes, lending libraries, and various types of private and state schools? How are the contents geared to the official requirements of school inspectors' reports and of examination boards, or the successive 'codes' laid down after 1870?
12. Are there differences between town and country, north and south?
13. How far is the special situation of learners in Scotland and Ireland taken into account? Is there any special regard paid to non-native speakers - also in America, or in books primarily meant for (or published in) countries of the Empire?
14. What is the relationship of numbers of copies printed and editions (if determinable), size and price; in particular, how does the reduction of the size of a book affect its contents?
15. How prescriptive is the grammar writer's attitude? (And, by contrast, is any account taken of usage, not only lip-service paid to the concept?) Are rules formulated without exceptions? Are these rules to be memo-

rized? (And, by contrast, how much emphasis is laid on inductive methods and the pupil's logical reasoning and judgement?) Is the structure of the argument underlined by typographical devices, with important rules printed in bold? Is the catechism method of question and answer used? What is the relation between teacher's guidance and self-study? How much use is made of 'native' terminology or Latin categories implicitly or explicitly?

16. Are there sections on erroneous spelling and false syntax, to be corrected by the pupils? Do these errors include 'vulgar' and obsolete features?
17. Are there exercises, integrated in the book or collected in a separate volume, and are there keys, for the teacher?
18. How much use is made of literary texts (or the Bible) to illustrate good usage and correct grammar? Are these texts and the rules based on them synchronically relevant?
19. What relation, if any, is seen between grammar education in the mother tongue and the learning of foreign languages? (e.g. is grammatical competence in English seen as a step for the proper acquisition of Latin?)
20. What major changes/disruptions can be found (in the 1840s? 1870s?) and how are such changes of paradigms related to developments in cultural, educational and social history?
21. How far do answers to the above questions help to explain the extraordinary number of new grammars published, some twenty per year? (cf. Michael 1991).

5. Reprints

English grammar books (and other works on language) before 1800 are exhaustively documented and made available in reprints by Alston (EL, 1967-72). By contrast, there is very little indeed on the 19th century which might save the scholar a trip to London (etc.) to study problems related to grammar books. For the U.S., Scholar/Delmar has put out a series of facsimiles with scholarly introductions, a laudable enterprise however small the number of books is compared to the total 19th-century output. For Britain, however, there is nothing comparable. From the beginning I therefore intended to have a small reprint series to accompany the bibliography. However, the plan proved to be impossible to put into practice - since the fees demanded of the libraries for photographies of their books were forbidding - for a project in which a publisher could not expect to sell more than a few hundred copies each.

The planned reprint series was to consist of some forty titles, covering all types of grammar books of all periods (though with a concentration on the mid-century which saw the greatest number of diverse grammars published).

The selection was made on inspection of some 700 titles, and biased towards British books since American titles are covered by the Delmar series. I here give the works in two sections, listing the most urgently needed titles first:

A) Most important titles

Alexander, Levy. 1833. *The young lady and gentleman's guide to the grammar of the English language. In verse.* London: the author. (No. 24).

Bain, Alexander. 1863. *An English grammar.* London. (No. 80).

Coghlan, John. ²1868. *Reformed English grammar; A critique and textual outline of English grammar, being an attempt to exhibit the true grammatical basis on which to develop the structure, simplify the treatment, and facilitate the acquisition of the English language.* Rev. impression. Edinburgh: William P. Nimmo. (No. 345).

Crane, George. Grammarian. 1843. *The principles of language; exemplified in a practical English grammar. With copious exercises. Designed as an introduction to the study of languages generally, for the use of schools, and self instruction.* London: Whittaker & Co. (No. 387).

Crombie, Alexander. 1802. *The etymology and syntax of the English language, explained and illustrated.* London: J. Johnson. (No. 390).

Duxbury, C. ³[1886]. *A new English grammar of school grammars.* London: W. Stewart & Co. (No. 473).

Earnshaw, Christopher. 1817. *The grammatical remembrancer: a short but comprehensive English grammar for the use of young students.* Huddersfield. (No. 478).

James, J.H. 1847. *The elements of grammar, according to Dr. Becker's system, displayed by the structure of the English tongue (With copious examples from the best writers); arranged as a practice for translation into foreign languages.* London: Longman etc. (No. 968).

Kigan, John. 1823. *Remarks on the practice of grammarians; with an attempt to discover the principles of a new system of English grammar.* London: Longmans & Co. (No. 1024).

Kigan, John. 1825. *A practical English grammar, agreeably to a new system. Adapted to the use of schools, and private students; containing copious examples of wrong choice of words, under etymology; and wrong arrangement of them under syntax. With a key ... and questions.* Belfast: Simms & McIntyre. (No. 1025).

Lennie, William. 1810. *The principles of English grammar briefly defined, and neatly arranged... etc.* Edinburgh. (No. 1077).

McArthur, Alexander. 1836. *An outline of English grammar for the use of schools.* (publ. anon.). Dublin: for the Commissioners of National Education, Ireland, sold by R. Groombridge, London. (No. 1135).

Meiklejohn, John Miller Dow. 1862-66. *An easy English grammar for beginners; being a plain doctrine of words and sentences.* (Herbert Series of Short School Books). 4 pts. Manchester/London. (No. 1210).

Meiklejohn, John Miller Dow. 1890. *A short grammar of the English tongue with three hundred and thirty exercises.* London: Simpkin & Marshall. (No. 1219).

Murison, Alexander Falconer. 1875. *First work in English: grammar and composition taught by a comparative study of equivalent forms.* London: Longmans, Green & Co., pr. in Aberdeen. (No. 1285).

Singleton, James Edward of Kendal. [1882]. *Notes on lessons on English grammar for the use of teachers in elementary schools.* (Jarrold's pupil teachers' series). London: Jarrold & Sons. (No. 1611).

Smart, Benjamin Humphrey. 1841. *The accidence and principles of English grammar.* London: Longman, Orme et al. (No. 1620).

Smart, Benjamin Humphrey. 1847. *Grammar on its true basis. A manual of grammar, containing questions, exercises in orthography, etymology, syntax, prosody ... auxiliary to the accidence and principles of English grammar, with a key.* 2 vols. London: Longman etc. (No. 1622).

Smart, Benjamin Humphrey. 1858. *An Introduction to grammar on its true basis, with relation to logic and rhetoric; submitted to teachers as well as learners.* London. (No. 1625).

Thring, Rev. Edward. 1851. *The elements of grammar taught in English; with questions.* Cambridge: Macmillan & Co. (No. 1745).

Thring, Rev. Edward. 1852. *The child's grammar: being the substance of "The Elements of Grammar taught in English"; adapted for the use of junior classes.* London: George Bell. (No. 1746).

Wiseman, Thomas John. 1846. *A school grammar of the English language.* (publ. anon. by "the Brothers of the Christian Schools of Ireland") Dublin: William Powell. (No. 1900).

Two variorum volumes of small booklets

B) Supplementary titles

Barnes, William. 1878. *An outline of English speech-craft.* London: Kegan Paul. (No. 99).

Bromby, Charles Henry. 1848. *The pupil-teacher's English grammar, and etymology of the English language, adapted to the use of normal schools.* London: Simpkin & Marshall. (No. 209).

Churchill, T.O. 1823. *A new grammar of the English language; including the fundamental principles of etymology, syntax, and prosody, etc.* London: for W. Simpkin & R. Marshall. (No. 310).

Jamieson, Alexander. 1818. *A grammar of rhetoric and polite literature:*

comprehending the principles of language and style, the elements of taste and criticism, with rules for the study of composition and eloquence, illustrated by appropriate examples selected chiefly from the British classics .... n.p. (No. 971).

Latham, Robert Gordon. 1843. *An elementary English grammar for the use of schools.* London: Taylor & Walton. (No. 1053).

Mason, Charles Peter. 1858. *English grammar; including the principles of grammatical analysis.* London: Walton & Maberly. (No. 1180).

Mason, Charles Peter. 1879. *A shorter English grammar with ... exercises.* London: G. Bell. (No. 1184).

Millar, James. 1855. *Outlines of English grammar; arranged for being taught on the intellectual system.* Edinburgh: Sutherland & Knox. (No. 1231).

Morell, John Daniel. [1852]. *The analysis of sentences explained and systematised: with an exposition of the fundamental laws of syntax. After the plan of Becker's German grammar.* London: Theobald. (No. 1249).

Murray, Gerald. 1847. *The reformed grammar, or philosophical test of English composition.* London: publ. for the author. (No. 1289).

Nesfield, John Collinson. 1898a. *English Grammar, past and present.* In 3 pts. N.Y. and London: Macmillan. (No. 1310).

Nesfield, John Collinson. 1898b. *Manual of English grammar and composition.* London: Macmillan & Co. (No. 1311).

Simmonite, William Joseph, of Sheffield. 1841. *The practical self-teaching grammar of the English language: (...). For the use of schools, local preachers, and young men.* Sheffield & London: Whittaker. (No. 1605).

Steel, G. 1894. *An English grammar and analysis for students and young teachers.* London: Longmans, Green & Co. (No. 1681).

White, Frederick Averne. 1882. *English grammar.* London: Kegan Paul & Co. (No. 1843).

A variorum volume of small booklets

6. *Conclusion*

Whereas the present bibliography cannot claim to be a comprehensive account of the surviving 19th-century grammar books, it is a compilation which covers much more ground than any previous book. It should be a useful starting-point from which to begin more proper research into the characteristic features of these grammars and the specific aims of their authors. Modern technology will make it possible to add all kinds of evidence overlooked, and it is my hope that readers of my list will write to me supplying corrections and additions, referring to the individual entries. This evidence could then be entered into the master list (with due acknowledgments) and made available to future researchers - whether in a second edition or on-line. I look forward to such additions -

and possibly to a co-author coming forward to supply descriptions of hundreds of grammar books published in America and found only in U.S. libraries.

There is unlimited scope for further study on authors, publishers, interdependences, structural developments and shifts of focus in the contents of grammar books, types of schools and the kinds of grammar teaching individually preferred, etc., all of which will hopefully be pursued topic by topic by Ph.D. students in need of a rewarding thesis. There have been far too few workers in the vineyard so far!

7. *How to read the annotated bibliography*

The data provided are to be interpreted as follows:

1 *Initial symbols*:

!	The book is mentioned in early grammars (esp. in Hunter, Lowres, Martin etc.), in contemporary advertisements, (rarely) in modern works or is known from personal communications, but no library location has been established so far. It is hoped to reduce the numbers of these entries by: a) identifying works with existing grammars incorrectly quoted ; b) tracing the book in question in libraries, especially collections not fully investigated.
$	(preceding entries). The book is certain (or at least likely) to have been printed in the United States. Since the number of such books which I was not able to inspect, and thus to confirm their provenance, is quite large, many corrections will be necessary, in particular, an $ will often have to be added to individual entries.
⇒	cross-reference (not counted in the numbering)
Number	Independent publications in alphabetical order are counted; the numbers were settled in early August 1997, so that a few deletions and additions (1807a) etc. had to be indicated.
2 Author:	Wherever possible, authors have been identified, with dates of birth and death, and their profession etc. (data taken from title pages and entries in library catalogues). Anonymous books are entered with the first main word of the title being alphabetized. Coauthors are normally included (and separately indexed, pp. ...).

3 Year of Publication: The first available year is quoted; if a later edition is extant only, its year is listed preceded by 'a.' (=ante, before).

4 Title: Titles are quoted as fully as was advisable - the subtitles often providing important indications to the author's purpose, contents,

intended audience, sources etc., which makes extensive descriptions of the book itself less necessary.

5 Place of publication and publisher: Again, the information is as full as possible, but copublishers (frequent in schoolbooks esp. after 1860) have generally been omitted.

6 Measurements: Given as precisely as possible, i.e. in cms (height by width), or height only, or octavo etc. Books inspected have normally the measurement in cms (which are more useful, even if books were cut down and existing sizes may therefore vary). Data are not repeated for later editions unless the size has changed.

7 Pages: Roman (for preliminary matter) and Arabic (as in the book); new data for later editions are given only if their number has changed.

8 Editions: Editions as listed in catalogues etc. are given as fully as possible, but information on the make-up of the book is drastically reduced if it seems certain or likely that it has not changed from the preceding edition(s). Only in a few cases have unchanged editions been summarized ("Another five editions between 1877 and 1892" etc.). Modern reprints are listed.

9 Locations: Available locations are fully listed (see sigils on p. 16-7, in a fixed sequence); the coverage is sadly incomplete, only London (B.L.) and Oxford (Bodleian) being reasonably comprehensively covered. Not all library holdings are accessible for electronic searches; those which are, and have been searched, are asteriksed. For the United States, @ indicates a mention in the *National Union Catalogue*, $ a reference in the online list - both sources not specifying the particular library.

In the case of books for which we have found no library location so far (see ! above), reference is made to the specific source of information. Mentions in 19th-century grammarians (see list on p. 17-8) are always included, sigils being italicized.

10 Annotations: The short texts combine descriptions by Michael and Görlach. An attempt was made to provide as much useful information about contents, purpose, sources etc. as was possible to abstract from a cursory look at the copies.

11 Literature: Discussions of individual grammars have been listed; this section needs to be greatly expanded - I have not made a systematic search for such titles but thought it better to include incomplete information than to omit it altogether.

A great amount of work will be necessary to check the correctness of the annotations (and to complement them by further investigations, e.g., on the interdependence of grammar and how far authors relied on authorities mentioned or quoted - and those passed over in silence).

8. *Sigils indicating locations in libraries*

Library catalogues which were searched electronically are marked by an asterisk:

$	=	US libraries (sources: online American libraries and other sources apart from *NUC*)
@	=	US libraries (source: *NUC* (*National Union Catalogue*); both $ and @ do not specify individual libraries but are here treated as equivalent to specific locations
A	=	Aberdeen University Library*
Aw	=	Wales, University College of Aberystwyth
B	=	Birmingham
Bd	=	Bedford College of Higher Education
Br	=	Bristol University
C	=	Cambridge University Library
D	=	Dublin
Dt	=	Trinity College, Dublin
E	=	Edinburgh, National Library of Scotland*
Ep	=	Edinburgh Public Library
Eu	=	Edinburgh University Library*
G	=	Glasgow University Library*
Gj	=	Glasgow, Jordanhill College
Gm	=	Glasgow, Mitchell Library
H	=	Hull University Library
L	=	London, British Library*
Lc	=	Leicester University Library
Le	=	University of London Institute of Education
Lf	=	London, Friends House
Li	=	London, Imperial College and Science Museum Libraries
Lm	=	Leeds University Museum of Education
L^M	=	London, Ministry of Education
Lo	=	London University Library
Lp	=	Leeds Public Library
Ls	=	Leeds City Library
Lu	=	Leeds University Library

Lv   = London, Victoria & Albert Museum
Lw   = London, Wandsworth Public Library
M   = Manchester
Mb   = Melbourne University
N   = Nottingham University Library
Nc   = Newcastle upon Tyne, University Library
O   = Oxford, Bodleian Library*
Rd   = Reading University Library
S   = Sheffield University Library
Sc   = Sheffield City Library
Sm   = Stockholm, Royal University
St   = Stafford Public Library

9. *Other sources*

Other sources are quoted in the case of 19th-century sources, otherwise only if individual grammar books were insufficiently attested:

(*Al*) Alwall (1970 & 1974) = Alwall, Ellen. 1970. *The Religious Trend in Secular Scottish School-books 1850-1861 and 1873-1882.* (Studies in English 38). Lund; and Alwall, Ellen. 1974. *The Religious Trend in Secular English-Irish School-books 1850-1861 and 1873-1880.* (Studia psychologica et paedagogica, 2nd series, 25). Lund.

(*Br*) Brown (1851) = Brown, Goold. 1851. *The Grammar of English grammars.* Boston.

(*Ch*) Alston, ed. (Chadwick-Healey, 1992) = Alston, R.A., ed. 1992. *The Nineteenth Century. Linguistics, Specialist Collection.* Cambridge: Chadwick-Healey.

(*Dk*) Dekeyser (1975) = Dekeyser, Xavier. 1975. *Number and Case Relations in 19th Century British English.* Amsterdam.

(*Dw*) Downey (1991) = Downey, Charlotte. 1991. "Trends that shaped the development of 19th century American grammar writing". In Gerhard Leitner, ed. *English Traditional Grammars.* Amsterdam: Benjamins, 27-38.

(*Gu*) Gumuchian (1967) = Gumuchian, K. A. 1967. *Les livres de l'enfance du XVe au XIX siecle.* Holland Press reprint.

(*Hu*) Hunter (1848) = Hunter, Rev. John, of Uxbridge. 1848. *Text-book of English grammar: A treatise on the etymology and syntax of the English language: including (...) a copious list of the principal works on English grammar. (...).* London.

(*Ke*) Kennedy (1927) = Kennedy, Arthur G. 1927. *A Bibliography of Writings on the English Language.* Harvard: University Press. (repr. New

York: Hafner, 1961).
- (*Lw*) Lowres (1863) = Lowres, Jacob. 1863. *Grammar of English grammars*. London: Longman & Green.
- (*Ma*) Martin (1824) = Martin, Thomas, of Birmingham. 1824. *A philological grammar of the English language; (...). Observations (...) on the comparative merits of more than 100 treatises on English Grammar (...)*. London: Rivingtons.
- (*Mc*) Michael (1991) = Michael, Ian. 1991. "More than enough English grammars". In Gerhard Leitner, ed. *English Traditional Grammars*. Amsterdam: Benjamins, 11-26.
- (*Mi*) Michael (1987 & 1993) = Michael, Ian. 1987. *The Teaching of English: from the Sixteenth Century to 1870*. Cambridge: UP; and Michael, Ian. 1993. *Early Textbooks of English*. Reading: University.
- (*Mp*) Michael, private communication: lists sent in privately (1994-7)
- (*Sk*) Skeat (1888) = Skeat, Walter William. 1888. "English Grammars". *Notes and Queries*. Series 7, 6. pp.120-2, 243-4, 302-3. Repr. in Skeat's *Student's Pastime*, 1896, pp.241-51.
- (*So*) South Kensington (^{5}1860) = South Kensington Museum, London, *Catalogue of the Educational Division*, ^{5}1860.
- (*Tm*) Karen Thomson catalogues
- (*Wa*) Watt (1824) = Watt, R. 1824. *Bibliotheca Britannica*. 4 vols. Edinburgh (Vol. 3).
- (*We*) Wells (1846) = Wells, William H. 1846. *Wells' School Grammar*. Andover, U.S.A. v-viii.
- (*Wm*) Walmsley, private communication

10. *References*

Aarsleff, Hans. 1967. *The Study of Language in England*. Princeton, N.J.: University Press.

Aarts, Flor. 1986. "William Cobbett: radical reactionary and poor man's grammarian". *Neophilologus* 70:603-14. Discusses other grammarians also.

Allibone, S. Austin. 1852. *A critical dictionary of English literature*. Philadelphia.

Allott, Stephen. 1991. *Lindley Murray, 1745-1826, Quaker Grammarian*. Yale.

Alston, R.C. ed. 1967-72. *English Linguistics 1500-1800*. A collection of facsimile reprints. Menston: Scolar Press. [= EL].

---. 1974. *A Bibliography of the English Language from the Invention of Printing to the Year 1800*. (Corrected reprint of volumes I-X). Ilkley: Janus; esp. vol. I.

Alwall, Ellen. 1970. *The Religious Trend in Secular Scottish School-books*

1850-1861 and 1873-1882. (Studies in English 38). Lund.
---. 1974. *The Religious Trend in Secular English-Irish School-books 1850-1861 and 1873-1880*. (Studia psychologica et paedagogica, 2nd series, 25). Lund.
Anon. 1874. "English grammars". *London Quarterly Review* 42 (April); repr. in Harris 1995:154-81.
Austin, Frances. 1996. "Lindley Murray's *Little Code of Elementary Instruction*". In Tieken-Boon van Ostade, 45-61.
Bailey, Richard W. 1996. *Nineteenth-Century English*. Ann Arbor: University of Michigan Press.
Barr, Bernard. 1996. "Towards a bibliography of Lindley Murray". In Tieken-Boon van Ostade, 217-29.
Bartine, David. 1989. *Early English Reading Theory: Origins of Current Debate*. Columbia, Sc.: University S. Carolina Press.
Benzie, W. 1972. *The Dublin Orator: Thomas Sheridan's Influence on Eighteenth Century Rhetoric and Belles Lettres*. (Texts and Monographs). Leeds.
Beyer, Arno. 1981. *Deutsche Einflüsse auf die englische Sprachwissenschaft im 19. Jahrhundert*. Göppingen.
Bryant, Margaret E. 1986. *The London Experience of Secondary Education*. London: Athlone Press.
Catlow, Samuel. 1818. *A Guide in the Selection and Use of Elementary School-books. By the Late Joshua Collins. Revised and enlarged by Samuel Catlow*.
CBEL = *Cambridge Bibliography of English Literature*. Cambridge 1940.
Chambers, Robert. 1832-35. *Bibliographical Dictionary of Eminent Scotsmen*. Reprinted, 3 vols. Hildesheim: G. Olms, 1971.
Collins, Joshua. 1802. *An Adress to Instructors and Parents, on the Right Choice and Use of Books in Every Branch of Education*. T. Reynolds. (L). (^{2}1802 as *A Practical Guide to Parents and Guardians, in the Right Choice* ...; ^{4}1805 as *A Practical Guide to Parents and Tutors, in the Choice* ... T. Hamilton. (G)).
see Catlow, above.
DeKeyser, Xavier. 1975. *Number and Case Relations in Nineteenth Century British English: A Comparative Study of Grammar and Usage*. Antwerp: De Nederlandsche Boekhandel.
DNB = *Dictionary of National Biography*
Downey, Charlotte. 1986. "The constants and variables which guided the development of American grammar writing in the 18th and 19th centuries." In Leitner, 334-50.

---. 1991. "Trends that shaped the development of 19th century American grammar writing." In Leitner, 27-38.
Emsley, Bert. 1888-89. "English grammars". *Notes & Queries*, 7th series, VI:121, 243, 302, 453; VII:54.
Eschbach, Achim. 1978. *Benjamin Humphrey Smart. Grundlagen der Zeichentheorie: Grammatik, Logik, Rhetorik.* Frankfurt am Main: Syndikat.
Girault-Duvivier, C.P. 1827. *Grammaire des Grammaires*. Paris.
Görlach, Manfred. 1995. "English in nineteenth-century England." In M.G. *New Studies in the History of English*. Heidelberg: Winter, 190-234.
---. fc. *English in 19th-century England*. Cambridge: University Press.
Graham, George Frederick. 1845. "On English grammars". *Classical Museum* 2:404-10.
Green, Emmanuel. 1902. *Bibliotheca Somersetensis*. Taunton.
Gumuchian, K. A. 1967. *Les livres de l'enfance du XVe au XIX siecle*. Holland Press reprint.
Harrington, Brian. 1989. "Alexander Bain: a reappraisal". *History of Education Society Bulletin* 44:46-51.
Harris, Roy ed. 1995. *English Language and Language Teaching 1800-1865*. London: Routledge/Thoemmes Press.
Higson, C.W.J. 1967 & 1976. *Sources for the History of Education*. Library Association.
Holtom = Holtom, Christopher, bookseller, England.
Howatt, A.P.R. 1984. *A History of English Language Teaching*. Oxford: University Press.
Huston, Jon Reckard. 1954. *An Analysis of English Grammars Used in American Schools before 1850*. Dissertation, University Pittsburgh. University Microfilm No. 8896.
Jones, Bernard. 1983. "William Barnes on Lindley Murray's *English grammar*". *English Studies* 64:30-35.
---. 1996. "The reception of Lindley Murray's *English Grammar*". In Tieken-Boon van Ostade, 63-80.
Jones, Stanley. 1987. "The suppression of Hazlitt's *New and Improved Grammar of the English Tongue*". *Library* 9:32-43.
Kearney, Anthony. 1959. "Leslie Stephen & the English Studies debate, 1886-7". *History of Education Society Bulletin* 43:41-47.
Keynes, Geoffrey. 1932. "Hazlitt's *Grammar abridged*". *Library* 13:97-99.
Kittredge, George Lyman. 1906. *Some Landmarks in the History of English Grammar*. Boston: Ginn.
---. 1911. *English Grammars of Five Centuries*. Boston: Ginn.
Leitner, Gerhard. 1986a. "English grammars - past, present and future". In Leitner 1986b, 409-431.

---, ed. 1986b. *The English Reference Grammar*. Tübingen: Niemeyer.
---. 1986c. "English traditional grammars in the nineteenth century". In Kastovsky, D. & A. Szwedek. *Linguistics Across Historical Boundaries. In Honour of Jacek Fisiak*. II:1333-55. Berlin: de Gruyter.
---. 1991a. *English Traditional Grammars. An International Perspective*. Amsterdam: Benjamins.
---. 1991b. "Eduard Adolf Maetzner (1805-1902)." In Leitner, 233-55.
Leonard, S.A. 1929. *The Doctrine of Correctness in English Usage, 1700-1800*. Madison.
Lyman, Rollo LaVerne. 1921. *English Grammar in American Schools before 1850*. Washington: Bureau of Education, Bulletin 12.
Marshall, Peter H. 1984. *William Godwin*. Yale University Press.
Michael, Ian. 1970. *English Grammatical Categories and the Tradition to 1800*. Cambridge: University Press. (ʳ1985).
---. 1987. *The Teaching of English. From the Sixteenth Century to 1870*. Cambridge: University Press.
---. 1991. "More than enough English grammars." In Leitner, 11-26.
---. 1997. "The hyperactive production of English grammars in the nineteenth century: a speculative bibliography". *Publishing History* 41:23-61.
McAlester, Charles J. 1961. *A Sketch of the Life and Literary Labours of the Late Robert Sullivan. Being a Lecture Delivered ... on March 7th, 1870*. Belfast: Graham & Heslip.
Monaghan, Charles. 1996. "Lindley Murray, American". In Tieken-Boon van Ostade, 27-43.
Moon, Marjorie. 1976. *John Harris's Books for Youth, 1801 to 1843. A Check List*. (enl. ed. 1992).
Mugglestone, Lynda. 1995. *"Talking Proper". The Rise of Accent as Social Symbol*. Oxford: University Press.
---. 1996. "'A subject so curious and useful': Lindley Murray and pronunciation". In Tieken-Boon van Ostade, 145-61.
NBL 1946 = National Book League, *Children's Books of Yesterday*. Catalogue of an exhibition arranged by Percy Muir, 1946.
NBL 1949 = National Book League, *The English at School*. Catalogue of an exhibition arranged by Arnold Muirhead, 1949.
NCBEL = *New Cambridge Bibliography of English Literature*. Cambridge, 1969-77.
Nietz, John A. 1961. *Old Textbooks*. Pittsburgh.
Osselton, N.E. 1996. "Lindley Murray and English spelling." In Tieken-Boon van Ostade, 135-44.
Pearl, William. 1953. *William Cobbett: a Bibliographical Account of his Life and Times*. n.p.

Percy, Carol. 1994. "Paradigms of their sex? Women's grammars in late eighteenth century England". *Histoire, Epistémologie, Langage* 16:2.
Quirk, Randolph. 1974. "The study of the mother tongue". In his *The Linguist and the English Language*. London: Arnold.
Read, Allen Walker. 1939. "The motivation of Lindley Murray's grammatical work." *JEGP* 38:525-39.
Reibel, David, ed. 1995. *Robert Lowth (1710-1781). The Major Works*. 8 vols. London: Routledge/Thoemmes Press.
Reibel, David, ed. 1996. *Lindley Murray: The Educational Works*. 12 vols. London: Routledge/Thoemmes Press.
Robins, Robert H. 1986. "The evolution of English grammar books since the Renaissance." In Leitner, 292-306.
Rosenbach, A.S.W. 1933. *Early American Children's Books*. Portland, Maine. (^{2}1971 New York).
South Kensington Museum, London, *Catalogue of the Educational Division*, ^{5}1860.
Smith, Henry Lester, *et al*. 1946. *The Hundred Fifty Years of Grammar Textbooks <1795-1945>*. (Bulletin of the School of Education). Indiana: University.
Smyth, A.L. 1966. *John Dalton. A Bibliography of Books by and about him*. Manchester: University Press.
Sundby, Bertil, Anne Kari Bjørge & Kari E. Haugland. 1991. *A Dictionary of English Normative Grammar, 1700-1800*. Amsterdam: Benjamins.
Swiggers, P. 1994. "Joseph's Priestley's approach of grammatical categorization and linguistic diversity". In Keith Carlon *et al*., eds. *Perspectives on English*. (Emma Vorlat Festschrift). Leuven: Peeters, 34-53.
Thomson = Karen Thomson, bookseller, Edinburgh.
Tieken-Boon van Ostade, Ingrid. 1996a. "Lindley Murray and the concept of plagiarism". In Tieken-Boon van Ostade 1996b, 81-96.
---, ed. 1996b. *Two Hundred Years of Lindley Murray*. Münster: Nodus.
Tilleard, J. 1859. "On elementary schoolbooks". *Trans. Nat. Assoc. for Promoting Social Science* 387-96.
Tyler, Priscilla. 1954. *Grammars of the English Language to 1850: with Special Reference to School Grammars Used in America*. Dissertation, Western Reserve University.
Vallins, G.H. 1954. "Cobbett's Grammar". *English* 10:48-53.
Vincent, David. 1989. *Literacy and Popular Culture: England 1750-1914*. Cambridge: University Press.
Vorlat, Emma. 1959. "The sources of Lindley Murray's *The English Grammar*". *Leuvense Bijdragen* 48:108-25.
---. 1975. *The Development of English Grammatical Theory. 1586-1737*. With

Special Reference to the Theory of Parts of Speech. Leuven.

---. 1996. "Lindley Murray's prescriptive canon". In Tieken-Boon van Ostade 1996b, 163-82.

Wächtler, Kurt. 1986. "Goold Brown - the American grammarian of grammarians in the nineteenth century." In Leitner, 351-62.

---. 1991. "W.D. Whitney's *Essentials of English Grammar. For the Use of Schools (1877).*" In Leitner, 39-55.

Walmsley, John. 1991. "E.A. Sonnenschein and grammatical terminology." In Leitner, 57-80.

Watts, Ruth. 1983. "Joseph Priestley and education". *Enlightenment and Dissent*, 2:83-88.

Welch, D'Alte A. 1972. *A Bibliography of American Children's Books Printed Prior to 1821.* Worcester, Mass.

Wells, William H. 1831. "Notes on English grammars". *Common School J.* 3. passim.

Welsh, Charles. 1885. *A Bookseller of the Last Century [Newbery].* London.

Williams, D.G. 1973. *The Educational Ideas of Alexander Bain, 1818-1903.* PhD Dissertation, Sheffield.

Cologne, May 1998

Englisches Seminar
Universität zu Köln
Albertus-Magnus-Platz
D-50923 Köln
FAX: ++49/221/470-5109
e-mail: Manfred.Goerlach@uni-koeln.de

Alphabetical List of 19th-century English Grammars by British and American Authors

1. $ Abbot, Elijah. 1803. *A short but comprehensive system of English grammar designed for the use of country schools.* n.p. 80pp.
   ($)
2. Abbott, Rev. Edwin Abbott (Head Master of the Philological School, Marylebone, London, 1838-1926). 1869. *A Shakespearian grammar. An attempt to illustrate some of the differences between Elizabethan and Modern English: for the use of schools.* London: Macmillan & Co. 17/18cm, viii+136pp. (Rev. and enl. ed. ^{3}1870, London: Macmillan & Co., 18cm, xxiv+511pp. ($ A L); anr. ed. 1870, 18cm, viii+143pp ($); at least seven further editions before 1897 which all left the text unchanged; ^{r}1966 of ^{3}1870, New York: Dover Publications, 21.5x13.5, xxiv+511pp.).
   ($ @ A Dt E L)
   [As the title says, the grammar is mainly a synchronic description of Shakespeare's language; "grammar" deals with adjectives, adverbs, articles, conjunctions, prepositions, pronouns, relatival constructions, verbs (forms, auxiliary, inflections, moods), participles and verbals, ellipses, irregularities, compound words, prefixes and suffixes (1-451). This is followed by "Prosody" (452-515). This survey makes clear that alphabetical treatment of items, intended to help with a better understanding of the texts, dominates over systematic exposition. The references to contemporary English are slight.]
3. ---. 1872a. *A handbook of English grammar.* n.p. (Rev. ed. ^{2}1874, augmented by William Moore, Headmaster of the Philological School, London: J. Martin, 19cm, iv+68pp. (@); ^{3}1879, rev. by William Moore, London: James Martin, 18x12, iv+77pp. (L)).
   (@ L)
   [On ^{3}1879: The first part (1-51) is on words, sentences, letters and sounds; this "was printed, nearly in its present form, some 25 years ago, for the use of the junior classes of the Philological School [=ca. 1845, not recorded]. The recent book is intended as "a complete *Elementary* work, suitable for English schools in which Latin forms an essential part of the regular course of instruction." "Most of the paragraphs printed in large type may with advantage be committed to memory; the observations and notes are intended to form the basis of examinations, both written and oral." The addition of part IV, on (modern) etymology, apparently mirrors the new interest in the discipline in the 1850s and 1860s. A few words on punctuation at end.]
4. ---. 1872b. *How to write clearly.* London: Seeley & Jackson. 78pp. (Anr. ed. 1880; anr. ed. 1891 (Dt); anr. ed. 1896 (H)).

(Dt H L)
[A grammar?]

5. ---. 1874. *How to tell the parts of speech or easy lessons in English grammar: an introduction to English grammar.* London: Seeley, Jackson, & Halliday. 8°, 144pp. (²1875 (L); rev. and enl. ed. 1880, 14th thousand, London: Seeley, Jackson & Halliday, 17cm, 169pp. (@); Am. ed. 1881, rev. and enl. by John G.R. McElroy, 18cm, xvi+143pp. ($ @); anr. ed. 1885 ($); anr. ed. 1887; rev. and enl. ed. 1890, 28th thousand, London: Seeley & Co., 169pp. (@); anr. ed. 1892, Boston: Roberts (@)).
($ @ L)

6.$ ---. 1874. *How to parse. An attempt to apply the principles of scholarship to English grammar. With appendixes on analysis, spelling, and punctuation.* Boston: Roberts Bros. (Anr. ed. 1875, London: Seeley, Jackson & Co., 17cm, xxxi+343pp.; anr. ed. 1876; anr. ed. 1877 ($); anr. ed. 1878, Boston: Roberts Bros. ($ @); at least another eighteen editions (Boston or London) by 1900, all apparently unchanged).
($ @ L)

7. Anon. 1848. *An abridgement of the pupil teacher's English grammar and etymology adapted to the higher classes of elementary schools. Published for the use of the model schools of the Cheltenham Training Institution.* London: Simpkin, Marshall & Co. / Cheltenham: Wight & Bailey. 16°, 54pp.
(L O)
["Technical expressions avoided and (!) explained ... all confusion with the principles of other languages avoided ... the means of correcting *bad* language, rather than of instructing a foreigner, kept in view"; "undertaken to the simultaneous or gallery system of education; parsing exercises omitted". OES (O and S very short) with long lists of prefixes and Latin roots of questionable value provided instead.]

⇒ Adair, James (pseud.) - see Phillips, Sir Richard, no. 1405 & 1407.

8.$ Adams, Rev. Charles. D.D. 1838. *A system of English grammar; constructed upon the basis of Murray's grammar and adapted to the use of schools, academies, and private learners.* Boston: D.S. King. 17x10, iv+[5]-172pp.
(@ L *Br*)
[A free adaptation of Murray intended to make grammar pleasant and inexpensive. Definitions and arrangement of Murray frequently changed; other (unnamed) grammars were consulted. OESP, with exercises in parsing added at end. A close comparison with Murray would be necessary to test Adams' claims.]

9.$ Adams, Daniel. Pseud. Dudley Leavitt (1773-1864). 1803. *The thorough scholar; or, The nature of language, with the reasons, principles, and rules of English grammar: rendered accessible to the understanding of youth; comprehending, I. the nature of the language ... II. the nature of sounds ... III. English grammar, punctuation, etc.* Leominster, Mass.: Adams & Wilder. 18/19cm, 100pp. ($ L). (^{2}1810, Boston: Thomas & William Parker, pr. by E. Oliver, 18cm, 106pp. ($ @); ^{3}1814, Montpelier, Vt.: L.Q.C. Bowles, 17cm, 103pp. (L); impr. ed. ^{4}1817, Montpelier, Vt.: L.Q.C. Bowles, 15cm, 131pp. ($ @); anr. ed. n.d., Boston: Parker, 196pp. (@)).
($ @ L)
[OES, preceded by general reflexions on language; descriptions and rules, with few footnotes and 'stories' with subsequent notes. The presentation of the material is somewhat confused (and confusing). Questions are printed in the margins.]

10.$ ---. ^{3}1814. *English grammar.* Montpelier, Vt. 12mo, 103pp. (Anr. ed. 1817 (@)).
(@ Br)

11.$! Adams, E. 1806. *English grammar.* Leicester, Mass. 18mo, 143pp. (^{5}1821).
(Br)

12. Adams, Ernest. 1858. *The elements of the English language.* London: Bell & Daldy. vii+183pp. (Enl. ed. ^{2}1862; anr. ed. 1865, 253pp. ($); anr. ed. 1866, London (@); new, rev. and cor. ed. 1870, London: Bell & Daldy, 20cm, vii+253pp. (@); at least another nine editions documented before ^{19}1883 (Le); anr. ed. 1889 ($); anr. ed. 1890, viii+326pp. ($); ^{25}1892, rev. by J.F. Davis; anr. ed. 1893 ($)).
($ @ C L Le)
[cf. Anon. 1874, Beyer 1981:386]
[Disappointed with previous grammars, Adams set out to combine historical aspects and comparative grammar with functional description, focusing on the verb. The two main chapters, 'accidence' and syntax, leave many categories badly accounted for. Some mixture of Latin- and English-based arguments, Latin structures, not very clear exposition, no apparent use of existing grammars.]

13. ---. 1868. *The rudiments of the English grammar and analysis.* London: Bell & Daldy. 17cm, viii+86pp. (rev. ed. ^{2}1871, London: Bell & Daldy, vi+114pp., 2s (L); anr. ed. 1875 (@); later editions to 1877).
(@ C L O)
[cf. Beyer 1981:386]

[Written "to familiarize the young student with the technical forms required in studying a foreign tongue", with Latin as a basis of description. Very brief definitions, with minimal exemplification, arranged under "Accidence, Syntax, Analysis". Abbreviated from Adams 1858?]

14.$ Adams, Frank P. 1882. *Grammatical diagrams and analysis.* (Normal Publications). n.p. 23cm, 130pp.
($)

15. Adams, Lionel Ernest. 1884. *A concise system of English parsing.* London: Bell & Sons. 61pp.
(@ L)

16. Adamson, James (1797-1875). 1846. *A manual of instruction for the South African College. Literature. Pt. I: The principles of grammar applied to the English language.* Cape Town: University of Cape Town. viii+140pp. (@ L). (Anr. ed. 1848, Cape Town: J.H. Collard, pr. by Pike & Philip for the South African College / Edinburgh: J. Johnstone 19cm, viii+272pp. (@)).
($ @ L)

17. Anon. [1881]. *Advanced English grammar: preceded by a sketch of the history of the English language. For the use of the higher forms of middle-class schools, pupil teachers, and students in training colleges.* (Blackie's Comprehensive School Series). London: Blackie. 16.5x11, 160pp.
(@ L O)
[OESP, detailed and very traditional account, with various excursions. Advertisements at end also mention related works: *[Blackie's] Elementary English grammar. Based on the Analysis of Sentences. Parts I. to V., for Standards II to V* (no. 493); *Complete English grammar and analysis*, 1s (no. 493); *Test-cards in grammar and analysis, based on the Complete English Grammar, for Standards II to VI*, 9d each.]

18.! Anon. 1815. *The adventures of Dame Winnifred, and her numerous family; or the infant's grammar.* London: G. Martin.
(*Gu*)
[cf. Gumuchian (1967: No.249)]

19.$ Ainsworth, Luther. 1837. *A practical system of English grammar (...) plainly and familiarly taught by questions and answers, and illustrated by a copious variety of practical examples.* Providence, R.I.: Cranston & Co. 19cm, 144pp.
($ @ Br)

20.$ Alden, Abner (1758-1820). 1811. *Grammar made easy, or, A practical grammar of the English language ... being the fifth part of a Columbian exercise, the whole comprising an easy and systematical method of teaching and learning the English language.* Boston. 17/18cm, 180pp. ($ *Br*)

21.$ Alden, Joseph (1807-1885). 1874. *Introduction to the use of the English language; grammar and rhetoric combined.* Albany: J. Munsell. (Anr. ed. 1875, New York: Potter, Ainsworth & Co., 18cm, 192pp. (@)). ($ @)

22.$ Alden, Rev. Timothy Jr. (1771-1839). 1808. *Practical questions on English grammar to be answered by those, who study Murray's abridgment: to which are added some directions for parsing.* Boston, Mass.: Manning & Loring. 14cm, 36pp.
($ @)
[Possibly identical with Brown's reference to 1811. *English grammar.*]

23.$ Aldrich, W. 1843. *Five lectures on English grammar: for common schools, academies, and private instruction.* Providence, R.I.: B.T. Albro. ($). (^{8}1845, 15cm, 71pp. ($); $^{9+10}$1846, 14cm, 72pp. ($); ^{11}1847, Boston, 16cm, 68pp. ($ *Br*); ^{6}1848 (@); ^{12}1848, title changed to *Lectures on English grammar and rhetoric for common schools, academics, and private instructions*, New York, 14.5x9, 68pp. (L)).
($ @ L *Br*)
[No orthography or prosody; eight parts of speech (include 'Connective' and 'Independent'; no 'Article', 'Participle'). Discursive exposition in clumsy style; many remarks are ill-informed and off the point, definitions often very poor. Ends with stylistic advice on how to structure sentences. Negligible.]

24. Alexander, Levy. 1833. *The young lady and gentleman's guide to the grammar of the English language. In verse.* London: the author. 119pp. (Anr. ed. 1835).
(C L *Hu*, *Lw*)
[Interesting experiment in doggerel verse with copious notes in prose; the content is highly traditional.]

25. Alexander, Samuel. 1822. *A practical and logical essay on the syntax of the English language.* n.p. (^{2}1830, Liverpool, 20cm; ^{3}1832, Manchester; enl. and amended ed. ^{4}1832, designed particularly for schools, quoted as *A practical and logical grammar of the English language*, London: Longman etc., 15cm, x+216pp.).
(@ C L *Hu*, *Br*, *Lw*)
[An outspoken plea for 'reason' (against usage, custom), organized to present rules followed by sections called 'reason' and 'exercises' and plentiful footnotes; vituperative but intelligent. An account of quite a high standard, on traditional lines, (OESP) and with many details dis-

cussed in footnotes; the fourth edition has many exercises added to make it more useful in schools.]

26.$ Alger, Israel Jr. A.M. (1787-1825). ?1824. *Alger's Murray. English grammar. Improved stereotyped edition ... Abridgment of Murray's English grammar, with an appendix, containing exercises in orthography, in parsing, in syntax, and in punctuation ... To which questions are added ... Revised, prepared and adapted to the use of the "English exercises"*. Boston, Mass.: Lincoln & Edmands. 14x8.5, viii+126pp. (L). (Anr. ed 1829, Boston; anr. ed. 1838, Boston: R.S. Davis & Co. (@ L); anr. ed. 1842, Boston (L)).
(@ L)
[(Publisher's advertisement): "As a cheap and compendious elementary work for general use, this is probably the best grammar extant. Though furnished at a cheap price, it is so copious, as in most cases to supersede the necessity of a larger work". Alger enlarged Murray to "assist the pupil in parsing and correction of the English Exercises", but otherwise left the *Abridgment* intact; a close comparison is necessary to verify his claims. Alger's abridgments appear to have been widespread, often preferred to Murray's own. References commonly do not indicate which of Alger's revisions is recommended.]

27.$ ---. 1824. *The English teacher, or private learner's guide: containing a new arrangement of Murray's exercises and key, with the various parts of which, the corresponding notes, rules, observations in Murray's grammar are incorporated: also references in promiscuous exercises to the rules by which the errours are to be corrected: revised, arranged, prepared, and particularly adapted to the use of instructors and private learners: designed to accompany and match with the Boston stereotype edition of Murray's exercises prepared for the use of schools*. Boston: pr. Lincoln & Edmands. 18x11, vii+240pp. (L). (Anr. ed. 1835 (L); anr. ed. 1836, Holtom, List 44).
($ L)
[Murray's Exercises and Key arranged "with a particular design to aid Teachers and Private Learners in their labours of teaching and learning the elementary principles of the English language"; incorporating "all the Rules, Notes, and Observations". Exercises referring back to rules. The book concentrates on parsing, syntax, punctuation and style, juxtaposing defective English with correct, or better, alternatives.]

28.$ ---. 1833. *Murray's English exercises: ... With which the corresponding notes, rules and observations in Murray's grammar are incorporated; also references in promiscous exercises to the rules by which the errours are to be corrected. Rev., prepared and particularly adapted to the use*

of schools; being a counterpart to the English teacher. Ed. I. Alger. Boston/Cincinnati. (Anr. ed. 1838 Boston: R.S. Davis (@)).
(@ L)

29. Allan, Louisa. 1813. *The decoy; or, An agreeable method of teaching children the elementary parts of English grammar by conversations and familiar examples.* First published anonymously in *A present for a little boy.* London: Darton, Harvey & Darton. (^{2}1814 (L); anr. ed. 1816, New York ($); ^{3}1817 ($); ^{4}1819 (L); ^{5}1823 ($); ^{6}1827 (Rd)).
($ L Rd)

30. Allen, Alexander (1814-1842) & James Cornwell (Ph.D). $^?$1841. *A new English grammar, with very copious exercises, and a systematic view of the formation and derivation of words.* London: Simpkin, Marshall & Co. 8°, xv+168pp. (^{3}1841; ^{7}1844; ^{9}1845; by ^{12}1847 London: Simpkin, Marshall & Co., its title had changed to *An English school grammar* (@); at least another eleven editions recorded before ^{37}1865; by ^{38}1866 *... of words, comprising Anglo-Saxon, Latin, and Greek lists, which explain the etymology of above seven thousand English words* has been added to title, thirty editions (of which six are recorded) up to ^{68}1878; anr. ed. 1888 (@)).
($ @ H L Lc O *Hu, Br, Lw*)
[A modest school grammar on traditional lines - the claimed innovations are very minor; accompanied by an even more elementary *Grammar for beginners*, and Cornwell's *The young composer.*]

31. --- & ---. [a1846]. *Grammar for beginners; being an introduction to Allen & Cornwell's English school grammar, by the same authors.* London. (^{8}1847; $^{10+11}$1848 ($); anr. ed. 1853, 14cm, vii+[9]-71pp. (@); ^{25}1855, London: Simpkin, Marshall & Co., 14x9.5, vii+71pp., 1s9p (L); ^{35}1860 (@); ^{56}1870 (@); anr. ed. 1873, London: Simpkin, Marshall & Co./Hamilton, Adams & Co./Whittaker & Co. / Edinburgh: Oliver & Boyd, 71pp. (*Wm*); twenty-five further editions to: ^{81}1888 (@)).
($ @ L O *Hu, Wm*)
[Modest abridgement. "One thing taught at one time ... The Rules or Definitions are in all cases inductions from given examples." Nine parts of speech defined and characterized; syntax and parsing exercises. "Clear examples, explanations, definitions and exercises" ... "to imprint onto the child's mind a strong, clear type of the leading essentials of English grammar."]

32. $ Allen, D. Caverno. 1847. *Grammatic guide, or common school grammar.* Syracuse, N.Y. 19cm, 94pp.
($ *Br*)

33.! Allen, Edward. 1835. *The pocket English explanator; or, A dive into grammar.* n.p.
(*Lw*)

34.$ Allen, Edward Archibald (b.1843). [a1897]. *Longman's school grammar.* Rev. ed. New York: Longmans, Green & Co. 19cm, xiv+264pp.
(@)

35. ---. n.d. *English grammar, viewed from all sides.* (Collected monographs). n.p. 12pp.
(@)

36. Allen, Rev. William (M.A. of Newbury, Berks). 1813. *The elements of English grammar; with numerous exercises, questions for examinations, and notes, for the use of the advanced student.* London: Geo. B. Whittaker. 17x10, vii+457pp. (^{2}1824, London: G. & W.B. Whittaker (@); rev. and shortened ed. ^{3}1824 as *An English grammar; with exercises, notes, and questions ...* , London: G. & W.B. Whittaker, 180pp, 2s6d. (L)).
($ @ L *Ma*, *Hu*, *Br*, *Lw*)
[Detailed and very traditional account; OESP, with many exercises appended; includes an article on political licenses and older English constructions "to invite the student to a more extensive research." Particularly praised by Martin 1824:272. The third edition is much revised by "shortening the rules" and by using smaller print on a smaller page. ^{2}1824 has about 95,000 words, reduced to 50,000 in ^{3}1824.]

37.$ ---. ^{2}n.d. *A grammar of the English language with exercises and questions for examination. Being a sequel to the Catechism of English grammar.* Newbury: Pinnock & Co. 287pp.
(@)

38. Allison, M.A. 1825. *First lessons in English grammar; for the use of the nursery, and for junior classes in schools. With questions for examinations at the end of each lesson.* n.p. (^{8}1848, London: Simpkin, Marshall & Co., 15cm, iv+[5]-90 (@); ^{9}1851, London: Longman, 9d).
(@ L *Hu*, *Lw*)
[Elementary work intended for eight- to ten-year olds; fifty lessons in Q/A form.]

39. Anon. 1876. *Analysis of sentences, with illustrated examples and numerous graduated exercises.* Glasgow. 64pp.
(L)
[Sentence and clause analysis; passages from literature for analysis.]

40.$ Anon. 1836. *An analytic grammar: being a concise exposition of the structure of the English language, and of speech in general, the manner and principles of which are in a large proportion new. Intended for self-*

instruction and for the use of schools. By an experienced reader ... Philadelphia: Massey & Boate. 15cm, 88pp.
(@)

41.$ Anon. 1869. *An analytical and practical grammar of the English language: with an appendix on prosody, punctuation, etc.* (Canadian National Series of School Books). Ontario: the Council of Public Instruction of Ontario. 18cm, 213pp.
($)

42. Anderson, Robert (Headmaster of the Normal Institution, Edinburgh). 1869. *The scholar's book of English: a handbook of grammar and etymology.* Edinburgh: J. Thin & Co. / London: Simpkin, Marshall & Co. 18x11, vi+90pp.
(L O)
[The sentence is made the basis of the grammar; (new) etymology takes up the second half of the book (47-88). Some attempts at philosophical and logical analysis, with plenty of exercises, some notes in smaller print. Although the coherence of the parts is not evident, the (limited) success in presenting grammar along new lines deserves mention.]

43. Andrew, James (LL.D., 1773-1833). 1817. *Institutes of grammar, as applicable to the English language; or as introductory to the study of other languages, systematically arranged, and briefly explained. To which are added some chronological tables.* London: Black, Parbury & Allen. 21cm, iv+129pp.
($ A L *Hu, Br, Sk, Lw*)
[A strange mixture of elementary grammar in form of a catechism, tables and definitions, most of this hearking back to 18th-century ideas of reason and propriety.]

44.$! Angell, Oliver. 1830. *English grammar.* Providence, R.I. 12mo, 90pp.
(*Br*)

45. Angus, Rev. J. 1805. *The English grammar unveiled, and adapted to the lowest capacity on an entirely new plan, for plainness and entertainment.* Workington: the author. 17x9, xii+93pp.
(O)
[Rejects Latin patterns; partly in Q/A form, rambling, selective and incoherent; "common errors" listed pp. 33-7; punctuation appended pp. 49-58 - possibly one of the poorest attempts in the field.]

46. Angus, Joseph (Examiner in English Language, Literature and History to the University of London, 1816-1902). 1861. *Hand-book of the English tongue. For the use of students and others.* n.p. 18x10.5, vi+504pp. (^{2}1862, London: Religious Tract Society. (@ L); anr. ed. 1864 ($); anr.

ed. 1866 (@); anr. ed. 1867 (@); anr. ed. 1869 ($); anr. ed. 1870 ($), anr. ed. 1872 ($); anr. ed. 1873).
($ @ L)
Lit.: Anon. 1874.
[The author combines "the history of our language, the principles of its grammar, and the elements of composition", focusing on etymological correctness, logical analysis of sentences and some diachronic data to explain present-day phenomena. He names a long list of works used, by Latham, Trench, Key, Marsh, Dasent, Craik, Rogers, Adams, and Morell, and another twenty authors to whom he is endebted for occasional suggestions. OESP in ch. 5-8 (= 96-365), eight parts of speech. Very thorough exposition, including a particularly extensive treatment of syntax (240-327), but marred by detail and the combination of description and historical/comparative data and arguments as well as doubtful generalizations and parallels. (The reading is much easier in the excellent sections on composition, 366-415). There is an extensive appendix with 745 questions or suggestions for active work (441-488) to check the readers' comprehension.]

47. Angus, William (M.A. of Glasgow, Teacher of English and author of "The Life of Christ"). 1800a. *An epitome of English grammar. Containing* [parts of speech; syntax] *violations of the rules of syntax; improprieties in the choice of words; errours, arising from redundancy* [etc.]. *In these errours are included, a variety of Scotticisms and vulgar Anglicisms ... On a new plan. Calculated for the use of schools*. Glasgow: D. Niven. 12°, xlviiipp. (A). (enl. ed. ²1807 as *An epitome of English grammar, with exercises on false syntax, erroneous punctuation, incorrect orthography, Scotticisms, vulgar Anglicisms and a key to the exercises, etc.*, Glasgow/Edinburgh etc.: W. Lang, sold by P. Hill, etc., 18cm, viii+255pp. (@ L)).
(@ A L *Br*)
Lit.: Sundby 1991.
[The modest work contains "a brief explication of the parts of speech, phrases for parsing, (violations of) the rules of syntax, improprieties in the choice of words and errors arising from redundancy, improper ellipsis, bad arrangement and ambiguity. In these errors are included, a variety of Scotticisms and vulgar Anglicisms". On a new plan, calculated for the use of schools. The 'Scotticisms' are not explicitly marked.]

48. ---. 1800b. *A pronouncing dictionary of the English language: exhibiting the most approved mode of pronunciation*. (To this edition is subjoined an epitome of English grammar). Glasgow: D. Niven. 116pp. (Gm L).

(^{4}1804 as *An English spelling and pronouncing dictionary* (Wa); ^{5}1814 (E L); ^{10}1821 (*Tm*, 21); ^{19}1830 (G)).
(E G Gm L *Tm*, Wa)

49. ---. 1812. *A new system of English grammar, with exercises, and questions for examination; interspersed with critical notes and explanatory observations, chiefly of a practical nature. Also, an appendix, containing an extensive collection of vulgar Anglicisms, Scotticisms, examples of bad arrangement, of ambiguity, &c; and elements of English composition, with a key to the exercises. The whole intended for the use of schools, and private teaching.* Glasgow: the author, sold by Brash & Reid / Edinburgh: P. Hill/A. Constable & Co. / London: G. Cowie & Co. 16.5x10, xii+431pp. (Impr. ed. ^{3}1817 Glasgow, 300pp.; anr. ed. 1819, *Supplement*, 224pp., bound with his *English grammar* ^{3}1817 (@); anr. ed. 1825 ($); anr. ed. 1829 (G); ^{5}1839).
($ @ A G L O)
[OESP. A very comprehensive and orderly traditional description based on (iv) Kames, Blair, Campbell, Beattie, Pickbourne, Priestley, Trusler (...); nine parts of speech; short rules, examinations, sentences to be corrected with a considerable number of observations and exceptions in small print, and footnotes. A sober early 19th century summary of 18th-century grammatical thinking. (Angus sees the treatment of Scotticisms as a particular achievement of his book.)]

50. ---. [a1813]. *An abridgement of Angus's grammar, for the use of beginners. For the use of younger classes.* Advertised in Angus 1812 as *An abridgement of the grammar* 1s. (Enl. ed. ^{2}1813, Glasgow: the author, 19cm, 70pp.; ^{4}1825; ^{5}1829; impr. ed. ^{6}1839).
($ C L *Lw*)
[The preface to the first edition, reprinted in the second, says it is 'an abridgement of a larger work published ... about two years ago'. Its structure is identical to that of a full grammar.]

51. ---. [a1825]. *English grammar; mnemonically arranged. Interspersed with critical notes and explanatory observations, chiefly of a practical nature: with exercises; a key; Anglicisms, Scotticisms, Iricisms, etc.* n.p. (Impr. and enl. ed. ^{4}1825, Glasgow: James Curll, 17cm, 288pp ($ @ A G); ^{5}1839, Glasgow: the author, sold in Glasgow/Edinburgh/Aberdeen, viii+[9]-208pp. (L)).
($ @ A G L)
[The structure is largely identical with the larger book; the text having many passages left after the necessary reduction. As a summary of no independent value.]

52. ---. [1828]. *Supplement to Angus's English grammar; containing the principles of English composition; additional scotticisms and exercises; remarks on letter writing; and on the analogy and anomalies of English pronunciation.* Glasgow. (^{2}1829, preface dated as Nov. 1828, Glasgow (G)).
(A G)

53. ---. 1840. *A brief analysis of the English language, showing the mode of its formation, and the principal sources whence it is derived.* Glasgow/London. xlviii+142pp.
(G)

54. Anthony, William Bennett. [1881]. *Essential memoranda of English grammar.* (signed W.B.A.). 3 parts. Part I & II: London: Relfe Bros. 23.5x 14.5. Part III: Manchester: Heywood. 25x15.5.
(O)
[Three parts of 2+4+2pp. = 4 cardboard pages, with elementary rules to be committed to memory; Part II "contains all necessary (!) memory work for the Cambridge Local and College of Preceptor's Examinations." Part III Anon. "The 'dot' parsing and grammar notes for pupil teachers and upper standards". The three parts are possibly not by one author.]

55.$ Armstrong, John Gilbert (b. 1826). 1861. *The student's guide to English grammar, or, the way to speak and write grammatically by a concise and comprehensive system, in which considerable improvements and corrections have been made throughout: comprising, in a plain and systematic compendium, practical lessons, illustrations, exercises, rules, questions, &c., for beginners.* n.p. 144pp.
($)

56.$ Armstrong, Joseph L. 1889. *A grammar of English: parts I and II.* Trinity College, N.C.: Trinity College Publication Society. 23cm, vii+[9]-59pp.
($ @)

57. Armstrong, Robert (English Master, Madras College, St. Andrews). 1868a. *The narrative English grammar, with exercises and questions. Illustrated.* (Chambers' Educational Course). Edinburgh: W. & R. Chambers. 8°, vi+54pp. (Anr. ed. 1878 (Chambers' Educational Course), London: Chambers, 17cm (@)).
(@ L O)
["Preparatory to the use of the more advanced *Practical English grammar* ... the illustrations introduced are designed as further aid to the Juvenile Grammarian". Eight parts of speech; sentence analysis; syntax

rules; examination papers; questions on literary passages; defective (progressive omitted) and not very precise.]

58. ---. 1868b. *The practical English grammar. With exercises and questions.* (Chambers's Educational Course). London/Edinburgh: Chambers. 17x 10, vi+120pp. (Anr. ed. 1877 (@); anr. ed. 1885, vi+122pp. (@)). ($ @ L O)
 ["Letters, words and sentences" treated in brief and not completely satisfactory definitions, with exercises; "rules of construction" (concord, government, ellipsis and arrangement of words) follows, with examination papers appended. Not a successful book. (Advertisements refer to *Introduction to English grammar*, 58pp., 6d; *English grammar and composition*, 184pp, 1s6d; *Elements of English grammar, in narrative lessons* in prep. by R. Armstrong, all in Chambers's Educational Course.)]

59. --- & Thomas Armstrong. 1858. *Introduction to English etymology.* Edinburgh: Sutherland & Knox / London: Simpkin, Marshall & Co. 19cm, 166pp.
 (L)

60. --- & ---. 1859. *Manual of etymology.* Edinburgh.
 (L)
 [Abridgment of their Introduction.]

61.! --- & ---. [a1862]. *Etymology for junior classes.* London: Robert Gordon.
 [Advertised by Robert Gordon, publisher, in 1862.]

62.$ Arnold, Helen. 1893. *Practice in parsing and analysis.* Philadelphia: J.B. Lippincott. 18cm, 69pp. (Anr. ed. 1895 (@)).
 ($ @)

63. Arnold, Rev. Thomas Kerchever (1800-1853). 1838. *An English grammar for classical schools. Etymology, by the editor of 'Eclogæ Ovidianæ'*. 2 parts. London. 18cm, 76pp. (enl. ed. ^{2}1841, with an add. of a syntax, London: J.G.F. & J. Rivington, xi+76pp.; ^{3}1843 subtitled: ... *with questions and a course of exercises: being a practical introduction to English prose composition*, 19cm, xi+143+76pp. ($ @); ^{4}1848 London (A); ^{5}1852; ^{6}1860, 19cm, vii+220pp. ($ @); ^{10}1872 as *A practical introduction to English prose composition. An English grammar for classical schools, with questions, and a course of exercises*, London etc.: Rivington, 19cm, vii+220pp. (@)).
 ($ @ A C G L O *Br, Hu, Lw*)
 [Very traditional, based on Latin structures.]

64. ---. 1853. *Henry's English grammar: a manual for beginners.* London: Rivington. 19cm, viii+219pp.
 (@ L O)

[The author was a classical and Biblical scholar of immense productivity. Very elementary exercises, increasing in difficulty; the underlying system is traditional but not made quite explicit.]

65. Arthington, Maria (of Leeds, d.1863). 1828. *The little scholar's first grammar; or grammar made easy to the capacities of young children and rendered pleasing by a variety of familiar examples; adapted to the use of private families.* London/Birmingham/Dublin/York: W. Alexander & Son. 16.5x9.5, iv+[5]-64pp., 1s.
(L O)
["Built upon the basis of L. Murray's Grammar"; OESP; "Etymology being the only part which can properly be introduced to the attention of a young child, the others are but slightly touched upon" (5) Though simplified, the grammar is still heavily dependent on traditional patterns with long lists of conjugated verb forms. Some specimens for easy parsing and questions at end.]

66. Atkin, John (Master of the Grammar School, Goole). 1845. *A practical and self-instructing English grammar, comprising the principles of that science with copiousness, perspicuity, and precision, containing various specimens of etymological and syntactical parsing; numerous exercises for correction; and copious elliptical lessons.* Hull: George Hunter. 14cm, 132pp.
(@ L O *Hu*, *Lw*)
["Interrogatory tuition being now so justly appreciated, generally taught, and universally approved, as it dismantles instruction of that mechanical irksome, and perplexing mode, and garbs it in a familiar, pleasing, and impressive style, has induced the author to adopt this plan. In order that deficiencies may be supplied and inaccuracies rectified, the author will consider it his duty to listen to critical observations." OESP, in Q/A form throughout, with a glossary of etymological explanations at end. Exercises include a great deal of false English. Ten parts of speech, six tenses - traditional pattern.]

67. Anon. 1827. *An attempt to elucidate the grammatical & critical construction of the English language; and to account for and explain various delicacies and peculiarities incident to elegant composition.* London. v+162pp.
(L)

68.! Anon. 1824. *An attempt to illustrate the rules of English grammar, and to explain the nature and uses of the several particles.* London: Longman & Co.
(*Lw*)
[An earlier form of Anon. 1827. *An attempt to elucidate* ...?]

69.$ B., J. 1869. *A primary English grammar, in familiar conversations, interspersed with object teaching, inductive and synthetic; presenting to the learner an easy mode of gradual combination; and at every step, reducing theory to practice: containing, also, analytic exercises.* Utica: Roberts. 6cm, iv+[5]-192pp.
(@)
70. B., L. (of Kensington). 1847. *The young lady's new grammar; or, A summary of the various rules of English grammar familiarly explained; with numerous exercises in etymological and syntactical parsing. By a lady.* London: James Madden. 17.5x10.5, v+105pp.
(C L O)
[OES, with parsing exercises and punctuation appended; traditional account, slightly simplified; otherwise indistinctive.]
71. Bachmaier, Anton. 1870. *Pasigraphical dictionary and grammar. (Pasigraphical English dictionary).* 2 parts. Augsburg: A. Volkhart. 188+169pp.
(@ L)
72.$ Bacon, Caleb, ed. 1818. *An epitome of the English language; or a catechetical grammar with an appendix. Being in substance Mr. Murray's English grammar put into questions and answers.* New York. 18mo, 108pp. (Anr. ed. 1819, New York: S. Marks, sold by J.A. Burtus (@); ^{5}1823 (*Br*); anr. ed. 1827 (*Br*); anr. ed. 1830 (*Br*); anr. ed. 1845).
(@ *Br*)
73.$ Badgley, Jonathan. 1837. *The principles of English grammar in familiar lectures: accompanied by amusing dialogues containing copious exercises in parsing and false syntax: adapted to the capacity of youth, and calculated to enable private learners to become their own instructors.* Whitesboro, N.Y.: the Office of the Friend of Man. 18cm, 191pp.
($ @)
74.$ ---. 1845. *An introduction to an easy practical system of philosophical grammar: unfolding the principles of our language in the inductive method, and reducing them immediately to practise by exercises for distinguishing every part of speech and each modification.* Utica, N.Y.: Bennett, Backus & Hawley. 19cm, 200pp.
($ @ *Br*)
[*Br*: "suppressed for plagiarism from G. Brown"]
75.$ ---. 1867. *English grammar, taught in plain, familiar conversations, by Uncle Jonathan.* (Pseud.). Utica: the author.
(@)

76.$ ---. 1875. *An English grammar, in familiar conversations, inductive and progressive, uniting and harmonizing theory and practice, and adapted to oral teaching.* New York: the author. 20cm, vi+[7]-384pp. (@)

77.$ ---. 1876. *A primary English grammar, adapted to oral teaching.* New York: the author. 18cm, 105pp. (@)

78.$ Bailey, Rufus William (1793-1863). 1853. *English grammar: a simple, concise, and comprehensive manual of the English language: designed for the use of schools, academies, and as book for (the) general reference in the language, in four parts.* Philadelphia: Clark & Hesser. 19cm, xv+239pp. (^{2}1853, 1854, 19cm, xv+[17]-240pp. ($ @); ^{10}1855, Philadelphia: Lippincott, Grambo & Co., 19cm, xv+[17]-239pp. ($ @); ^{10}1856 Portland, Me.: Merrill & Whitman, 19cm, xv+[17]-239pp. (@); anr. ed. 1857, 19cm, xv+[17]-240pp. ($)). ($ @)

79.$ ---. 1854. *Primary English grammar: introductory manual of the English language.* Philadelphia: Clark & Hesser. 14cm, viii+[9]-144pp. ($ @)

80. Bain, Alexander (Professor of Logic in the University of Aberdeen, 1818-1903). 1863. *An English grammar.* London. (^{2}1864, London: Longman (@); new ed. 1866, London: Longmans, Green, Reader & Dyer, 17x10, xvi+219pp., also published under title *A higher English grammar* (@); new ed. 1869 ($); rev. ed. 1872, as *A higher English grammar*, London/New York: Longman (@); ^{2}1875, 16cm; anr. ed. 1877, London; ^{3}1879, London: Longmans & Co., 17cm, xxiii+359pp. ($); anr. ed. 1879, 16cm, xvi+219pp. ($); anr. ed. 1880 (Handbooks for Students and General Readers), 16cm, xxiii+358pp. ($); anr. ed. 1891, London (A)). ($ @ A C L O)
Lit.: Anon. 1874, Williams 1973.
[A very detailed grammar containing, apart from clear definitions and appropriate illustrations, a host of insightful observations on usage (including Scotticisms) in a clear if discursive style. The great care with which the book was compiled is illustrated by the number of sources used: Bain mentions on p.v C.P. Mason, Angus, E. Adams, Latham, C.W. Connon, Crombie, Dr. Morell, O. Allen Ferris, (E. Ety), T.K. Arnold, A.J.D. D'Orsey, Brandon Turner, Matthew Harrison, H.H. Breen.]

81.$ ---. 1872a. *A brief English grammar on a logical method.* New York/London: Holt & Williams. 16cm, xii+186pp. (@). (Anr. ed. [1873],

New York: H. Holt & Co. / Boston: Schönhof & Möller ($ @); anr. ed. 1890, London: Longman & Co., 14cm (@)).
Key 1872.
($ @)

82. ---. 1872b. *A first English grammar.* London: Longmans. 14/15cm, xii+186pp. (^{3}1877, London (@); ^{4}1880, London: Longmans, Green & Co. (@); new and rev. ed. 1882, London: Longman & Co., 15cm, xii+200pp. ($ @); new and rev. ed. 1891, London: Longmans (@)).
Key 1872, with additional exercises, London: Longmans & Co., 14/15cm, 186pp.
($ @ L O)
[Preparatory explanations; seven parts of speech; syntax treated in a 'scientific' way, i.e. by definition; the small book refers back to his *Higher English grammar*; it is accompanied by a key published separately.]

83. ---. 1874a. *A companion to the Higher English grammar.* London: Longmans, Green & Co. 15.5x10, xxiv+358+16pp. (^{2}1877, London, 17/18cm, xxiv+358pp. ($ @ A)).
($ @ A L O)
[Parts of speech, derivation and syntax, discussed in somewhat discursive style, but careful reasoning and plentiful illustrations from English literature. Refers to treatises and grammars by Earle, Findlater, Latham, Lennie, Mansel, William Smith and Stoddart.]

84.$ ---. 1874b. *English grammar: as bearing upon composition.* New York: H. Holt & Co. 19/20cm, xxiv+358pp.
($)

85.! Baird, W. 1886. *An exercise book for analysis.* Belfast.
[Recorded in BL Subject Index, 1881-1900, 923\33(b), but not in present printed catalogue.]

86.$ Balch, William Stevens (1806-1887). 1829. *Inductive grammar. By an instructer.* Windsor, Vermont: S. Ide / Boston: Carter & Hendee. 15cm, vii+[7]-54pp.
(@ L)

87.$ ---. 1839. *A grammar of the English language; explained according to the principles of truth and common sense, and adapted to the capacities of all who think. Designed for the use of schools, academies, and private learners.* Boston: B.B. Mussey. 19cm, vii+140pp. (^{2}1840, 19cm, xii+160pp. ($); ^{4}1841, 19cm, xii+160pp. ($)).
($ @ L *Br*)

[Criticises current teaching of grammar; there have been 78 attempts in the USA to improve L. Murray. Advises to use reasoning, not rules; three parts of speech. Thoughtful and sensible.]
⇒ Baldwin, Edward (pseud.) - see Godwin, William, no. 643
88.$ Ballard, Harlan Hoge (1853-1934). 1878. *Words, and how to put them together*. New York: D. Appleton, 16cm, 83pp. (@). (Anr. ed. 1879, New York: D. Appleton, 16cm, 83pp. (@); ²1880 ($)).
($ @)
89. Bankes, Roden. 1898. *A story book for lesson time, or: A child's first English grammar*. London: Archibald Constable & Co. 8°, 128pp.
(L O)
[Language, parts of speech, and sentences discussed in a cramped dialogue between a teacher, a young girl and her dolls, "with information from the best school grammars now in use".]
90. Banks, William. 1823. *The English master, or student's guide to reasoning and composition. Exhibiting on analytical view of the English language, of the human mind and of the principles of fine writing*. London: Longman/Hurst, Rees, Orme & Brown. 8°, lii+399pp. (@). (²1829, London: Smith, Elder & Co., 21cm, xvi+456pp. (@)).
(@ L *Hu*, *Ma*, *Lw*)
[Devoted to philosophy, education and universal grammar, English is treated in discursive style in Part I (1-121); quite fanciful etymologies; Part II is on "Intellectual philosophy", Part III on "Composition".]
91. Barber, E. (of Glasgow), comp. [1881]. *English grammar*. Glasgow: William Collins & Co. 93x70, 14 sheets.
(L)
[Large sheets to be hung up in classrooms; rules and exercises (often insertion texts) on right side, questions on left. Only etymology and sentence analysis covered; eight parts of speech (no articles, participles); nouns used, as adjectives, as in *an iron safe*. Short definitions, generally adquate for the purpose; Latin terms accompanied by translations. There is no indication as to which grammar book should be used with the sheets.]
92.$ Bardeen, Charles William (1847-1924). 1884. *Outlines of sentence-making. A brief course in composition*. New York: A.S. Barnes. 19cm, 187pp.
($)
93.$ Barnard, Frederick Augustus Porter (President of Columbia University, 1809-1889). 1836. *Analytic grammar; with symbolic illustration*. New York: E. French. 12mo, 264pp.
(@ L *Br*, *Lw*)

[The elaborate, coherent but impractical symbolism is derived from the teaching of the deaf and dumb. *NUC* adds "The author, who was president of Columbia University the last twenty-five years of his life, suffered from hearing impairment and was a teacher in the American Institution for the Deaf and Dumb at Hartford and in the New York Institution for the Deaf and Dumb."]

94.$ Barnard, Samuel (of Philadelphia). 1825. *A polyglot grammar of the Hebrew, Chaldee, Syriac, Greek, Latin, English, French, Italian, Spanish, and German languages, reduced to one common rule of syntax and an uniform mode of declension and conjugation as far as practible.* Philadelphia: Abraham Small. 23cm, 312pp.
(@ L)
[The impractibility of the plan described in the title is apparent; as far as the traditional OESP account considers English, its explanatory value is slight.]

95.$ Anon. 1887. *Barnes' working lessons in English, or, Short studies parts II & III.* New York: A.S. Barnes & Co./American Book Co. 20cm, 147pp.
($ @)

96. Barnes, William (Dorsetshire poet, 1801-1886). 1840. *An investigation of the laws of case in language, exhibited in a system of natural cases; with some observations on prepositions, tense, and voiced, being, as it is conceived, the first step towards a system of universal grammar.* London: Longman/Whittaker/Hamilton & Adams. 18x10, 49pp.
(L)
[A kind of universal case grammar based on the author's comparison of twelve to fourteen languages; speculative in mixing deep and surface categories.]

97. ---. 1842. *The elements of English grammar, with a set of questions and exercises.* London/Dorchester: Longman. 15cm, viii+112pp.
($ L O *Br*)
[An unassuming, but competent and clearly expressed summary of traditional concepts (OESP), focusing on "the common principles of articulation, derivation, case and mood" (vi).]

98. ---. 1854. *A philological grammar, grounded upon English, and formed from a comparison of more than sixty languages. Being an introduction to the science of grammar, and a help to grammars of all languages, especially English, Latin, and Greek.* London: John Russell Smith. 8°, x+312pp.
(C L *Sk*)

[Highly speculative - as any attempt based on 60 languages is likely to be: a curiosity.]

99. ---. 1878. *An outline of English speech-craft*. London: Kegan Paul. 19x 12.5, viii+92pp.
($ @ L Nc)
[The grammar is neither systematic nor comprehensive. Barnes focuses on individual phenomena from pronunciation, lexis and syntax stressing topics like ambiguity, transparency, logic and etymological correctness, using evidence from comparative philology (especially other Germanic languages, Welsh and Greek). Much of the fascination of the book lies in Barnes' attempt to avoid loanwords as far as possible, coining more than a hundred replacements from 'Saxon' roots - not all of these convincing. The second half of the book (47-83) is taken up by a list of some 300 of his coinages entered after the Latinate headword (a complementary list of 'Saxon' headwords would have been helpful).

100. Barnett, Percy Arthur (Principal of Borough Road Training College, b.1858). 1893. *The new Morell: being a grammar of the English language, together with an exposition of the analysis of sentences, based on the work of the late J.D. Morell*. London: Allman & Sons. 18.5x11.5, viii+256pp.
(O)
[Stresses the new insights gained by comparative Isleworth philology and phonology and revisions made under 'verb'; the OESP pattern of Morell is otherwise retained. A comparison of the 'Old' and 'New' Morell would be necessary to test the author's claims as to innovation; for 1893, the revision looks quite traditional. "Selection from examination papers" (set for various groups of students) are appended, pp. 231-56.]

101.$ Barrett, John (Teacher of the Greek, Latin & English Languages). 1813. *A grammar of the English language containing a variety of critical remarks, the principal part of which are original*. n.p. 15cm, 108pp. ($) (²1819, Boston: the author. 14x8, viii+214pp. ($)).
($ L *Br*)
[Relies on Latin for parsing English. OESP, ten parts of speech, very traditional, barren definitions. No sources mentioned apart from "Mr Adam's Latin Grammar".]

102.$ Barrett, Solomon Jr. 1837. *The principles of language: containing a full grammatical analysis of English poetry, confirmed by syllogistical reasoning and logical induction; with corrections in syntax, and copious examples in prosody*. Albany: O. Steele. 19cm, ix+120pp. ($). (Anr. ed. 1840 ($); anr. ed. 1842, titled as *The principles of language: The self instructor containing a full grammatical analysis of English poetry, with*

corrections in syntax and examples in prosody, on the inductive system of reason and philosophy accompanied by a plate and illustrations, 132pp. ($); rev. ed. [10]1845, as *The principles of English grammar, or, The self instructor: being a treatise on the constructive principles of the language. Showing the actual relation which the words and sections sustain to each other on inductive principles. Thereby enabling the student to parse and correct every word, and punctuate every sentence in the language*, Utica: R.W. Roberts, 16cm, viii+[9]-96pp. (@)).
($ @ L *Br*)
[Too much pretentious theory. Three primary parts of speech (noun, verb, interjection) and six secondary ones. Good literary passages extravagantly coded for parsing.]

103.$ ---. 1845. *The principles of grammar: being a compendious treatise on the languages, English, Latin, Greek, German, Spanish, and French. Founded on the immutable principle of the relation which one words sustains to another*. n.p. (Anr. ed. 1848, Albany: J. Munsell, 19/20cm, 204/3-312pp. ($ @); rev. ed. 1849 (@); anr. ed. 1849, 20cm, 240pp. ($ @); anr. ed. 1850 (from 1848 ed.), 20cm, 239pp. ($); rev. ed. 1851 (from 1848 ed.), Philadelphia: King & Baird, 20cm, 312pp. ($ @); rev. ed. 1852, Philadelphia: King & Baird (@); rev. ed. 1854, Cambridge, Mass.: Metcalf, 407pp. (@); rev. ed. 1855, Cambridge, 3 p.l., 20cm, 3-312pp. (@); rev. ed. 1856, Cambridge, 20cm, 407pp. (@); rev. ed. 1857, 20cm, 407pp. (@); anr. ed. 1857, 552pp. ($); rev. ed. 1858, Boston: Geo C. Rand & Avery, 22cm, 552pp. ($); rev. ed. 1859, Boston (@); rev. ed. 1860 (from 1848 ed.), Boston, 23cm, xii+576pp. ($ @); rev ed. 1861, Boston (@); rev. ed. 1862, Boston (@); rev. ed. 1863 *with polyglot arrangement of a part of the Gospel of Matthew, and: International and commercial dictionary*, pt. 2, Boston/Buffalo, 8° (@); rev. ed. 1865, Boston, 312pp. (@); anr. ed. 1866, 20cm, 576pp. ($); rev. ed. 1868 (from 1848 ed.), Boston: J. Bradley & Co., 22cm, xii+576pp. ($ @); rev. ed. 1872 ($ @); rev. ed. 1873, New York, 23cm, 236pp. (@)).
($ @ L)
[It is uncertain whether the book consists of two parts 312+240=552pp. Also there are a couple of double eds. in one year. The history of the book needs further investigation. Eight parts of speech; for adults; rather naive.]

104.$ ---. 1858. *A new inductive grammar of the English language: founded entirely on the principle of relations*. Boston: Higgins, Bradley & Dayton. (Anr. ed. 1859, 20cm, 236pp. ($)).
($ @)

105.$ ---. 1876. *A signal grammar of the English language for the use of all classes of learners and grades of schools.* New York: Press of Pinckney Brothers. xxv+80+112pp.
(@)
106. entry deleted
107. ---. 1800. *The tyro's guide to wisdom and wealth, designed for the moral instruction of the youth. With exercises in spelling intended as an introduction to the author's collection, to which are now subjoined the principles of English grammar.* n.p. (Gj). (^{2}1802 Edinburgh (L); ^{3}1804, Edinburgh (*Tm*); ^{4}1807 (E); ^{5}1808, Edinburgh. (A); ^{9}1815, Edinburgh: J. Moir, pr. for P. Hill, 252pp. (@ G)).
(@ A E G Gj L *Tm*)
[It is not clear to which edition the grammatical material was first added.]
108. Bartle, Rev. George W. (Principal of Freshfield College, Formby, Liverpool). 1858. *An epitome of English grammar. Intended for schools and private families.* London: Piper, Stephenson & Spence / Liverpool: Edward Howell. 14cm, iv+76pp.
(L O)
[Rudimentary, in Q/A form, ES only; some rules; miscellaneous observations and punctuation at end. The author tried "to hold the substance and reject the shadow; to keep the corn and reject the chaff".]
109. ---. 1878. *A new grammar of the English language with the principles of analysis. Expressly designed for students preparing for the Oxford and Cambridge local examinations, the civil service, and other competitive tests; and also for the use of colleges, schools, and private families.* Edinburgh, etc.: Thomas Laurie. 8°, 208pp. (new ed. 1879, London: Longmans, 16cm, 208pp. (@)).
(@ L O)
[OESP, eight parts of speech (formerly reckoned nine), rules and many notes for exceptions with lists of Anglo-Saxon, Latin and Greek stems (107-40); deliberate omission of "progressive exercises".]
110.$ Bartlett, Albert Le Roy (1852-1934). 1899a. *The essentials of language and grammar.* (The Silver Series of Language Books). New York/ Boston: Silver, Burdett & Co. 20cm, 318pp. (Anr. ed. 1900, 332pp. (@)).
($ @)
111.$ ---. 1899b. *First steps in English.* (The Silver Series of Language Books). New York/Boston: Silver, Burdett & Co. 20cm, 173pp.
($)
112.! Bartlett, B.R. 1872. *English grammar.* London: Allman. 32pp.

(*Al*)
[cf. Alwall 1974:165]

113.$ Bartlett, Montgomery Robert. 1827. *The common school manual: a regular and connected course of elementary studies: embracing the necessary and useful branches of a common education compiled from the latest and most approved authors.* (called in the Third or Philadelphia Edition *The national school manual.*) Utica: W. Williams, Northway & Bennett. 4 vols. 19cm. ($). (Anr. ed. 1830, New York: the author, 19cm, 300pp. ($ @); anr. ed. n.d., New York, 19cm, I:103pp., II:302pp., III:379pp., IV:450-500pp. (*Br*)).
($ @ *Br*)
[*Br*: "A miserable jumble, in the successive pages of which, Grammar is mixed up with Spelling-columns, Reading-lessons, Arithmetic, Geometry, and the other supposed daily tasks of a school-boy!"]

114.$ Barton, John Graeff. 1855. *An outline of the general principles of grammar. With a brief exposition of the chief idiomatic peculiarities of the English language.* New York: Harper & Brothers. 16.5x10.5, (vii)-xii+[13]-155pp. (Enl. ed. 1856, New York: Harper, xii+[13]-155pp. ($ L); anr. ed. 1867 ($)).
($ L)
[The book is in three parts: an introduction (13-33, mainly devoted to style and historical texts) is followed by sections on universal grammar (34-47), before English grammar is treated (48-137). This concentrates on parts of speech, especially the verb (67-110), followed by syntax (116-37: traditional and somewhat Latinate). Questions are appended, referring back to individual pages (139-55). Not quite coherent and not always clear; impaired by frequent comparisons with Old English and Latin categories. Cf. no. 1353.]

115.$ Barton, William Sumner (1824-1899). 1855. *A new system of English grammar, progressively arranged: concisely embodying the principles of analysis and synthesis.* (Intermediate Grammar). n.p. 19/20cm, 256pp. (Rev. ed. ^{5}1859, Boston: Gould & Lincoln / New York: Sheldon ($ @); anr. ed. 1860 ($)).
($ @)

116.$ ---. 1859. *Easy lessons in English grammar for young beginners.* n.p. 20cm, 152pp. (Anr. ed. 1860, Boston: Gould & Lincoln (@); anr. ed. 1871 (35th hundred), Boston: Gould & Lincoln (@)).
($ @)

117.$ ---. 1859. *High school grammar, or, An exposition of the grammatical structure of the English language.* n.p. (Anr. ed. 1860, 2nd thousand, Montgomery, Ala.: Teachers' Exchange, 20cm, 373pp. ($ @); anr. ed.

1860, Boston: Gould & Lincoln / New York: Sheldon & Co. (@); anr. ed. 1862, Boston: Gould & Lincoln (@)).
($ @)

118.$ Baskervill, William Malone (1850-1899) & Sewell, J.W. 1895. *An English grammar for the use of high school, academy and college classes*. n.p. (Anr. ed. 1896, New York, etc.: American Book Co. 394pp.).
($)

119. Baskerville, Alfred. 1859. *An English grammar for the use of Germans*. Cologne: M. Dumont-Schauberg. 22.5x13.5, vi+170pp. (^{2}1866, viii+182pp. (@)).
(@ L)
[PronES on a contrastive level, with Latin grammar shining through; some specimens accompanied by translations into German. No sources given.]

120.$ Bates, Edward P. 1862. *English analysis: containing forms for the complete analysis of English composition, together with selections for analysis from the best English authors: designed to accompany the study of English grammar in high and grammar schools*. Boston: Crosby & Nichols. 20cm, 107pp.
($ @)

121. Bathurst, Charles (Under-Master of Sir J. Williamson's Free School, Rochester). 1846. *Outlines of English grammar, for the use of schools*. Rochester/London: H.V. Scriven. 12°, 71pp.
(L O)
[Letters, nine parts of speech (note 'adjective pronouns'), stops, syntax (= concord, government); exemplifications are glossed for hard words. Unsatisfactory, for local use.]

122. Bayley, R.S. 1843. *The textbook of the People's College on English grammar, for the use of students*. Sheffield: People's College. 34pp.
(Sp)

123.$ Bazeley, Charles W. 1835. *The juvenile scholar's English grammar: in which the principles of the language are methodically digested into plain and easy rules ... To which are added .. some easy parsing lessons, as an exemplification of the rules with a synopsis of rhetoric, and logic, and a glossary of the grammatical terms: for the exercises of the learner ...* Brooklyn: the author. 15/16cm, 240/285pp.
($)

124. Beach, George. 1891. *The elements of English*. London?: J. Hughes. iv+257pp.
(L)

[Contains "a whole apparatus of official questions, a complete series of model answers, and a considerable number of government papers." Drearily conventional.]
125. ---. [1898]. *Dr. Beach's scholar's grammar, for the upper standards of primary schools. Contains everything required, including accidence, analysis, composition, parsing, prefixes, affixes, and examination questions.* Luton: The School Teacher Publishing Co. 17.5x11, 33pp. 3s2d.
(L)
[Succinct definitions of forms and functions of parts of speech leading on to parsing; word-formation with native and foreign elements. Exercises at end. Not original, but generally competent as far as the short treatment allowed.]
126. Beal, William J. [1894]. *Exercises for parsing, analysis and paraphrasing.* 2 parts. (Brown's School Series). Hull.
(L)
127.$ Beale, Solon. 1833. *The child's first book of grammar.* Bangor, Maine. 18mo, 27pp.
($ Br)
[The book was published anonymously, but is attributed by Goold Brown to Solon Beale, and the Columbia University copy agrees.]
128.$ Beall, Alexander. 1841. *Beall's new grammar. English grammar on the analytic and inductive method of instruction designed for the use of schools and private learners.* Cincinnati, Ohio: Kendall & Barnard. 19cm, 241pp.
($ @ Br)
129.! Beard, George. 1826. *An introduction to grammar, with notes.* Taunton. (Green 1902:II.151.)
130. Beard, John Relly. 1854. *(Cassell's) lessons in English; containing a practical grammar, adapted for the use of the self-educating student ... From the "Popular educator".* (Cassell's Educational Works). London: John Cassell, Petter & Galpin. 17x10, vi+342pp.
(@ L)
[Although the book contains general reflections and has (slightly speculative) treatments of the major fields of grammar, the greater part is taken up by lexis, esp. unreliable etymologies. In the grammar sections, historical and comparative evidence is always present so that the author does not arrive at a coherent description of 19th-century grammar.]
131. entry deleted
132.! Beaumont, John. 1871. *The syntactical structure of sentences.* n.p. [Edinburgh or London]: Chambers.
(Mp)

133. ---. ²1872. *The grammatical looking-glass, improved.* Manchester: A. Heywood. 18cm, 32pp.
(@)

134. Beaumont, John (Head Master of Kirkwall Burgh Schools). 1875. *Analysis of sentences.* Edinburgh: John Menzies. 56pp.
(O)
[Rules followed by copious exercises; appendix (39-56) is on etymology; eight parts of speech; matter which "a boy should have committed to memory by... the Fifth Standard".]

135.! Beck, William. [a1829]. *Outline of English grammar.* London. 34pp. (³1829).
(*Br*)

136. Bedford, Edward Henslowe. 1873-4. *A digest of the preliminary [law] examination questions in English grammar, history, geography, Latin grammar, arithmetic and French grammar. With the answers.* 2 parts. Pt. 1: *English grammar.* Pt. 2: *Latin grammar.* London: Stevens & Sons. 8°, 98pp. (Anr. ed. 1875, London: Stevens & Sons, 421pp. (L); ²1882, London: Stevens & Sons, 23cm, viii+635pp. (@ L)).
(@ L O)

137. Bedford, Frederick William. 1852. *Basis of English grammar for the use of schools.* (Elementary School Series). London: Millington, Webb & Co. 14x9, iv+41pp. (Ster. ed. 1852, sixth thousand, London/Yorkshire: J.S. Pub. & Stationary Co. (@)).
(@ L)
[ES; Inflexion fully treated and "rules of Syntax (...) classified in a novel manner". Traditional account: rules, questions, no footnotes or exceptions noted. Of no original value.]

138. ---. 1858. *Canons of punctuation, based on the analysis of sentences.* London: Nelson.
(L)

139.$ Beecher, Catharine Esther (1800-1878). 1829. *Exercises in grammar: prepared for the use of the Hartford Female Seminary.* Hartford, Conn. 19cm, 49pp. (Anr. ed. 1829, 19cm, 74pp. ($ *Br*)).
($ *Br*)

140.$ Beede, Samuel. 1831. *Questions, designed to assist the pupil in acquiring a knowledge of English grammar, particularly adapted to Putnam's grammar.* Concord: Hoag & Attwood. 12pp.
(@ L)
[The booklet is also appended to Putnam 1831, no. 1462.]

141. Belcher, William. ²1813. *Observations on the use of the words shall and will, chiefly designed for foreigners and persons educated at a distance*

from the metropolis, and also for the use of schools, containing XXXV rules. Canterbury: the author. 17x10, 60pp.
(L)
[Belcher argues that "the Verb, in itself, forms the cement of Language, and may be considered as the basis of Grammatical Construction" (1815:4). This and the apparent difficulties in usage, lead him to concentrate fully on this one part of grammar. The three books by Belcher, of the same format, are bound together in B.L.236.c.3]

142. ---. 1814. *Remarks on the incidental ambiguities and false imports, attendant on the use of the auxiliary signs in the English language, the whole being designed to facilitate the acquisition of correctness in this most difficult part of the English language.* Canterbury: the author. 16.5x9.5, 47pp.
(L)
[Almost exclusively devoted to the usage of *will/shall, would/could,* with errors pointed out in eminent writers. Part of a larger discussion of *A grammar of the English verb* (see no. 143).]

143. ---. 1815. *A grammar of the English verb, founded on the remarks already published by the same author, on the auxiliary signs.* 2 parts. Canterbury. 17x10, 12+11pp.
(L *Sk*)

144.$ Bell, Goodloe Harper (1832-1899). 1881. *Natural method in English: consisting of a series of graded lessons for the use of schools. Arranged for the convenience of teachers, and especially adapted to private study.* Battle Creek, Mich.: Student's Publishing Committee. 21cm, xvi+416pp. (^{2}1882, Battle Creek: Giles & Nelson, 416pp. (@); anr. ed. 1887, 21cm, xvi+416pp. ($); anr. ed. 1893, 21cm, 416pp. ($)).
($ @)

145.$ ---. 1882. *Guide to correct language: a book of ready reference in three parts. Pt. I: Practical grammar ... Pt. II: Punctuation ... Pt. III: Use of capitals.* Battle Creek, Mich.: the author. 24cm, 98pp. (rev. and enl. ed. 1886, Battle Creek, Mich.: the author, 24cm, 111pp. ($ @); anr. ed. 1895, 112pp. ($)).
($ @)

146.$ ---. 1885. *Familiar talks on language: a special work on practical & theoretical grammar, carefully adapted to a shorter course of private study.* (Pocket Ed., 1). Battle Creek, Mich.: D.O. Bell. 16cm, viii+203pp.
($)

147.$ ---. 1896a. *Complete grammar*. (Bell's Language Series, Book 3). Chicago, Ill./Battle Creek, Mich.: International Tract Society. 20cm, viii+281pp.
($ @)

148.$ ---. 1896b. *Elementary grammar*. (Bell's Language Series, Book 2). Chicago, Ill./Battle Creek, Mich.: International Tract Society. 20cm, viii+224pp.
($)

149.$ ---. 1896c. *Grammar manual: to accompany Bell's 'Natural method in English'*. n.p. viii+224pp.
($)

150.$ ---. 1898. *Primary language lessons from life, nature, and revelation*. (Bell's Language Series, Book 1). Battle Creek, Mich./Chicago, Ill.: Review & Herald Publishing Co. 20cm, 272pp.
($ @)

151.! Bellamy, Elizabeth. 1802. *English grammar*. London. 12mo.
(*Br*)

152.$ Benedict, H.T.N. 1820. *An epitome of the American common school grammar, containing such alterations and emendations as forty years' experience in teaching and a critical analysis of the production of authors, ancient and modern, have suggested; adapted to the author's inductive system of instruction*. Louisville: Kellog. 16cm, 152pp. (Undated ed. Louisville, Ky. ($)).
($ @)

153.$ ---. 1832. *Murray's English grammar, revised, simplified and adapted to the inductive and explanatory mode of instruction*. Frankfort, Ky.: A.G. Hodges.
(@)

154. Benson, Wilfrid (Vicar of Leaton). 1900. *The preparatory English grammar*. London: G. Bell. 17x11, iv+51pp., 8d.
(O)
[Grammar is here reduced to a definition of parts of speech and inflexion, with a short section on parsing and analysis and a few exercises at end. Disappointing; it is remarkable that such a book had a market in 1900, even with 'preparatory' in its title.]

155.$ Berry, Jacob (1834-1881). 1871. *A parsing book, or analysis and parsing in tabular forms: with examples for practice*. n.p. 17cm, 84pp. (Anr. ed. 1877 ($)).
($)

156. Best, D.J. ³n.d. *Difficulties of English grammar removed*. n.p.
(Lm)

157. Best, Hon. Samuel. [a1852]. *Elementary grammar for the use of village schools*. London. (^{3}1852; ^{4}1857, London: Darling etc., 14cm, viii+[9]-72pp. (@); ^{5}1862).
(@ L Lm O)
[Conventional, Latinate and lordly: "The classically educated man cannot ... so ignore his education as to address a congregation in the jargon and patois of the village ... We may and ought to raise them to our standard; we cannot, without profaneness in sacred things, descend to theirs."]

158.$ Bethune, Joanna (Graham) (1770-1860). 1830. *The infant school grammar, consisting of elementary lessons in the analytical method, illustrated by sensible objects and actions*. New York: Jonathan Seymour. 18mo. 132pp. (^{2}1832, New York: sold by R. Lockwood & A.W. Corey, 15cm, x+12+9-140pp. (@)).
(@ L *Br*)
["The cuts are copied from an English work by the Rev. Ingham Cobham", i.e. Ingham Cobbin. p.x. *NUC* adds "Originally composed for Infant School no. 1 in New York."]

159.! Anon. [a1845]. *The Bible word-book; or, The rudiments of English grammar taught by the words of the Old and New Testament, classed according to the parts of speech, and arranged according to the number of syllables*. London. (^{2}1845).
[Advertised in Bennett George Johns, *Hints to teachers of the children of the poor*, 1845.]

160. Bidlake, John Purdue. 1863. *A new English grammar, comprising the substance of Lennie's Principles of English grammar, with extensive alterations and improvements, and additional chapters on derivation, analysis and composition*. London: T.J. Allman. 14x9, 216pp.
(L O)
[Revision of Lennie, incorporating Sullivan, Keane, Mason, Morell, Angus. OESP, nine parts of speech, parsing. Syntax consisting of analysis, composition and punctuation. Many exercises. No independent value apparent.]

161. ---. [1884]. *The Oxford and Cambridge examiner, English grammar, parsing and analysis, comprising the Oxford and Cambridge examination papers from 1858 to the present, and a selection from the papers of the Royal College of Preceptors. [With] Answers to the Oxford and Cambridge English grammar*. (Publ. anonymously). London. 16/18cm.
(O)

162. ---. [1887]. *Answers to the Oxford and Cambridge and College of Preceptors examination questions in English grammar, parsing and analysis*. London: Allman & Son. 8°, 167pp.

(L O)
163. Biggs, Charles Henry Walker. 1871. *The class and home-lesson book of English grammar.* London: T.J. Allmann. 16°, 72pp.
(L O)
[OE, words, S, composition; unoriginal brief account, includes exercises and questions.]
164.$ Biglow, William (1773-1844). 1800. *The child's library.* Salem, Mass.: Joshua Cushing. 15cm.
(@)
[Second part containing a selection of lessons for spelling, reading and speaking.]
165.$ ---. 1802. *The rudiments of English grammar.* n.p. 35pp.
($)
166.$ Bigsby, Bernard. 1874. *Elements of the English language: an introduction to the study of grammar and composition. For common schools.* n.p. 17cm, xiv+155pp.
($)
167.$ Bingham, Caleb (1757-1817). 1808. *The young scholar's accidence, or, A short introduction to the English grammar: collected and abridged from the most celebrated modern authors.* n.p. 15cm, 54pp.
($)
168.$ Bingham, William (1835-1873). 1867. *A grammar of the English language: for the use of schools and academies. With copious parsing examples.* Philadelphia: E.H. Butler. 19cm, 207pp. ($ @). (Anr. ed. 1868 (@); anr. ed. 1870 ($); anr. ed. 1871 ($ @)).
($ @)
[Cf. no. 705]
169. Binns, John (Schoolmaster) & Thomas Coar. 1800. *An essay towards an English grammar for Ackworth School.* York: T. Wilson & R. Spence. 17x10, ii+27pp.
(B C L)
[A part of a larger work composed for Ackworth School". Almost exclusively on parts of speech (prescriptive, elementary) with a few rules on concord added. Condensing what "is needful to be committed to the memory"; very basic rules, with exceptions in footnotes; based on (?). *A grammar of the English tongue.* London: James Phillips. 1796.]
170. Binns, John (1772-1860). [7]1802. *Exercises, instructive and entertaining, in false English: written with a view to perfect youth in their mother tongue: as well as to enlarge their ideas in general: and give them a relish for what is ornamental, useful and good.* Leeds. (N). ([10]1803, Leeds (L^M); [11]1805, Leeds, 18cm, viii+111pp. ($ L); anr. ed. 1806,

17cm, viii+111pp. ($); [12]1808, Leeds (L); [13]1809; [14]1811; [15]1813; [18]1823; [20]1831; [21]1841; [22]n.d. London).

($ L^M N)

171.$ Black, James. 1829. *Little grammarian, or, an easy guide to the parts of speech: designed for the young person in general, but more particularly adapted to facilitate instruction in preparatory schools (By a teacher).* (Publ. anonymously). n.p. 16cm, 108pp. ([2]1829, Boston: Munroe & Francis, 18mo, 108pp. ($ @)).

($ @ Br)

172.$ Blackmar, J. [3]1847. *A practical grammar of the English language: designed to amuse the curious and to benefit all. This work corrects several hundred improprieties in common conversation.* Providence, R.I.: J.F. Moore. 15cm, 36pp.

($)

173. Blackwood, William (and sons). [1889]. *Blackwoods' English grammar and analysis. Standard II (-VII).* 10 parts. London/Edinburgh: William Blackwood & Sons. 17x10.5, II:24pp., 1.5d; III: 32pp, 1.5d; III Scotch Code: 32pp., 1.5d; IV: 48pp., 2d; IV Scotch Code: 56pp., 2.5d; V: 64pp., 3d; V Scotch Code: 56pp., 2.5d; VI: 64pp., 3d; VI Scotch Code: 64pp., 3d; VII: 64pp., 3d.

(L O)

[The series builds up grammatical competence in steps explained in the inner covers: II "Recognize nouns and verbs", III "further on parts of speech", IV "the parsing of single words", combined with analysis, IV Scotch and V "grammar and analysis", V Scotch and IV "The complex sentence", VI Scotch and VII "Compound sentences, word-formation, Latin and Greek elements". Carefully geared to the English and Scotch codes, the booklets provide traditional, prescriptive and generally reliable rules and definitions with plenty of exercises (some of which use Scottish examples in the Scotch versions).]

⇒ Blair, David (pseud.) - see Phillips, Richard nos. 1403 & 1408

174.$! Blair, John. 1831. *English grammar.* Philadelphia. 12mo, 145pp.

(Br)

175.$ Blaisdale, Silas. 1831. *Murray's English grammar.* Boston: Marsh, Capin & Lyon. 18mo, 88pp.

(@ Br)

176.$ Blanchard, Rufus (1821-1904). 1853. *The grammatical tree showing the classification and properties of English parts of speech.* New York: J.H. Colton. 1 sheet.

($)

177. Blezard, Robert & R. Thompson (both of Guisborough). [1856]. *Textbook of English grammar, for the use of schools.* London: Judd & Glass. iv+39, 14x9, 9d.
(L)
[Words and sentences instead of OESP, eight parts of spech. Attempts to combine brevity and simple phrasing with moderately new methods. A misleading list of roots (25-38) to suggest universal stems to which inflexions are added.]

178.$ Bliss, Leonard Jr. (1811-1842). 1839. *A comprehensive grammar of the English language: introductory lessons.* Louisville, Ky.: Morton & Griswold. 16cm, 73pp. (^{2}1840 as *A practical grammar of the English language: introductory lessons,* (Comprehensive School Series), Louisville, Ky.: Morton & Griswold (@)).
(@ Br)

179.$ Boardman, John. 1825. *English grammar, methodically arranged and familiarly explained; containing exercises adapted, with violations, to the rules of syntax; and a key to the exercises. Designed for the use of private learners as well as for the use of schools.* Richmond, Va.: the author. 144pp.
($ @)

180. Bobbit, A. 1833. *Elements of English grammar: familiarly illustrated, for the use of young people.* London: John Souter. 12mo, viii+136pp.
(C L Br, Sk)
["In a colloquial form, suited to the capacities of junior classes" - an elementary grammar, traditional, with rules interspersed with questions and answers; largely a catechism, with a few exercises appended; no scholarly interest.]

181. Bond, Francis (Head-Master of the Hull and East Riding College). [1893]. *An introduction to English grammar and analysis.* (Arnold's School Series). London: Edward Arnold. 17cm, viii+166pp.
(L O)
[Parts of speech, inflexion, analysis of simple and complex sentences; the alphabet, structure of words, punctuation, etymology and syntax, (inductive) parsing relegated to appendices. Six parts of speech (substantive = noun, pronoun; interjection not really part of a sentence). Attention given to method, yet some doubtful solutions proposed.]

182. Bonthron, William (Schoolmaster of Kilrenny). 1845. *Elements of English grammar, for the use of junior classes.* Edinburgh: Oliver & Boyd, for the author. 15cm, 24pp.
(O)
[Rudimentary ES, with footnotes, and appendix with additional material.]

182a. Bonwick, James (Inspector of denominational schools, Victoria). 1857. *First grammar for young Australians*. Melbourne: Goodhugh & Gough. 13.5x8.5cm, 37pp. (Anr. ed. ²1858).
(L)
[Intended "for junior classes at schools, and as a mother's help for children at home", this modest booklet (in a series of items called "X for young Australians") is remarkable as an early colonial publication. Nine parts of speech discussed in language considered appropriate for very young pupils; verbs treated very extensively (20-34).]

183.! Anon. 1813. *A book case of instruction*. 10 vols. London: John Wallis. (Vol. 10 *Grammar* 1813).
(*Gu*)
[cf. Gumuchian (1967: No.800)]

184.! Anon. 1801. *The book case of knowledge. Vol. 8, grammar and letters*. London: John Wallis.
(*Gu*)
[cf. Gumuchian (1967: No.801)]

185. Booth, David (1766-1845). ²1814. *Introduction to an analytical dictionary of the English language ... containing a new grammar of the language ...* London: Gale, Curtis & Fenner. 21cm, 158+xpp., 8s. (Anr. ed.? [1822] (@); anr. ed. 1830 (from [1822] ed.), London: J. & C. Adlard, 30cm (@ O); anr. ed. 1835, London: J. Cochrane & Co., 29x23, vii+ccxxii+455pp.; cor. ed. 1836, ... *with an appendix on the metaphorical genders of English substantives*, London: Simpkin, Marshall & Co. (@)).
($ @ L O)
["Originally announced for publication in twelve successive parts, six of which are here produced. These, though not including the whole of the English vocabulary, complete a volume that ... may be ... consulted as an independent work." - Pref. Contains (pp. i-ccxxx) "a new grammar of the language". The introduction discusses the classification of letters, of words and various syntactical features (auxiliary verbs, the future tense and *shall/will*, moods, individual parts of speech, and derivation in discursive style - only partially a grammar of English.) (cf. revised ed., no. 186).]

186. ---. 1837. *The principles of English grammar*. London: Charles Knight. 19cm, viii+343pp.
($ L O *Hu, Br, Lw*)
["In the composition of this work, I have made liberal use of the Introduction to my Analytical Dictionary. I have borrowed very little from any other source". Letters and sounds, parts of speech individually

treated; very short on syntax (concord and government, ellipses, 313-43). The book is a revision of no. 185.]

187.$ Booth, E. R. 1889. *Practical English for intermediate and high schools and teachers' institutes. Pt. I: Pronunciation. Pt. II: Spelling. Pt. III: Lexicology. Pt. IV: Etymology. Pt. V: Syntax. Pt. VI: Composition. Pt. VII: Literature.* Chicago: A. Flanagan. 20cm, 313pp. (@). (Anr. ed. 1890, 20cm ($)).
($ @)

188.! Bowden, Thomas Adolphus (Late Government Inspector of Schools, 1825-1906). [c1876]. *An English grammar for beginners with analysis and exercises.* Wellington: T.A. Bowden & Sons. 15cm, 61pp. (Anr. ed. [c1888] (Bowden's Explicit Series), Christchurch: Whitcombe & Tombs, 64pp.).
(Colin McGeorge p.c.)

189.! ---. [c1876]. *Key to English grammar for beginners with analysis and exercises.* Wellington: T.A. Bowden & Sons. 15.5cm, 45pp.
(Colin McGeorge p.c.)

190. Bowen, Francis. 1873. *English parsing and the analysis of simple sentences simplified. Suited to the requirements of the higher standards of the New Code of Education (1871).* Manchester: John Heywood / London: Kent. 16x10, 56pp., 8d.
(L)
[Minimal definitions, exercises (also for 'home lessons') reduce competence to mechanical application.]

191. Bowen, Herbert Courthope (Head Master of the Grocer's Company's Schools, Hackney Down, 1833-94). 1879. *English grammar for beginners.* London: Kegan Paul & Co. 17cm, 124pp. (Anr. ed. 1880 (@)).
(@ L O)
[On words, classes of words, sentences, inflexion and functions of words in syntax, parsing - all in a narrative style, with definitions, in bold, interspersed; well-meant, but not well arranged, or precise.]

192.$ Boyd, James Robert (1804-1890). 1860. *Elements of English composition, grammatical, rhetorical, logical, and practical. Prepared for academies and schools.* New York: A.S. Barnes & Burr. 19cm, 406pp. (Anr. ed. [c1867], New York/Chicago: A.S. Barnes & Co. (@); anr. ed. 1868, New York (@); anr. ed. 1869, New York (@); anr. ed. 1871 (@); anr. ed. 1874 (@); anr. ed. 1876 (@); anr. ed. [1888] (@)).
($ @)

193.$ Brace, Joab Jr. (Grammarian). 1839. *The principles of English grammar ... With copious exercises in parsing and syntax. Arranged on the princi-*

ples of Lennie's grammar. Philadelphia: H. Perkins / Boston: Perkins & Marvin. 16cm, 144pp. (Anr. ed. 1840, Boston: Nes & Dennet ($ @)). *Key* 1840 Philadelphia: Henry Perkins / Boston: Nes & Bennet, 16cm, 108pp. (@ L).
($ @ L *Br*)
[*Br*: "vile theft from Lennie". Nine parts of speech; syntax rules; exercises in false English, for correction. Scarcely improves Lennie.]

194.$ Bradbury, Charles W. 1856. *First lessons in English grammar, with a new and comprehensive arrangement of the verb*. Boston: Higgins & Bradley. 25x19, 123pp.
($ @)

195.$ Bradford, Henry M. (Headmaster of St. Andrew's School, Annapolis, N.S., Late Foundation Scholar of St. John's College Cambridge, 21st Wrangler, 1886). 1899. *Notes on grammar*. Halifax, N.S.: A. & W. Mackinlay. 18x12.5, vi+32pp.
(L)
["The basis of a series of lessons for junior classes" ... "very little knowledge is required for ordinary parsing and analysis." Traditional, selective and not well arranged, successful parsing being the only aim.]

196. Bradley, Charles (Vicar of Glasbury and Principal of Wallingford School, 1789-1871). 1809. *Grammatical questions adapted to the grammar of Lindley Murray: with notes*. Banbury: J. Rusher. vii+82pp. (^{2}1810, York: T. Wilson & Son / London: Longman & Co., 18cm, xi+107pp. ($ @); ^{3}1813, London: Longman, Hurst, Rees, Orme & Brown / York: Wilson & Sons, 18cm, viii+112pp. (@ *Br*); anr. ed. 1816, Salem: Cushing, vi+107pp. ($ @); anr. ed. 1817, 17cm, 24pp. ($); ^{4}1818, York: Wilson & Sons / London: Longman & Co., viii+111; anr. ed. 1818, 24pp. ($); rev., cor. and enl. ed. 1819, with notes by J. Webber, Sr., Georgetown, D.C., repr. from the second ed. by J. Webber, Jr., 18cm, ix-xi+106pp. (@); anr. ed. 1820 (@); anr. ed. 1823 (@); ^{6}1825, York: Wilson & Sons, viii+111pp.; ^{7}1830, York: Wilson, viii+111pp. ($ @); ^{8}1835, York: Thomas Wilson & Sons, 19cm, vii+111pp. ($ @); anr. ed. 1840, 16cm, 108pp. ($)).
($ @ L *Br*)
[Popular work, of pedagogic rather than linguistic importance. Draws on Tooke, Valpy, Crombie, Dalton, Kett. A short version of 24pp. is recorded in 1817 and 1818; its relation to the longer book remains to be established.]

197.$ Bradley, Joshua (1773-1855). 1815b. *An improved spelling book, or, youth's literary guide; containing an easy system of spelling and pronunciation, a short system of polite learning, and an English grammar;*

being selected from the most approved authors on education, and arranged in such order, as to render it a useful book for schools and private families, throughout the American government. Windsor, Vt.: Oliver Farnsworth. 17cm, vi+[7]-192pp.
(@ Br)

198. Brady, John Henry. 1838. *The writer's and student's grammar of the English language; after the model of that written by William Cobbett, Esq., but divested of all political illustrations and offensive personal allusions. In a series of letters from a father to his son.* (Publ. anonymously "by the author of 'The writer's and student's assistant'."). London: Whittaker & Co. 17cm, ii+160pp.
(L O *Hu, Lw*)
[The text is (apparently) virtually identical with Cobbett, apart from omissions; further checking necessary.]

199.$ Branson, Levi (b. 1832). 1863. *First book in composition: applying the principles of grammar to the art of composing: also giving full directions for punctuation: especially designed for the use of Southern schools.* Raleigh, N.C.: Branson, Farrar & Co. 20cm, vi+139pp.
($ @)

200.$! Breene, Roscoe G. 1833. *A grammatical text-book, being an abstract of a practical grammar, etc.* Boston. 12mo, 69pp.
(Br)

201. Brewer, Robert Frederick. 1869. *A manual of English grammar, including the analysis of sentences, with copious exercises.* London/Liverpool: G. Philip & Son. 16x10, iv+78pp.
(L O)
[OESP, to be committed to memory; "What is old and well-known has been adhered to (...) strict logical accuracy in definition and division has not been attained, nor even aimed at (...)." Short rules and definitions often quite adequate, few footnotes. Exercises in all sections (63-78).]

202. ---. 1872. *An elementary English grammar, including the analysis of simple sentences.* London: George Philip. 16cm, 52pp. (Anr. ed. [1875], London etc. (@)).
(@ L O)
[Non-technical, short definitions with examples; eight parts of speech; ES only, with exercises, 41-52.]

203.$ Brewster, Francis Augustus (1817-1890). 1841. *English grammar.* Brooklyn, Conn.: Carter & Foster. 18cm, 48pp.
(@)

204. Anon. 1890. *The brief English grammar and analysis.* (Royal English Class Books). London: Nelson. 16x11, 48pp., 4d.

(L O)

[Grammar (= letters and words, eight parts of speech, syntax and parsing) is followed by Analysis and Derivation. Short definitions, clear and competent though dry.]

205.$ Bright, Orville T. [c1881]. *Graded instruction in English. For the use of teachers* ... Oshkosh, Wis.: C.M. Bright. 15cm, 47pp. (@). (Anr. ed. 1882 ($); anr. ed. 1883, New York: D. Appleton & Co., 16cm, 80pp. ($ @); anr. ed. 1884, New York (@); anr. ed. 1885 (from 1882 ed.) (@); anr. ed. 1886 ($); anr. ed. 1890, New York: American Book Co. (@)).
($ @)

206. Brockie, William (of Southfield, 1811-1890). 1850. *The elements of universal grammar. Pt. 1.: Orthography and etymology, for the use of schools and young men's improvement societies.* Newcastle on Tyne: T.P. Barkas. iv+[5]-35pp., 14x8, 2d.
(L)

[OESP, 335 short but very conventional definitions, largely based on Latin categories (e.g. six cases), often quite misleading where applied to English, followed by a list of examples illustrating the rules.]

207.$ Brockington, Alfred Allen. 1895. *Notes on English grammar.* Toronto: Copp, Clark Co. (²1897, with additional exercises, London: Relfe Bros., 8°, viii+111pp.).
(L O)

[Inductive method focusing on parsing, with omission of 'abstract noun' and neglect of subjunctive which is "rapidly disappearing from English". Parsing, accidence, syntax, analysis of sentences are followed by appendices. Rather critical on parts of speech (because of polyfunctional *back* etc.); somewhat naive 'definitions'.]

208. Brockwell, A.B. [1890]. (Lecturer and examiner in schools). *A short abstract of the history and science of the English language.* London: Simpkin Marshall / Scarborough: Dennis. 18x11.5, 75pp.
(L)

[Based on Angus, Bain and Morris, with small changes, and arranged in definitions accompanied by tables (paradigms). The definitions are often dubious and misleading; the catechism (39-55) meant for repetition of the preceding grammar. Model sentences and exercises for parsing at end. The grammar is incomplete and not well arranged. The book is possibly a re-edition of no. 1596a (but the interrelationship needs investigation).]

209. Bromby, Charles Henry (Bishop of Tasmania, 1814-1907). 1848a. *The pupil-teacher's English grammar, and etymology of the English language, adapted to the use of normal schools.* London: Simpkin & Mar-

shall. 19x11, 138pp. (⁴1852; rev. ed. 1853, as *The history and grammar of the English language: adapted to the use of pupil teachers and normal schools, revised and partly re-written by I.L. Reynolds*, London: Simpkin, Marshall & Co., iv+175pp.; rev. ed. ²⁰1863, 18cm, viii+[9]-196pp. (@); abridgment 1868; anr. ed. 1876 (from ²⁰1863 ed.), London; 2nd rev. ed. 1881, rev. and partly rewritten by J.L. Reynolds, London: Moffatt & Paige, 18cm, iv+188pp. (@)).

($ @ C L O *Lw*)

[Introductory, somewhat burdened with data, but concentrating on teaching methods (includes "Hints for teachers"); praises Latham (no. 1053.). Some 25 editions.]

210.! ---. 1848b. *Abridgment of the pupil teacher's grammar: published for the use of the model schools*. Cheltenham. 6d/8d.

[Advertised in Bromby 1848a.]

211. ---. 1853. *An abridgment of the history and grammar of the English language: adapted to the higher classes of elementary schools. Published for the use of the Cheltenham Normal Training College*. n.p. 14cm, iv+[5]-65pp. (Enl. and impr. ed. 1858, 17th thousand, London: Simpkin, Marshall & Co. (@)).

($ @)

212.$ Bromley, Walter. 1822. *The English grammar made easy, by being reduced to the form of a catechism, for the mutual instruction of youth; either on the old or new system of education*. Halifax, N.S.: Royal Arcadian School. 14cm, 104pp. ($). (Anr. ed. 1832, Halifax, N.S.).

($ *Br*)

213.$ Brown, Goold (1791-1857). 1823a. *The institutes of English grammar, methodically arranged, with forms of parsing and correcting with examples for parsing, questions for examination, false syntax for correction, exercises for writing, observations for the advanced student, five methods for analysis, and a key to the oral exercises, to which are added four appendixes: designed for the use of schools, academies and private learners*. Ster. ed. New York: the author. 8°, 311pp. (Anr. ed. 1823, 19cm, viii+219pp. ($); rev. and enl. ed. ²1825, 18/19cm, xi+297pp. ($); ³1827 (from 1825 ed.), 18/19cm, vii+304pp. ($); ⁴1830, New York: S. Wood & Sons, 19cm, xii+311pp. ($ @); rev. ster. ed. 1832 (from 1825 ed.), New York: S.S. & W. Wood / Boston: W.D. Ticknor & Co., 19cm, xiv+[15]-311+[1]pp. ($ @); rev. ster. ed. 1833 (from 1825 ed.), New York: S. Wood & Sons ($); rev. ster. ed. 1836 ($ @); anr. ed. 1840 ($ @); anr. ed. 1844; anr. ed. 1845 (from 1825 ed.) ($); rev. ster. ed. 1846 ($ @); ster. ed. 1847, rev. by the author ($); anr. ed. 1848 ($ @); anr. ed. 1849 ($ @); anr. ed. 1850 ($ @); anr. ed. 1851 ($ @);

ster. ed. 1852, New York: Samuel S. & W. Wood, 20cm, xii+[13]+ 311pp. ($ @); anr. ed. 1854 ($ @); anr. ed. 1855 (@); new ster. and rev. ed. 1856 as *The institutes of English grammar with forms of parsing and correcting, methodically arranged*, with exercises by Henry Kiddle, N.Y.: Samuel S. & William Wood, 19/20cm, xvi+[17]-335pp. (@ L); between 1857 and 1893 at least two editions with 311pp. and twenty-six editions with 335-43pp.; further editions to 1923; repr. Delmar: Scholars' Facsimiles & Reprints, 1983).
($ @ L O *Hu, Br, Lw*)
[One of the most detailed smaller American grammars exhibiting a great deal of sound judgement and learnedness, but burdened with a succession of Rules, Exceptions to Rules, Observations to Rules and Notes to Rules and Examples under Notes, all in small print which make it very difficult to properly understand the intricate argument. This was the first publication by Brown in the field [the accompanying *First Lines* is of 1826]; he had it thoroughly revised in 1855, the basis of the standard edition (often reprinted), which he believed to be "the best common school grammar now extant" (1856:xiii). OESP, succinct definitions, examinations on preceding matter. A few footnotes (some extensive, as pp. 72-73 on Quaker *thou*). Quotation from 1856 ed.: "This treatise being intended for general use, and adapted to all classes of learners, was designed to embrace in a small compass a complete course of English Grammar, disencumbered of everything not calculated to convey direct information on the subject" (iii). According to Nietz (1961:116), in New York State, in 1850, one academy used Lindley Murray, fifteen used Kirkham, and 72 used Goold Brown.]
Lit: Wächtler 1986.

214.$ ---. 1823b. *The first lines of English grammar: being a brief abstract of the author's larger work: designed for the young learner.* (Brief Abstract of *The institutes of English grammar*). New York. 15cm, 90pp. ($) (Anr. ed. 1824, 15cm, iv+108pp. ($); ²1826, New York: S. Wood & Sons ($ @); anr. ed. 1827 (@); anr. ed. 1831, 20cm, iv+[5]-108pp. ($); anr. ed. 1836 (@); anr. ed. 1840, New York: Samuel S. & W. Wood / Philadelphia: E.C. Biddle; anr. ed. 1843 ($); anr. ed. 1844 (from 1824 ed.), 19cm, xiv+[15]-311pp. ($); anr. ed. 1845, 19x11.5, iv+[5]-108pp. (L); anr. ed. 1846 ($); anr. ed. 1848, 20cm, 108pp. ($); anr. ed. 1851 (@); anr. ed. 1852 (from 1851 ed.) ($); anr. ed. 1854 (@); new ster. ed. 1856, carefully revised by the author, New York: Samuel S. & William Wood, viii+122pp. ($ L); anr. ed. 1857, 108pp. ($); new ster. and rev. ed. 1859, New York: Samuel S. & William Wood, 20cm, 122pp. ($); anr. ed. 1861 (from 1856 ed.) ($); anr. ed. 1862 (from 1856

ed.) ($); anr. ed. 1867 (from 1862 ed.) ($); anr. ed. 1868 (@); anr. ed. 1870 ($); anr. ed. 1871 (@); anr. ed. 1872 (@); anr. ed. 1873 ($); anr. ed. 1877 (@); anr. ed. 1879 ($); anr. ed. 1883 ($); anr. ed. 1884 (Brown's Series of Grammars), 19/20cm, iv+[5]-156pp. ($); anr. ed. 1885 ($); anr. ed. 1888 (@)).
($ @ L O Br, Hu)
[Quotation from preface from 1845 ed. (dated 1826): "Definitions and explanations here given are necessarily few and short. The writer has endeavoured to make them as clear as possible, and as copious as his limits would allow (...) The only successful method of teaching grammar, is, to cause the principal definitions and rules to be committed thoroughly to memory, that they may ever afterwards be readily applied."]

215.$ ---. 1825. *A key to the exercises for writing, contained in the Institutes of English grammar. Designed for the aid of teachers and private learners*. New York. 18cm, viii+[9]-51pp. (Anr. ed. 1832 (@); later edition contained in the *Institutes of English grammar* [1842] as *A key to the exercises for writing, contained in the Institutes of English grammar, designed for the aid of teachers and private learners*, New York: Samuel S. & William Wood, 19x11.5, vi+[8]-48pp. (L)).
($ @ L Br)
[Solutions to the exercises only.]

216.$ ---. 1827. *A catechism of English grammar; with parsing exercises. Designed for the youngest class of learners in common schools, and particularly adapted to the method of monitorial instruction*. New York: S. Wood & Sons. 15cm, 72pp.
($ @ Br)

217. entry deleted

⇒ ---. 1840. *A new English grammar* ... - see Turner, Rev. C. Brandon. no. 1772.

218.$ ---. 1850-51. *The grammar of English grammars, with an introduction historical and critical: the whole methodically arranged and amply illustrated; with forms of correcting and of parsing, improprieties for correction, examples for parsing, questions for examinations, exercises for writing, observations for the advanced student, decisions and proofs for the settlement of disputed points, occasional strictures and defences, an exhibition of the several methods of analysis, and a key to the oral exercises: to which are added four appendixes, pertaining separately to the four parts of grammar*. Boston/New York: Samuel & William Wood / London: Delf & Trübner. 24cm, xix+1028pp. (Anr. ed. 1851, 25cm, xx+1102pp. ($); rev. and impr. ed. ^{2}1857, A.M., New York: W.

Wood, 25cm, xx+[21]-1102pp. (@); rev. and impr. ed. ^{4}1856, xix+ 1028pp. ($ @); anr. ed. 1857, 25cm, xx+[21]-1070pp. ($); ^{2}1858, 25cm, xx+1070pp. ($ @); rev. and impr. ed. ^{4}1859, London: Sampson & Low ($ @); new ed. ^{5}1860 (from 1851 ed.) ($ @); anr. ed. 1861 ($); rev. and impr. ^{6}1862, enl. by the addition of a copious index of matters by Samuel U. Berrian, A.M., New York/Boston; repr. in 1862, 1864, 1865 and 1868, all from the 1851 ed. ($); rev. and impr. ed. ^{10}1869, New York: W. Wood (@); anr. ed. 1871 ($); rev. and impr. ed. 1872 (@); anr. ed. 1873 ($ @); anr. ed. 1875; anr. ed. 1878 ($ L @); rev. and impr. ed. 1880 ($); anr. ed. 1882 ($); anr. ed. 1884 ($)).
($ L O *Br*)
[The numbering of editions is contradictory. Rightly considered the most important American grammar of the 19th century. The "catalogue of grammars and grammarians", pp. xi-xix, with its more than 400 titles is truly impressive - even if not all have really been used, and the four parts (orthography 134-270, etymology 271-438, syntax 439-741, prosody 742-874, followed by keys to the exercises, 875-1028) cover every conceivable topic. Its enormous size made abridgments for the ordinary reader necessary].

219.$ Brown, James. (Grammarian). 1815. *A treatise on the nature and reasons of the English grammar illustrated by a machine constructed for that purpose.* Boston: W.W. Clapp. 20cm, 40pp.
($ @)
[Quoted as *An explanation of English grammar as taught by an expensive machine* by Brown. Sixty entries for James Brown in the National Union Catalogue represent between 30 and 35 different works and their abridgments. Titles resemble each other so much that it is difficult to tell which are separate works and which new editions. It would be worth studying Brown in case he is more than a productive eccentric.]

220.$ ---. 1819. *A grammatical treatise being an exposition of the difficulties found in the present system of English grammar, and of the principles of a new system, soon to be published.* Albany: Jeremiah Tryon. 22cm, xii+[9]-40pp.
($ @)

221.$ ---. 1820. *An American grammar, developing the principles of our language, and impressing them upon the memory by exercising the judgment of the learner: designed for the schools in the United States.* Troy: Adancourt. 17cm, 80pp./60+108pp. ($ @). (Anr. ed. 1821, New York: C.N. Baldwin, for the author, 15cm, 162pp. ($ @ *Br*); anr. ed. 1822, New York: the author, 14cm, 252pp. (@); anr. ed. 1825, Baltimore; anr. ed. 1826, Washington).

($ @ *Br*)
[The relationship of these texts needs further investigation; note different sizes and numbers of pages. Probably related to the following two entries.]

221a. ---. 1821a. *The American grammar.* A Pamphlet. Salem, N.Y. 12mo, 48pp. (*Br*). (Anr. ed. 1831 Philadelphia: Clark & Raser, 19cm, 192pp. ($)).
($ *Br*)

221b. ---. 1821b. *Preface to the American grammar designed to aid its introduction by exposing the defects of the European system.* New York. 17cm, 90pp.
(@)

222.$ ---. 1823. *An abridgment of the American system of English grammar: developing the principles of the English language, and impressing them upon the memory by exercising the judgment of the learner. Designed for the use of schools.* Washington: I.G. Hutton. 16cm, xii+[13]-234pp. (^{2}1823, with additions and improvements, New York: J. Seymour, 15cm, xii+[13]-234pp. (@); anr. ed. 1826 (@); anr. ed. 1829, Philadelphia: J.C. Clark; anr. ed. 1835).
($ @)

223.$ ---. 1824. *A practical English grammar, designed to enable all who cannot attend to this subject, as presented in the voluminous works of the day, to become practical grammarians without an instructor, as well as to aid those who, after attending to the study as laid down in the common system, are unable to speak, write, or punctuate with grammatical precision.* Philadelphia: W. Brown. 15cm, vi+[7]-126pp.
(@)

224.$ ---. 1825a. *An American system of English grammar developing the principles of the English language, and impressing them upon the memory by exercising the judgment of the learner.* Baltimore: W. Woody, for the author. 18cm, xii+[13]-228pp. (Rev. and enl. ed. 1826 as *An American system of English grammar. Rev. and enl. to which will soon be appended a key and exercises, developing the constructive principles of the English language ...*, Washington: P. Force, for the author, 19cm, 252 (i.e. 276)pp. (@)).
($ @)
[Adversely criticised by Goldsbury (1846:14-18), no. 666.]

225.$ ---. 1825b. *An appeal from the present popular system of English philology, to common sense. Designed to aid the introduction of the American system of English grammar.* Baltimore: B. Lundy. 20cm, 52pp. (Anr. ed. 1828, Carlisle: "Herald" Office, 18cm, xvii+[19]-432pp. ($ @);

anr. ed. 1836 quoted as *An appeal from the British system of English grammar to common sense. Designed to aid the introduction of the American system of English syntax*, Philadelphia: J. Fennemore etc., 19cm, xxxv+[37]-336pp.).
($ @ Br)
[(On 1836 ed.) In spite of his rhetoric and his passion for new terminology, Brown's approach is sensible: inadequacy of traditional definitions; different parts of speech express the same idea (e.g. *of, my, John's, owns*); the relations between words are more important than their classification; diagrammatic representation of his innovative terminology.]

226.$ ---. 1827. *The American grammar: abridged and simplified*. Baltimore: J. Robinson. 18cm, 108pp. (Anr. ed. 1828 Chamberburg: the author, 18cm, 144pp. ($ @)).
($ @)

227.$ ---. 1837. *The American system of English syntax: developing the constructive principles of the English phrenod or language*. Philadelphia: J. Blackman. 19cm, xxxii+[33]-442pp. ($ @). (Anr. ed. 1838, Philadelphia: T.K. & P.G. Collins, 19cm, 216pp. (*Br*)).
($ @ Br)

228.$ ---. 1838. *The American grammar defended against the recent attack of the Rev. Robert J. Breckinridge, of Baltimore* ... Philadelphia: T.K. & P.G. Collins. 19cm, 12pp. (With his *The American system of English syntax*, Philadelphia 1838).
(@)

229.$ ---. 1839. *An English syntascope, developing the constructive principles of the English phrenod, or language, and impressing them on the memory by pictorial, and scenical demonstration*. Philadelphia: J. Kay, Jr. & Brother. 19cm, iv+[5]-236+12pp.
($ @)
[He describes a syntactascope as "a large map giving a symbolic view of the *syntax* of the English language" and defends his increasingly elaborate terminology, but his main aim seems to be a generalised symbolic system, algebraic in character, which would indicate the structure of sentences. The syntactical relationships he displays are not, of course, new.]

230.$ ---. 1840a. *An exegesis of English syntax, designed to enable teachers, pupils, and others to comprehend fully, the present popular system of English grammar, as presented by Murray, and simplified by later writers*. Philadelphia: J. Kay & Brother. 19cm, xii+[4]-135+12pp. (Anr. ed. 1840 ($ @)).
($ @ L Br)

["In spite of its title the book is hostile to Murray and advocates 'the American system'". The author lists the 16 ways in which "the American system" of teaching grammar differs from the old (British) system. Included is a "Verbatory" in which more than 50 of his new terms are explained.]

231.$ ---. 1840b. *The English syntascope. Consisting of diagrammic illustrations of the constructive principles of the English language: with a technical verbatory, defining the new words, used in the American system of English syntax and explaining the process of their formation from the Greek and Latin.* Philadelphia.
(@)

232.$ ---. 1841. *The first part of the American system of English syntax, developing the constructive principles of the English language or phrenod.* In 3 parts. Boston: G.A. & J. Curtis. 19cm, 195pp.
(@ Br)
[Br: "'An English Syntascope,' a 'Chart,' and other fantastical works".]

233.$ ---. 1842. *An English syntithology: in three books: developing the constructive principles of the English language, by appropriate polymorph terms, used in this science only, and each having but one meaning.* Philadelphia. 3 vols. 18cm. ($). (Anr. ed. 1843, Boston/Philadelphia: G.A. & J. Curtis, 19cm (@); anr. ed. 1845, Philadelphia: Grubb & Reazor, Vol. I: 3rd ster. ed., 19cm ($ @); anr. ed. 1847, Philadelphia, Vol. I & II: 2nd ed., 20cm, 255pp. ($ @)).
($ @)
[NUC has: *An English syntithology, in three books. The whole developing the new science, made up of those constructive principles which form a sure guide in speaking, and writing the English language, but which are not found in the old system of English grammar.*]

234.$ ---. 1843. *An abridgment of Brown's second book on English syntithology, to which is appended a technical concordance: to enable those who desire it, to become familiar with the old nomenclature with little or no trouble.* Philadelphia. 18/19cm, 124pp.
($)

235.$ ---. 1845. *An appeal from the old theory of English grammar, to the true constructive genius of the English language: developed in three books: the whole entitled: an English syntithology.* Philadelphia: Grubb & Reazor. 19cm, xxi+[5]-622pp. (^{2}1845 (@)).
($ @)

236.$ ---. 1850a. *An appeal from the absurdities and contradictions which pervade, and deform the old theory of English grammar, to the true*

constructive principles of the English language. Philadelphia: J.T. Lange. 25cm, x+209pp.
($)
237.$ ---. 1850b. *An exegesis of the true way of analyzing the words, and constructions of difficult solution, as well as all anomalies.* Philadelphia: J.T. Lange. 19cm, v+[7]-144pp.
(@)
238.$ ---. 1850c. *A system of analyzing notation, designed to enable all who desire to teach or learn English grammar from James Brown's new system, to accomplish the object of their wish with unexampled rapidity, ease and accuracy.* Philadelphia: J.T. Lange. 19cm, 4+20pp.
(@)
239.$ ---. 1851. *A supplement to the common theory of English grammar ... The whole developing the constructive principles of the English language, not found in the old theory of English grammar.* Philadelphia. 19cm, viii+[9]-91pp.
(@)
240.$ ---. 1852. *Supplement to the English grammar.* Philadelphia: Wyeth.
(@)
241.$ ---. 1853. *System of analysing forms, designed to enable all who desire either to teach or to learn English grammar.* Philadelphia: Brown. 23pp.
(@)
242.$ ---. 1853-56. *The first [second and third] book of the rational system of English grammar ... (Vol. II: designed to enable one to parse the words of an English sentence with sound judgment, and to use the English language with grammatical propriety. Vol. III: designed to enable one to understand and use the prepositions with perfect accuracy; including English style).* n.p. 20cm, vi+[7]-138pp, 170pp., vii+223pp. (Anr. ed. 1855? ($); anr. ed. 1856 (from 1855 ed.), v+198pp. ($); anr. ed. Vol. I-III: 1856-62, Philadelphia: P. Griffee, 19cm (@); anr. ed. Vol. I: 1859, as *The first book of James Brown's system of English grammar. Simplified for the use of schools and private learners by Leonard F. Bittle*, Philadelphia: P. Griffee, 19cm, iv+[5]-69 (@)).
($ @)
243.$ ---. 1854?. *The grammatical reader: a class book of criticism on the old theory of English grammar and on the writings of its compilers: designed for private readers, advanced schools and colleges.* n.p. (Anr. ed. 1856, 19/20cm, 202[+19]pp. ($)).
($)
244.$ Brown, James (of Philadelphia). 1849. *An English grammar in three books, developing the new science, made up of those constructive princi-*

ples which form a sure guide in using the English language; but which are not found in the old theory. Philadelphia: John T. Lange. Part I: 17.5x11, iv+116pp. Part II: 18x11, xix+387pp. (All three parts mentioned in reviews, p.3).
(L @)
[Same writer as above? On Part I: OESP, with excessive innovative terminology ("Monology respects the division of a syllabane into *monos*", p.7, etymology is made up of "symmonology, bemaology, cardiology, monology, tropology and gnom-ology", p.6). At least a hundred new terms which were probably never heard of again. In Part II he returns to the old names of parts of speech to make the new system more palatable, but which remains unnecessarily complicated, with dozens of newly coined words (e.g. "nepos pluror" = new-word pluralisation in *I:we*).]

245. Brown, John (Teacher of English at Göttingen). 1802. *A new English grammar, containing the nine parts of speech with compleat vocabulary, dialogues, anecdotes, letters moral and mercantile*. Göttingen: Vandenhoek & Ruprecht. viii+227pp.
($ @)

246. Brown, John (Master of an academy, at Kingston, Surrey). 1809. *The elements of English education, containing an introduction to English grammar, and a concise English grammar*. London: Benjamin Crosby.
(L *Lw*)
[Conventional elementary grammar; ten parts of speech; parsing; twelve pages of syntax.]

247. Brown, M. Morgan. 1900. *A first form grammar*. London: Longman. viii+80pp. 18.5x13.5.
(L)
[The grammar treats the parts of speech individually, then cases and moods/tenses, and finally syntax. It teems with vague and misleading definitions, and a mixture of Latin categories; in addition, the categories are presented in dubious order - because there was no unifying principle behind the author's approach.]

248. $ Brown, W. 1855. *A practical school grammar*. Halifax, NS. (Anr. ed. 1856 (L Eu)).
(C L Eu)

249. Browne, William James (of Londonderry). 1875. *Junior English grammar*. Dublin: Sullivan. 8°, 147+20pp. (Anr. ed. 1900, Dublin: Sullivan, A. Thom / London; Simpkin etc. / Manchester: John Heywood, viii+144pp., 16.5x10.5cm. (L)).
(L O)

[OESP, framed by general introduction and "History of the English Language". Quite traditional account, with exercises inserted; definitions not always satisfactory. Eight parts of speech.]

250. Bruce, Robert H. [1894]. *A notebook of English grammar*. London: Relfe Bros. 18.5x12.5, 24pp.
(L O)
[Most drastically curtailed definitions and rules apparently for memorizing, not unintelligent, but suffering from the extreme brevity; concentrates on parts of speech.]

251.$ Brunner, David B. (1835-1903). 1877. *Elements of English grammar and analysis*. Reading, Pa.: The Spirit of Berks Publishing Company. 18cm, 59pp. (Anr. ed. 1882 ($)).
($ @)

252.$ Bryant, James H. 1892. *Plain English: a practical work on the English language: for use in public and private schools, academies, commercial colleges, and for private learners*. n.p. 21cm, viii+224pp.
($)

253.$ Buck, Martha. 1895a. *Elements of English grammar*. Cambridge: J. Wilson & Son, for the author. 19cm, xii+163pp.
($ @)

254.$ ---. 1895b. *English grammar and analysis*. Cambridge: J. Wilson & Son, for the author. 19cm, xii+173pp.
(@)

255.$ ---. 1900. *Grammar and analysis of the English language*. Chicago: Clinic Publishing Company. 19cm, x+188pp.
(@)

256. Bucke, Charles (1781-1846). 1829. *A classical grammar of the English language, with a short history of its origin and formation*. London: Baldwin & Cradock. 17cm, vii+152pp.
(L *Hu*, *Br*, *Lw*, *Sk*)
[Elementary grammar, with a focus on 18th-century correctness and good style to be learnt from the best authors. Letters, pronunciation, punctuation, parts of speech, syntax, prosody, with a few minor points, and an account on the history of English appended.]

257.$ Buckham, Henry B. 1881. *The analysis of sentences*. New York: American Book Co. / New York/Chicago: Ivison, Blakeman, Taylor & Co. 18cm, 251pp.
($ @)

258.$ Buehler, Hubert Gray (English Master in the Hotchkiss School). [1900]. *A modern English grammar*. New York: Newson & Co. 18x11.5, vii+291pp.

(O)
[Argues for an analytic treatment based on native competence, starting from the sentence, and then turning to the (nine) parts of speech. "The pupil is not only led to observe for himself; he is also guided to the right inferences." (iv) Discussions leading up to succinct definitions (generally adequate), followed by queries and exercises, and a few hints to the teacher (p. 31: aim not at knowledge but insight). Quite well planned and carried through; no mention made of spelling, pronunciation, punctuation and prosody.]

Buehrle, Robert K. 1877. *Grammatical praxis in American literature.* Philadelphia: Cowperthwait & Co. 18cm, 80pp.
($ @)

Bullen, Rev. Henry St. John. 1853. *Linguae Anglicanae Clavis; or, Rudiments of English grammar, so arranged for the use of schools, as to form a new and easy introduction to Latin and other classical grammars,* originally published by [HB], late headmaster of the grammar school at Leicester. Now edited, with a Preface by the Rev. Charles Heycock [Perpetual Curate of Owston, and Rector of Withcote, Lincs.]. London: Arthur Hall, Virtue & Co. 12°, xliv+244pp. (^{3}1870, London: Longmans & Co., 8°, xii+192).
(L O)
[First published in 1797 as *The rudiments of English grammar* (^{3}1813). Very verbose, and sometimes muddled, especially where C.H.'s semi-learnedness interferes; strongly Latin-based. Refers to Connon, Crombie, Wall, Murray, Walker, Harris. Identical with the work reviewed by Martin 1824:271-2? He says: "Rudiments of English Grammar for the use of schools by the Rev. Henry St. John Bullen, Head Master of the Grammar School, Leicester. ^{3}1809. The plan of Mr Bullen's Grammar is entirely original and comprehensive; and where he has found a disputed point, he has endeavoured to found his opinion on the best authority. Each lesson is attended by a brief Analysis, and the notes inserted in the appendix are suitably arranged".]

Bullions, Peter (Late Professor of languages in the Albany Academy, and author of the series of grammars, Greek, Latin, and English, on the same plan, etc., 1791-1864). 1834. *The principles of English grammar: comprising the substance of the most approved English grammar extant, with copious exercises in parsing and syntax: and an appendix of various and useful matter: for the use of academies and common schools.* New York: Clement & Packard / Albany: O. Steele. 18cm, xii+195pp. (@). (rev. and corr. ed. ^{2}1837, New York, xii+187pp.; rev. and corr. ed. ^{3}1841, Albany: Oliver Steele ($ @); rev. and corr. ed. ^{4}1842, New

York: Clement & Packard ($ L); anr. ed. 1842, New York: C.C. Clement, 19cm, xii+216pp. ($ @); new, rev. and corr. ed. ^{5}1843 (@); anr. ed. 1843, 1844 (from 1842 ed.), ($); $^{11+12+13}$1845 (from 1842 ed.), New York: Pratt, Woodford & Co. ($ @); $^{15+16+19}$1846 (from 1842 ed.) ($ @); $^{22+23}$1847, xii+216+12pp. ($ @); $^{27+29}$1848 (from 1846 ed.) ($ @); $^{32+34}$1849 (from 1846 ed.) ($ @); ^{52}1850 ($ @); new ed. 1851, 225pp. ($ @); anr. ed. 1851 (from 1846 ed.), xii+216pp. ($); anr. ed. 1852 (from 1851 ed.), xii+225pp. ($); $^{60+62}$1854, New York: Pratt, Woodford, Farmer & Brace ($ @); $^{65+70}$1855, New York: Pratt ($ @); rev. ed. ^{21}1856 (@); rev. ed. ^{23}1856 (@); anr. ed. 1857 (from 1851 ed.) ($); rev. ed. $^{25+27}$1857 (@); anr. ed. 1857 (@); rev., re-arranged and impr. ed. 1858 (from 1851 ed.); new and rev. ed. ^{30}1858, New York: Pratt, Oakley & Co. (@); anr. ed. 1859 (from 1851 ed.) ($); rev. ed. ^{31}1859 (@); new, rev, re-arranged, impr. ed. 1860 (from 1851 ed.), 18cm, xii+225pp. ($); rev., re-arranged and impr. ed. 1864 (from 1851 ed.), New York: Pratt, Oakley & Co. ($ @); rev. ed. ^{35}1862, New York: Sheldon & Co. (@); repr. of ^{35}1862 ed. in 1864, 1867 and 1871; anr. ed. 1872 ($); rev. and impr. ed. 1873, 19cm, viii+344pp. (@); repr. Delmar: Scholars' Facsimiles & Reprints, 1983).
($ @ L *Br*)
[Born in Perthshire and educated at Edinburgh, Bullions absorbed much of the prescriptive grammar of his time before he became one of the most widely read grammarians of the New World. Brown accused him of copying from Lennie; he is aware of the dominating position of Murray, but also very critical, as he explains in his preface. OESP. Wants to find a middle way between the detailedness of Murray's original and the meagreness of most abridgments. "Utility, not novelty has been aimed at." Mentions Lennie, Murray, Angus, Connel, Grant, Crombie, Hiley and Webster among authors consulted. "Copious exercises in false syntax follow each rule." The work should also be "a profitable introduction to classical studies"; he envisaged parallel grammars for English, Latin and Greek "as nearly in the same words as the genius of the languages would permit" (1846:vi).]

262.$ ---. 1844. *Practical lessons in English grammar and composition; for young beginners: being an introduction to "The principles of English grammar" with copious exercises, and directions for their use.* New York. 19cm, 132pp. (Anr. ed. 1845, 18cm, vi+[7]-132+12pp. ($); anr. ed. 1846 ($); ^{11}1849 (from 1846 ed.), New York: Pratt, Woodford & Co. ($ @); anr. ed. 1851 (from 1846 ed.) ($); at least six further new, rev. and corr. editions between 1852 and 1871 ($)).
($ @ L *Br*)

[In the 1853 edition he regards as a "peculiar feature" the combination of grammatical analysis with the composition of short sentences. Nine parts of speech.]

263.$ ---. 1849. *An analytical and practical grammar: A practical grammar of the English language: with analysis of sentences.* New York: Pratt, Woodford & Co. 18x11, 240pp. (@). (Anr. ed. 1850; $^{15+17}$1852 ($ @); rev. ed. $^{19+21+22}$1853, preface dated 1849 (L @); $^{27+28+29+31}$1854 (from 1853 ed.) ($ @); $^{33+34}$1855 (from 1853 ed.) ($ @); rev. eds. $^{36+37}$1856 (from 1853), New York: Farmer, Brace & Co., 244pp. ($ @); rev. eds. $^{39+40}$1857, New York: Pratt, Oakley & Co., 244pp. (@); $^{42+46}$1858, 19cm, 244pp. ($ @); rev. ed. $^{47+48+50}$1859 ($ @); rev. ed. ^{52}1860 (from 1853 ed.) ($ @); rev., corr. and impr. ed. ^{17}1862, New York: Sheldon & Co., 19cm, iv+[5]-258pp. (@); $^{52+70}$1862 (from 1853 ed.), New York: Sheldon & Co. 244pp. ($ @); anr. ed. 1863, New York: Sheldon (@); anr. ed. 1864, rev. by R.B. Craven, D.D. Raleigh: The N.C. Christian Advocate Publishing Company, 18cm, 192pp. ($ @); rev., corr. and impr. ed. ^{70}1864, New York: Sheldon & Co. (@); rev., corr., and impr. ed. 1865 (from 1862 ed.), iv+258pp. ($); rev. ed. 1866, quoted as *Revised edition of Bullion's Analytical and practical grammar of the English language containing, in addition to other new matter, a section on the structure of words, a vocabulary of Saxon, Latin and Greek roots, extensive selections in prose and poetry, for analysis, and a complete course of instruction and exercises in English composition*, 324pp. ($); rev. ed. 1867, New York: Sheldon, 20cm, x+336pp. ($ @); anr. ed. 1868 (from 1862 ed.), 20cm, x+336pp. ($); anr. ed. 1869 (from 1867 ed.) ($); anr. ed. 1870 ($); anr. ed. 1872 (from 1867 ed.) ($); rev. ed. 1873 ($ @); rev. ed. 1877 (@); anr. ed. 1878 (from 1867 ed.) ($)).
($ @ L *Br*)
[Quotation from ^{21}1853: "designed for the more advanced classes in schools and academies, prepared on a more extended plan than (*Principles*), though not essentially different from it. The arrangement (except in syntax), the definitions and rules, are the same, but with much greater fulness in the illustrations and exercises, intended to lead the student into a thorough and critical acquaintance with the structure and use of the English language." OESP, with great attention given to analysis (not in *Principles*) and parsing; traditional, sober; definitions, rules and special rules with many observations, remarks and footnotes covering exceptions etc. Exercises for recapitulation, including "to be corrected". The amount of data is somewhat much for a school grammar.]

264.$ ---. 1851. *Progressive exercises in analysis and parsing, containing selections in prose and poetry, with directions and notes adapted to Bullion's English grammars.* New York: Pratt, Woodford & Co. 16cm, [5]-120pp. (@). (^{5}1854, New York: Pratt, Woodford, Farmer & Brace (@); ^{10}1856 (@); ^{14}1858, New York: Pratt, Oakley & Co. (@); repr. of ^{14}1858 in 1860 (@); ^{15}1862, New York: Sheldon & Co. (@); repr. of ^{15}1862 in 1864, 1868, 1869 and 1870 (@); anr. ed. 1863 ($); anr. ed. 1881, New York: Sheldon (@); anr. ed. 1882, New York: Sheldon (@)).
($ @)

265.$ ---. 1853. *Introduction to the Analytical and practical grammar of the English language, with exercises in analysis and parsing, being practical lessons in English grammar and composition for young beginners, with copious exercises, and directions for their use.* New York: Pratt, Woodford & Co. 17.5x10.5, vi+[7]-141pp. ($ L). (Anr. ed. 1854; ^{4}1855 ($); anr. ed. 1858 (@); ^{8}1859 (@); anr. ed. 1862, New York: Sheldon & Co., 139pp. (@); anr. ed. 1863, New York: Sheldon & Co. (@); anr. ed. 1865 ($); anr. ed. 1866, 150pp. ($)).
($ @ L)
[Explicitly intended as an introduction to the *APG*, for learners up to 12-14; older pupils should start with *APG* which "is sufficiently simple for pupils of that age". Features mentioned: "With the principles of Grammar, at every step, are combined instructions and exercises in the elementary principles of Composition." OESP, as in *APG*.]

266.$ ---. 1862. *Bullion's common school grammar: an introduction to the analytical and practical grammar: with practical lessons and exercises in composition.* n.p. (Anr. ed. 1865, New York: Sheldon, 19cm, 142pp. ($ @); anr. ed. 1866 ($); anr. ed. 1867 ($); anr. ed. 1868, 18cm, 142pp. ($); anr. ed. 1871 (@); anr. ed. 1879 (@); further editions to 1884).
($ @)

267.$ ---. 1864. *A practical grammar of the English language: with analysis of sentences.* New York: Sheldon. (@). (Anr. ed. 1867 (@); rev. ed. 1868 ($ @); rev. ed. 1869, 19/20cm, x+336pp. ($ @); rev. ed. 1870 (@); anr. ed. 1871 ($ @); anr. ed. 1872 (@); anr. ed. 1873 (from 1867 ed.) ($); anr. ed. 1874 (@); anr. ed. 1877 (from 1867 ed.) ($); anr. ed. 1880 (@); anr. ed. 1881 (@)).
($ @)

268.$ ---. 1870. *Bullion's school grammar: with practical lessons and exercises in composition and analysis. A rev. ed. of the common school grammar, and introductory to the practical grammar.* (Bullion's Grammatical Series). New York: Sheldon & Co. 18cm, xvi+172pp. (Anr. ed. 1872

(@); anr. ed. 1874 ($); anr. ed. 1877 ($); anr. ed. 1884, Montreal: Danson Brothers, xvi+1+180pp. ($ @); anr. ed. 1899 ($)).
($ @)

269. Bullock, Thomas Austin. [1871]. *Classbook of English grammar. The young student's English grammar for schools, including the formation and derivation of words, the analysis of sentences and numerous exercises*. Manchester: John Heywood. 17cm, vi+[7]-126pp. (@). (New, rev. and enl. ed. [c1880] (Dr. Bullock's Series of Educational Works), London: Simpkin, Marshall (@)).
(@ H)

270. ---. [a1874]. *The youth's English grammar, for use in junior schools, including the analysis of sentences and numerous exercises; an introduction to "The young student's English grammar"*. New, corr. and much enl. ed. (Dr. Bullock's Educational Works). London: Simpkin, Marshall & Co. 17cm, 64pp.
(@)
[Advertised by Heywood and by Simpkin Marshall (publishers) in 1874.]

271.$ Burns, Elijah A. [a1859]. *Principles of English grammar defined and illustrated*. n.p. (^{2}1859 Cincinnati; anr. ed. 1859; anr. ed. 1864; anr. ed. 1865 quoted as *Principles of English grammar, defined and illustrated, to which are added copious exercises in parsing, and false syntax for correction. Designed for the use of schools and private learners*, Cincinnati: Applegate & Co., 19cm, viii+[9]-264pp. (@); impr. and rev. ed. ^{8}1867, Cincinnati: Applegate, Pounsford & Co., 264pp. (@); impr. and rev. ed. ^{10}1870 (@); anr. ed. 1875).
(@)

272. Burton, James (First English Master in the High School of the Liverpool Institute). 1878. *The beginners' drill-book of English grammar. Adapted for middle-class and elementary schools*. London: Rivingtons. 16x10, 113pp.
(L O)
["To conduct pupils as far as the analysis and parsing of ordinary constructions"; the author provides "a bare framework of instruction, and a large body of really workable exercises." The book starts with the Analysis of simple sentences, moves on to Inflexion and Syntax: Analysis of complex sentences, and then gives a sketch of the alphabet and pronunciation. The Appendix contains exercises only.]

273.$ Burtt, Andrew. [c1846]. *Elements of English grammar, synthetic and analytical*. Rev. and ster. ed. Louisville: J.P. Morton & Griswold, 16cm, 71+1pp. (Rev. and ster. ed. 1851, Louisville: J.P. Morton & Griswold (@); anr. ed. 1859 as ... *Designed for the use of schools,*

academies, and private learners, Pittsburgh: A.H. English & Co., 20cm, 223pp. (@); from 1868 on as *A practical grammar of the English language, synthetic and analytical, adapted to the wants of public schools, academies and private learners*, New York/Pittsburgh/Chicago: Taintor Brothers & Co., 320pp. (@); anr. ed. 1869; anr. ed. 1871 (American School Series), Louisville: J.P. Morton & Griswold, 18cm, 78pp. (@); rev. ed. 1874, 20cm, 256pp.).
(@)
[cf. Nietz 1961:130]

274.$ ---. 1873. *A primary grammar of the English language, designed for the use of schools and private learners*. Pittsburgh: A.H. English & Co. 20cm, 160pp.
(@)

275.$! Butler, Noble (1819-1882). 1845a. *Introductory lessons in grammar*. Louisville, Ky. (Anr. ed. 1846; anr. ed. 1851; anr. ed. 1871).
(*Br*)

276.$ ---. 1845b. *A practical grammar of the English language*. (Comprehensive Series of School Books). Louisville, Ky.: Morton & Griswold. 20cm, vi+[5]-216pp. (@). (electrotype ed. ²1846 (American School Books), 19cm, 254pp. (@); ster. ed. 1846, 18cm, 235pp. (@); ster. ed. 1849 (from 1846 ed.) (@); ster. ed. 1850 (from 1846 ed.) (@); anr. ed. 1864, 235pp. (@); anr. ed. [1874], as *A Practical and critical grammar of the English language*, Louisville: John P. Morton & Co. 18.5x13.5, 312pp. (L); electrotype ed. 1875 (from 1846 ed.) (American School Series), Louisville: John P. Morton & Co. (@); anr. ed. [c1879] (@); anr. ed. [c1880], 20cm, 288pp. (@)).
(@ L *Br*)
[On 1874 ed.: O(+Phon)ESP; technical discussion and numerous remarks and footnotes; cf. 632]

277.$ Butter, Henry (1794-1885). 1836. *The scholar's companion; or, A guide to the orthography, pronunciation, and derivation of the English language ... Arranged on the basis of the 15th London ed. of Butter's Etymological spelling book and expositor*. By Richard W. Green. Philadelphia: H. Perkins, Marvin & Co. 19cm, 190pp.
(@)
[Many more editions in *NUC* vol. 87, p. 537.]

278. ---. ⁵1841. *Inductive grammar: being a simple and easy introduction to a grammatical knowledge of the English language. Designed for the use of beginners. By an experienced teacher*. (Publ. anonymously; attribution is by British Library, London). London: James Shirley Hodson. (Anr.

ed. 1843, London: James S. Hodson, 13.5x9, vi+[7]-54pp., 6d, s.v. *English language* (L); anr. ed. 1848).
(L Lw)
["The pupil is led forward in such a manner as to make his own deductions from the nature of the language"; an unassuming attempt to counteract the prevailing memorizing tradition. Few definitions followed by educational specimen sentences for application of grammatical analysis.]

279. Byrne, James (1820-1897). 1885. *General principles of the structure of language*. 2 vols. London: Trübner & Co. (@ L). (²1892, with an appendix *Comparison of the mental powers of man with the intelligence of lower vertebrate animals* (pp. 387-404), London: Kegan Paul/Trench/ Trübner & Co., 23cm (@ L)).
(@ L)

280. Bysh, John. 1843. *The keystone of grammar laid; or, The governess's assistant in simplifying that science*. London.
(L O)

281. Campbell, David (Rector of Melrose Academy). 1881. *A first course of English grammar and analysis*. London: T. Laurie. (Laurie's Kensington Series). 16cm, 4+74pp.
(@)

282. ---. [c1885]. *A complete course of English grammar and analysis. Part I: A series of graduated exercises. Part II: A synopsis of grammatical principles*. (Laurie's Kensington Series). London: T. Laurie. 16cm, 6+156pp.
(@)

283. ---. 1895a. *Higher English: An outline of English study for the middle and upper forms of schools*. (Also quoted as: *Higher English grammar: a textbook for secondary schools*). London: Blackie. 8°, 186pp., 1s6d.
(@ L)
[The contents range from language history to literature and prosody; English grammar is reduced to "Brief notes" (149-60) intended "to aid in revisal", under "grammatical analysis" D.C. states "The methods employed to set forth in tabular form the analysis of a sentence are as varied as are the verb paradigms of grammatical text-books" (160). Insignificant for grammar.]

284. ---. 1895b. *Lower English. A textbook for intermediate classes*. London: Blackie. 16.5x11, 155pp.
(L)
[OES followed by Phonetics and Prosody, eight parts of speech; technical definitions aiming at descriptive adequacy, well organized; some interference from Latin categories. A short history and reflections on

loanwords are inserted (70-103], followed by an outline of English literature (104-12). Apart from the irrelevant insertions a clear synopsis of late 19th-century grammar.]

285. ---. 1896. *Lessons in English for beginners.* London: Blackie. 131pp.
(L)

286. Campbell, J. [a1860]. *Principles and practice of English grammar, according to the lesson system.* London/Edinburgh: Gall & Inglis.
(L)

287. Campbell, Mrs. Graham. 1861. *Louisa's metrical English grammar. Published for the authoress, to be had also for Messrs.* Cheltenham/London: Longman & Co. 8°, iv+73pp.
(L O)
[Very basic grammar, reduced from Latham, in very bad verse by a lady who "wished to avoid frightening by the sight of a large book (trying) to combine, with brevity and simplicity, real information in an easy rhyme".]

288. Capp, Mrs. [a1866]. *An easy grammar, for the use of schools.* n.p. iv+66pp. (^{3}1866, Lincoln).
(O)
[Entirely derivative and conventional at a deliberately simple level.]

289.$ Cardell, William Samuel (1780-1828). 1825. *An essay on language, as connected with the faculties of the mind, and as applied to things in nature and art ...* New York: C. Wiley. 18cm, 203pp.
(@ Br)

290.$ ---. 1826. *Elements of English grammar, deduced from science and practice, adapted to the capacity of learners.* New York. 14/15cm, 141pp. (^{3}1827, Hartford: H. & F.J. Huntington / New York: White, Gallaher & White, xiii+[15]-135pp (@); ^{4}1828, Philadelphia: Russell & Martin, xiii+[14]-144pp. (@); anr. ed. 1828 (1st Vt. ed.), Windsor, Vt.: S. Ide (@)).
(@ Br)

291.$ ---. 1827. *Philosophic grammar of the English language, in connection with the laws of matter and thought.* Philadelphia: U. Hunt. 18cm, xiii+[15]-236+[2]pp.
(@ Br)

292.$ Carpenter, George Rice (Professor of Rhetoric and English Composition in Columbia University). 1898. *Principles of English grammar, for the use of schools.* New York/London: Macmillan. 18x11.5, x+254pp. (Repr. in 1898, 1899 and 1900).
(L O)

["Essential facts and principles of Modern English inflection and syntax for use in high-schools (...) to present the theory or system of the modern language in accordance with the results of philological research", with an appendix on phonology by E.H. Babbitt. A student "must know, first, the logical method by which we classify words; second, the simple English systems of inflection; third, the main principles of English syntax. Fourth, he must understand thoroughly the structure of the English sentence." Argues for a recognition of varieties and diversity of usage; leaves orthoepy and orthography to the dictionaries. The book is well organized; clear definitions accompanied by examples, with exercises interspersed. In spite of its narrative style quite an 'academic' grammar.]

293.! Carrie, J. [c1856]. *Rudiments of English grammar*. London: Constable. 62pp.
(*Al*)
[cf. Alwall 1970:165]

294. Carter, George (Headmaster of New College School, Oxford). [1892]. *Explanation of grammatical terms (arranged alphabetically) for the use of candidates preparing for the Oxford and Cambridge local and other examinations*. London: Relfe. 29pp.
(L O)
[The arrangement leaves room for short definitions, in order to provide rules for checking and memorizing; eight classes, six tenses. No specific grammar referred to.]

295. Anon. 1852. *A catechism of English grammar, especially adapted for a class book. For the use of schools*. (By "A Lady"). Wymondham: T. Colman / London: Roulston & Stoneman. 14x8.5, 31pp., 4d. (Anr. ed. 1859, n.p.: Houlston & Stoneman, 32pp.; anr. ed. [1866/67], London: Burns, Lambert & Oates, 15cm, 31pp. (@)).
(@ L *Al*)
[cf. Alwall 1974:163]
[Very brief Q/A, with many inadequate definitions; nine parts of speech, much room given to conjugation; short sections on prosody and punctuation at end.]

296. Anon. [12]1820. *A catechism of the principles of English grammar, to which are added for the exercise of the learner, some easy parsing lessons ... By a friend to youth*. (Pinnock's Catechisms of the Arts and Sciences). London. 13x8, 70pp. ([c[3]1820], Newbury; [c[4]1821], Newbury: W. Pinnock, 69pp. (L); [18]1825, 15cm, 71pp. ($); [20]1828; [21]1829, London: Whittaker, Treacher & Co. 72pp.; anr. ed. 1840).
($ L O *Br, Ma*)

[Reviewed by Martin 1824:227. Very brief Q/A, often insufficient definitions; very traditional, with great care devoted to the verbal system and to parsing.]

297.$ Anon. [1823]. *A catechism of English grammar, with practical exercises; prepared for the use of the School of Mutual Instruction in Boston by the instructor.* Boston: Wm. B. Fowle. 16.5x10, 67pp.
(L)
[Simplest form of Q/A. Nine parts of speech, rudimentary definitions; Murray is quoted in some footnotes, where also some arguments relating to the history of English are found.]

298. Chamberlain, Rev. Thomas (Student of Christchurch, and Vicar of S. Thomas the Martyr, Oxford). ³1856. *English grammar, and how to teach it: together with a lesson in spelling and reading.* London: Joseph Masters / Oxford/Cambridge/Derby/New York. 15x8.5, 24pp.
(L)
[Accidence (*not* English) and syntax; very rudimentary and not convincing, definitions being often vague or contradictory or too much dependent on Latin.]

299.$ Champlin, James Tift. 1850. *A concise practical grammar of the English language, with exercises in analysis and parsing.* New York: D. Appleton. 16x10, xii+219pp.
(@ L)
[Follows "the most eminent grammarians of the present day ... such as Becker, Kühner, Kritz etc. But all unnecessary novelties have been studiously avoided". Divided into Etymology (=OE) and syntax, in 60 chapters; Q/A form, with exercises interspersed. Parsing seen as useful for analysis, otherwise for English "deficient as it is in inflection, it must be comparatively fruitless".]

300.$ Chandler, Joseph Ripley (1792-1880). 1821. *A grammar of the English language adapted to the use of schools.* Philadelphia: J. Crissy & G. Goodman. 19cm, xii+[13]-180pp. (Anr. ed. 1847 (Chandler's Common School Grammar), Philadelphia: Thomas, Cowperthwait & Co., 19cm, vi+[7]-208pp. (@)).
(@ Br, Lw)

301.$ Chapin, Joel. 1842. *An analytical and philosophical grammar.* Springfield, Mass.: Wood & Rupp. 19cm, ix+[2]+[13]-252pp. (Anr. ed. 1844, New York: Collins, Brothers & Co., 15cm, xi+[13]-108pp. (@); ster. ed. 1851, New Haven, N.Y. 19cm (@)).
(@ Br)

302.$ ---. 1861. *Chapin's practical grammar for beginners.* New Haven, N.Y. 16cm, 90pp.

(@)
303.$ Chessman, Daniel (Pastor of the Baptist Church in Hallowell, Me., 1787-1839). [a1821]. *A compendium of English grammar; comprising all that is necessary to be committed to memory by students: abridged from Lindley Murray's excellent treatise.* n.p. (Corr. ed. ³1821, Hallowell, Me.: Goodale, Glazier & Co., 13x8, 24pp. (L)).
(@ L *Br*)
[Very elementary abstract (OESP) in Q/A form, with footnotes added for specification; definitions often misleading.]
304. Anon. [1823?]. *The child's first ... [to fifth] ... grammar lessons ... contracted into a table for the improvement of young children.* Printed originally for the use of the Misses Wilmshurst's Seminary, Cromwell House, Malden. 5 parts. Maldon: The Misses Wilmhurst's Seminary. 31.5x26, 20pp.
(L)
[Five tables illustrating parsing, with accompanying notes. The pupils are then asked to continue with Murray. A poor attempt at popularizing grammar.]
305. entry deleted
306.$ Choate, Isaac B (1833-1917). 1884. *Elements of English speech.* New York: D. Appleton. 18cm, 220pp.
($ @)
307. entry deleted
⇒ Christian Brothers (publ. anon.) - see Wiseman, Thomas John, no. 1900
308.$ Christian Brothers. 1885. *Lessons in English: intermediate course.* n.p. 19cm, xiv+488pp.
($)
309.$ ---. 1889. *Lessons in English: elementary course.* New York/Chicago: W.H. Sadler. 21cm, viii+236pp.
($ @)
310. Churchill, T.O. 1823. *A new grammar of the English language; including the fundamental principles of etymology, syntax, and prosody, with notes and illustrations, critical and explanatory.* London: W. Simpkin & R. Marshall. 18cm, xii+454pp.
(C L *Hu*, *Br*, *Lw*, *Ma*, *Sk*)
[Traditional account based on Lowth, but with many additions in orthography and word-formation, improving him in the grammar of the verb, punctuation, and a few details to show that the author was "not guided by caprice, or a wanton spirit of innovation". He also adds a fuller treatment of syntax and includes prosody. Martin 1824:274: "The real character of this Grammar is an equipoise of good and ill; the critical

exactness of the author sometimes inclines to the right of the fulcrum, and sometimes to the left, but never so far as to produce preponderance".]
311.! Clapham, Samuel. 1810. *English grammar, taught by examples rather than by rules of syntax.* London.
(*Br*, *Mi*)
312. Clare, Thomas. 1838. *English parsing exercise book.* St Albans.
(L C)
313. Clark, David (Headmaster of the Board School, Pensnett, Dudley. Principal of Albion House School, Brierly Hill, Staffs). 1871. *The comprehensive English grammar, theoretical and practical.* London etc.: Educational Trading Co. 14.5x9, viii+68pp.
(L O)
[Advertised by Blackie (1887). Traditional account of OESP, with "The English Language" appended; generally clear definitions, with tables, exercises and remarks interspersed, but little justification of the claims voiced in the preface for the need of such a book.]
314. ---. [1896]. *The young student's complete English grammar.* (Publ. anon.?). Redditch: Thomas Evans. 17.5x11.5, 223pp.
(L O)
[Introduction to the grammar and history of the English language, especially for students preparing for Oxford and Cambridge local and other examinations; refers to Mason, Morris, Daniel, Meiklejohn, Bain, Adams, Angus, Marsh, and Trench for further information. OESP plus History and Derivations, with examination questions appended (207-20). Quite an 'academic' grammar, with clear definitions and rules illustrated by examples, footnotes, and questions and exercises interspersed, and references to the larger grammars provided.]
315.$ Clark, Schuyler. 1830. *The American linguist, or natural grammar. Explaining in a series of social lessons, the first elements of language ... The whole interspersed with directions and questions, for the assistance of teacher and pupil. Designed to be a guide to a perfect command of voice and proper use of words.* Providence, R.I.: Cory, Marshall & Hammond. 19cm, 240pp.
(@ *Br*)
316.$ Clark, Stephen Watkins (Principal of East Bloomfield Adademy, 1810-1901). 1847. *Science of the English language. A practical grammar: in which words, phrases, and sentences are classified acccording to their offices, and their relations to each other. Illustrated by a complete system of diagrams.* New York: A.S. Barnes & Co. / Cincinnati: Derby, Bradley & Co. 19cm, iv+218pp. ($^{2+4}$1848, New York: A.S. Barnes

(@); [5]1849 (@); anr. ed. 1853; [6]1851, New York: A.S. Barnes & Co., 12°, iv+218pp. (@); repr. of [6]1851 in 1852, 1853, 1853 and 1854, all New York: A.S. Barnes & Co. / Cincinnati: H.W. Derby & Co., 18.5x 11.5, iv+218pp. (plus 5 pages of reviews and commendatory notices at end), 50 cts. (@ L); rev. ed. 1855 (@); rev. eds. in 1857, 1858 and 1860, all New York: A.S. Barnes & Co. (@); anr. ed. 1862 (@); rev. ed. in 1863 and 1864 both New York: A.S. Barnes & Co. (@); rev. ed. [40]1865, New York: A.S. Barnes & Burr / Chicago: G. Sherwood, 19cm, x+[11]-309pp. (@); at least five repr. of 40th ed. until 1875 (@); rev. ed. 1877, New York: A.S. Barnes & Burr / Chicago: G. Sherwood (@)).
($ @ L *Br*)
[Inductive method, traditional terminology, innovative diagrams. OESP accepted, but not used in the book. The author prides himself on diagrams illustrating constituent structures of sentences and a folding chart following p.110. The seeming rationality of his approach, signalled by the uses of numbered definitions, principles, explanations and remarks (= notes) is not fully convincing, and the diagrams perplexing rather than helpful and definitions often not satisfactory. Clark concentrates on sentence analysis, preferring religious or educational specimens. No sources are indicated. Five pages of reviews and commendatory notices printed at end.]

317.$ ---. 1851. *Analysis of the English language, with a complete classification of sentences and phrases according to their grammatical structure; designed as an introduction to English grammar.* (National School Series). New York: A.S. Barnes & Co. / Cincinnati: H.W. Derby & Co. (Anr. ed. 1860 (National School Series), New York: A.S. Barnes & Burr, 19cm, iv+[5]-168+14pp. (@); anr. ed. 1867 (from 1854 ed.), New York: A.S. Barnes & Burr / Cincinnati: H.W. Derby & Co. (@); anr. ed. 1874 (from 1851), New York/Chicago: A.S. Barnes & Co., 168pp. (@); anr. ed. 1876, New York/Chicago: A.S. Barnes & Co., 19cm, iv+[5]-168+14pp. (@)).
(@)
[cf. Nietz 1961]

318.$ ---. [c1856]. ... *First lessons in English grammar.* (National Series. Science of the English language). New York: A.S. Barnes. 18cm, 156pp. (@). (Anr. ed. 1857 (@); anr. ed. 1864 (@); at least three further editions to 1889 (@)).
(@)

319.$ ---. 1857. *Science of the English Language. First lessons in English grammar.* New York: A.S. Barnes & Co. 156pp.

(L)

320.$ ---. 1859. *Key to Clark's grammar, in which the analysis of the sentences in the grammar are indicated in diagrams.* New York: A.S. Barnes. (Anr. ed. 1866, 16cm, 100pp. (@); anr. ed. 1869 (@); anr. ed. 1871 (@)).
(@)

321.$ ---. 1870a. ... *The normal English grammar, analytic and synthetic. Illustrated by diagrams.* (The Science of the English Language). New York/Chicago: A.S. Barnes & Co. 19cm, 334pp. (Anr. ed. 1875 (@); anr. ed. 1876 (@)).
(@)

322.$ ---. 1870b. *Key to Clark's normal grammar in which the analysis of the sentences in the grammar are indicated by diagrams, and the examples of grammatic fallacies are corrected.* New York: A.S. Barnes & Co. 19cm, 93pp.
(@)

323.$ ---. 1871. *A critical grammar.* New York. 309pp.
(@)

324.$ ---. [a1874]. *English grammar for beginners, with illustrations and diagrams.* (National Series). New York/Chicago: A.S. Barnes & Co. 18cm, viii+[9]-192pp. (@). (Anr. ed. 1874 (National Series), New York: A.S. Barnes & Co. (@)).
(@)

325.$ ---. 1875. ... *Easy lessons in language; with illustrations and diagrams.* (National Series). New York/Chicago: A.S. Barnes & Co. 18cm, 96pp.
(@)

326.$ ---. 1876. *Brief English grammar with illustrations and diagrams.* (National Series). New York/Chicago: A.S. Barnes & Co. 18cm, viii+[9]-192pp.
(@)

327. Clark, William (Conductor of an Academy at Wisbech). [a1835]. *A companion to [an English grammar], or book of exercises.* Wisbech.
(G L O)

328. ---. 1835. *An English grammar systematically arranged in a series of easy lessons appropriately designated; and characterized by many new and important features: adapted to the capacities of youth at school, and adults desirous of becoming acquainted with the principles requisite to speak and write the English language correctly; compiled from the best authorities.* Wisbech: N. Walker, for the author. 8°, iv+93pp.
(L O)

["For class reading, as well as committal to memory". OESP, with additional hints on perspicuity and elegance, plus orthoepy and punctuation, clearly arranged. Nine parts of speech, traditional, with critical remarks on classification of cases, conjugation, verb classes and 'adjective pronouns'. Mentions Murray, Lennie; no exercises.]
329. Clarke, Hyde (1815-1895). 1853. *A grammar of the English tongue, spoken and written; for self-teaching and for schools.* London: John Weale. 8°, iv+466pp. (^{2}1859, London: John Weale, 18cm, iv+152pp. (@); new ed. [1860], ... *with an introduction to the study of comparative philology,* (Weale's Educational Series II), London: Virtue / New York: Virtue & Yorston (@); ^{3}1874, London: Lockwood & Co., 18cm, 152pp. (@); ^{4}1879, 1s6d (@)).
(@ G L O)
[Somewhat rhapsodic account, claimed to be based on spoken English and drawn from writers as widely apart as Aelfric and Horne Tooke, Skinner and Adelung, Ben Jonson and Raske; mixing comparative philology with Latin-based analysis and various tables and word-lists: unsatisfactory in method and content.]
330. Clarke, Robert (Schoolmaster). 1834. *A poetical grammar of the English language and an epitome of the art of rhetoric.* London: Houlston & Co. 8°, viii+172pp. (Anr. ed. [1854] (C); ^{2}1855 (C Dur L O); [^{3}1855] (E)).
(C Dur E L O)
[The first parts, including prefaces to the second and third editions, are in pitiful rhyme, the poet not managing to squeeze grammatical information mixed from various sources, with alternative terms provided into regular rhyme and metre. Orthography has a 'grammar chant' with notes to it. From p.29, on Elocution, the text is in prose.]
331. Clarke, William Esdail Cattley (Inspector of Schools, Cape Colony) & Aldoph Conrad Muller (English Master, Grahamstown). 1897. *A class book of English grammar, including notes on figures of speech and the scansion of English verse.* Cape Town/Port Elizabeth/Johannesburg: J. C. Juta & Co., pr. in London, xi+303pp. (At least six editions in the twentieth century).
(L)
[OESP, eight parts of speech, a comprehensive account which includes some language history and word origins. Definitions followed by exposition including a great amount of detail; some exercises. Quite ambitious for its size, insightful and successful; remarkable for being one of the grammars produced in a colony.]

332. Clere, Rev. Henry & Alexander M. Shaw (of Southport). 1864. *English grammar for junior classes*. London: Longman, Roberts & Green. 14.5x9, vi+43pp.
(L O)
["... To teach in a *simple* and *entertaining* manner [...] to distinguish the parts of speech, particular of these, and [...] various errors in speaking, frequent among young people, are pointed out and corrected." Dominated by elementary definitions and long exercises, incl. parsing. The author's "English grammar for higher classes" announced p. vi has not been traced.]

333. entry deleted

334.$ Cobb, Enos. 1820a. *Elements of the English language containing illustrations of etymology and syntax: being a fair delineation of a new system of teaching English grammar*. Boston. 19cm, vi+[7]-108pp.
(@ Br)

335.$ ---. 1820b. *A self-explaining grammar of the English language, for the use of schools and academies, also calculated for those who wish to acquire a correct knowledge of English grammar, by private application. Containing rules for parsing ... rules for writing composition, and a complete system of punctuation, entirely original*. 18cm, ix+[10]-108pp. (^{2}1821, Boston: Richardson & Lord).
(@ L)
[This is the second edition of no. 334. Cobb takes definitions out of the earliest stage of learning; combines etymology and syntax under each part of speech; he records how an audience walked out because of the vulgarity of the sentence "The cow runs round the barn", used to illustrate the preposition.]

336. Cobbett, William (1763-1835). M. P. 1818. *A grammar of the English language, in a series of letters. Intended for the use of schools and of young persons in general; but more especially for the use of soldiers, sailors, apprentices, and ploughboys*. New York/London: Clayton & Kingsland, for the author, sold by T. Dolby. 184pp. (^{2}1819, London, 17/18/20cm, iv+[5]-186pp. (@ A); ^{3}1819, London: Thomas Dolby, 186pp.; ^{4}1820, London: William Benbow, 17cm, ii+186pp.; rev. and new ed. 1823, as *A grammar of the English language, in a series of letters. To which are added, six lessons, to prevent statesmen from using false grammar, and from writing in an awkward manner*, London: J.M. Cobbett, 19cm, vi+230pp. (A); new ed. 1824, London: C. Clement (A); new ed. 1826 (of 1823 ed.), London, 17cm; anr. ed. 1824, London: C. Clement, unnumbered pages; anr. ed. 1829, London: the author, 18cm, [240]p; anr. ed. 1831, London: the author, 17cm; anr. ed. London,

20cm, unnumbered pages; anr. ed. 1832, New York: John Doyle / Providence, R.T.: T. Doyle *et al.*, 16cm, 213pp. (@); anr. ed. 1833, London: Thomas Dolby, 12mo, 186pp.; anr. ed. 1833, New York: J. Doyle, 16cm, 213pp. (@); anr. ed. 1835, London: W. Cobbett, 20cm, 240pp. (@); anr. ed. 1836 (@ A); anr. ed. 1837 (@); anr. ed. 1838; anr. ed. 1840 (@); anr. ed. 1842; anr. ed. 1844 (@); anr. ed. 1847 (@ L); ster. ed. 1852, London, 18cm (A); anr. ed. 1854, Philadelphia: J.L. Gihon, 16cm, 213pp. (@); anr. ed. 1859, London: Simpkin, 289pp. (@); anr. ed. 1860; new ed. 1861; new ed. 1863, London: Griffin & Co., 15cm, 191/239pp. (@); new ed. 1866 with an additional chapter by J.P. Cobbett, London: G. Routledge & Sons, 8°, vi+151pp.; new ed. 1868 (from 1866 ed.), London: C. Griffin & Co., 16cm, 255pp.; new ed. [c1870] (from 1868 ed.), London, 12cm.; anr. ed. 1875, London: Griffin, 255pp. (@); new ed. [1880] (from [c1870] ed.), annotated by J.M., London: Ward, Lock & Co., 16cm, 163pp.; anr. ed. 1882; repr. 1883, with notes by Robert Waters as an appendix to *How to get on in the world as demonstrated by the life and language of William Cobbett*, New York: J.W. Pratt, 20cm, xiv+272pp. (@); carefully rev. and annotated ed. 1884 by Alfred Ayres [Thomas E. Osmun], New York: Appleton, 254pp.; repr. of 1833 ed. by William Cobbett as *A grammar of the English language*, London, 17cm, xvii+232pp. (E)).
(@ A C E L O Br, Hu, Lw, Ma, Sk)
Lit.: Aarts 1986; Vallins 1954; Vincent 1989.
[Reviewed by Martin 1824:5-7. In his review of anon.'s n.d. "A critical examination of Cobbett's English Grammar" Martin gives a very ironic and critical comment on Cobbett's grammar. Quotation from Lyon 1832:2 on Cobbett: "nor in fact, is it very easy to discover in what respects it differs from other grammars, excepting that it repeats their errors in plainer language, and in so doing, only tends to give them greater currency and perpetuity. (...) There is indeed another object in the publication of this book (whether the principal, or only a secondary one, I pretend not to decide), namely, the propagation of treason and libel, and a wanton use of the constituted authority of the country. Cobbett may thank his stars that he is a Englishman; for such a publication would not be tolerated in any other country under the sun, not even in America." Written to 14-year old James, 1817 from Long Island, with due regard for the boy's capacity, in non-technical language and dialogue form; appended: errors in great writers ("errors and nonsense in a King's speech" etc). The work was one of the most-quoted 19th-century grammars; criticism was frequently levelled against Cobbett's radical persuasions rather than his grammar (although some details came under severe

fire). The 1866 revision by his son has substantial changes regarding pronunciation in particular. There are two modern editions: Nickerson & Osborne, Amsterdam: Benjamins, 1983, gives everything; Burchfield's (OUP, 1984) is adequate.]

337. ---. 1831. *A spelling book, with appropriate lessons in reading, and with a stepping-stone to English grammar.* London: the author. 185pp. (^{2}1831, London, 19cm, 185(i.e. 195)pp. (@); ^{3}1832, London: Mills, Javett & Mills, 19cm, vi+[7]-192pp. (@); ^{4}1834; price in 1838: 5s; ^{7}1843, London, 12°, 175pp. (@); ^{9}1845, London: A. Cobbett, 19cm, 175pp. (@)).
(@ L)
[Traditional in form, except for exclusion of religious matter; includes "Stepping stone to Cobbett's English grammar" and "Advice to the learner of grammar".]

338. ---. 1860. *An abridgment of Cobbett's English grammar.* London: Charles Cooke.
(L)

339. ---. 1884. *The English grammar for W.C. Carefully rev. and annotated by Alfred Ayres [i.e. Thomas E. Osmun].* n.p. (Anr. ed. 1884, New York: D. Appleton & Co., 16cm, 254pp. (@); anr. ed. 1888 (@); anr. ed. 1890 (@); anr. ed. 1895 (from 1883 ed.), 254pp. (@)).
(@)
[cf. no. 336. above]

340. Cobbin, Ingram (Writer of school books, 1777-1851). [a1828a]. *Elements of English grammar; being an improved edition of Grammar for children ... illustrated with cuts by Branston.* n.p. (^{7}1828, London: F. Westley & A. H. Davis, 72pp.; ^{20}1845 as *Elements of English grammar, designed for young persons in general, particularly for preparatory schools. Illustrated with engravings*, London: T. Ward & Co., 15cm, vi+[7]-72pp. (@); ^{33}1864 as *Elements of English grammar: expressly designed for the juvenile students, either at home or in preparatory schools. Illustrated*, London: William Tegg, 16.5x10, vi+[7]-84pp. (@ L)).
($ @ L O *Br*)
[Greatly simplified account omitting "niceties" and using simple drawings for mnemonic support; conversational style, with recapitulations and practices inserted. "In sketching this grammar, the order of *nature* is followed, and not that of *art*" (30). Although there is the admitted lack of precision, the book is adequate for its needs - and was apparently successful.]

341. ---. [a1828b]. *Grammar for children.* n.p. (^{20}1844).
(*Br*)

[Mentioned on the title page of his *Elements*, no. 340; *Grammar for children* was probably the original title of *Elements*]
342. ---. ²1830. *The grammatical and pronouncing spelling book, on a new plan: designed to communicate the rudiments of grammatical knowledge, and to prevent and correct bad pronunciation, while it promotes an acquaintance with orthography.* London: Westley & Davis. (@). (⁸1838, London: Simpkin, Marshall & Co., 18cm, vii+[7]-172pp. (@)). (@)
343.! Cobbin, J. [1820?]. *Lessons in grammar, designed more especially for the use of Sunday schools.* London.
(*Mi*)
[Advertised in *Gentleman's Magazine* (Sept 1819) 89/ii:251, as nearly ready for publication.]
344.$ Cochran, Peter. 1802. *The Columbian grammar; or, A concise view of the English language.* Boston: the author. 71pp.
(@ L *Br*)
[Nine parts of speech; parsing exercises taken from Chesterfield's Maxims (*sic*).]
345. Coghlan, John. ²1868. *Reformed English grammar; a critique and textual outline of English grammar, being an attempt to exhibit the true grammatical basis on which to develop the structure, simplify the treatment, and facilitate the acquisition of the English language.* Rev. impression. Edinburgh: William P. Nimmo. 18.5x12, 56pp., 1s6d.
(L O)
[Thoughtful criticism of earlier grammarians - Coghlan analyses methods and terms praising (but disagreeing with) Bain, Latham and McCulloch; pp. 1-24 lead up to a Textual Outline of English Grammar in which 181 succinct and adequate rules are followed by examples.]
346.$ Colburn, Warren (1793-1833). 1832. *First lessons in reading and grammar, for the use of schools; chiefly from the works of Miss Edgeworth.* Boston: Hilliard, Gray & Co. xii+82pp. (Anr. ed. 1836).
1831 *Second lessons* ... Boston. (Anr. ed. 1832; anr. ed. 1833).
1832 *Third lessons* ... (Anr. ed. 1836; anr. ed. 1838).
1833 *Fourth lessons* ..., 16cm, xxiv+174pp. (@). (Anr. ed. 1838; anr. ed. 1841, Boston: Hilliard & Gray, 16cm, xii+82pp (@)).
(@ L)
[Sensible combination of reading and grammar. "It is better to teach English grammar orally than to require the scholars to study the rules in books."]
347.$ Colegrave, William (b.1824). 1878. *A complete scientific grammar of the English language, with an appendix containing a treatise on composi-*

tion, specimens of English and American literature, a defense of phonetics, etc. for the use of colleges, schools and private learners. New York: The Authors' Publ. Co. 19cm, 362pp.
(@)

348.$ Colegrove, Rev. W. 1852. *Multum in parvo. An improved grammar of the English language.* Cleveland: Smith, Knight & Co. 18cm, xi+89pp.
(@ L)
[Very brief, and sometimes objectionable, definitions; OESP with appendix supplementing the discussion in main text.]

349. Coles, James (Schoolmaster) & John Hewitt Tomlin. [1880]. *Second/third standard grammar. Adapted to the code of 1880.* (Coles' & Tomlin's School Series). 2 parts. Pt. I: *Second standard grammar and geography.* Leeds: J.W. Bean/E.J. Arnold / London: Simpkin, Marshall & Co. etc. 16x10, 32pp., 1d each.
(O L)
[Very short definitions, mostly not satisfactory, with Exercises (finding and underlining parts of speech).]

350. --- & ---. 1881. *An English grammar for first classes in elementary schools.* (Coles' & Tomlin's School Series). Standards IV, V, VI. Leeds: J.W. Bean & Son / London: Simpkin, Marshall & Co. / Manchester: Hull & Educational Trading Companies. 16.5x10.5, 54pp., 3d.
(O L)
[Definitions in boxes suggest orderliness, but are very elementary and often misleading; derivative at best.]

351. Collier, Henry, Gent. 1820. *An epitome of English grammar.* London: the author. 16.5x10, 42pp., 2s.
(@ L *Hu, Lw*)
[A very brief discussion of eight parts of speech (5-36), with a few remarks on syntax, 37-42. Disappointing. Verb forms on a strictly Latin pattern; based on 18th-century traditions.]

352. Collier, William Francis. 1866. *A grammar of the English language, with a sketch of its history for schools.* (Constable's Education Series). London: Simpkin, Marshall / Edinburgh: Thomas Laurie. 18x11.5, viii+126pp., 1s6d. (new ed. 1870, Edinburgh: T. Laurie, 19cm, iv+124pp. (@)).
(@ L O)
[OES with an appendix on prosody and a history of the English language at end; eight parts of speech. A competent and well-arranged summary of traditional knowledge reduced to the capacities of school children; references to Old English, slightly more than appropriate - the appended

history does not belong, either. Definitions, rules and a few notes; few parsing exercises.]
353. ---. 1867. *First lessons in English grammar*. Edinburgh: Adam & Charles Black. 14.5x10, iv+58pp., 6d. (Anr. ed. [1876], Edinburgh: Thomas Laurie).
(L O)
[Introductory to his *GEL*, in simple language and conversational style: expository passages alternating with exercises. The method did not permit precision - *GEL* is much more substantial.]
354. ---. [1874]. *The new practical English grammar, with exercises*. (Laurie's Kensington Series). Edinburgh: Thomas Laurie. 16.5x10.5, iii+124pp., 1s/1s6d.
(L O)
[A practical work based on experience, accuracy of definitions aimed at, with a complete order of parsing and many exercises appended, OESP, nine parts of speech; unexciting, but quite competent.]
355. Colquhoun, John Stuart. 1871. *A compendious grammar and philological hand-book of the English language for the use of schools and candidates for the army and civil service examinations*. London: Griffith & Farran. 8°, vii+202pp., 2s6d.
(L O)
[A somewhat learned compilation made from Horne Tooke, Hallam, and Latham; short definitions and illustrations, with etymological/historical explanations where appropriate. The same book as the one advertised in Parry Gwynne, *A word to the wise*, of 1852?]
356.! Anon. [c1830]. *Comic grammar*. London. 28 plates.
(*Gu*)
[cf. Gumuchian (1967: No.1823)]
[Not the same as Leigh, no. 1703.]
356a. Anon. 1871. *The comic Lindley Murray; or, The grammar of grammars. With illustrative sketches*. Dublin: A. Murray & Co. (Facs. repr. London: Routledge/Thoemmes Press, 1996 (In: Reibel 1996, vol. II, *Lindley Murray's Grammar in caricature: Four Parodies*).
(Reibel 1996)
["It looks at first more like the beginnings of a parody [of Lindley Murray's *English Grammar*] rather than a complete effort, as if the author had run out of steam or conviction before the task was completed. but on closer perusal we see that the work is a vehicle for a range of humorous puns and passages, the 'illustrative sketches', that in fact have very little to do with grammar, and with an Irish slant that is self-explanatory". Reibel (1996:xvif.).]

357.$ Comly, John. 1803. *English grammar made easy to the teacher and pupil. Principally compiled for the use of West-town boarding school, Pennsylvania.* Philadelphia. 18mo, 192pp. (Corr. and enl. ed. ^{2}1805, 15cm, iv+[5]-230pp. (@); ^{3}1808, Philadelphia: Kimber, Conrad & Co., 228pp. ($ @); corr. and enl. ed. ^{4}1810, 215pp. (@); corr. and enl. ed. ^{5}1812, 214pp. (@); corr. and enl. ed. ^{6}1815, Philadelphia: Emmor Kimber (@); ^{8}1818 Philadelphia (@); ^{15}1826).
($ @ *Br*)
[From ^{5}1812: Ten parts of speech; emphasises parsing and correction of false English; routine, nothing significant. 1821 edition revises definitions; 1825 edition unchanged. Nevertheless a much used book.]

358.! Anon. [a1898]. *Companion exercise book for analysis and parsing.* London: Relfe.
[From advertisement]

359. Anon. [p1836]. *Compendious English grammar, preceded by a sketch of the history of the English language.* (Blackies School Series). London: Blackie.
(@)

360. entry deleted

361.$! Anon. 1807. *Compendium of Ash's Grammatical Institutes; or, An easy introduction to Dr. Lowth's English grammar; etc.* Washington City: J.D. Westcott & Co. 72pp.
(*Ke*)

362. entry deleted

363. Anon. 1840. *A compilation of English grammar rules for the use of Maize Hill School, London.* London: W. Annan. 16cm, 59pp.
($ @ L)
[Very brief grammar rules with few examples; with remarks on composition, "faulty examples", and abbreviations appended. A minimal grammar.]

364. Anon. [1890]. *Complete grammar for pupil teachers and middle-class scholars.* (The Jubilee Series). n.p.
(L)

365. Anon. ^{3}1855. *The complete grammar summary, including analysis, derivation, letter-writing, composition, paraphrase & exercises.* (Heywood & Newton's Derby Series). Derby: Heywood & Newton. 18cm, 32pp.
(@)

366. Anon. 1879. *A comprehensive grammar or ðe Iŋgliʃ laŋgwɛj in fonetik speliŋ.* London: Frederick Pitman / Bath: Isaak Pitman. 16x10, 48pp.
(O)

[Drawn from short OESP accounts "found in the best modern grammars". The interest is purely in the use of Pitman's reformed spelling throughout. Includes punctuation and prosody at end. Also cf. no. 528.]
367.$ Anon. 1825. *A concise grammar of the English language, attempted in verse for the sake of the memory, and designed for the use of common schools.* New York. 18mo, 63pp.
(@ *Br*)
368. Connel, Robert (Teacher of English). 1831. *An improved system of English grammar, with copious exercises and explanatory observations adapted alike to the use of schools, and to the purpose of private tuition.* Glasgow: Atkinson & Co. 15cm, xiii+162pp. (^{2}1834, Glasgow: A. Rutherglen & Co. (@); rev., impr. and greatly enl. ed. ^{3}1839, Glasgow: A. Rutherglen, 15cm, 200pp. (@); ^{4}1843).
(@ L *Br*)
[Relates grammar to oral and written expression; nine parts of speech (no participle); recommends Tooke; conventional but discriminating and typographically sophisticated.]
369. Connell, Jessie. 1854. *The heart's-ease, or, grammar in verse. With easy exercises in prose. For very young children. By a lady teacher.* (Publ. anon). London/Glasgow: Richard Griffin. xv+160pp.
(C O)
[Doggerel verse used to put across very insufficient definitions and methods. Written in conversational style between mother and child, the quality of the verse being about as bad as that of the explanations; examples and exercises ("fill in ..."). Her address to teachers includes "I learned myself from Lennie's book / But O! the trouble that it took / To make me comprehend!"]
370. Connon, Charles Walker. 1845. *A system of English grammar, founded on the philosophy of language and the practice of the best authors. With copious exercises. For use in schools and private study.* Edinburgh: Oliver & Boyd. 18cm, 168pp., 2s6d. (A). (^{2}1852, 199pp.; ^{4}1854 (A); ^{5}1855, 199pp. (@); ^{8}1863, Edinburgh: Oliver & Boyd / London: Simpkin, Marshall & Co., 17cm, 199pp. (@); price in 1870: 2s6d).
(@ A C L O *Hu*, *Lw*)
[Traditional account, with parsing exercises and many study questions.]
371. Constable, Thomas. 1857. *A series of graduated exercises adapted to Morell's Grammar and analysis.* Edinburgh: Constable.
(L)
372. Contractor, Hasum Alidina. 1887. *The English teacher. Containing English grammar, words and proverbs, idioms, essays, letters, petitions,*

invitations, cards, &c and many matriculation questions up to 1886. Bombay: Erachshah Karani & Co. 97pp.
(L)
[The grammar (mainly on eight parts of speech) takes up pp. 1-21; though unexciting it illustrates the English input on the Indian subcontinent; quite adequate for the intended purpose.]

373. Cooper, Alice J. (Head Mistress of the Edgbaston High School). 1889. *An English grammar for schools.* (Parallel Grammar Series). London: Swan Sonnenschein. 24pp.
(L)

374.! ---. 1890. *English examples and exercises. Part 2: Analysis.* (Parallel Grammar Series). London: Swan Sonnenschein. 58pp.
(Nietz 1961:130)
[Part 1 is by Mary A. Woods.]

375.$! Cooper, Rev. Joab Goldsmith. 1828. *An abridgment of Murray's English grammar.* Philadelphia. 12mo, 200pp.
(*Br*)
[*Br*: "largely stolen from G. Brown".]

376.$ ---. 1831. *A plain and practical English grammar: in which the principles of our language are simplified, and more fully explained than in any work of the kind. With suitable parsing lessons, and copious critical and explanatory notes. Designed for students in the schools, academies and colleges of the United States.* Philadelphia: Judah Dobson. 18cm, iv+210pp.
(@ *Br*)

377. entry deleted

378.$! Cornell, William. 1840. *English grammar.* Boston. 4to, 12pp.
(*Br*)

379. Corner, Julia (1798-1875). [1848] *The play grammar; or, The elements of grammar, explained in easy games.* London: Thomas Dean & Son. 8°, 113pp., 1s6d. (Anr. ed. 1848; enl. and impr. ed. [6]n.d., London: Thomas Dean & Son, 109pp. (@); enl. and impr. ed. [27][1875?], *with conundrum exercises*, London: Dean & Son, 18cm, 116pp., 1s6d/1s (@)).
(@ L *Hu*)
[Basic terms and concepts are introduced in a conversation between a mother and her two children: parts of speech, 'cases', gender.]

380. ---. [1857]. *Round games and amusing exercises upon grammar. An addendum to Corner's Play grammar and all other grammars.* London: Thomas Dean & Son. 16x10, vi+76pp.
(Eu L)

[Common games filled with grammatical questions and exercises, some in rhymes adapted to beginners' comprehensions so that rules might "be impressed upon and retained in the memory of young students". Nine parts of speech.]

381. Cornwallis, Caroline Frances (1786-1858). 1847. *General principles of grammar.* (Publ. anon.). (Small Books on Great Subjects - No. XII). London: William Pickering. 17x11, iv+118pp. (Anr. ed. 1847, Philadelphia: Lea & Blanchard, 17cm, 76pp. (@); ²1854).
(@ L *Hu*, *Lw*)
[Very selective remarks on the nine parts of speech are embedded in the author's reflexions on general grammar and linguistic diversity; some references to Anglo-Saxon.]

382.$ Covell, L.T. 1852. *(Covell's) Digest of English grammar, synthetical and analytical, classified and methodically arranged ... and adapted to the use of schools.* New York: D. Appleton. 18.5x11.5, 218pp. (L). (²1853, New York: D. Appleton & Co. (@); ³1853, New York: D. Appleton & Co. (@); anr. ed. 1854, New York: D. Appleton / Pittsburgh: A.H. English & Co., 20cm, 218pp. (@); at least five more editions until 1866, price in 1864: 63c).
(@ L)
[OESP, eight parts of speech; succinct and generally precise definitions and rules followed by examples and exercises; self-study questions at the bottom of the page; some "false syntax". More detailed advice is given in "Remarks" in small print. A well-planned, if sober description.]

383.$ ---. 1853. *Primary grammar; being a brief abstract of the author's digest of English grammar; and designed for beginners.* Pittsburgh: A.H. English & Co. 16cm, viii+[9]-120pp.
(@)
[cf. Nietz 1961:130]

384. Crabb, George (Master of the Commercial and Literary Seminary, Walworth, 1778-1851). 1807. *The preceptor and his pupils; or, dialogues, examinations, and exercises on grammar in general, and the English grammar in particular. For the use of schools and private students.* [Part 1]. London. 20cm.
(@ H L)
[cf. *Gent. Mag.* 77 (Aug. 1807) ii.751.]
[Interesting for the fact that Crabb discusses, and rejects, learning the functions of the parts of speech through familiarity. They should be learnt by studying "the relations and dependencies of words". Light-hearted illustrations.]

385.! ---. 1808. *The preceptor and his pupils, part the second; containing the syntax of all languages, together with special rules, dialogues, examinations, and exercises on the English language; to which are added a practical system of English composition, and a concise history of the formation of all languages.* London.
(Mi, Mp)
[Links grammar with composition; offers innovation in his treatment of government, and acknowledges obligations to Adelung for much on the sentence. Part 3, 1810, is a volume of synonyms "etymologically illustrated".]

386. Cramp, William. 1838. *The philosophy of language, containing practical rules for acquiring a knowledge of English grammar, with remarks on the principles of syntax and composition.* London: Relfe & Fletcher. 21x13, xvi+241pp.
(Dt L O *Hu, Lw*)
["... To render the principles of grammar easy, and the rules of syntax useful, to those who have in early life neglected the theory of speech [...]. To blend the philosophy of language with the best instructions of the best teachers is perhaps the surest means of attracting the attention of the self-educated reader" (iv-v). An ambitious discursive grammar which draws freely on Lowth, Harris, Tooke, Murray, M'Culloch, Lennie, and Crombie in particular, stressing the logical background of grammar; loosely organized, it argues with the reader rather than instructs him. Cramp rejects what he refers to as an opinion generally held, that "the province of the grammarian is not to dictate what usages ought to be, but simply to discover what they are."]

387. Crane, George (Grammarian). 1843. *The principles of language; exemplified in a practical English grammar. With copious exercises. Designed as an introduction to the study of languages generally, for the use of schools, and self instruction.* London: Whittaker & Co. 18x10.5, xii+264pp.
(C L O *Hu, Br, Lw*)
[Important as an exponent of Becker's views about analysis. Crane was an earlier influence on English grammar than is commonly realised. More interesting pedagogically than most grammars. Very careful exposition of traditional grammar (some influence of Latin structures), moderately prescriptive.]

388. Anon. [a. 1824]. *A critical examination of Cobbett's English grammar, in a letter to a friend: shewing the errors and inconsistencies contained in that work, and the absurdity of the author's proposed changes in the established grammatical terms and ...* n.p.

(@ *Ma*)
["A critical examination of Cobbett's English Grammar", by X. This gentleman evidently understands Grammar; why therefore, has he not published his name?" The greater part of the book is taken up by four chapters on the sentence: Categories like number, gender, tense, case, word order being discussed in I, complements, passive voice and adverbs in II, compound sentences in II, and complex ones in IV. Eleven parts of speech are discussed in V under 'Etymology'. The author openly professes to be an admirer of Becker, basing his views on his experience as a teacher of English on the Continent. Account based on Martin 1824:273.]

389.$ Anon. 1854. *Criticisms in etymology and syntax, or, a supplemental grammar: containing much that is new, original, and important* ... n.p. 20x21, 48pp.
($)

390. Crombie, Alexander (1762-1840). 1802. *The etymology and syntax of the English language, explained and illustrated.* London: J. Johnson. viii+302pp. (^{2}1809, as *A treatise on the etymology and syntax of the English language*; corr. and enl. ed. ^{3}1830, London: Taylor, 23cm, 430pp. (@); ^{4}1836, London: Taylor & Walton, 22cm, xii+335pp. (@); ^{5}1843 (@); ^{7}1853 (@); ^{8}1856 (@); ^{9}1865; price in 1848: 7s6d).
(@ C L *Hu, Br, Lw, Ma, Sk*)
[Crombie's conservatism is usefully critical and is frequently commended by later writers (at least 26 references); his book had nine editions to 1865. Discursive traditional account, largely indebted to Harris, Lowth, Priestley, Murray etc., some classical ballast ('aorist' p.125). Ten parts of speech treated one by one, with syntax (= concord and government) in Part II, 175-233) and useful "critical remarks" and illustrations appended, 234-. Very conservative '18th-century' treatment in structure, content and attitude. Martin 1824:271: "This work is allowed to rot in obscurity on account of its price, which is much below its internal worth. Dr CROMBIE was not a scribbler, but a man who dived to the depths of the language, and founded all his rules on demonstrative principles." The grammar was praised and/or used by more than 25 nineteenth-century grammarians.]

391. Currey, Rev. George (Preacher at the Charterhouse, London). 1856. *An English grammar for the use of schools.* (Published under the direction of the Committee of General Literature and Education, appointed by the Society for Promoting Christian Knowledge). London: SPCK. 16x10, 216pp. (in large print). (Anr. ed. [1863]; the easier parts of the book

were published separately as *A grammar for beginners*, London, 127pp. (O); anr. ed. 1865 (E)).
(E L O *Lw*)
[Grammar is defined as accidence (the formation and classification of words) plus syntax (how to put words together); nine parts of speech; adequate definitions, quotations mostly from the Bible (note exceptions in *Believest thou this?*). Parts of speech and syntax treated, with much attention paid to parsing; the exercise is seen as a preparation for foreign languages since "The logical basis is the same in all languages, and the construction of the different languages is in many respects alike".]

392. Currie, James (Principal of the Church of Scotland Training College, Edinburgh, 1828-1886). [1866]. *Rudimentary English grammar*. (Constable's Education Series). Edinburgh: Thomas Laurie. 16°, ii+62pp.
(L O)
[Eight parts of speech, with inflexion and syntax: illustration, definition, exercises - "the natural method for the instruction of children". Six tenses, including past (perfect).]

393. ---. [1870]. *The practical school grammar including analysis of sentences, with an appendix of exercises in composition*. Edinburgh/London: W. Stewart. 17cm, 75pp.
(@ L)
[Eight parts of speech; three kinds of subordinate clause; up-to-date in a narrow way; mechanistic view of composition.]

394. Curtis, John Charles (Principal of the Training College, Borough Road, London). 1867. *Outlines of English grammar. For school and home use*. London: Simpkin & Marshall & Co. 16.5x10.5, 48pp. (^{29}1878 London: Simpkin & Marshall (@); undated ed. in Jill Grey collection).
(@ L O)
[cf. Dodwell 1993:64]
[A pattern of definition, examples, explanations, exercise is rigorously carried through in the introductory part, whereas the second, dealing with classification, inflection and syntax has rules and notes interspersed. Curtis regards it as an innovation that syntax is distributed amongst parts of speech. Tightly organized and very solidly adequate. Indebted to Becker and his followers Morell, Mason and Green.]

395. ---. 1871. *A manual of the analysis of sentences*. London: Simpkin & Marshall. 16x10, ii+48pp. (^{9}1878 (@); ^{17}1887 (@)).
(@ L)
[Syntax explained analytically in short definitions, explanatory notes and plentiful exercises; C. says he is indebted to the works of Becker and his followers Morell, Mason and Green. Quite a clear exposition, with

plentiful exercises, and many notes devoted to details. Technical, but adequate.]

396. ---. 1875. *A first book of grammar and analysis*. (Curtis's Educational Series). London. Simpkin & Marshall. 24pp. (^{4}1877, London: Simpkin & Marshall, 16x10, 24pp., 3d. (@ L); ^{6}1885).
(@ L)
[The booklet consists of very brief definitions and explanations followed by extensive exercises; meant as an introduction to C's *Outlines* (no. 394) and his *Manual* (no. 395) it is exclusively a poor exercise book for the classroom.]

397. Curtis, John Charles (Principal of the Training College, Borough Road, London). 1876. *An English grammar for schools*. (Curtis's Educational Series). London: Simpkin, Marshall & Co. 17cm, vi+122pp. (^{2}1877, London: Simpkin & Marshall (@)).
(@ L O)
[The alphabet, etymology (eight parts of speech, 'demonstrative adjectives', three tenses combined with 'indefinite', 'imperfect', 'perfect' and 'perfect continuous'), syntax and analysis, with notes and exercises, especially for parsing.]

398.$ Cutler, Andrew. 1841. *English grammar and parser, made up of proverbs, interesting anecdotes, prose and poetical selections: addressed to school examining committees; teachers and scholars a little advanced in understanding*. Plainfield, Ct.: W.A. Bennet & J.S. French. 12mo, 168pp.
(@ Br)

399.$ Dagg, John Leadley (1794-1884). 1864. *The grammar of the English language: book first; progressive lessons in English grammar*. Macon, Ga.: Burke, Boykin & Co. 17cm, 164pp.
($ @)

400.$! Dale, William A. Tweed. 1820a. *A small English grammar*. Albany, N.Y. 18mo, 72pp.
(Br)

401.$ ---. 1820b. *The teacher and pupil's assistant, in grammar and pronunciation: with rules for rhetorical pausing, inflecting the voice, and placing the emphasis on the principles of Walker*. Albany: Packard & Van Benthuysen. 16cm. 168pp.
(@)

402. Dalgleish, Walter Scott (1834-1897). Vice-Principal of Dreghorn College. ^{3}1865. *English composition in prose and verse based on grammatical synthesis*. Edinburgh: Oliver & Boyd. 2s6d. (^{2}1866; ^{3}1868; anr. ed.

1872; ⁵1878, Edinburgh: Oliver & Boyd, London: Simpkin & Marshall, 15cm, 76pp. (@)).
Key 1863
(@ L)
[Composition is "the exact counterpart of grammatical analysis". The view damages his teaching of composition.]

403. ---. 1865. *Grammatical analysis, with progressive exercises*. Edinburgh: Oliver & Boyd. 17x12, 66pp. (L). (Anr. ed. [²1865], New York: American Book Co. (@ L); anr. ed. 1868 (@); anr. ed. 1869 ($); anr. ed. 1870 (@); anr. ed. 1871, 20cm, 66pp. ($); anr. ed. 1874 ($); at least nine editions to 1883).
Key 1865 (at least seven editions to about 1870).
($ @ L)
[Meant as an introduction to *English composition* (no. 402); refers to Morell, Bain and Adams. "The sentence and its parts; the simple sentence; the complex sentence; the compound sentence" with copious exercises inserted. Though not original, quite competent and clear.]

404. Dalgleish, Walter Scott (Vice-Principal of Dreghorn College, 1834-1897). 1866. *The progressive English grammar. With exercises*. Edinburgh: Oliver & Boyd / London: Simpkin, Marshall & Co. 17x11, 152pp., 2s. (rev. ed. ²1868; rev. ed. ³1871; rev. ed. ⁴1873; ⁵1876 (@); rev. ed. ⁶1878; rev. ed. ⁸[1892]; anr. ed. 1898).
Key 1867 Edinburgh: Oliver & Boyd / London: Simpkin, Marshall & Co., 95pp. (rev. ed. ²1869 (L)).
(@ L O)
[Stresses the practical, simple, progressive method; eight parts of speech related to parsing; syntax explained as the relations of words, with final sections on word-formation, language history and punctuation. Many parsing exercises interspersed. Solid but unexciting.]

405. ---. 1867. *Outlines of English grammar and analysis, for elementary schools. With exercises*. Edinburgh: Oliver & Boyd / London: Simpkin, Marshall & Co. 8°, 76pp., 8d. (L). (²1868 (L); ³1870 (L)).
Key 1867 Edinburgh: Oliver & Boyd / London: Simpkin, Marshall & Co., 15x10, 55pp., 1s. (L). (Anr. ed. 1871? (@)).
(@ L O)
[The key is purely complementary, and of no independent value apart from the (unexciting) hints to teachers on methods.]

406. Dalton, John (Teacher of Mathematics and Natural Philosophy, and secretary to the Library and Philosophical Society, Manchester, 1766-1844). 1801. *Elements of English grammar; a new system of gram-*

matical instruction, for the use of schools and academies. London: W.J. & J. Richardson. 16x10, xvi+122pp. (Lu). (²1803 London: T. Ostell).
($ L Lu Sm *Hu, Br, Lw, Ma*)
Lit.: Smyth 1966.
[The author has "long thought that elementary books on grammar were more remarkably defective than others." Dedicated to Horne Tooke, whose system is followed with some modifications; the author summarizes his deviances from the grammatical tradition, i-xiii, and significantly starts with "On the origin of ideas; and their relation to language" (1-4). Etymology and syntax, with few remarks on punctuation.]

407. Dalziell, Allan (First class certificated teacher, Causewayhead Public School). [1882]. *Hand-book of English grammar and grammatical analysis*. Edinburgh/Glasgow: John Menzies & Co. 17x11.5, vi+[7]-79pp., 1s.
(L O)
[Emphasis on sentence analysis. Nine parts of speech with verbs described in particular detail. Short definitions (not always satisfactory) and plenty of notes, with exercises on letters, words, sentences, punctuation and parsing; prosody and "lexical meanings and verbose definitions" are omitted in order to provide "what is absolutely necessary". Too traditional for 1882 to be remarkable.]

408. Daniel, Evan (Principal of the National Society's Training College, 1837-1904). 1881. *The grammar, history, and derivation of the English language with chapters on parsing, analysis of sentences, and prosody*. London: National Society's Depository. 18x11.5, vii+383pp., (New and rev. ed. 1885 ($ @); new and rev. ed. 1890, vii+[1]-401pp. (@); anr. ed. 1891, vii+456pp. ($); new rev. ed. 1894 (@ L); new rev. ed. 1898 (@ L)).
($ @ H L O)
[Leisurely exposition leading up to definitions in bold print; exercises at end of subchapters. Great attention paid to analysis and parsing. Accidence (1-126), Analysis of sentences (127-58), Syntax (159-220), Prosody (221-36), History (237-374; a very mixed section). Although a serious attempt at summarizing the grammatical knowledge of the time, Daniel fails to organize his material in a totally convincing way.]

409. Darnell, George (Schoolmaster, Islington, 1798-1857). [1846]. *Grammar made intelligible to children: being a series of short and simple rules, with ample explanations of every difficulty, and copious exercises for parsing, in language adapted to the comprehension of very young students*. London: Griffith & Farran. vi+88pp. (Ster. ed. 1855; anr. ed.

1860 (*Tm*, 50); anr. ed. 1861 (@); ster. ed. 1864, 18cm, iv+[7]-88pp. (@); ster. ed. n.d., 18cm, vi+[7]-34pp. (@); price in 1869: 1s).
(@ L *Hu*, *Lw*, *Tm*)
[Part I was issued separately as *An introduction to English grammar, being the first part of "Grammar made intelligible to children"; consisting of a graduated series of easy lessons, in language adapted to the comprehension of very young students; with ample explanations of every difficulty, questions for examination, and copious exercises for parsing ... Stereotype edition*. London: Grant & Griffith [1855?], 32pp. (L). The whole work is written for 8 to 9-year-old boys, departing from the common system of arrangement in placing spelling together with prosody at the end; particular attention given to verbs.]

410. Darnell, Thomas. 1865. *Parsing simplified. An introduction and companion to all grammars: consisting of short and easy rules, with parsing lessons to each, whereby very young students may* [understand] *the grammatical construction of the most complex sentences of our ordinary authors*. London: Griffith & Farran. 18cm, 76pp. (⁴a1876).
(@ L)
[An unsophisticated work.]

411. Dasent, Charles Underwood (1824 or 25-1895). 1877. *A grammar of the English language, for middle and higher class schools*. Ed. by Leonhard Schmitz. (Collins' School Series). Glasgow: William Collins, Sons & Co. 18cm, viii+203pp.
(@ C L O)
[Not very systematic, and with a strong historical bent totally unjustified by the purpose. Dasent mentions Abbott, Morris, Adams, Mason, Latham and Mätzner, Fiedler, Sachs.]

412.$ Davenport, Bishop. 1830. *English grammar simplified on philosophical principles*. Wilmington, Del.: the author. 14cm, 139pp.
($ @)

413.$ Davenport, Herbert J. (1861-1931) & Anna M. Emerson. 1898. *The principles of grammar, an introduction to the study of the laws of language by the inductive method*. New York/London: Macmillan. 19cm, xiv+268pp. (Anr. ed. 1899 (@)).
($ @ L *Br*)

414.$ Davidson, Alexander (1794-1856). 1850. *The Canada spelling book intended as an introduction to the English language, consisting of a variety of lessons, progressively arranged in three parts: with an appendix, containing several useful tables, the outlines of geography, a comprehensive sketch of grammar, and morning and evening prayers for every day in the week: the words divided and accented to the purest*

mode of pronunciation. n.p. 179pp. (Anr. ed. 1845 ($); anr. ed. 1850 ($); anr. ed. 1860 ($)).
($)

415. Davidson, David. 1815. *An arrangement of English grammar; with critical remarks, and a collection of synonymes.* Edinburgh: Michael Anderson / London: Longman, Hurst, Rees, Orme & Brown. 19cm, xii+303pp.
($ A G L)
[The title is suggestive: the book seems even more of a compilation than is usual. His use of *adnoun* and of *grammatical resolution* for parsing are from an older tradition than are his 31 forms of poetic licence.]

416. ---. 1823. *A syntactical English grammar, in which the rules of composition are briefly exemplified: the sentences are construed and parsed, and the whole is divided into short and easy lessons.* London: Baldwin, Cradock & Joy. 20cm, 150pp.
(@ Br, Lw, Ma)
[Martin 1824:275: "certainly deserves a share of public patronage; his division of the Verb into Tenses is adopted in the present treatise as the most correct".]

417. Davidson, Ellis A. [1870]. *Our first grammar. With 100 exercises for home work, and questions for examination.* London/New York: Cassell, Petter & Galpin. 16x10, vi+[7]-120pp., 1s.
(@ L O)
[Nine parts of speech introduced in childlike style, with exercises interspersed; a consistent attempt at simplifying grammar.]

418. Davidson, John Best. 1839. *The difficulties of English grammar and punctuation removed. For beginners and unsuccessful learners.* London: Simpkin etc. 17.5x10.5, 114+74pp. (unpagin.). (^{3}1846 as *The difficulties of English grammar and punctuation removed; or English grammar simplified. Adapted for schools and self-instruction. To which is added a treatise on punctuation*, London: Simpkin & Marshall / Leeds: J. Buckton, 14cm, 140pp., 1s6d).
(C L Lu O *Hu, Lw*)
[An interesting example of unsophisticated attempts at reform, especially in his "new theory of the verb". Davidson is caught in the system, but it is critical of it, and struggles. After critical discussion of definitions and methods of earlier grammarians the parts of speech are discussed one by one, often with new (easier?) terms suggested (*forename, describing word* = pronoun etc.).]

419. Davidson, William (B.A.) & Joseph Crosby Alcock (Headmaster of Gosforth School). [1873]. *A complete manual of parsing, including also*

a synoptical table of the system: a full elucidation of English idioms; a discussion of words difficult to classify; and a glossary of grammatical terms. Manchester: John Heywood. 16.5x10, viii+[9]-160pp. (^{2}1875; ^{6}1878, 1s6d; rev. and enl. ed. ^{7}1880, London: Allman, 17cm, vii+[8]-204pp. (@); ^{15}[1899]).
(@ L)
[A systematic account of parsing; arrangement claimed to be novel; "a necessary supplement to the common text-books of grammar." Nine parts of speech are illustrated in subchapters (9-91), part II (95-139) being devoted to idiomatic words and phrases presenting particular problems.]

420. --- & ---. 1876?a. *A first English grammar and analysis.* London: T.J. Allman. 17cm, 32pp.
(@)

421. --- & ---. [1876]b. *Intermediate English grammar and analysis.* London: T.J. Allman. 16x10, 80pp. (Anr. ed. n.d., New York: Schwartz, Kirwin & Facess (@); reissue [1899], London: Allman & Son (L)).
(@ H L O)
[OES, eight parts of speech, brief and often unprecise definitions with plentiful exercises added; study questions at end of chapters.]

422. --- & ---. 1876c. *English grammar and analysis.* London: T.J. Allman. 18x12, viii+[9]-256pp., 2s. (L). (Anr. ed. 1878, with a new chapter on phonology & phonetics by authors & Ethel Maria Alcock; new ed. 1889 (Davidson and Alcock's Educational Works, 3), with considerable additions, London: Allman, 19cm, 288pp. ($ @); anr. ed. 1897 ($); new ed. 1899, with considerable additions, 300pp. (L); new ed. 1900, with considerable additions and complete index, London: Allman & Son, 300pp. (L); many later editions, in various forms).
Key [1878] London: T.J. Allman, 19cm, viii+[9]-268pp.
($ @ L O)
[OESP, with Punctuation and History added at end. Concise rules, with very many observations and exceptions; exercises and questions referring back. The arrangement is clear in principle but suffers from excessive detail. Great care is devoted to syntax and the analysis of sentences.]

423. --- & ---. [1877]. *Complete manual of analysis and parsing.* London: T.J. Allman. 232pp., 2s. (L). (Anr. ed. [1899] (L)).
(@ L)

424.$ Davies, E. F. 1859. *The word-work, and analytical grammar and dictionary; a new and improved system of ethnology and English grammar, rendering a classic turn to the English language. For the use of schools, academies and colleges, and as a book of reference to each rank position of society. Together with a system of penmanship, bookkeeping and*

arithmetical rules, with examples for the student, teacher and practical business man. n.p. 23cm.
($)

425.$ Davies, Henry William (Second Master of Normal School, Province of Ontario, 1834-1895). 1868. *An analytical and practical grammar of the English language with an appendix on prosody, punctuation.* (Canadian National Series School Books). n.p. viii+240pp. (Anr. ed. 1869, viii+213pp. ($)).
($)

426.$ ---. 1869. *An English grammar for the use of junior classes.* (Canadian National Series School Books). Toronto: Adam Miller. 15.5x10, xxii+124pp. (Anr. ed. 1877 ($); anr. ed. 1886 ($)).
($ L)
[Arranged in two parts, "First steps in grammar" (i-xxii) and "English grammar" (23-124) which cover similar ground at different levels of abstraction; otherwise traditional OESP, unexciting - remarkable for being one of the few grammar books published in the colonies.]

427. Davis, George W. & William Moughton. [1885] *The guide series of standard grammars.* 4 vols. London: Simpkin, Marshall & Co. 16+20+48+56pp., 1+1+2+3d.
(O)
[Traditional, and not fully convincing. "An outline of the way the lessons should be presented to the children. The difficulties are dealt with step by step, and in simple language." The authors also figure as publishers (Birmingham).]

427a. Davis, Rev. John. A.M. [c1820]. *Abridgment of Murray's English grammar, improved and illustrated, with copious explanatory observations... A new edition, thoroughly revised... by a member of the university.* London/Guildford. 24°. (Anr. ed. 1872 Belfast: William Mullen, 182pp., 9d).
Key 1820 (L).
(L O)

428. Davis, Rev. John. A.M. 1830a. *Murray's English exercises, adapted to his English grammar: consisting of exercises in parsing; instances of false orthography; ... violations of the rules respecting perspicuous and accurate writing. Designed ... for the use of schools. Enlarged by the Rev. John Davis, A.M.* Belfast. 18cm, 212pp.
(L O)
[Davis considerably expands Murray on composition.]

429. ---. 1830b. *Murray's English grammar, adapted to the different classes of learners, enlarged by J. Davis.* Belfast. 17cm. (C O).

Key 1830 Belfast (L).
(C L O)
[Davis's introduction is a defence of exercises in false English. His additions deal with narrative and themes. Possibly identical with *Br*'s reference: Davis, J. 1832. *English grammar*. Belfast. 18mo, 188pp. (*Br*)]

430.! ---. [a1872]. *Murray's first grammar for junior classes. By the Rev. John Davis*. Belfast: William Mullan. 6d.
(*Mi*)
[Advertised]

431.$ Davis, Pardon. 1818. *A philological epitome. Designed for the use of the elect didactic seminary*. Philadelphia: Thomas Town, for the author. 18cm, 56pp.
($ @ *Br*)

432.$ ---. 1845. *(Davis's) Modern practical English grammar: adapted to the American system of teaching*. Philadelphia: U. Hunt & Son. 19/20cm, xviii+175pp.
($ @ *Br*)

433. Davis, William. 1867. *Examples and exercises in English parsing, syntax, and the analysis of sentences, together with a brief outline of etymology, syntax and analysis*. London: Longmans, Green & Co. 16.5x10.5, v+63pp.
(L O)
[Etymology (='morphology') and Syntax (incl. analysis) treated briefly; the main section is devoted to parsing exercises and the analysis of sentences (14-63), with specimens taken from standard authors. "Not intended for mere beginners" - grammar and parsing methods here being only recapitulated.]

434. ---. 1877. *The complete grade parsing and analysis. A book of exercises for home and school use*. 2 parts. I: *Containing parsing, and the analysis of simple sentences*. II: *Containing the analysis of compound, complex, and miscellaneous sentences*. n.p. 4d each.
London: Simpkin, Marshall & Co. 16x10, 218pp., 2s6d. *Key* 1878
(L)
[The volume is purely complementary - solutions "to the copious and graduated collection of exercises taken from standard writers, and interspersed with such brief notes as are calculated to aid and refresh the memory". Its size documents the great weight given to parsing at the time.]

435. Dawnay, William Henry (7th Viscount Downe). 1857. *An elementary English grammar. By the Viscount Downe*. London: Longman, Brown, Green, Longmans & Roberts. 8°, xii+150pp.
(L O *Lw*)
[OESP, nine parts of speech, giving special weight to the verb (progressives, tenses, participles) as being problematic; many quotations from the Bible, Shakespeare, Milton and Addison; some historical and comparative arguments; praises Latham, T.K. Arnold and Sullivan. Preface is signed B.G.]

436. Dawson, Benjamin, B.A. [a1867]. *Text book of English grammar, with exercises thereon*. 3 parts. n.p. (Part 2: ^{3}1874, London: C. Jaques, 48pp. (L); Part 3: ^{2}1867, London: C. Jaques, 18x10, 48pp. (L O)).
(L O)
[Succinct definitions; exercises geared to the *Grammar*.]

437.$ Day, Henry Noble (1808-1890). 1870. *The young composer: a guide to English grammar & composition*. New York: C. Scribner & Co. 19cm, xiv+203pp. (Anr. ed. 1874 (@)).
($ @)

438.$ Day, Parsons E. 1843. *District school grammar: the elementary principles of English grammar accompanied by appropriate exercises in parsing: with an appendix*. Ithaca, N.Y.: Andrus, Woodruff & Gauntlett. 18cm, 112pp. (@). (Anr. ed. ^{2}1844, 16cm, 120pp. ($ *Br*); ^{4}1845, Ithaca, N.Y.: Andrus & S. Spencer, 16cm, [vii]-xiv+[15]-142pp. (@); ^{5}1846 (@); anr. ed. 1849, 16cm, 144pp. ($)).
($ @ *Br*)

439.$ ---. 1844. *Elementary principles of English grammar*. Rochester, N.Y.: Sage & Brother / Ithaca, N.Y.: Andrus, Woodruff & Gauntlett. 16cm, xiii+[14]-138pp.
(@)

440.! Deakin, R. [a1898]. *The universal parsing book*. London: Relfe Bros.
[Advertised by Relfe in 1898.]

⇒ Anon. 1820. *The decoy. An English grammar with cuts* - see Allan, Louisa, no. 29

441.$ De Garmo, Charles (1849-1934). 1897. *Language lessons*. (De Garmo Language Series). 2 vols. New York/Chicago: Werner School Book Company. 20cm, 256pp.
($ @)

442. Del Mar, Emanuel. 1842. *A grammar of the English language in which the rules of etymology and syntax are clearly expounded, in a series of familiar lectures: designed for the use of schools and selfteaching; and*

particularly adapted for those who learn foreign languages. London: Cradock & Co. 16.5x10.5, vii+115pp.

(@ C L O *Br, Hu, Lw*)

[Leisurely exposition of OESP organized in twenty 'lectures' (= chapters) with Parsing and Exercises, and a chapter on Punctuation at end. Competent, but quite conservative, and Del Mar's depending on Latin can be misleading and inadequate for English (as in his treatment of cases). Nine parts of speech. Some references to views of "some respectable grammarians". Del Mar also wrote books on Spanish, but his intention that the English grammar is for "the use of schools and self-teaching; and particularly adapted for those who learn foreign languages" is not apparent.]

443. Demaus, Robert (Master of the West End Academy, Aberdeen, 1829?-1874). 1858. *The analysis of sentences, with applications to parsing, punctuation, and composition.* Edinburgh: Oliver & Boyd. 16x10, 32pp., 6d. (L). (^{2}1860 (L); ^{4}1871 (*DNB*); enl. and impr. ed. ^{4}1873, Edinburgh: Oliver & Boyd / London: Simpkin & Marshall (@)).

(@ L *DNB*)

["Intended to serve as a supplement or appendix to those grammars in which the analysis of sentences is either entirely omitted, or treated in a cursory and unsatisfactory manner"; sober description of sentence structure; ^{2}1860 has a few exercises and notes added.]

444. De Mornay, A.A. 1873. *A grammar of the English language, based on organic principles.* Melbourne: Mason, Firth & M'Cutcheon. 18.5x12, vi+123pp.

(@ L O)

[Based on Becker's *German grammar*, which the author first saw in 1844; abandoned his adaption to English when he "found that Morell, who had learned from the same master, had made a similar attempt and failed", which made him "to work with renewed vigour". Promises a "course of exercises in preparation" (unidentified). A worthwhile attempt to get away from traditional grammar, basing much of the argument on logical relations and functions, but with numerous infelicities (adverbial case in nouns, supines p. 80, genitive object and ablative object p. 91.]

445.! Denny, Dr. E.E. & Lyddon Roberts. n.d. *Knotty points in analysis and parsing.* London: Normal Correspondence College. 76pp.

(*Wm*)

[Contents: Knotty points in analysis (eight sections); Knotty points in parsing (18 sections). "... written with a view of assisting Pupil Teachers and others in preparing for the scholarship and Certificate Examinations."]

446.$ Deuel, A. C. 1873. *Exercises in parsing, for beginners.* Cincinnati: J. Tanner & Co. 19cm, 39pp.
($ @)
447. Dewe, Rev. Joseph Adalbert (Ikley College). 1897. *Grammar, explained according to the order of ideas, especially intended for masters and senior students.* London: Elliot Stock. vi+58pp.
(O)
[Philosophical treatment starting from the language ~ thought correlation, arrives at a few 'modern' non-traditional definitions and concepts, not all of them convincing; parts of speech and syntax/analysis covered.]
448. Dick, Thomas, F.R.P.S. 1898. *The rudiments of English grammar.* (Oliver & Boyd's Educational Series). Edinburgh: Oliver & Boyd / London: Simpkin, Marshall & Co. 18.5x12, iv+88pp. (Rev. ed. ^{2}1900, iv+95pp.).
(L O)
[Simple definitions, with an attempt at plain language, OES plus punctuation, eight parts of speech; sentence analysis; with exercises interspersed; sober, but unexciting for 1898.]
449. Dickinson, W.J. (Formerly Normal Master and Lecturer on Grammar and Analysis at the Battersea Training College). 1878a. *The difficulties of English grammar and analysis simplified; with a brief sketch of the history of the language.* (Hughes's Educational Course). London: Hughes & Co. 16x10, vii+125pp., 2s. (Anr. ed. 1879 ($); ^{6}1891 rev. and ed. by Charles James Dawson, London, 18cm).
($ L O)
[Focuses on difficulties derived from questions in public examinations. Obligations to Morris's *Historical outlines*, Adam's *Elements* and Mason's *English grammar*. With all its claims to originality a traditional and not well arranged book.]
450.! ---. 1878b. *How to teach the rudiments of grammar and analysis successfully, being a series of model lessons for teachers.* London: Hughes & Co. 1s.
[From advertisement in Dickinson 1878a; review by *The schoolmaster*: "It contains a clear explanation of the outlines of Grammar and Analysis, and forms a good foundation for a more extended grammatical course".]
451. ---. 1878-9. *A practical English grammar and analysis. With ... exercises.* 5 parts. For Standard II (L), 1878; For Standard III, 1879; For Standard IV, 1879; For Standard V, 1878; For Standard VI, 1878 (O). In one vol. (Hughes's Educational Course). London: Hughes & Co. 16x10, viii+185pp. (run-on pagination), 3d each, 1s.
(L O)

[Short definitions, with exercises; the volumes cover parts of speech, syntax up to complex sentences; note 'noun sentence' and 'adjectival sentence' for types of relative clauses. Review of *The School Guardian* (advertisement in Dickinson 1878): "The Exercises are numerous, and there are some features which deserve special notice, e.g. the Summary, to be learnt by heart, which is placed at the end of each part [...] The subject of Analysis of Sentences is very fully treated."]

452. ---. 1879. *A complete set of pupil teachers' government examination questions in English grammar, paraphrasing, parsing, analysis, composition, and notes of lessons, to September 1879 (inclusive) Collected, arranged, and graduated by W. J. Dickinson*. (Hughes's Pupil Teachers' Examination Manuals). London: Joseph Hughes. 18x11.5, 72pp. (^{2}n.d., 72pp.).
(L O)
[Some 750 questions (without key) illustrate what pupil teacher's qualifications were expected; complementary to a grammar (but none is mentioned).]

453.$ Diebel, John Henry (b. 1862). 1891?. *New methods with the common branches*. (Anr. ed. 1897 (from 1891 ed.), 5 v. in 1; 20cm ($)).
($)

454.$ ---. 1896. *A new method with English grammar*. ... West Unity, Ohio: the author. 19/20cm, 64/80pp.
($ @)

455. Direy, Louis & A. Foggo. 1858. *English grammar*. London: Chapman & Hall. 12°, 136pp.
(C L O)
[Somewhat rhapsodic account based on a unique and somewhat strange system.]

456.$ Doane, Hiram H. 1841. *Doane's new grammar, in familiar lectures: embracing a new systematic order of parsing: exercises in false syntax: and a key to the oral exercise: designed for the use of schools and private learners*. Watertown, N.Y.: Knowlton & Rice. 18/19cm, 120pp.
($ @)

457. Dodd, James Philip. 1855. *Two lectures on the philosophy of language*. North Shields.
(Dt)

458. Doherty, Hugh (Miscellaneous Writer, d.1891). 1841. *An introduction to English grammar on universal principles*. London: Marshall & Co. 21.5x13.5, viii+240pp. (Anr. ed. 1878 (*Al*)).
(C L O *Al, Br, Hu, Lw*)
Lit.: Beyer 1981.

[cf. Alwall 1970:165]
[Polemic attack on traditional grammar in which he blames "schoolmasters to perpetuate those difficulties which render their assistance absolutely necessary", replacing it with a system "derived from a more scientific work, which remains unpublished, because the subject is too serious and voluminous to meet with an extensive demand" (p.1). Although his system is somewhat abstruse, it is an authentic attempt to break out of the tradition, and there are few such.]

459. Donaldson, David (English Master, Grammar School, Paisley). 1873. *Principles of English grammar, including analysis of sentences*. London/ Edinburgh/Glasgow: Collins. 1s.
(L)

460. ---. 1878. *Outlines of English grammar, including analysis of sentences. For the use of junior pupils*. (Collins School Series). London/Glasgow: Collins. 16.5x10.5, 64pp., 6d.
(L O)
[The alphabet, classifications of words, syntax rules, analysis of sentences and exercises (also interspersed), brief definitions; sober, but unoriginal.]

461. Donatti, Louis Anthony (Professor of Languages). 1839. *Elementary English reading book and grammar, strongly recommended to parents, tutors, and governesses*. London: Joseph Mallett. 12°, iv+36pp. (^{2}1839, 39pp.; ^{3}1842).
(L O)
[Very brief and incompetently done; apparently intended for foreign learners - with a long section on how to pronounce individual letters.]

462. D'Orsey, Alexander James Donald (Master of the English department, Glasgow High School). 1842. *English grammar and composition. Part 1: Orthography and etymology*; Part 2: *Syntax and prosody*. (Chambers's Educational Course). Edinburgh: Chambers. 18cm, 1s6d each. (Anr. ed. 1851; anr. ed. 1873).
(@ L *Br*, *Hu*, *Lw*)
[cf. Mugglesone 1995:228-9]
["A complete revision of the book was issued anonymously in 1853, under the same title." cf. Anon. 1853, no. 522. Grammatical content conventional but there is much of interest in his methods of applying grammar to composition. Cf. W.J. Unwin. 1851. *Reading in primary schools*, p. 12.

463. ---. 1845. *Introduction to English grammar*. (Chambers's Educational Course). Edinburgh: Chambers. 18cm, 104pp.
(L *Br*, *Lw*)

[A shorter version of no. 462.]
464. Douglas, James (Ph.D., Teacher of English, Queen Street Academy, Edinburgh). [c1850?]. *An initiatory grammar for the use of junior pupils, intended as an introduction to the Principles of English grammar.* n.p. (^{86}1867, Edinburgh; ^{109}1871 (L); ^{111}1874 (*Al*)).
(E L *Al*)
[cf. Alwall 1970:167]
465. ---. 1850. *The principles of English grammar, with a series of progressive exercises for the use of schools.* Edinburgh/London: Adam & Charles Black, etc. 14cm, ii+168pp. (rev. ed. ^{2}1851, pr. in Edinburgh/London (A E L); ^{97}1871, Edinburgh/London (L); ^{98}1872, Edinburgh (L); ^{101}1874, Edinburgh (L); ^{112}1891, with improvements as *English grammar and analysis with a series of progressive exercises. For the use of schools,* Edinburgh, 12°; price in 1870: 1s6d).
(A E L O)
[An expansion of no. 464. and itself expanded in later editions, Latinate; OESP, nine parts of speech; traditional - competent but unexciting; many exercises (parsing in syntax) interspersed.]
466.$ Dowd, J. N. 1830. *English grammar, exhibiting a new and improved system of teaching grammar, in the form of questions and answers with explanatory examples, adapted to the capacity of children, intended greatly to facilitate the progress of learners, including rules for syntactical parsing, exercises in false syntax, etc. Designed for the use of common schools.* Middleton, Conn.: E.T. Greenfield. 15cm, v+[6]-54/72pp.
($ @)
⇒ Downe, The Viscount (personal title) - see Dawnay, William Henry, no. 435
467.$ Duggan, William B. 1835. *A primer of English grammar: in which etymology alone is considered: designed for primary schools.* Boston: Beals & Greene. 15cm, 34pp.
($ @)
468. Dunlop, William Wallace (Headmaster of Daniel Stewart's College, Edinburgh). 1893. *Principles of English grammar, with analysis of sentences and and exercises.* London/Edinburgh: Chambers. 17.5x11.5, 144pp.
(L O)
[Parts of speech and their inflection and analysis of sentences; with exercises for analysis and parsing, rules of syntax and exercises, punctuation, paraphrasing, and lists of prefixes and suffixes and roots at end.

Short definitions (generally adequate), with exercises interspersed. The arrangement should be noted, otherwise dry and unoriginal.]
469. Dunnock, Richard. 1836. *An elementary grammar of the English language.* Sheffield: Whittaker. 22pp.
(Sc)
[Conventional, but aims to be as short as possible. Syntax therefore occupies only 33 lines.]
470.$ Du Pont, B. 1898. *An essay on the classification of words into parts of speech.* Johnston, Pa. 23cm, 23pp. (Anr. ed. 1898, London, 22pp. (@)). ($ @)
471. Duval, M.V. [1825?]. *Graphical model of the conjugation of verbs.* n.p. (L)
472. Duxbury, C. [a1884]. *The advanced grammar of school grammars.* n.p. (^{5}1884, viii+254. (L); enl. ed. ^{7}[1886], London: Duxbury (@ H); ^{9}1888; ^{10}1891; ^{12}1894 adds ... *with word-building, derivation, composition. Analysis of sentences, and history of the language, also copious exercises and questions for examination,* London: Simpkin & Marshall, viii+287pp. (@); ^{14}1901 (L)).
(@ H L)
[By 1891 the sections on etymology and on the history of the language had been increased; included are a list of 93 subscribers and sixteen press reviews.]
473. ---. ^{3}1886. *A new English grammar of school grammars.* London: W. Stewart & Co. Impr. ed. 8°, 174pp.
(C L O)
[A good representative of the end-of-century style of grammar, incorporating history of the language, derivation and composition. Its relation to no. 472. needs to be sorted out. Popular work; representative, not innovative. Duxbury consulted for his OESP account a long list of established grammars; he mentions those by Murray, Latham, Beard, Angus, Morell, F.W. Bedford, Allen & Cornwell, Alford, Trench, Lennie, T.K. Arnold, Cobbett, Connon, Sullivan, Lewis, Dalgleish, Currie, Bromby and W. Smith.]
474. Dymond, Jonathan. 1829. *Essays on the principles of morality, and on the private and political rights and obligations of mankind.* London. (^{3}1836 (Br)).
(@ Br)
[Essay II, chapter xi, is an attack on the predominance of classical teaching, with observations on English grammar, of which "a boy learns more by joining in an hour's conversation with educated people, than in poring for an hour over Murray or Horne Tooke.]

475. Dyson, John (First Assistant Grammar-Master at Christ's Hospital, Hertford). [a1890]. *The plain facts of grammar and analysis.* n.p. (²1890, Hertford: Simson, ii+18pp., 17.5x11.5 (L)).
(L)
["Contains in condensed form the first principles of Grammar ... definitions to be learnt by heart". Crude definitions, interspersed with exercises; very poor.]

476.$ Earl, Mary. 1816. *A short but comprehensive English grammar: rendered simple and easy by familiar questions and answers adapted to the capacity of youth.* Boston: Wells & Lilly. 14.5x9, 88pp.
($ L *Br*)
[OESP. Crude definitions elicited in a mechanical Q/A style summarizing 18th-century knowledge from established grammarians (not named). Very slight.]

477. Earle, John (Rector of Swanswick, Formerly Fellow and Tutor of Oriel College, Professor of Anglo-Saxon in the University of Oxford, 1824-1903). 1892. *A simple grammar of English now in use.* New York: G.P. Putnam's Sons. 297pp. (@). (Anr. ed. 1898, New York: G.P. Putnam's Sons / London: Smith, Elder & Co., 18.5x12, xiv+297pp., $1.50. ($ E); anr. ed. 1899 ($)).
($ @ C L O)
["A book not of Philology but of Grammar ... not the mechanism of the mother tongue, but its mental action in practical use." I. Parts of speech; II Syntax; III Prosody. For the teacher rather than the pupil? Discursive and careful introduction which makes the reader *discover* the rules of English; remarkably little use is made of the author's excellent historical knowledge to explain ModE features. Insightful distinctions, as in the twelve verb types (125-7); plain syntax distinguished from 'graphic' syntax (which treats rules somewhat cavalierly, 125); valuable remarks on idiom (143-6); poetic diction and figured diction. The book ends with a thorough discussion of prosody and prose composition. An appendix contains punctuation, parsing, passages to modernise etc. A well-considered treatment of grammar.]

478. Earnshaw, Christopher. 1817. *The grammatical remembrancer: a short but comprehensive English grammar for the use of young students.* Huddersfield. 15x12, 84pp., 2s6d.
(C L Lu *Hu, Lw*)
[Not entirely traditional: his twelve parts of speech are unique, but he does not do much with them. An example of a well judged, thoughtful grammar.]

479. Easton, William (Schoolmaster, Hereford). 1868. *A short introduction to English grammar. Part 1*. London: Groombridge & Sons. 14x9, 24pp. *Parts 1 & 2*: 44pp. (Anr. ed. 1870, London: Simpkin, Marshall & Co., & J. Martin, 44pp.).
(L E)
[OE(SP in part II?), nine parts of speech. Very brief definitions, with exercises added. Too modest and unsophisticated to be of any relevance.]

480. Anon. [1873]. *An easy English grammar for young children*. Edinburgh: Thomas Laurie. 16x10, 32pp., 3d.
(L O)
[Naive formulations ending in rules; divided into lessons with exercises at end. Nine parts of speech; almost completely devoted to parsing.]

481. Anon. [a1845]. *Easy grammar for children*. (By a lady). London: John William Parker. 14cm, 63pp., price in 1845: 9d.
(@)

482. Eaton, A. (Teacher of Languages). 1828. *A reasoning grammar, with the addition of the employment of all the English monosyllable sounds, in the form of treatises, which are the commencement of an attempt to make a year's routine-study of language the study of a day*. London. 12°.
(C G L O)
[Discursive, no rules, but tables of verb forms; strange classification in: "The English language has likewise the potential active participle, terminating with *ic* or *ive*, the potential passive with *ble*, the official passive with *dum*, and the future participle with affix of *ture*" p.6; 16-34 are lessons for reading.]

483. Edmonds, George (of Birmingham, Attorney of London, 1788-1868). [183-?]. *George Edmonds' English grammar; a guide to the arts of speaking, reading, and writing the English language*. n.p. 19cm, 16pp.
(@)

484. ---. ^{5}1837. *(G.E.'s) Complete English grammar, with a supplemental grammar of etiquette*. London: the author. 16pp.
(L)
[Not a proper grammar of English, apart from parts of speech illustrated from one sentence, or a brief discussion of the verbal system; the pamphlet does contain valuable remarks on sociolinguistics and style - and etiquette.]

485. ---. ^{2}1837. *Three-halfpenny English grammar*. London. 8°.
(O E)

486. ---. 1855. *A universal alphabet, grammar, and language: comprising a scientific classification of the radical elements of discourse: and illustrative translations from the Holy Scriptures and the principal British clas-*

sics: to which is added, a dictionary of the language. London: R. Griffin & Co. 4°, [256]pp. (Anr. ed. 1856, 29cm, 409pp. (@)).
(@)

487.! Edmonds, Mrs. 1845. *Notes on English grammar; for juvenile pupils.* London. (^{2}1847).
(*Hu, Lw*)
[Possibly identical with no. 1333.]

488.$! Anon. 1843. *Edward's first lessons in grammar.* Boston: T.H. Webb & Co. 18mo, 108pp.
(*Br*)

489. Edwardes, Lionel. ^{3}1877. *Easy lessons in English grammar, designed for use in primary schools, and for the junior classes in seminaries and colleges.* Dublin: A. Thom. 14.5x9, viii+120pp.
(L O)
[46 lessons, OESP, with idioms, vulgarisms, *will/shall*, and punctuation at end. Simple definitions, some inadequate and misleading. No reference made to L2 problems in Ireland except for "vulgarisms" discussed on pp. 106-8.]

490. Edwards, F. 1884. *Examples for analysis, in verse and prose, from well-known sources selected and arranged.* Belfast. 16.5x10, 28pp. (Anr. ed. advertised in 1888; ?1889, 59pp.).
(L)
[Examples only, without explanations or key; not itself a proper grammar.]

491.! Anon. 1876. *An elementary English grammar.* London: Simpkin, Marshall & Co. 62pp.
(*Al*)
[cf. Alwall 1974:161]

492.$ Anon. 1891. *Elementary English grammar.* (Indiana State Series). (Copyright 1891 by Josephus Collett). Indianapolis: Indiana School Book Company. 18cm, 160pp.
(@)

493. Anon. 1880. *[Blackie's] Elementary English grammar complete, based on the analysis of sentences.* (Blackie's Comprehensive School Series). London: Blackie. 16.5x10.5, 80+64pp. Each part 2d/3d.
(L)
[Called *Complete English grammar and analysis* on the title-page. Part III mentions as "now ready" *Elementary English grammar* in three parts (24+24+32pp., each 2s3d) and parts IV-V *Analysis of sentences* (each 32pp., 2s3d) which are identical with the collection in one volume. (Cf. no. 17). Short definitions, with plenty of illustrations, exercises and

recapitulations, but dry and unoriginal; the space devoted to analysis deserves mention.]

494. Anon. 1873. *Elementary English grammar; containing a large selection of graduated exercises.* (Collins' School Series). Glasgow: Collins. 12°, 48pp.
(O)
[Nine parts of speech with one chapter on each; no syntax; unoriginal.]

495. Anon. [1883]. *Elementary English grammar founded on the principle of analysis of sentences.* Glasgow: Orr & Sons. 16cm, 80pp. (Anr. ed. 1883, Glasgow: Orr & Sons, pt. 1: 24pp.).
(L)
[An edition, or a rival, of no. 493?]

496. Anon. [1891]. *Elementary grammar, based on the analysis of sentences.* London/Edinburgh: William Blackwood & Sons.
(L)
[Preface states "it is now generally admitted that in the elementary stages of education, grammar and composition are the complements of each other."]

497.$ Anon. [1891]. *Elementary grammar of the English language.* (The Popular Series). New York/Cincinnati etc.: American Book Company. 18cm, 160pp. (Anr. ed. 1895 (@)).
(@)

498. Anon. [1876]. *Elements of analysis of English grammar.* (Gill's School Series). London: Gill. 16x10.5, 64pp.
(L)
[Outlines of analysis with exercises, followed by "Analysis of [complex] sentences". Sober rules and definitions, very dry.]

499.! Anon. 1843. *The elements of English grammar.* London: Chester Diocesan Schools. 4d.
(*Hu, Mi*)

500. Anon. [1860?]. *The elements of English grammar, etc. English and Bengali.* Calcutta?. 83pp.
(L)

501. Anon. 1842. *The elements of English grammar, for the use of the Philological School.* London: James Martin. 16.5x10, 36pp.
(L)
["An outline to be filled up and illustrated by oral instruction (...) should be committed to memory." Crude and often misleading definitions. Some reference to Latin made. Insignificant.]

502. Anon. 1868. *Elements of English grammar interpaged with a Canarese translation.* Bangalore: Catholic Press. 137pp.

(L)
503. Ellis, Rev. John Jr. (Vicar of Ebberston). 1837. *An abridgment of Murray's English grammar, in the way of question and answer, with explanatory notes, accompanied by an appendix containing exercises in parsing and syntax. Designed chiefly for his own pupils, by J. Ellis.* London. 14x9, iv+[5]-144pp. (Anr. ed. 1839, 58th thousand, London: Webb, Millington & Co., 14x9, iv+[5]-144pp., 1s (L); anr. ed. 1853, London: Webb, Millington & Co., pr. in Leeds, 144pp. (L)).
(L O)
[This Q/A revision has the answers "cautiously given in the author's own language". Various footnotes, mainly translating the Greek/Latin terms. OESP (5-85); an appendix contains exercises in orthography, in parsing, in syntax and in punctuation (86-144) - but without instructions (which apparently have to be supplied by the teacher). Apparently close to Murray, published at a time when his fame was declining.]

504. Ellison, Seacome. 1854. *A grammar of the English language for the use of schools and students: with copious examples and exercises.* London: Nathaniel Cooke. 21cm, xii+103pp.
(@ C L O *Lw*)
[Traditional, adequate but unexciting; with many classical passages used for exercises and analysis; a few flaws (*do*, emphatic p.30-1), no 'faulty' English - but plenty of quotations from best authors.]

505.$ Ells, Benjamin Franklin (1805-1874). 1834. *The dialogue grammar, or, Book instructor: designed to teach the science of English grammar without a teacher.* South Hanover, Ind.: the Hanover College Press. 19cm, 252pp. ($) (rev. and cor. ed. ^{2}1835, Dayton: B.F. Ells & E.M. Strong, 16cm, 216pp. ($ @)).
($ @)

506.$ Elmore, D.W. 1830. *English grammar, or, A natural analysis of the English language.* Troy, N.Y.: Tettle & Gregory. 14x8.5, 19pp.
($ @ L *Br*)
[*Br*: "A mere trifle". Modest sketch, "written in haste for a class of my own amidst the bustle of multiplied concerns". Idiosyncratic, not well arranged, definitions largely inadequate, with some unique explanations. Elmore proposes three primary parts of speech: noun, relative word and particle, but loses his way among their subdivisions. Three pages of exercises in parsing at end. An "enlarged and improved" version promised (if successful) on p.2 does not appear to have been published.]

507. Emblow, William. 1847. *An English school grammar.* Grantham/London: Simpkin & Marshall. 16°, 36pp., 6d.
(L *Hu, Lw*)

[A most rudimentary collection of rules, apparently meant to be memorized, often in misleadingly simple form.]

508.$! Emery, J.A.B. 1829. *English grammar.* Wellsborough, Pa. 18mo, 39pp.
(Br)

509.$ Emmons, Samuel B. 1832. *The grammatical instructer, containing an exposition of all the essential rules of English grammar.* Boston: Waitt & Dow. 18x11.5, 160pp.
(L Br)
[Br: "Worthless". ES only, O and P being intentionally omitted; includes a vocabulary of technical words (89-90), remarks on punctuation, ellipsis, false grammar and observations on writing with perspicuity. Ten parts of speech. Barren, dry and inelegant style; definitions often inadequate.]

510.! Anon. 1813. *English grammar ("By T.C.").* London. 18mo, 104pp.
(Br)

511.! Anon. 1817. *English grammar.* Huddersfield. 81pp.
(Br)

512.$! Anon. 1819. *English grammar.* Albany, N.Y. 18mo, 131pp.
(Br)

513.! Anon. 1838. *English grammar.* London. 161pp.
(Br, Mp)

514. Anon. 1850. *English grammar.* (Elementary Catechisms). London: Groombridge & Sons. 13.5x8, 63pp., 4d. ("a liberal allowance to schools").
(O)
[OESP in Q/A form, somewhat too abstract for the purpose, even discussing the Latin model falsely prevailing in other grammars (p.39) although the editors purpose that "the information conveyed will be suited to the capacity of children, and the subjects treated in an inviting and familiar style". Parsing and 'cautions'(= improper English) at end.]

515. Anon. 1856. *English grammar.* Edinburgh: Chambers.
(L)

516. Anon. ^{5}1874-75. *English grammar.* Rev. under the editorship of Andrew Findlater. London: Chambers.
(Detached from Chambers' Information for the People).
(@)

517. Anon. 1881. *English grammar.* 3 parts. (Part I: for Standards II and III, 34pp.; Part II: for Standard IV, 39pp.; Part III: for Standards V and VI, 27pp.). London: Marshall Japp & Co., each 3d.
(L)

[Traditional and unexciting account; OESP; eight parts of speech. Short definitions (often inadequate) followed by simple exercises. Latin terms translated, and explanations of other hard words in footnotes. Part III is devoted to sentence analysis.]

518.$ Anon. 1888. *English grammar.* (California State Series of School Textbooks). n.p. 19cm, 292pp.
($)

519. Anon. 1889. *English grammar and analysis.* London: Blackwood.
(L)

520. Anon. 1866. *English grammar and analysis ... arranged in a series of lessons.* London: Gill. (^{2}1868).
(L)

521.! Anon. 1857. *English grammar and analysis of sentences.* London: Constable. 65pp.
(*Al*)
[cf. Alwall 1970; Also advertised by Constable]

522. Anon. 1853. *English grammar and composition.* (Chambers' Educational Course). Edinburgh: W. & R. Chambers. 8°, 176pp., 2s. (Anr. ed. 1854 (L); anr. ed. 1855 (L); anr. ed. 1857 (L)).
(C L O *Lw*)
[A revision of Alexander D'Orsey's book of the same title, 1836.]

523. Anon. [a1810]. *English grammar epitomised, for the use of schools.* n.p. (^{3}1810, Halifax: J. Fawcett, Ewood Hall, 84pp. (L)).
(L)

524. Anon. ^{2}1877. *English grammar for elementary schools.* (Public School Series). London: William Isbister. 8°, 96pp., price in 1879: 6d-9d.
(L O)
[Historical summary; word formation; sentence and clause analysis; parsing.]

525.$ Anon. ^{2}1886. *An English grammar for schools. Prescribed for use in the public schools of Nova Scotia.* Halifax: Mackinlay. 17cm, xxxiv+172pp.
(@)

526.$ Anon. 1879. *An English grammar for the use of schools and academies: arranged according to Dr. Sullivan's "Attempt to simplify English grammar" with revisions and addenda. By a practical teacher.* New York/Cincinnati: Benziger Brothers. 18cm, iv+[5]-83pp.
($ @)

527. Anon. 1881. *English grammar. Part 1, for Standards II and III. Part 2, Standard IV. Part 3, Standards V and VI.* 3 parts. London: Marshall Japp & Co. 16.5x10, 34+39+24pp.
(L O)

[Traditional OESP accounts; short (and often dissatisfactory) definitions, with exercises (parsing in part III).]

528. Anon. 1856. *An English grammar, printed phonetically from the Phonetic Journal*. London, pr. in Bath. 8°.
(L O)
[Same as: Anon. 1856. *An Iŋglic Gramar Printed Fɔnetikali. From De "Fɔnetik Djūrnal."* London: Fred. Pitman. 72+4pp.]
(O)
[Traditional OESP treatment - the present text may be original (or just transliterated to exemplify the revised spelling?). Also cf. no. 366.]

529. Anon. 1810. *English grammar, taught by examples, rather than by rules of syntax, etc*. London: Darton, Harvey & Darton. 17x10.5, viii+88pp, 2s/2s6d, with blank leaves.
(L)
[Discursive treatment of parts of speech with ideas taken from Murray who receives unreserved praise (and whose *Grammar* is frequently referred to for further information). Some use of false syntax, but otherwise no exercises which "weary the attention, and exhaust the patience". Dry and not well organized.]

530.! Anon. [a1844]. *An English grammar, together with a first lesson in reading*. n.p. (^{2}1844 London: James Burns. 16pp.).
(*Br, Mi*)
[*Br*: "not worth a pin"]

531.! Anon. 1820. *An English grammar, with engravings*. London. 18mo, 16pp.
(*Br*)

532. Anon. 1879. *The English language: its history and structure. With chapters on derivation, paraphrasing, sentence-making, and punctuation*. (Royal School Series). London: T. Nelson. 89pp. (Anr. ed. 1882, 96pp.).
(@ H)

533. Anon. [c1840]. *English parsing made easy, in a progressive series of plain and familiar examples adapted to the capacities of children, and intended as a companion to Murray's abridgment of his grammar*. London: Woodbridge Pr., sold by J. Munro. 14cm, [2]-116pp.
($ @)

534.! Anon. 1844. *English school grammar; with explanatory questions*. London: Society for the Promotion of Christian Knowledge. (Anr. ed. 1853, 2d).
(*Hu*)

535. Anon. [1859]. *An English spelling-book ... carefully arranged in lessons of progressive difficulty. To which are added first lessons in grammar (etc.)* Published under the direction of the Committee of General Literature and Education. London. 16x10.
(L O)
[The First Lessons in Grammar are in II: 25-66; they consist of ten pages of morphology, the remainder being devoted to vocabulary - apparently of greater interest in a speller. Negligible.]

536. English, Thomas. [1853]. *Grammatical definitions and distinctions.* Sold at the Stoke Newington Schools. 11.5x7, 12pp.
(L)
[Very short definitions of nine parts of speech to prepare parsing lessons in class; one of the smallest books of its types, without independent value.]

537. Espin, T. (Master of the English and Commercial Academy, Lowth, Lincs) 1854. *Rudiments of English grammar* compiled by the late T.E., J.H. (Master of the Commercial Academy, Grantham), enlarged by J. Hardwick. Grantham: T. Busby. 15x9, 52pp.
(O)
[Short definitions of parts of speech, with examples, and rules of syntax, not very satisfactory; the genesis of the book is not explained.]

538. Anon. 1808. *The essentials of English grammar; for classical and French schools.* (By a Member of the University of Oxford). London. 14cm, 108pp. (^{3}1821 as *The essentials of English grammar, on a practical plan, for the use of classical and French schools, and private learners: with an appendix ...*, London: Clement Chapple, 14cm, 108pp. (@); anr. ed. 1825 as: *The essentials of English grammar, containing a key to the syntactical parsing lessons*, London: Souter, for the editor, pt. 1., no further parts published, 13cm, 108pp.).
Key: 72pp. (L O).
(@ L O *Hu, Br, Lw*)

539. Evans, Leslie Charles. [1868]. *Parsing tables.* London.
(O)

540. Evans, Thomas. 1887. *A Midland grammar for the standards with examinations.* London: Simpkin, Marshall & Co. 18x12, 32pp.
(L)
[Rudimentary and unassuming, with many specimens interspersed for illustration, but notably weak on definitions. Eight parts of speech, Examination questions for analysis and parsing (Standards V & VI) at end.]

541. ---. 1888. *The Midland hand-book of grammar questions. With answers after each question for all the standards II to VII.* London: Simpkin, Marshall & Co. etc. 64pp.
Key 1889.
(L O)
[The definitions, etc. used in this book are similar to those in "Evans's Midland Grammar for the Standards". ("The most complete and cheapest school Grammar ever published. 100,000 already sold" - back cover). Hundreds of short questions mostly followed by answers in italics; no discussion. Eight parts of speech, three tenses.]

542. Evans, Thomas. 1890. *Evans grammar test cards. Grammatical test cards, containing two complete grammar examinations etc. Standards IV [-VI].* 3 parts. London: Simpkin, Marshall & Co. 36 cards, pr. on both sides. 10x8, 1s.
(L)
["Containing two complete grammar examinations set out by H.M.I.'s - one difficult and one easy ... Before using these cards work carefully through 'Evans Midland grammar', 2d." Questions on sentence analysis and prefixes.]

543. ---. 1897. *Evans grammar cards for the standards.* Redditch. 18x10, 4pp.
(L)
[Definitions only, apparently abstracted form the *Midland Grammar*.]

544.$ Evans, William M. (1859-1904). 1894. *A manual of grammar.* n.p. 19cm, 124pp. (^{2}1899, Syracuse, N.Y.: Bardeen, 126pp. (@)).
($ @)

545.$ Everest, Cornelius Bradford (1789-1870). 1835. *An English grammar: in which the principles of the language are methodically arranged, and practically illustrated; with examples for parsing, and questions for examination: Designed for schools, academies, and private learners.* Norwich, Ct.: J. Dunham. 19cm, 270pp.
($ @ L *Br*)
[*Br*: "Suppressed for plagiarism from G. Brown".]

546. Everill, George. 1850. *Recapitulation of English grammar in questions and answers by George Everill. Adapted to the author's book of instructions.* Munich: Georg Franz. 14x8.5, iii+75pp.
(L)
[Remarkable for a book all in English published in Bavaria in 1850. 250 questions, many contrasting German structures (1-50) followed by answers (51-75). The questions relate to the author's *Lehrbuch der englischen Sprache* in four parts, of which part I is the *Grammatik*. They are partly explained in 143 footnotes providing additional grammatical

information and some contrasts with German, and answered in very brief form. No English grammarian is mentioned.]
547. Eves, Charles. 1852. *The school examiner, containing nearly 4000 exercises on sacred history; geography; English grammar, the histories of England and Rome; sacred geography; and arithmetic.* London: Simpkin, Marshall & Co. etc. 14.5x9, iv+104pp. (Anr. ed. 1881, London: Simpkin, Marshall & Co., for C.W. & O. Eves, 24°, 104pp. (@); anr. ed. 1882, 4 parts in 1 vol., 12° (@)).
(@ L)
[Mixed questions on all sections of grammar, "so formed that, with very few exceptions, the Pupils may obtain answers form any History, Grammar &c., in their possession; but when Questions occur which cannot be answered by reference to the usual School-books, the Teacher can refer (if requisite) to the Key and dictate the reply". Didactically questionable.]
548. ---. n.d. *Key to the School examiner,* ... London: Relfe. 24pp.
(@)
549. ---. 1872. *School examiner containing* ... London: Simpkin. 104pp.
(@) [identical with no. 547?]
550. Eves, Mrs. (of Crescent School, Birmingham). 1800. *The grammatical plaything; or Winter evening's recreation for young ladies from four to twelve years old.* Birmingham: Marshall, Seeley & Co. 19cm, xiii+65pp.
(@ B N *Lw*, *Ma*)
[Conventional, except that she puts linguistic illustrations into complete sentences. Praised by Martin 1824:161: "employs simple cards, on which she writes the names of the different parts of speech, and the classes of each."]
551. Anon. 1886-91. *Examination papers in English grammar ... 1876 ... to 1886.* (By "College of preceptors"). 2 parts. London. 21 cm.
(L O)
552. Anon. 1804. *Examinations composed for the use of the pupils, at Ormskirk Classical and Commercial School. Vol. I. English grammar.* Ormskirk: T. Tasker. 182pp.
(G L)
[A series of examinations graded according to classes and including prosody, and false syntax for correction. A second title page reads: *Examinations adapted to L. Murray's Grammar and exercises, Dr Crombie's Etymology and syntax, and Irving's Elements of English composition.*]

553.! Anon. [a1817]. *Examples of parsing, for children, intended as an introduction to the parsing of those parts of sentences &c. given in Lindley Murray's small grammar, as parsing exercises.* London: Darton, Harvey & Darton.
(*Mp*)
[Advertised in 1817.]

554. Anon. 1896. *Exercises in analysis, parsing, and correction of sentences.* n.p.
(L)

555.! Anon. [a1887]. *Exercises in English grammar and composition.* London: Moffatt & Paige.
(*Mp*)
[Advertised in 1887.]

556.$ Anon. 1829. *Exercises in grammar: prepared for the use of the Hartford Female Seminary.* n.p.: Philemon Canfield. 19cm, 49pp.
($ @)

557. Anon. n.d. *Exercises for "Lower grade English". Grammar, analysis, derivation, paraphrasing.* (Royal English Class-Books). n.p. 16.5x11, 48pp.
(O)
[Questions only, without key; occasional reference is made to "Brief English Grammar" (?which) and to "Lower Grade English". Questions relate to grammar, parsing and paraphrase.]

558. F. 1838. *The grammarian: or the English writer and speaker's assistant, comprising* shall *and* will *made easy to foreigners, with instances of their misuse on the part of the natives of England.* (The dedication is to the "inhabitants of the Athens of Ireland" by their "dear countryman"). n.p. [Dublin?]
(L)

559. Fallon, D. (Professor). 1889. *Elementary English grammar including analysis of sentences and first steps in composition.* Malta: G. Muscat. 107pp. (^{2}1893, Malta: G. Muscat, 17.5x11.5, 115pp.).
(L)
[On ^{2}1893: OES. Eight parts of speech. Short definitions interspersed with exercises and questions, obviously unoriginal. The grammar (1-88) is followed by "exercises in English and Italian translation" - no other indication of English as a second language being found.]

560. Fallon, John A. (Master of Richards's Endowed School, Silverton, Devon). [1883]. *Analysis of sentences with copious exercises. Compiled for use in elementary and middle class schools, and for Oxford and*

Cambridge Local Examinations, and pupil teachers. Exeter: Wheaton. 17.5x11, 18pp., 2d.
(L)
[Very brief explanations on the structures of sentences, with many exercises. Dry and unoriginal.]

561. Farnell, William Keeling. [1858]. *A practical English grammar and parsing expositor; containing clear definitions, concise rules* [etc.]. *Adapted to schools, private teachers, and self-instructors*. London. 36pp. ([²1860], London: Jarrold, 14cm, iv+[5]-33pp. (@)).
(@ L)
[Farnell is afraid that "*pedantic* and hypercritical philologists" will think it perfunctory. There is nothing novel in it.]

562.$ Farnum, Caleb Jr. 1842. *Practical grammar; a grammar of the English language on an improved plan: in which the principles of the science are clearly and briefly stated, and their application in practice is made familiar by copious and appropriate exercises*. Providence, R.I.: B. Cranston & Co. 19cm, iv+[5]-124pp. (L *Br*). (²1843, Boston: B. Mussey ($ @); ³1843 (@); ster. ed. 1848, n.p.: pr. by J. Knowles (@)).
($ @ L *Br*)
[*Br*: "1st ed. suppressed for petty larcencies from G. Brown; 2nd ed. altered to evade the charge of plagiarism"]

563.$ Farrell, Edward D. 1877. *The grammar school speller and definer: embracing graded lessons in spelling, definitions, pronunciation, and synonymes; proper names and geographical terms; a choice selection of sentences in dictation; and a condensed study of English etymology*. New York: The Catholic Publication Society. 19cm, [11]-225pp. (⁴1878 ($ @)).
($ @)

564.! Faulkner, W. (Head master of Queen Elizabeth's Grammar School, Worcester). [c1800]. *Elements of grammar, or an introduction to the English language*. London.
(*Ma, Mi*)
[cf. Martin 1824:271]

565.$ Felch, Walton. 1821. *A concise grammar of the English language; adapted to the memory, and designed as an improvement upon ... Murray and others*. Southbridge, Mass. 14cm, viii+[9]-72pp. (Anr. ed. 1831 (@)).
(@ L)
[Relaxed about the number of parts of speech, suggests seven (pronoun within noun).]

566.$ ---. 1837. *A comprehensive grammar: presenting some new views of the structure of language: designed to explain all the relations of words in English syntax, and make the study of grammar and composition one and the same process: abridged from a work preparing for publication.* Boston: Otis, Broaders & Co. 18cm, xvi+[17]-122pp. (Anr. ed. 1873, New York: Taintor Brothers (@)).
($ @ *Br*)
[*Br*: "This author can see others' faults better than his own."]

567.$ Fellows, Aaron N. 1872. *First steps in English grammar. On the "Catechetical plan".* n.p. 18cm, 62pp. (Anr. ed. 1873, East Millstone, N.J.: Vanderhoef's Press (@)).
($ @)

568.$ Felton, Oliver C. 1843. *The analytic and practical grammar. A concise manual of English grammar: arranged on the principle of analysis: designed for the use of common schools containing the first principles and rules, fully illustrated by examples ... and a series of parsing lessons in regular gradation from the simplest to the most abstruse.* Ster. ed., rev. by the author. Salem, Mass.: W. & S.B. Ives / Boston: B.B. Mussey. 18cm, 145/147pp.
($ @ L *Br*)

569.! Fenn, Lady Eleanor. (1743-1813). [c1809]. *Sportive exercises in grammar.* [Mrs. Lovechild]. London.
(*Mi*)
[Advertised in c.1809.]
[cf. Moon (1976: No. 1023)]

570. ---. 1809. *The teacher's assistant, in the art of teaching grammar in sport. Designed to render the subject familiar to children.* [Mrs. Lovechild]. London: John Harris. 36pp.
(L)
[A commentary on how to use not only the apparatus in the accompanying box but also Lady Fenn's seven other books.]

571. ---. 1831. *... being a new and infallible method of acquiring languages ... part of a series for teaching.* [Mrs. Lovechild]. n.p. 15cm, viii+64pp.
($)

572. entry deleted.

573. Fenwick, Elizabeth. 1808. *Rays from the rainbow. Being an easy method for perfecting children in the first principles of grammar, without the smallest trouble to the instructor.* London. (^{2}1812, 15cm, xii+58+[2]pp. ($)).
($ @ L Ph)

[Uses a colour-coding to teach the parts of speech; tries to be empirical and avoid definitions at first.]

574.! Fenwick, John. 1811. *A new elementary grammar of the English language*. London: Watt. (Anr. ed. 1814, London, 12mo (*Br*)).
(*Br*, *Lw*, *Wa*)

575. Fergie, Thomas Francis. 1858. *The elementary school grammar*. London: Simpkin, Marshall & Co. & Wigan. 14x9, 40pp.
(L)
["A Text Book for *Home Use* in the simplest and most condensed form." Short definitions, OES, and a parsing exercise; no observations, exceptions or footnotes. Though reduced to minimal information, generally clear.]

576. Fernald, Frederick A. (pseud./perpetrated by Fritz Federheld). [1885]. *Ingglish az she iz Spelt*. London/New York: G.W. Carleton & Co. 15x12, 93pp.
(@)

577. Ferris, Achilles. [1888-91]. *First elements of English grammar for the use of the Government Primary Schools (in Malta)*. 2 parts. Malta: C. Busuttil. 16.5x11cm. 36+114pp.
(L)
[Part I is a short description of the nine parts of speech with glosses in Italian; Part II contains fuller definitions, examples and exercises, again with some glosses. OES, traditional but not ineffective; no mention of special TEFL concerns. Though unoriginal, probably adequate for the purpose.]

578.$ Fewsmith, William & Edgar A. Singer. 1866. *A grammar of the English language*. Philadelphia: Sower, Barnes & Potts. 19cm, 228pp. (Anr. ed. 1867 ($ @); anr. ed. [1868] (@); anr. ed. 1869 (from 1867 ed.), 19cm, 228pp. ($ @); anr. ed. 1872 (from 1866 ed.) ($ @); anr. ed. 1873 (from 1866 ed.), 146pp. ($ @); rev. ed. 1874, 228pp. (@); anr. ed. 1882 (from 1867 ed.), 146pp. ($); anr. ed. 1883 (from 1867 ed.), 146pp. ($)).
($ @)

579.! Findlater, Andrew. [c1860]. *Outline of English grammar*. (Chambers's Information for the People). [Edinburgh or London]: Chambers.
[Quoted in Bain 1863.]

580. Anon. 1842?. *First elements of English grammar*. Edinburgh: Oliver & Boyd. 12pp.
(L *Mi*)

581.! Anon. [1876]. *A first English grammar*. London: W. Stewart. 32pp.
(*Mp*)
[Advertised in 1876.]

582. Anon. [1890]. *First lessons in English grammar with sentence building and copious and well graduated exercises.* (Guide Series). London: Simpkin, Marshall & Co. 17x10, 103pp., 9d.
(O)
[Uses and kinds of (eight) parts of speech followed by their inflections; three pages on syntax, but some thirty on analysis; no orthography, vocabulary or prosody. Barren and unexciting.]
583. Anon. n.d. *First lessons in English grammar and analysis.* Birmingham: Davis & Moughton. 72pp.
(O)
584.$ Anon. 1890. *First lessons in English grammar: used by the Brothers of the Christian Schools.* (Excelsior Series). New York: W.H. Sadlier. 20cm, 108pp. (Anr. ed. 1892, 18cm, 108pp. (@)).
($ @)
585. Anon. 1881. *First lessons in grammar. Arranged as home lessons.* 2 parts. Part One: For Standards II and III. (The London School Series). London: William Isbister. 31pp.
(@ O)
[Eight parts of speech explained; sections divided into "Read carefully", "Learn", "Exercises".]
586.$ Anon. 1842. *First lessons in grammar. For the use of young pupils, in school and families.* (Boston Grammar Lessons, Copyright by T.H. Carter). Boston: H.J. Weeks. 16cm, 90pp.
(@ Br)
587. Anon. [c1855]. *First steps in grammar for very young children, in amusing lessons.* London: Darton & Co. 16pp.
(@)
588.$ Fisk, Allen (1789-1875). 1821. *Murray's English grammar simplified: designed to facilitate the study of the English language by enabling the instructor to teach without the aid of his birch, and the student to learn without the drudgery of committing to memory what he does not understand. On a new plan.* n.p. 22/23cm, 56pp. ($). (Anr. ed. 1822, as *Murray's English grammar simplified: designed to facilitate the study of the English language: comprehending the principles and rules of English grammar, illustrated by appropriate exercises: to which is added a series of questions for examinations: abridged for the use of schools*, Troy, N.Y., 23cm, vii+176/178pp. ($); anr. ed. 1822, *For the use of the more advanced learners*, 23cm, 232pp. ($); anr. ed. 1824, same title as 1822 ed., Hallowell, Maine: Glazier & Co., 176pp. (@ L); anr. ed. 1833, 15cm, 124pp. ($); anr. ed. 1834, Hallowell, Maine: Glazier, Maters &

Smith (*Dw*); anr. ed. 1836, 23/24cm, 176pp. ($); anr. ed. 1840, Hallowell, Maine ($ L); anr. ed. 1846).
($ @ L *Br*)

589. Fitch, Joseph. [c1820?]. *A poetical grammar of the English language, with one hundred questions for examination.* n.p. (²1841 *With ... questions for examination ...*, rev. by R.D. Markham, Principal of the Grammar School in Edmonton, London: Teulon, Harvey & Darton, 8°, vi+70pp. (L)).
(L O)
[Traditional OESP account, all in skilful verse, with exercises on faulty English, notes on parsing and questions appended.]

590. Anon. 1855. *Five hundred mistakes of daily occurrence, in speaking, writing and pronunciation, corrected.* London: John Farquhar Shaw. 6d. (Anr. ed. 1856, New York: D. Burgess & Co. / Philadelphia: J.B. Lippincott & Co. 19cm, v+[7]-73pp. (@); ³²1875, New York: J. Miller, 20cm, 73pp. (@)).
(@ C E L)
[The title is sometimes preceded by 'Never too late to learn']

591. Fleay, Frederick Gard (Head Master of Hipperholme Grammar School, 1831-1909). 1859. *Elements of English grammar: relations of words to sentences (word building).* 2 parts. London: Edward Stanford. 25pp.
(L)
[Fleay regards as novelties in his grammar: that the theory of sentences precedes that of words; that words are classified etymologically and logically (the parts of speech are "manifestly unphilosophical"); the logical nature of prepositions, conjunctions, interjections and relatives is pointed out for the first time.]

592. ---. 1884. *The logical English grammar.* London: W. Swan Sonnenschein. 12°, 96pp.
(L O)
[Treats "Syntax before accidence; binary classification of words, logical and etymological; new arrangements for analysis of sentences, parsing, paraphrasing, and analysis of sounds (spelling) suggested; analysis to elementary word-components" - an original and new approach even though not fully convincing.]

593. Fleming, Isaac Plant. 1869. *Analysis of the English language in three parts: grammar, etymological derivations and praxis.* (Papers set at the Oxford and Cambridge local examinations for seven years). London: Longman. xii+306pp. (Anr. ed. 1872, 19cm, xiv+306pp ($); anr. ed. 1875, *Part I ... II ... III... Containing a systematic course of examination-questions; all the questions on grammar and etymology proposed at*

the Woolwich competitive examinations from 1854 to 1869. The papers set at the Oxford and Cambridge local examinations for several years, repr. from the latest ed. with corrections, additions, and copious indices, Buffalo: Courier Co., xiv+350pp. (@); anr. ed. 1875, 19cm, 349pp. ($); anr. ed. 1877 ($); anr. ed. 1888, 19cm, xiv+349pp. ($)).
($ @)

594.$ Fleming, Mrs. (Ann Cuthbert) (1788-1860). 1844. *The prompter: containing the principles of the English language, and suggestions to teachers with an appendix, in which are stated the opinions of different grammarians on disputed points*. Montreal: Lovell & Gibson. 19x11, 168+46pp.
($ @)

595.$! Fletcher, Levi. 1834. *English Grammar, or: First steps to analysis*. Philadelphia: J. Kay, Jr. & Brother / Pittsburgh: J.J. Kay & Co. 18cm, 83pp.
(*Br*)

596. Fletcher, Rev. William (Vicar of Stone, Bucks). 1828. *The little grammarian; or, An easy guide to the parts of speech, and familiar illustrations of the leading rules of syntax: in a series of instructive and amusing tales*. London: John Harris. 14x9, ii+175pp., 3s. (Anr. ed. 1829, 132pp. ($); anr. ed. 1830, title has changed to *Little grammarian; or, An easy guide to the parts of speech designed for young persons in general but more particularly adapted to facilitate instruction in preparatory schools, by a teacher*, Boston: Munroe, 108pp. (@); ^{2}1833, title has changed to *The little grammarian; in a series of instructive tales, forming an easy guide to parts of speech, and rules of syntax*, London: J. Harus, 15x10cm (@)).
($ @ L *Br, Lw*)
[Conversational style of introduction followed by definition of parts of speech, each of which is then given a tale in which the respective tokens are italicized (a method allegedly copied from Abbé Gaultier). Precision or comprehensiveness not aimed at - a well-meant didactic effort of questionable efficiency.]

597.$ Flint, Abel (1765-1825). 1807. *Murray's English grammar abridged*. Hartford, Ct. 12mo, 204pp. (^{5}1821, title has changed to ... *to which is added under the head of prosody, and abridgement of Sheridan's lectures on elocution. Also Murray's treatise on punctuation at large. Together with a system of exercises, adapted to the several rules of syntax and punctuation. Designed for the use of schools*, pr. and sold by Peter B. Gleaso & Co. (@); ^{6}1826, 214pp.)
(@ *Br*)

598.$ Flint, John (Grammarian). 1834. *First lessons in English grammar, upon a plan inductive and intellectual.* New York: N.B. Holmes. 14cm, vi+107pp. (Anr. ed. 1837, title has changed to ... *adapted to oral instruction*, New York: Doolite & Vermilye, 16cm, vi+[7]-125pp. ($)). ($ @ *Br*)

599.! Flower, Marmaduke & Rev. William Balmbro' Flower. 1844. *A practical English grammar, containing a complete new class of exercises, adapted to each rule, and constructed on a plan entirely new.* London: Simpkin & Co. 16cm, [5]-170pp.
(*Br, Hu, Lw*)

600.$! Folker, Joseph. 1821. *An introduction to English grammar.* Savannah, Ga. 12mo, 34pp.
(*Br*)

601.$ Folsom, Silas. 1837. *Practical American grammar of the English language: exhibiting on charts a new and full conjugation of the verb, and a compendium of etymology and syntax: the whole adapted to the understanding of children, in concise language: with theoretical questions and definitions.* n.p. (Anr. ed. 1838, Hartford, 20cm ($ @)).
($ @)

602. Forbes, John. (Master in the Normal Institution, Edinburgh). 1843. *A double grammar, of English and Gaelic, in which the principles of both languages are clearly explained; containing the grammatical terms, definitions, and rules, with copious exercises for parsing and correction, (...) adapted to the improved mode of tuition. For the use of schools and private students.* Edinburgh: W. Whyte & Co. 16.5x10.5, xii+[13]-377pp., 4s. (^{2}1848).
(@ L)
[OESP, based on M'Culloch, but changed where the comparative treatment made this necessary; expressed in plain words and omitting dubious points. In two columns, with general remarks printed across the page; exceptions, queries inserted. The fact that two languages are treated in both English and Gaelic makes the arrangement quite difficult; the contrastive treatment leads to some questionable generalizations. Ten parts of speech, some parsing exercises and false grammar for correction, punctuation and model letters. In contents and method an ambitious undertaking.]

603. Ford, E.B. 1801. *A short and easy introduction to English grammar.* London: Beverley. 56pp.
(L)
[Conventional; ten parts of speech; five moods, five tenses; standard definitions.]

604. Ford, James. 1870. *Ford's home lesson and school class grammar of the English language, with questions and exercises to follow every subject and rule, esp. adapted for class teaching*. Sheffield: Loxley. 16.5x10.5, 82pp.
(L)
[Similar to his *Lessons*: short definitions, questions and exercises, with a one-page "poetical grammar" in rhyme, some idiosyncracies (p. 37 "Radicative Mood" of BE).]

605. ---. [1877]. *Lessons in English Grammar. I. The parts of speech. II. The inflection of the parts of speech. III. Syntax and analysis of sentences. With numerous questions of examination, and exercises after each lesson*. 3 parts in 1 vol. (The Empire Educational Series). London: Jarrold & Sons. 16.5x10, i+45pp. (Anr. ed. [1880] (Jarrolds' Educational Series, for School and Home) (@)).
Key to the lessons in English grammar. Part I ... (Jarrolds' Series of Special Subject and Home Lesson Books). London: Jarrold. 16cm, 4pp. (@).
(@ L)
[Parts of speech, inflections, and syntax and analysis of sentences treated in short definitions in bold print with questions and exercises interspersed. Punctuation and prosody appended at end. Solid, but unexciting.]

606. [Ford, Thomas]. 1855. "Compositor". *Reminders in grammar and orthography; or, Rules and examples by which many of the doubts constantly arising may be set at rest selected, rev. and made familiar to present usage*. London: Simpkin Marshall. 16x10, 60pp. (^{2}1856).
(L)
[Almost exclusively an orthography, with a few remarks on morphology (*a* vs. *an*, plurals). Certainly not a full grammar.]

607. Forrester, Alfred Henry (1804-1872). 1825 [1824?]. *The holiday grammar, a Christmas present for the present Christmas, passing Murray, Dilworth, and all past grammarians in simplicity and as fitting for the future as the present generation; where in each article is hieroglyphically and laconically defined, and adapted to the capacity of all degrees whether positive, comparative, or superlative*. [published under pseud. Alfred Crowquill]. London: S. Knights. 4°.
($ @)

608. Forrester, Charles Robert (1803-1850) & Alfred Henry Forrester (illustr.). 1842. *The pictorial grammar*. [published under pseud. Alfred Crowquill]. London: Harvey & Darton. 16.5x11, [iv]+75pp. (L O N Ph). (Anr. ed. 1851 (Bd); c1860 (Mb); anr. ed. 1872 ($); anr. ed. 1873

(*Gu*); anr. ed. 1875, London: Harvey & Darton (@); anr. ed. 1876, London: W. Tegg ($ @ Bed); facs. repr. London: Routledge/Thoemmes Press, 1996 (In: Reibel 1996, vol. II, *Lindley Murray's Grammar in Caricature: Four Parodies*).
($ @ Bd L O Mb N Ph, *Gu*)
[cf. Gumuchian (1967: No.1955); Reibel (1996:xiii-xvi)]
[As other children's books published by the same firm (cf. the 16pp. of advertisement added at end) the text is meant for beginners; its attractiveness lies in the illustrations - the grammatical rules on articles, substantives and pronouns being very elementary.]

609. Foster, Edward Ward. 1840. *The elements of English grammar in which the complicated matter of the other grammars is expunged, and the whole simplified and rendered more easy to be acquired by a pupil*. London: Harvey & Darton. 12°, vii+31pp.
(L O *Hu*, *Lw*)
[For native speakers "the art of correct speaking will be obtained by an intercourse with genteel society: the principles of writing must be acquired by a knowledge of the elements of the grammar" - here extended in reduced form based on a modified Latinate pattern. The rules (as in Syntax) are obviously intended for memorization.]

610. Foster, Henry Thomas. [1877]. *A practical manual of analysis for the use of schools, private teachers, and students*. London: Simpkin, Marshall & Co. / Lincoln: C. Akrill. 46pp.
(L O)
[Exercises in logical analysis (as contrasted with parsing), by division of clauses. Supplement to a grammar book - but no title is mentioned or implied by the procedure adopted.]

611. Foster, John M.A. 1896. *A companion to English grammars*. London, etc.: T. Nelson. 90pp. (Anr. ed. 1898 (Royal English Class-Books), 19cm, 90pp. ($ @)).
($ @ L O)
[Assumes that initial teaching has been received; notes and exercises on parsing and analysis.]

612.$ Fowle, William Bentley (1795-1865). [1823]. *A catechism of English grammar with practical exercises, prepared for the use of the School of Mutual Instruction in Boston by the Instructor* [i.e. William B. Fowle]. (Publ. anon.). Boston: Wm. B. Fowle. 17cm, 68pp.
(@ L)
[At the age of six W.B. Fowle had memorised Bingham's *Young ladies accidence* but at the age of 13 he could not give the past participle of *love*.]

613.$ ---. 1827. *The true English grammar; being an attempt to form a grammar of the English language, not modelled upon those of the Latin, Greek and other foreign languages.* (Part I). Boston: Munroe & Francis. 18mo, 180pp. (Anr. ed. 1829).
($ L *Br*)
[Based on Tooke and Gilchrist; three parts of speech (noun, adjective, verb) and "contractions" (words which are none of the three)]

614.$ ---. 1829a. *The true English grammar founded on authority as well as propriety; being the second part of an attempt to form a grammar of the English language not modelled upon those of Latin, Greek, and other foreign languages.* Part II. Boston: Hilliard, Gray *et al.*/Munroe & Francis. 97pp.
(@ L *Br*)

615. ---. 1829b. *Inductive grammar, designed for beginners, by an instructor.* Boston, Mass.: Hilliard, Gray, Little & Wilkins.
($ @)
[Cf. no. 942; same book?]

616.$ ---. 1833. *An etymological grammar of the English language in which the arbitrary and unnatural grammar of Murray and his followers is contrasted with the rational grammar proposed by Wallis, Harris, Horne Tooke, Gilchrist, Dr. Crombie, and other philologists.* [Boston, Mass.]: Munroe & Francis, publ. for the use of the Monitorial School. 15x9, iv+105pp.
(L)
[Brief expositions "intended for the use of Monitors, who have studied the first part of the True English Grammar of the author .. and who are acquainted with the Second Part" which is mentioned for further reference. A very clear exposition with Murray's statements summarized at the top of each page, contrasted with the author's rational grammar below: an exemplary short survey of the main tenets of the two traditions. Discussion of the three classes of words followed by syntax, practical exercises on the rules and false syntax.]

617.$ ---. 1842. *The common school grammar, being a practical introduction to English grammar with illustrative engravings, designed for preparatory schools.* (Part I & II). Boston: W.B. Fowle & N. Capen. I: 18/19cm, vi+46pp. II: 19/20cm, 108pp. (Anr. ed. 1847 ($)).
($ @ *Br*)

618.$ Fowler, William Chauncy (1793-1881). 1850. *English grammar. The English language in its elements and forms: with a history of its origin and development, designed for the use in colleges and schools.* New York: Harper & Brothers. 24cm, xxiii+[17]-675pp. (Anr. ed. 1851 ($);

619. Fowler, William Chauncy

anr. ed. 1852 ($); rev. and enl. ed. 1855, [ix]-xxxii+[33]-754pp. ($ @); rev. and enl. ed. 1856 ($ @); rev. and enl. ed. 1857 (from 1855 ed.) ($); anr. ed. [1858], title has changed to *Abridged from the octavo edition. To which is added: Professor March's method of philological study of the English language*, New York: Harper & Brothers, 20cm, xiv+381+iv+[5]-118pp./(x)-xxxii+[34]-754pp. ($ @); rev. and enl. ed. 1859, 24cm, xxxii-754pp. ($ @); anr. ed. 1859, as *Elementary grammar, etymology and syntax. Abridged from the octavo ed. of the "English language in its elements and forms." Designed for general use in common schools*, New York: Harper & Bros., 18cm, viii+[9]-224pp. ($ @); anr. ed. 1860, 24cm, (ix)-xxxii+[33]-754pp. ($ @); anr. ed. 1860, 20cm, xiv+381pp.; anr. ed. 1861 (from 1858 ed.), 20cm, xiv+381pp. ($); anr. ed. 1864 (from 1855 ed.), 24cm, [ix]-xxxii+[33]-754pp. ($ @); rev. and enl. ed. 1865, 796pp. (@); anr. ed. 1866 (from 1858 ed.), 24cm, xiv+381+118pp. ($); anr. ed. [1867], 24cm, 796pp. (@); anr. ed. 1868 (from 1855 ed.?), 24cm, 4, [2], [v]-vi,[ix]-xxxii+[33]-796pp. ($ @); anr. ed. 1868, *Abridged from the octavo edition. For general use in schools and families. To which is added: Professor March's method of philological study of the English language*, 20cm, xiv+381pp. ($); eleven further editions between 1870 and 1899, all 23/24cm, 796pp.; abridged ed. in 1873, 19cm, xiv+381, iv+118pp.).
($ @ L *Br*, *Lw*)
[A monumental reference book for teachers in nine parts: historical; phonetic; orthographical; etymological; logical; syntactical; rhetorical; poetical; punctuation. The three different sizes of 224/381/675-796 pages suggest three coexisting editions of the work which appear to have been independently revised; a detailed study of the publishing history is necessary.]

619.$ ---. 1870. *Common school grammar. Easy lessons in etymology and syntax. Abridged from the octavo ed. of the 'English language in its elements and forms'. Prepared for general use in common schools.* New York: Harper & Brothers. 18cm, vii+[9]-258pp. (Anr. ed. 1875, title has changed to *... forms'. To which is annexed a parser and analyzer, by F.A. March, with diagrams and suggestive pictures*, New York: Harper & Brother, 16°, vii+[10]-258, vii+88pp; anr. ed. 1876 (@); anr. ed. 1881, 11cm (@)).
(@)
[The relationship to the preceding grammar needs investigation.]

620.$ Frazee, Bradford. 1843. *An improved grammar of the English language, on the inductive system: with which elementary and progressive lessons in composition are combined: for the use of schools and academies, and*

private learners. Philadelphia: Sorin & Ball / New York: M.A. Newman. 19cm, viii+[9]-192pp. (Ster. ed. 1845, Philadelphia: Sorin, 19cm, 192pp. ($ @); anr. ed. 1846, Philadelphia: Sorin / New York: M.H. Newman etc. (@)).
($ @ L *Br, Hu, Lw*)
[Deplores reliance on memory; preface stresses the importance of "induction" but the text shows little application of it. Grammatical content conventional.]

621.$ Frazer, T. 1884. *First lessons in grammar and how to teach them.* n.p. 94pp.
($)

622.$ French, D'Arcy A. 1831. *Parsing made easy, an English grammar unfolding the principles of the English language.* Baltimore. 168pp.
($)

623.$ ---. 1846. *English Grammar simplified in which it is clearly proved that in the exercises, adapted to Murray's English grammar ... Designed for ... important construction, are grossly erroneous and defective: and in which some plain and very useful rules are laid down, for the direction of persons who have not sufficient leisure to enter into a minute study of this subject.* n.p. 10.5x14.5, 46pp.
($)

624.$ French, Rev. John William (1810?-1871). 1863. *Grammar: part of a course on language, prepared for the instruction in the U.S. corps and cadets.* New York: D. Van Nostrand. 20cm, 467pp. (Anr. ed. 1865 ($)).
($ @)

625.$ Frost, John. LL.D. (1800-1859). [a1828]. *Five hundred progressive exercises in parsing. Adapted to Murray's and other approved treatises of English grammar.* n.p. (^{2}1828, Boston: Hilliard, Gray, Little & Wilkins, 15cm, 36pp.; ^{3}1833 (@)).
(@ L)
[Frost sees the main difficulties as: ascertaining the rules of syntax under which a particular form of construction falls; completing elliptical sentences; paraphrasing inverted sentences.]

626.$ ---. [1828]. *Elements of English grammar, with progressive exercises in parsing.* Boston: Richardson & Lord. 15cm, iv+108pp. (^{2}1830 ($ @); 1831 (@); 1833, Boston: Carter, Hendee & Co. ($ @); ster. ed. 1838, Boston: C.J. Hendee (@); ster. ed. 1842, Boston: Jenks & Palmer (@); ster. ed. 1845 (@); anr. ed. 1846).
($ @ L *Br*)
[Etymological and syntactical parsing; exhaustive; ellipsis and false English. Ordinary.]

627.$ ---. 1842. *(Frost's practical grammar) A practical English grammar; with progressive exercises in orthography, analysis, and grammatical composition: adapted to the use of schools and private learners/ students(@).* (With 89 cuts). Philadelphia: Thomas, Cowperthwait & Co. 20cm, xi+[13]-204pp.
($ @ *Br*)

628. Fuglsang, N.S. 1816. *An easy and short English grammar, compiled for the use of young persons.* Pt. 1. (No more published according to L). Slagelse: Petr. Magnus. 17x10, iii+68pp.
(L)
[Direct method used for teaching Danish (?) pupils; OES, very traditional, 18th-century methods. ("The english Language has so little inflexion, or variety of terminations, that its constructions neither requires nor admits many rules", p. 62). Remarkable for the number of printer's errors.]

629.$ Fuller, Allen. 1822. *Grammatical exercises, being a plain and concise method of teaching English grammar. Original and selected.* Plymouth, Mass.: A. Danforth. 18cm, 108pp.
($ @ *Br*)
[*Br*: "A book of no value"]

630. Fuller, H. 1820. *A grammar of the English language, designed for the use of schools and private families.* Chelmsford: R.H.Kelham, for the author. 133pp.
($ A C)

631. Fulton, George (Master of a private school in Edinburgh, 1752-1831). 1826. *A pronouncing vocabulary; with lessons in prose and verse and a few grammatical exercises.* Edinburgh: Oliver & Boyd. 17cm, vi+212pp.
($ @)
[If children are enjoying their lessons, parents and teachers may be deceived into overestimating progress. First two-thirds of book on pronunciation and spelling; rest on grammar, standard.]

632.$ Gaines, John T. 1893. *Inductive grammar: a manual of directions for the study of English. Based on the practical grammar of Noble Butler, A.M.* Louisville: J.P. Morton & Co.
(@)

633. Gardiner, Alfonzo. [1873]. *John Heywood's standard lesson series in grammar. For standard IV-VI, New Code 1871.* (Home Lessons Books). Manchester: John Heywood / London: Simpkin & Marshall. 3 vols. in 1. 16.5x10, 22pp., 1d.
(@ O)

[47 lessons of definitions and exercises.]
634.! ---. n.d. *Grammar for standard IV*. Manchester: Heywood. 32pp.
(*Mp*)
[Conventional exercises.]
635.! Gardiner, Jane (of Beverley, Mistress of a school in Beverley, Yorks). 1801. *English exercises: adapted to the young ladies' grammar, lately published by the same author*. 2 vols. York.
(*Mp*)
[Copy in unidentified library now lost; exercises based on: 1799. *The young ladies' English grammar: adapted to the different classes of learners. With an appendix*. n.p.]
636. Gardner, William (Headmaster of St. Crysostom's School, Liverpool) & T.T. Sharpe. [c1870]. *An elementary English grammar, arranged in lessons*. (Gardner & Sharpe's Series of Home Lessons). London: The Educational Trading Co. etc. 16x10, 56pp., 4d & 6d.
(@ O E)
[Very succinct definitions, but exercises predominate; OESP, sober, traditional; largely inadequate because of its brevity.]
637. --- & ---. n.d. *Lesson series for home & school use. The fourth standard grammar. Arranged in lessons*. London: George Philip, etc. 17x10, 32pp., 1d.
(O)
[60 lessons of elementary definitions and exercises. "The Third Standard Grammar, arranged in Lessons, 1d" is advertised on the back.]
638. Gartly, G. 1831. *Murray's grammar and exercises abridged, comprising the substance of his large grammar and exercises. With additional notes and illustrations*. London. 18mo, 225pp. (Anr. ed. 1859 (Lm)).
(L Lm)
[He says this abridgment of Murray is fuller than Murray's own.]
639.$ Gauss, Charles & B.T. Hodge. 1889. *A comprehensive English grammar for schools, colleges, families and private students*. n.p. (Anr. ed. 1890, Baltimore: Pan Publication Co. 22cm, xii+[13]-393pp. ($ @)).
($ @)
640.$ Gauthier, Marc. [1888]. *French and English at a glance: a new system on the most simple principles for universal English and French self-tuition: with complete French and English pronunciation of every word*. [Providence, R.I.]: J.A. & R.A. Reid. 19cm, 157pp. (Anr. ed. [1890], ... *French and English Library*, 12°, 160pp. (@)).
($ @)
641.$ Gengembre, Philippe W. (Professor of foreign languages in the Girard College) & J. H. Brown (Principal of the Zane Street Grammar Schools,

late President of the Association of Principals of the public schools of Philadelphia, etc.). 1855. *Brown and Gengembre's English grammar. Elements of English grammar, on a progressive system; with copious exercises in parsing and syntax, and an application of short-hand, or symbols, to grammatical analysis.* By P. W. G. and J. H. Brown. Philadelphia: Hayes & Zell. 17.5x11, xii+[13]-213pp.
($ @ L)
[ESOP (with orthography and punctuation moved to the end), plus "Common errors to be avoided" (listed on 129-41) and Punctuation. Versification etc. in Q/A form. Nine parts of speech (no participle). Short definitions, generally adequate, followed by plenty of exercises, many for correction. The graphic system ('shorthand') used to visualize parsing is unnecessarily complex and unconvincing. Advertises Gengembre & Brown's *New English grammar* for 38c.]
642. Ghosha, Ramanatha. ?1880. *An elementary practical grammar of the English language* ... Rev. ed. Dacca. 56pp.
(L)
643.$ Gibbs, Josiah Willard (1790-1861). 1857. *Philological studies: with English illustrations.* New Haven: Durrie & Peck. 19cm, vii+244pp.
($ @)
644. Gibson, John. 1888. *A manual of the English language.* London: James Cornish & Sons. 88pp.
(L)
[Expresses obligations to Adams, Morris and Mason; five pages of comparative philology; poorly organised. Gibson was a crammer, with three branches in London, others in Versailles, Bonn and Seaford.]
645. Gibson, William Thomas. 1868. *A parsing book; or, blank forms for grammatical analysis.* n.p.
(L)
646.$ Gilbert, Eli. 1834. *The youth's catechetical grammar or: A simple illustration of the principles of the English language, adapted to the capacity of the juvenile mind, comprising a philological view of orthography, etymology, syntax, and prosody. Illustrated by appropriate exercises, designed for the improvement of youth.* New York/Bridgeport, Conn.: J. Nichols & Co. 14cm, 124/128pp. (^{2}1835, New York: W. Mitchell, 14cm, 128pp. (@)).
(@ *Br*)
647. Gilchrist, James (1783-1835). 1816. *Philosophic etymology, or rational grammar.* London: George Smallfield, for Rowland Hunter. 24cm, viii+xxii+[23]-269pp.
($ @ G L E *Ma*)

[Quotes Whiter, *Etymologicon Magnum*, and Horne Tooke. Part 4 is "The common system of English grammar considered." *Mon. Rev. N.S. 84, 304-11*. Martin 1824:273: "another grammatical professor from the school of Gamaliel the Pharisee".]

648. ---. 1824. *The etymological interpreter, or, An explanatory and pronouncing dictionary of the English language: to which is prefixed an introduction containing a full development of the principles of etymology and grammar* ... London: Roland Hunter. 24cm, viii+274pp.
($ @ L)
[This is only the introduction to the dictionary. No more was published.]

649. Giles, James. 1803. *English parsing: comprising the rules of syntax, exemplified by appropriate lessons under each rule; with an index, containing all the parts of speech in the different lessons unparsed ... For the use of schools, private teachers, and elder students*. Gravesend. 17cm, 136/152pp. ($). (^{2}1810, London: the author, 17/18cm, xi+152pp. (@); ^{4}1817; ^{9}1834, London: Darton & Harvey (@); ^{10}1839, London: Harvey & Darton (@); 1842 ($); ^{15}1855 (Lm); 17th ed. advertised in 1859).
($ @ L Lm)
[Rules and method of parsing taken from Murray. Pedantically detailed: the parsing of *I look* takes 67 words and further requires *look* to be conjugated through all its moods and tenses.]

650. Giles, Rev. John Allen (1804-1884). 1839. *An enlarged edition of Murray's Abridged English grammar* by Dr. J. A. Giles. London: Harvey & Darton. 14x8.5, iv+212pp.
(L O)
[The volume testifies to the unbroken popularity of Murray; Giles reports 127 editions of Murray's *Abridgement* by 1839. This is here expanded by copious exercises. The authenticity of the Murray text needs to be checked.]

651. ---. [a1852]. *English grammar in question and answer*. n.p. (^{2}1852 London).
(L)
[His attitude and reasoning are deplorable: "Grammar is perhaps the ... least interesting of all the things which children are obliged to learn. This ... will explain the extraordinary number of treatises already written on the subject ... It is to be feared that in grammar much must be learnt at first without being understood.]

652. ---. [a1879]. *First lessons in English grammar; for the use of beginners*. New ed. London: Edward Stanford. 14cm, 7-80pp.
(@)

653. Giles, T.A. ²1838. *Elements of English grammar, for the use of schools.* London: William Pickering. 18cm, 34pp.
(@ Br, Hu, Lw)
654. Gill, George (Schoolmaster, Hope Street Schools, Liverpool, Publisher). 1866. *A series of lessons in English grammar.* Pt. 1. London, pr. in Liverpool. 16.5x10.5, 32pp., 3d. (Cheap ed. 1868, as *English grammar and analysis. Expressly arranged in a series of lessons for home use* (Gill's School Series), London: Philip & Son, 16cm, 64pp. (@)).
(L O)
[Part I: OES. Inductive method, definitions in bold (to be committed to memory), exercises and explanatory notes rudimentary; definitions often inadequate.]
655. entry deleted
656. ---. 1866. *A series of lessons in English grammar and analysis. Expressly arranged in a series of lessons for home use.* (Gill's School Series). 2 parts. London: Philip & Son, etc. 16x10, 64pp., 3d each. (Anr. ed. 1868, in one vol, 6d/8d).
(@ L O)
[Very elementary grammar, OES plus Derivation, in which "the facts are introduced in the order of their importance" (e.g. verb before adjective, analysis of simple sentences quite early on). Inductive method. Short definitions in bold (to be memorized) accompanied by exercises and explanatory notes in various founts which make the page difficult to survey and restrict the usefulness in teaching.]
657. ---. [1874?]. *The 'Oxford and Cambridge' grammar and analysis of the English language ... especially compiled for the use of middle-class schools.* (Gill's School Series). London etc.: Geo. Gill & Sons. (New ed. [c1890], rev. by? Charles Brook, 17x11, 156pp.)
(L O)
[Traditional OESP account in simple language, with short definitions; notes and exercises in smaller print interspersed. Syntax divided into Analysis and Synthesis. Gill "treated our language just as it is, and not as it should be, to harmonize with the Latin or any other model." Quite a successful attempt within the self-imposed restrictions.]
658. ---. [1875]. *Second Standard English grammar.* "The noun"; *Third Standard* "Nouns-verbs-adjectives". *Adapted to the standard requirements of the English and Scotch Codes.* 5 parts. London: John Hempster/ George Philip & Son etc. 16pp. each.
(L O)

[These booklets, meant to memorize essential facts of grammar in easy form, are part of five adapted for standards II to VI, as advertised on back covers.]

659. Gill, J.W. [1854]. *First steps in English grammar: to be committed to memory. Compiled for the purpose of enabling teachers to put into the hands of their pupils a book containing only such parts as should be committed to memory.* London: Varty & Owen, Educational Depository. 15x9, iv+[5]-32pp., 4s a dozen.

(L O)

[Gill "has purposely omitted all explanations, leaving them to the teacher, and carefully avoided speculative theory, as belonging to the more advanced student". OESP; note that present perfect is 'present tense complete'. Puts great weight on memorizing.]

660. Gilleade, G. 1816. *A compendious English grammar, in twenty-eight praxes or lessons, comprising above one thousand six hundred examples, at full length.* Spalding: T. Albin. 12mo, viii+206pp.

(L *Br*)

[Laborious, but not commendably. Uses Hornsey and Murray. Nine parts of speech; transposition; false English.]

661.$ Gilmore, Joseph Henry (1834-1918). 1875. *Outlines of the art of expression.* Rochester/New York: the Evening Express Printing Co., for the author. 17x13.5, 103/117pp. (@). (Enl. and rev. ed. ^{2}1876 ($ @); anr. ed. 1878, Boston: Ginn ($ @); ^{3}1880, Boston: Ginn & Heath ($ @); anr. ed. 1883 ($); anr. ed. 1887, Boston: Ginn & Co. (@); anr. ed. 1890 (@)).

($ @)

662. Gleig, George Robert (Inspector General of Military Education, 1796-1888). [a1853]. *An explanatory English grammar.* (Gleig's School Series). London: Longman.

(L)

663. Godwin, William (1756-1836). 1809. *A new guide to the English tongue.* First prefixed to the 2nd ed. of W.F. Mylius' *The Christ's Hospital dictionary of the English tongue*, which Godwin had revised as *Mylius' school dictionary*, 1809. (Anr. ed. 1810, issued together under the pseud. 'Edward Baldwin' with Hazlitt's *A new and improved grammar of the English language*, pp. 160-205; rev. ed. 1810, as *Outlines of English grammar, partly abridged from Hazlitt's New and improved grammar of the English tongue*; anr. ed. 1817 (*Lw*); anr. ed. 1824, as *Outlines of English grammar. Containing, in addition to the explanation usually given in similar works, a full development of the etymology of the conjunctions, an an analytical statement and elucidation of the rules of*

syntax, n.p. 14cm, xiii+148pp. ($); new ed. 1824, based on William Hazlitt's *New and improved grammar of the English tongue* (@); anr. ed. 1833, Montreal: Workman & Bowman, for Ariel Bowman, 14cm, 36pp. (@)).
($ @ L *Lw*)
Lit.: Jones 1987; Keynes 1932; Marshall 1984.
[This interesting work presupposes knowledge of the parts of speech but aims to replace Latinate declensions and conjugations with tables showing how words are varied in form and meaning by affixes. The preface discusses the defects of a Latinate approach and considers previous grammarians. Cf. Davidson, J.B. (no. 418) ^{3}1846:50 and Lennie (no. 1078) Introduction to ^{13}1843.]

664.$ Goldsbury, John (1795-1890). 1841. *The common school grammar, a concise and comprehensive manual of English grammar: containing, in addition to the first principles and rules briefly stated and explained, a systematic order of parsing, a number of examples for drilling exercises, and a few in false syntax: particularly adapted to the use of common schools and academies*. Boston: James Munroe / New York: Collins, Keese & Co. 20cm, vi+[7]-94pp. (^{6}1843, Boston/New York: Collins, Brother & Co. (@); ^{r}1845, Boston: J. Munroe ($ @); ^{6}1846, title has changed to *A Concise and Comprehensive manual of English grammar*, Boston: J. Munroe & Co. (@); anr. ed. 1849, 12° (@)).
($ @ *Br*)

665.$ ---. 1842. *Sequel to the common school grammar: containing, in addition to other materials and illustrations, notes and critical remarks on the philosophy of the English language, and explaining some of its most difficult idiomatic phrases: designed for the use of the first class in common schools*. Boston: James Munroe. 19/20cm, 110pp.
($ *Br*)

666.$ ---. 1846. *New theories of grammar. A brief review of four different theories of English grammar, opposed to that of Murray. With an appendix, giving some account of particles, combinations, auxiliaries, ellipses, idiomatic phrases, etc.* (New Theories of Grammar). Boston: James Munroe & Co. 19x11.5, x+[11]-82pp.
($ L)
[Wants to *improve* Murray's system rather than discard it. Discusses, as alternatives to Murray, the approaches by James Brown, William Balch, Oliver B. Peirce and Smith B. Goodenow. The book is not in itself a grammar.]

667.$ ---. 1847. *Exercises and illustrations on the black-board: furnishing an easy and expeditious method of giving instruction: designed for the use of common schools.* Keene, N.H.: G. Tilda. 18/19cm, 144pp.
($ @)

668.$ Goodenow, Smith Bartlett (1817-1897). 1839. *New England grammar. A systematic text-book of English grammar on a new plan, with copious questions and exercises.* Portland: W. Hyde. 18cm, vii+[8]-144pp. (Enl. and impr. ed. ²1843, Boston: Lewis & Sampson, 20cm, vii+[8]-142pp. ($ @); ⁵1831, Philadelphia).
($ @ L *Br*)
[Regards the fashion of an "inductive" approach as only a "plastering up" of Murray. He wants four parts of speech: substantive, verb, adjective, and particle.]

669.$ ---. [a1843]. *An essay on English grammar; designed as an introduction to the New England Grammar and exhibiting fully its character and advantages.* n.p. (Enl. and impr. ed. ²1843, Boston: Lewis & Sampson, 20cm, 78pp. ($ @)).
($ @ L)
[Praises Harris's *Hermes* and has himself tried to give "philosophical definitions." Discusses defects in contemporary grammars.]

670.$ ---. 1850. *A systematic text-book of orthoepy & orthography, or, Manual of reading and writing: for schools and seminaries: fitted as a substitute for the spelling-book, or, A companion of any series of reading-books, speakers, composers, grammars.* n.p. 19cm, 66pp. (Ster. ed. ³1850, Boston: Phillips, Sampson & Co. (@)).
($ @)

671. Goodwin, Thomas (Headmaster of the Greenwich Proprietary School). 1855. *The student's practical grammar of the English language; together with a commentary on the first book of Milton's Paradise Lost.* London: Charles Henry Law. 18cm, viii+309pp.
(@ C O *Lw*)
[Traditional account, with a history and with Milton used for analysis; argues for two word classes, based on Locke. Plenty of questions for repetition.]

672. Gostwick, Joseph (Writer on German Literature, 1814-1887). 1878. *English grammar, historical and analytical.* London: Longmans, Green & Co. 8°, ix/xiv+472pp.
(@ C L O)
[A very detailed grammar in which the historical elements clearly predominate.]

673. Gow, James (1854-1923). 1892. *A method of English for secondary schools. Part I: Grammar chiefly*. London/New York: Macmillan & Co. 18cm, [v]-xii+178pp. (Anr. ed. 1893, London (@); anr. ed. 1896 ($); anr. ed. 1899 (@)).
($ @)
[Cf. no. 784 for *key*.]

674. Anon. 1852. *Graduated grammar*. (National Education, or, Illustrated Two-Penny School Books). London.
(O)
[The only copy at Oxford has been "missing since 1883".]

675. Anon. 1898. *Graduated grammar hand-books for teachers. Book I. For standards I and II. By a Sister of Notre Dame*. Manchester: James B. Ledsham. 16x10.5, 27pp.
(O)
[Elementary lessons, as a reaction to the Code of 1891. Notable for the structure of lessons, divided into: Aim, 1st Step, 1st Thing learned, 2nd Step ... Exercises.]

676. Graham, George Frederick. 1843. *Helps to English grammar; or Easy exercises for young children*. London: Longman, Brown, Green & Longmans. 18cm, xi+134+[18]pp. (Anr. ed. 1851; anr. ed. 1855; new ed. 1864 (@)).
($ @ L Lu *Br, Hu, Lw*)
[Preface discusses the psychology of learning grammar: pupil can begin as soon as "his mind has attained the faculty of classification." He will then "have no difficulty in distinctly perceiving the difference between *things*, *qualities*, and *actions*.]

677. ---. 1862. *English grammar practice; or, Exercises on the etymology, syntax, and prosody of the English language. Adopted to every form of tuition*. London: Longman, Green, Longman & Roberts. 17cm, viii+264pp., 4s6d.
(@ L *Lw*)
[Nine parts of speech; generally conservative, but relies on the completion of blanks for the teaching of most aspects of grammar, including prosody.]

678. Anon. [1896]. *Grammar and composition: sentence forming*. Leeds: Arthur Padley. (40 cards in four packets).
(L)

679. Anon. 1885. *Grammar exercises*. n.p. Reprinted from "Notes of Grammar Lessons". London: National Society's Depository.
(L)

680. Anon. [a1854]. *Grammar explained in verse*. London.

(L)
681. Anon. 1850. *Grammar for beginners: being an introduction to a correct knowledge of the English language.* Sydney: J. Moore. 13.5x8.5, 71pp. (Anr. ed. 1859, London, 32pp.):
(L)
[Nine parts of speech and syntax treated, examples followed by explanations, "a rule of definition, which is an induction from the examples and an exercise, partly to be memorized". Rudimentary and not original, noteworthy for being one of the earliest of such books published in Australia.]

682.$ Anon. [1813]. *Grammar in the grades, its relations to constructive English.* Boston/New York: Silver, Burdett & Co. 17cm, 45pp.
(@)

683.$ Anon. [1870?]. *Grammar in use ...* Chicago etc.: Lyons & Cornahan. 26/28cm. Book 3 by Lydia M. Schwegler & Emma J. Wilson, Book 4 by Evalin Pribble.
(@)

684.! Anon. 1842. *Grammar lessons by a lady. Designed as a supplement to Mary's Grammar.* London: John Rodwell. vi+177pp.
(Mi)
[The preface is signed M., but the writer is not Mrs. Marcet.]

685. entry deleted

686. Anon. 1837. *A grammar of the English language: suited to the capacities of children.* Bicester: J. Smith. 16x10, 78pp.
(O)
[Simple form of traditional material. OESP; nine parts of speech; extensive tables of verb forms. Short chapter on syntax, punctuation and prosody at end.]

687.$ Anon. 1876. *Grammar rules for the public schools of Erie City and County.* Approved by Prof. H.S. Jones, City Sup't, and Prof. C.C. Taylor, County Sup't. Erie, Pa.: W.J. Sells. 22cm, 20pp.
(@)

688.$! Anon. 1830. *Grammar with cuts.* Boston. 18mo, 108pp.
(Br)

689. Anon. 1815. *Grammatical errors, which occur in conversation and writing, pointed out and corrected, by a simple and familiar method agreeably to the rules of Murray's grammar.* London: W. Arding. ii+38pp.
(L)
[A very modest booklet listing mistakes; "aided by the writings of Dr. Lowth, Mr. L. Murray and others; but their valuable treatises may not,

perhaps, be so likely at first to attract the attention of that description of persons which it is the object of these papers to improve".]
690.! Anon. 1802. *A grammatical game in rhyme. By a lady.* London.
[cf. NBL (1946: No. 417); NBL (1949: No. 266)] (*Gu*)
[A book, counters & pictures.]
691. Anon. [c1830]. *Grammatical preceptor in verse; or rules condensed & expressed in verse so as to furnish the youthful mind with a knowledge of the principles and elements of the English language. If young persons get these rhymes by heart, the reason of the thing will soon follow. Designed and written by an eminent academician.* Liverpool: Snow Publisher.
(Dt)
[Not traced in any of the bibliographical sources.]
692. Anon. [a1860]. *Grammatical primer.* (Chambers's Minor Educational Series). Edinburgh: Chambers.
(L)
692a. Anon. 1865. *Grammatical primer; with exercises.* Madras: The Christian Vernacular Education Society. 13.5x8.5cm, 36pp. (Total copies 20,000).
(L)
[OESP. Nine parts of speech (properly only eight, the article being an adjective). Short rules (complemented by special rules), specimen sentences, exercises (including corrections of false English). Traditional, dry and sometimes misleading. This unassuming booklet is remarkable as one of the early books produced for India, but there is no regard for ELT problems, and Indian context found only in a few specimen sentences. (The series includes spellers and easy readers).]
692b. Anon. n.d. *Grammatical primer, with exercises.* London: The Christian Vernacular Education Society for India. 13.5x8.5cm, 47pp.
(L)
[Different from the Madras edition. OESP, eight parts of speech (no article, which is part of 'demonstrative adjectives'). Descriptions of grammatical phenomena or short definitions, often inadequate, followed by examples and exercises; disproportionate attention given to verbs. Syntax summarized in fifteen rules, with parsing exercises. Though this is promised in the inner covers, the exposition is not adapted to the Indian context.]
693.! Anon. 1857. *Grammatical reform, a new grammar, in which the irregularities of the verbs, the useless rules, the difficulties of genders, participles, &c. are removed.* London: Joseph Thomas.
(Advertisement in: *Arithmetical reform.* London: Joseph Thomas 1837.)
694. entry deleted

695. Grant, John (of Crouch End). 1813. *A grammar of the English language: containing a complete summary of its rules, with an elucidation of the general principles of elegant and correct diction, accompanied with critical and explanatory notes, questions for examination, and appropriate exercises.* London: Sherwood, Gilbert & Piper/R. Taylor & Co. 18cm, xix+410pp. ($ @). (Anr. ed. [c1824]).
($ @ L *Br, Hu, Lw, Ma*)
[On [c1824]: Discusses recent improvements in English grammar: six cases reduced to three; why not a similar reduction in voices and moods? Classification of the parts of speech is "partly arbitrary"; he uses ten parts of speech but only noun and verb are essential. Praises Crombie. Reviewed by Martin 1824:272: "... also *Abridgment*, 1813. Had Mr. Grant weighed the subject of Grammar to a greater nicety, he would have been less inclined to heap loads of censure and declamation on Murray, and less solicitous to found his own empire on the downfall of another." Grant is praised by 'L. Murray' (no. 1293) ?1824:37, by Lewis (no. 1091) 1821:40, and adversely criticised by G. Murray (no. 1289).]

696.! ---. [a1815]. *An abridgment of A Grammar of the English language. For the use of junior classes.* London?: Sherwood.
(*Mp*)
[Reviewed as a new publication in *Gentleman's Magazine* 85.i.345 (April 1815).]

697.! ---. [a1824]. *A guide to the exercises* [in his grammar], *with notes and explanations. Intended chiefly for private learners.* n.p.
(*Mi*)
[Advertised in 1813.]

698. Granville, George. [a1827]. *Imperial school grammar.* n.p. (Anr. ed. 1827, London, 12mo (*Br, Lw*); anr. ed. 1827, title has changed to *The imperial grammar of the English language in familiar question and answer, with exercises in false spelling, parsing, etc., and an easier and more methodical system of parsing than has hitherto been introduced*, Devonport: R. Williams, 18cm, [11]-105pp.
(@ *Br, Lw*)
[From the *Plymouth Journal* May 3, 1827 quoted in *Key* p.vi: "will be found of great use in facilitating the study of the fundamental principles of the English Language. It is arranged in the interrogative form, upon a system which has been successfully tried by Mr. G. in his own school - that of parsing by *formulæ*. It is written in a plain and easy style, and is calculated to diminish the labour both of the teacher and the pupil."]

699. ---. 1827. *A key to the orthographical lessons, and parsing exercises, contained in Part I. of The imperial school grammar: executed according*

to the new and improved system of parsing, by formulae, in a series of six classes, as therein proposed. London: J. & C. Evans etc. 16x10, vi+some 50 unpaginated pages.
(L)
[Answers to exercises on false orthography and on parsing, which allow no judgement on the grammar they relate to.]

700. Gray, James (1770-1824). 1818. *Elements of English grammar, deduced from the English language alone; without regard to the grammatical principles of other languages* ... n.p. 15cm, 144pp.
($)

701. Green, Charles B. 1821. *A compendium of grammar: designed as a companion for the student, while attending a course of lectures on English etymology and syntax: in which are comprised rules, definitions, and necessary examples for parsing, with exercises in false syntax, accompanied with notes and remarks: to which is added a short system of punctuation.* n.p. 20/21cm, 44pp.
($)

702. Green, Matthias. 1837. *An English grammar: given in the simplest and most attractive method ever propounded; with copious examples and exercises, particularly well adapted to schools.* London, pr. in Birmingham. 16x10, v+168pp. (New and rev. ed. ^{2}1866 London: Sampson Low, Son & Marston, pr. in Birmingham (@); anr. ed. 1868).
(@ L O *Hu, Br, Lw*)
[The author tries to simplify learning by delaying the introduction of technical terms. He claims originality in treating nouns and verbs first in Etymology and Syntax; otherwise a traditional account of OESP (with prosody and punctuation subsumed under syntax; nine parts of speech. Not fully satisfactory definitions followed by examples and exercises.]

703.$ Green, Richard W., of Philadelphia (Teacher). 1829. *Inductive exercises in English grammar: designed to give young pupils a knowledge of the first principles of language ... The whole intended to inculcate habits of thinking, reasoning, and expressing thought.* New York: R. Lockwood / Boston: Gray & Co., etc. 16cm, vii+[8]-108pp. (^{2}1830, New York, M'Elrath & Bangs / Boston: Hilliard, Gray & Co., etc. [iii]-vii+119pp. (@); enl. and impr. ed. ^{3}1831, Philadelphia: U. Hunt, 16cm, xii+[13]-180pp. ($); ^{5}1834 Philadelphia).
($ L *Br*)
[Defends inductive methods: "the pupil is compelled *to make his own grammar*". There are philosophical divisions in language, but the divisions over which grammarians disagree are caused by uncertainty on how far to carry the process of subdividing.]

704.$ Greene, Frank Bartlett. 1888. *First lessons in English.* Philadelphia: Cowperthwait & Co. 18cm, 144pp.
($ @)
705.$ Greene, George Washington (1811-1883). 1881. *Bingham's elementary English grammar: an introduction to Bingham's English grammar.* n.p. 17cm, 63pp.
($)
[cf. no. 168]
706.$ Greene, Harris Ray (1829-1892). 1862. *Outlines of the analysis, or logical elements of the English language. A mere prospectus of a work now in progress of preparation.* Worcester, Mass.: C. Hamilton.
(@)
707.$ ---. 1867. *Grammatical and logical analysis of the English language: for the use of grammar schools, high schools, normal schools and academies. In two parts.* Worcester: Tyler & Seagrave. 18/19cm, x+[11]-111pp.
($ @)
708.$ ---. 1879. *The English language: its grammatical and logical principles; for the use of grammar high schools and academies.* Boston: Houghton, Osgood & Co. 19cm, xvii+347pp.
(@)
709.$ ---. 1888. *Inductive language lessons: elementary grammar and composition: with a new, simple, and effective system of diagraming.* (Greene's Language Series). New York: A. Lovell & Co. 19cm, 227pp. (pp.222-227 advertisements). (Anr. ed. 1889, 19cm, xiii+212pp. ($)).
($ @)
710.$ Greene, Roscoe Goddard. 1826. *A compend of English grammar; designed for the use of the student, while attending a course of lectures on ethymology and syntax; containing emblematical charts of the several modes and tenses, arranged on the principles of locality and association.* Portland: J. Adams, Jr. 54pp.
(@)
711.$ ---. 1829. *A practical grammar of the English language: in which the principles established by Lindley Murray, are incalculated, and his theory of the modes is clearly illustrated by diagrams, representing the number of tenses in each mode - their signs - and the manner in which they are formed: with an appendix.* (With diagrams of moods). Portland: Shirley & Hyde. 12mo, iv+111pp. (Anr. ed. 1830, 22cm, viii+[9]-111pp. ($); rev. and impr. ed. ^{3}1832 (@); anr. ed. 1835, 20cm, 132pp. ($); 1st stereotype ed. 1839 (@); ^{10}1840, with an appendix, 20cm, 140pp. ($ @); anr. ed. 1842, 138pp. ($); anr. ed. 1844, 19cm, 140pp.

(@); four further editions between 1846 and 1856 (all from 1840 ed.) ($ @)).
($ @)

712.$ ---. 1833. *A grammatical text-book: in which the several moods are clearly illustrated by diagrams, representing the number of tenses in each mood, their signs, and the manner in which they are formed: being an abstract of A practical grammar, etc.: designed for the use of schools.* n.p. 20cm, 60pp.
($)

713.$ ---. ³1835. *A grammar for children, with emblematic illustrations.* Boston: S. Colman, successor to Lilly, Wout & Co. 14cm, 63pp.
(@)

714.$ Greene, Samuel Stillman (1810-1883). [1846]. *Greene's analysis: a treatise on the structure of the English language; or, the analysis and classification of sentences and their component parts with illustrations and exercises adapted for the use of schools.* Philadelphia: T. Cowperthwait & Co. 19cm, 258pp. ($ @). (Anr. ed. 1848 ($); at least thirteen further editions between 1849 and 1868 ($ @).
($ @)
[The work is probably identical with Brown's mention "*Analysis of sentences.* Philadelphia. 12mo, 258pp. 1848". The first of Greene's prolific writings on English grammar in which "he made some daring innovations in grammar teaching, especially the sentence ... which presented a challenge to ... traditional methods" (Downey in no. 720.: 5-6.) After revision, Greene called his books "Greene's New Series of Grammars": *New Introduction* ($.56), *New English Grammar* ($1.05) and *New Analysis* ($1.20) according to his advertisement of 1874.]

715.$ ---. 1848b. *Greene's first lessons in grammar. First lessons in grammar, based upon the construction and analysis of sentences; designed as an introduction to the "Analysis of sentences".* Philadelphia: Thomas Cowperthwait. 17/18/19cm, 171/192pp. ($). (Anr. ed. 1849, 19cm, 171pp. ($); anr. ed. 1855, title has changed to *First lessons in grammar, based upon the construction and analysis of sentences; designed as an introduction to the "Analysis of sentences"* (@); seven further editions between 1858 and 1868, all 17/18cm, 192pp. ($ @)).
($ @ Br)

716.$ ---. 1850. *A treatise on the structure of the English language; or, The analysis and classification of sentences and their component parts with illustrations and exercises adapted to the use of schools.* Philadelphia: Thomas Cowperthwait & Co. (Ten further editions between 1852 and 1866 (@)).

(@)
717.$ ---. 1852. *The elements of English grammar; so arranged as to combine the analytical and synthetical methods: with an introduction for beginners, and various exercises, oral and written, for the formation, analysis, transformation, classification and correction of sentences.* 19cm, xxxvi +220pp. ($). (Anr. ed. 1853? ($); anr. ed. 1854, Philadelphia: Cowperthwait, Desilver & Butler ($ @); anr. ed. 1855 ($); anr. ed. 1856 ($); anr. ed. 1857, Philadelphia: Cowperthwait / Boston: Shepard, Clark (from 1853 ed.), 19cm, xxxvi+220pp. ($); anr. ed. 1858, title has changed to *The elements ... for beginners*, Philadelphia: Cowperthwait & Co. (@); eight further editions between 1858 and 1866 ($ @)).
($ @ L)
[An interesting preface wrestles with the relation between thought and language; "it is the study of the *language*, rather than the technical forms of grammar, that should claim the first attention of the teacher."]

718.$ ---. 1856. *Greene's introduction: An introduction to the study of English grammar.* Philadelphia: H. Cowperthwait & Co. 18cm, 192pp. ($). (At least eleven editions between 1857 and 1867; anr. ed. 1868 (Greene's Grammar and Language Series), 18cm, 224/240pp. ($); at least seven further editions between 1869 and 1890 ($ @)).
($ @)

719.$ ---. 1860. *A grammar of the English language: adapted to the use of schools and academies.* Philadelphia: H. Cowperthwait & Co. 19cm, xii+[13]-264pp. ($ @). (At least six editions between 1861 and 1866 ($ @); anr. ed. 1867, Philadephia: Cowperthwait & Co., 19/20cm, 264/ 320/323pp. ($); anr. ed. 1868, 19x12, 323pp. ($); anr. ed. 1869 (@); anr. ed. 1870, 19x12, 323pp. (L); anr. ed. 1871 (from 1867 ed.), 19cm, 323pp. ($); five further editions between 1872 and 1887 ($ @)).
($ @ L)
[On 1870 ed.: OESP, eight parts of speech. Short definitions, often inadequate; examples, remarks, notes, questions interspersed; remarkable amount of space given to syntax (164-311, includes Rhetoric and Punctuation). Very detailed in parts, but badly organized and didactically questionable.]

720.$ ---. 1873?. *An analysis of the English language; or, The elements of sentences, in their forms, combinations, and relations: with methods for determining their grammatical, logical, and rhetorical uses: designed for the higher grades of schools.* n.p. (Anr. ed. 1874, Philadelphia: Cowperthwait Co. 20/21cm, 323pp. ($); repr. Delmar: Scholars' Facsimiles & Reprints, 1983).
($ @)

[Cf. no. 954. Stresses the importance of thought; "language becomes ... the *organ* and *instrument* for (the thought's) manifestation to the senses" (1873:3). Somewhat idiosyncratic terminology, but otherwise clearly structured; succinct definitions, with exercises, suggestions, examples and notes in small print interspersed. "Logical and rhetorical elements" at end (227-96).]

721.$ ---. 1879. *Outlines of English grammar as evolved from the language itself.* Philadelphia: Cowperthwait & Co. 19cm, 264pp.
(@)

722.$ Greenleaf, Benjamin (Preceptor of Bradford Academy, 1786-1864). ^{2}1822. *A concise system of grammatical punctuation and rules of syntax, selected from various authors for the use of students.* Haverhill: Burrill & Hersey. (@). (^{3}1825 (from 1822 ed.), Haverhill, Mass.: E.W. Reinhart, 17cm, 16pp. ($); anr. ed. 1829, 17/18cm, 24pp. ($); ^{5}1835 (from 1822 ed.), Boston: Robert S. Davis, 14.5x9, 18pp. ($ L)).
($ L @)
[The succinct exposition presupposes syntactical knowledge, but thirteen "rules of syntax" are also provided on pp. 16-18. For other rules Alger's, Murray's and Perley's Grammars are recommended.]

723.$ Greenleaf, Charles Edward. 1853. *Criticisms in etymology and syntax; or, a supplemental grammar: containing much that is new, original, and important.* By a North American Teacher. Gardiner, Me.: Morrell & Heath, for the author. 21x21, 48pp. (Anr. ed. 1854, 19x20, 48pp.).
(@)

724. $ ---. 1855. *An improved and comprehensive school grammar: in which are equally regarded both the wants of the beginner and those of the advanced and critical student, with an addition of much that's new, critical, and highly approved by competent judges.* By a North American Teacher. Gardiner, Me.: A.M.C. Heath, for the author. 19x20.
($ @)

725.$ ---. 1857. *An appendix in English grammar; including a great variety of important matter directing to good language ... designed for a third part to the work entitled 'An improved and comprehensive school grammar,' but can be used to good advantage alone, or in connection with any other work.* By a North American Teacher. Gardiner, Me.: A.M.C. Heath, for the author. 19x20, 24pp.
(@)

726.$ ---. 1861. *An accompaniment to English grammars, including a thorough course of questions in etymology and syntax, with exercises to be performed by the pupil; to which is added a variety of new, important and*

critical matter not given elsewhere. By a North American Teacher. Portland, Me.: B. Thurston. 14x12, 40pp.
(@)

727.$ Greenleaf, Jeremiah (1791-1864). 18... *The self-taught grammarian: or, family grammar.* n.p.
(@)

728.$ ---. 1819. *Grammar simplified; or an ocular analysis of the English language.* Brattleborough: John Holbrook. 35x20.5, 28pp. (@). (Cor., enl. and impr. ed. ^{2}1820, New York: Southwick & Vom Pelt, 31x22, 36pp. ($ @); ^{3}1821, New York: C. Starr, 28/29cm, 48/50pp. ($ @).; ^{4}1822, 28x23, 2 p.l., [7]-48/50pp. ($ @); anr. ed. 1824, New York, 4to, 48/[7]-50pp. (@); ^{10}1826, 29cm, 50pp. ($ @); ^{10}1827, ster. by E. White, 28cm, 50pp. ($ @); ^{20}1828, Brattleboro, Vt.: Holbrook & Fessenden, 28x23, [7]-50pp. ($ @); anr. ed. ^{20}1831, Hartford, 28cm, 50pp. ($ @); ^{20}1834, Hartford: D.F. Robinson (@); cor., enl. and impr. ed. 1835, ster. by James Conner, New York: Robinson, Pratt & Co. (@); ^{20}1837, 29cm, 50pp. ($ *Br*); anr. ed. 1839, 29cm, 50pp. ($); anr. ed. 1851, 29cm, 50pp. ($)).
($ @ *Br*)

729.$ ---. 1841. *The labor saving system of English grammar: designed for schools, families and private learners. By the author of Grammar simplified.* Boston. 33.5x26.5, 23pp. (@). (Anr. ed. 1843, Boston: D.S. King, 27x17.5, 32pp.; enl. and impr. ed. ^{4}1855, New York: Pratt ($ @).
($ @)

730.$ Greenwood, James Mickleborough (b. 1836). 1892/1893. *Studies in English grammar.* Boston: Silver, Burdett & Co.
(@ H)
[Same as no. 1836 where the editor is given as Greenbaum.]

731. Greenwood, R. [187-]. *Lessons in English grammar and analysis of sentences.* London: Wesleyan Training College, Rochdale. ii+40pp.
(H)

732.! Gregory, George (1754-1808). [c1802?]. *A grammar of the English language.* n.p.
(*Mi*)
[Advertised at 1s6d in 1801 by R. Philips; it may never have been published.]

733.$ Grenville, A. Samuel (Headmaster of the Wesleyan Academy, Kingswood). 1822. *Introduction to English grammar. To which are added exercises in parsing ... designed for the use of our schools ...* Boston: E.W. Davies. 19cm, 63pp. / London: Hamilton Adams. 35pp.
($ O *Br*)

[Reads universality into the features of languages he knows. "The design of all languages is the same ... All words are essentially nouns".]

734.! Griffith, S. 1850. *The theory of grammar.* n.p.
(*Lw*)

735.$ Griscom, John (1774-1852). 1810. *Questions in some of the most useful branches of education: calculated for the exercise of students.* n.p. 14cm, 107pp.
($)

736.$ ---. 1821. *Questions in English grammar for the use of schools.* New York: Wood. 14cm, 42pp.
($ *Br*)

737. Grover, Albert. 1877. *A new English grammar for the junior classes in schools.* London: Relfe Brothers, pr. in Guildford. 16x10, [vii]+132pp.
(L O)
[Parts of speech only, treated in 67 lessons in which rules, illustrations and exercises are in unskilful rhymes, a form which also impairs the precision and general intelligibility. Whether the book that the author "has in store" for older children is a published grammar can not be established.]

738. Gubbins, Bruce (Classical professor, Jersey). 1849. *A new Latin and English grammar, with many improvements and additions; methodically, carefully and systematically arranged for the use of schools.* Jersey: R. Gosset. 18x10.5, 82pp.
(L O)
[Although English examples are used for illustration, and a few rules to explain divergent structures, this is mainly a grammar of Latin - in spite of the author's claim that it is meant "to answer a double end".]

739.$ Guernsey, Sarah L. 1852. *Grammar made easy, for beginners.* New York: G. Savage. 18cm, 108pp.
($ @)

740. Anon. n.d. *The guide series of standard grammars. First and second standards.* London: Simpkin, Marshall & Co., etc. 16pp.
(O)
[Very elementary definitions, examples, exercises.]

741. Anon. [1860]. *A guide to English parsing.* Birmingham.
(L)
[A single card.]

742.$! Gurney, David (1759-1815). 1804. *English school grammar.* Boston. 18mo, 72pp. (^{2}1808).
(*Br*)

743.$ Gurney, David (1759-1815). 1801. *The Columbian accidence: or, A brief introduction to the English language, attempted on a new plan, for the use of children, with an appendix, containing a list of irregular nouns and verbs, observations on punctuation, rules for the use of capitals, observations on forming derived words, and examples of parsing.* Boston: Manning & Loring. 14cm, vi+[7]-70pp. ($ @). (^{2}1808, Boston, 15cm, v+[6]-72pp. ($ @)).
($ @)

744.! Gurrier, S. 1827. *Dr Priestley's English grammar improved.* n.p.
(Lw)

745. Guy, John (Schoolmaster). [1840?]. *Stepping-stone to grammar, for the use of schools and private families.* London. (^{20}1854; ^{27}c1860; ^{32}18-? [pref. 1840], London: T.J. Allman, 14cm, 72pp. (@)).
(@ L)
[A simplified version of his *Lindley Murray simplified*. Question and answer; ten parts of speech; thirty words on prosody.]

746. ---. 1846. *Mother's own catechism of grammar, for the use of schools and private families ...* Impr. ed. London: T.J. Allman, 14cm, 72pp., 9d. (@). (Anr. ed 1854; anr. ed 1868).
(@ L Lw)

747. ---. [a1854]. *Lindley Murray simplified; or English grammar adapted for the use of junior classes and private families.* n.p.(^{19}1854, London: Allman, 107pp., 1s).
(L)
[Murray is praised but his exercises are found defective because of his lack of teaching experience. By 1868 the publisher says the book is "on the plan of Lennie".]

748. Guy, Joseph Jr. (1784-1867). 1813. *Guy's English school grammar: in which practical illustration is, in every step, blended with theory, by rules, examples, and exercises: adapted throughout to the use of schools, and private teachers.* Enl. and very considerably improved. London. (^{4}1816, 15cm, x+146pp. ($); ^{5}1819, 15cm, x+143pp. ($); enl. and impr. ed. ^{9}1833, London: Baldwin & Cradock/Whittaker, Treacher & Arnot, xviii+144pp.; ^{12}1845, 1 p.l., 15cm (@)).
Key [a1830].
(@ L *Br, Hu, Ma*)
[Martin 1824:273: "This work has a considerable share of patronage, and it deserves it; but he is not a *philosophical* grammarian".]

749. ---. 1829. *(Guy's) New exercises in English syntax.* London. 1s6d.
(L)

750.! ---. [1831]. *Guy's first English exercises, in parsing, orthography, syntax and punctuation; to supply the junior classes in ladies' and gentlemen's schools, and private families, with rules and exercises for perspicuous and accurate writing, on the plan of Lindley Murray.* n.p.
[Advertised in no. 752 as "just published 1s"]

751. ---. 1850. *(Joseph Guy's) Preparatory English grammar, for very young children; containing the essentials of the study proper to be first known by them.* London: Cradock & Co. 15cm, 60/69pp. (^{2}1851 (@)).
(@ L)

752. Guy, Joseph Sr. (Writer of several school-books). 1839. *(Guy's) First English grammar for junior classes in schools and for the use of private families, in which practice is blended with theory, by having the rules illustrated by examples.* London: Cradock. 14x9, 72pp., 1s.
(L *Hu*, Lw)
["Upon the plan proposed by Dr. Lowth", but "In the use of this Grammar, teachers may find a great convenience, as *the work needs no Key*; for they may find almost every sentence of the examples to be corrected, in Mr Murray's larger Grammar, under *the same article*." OES, traditional; with some parsing exercises and rules followed by exercises for correction.]

753. Gwynne, Parry. 1855. *A word to the wise, or: hints on the current improprieties of expression in writing and speaking.* London: Griffith & Farran. 6d. (^{2}1879; ^{2}1884, 13.5x9, 70pp.).
(@ L)
["Does not presume to undertake the elaborate task of teaching Grammar to persons totally ignorant of it; but is simply intended to correct the inaccuracies. Arranged in 22 chapters devoted to "solecisms of daily occurrence".]

754. Gyll, Gordon Willoughby James (1818-1878). 1859. *A tractate on language.* London: Longman/H.G. Bohn. 23cm, vi+266pp./v+264pp. (^{2}1860).
(@ L)
[Cultivated, amateurish, quirkish]

755. H., C.W. 1841. *The principles of English grammar applied to the interpretation of scripture: Principally adapted to the use of Bible classes, and of persons who have not obtained a thorough knowledge of the principles of grammar in early life.* Romsey: John Gray. 8°, 42pp.
(L O)
[Set out in 70 easy rules, OES, with questions appended p.27ff; very rudimentary, as adapted to audience. Some individual terminology, e.g. *actor* for *subject*, *objective* for *transitive*.]

756.$ H., H. J. 1834. *An explanatory treatise on the subjunctive mode, being the substance of Mr. Noah Webster's fourth dissertation on the English language.* n.p. vi+63pp.
($)
757. H., R.J. 1882. *Grammar for the million, based on Cobbett's grammar in ten lessons; giving plain instructions for acquiring a knowledge of English Grammar.* London: John Heywood. 24pp.
(L)
[The briefest abridgment of Cobbett; OEPS. Clear but doing away with examples and exercises, leaving bare rules with little discussion.]
758.$ H., S. G. 1835. *Murray's grammar of the English language, altered and abridged. Printed at the New England Institution for the Education of the Blind.* Ed. by S. G. H. [Boston, Mass.].
(L)
759.$ Haas, Clara. 1865. *English grammar in its elements and forms: or an exposition of the principles and usages of the English language; with exercises in analysis, parsing and composition, adapted to the use of schools and families.* n.p. 19cm, xii+178pp.
($)
760. Hack, Maria. 1812. *First Lessons in English grammar, with questions and exercises, adapted to the capacities of children, from six to twelve years old; designed as an introduction to the abridgment of Murray's grammar.* Chichester. 9d. (Rev. ed. ^{6}1815, publ. anon. "By a Lady", London: Longman, Hurst, Rees, Orme & Brown, 13.5x8.5, 72pp. (L); ^{7}1834 London (Hu); new, rev. and enl. ed. 1848, London: Longman, Brown, Green & Longmans, 14cm, vi+[7]-72pp. (@)).
(@ L *Hu, DNB*)
[Elementary introduction in plain language, mainly based on Murray, Priestley and Crombie; revised ed. now includes all parts of speech. Aim: "Lowering the style of grammarians [...] to be simple and intelligible"; pupil may proceed to the *Abridgment of Murray's grammar*. Nine parts of speech; etymology only.]
761.$ Hackett, Frederick H. & Earnest A. Girvin 1884. *Pure English; a treatise on words and phrases, or practical lessons in the use of language.* San Francisco: A.L. Bancroft & Co. 19cm, vii+205pp. (Anr. ed. 1886, n.p. 19cm, xi+205pp.).
($ @)
762.$ Hadley, Hiram (1833-1922). 1871. *Lessons in language: an introduction to the study of English grammar.* Chicago: Hadley Brothers. 19cm, vi+[7]-138pp. (@). (Anr. ed. 1872, 19cm, vii+143pp. ($); anr. ed. 1873, 19cm, vii+143pp. ($); anr. ed. 1874, 19cm, vii+143pp. ($); anr.

ed. 1875, 19cm, vii+143pp. ($); anr. ed. 1876, 19cm, 108pp. ($); anr. ed. 1877 (from 1876 ed.), 19cm, 108pp. ($); anr. ed. 1878, Pittsburgh: H.J. Gourley, 20cm, iv+144pp. ($ @) anr. ed. 1879, Chicago: Hadley, 108pp. (@)).
($ @)
[Said by Nietz, 1961:133, to attempt "to teach grammatical matters without using the regular grammatical terminology". The book is complemented by Lee & Hadley (1873, no. 1072). From the advertisement in Lee & Hadley (1873:309): "*the* pioneer in the great reform in teaching language. Experience has shown that it is the most popular book on that subject. It is designed for children from nine to thirteen years of age, and intended as a substitute for the ordinary Primary English Grammar. It proceeds on the plan of teaching the *science* of the English language through the *use* of it, rather than the *use* of the language through the *science* of it."]

763.! Haigh, J. [a1817]. *A rational and practical instruction to parsing, by means of which children of nine or ten years of age, may, in a few months ... distinguish the part of speech of any word [etc.].* London: Darton, Harvey & Darton. 6d.
(*Mp*)
[Advertised in 1817]

764.$ Hale, Salma (1781-1866). 1831. *A new grammar of the English language.* New York: Collins and Hannay. 18cm, 78pp. (@). (²1834, ... *prepared for use in academies and schools*, Boston: Russell, Odiorne & Metcalf, 19cm, viii+124pp. ($ @); anr. ed. 1837).
($ @ Br)

765. Hall, Henry. 1838. *Evening amusements in English grammar; being a new and purely intellectual mode of instructing and exercising youth in this important science.* 3 vols. Part I: *The Grammar*; Part II: *History of Rome*; Part III: *Key to the History of Rome*. London: John Souter. (Anr. ed. 1839, n.p.: W. Ball & Co., 12mo, viii+43pp., xii+70pp., [iv] +64pp.).
(L)

766. Hall, Joseph (Head Master of the Hulme Grammar School, Manchester, b.1854), Edward Adolf Sonnenschein & Alice J. Cooper (Head Mistress of the Edgbaston High School). 1890-91. *An English grammar for schools, based on the principles and requirements of the Grammatical Society.* Pt. 1 by J. Hall & E.A. Sonnenschein; Pt. 2 by A.J. Cooper & E.A. Sonnenschein. (Sonnenschein's Parallel Grammar Series). London: Swan Sonnenschein. 19cm. (Anr. ed. 1894, 63pp. ($)).
($ O)

[Five kinds of sentence; five forms of predicate; noun etc. equivalents and clauses. A sensible, teacherly book.]

767.$ Hall, Samuel Read (1795-1877). 1832. *The grammatical assistant: containing definitions in etymology, rules of syntax, and selections for parsing.* Springfield, Mass.: Merriam, Little & Co. 18cm, 131pp. (@ Br). (Rev. and enl. ed. ^{2}1833, 18cm, 148pp. ($ @); ^{3}1836, 19cm, iv+[5]-148pp. ($)).
($ @ Br)

768. Hall, Theophilus Dwight. 1873. *A primary English grammar for elementary schools. With exercises and questions.* (Dr. William Smith's English Course). 16x10, iv+76pp. (New ed. 1874 London: J. Murray, 17cm, 76pp. (@); anr. ed. 1876 ... with eighty-four exercises (@); enl. ed. 1881, London, 16cm, 151pp. (L); ^{12}1892).
Key: London: J. Murray 1873, 16cm, 52pp.
(@ L O)
["Not a mere abridgement of the *School manual*"; written for children of 7-8. Alphabet, Classification of Words, nine parts of speech, Syntax rules, Easy lessons in analysis (can be omitted), Exercises, Parsing, Punctuation; somewhat conservative and certainly too detailed for the age group. *Key* published separately.]

769. !---. a1873, ^{6}1881. *A school manual of English grammar. With historical introduction, copious exercises, and appendices.* n.p. 12mo, 256pp., 3s6d.
["The rules are simple, and the explanations, though brief, are always clear ... The great number of examples, a slight sketch of English Philology, a chapter on Prosody, and a good selection of Exercises" (*Educational Times*, from advertisement in no. 768.)]

770.$ Hall, William. 1849. *Encyclopaedia of English Grammar: designed for the use of schools, academies and private learners: embracing grammar, elocution, rhetoric, logic and music, upon a plan with copious exercises.* Wheeling: J. Wolfe. 20cm, viii+502pp. (Anr. ed. 1850, title has changed to *Encyclopaedia of English grammar: designed for the use of schools, academies and private learners: embracing what is generally distinguished by the separate titles of grammar, elocution, rhetoric, logic and music, upon a plan not before introduced: with copious exercises in prose, and specimens from the pens of the most distinguished poets of Europe and America*, (by report), Columbus, Ohio: Scott & Bascom (@)).
($ @ Br)

771.$ Hall, William D. 1897. *Rand-McNally primary grammar and composition: principles and definitions by induction. For pupils of the sixth*

grade. Chicago/New York: Rand, McNally & Co. 19cm, 182/207pp. (Anr. ed. [1898], 19cm, 207pp. (@)).
($ @)

772.$ Hall, William D. 1898. *The Rand-McNally English grammar and composition*. Chicago/New York: Rand, McNally & Co. 19cm, 312pp.
($ @)

⇒ Hallidie, A.R.S. (collaborator) - see Turner, James Arnold, nos. 1773 & 1774

773.$ Hallock, Edward John. 1812. *A grammar of the English language: for the use of common schools, academies and seminaries*. New York. 12mo, 251pp. (Anr. ed. 1842, New York: Dayton & Newman / Boston: Tappan & Dennet, 19cm, xii+[13]-251pp. ($ @ L); ²1849, New York: M.H. Newman, 19/20cm, 250pp. ($); anr. ed. 1855 (from 1849 ed.), 19cm, xii+[13]-250pp. ($)).
($ @ L Br)
[Br: "A very inaccurate book, with sundry small plagiarisms from G. Brown". Expounds both logical and grammatical analysis; acknowledgments to L. Murray, Webster and Andrews & Stoddard's Latin grammar.]

774.$ Halsey, Charles Storrs (b.1834). 1865. *The definitions and principles of English grammar*. Rochester/New York: Steam Press of Curtis, Morey & Co. 19cm, 23pp.
($ @)

775. Hamilton, R. [1806?]. *Lowth's introduction to English grammar simplified*. Aberdeen.
(A)

776. Hamlin, Lorenzo F. 1831. *English grammar in lectures: designed to render its principles easily adapted to the mind of the young learner, and its study entertaining*. Boston: Munroe & Francis / New York: Lockwood & Philadelphia. 16cm, 108pp. (Ster. ed. 1832, Brattleboro, Vt.: Peck, Stan & Co., 17/18cm, 108pp. ($); anr. ed. 1833 ($ @); anr. ed. 1834 (@)).
($ @ L Br)

777. Anon. 1890. *A handbook of analysis of sentences*. Edinburgh.
(L)

778. Anon. 1893. *Handbook of English, consisting of grammar, analysis and wordbuilding ... By a graduate and head-teacher*. Blackburn: Denham & Co. / London: Simpkin, Marshall, Hamilton, Kent & Co. 17x10.5, 56pp., 4d.
(L)

["This little work covers all the code requirements in English for day and evening schools, and the greater part of the English set for P.T. examinations, and the professional preliminaries". Mainly on (eight) parts of speech and word-formation; very little on pronunciation and syntax; brief definitions often inadequate, arrangement difficult to follow.]

779. Anon. 1842. *The hand-book of English grammar. Comprising, in a concise and simple form, the substance of all the most approved English grammars extant; with questions for exercise, and copious examples for parsing, &c. Also, an extensive glossary of the principal words made use of in this treatise.* Dublin: Machen. 15cm, 151pp.
(@ Hu, Lw)

780. Anon. 1841. *The handbook of grammar; for English, German, French, and Italian students. Shewing, at one view, the construction peculiar to each language.* London: Rodwell. 16x10, 230pp.
(C L O)
[Comparative treatment without any more thorough discussion of features; useless for English]

781.$ Hanser, Otto. [1897]. *English grammar in a nutshell.* Rockville, Conn. 18cm, [6]pp.
(@)

782. Hardwick, John. 1852. *A selection of moral sentences for parsing lessons, selected for the use of J. Hardwick's school.* Grantham.
(O)

783. Hardy, John Elvy. 1862. *Linear analysis of sentences.* Chester. 24pp.
(C E O)
[Thoughtful but impractical innovation: twelve typographical "signs" are used to indicate syntactical features, and numerical indices to indicate the nine parts of speech.]

784. Hardy, T.B. 1897. *A key to Dr. Gow's Method of English for secondary schools.* n.p. xvi+224pp.
($)
[For the grammar cf. no. 673]

785.$ Harper, William Rainey (1856-1906). 1894. *Inductive studies in English grammar.* New York/Cincinnati etc.: American Book Company. 19cm, 96pp.
($)

786. Harris, James (Private teacher). 1830. *The verb of the English language explained, in which the words commonly called auxiliaries are traced to their respective etymons.* London: Whittaker, Treacher & Co. 21x13, 62pp.
(G L)

[Exposition of the verbal system, including auxiliaries and modal verbs, to make pupils understand what they failed to get from Murray and Ash. Discursive, with some historical information and discussion of 18th-century grammarians. The book is itself not a full grammar.]

787. Harris, James (Head Master of the Cathedral Grammar School, Chester). 1862. *Easy exercises in English grammar and composition.* London, pr. in Manchester. 14.5x9, 115pp. (Rev. ed. ^{2}1865, London: Hamilton, Adams & Co., 14cm).
(L O)
[Exercises only; no grammatical explanations. For ages 10-12; conventional but sensible.]

788. Harrison, Elizabeth. ^{4}1853. *The child's first catechism of English grammar.* London: Relfe Bros. 54pp. 9d.
(L)
[Naive and rudimentary information in Q/A form, almost exclusively on words/morphology. Still advertised in 1898.]

789. Harrison, Rev. Matthew (1792?-1862). 1848. *The rise, progress and present structure of the English language.* London/Philadelphia: Longman, Longman, Brown, Green & Longmans. 20cm, xvi+382pp. (Anr. ed. 1849, London/Philadelphia (@); anr. ed. 1850, Philadelphia: E.C. & J. Biddle, 20cm, xii+[13]-393pp.(@); ^{2}1861 (2nd Am. ed.), Philadelphia: E.C. Biddle & Co. (@); 4th Am. ed. [^{4}187?], Philadelphia: W.J. Fortes, 19cm, xiv+[15]-395pp. (@)).
(@ L *Br*, *Lw*)
[In three parts: "Historical; Philological; Grammatical." Pedantic pursuit of grammatical errors.]

790. Harrison, William (Schoolmaster of Bradford). ^{3}1834. *Lines on English grammar, descriptive of the different parts of speech and illustrative of the leading particulars to be observed in reference to each; to which are appended prose definitions of their technicalities: accompanied with tables for etymological parsing.* Enl. ed. London. 16pp.
(L)
[These verses, to be repeated simultaneously in class, offer the barest information, not much improved by the definitions in prose, pp. 9-14.]

791.$ Hart, John. 1898a. *Advanced English grammar.* Richmond, Va.: B.F. Johnson Publ. Co. 19cm, 200pp.
($ @)

792.$ ---. 1898b. *Primary English grammar.* Richmond, Va.: B.F. Johnson Publ. Co. 19cm, 103pp.
($ @)

793.$ Hart, John Seeley (1810-1877). 1845. *English grammar, or, An exposition of the principles and usages of the English language*. Philadelphia: E.H. Butler. 12mo, [7]-192pp. (Anr. ed. 1846, 19cm, 12+21-192pp. ($); anr. ed. 1848, 19cm, 12+21-192pp. ($); anr. ed. 1849 (@); anr. ed. 1857 (@); anr. ed. 1858 (@); anr. ed. 1860 (@); anr. ed. 1861, 102pp. (@); 1862 ?; anr. ed. 1864 (from 1862 ed.), 19cm, 199pp. ($); anr. ed. 1868, 200pp. (@); anr. ed. 1869, 199pp. (@)).
($ @ Br)

794.$ ---. 1862. *Hart's English grammar: part first: an introduction to the grammar of the English language*. Philadelphia: E.H. Butler & Co. 18cm, 125pp. ($ @). (Anr. ed. 1872, 19cm, 199pp. (@); anr. ed. 1873 (@); anr. ed. 1877, 18cm, 125pp. ($ @)).
($ @)

795.$ ---. 1874a. *A grammar of the English language, with an analysis of the sentence*. Philadelphia: Eldredge & Brothers. 19cm, viii+[9]-220pp. ($). (Anr. ed. 1875, Philadelphia, 19cm, 232pp. ($ L); anr. ed. 1877, viii+[9]-239pp. (@); anr. ed. 1878, 20cm, 232pp. ($); anr. ed. 1879 (@); anr. ed. 1881 (@); anr. ed. 1882 (@); anr. ed. 1885 (@); anr. ed. 1899 (@)).
($ @ L)

796.$ ---. 1874b. *Language lessons for beginners*. Philadelphia?. 17cm, iv+[5]-80pp. (@). (Anr. ed. 1875, 18cm, 80pp. ($ @); anr. ed. 1878 (@); anr. ed. 1880 (@)).
($ @)

797.$ ---. 1878. *An elementary grammar of the English language*. Philadelphia: Eldredge & Brothers. 19cm, 147pp./vi+[7]-128pp. (@). (Anr. ed. 18cm, 128pp. ($); anr. ed. 1879 (@); anr. ed. 1880 (@); anr. ed. 1900, title has changed to ... *with an analysis of the sentences*, 18cm, 159pp. (@)).
($ @)

798. Hartley, Cecil. 1818. *Principles of punctuation or the art of pointing familiarized. Composed for the use of seminaries of education, and for all who aspire to accuracy in composition*. London: Effingham Wilson. 11.5x9, 144pp.
(@ L)

[Not a proper grammar, though closely connected with syntax: "The Principles of Grammar form a solid foundation for Elements of Punctuation; but Grammar, which ought to be the basis, has seldom been considered as adequate to the purpose" (p. 6). In Q/A form.]

799. Hartley, Charles. 1871. *The grammatical remembrancer. Aids to correct speaking, writing and spelling, for adults, original and compiled.* London: Groombridge & Sons. 16x10, iv+[5]-56pp.
(@ L)
[Although concentrating on more obvious rules and giving attention to problematic cases of uncertain and divided usage, the book is almost a comprehensive grammar book. OESP, nine parts of speech, generally clear, not following any particular school, but quoting from Murray, Smart, Walker, D'Orsey; quite short on syntax (41-7).]

800. ---. 1879. *Frequent faults in speaking and writing explained and corrected.* Brighton: the author. 16.5x10, 32pp., 6d.
(L)
["Intended to explain and correct the common errors in speaking and writing, not only of the uneducated, but of those who have not looked into a Grammar since they left school". Specimens taken from spelling, morphology, prepositions/conjunctions, and semantics.]

801. Harvey, J. 1821. *Key to the parsing exercises, contained in Lindley Murray's Grammatical exercises and in his Abridgment of English grammar... with notes.* Halesworth: T. Tippell. (^{2}1829, London, Halesworth: Longman & Co., vi+143pp.).
(L)
[Solid parsing throughout; acknowledgments to J. Harris, Blair, Crombie, Bradley, Lowth and Valpy.]

802. Harvey, J. (of Halesworth). 1841. *Abridgment of Murray's English grammar. Improved: with an enlarged appendix. Containing exercises in orthography, parsing, syntax, and punctuation, much more numerous than in former editions of this grammar.* London: Simpkin, Marshall & Co., pr. in Ipswich. 14x9, 125pp.
(L O *Br*)
[The alterations claimed as improvements of Murray appear to be minor - a modified way of cribbing and using a famous author's name.]

803. Harvey, Reuben. 1851. *A common sense grammar of the English language.* Dublin: I. & E. MacDonnell, for the author. 18x10.5, xxxi+65 +7pp.
(C L O)
["To overthrow the whole fabric of a system raised upon a false and artificial basis" - since "The grammarian is not the legislator of language but the interpreter of its laws". Promises to proceed from Universal Grammar to the "accidental peculiarities of English particular grammar", but quibbling mainly with 18th-century authors, he has no coherent system of his own to offer. In spite of large claims in the introduction,

the text is rather weak, simple and sometimes trivial. Seven parts of speech, six tenses; short prescriptive rules with little exemplification, no exercises.]

804.$ Harvey, Thomas Wadleigh (1821?-1892). 1868. *Harvey's English grammar. A practical grammar of the English language for the use of schools of every grade.* New York/Cincinnati: Wilson, Hinkle & Co. / Philadelphia: Claxton, Remsen & Haffelfinger. 19cm, vi+[7]-264pp. ($ @). (Anr. ed. 1868 (Harvey's Language Course), 19cm, vi+[7]-272pp. ($); anr. ed. [187?], Cincinnati/New York: Van Antwerp, Bragg & Co. 19cm, vi+[7]-264pp. (@); rev. ed. 1878, New York: van Antwerp, Bragg & Co. 19cm, 264pp.; anr. ed. 1878 (Harvey's Language Course), 19/20cm, vi+[7]-272pp. ($); rev. ed. 1896 (Harvey's Language Course), 19cm, vi+[7]-272pp. ($); repr. Delmar: Scholars' Facsimiles & Reprints, 1987).
Key 1881, 15cm, 112pp. ($). (rev. ed. 1885, 16cm, 200pp. ($)).
($ @)
[Cf. no. 954. OESP account (one of the last to use this division) avoiding "the discussion of mere theories; preferring, rather a plain, didactic statement (and) intelligent, systematic drill in the class room". Eight parts of speech; ample room for parsing and detailed analysis of sentences; extensive treatment of figures of language and punctuation at the end of "syntax". Traditional, somewhat prescriptive treatment including false syntax; but innovative in the use of straight-line diagrams to illustrate sentence structure.]

805.$ ---. 1869a. *Elementary grammar and composition.* 18cm, 160pp. ($). (rev. ed. ?1880 (Harvey's Language Course), Cincinnati/New York: van Antwerp & Bragg, 18cm, 160pp. ($); anr. ed. 1897 (Harvey's Language Course), 19cm, vi+[7]-160pp. ($)).
($)

806.$ ---. 1869b. *Harvey's elementary grammar: An elementary grammar of the English language, for the use of schools.* (Eclectic Educational Series). Cincinnati: Wilson, Hink & Co. / Philadelphia: Claxton, Remson & Haffelfinger, etc. 18cm, vi+[7]-160pp. (@). (Anr. ed. 1879, Cincinnati etc.: van Antwerp, Bragg & Co. (@)).
($ @)

807.$ ---. 1875. *First lessons in the English language, by Thos. W. Harvey.* (Harvey's Language Course). Cincinnati, etc.: Van Antwerp, Bragg & Co. 18cm, vi+[7]-80pp.
($)

808.$ Haskins, David Greene (1818-1896). 1858. *The French and English first-book; or, the rudiments of French and English grammar combined:*

with exercises for reading and translation. Boston: Jewett & Co. 18/ 19cm, iv+146pp. ($ @). (Anr. ed. 1864, New York: Barnes & Burr, 17.5x12, iv+168pp. (L)).
($ @ L)
[Rudimentary statements in Q/A form in 43 lessons which most often do not do justice to either English or French; proper contrasts would have been beyond the pupils' capacities - still it is doubtful whether one can properly learn the grammars of the two languages at a time.]

809. entry deleted

810.$ Hassam, John H. 1810. *Introduction to the principles of English grammar: with an appendix containing exercises corresponding with the rules of syntax.* New Brunswick. 19cm, 48pp. (Anr. ed. 1816, 19cm, 48pp. ($ @)).
($ @)

811. ---. [181?]. *English grammar abridged, for classes, according to (his) system.* n.p. 12°, 24pp.
(@)

812.$ Hathaway, Benjamin Adams (b.1852). 1884. *1001 questions and answers on English grammar.* Cleveland, Ohio: Burrows Brothers Co. / Lebanon, Ohio. 17cm, 126/136pp. (Anr. ed. 1884, 17cm, 136pp. ($); anr. ed. 1886, 17cm, 126pp. ($); rev ed. [c1895], Cleveland, Ohio: The Burrows, 17cm, 128pp.).
($)

813. Hawley, John Hugh. 1869. *A first book of English grammar.* London: Charles Bean. 15x9.5, 84pp.
($ @ E O)
[Discussion of parts of speech followed by subclassification, inflexion and syntax (no orthography or prosody). Somewhat idiosyncratic arrangement, but quite successful definitions, interspersed with exercises.]

814. ---. [a1889]. *English grammar for beginners.* Rev. ed. 3 parts. Part I: *The parts of speech*, 29pp., 6d; Part II: *The accidence*, 64pp., 6d; Part III: *Syntax and analysis*, 16x10, 109pp. London: Relfe Bros.
(L O)
[Conversational tone, sometimes in Q/A form, but lacking definitions, and in consequence, precision. Questions for repetition and exercises interspersed; the book becomes even more inadequate and confusing in part III. Recast from the author's *First book of English grammar* "written many years ago" (II:i) (untraced).]

815.$ Haynie, Mrs. Martha D.L. 1884. *English syntax and analysis simplified: designed for the use in common schools, high schools and normal*

schools. Chicago: G. Sherwood & Co. 19cm, 271pp. (Anr. ed. 1888 (@)).
($ @)
816.$ ---. 1889. *A new English grammar*. Chicago: A. Flanagan. 19cm, 244pp.
($ @)
817.$ Haywood, J. 1800. *A short introduction to the English tongue in two parts. Wherein declension and government are concisely explained, and simplified to the capacities of children; with notes, etc*. Sheffield: J. Montgomery. (Sp). (^{2}1805 (L)).
(L Sp)
[Conventional but thorough; second edition much improved; nine parts of speech.]
818.$ Hazen, Edward. 1842. *A practical grammar of the English language; or, an introduction to composition: in which sentences are classified into verbal forms and phrases*. New York: Huntington & Savage. 12mo, 240pp. (Anr. ed. 1842, 19x11, vi+[7]-240pp. ($); anr. ed. 1843 ($); anr. ed. 1844, modifies ... *in which the constructions are classified into predications and phrases*, New York: Huntington & Savage ($); anr. ed. 1847 (from 1844 ed.) ($); anr. ed. 1849, title has changed to *A practical grammar of the English language*. (@)).
($ @ L *Br*)
[Nine parts of speech explained, together with their syntactical uses, and parsing exercises added. Hazen prides himself on reducing syntactical patterns to 28 types of 'predications' (verbs and their complements, with transformations), otherwise quite traditional.]
819.$ ---. 1845. *The grammatic reader, no. I*. New York: J.S. Redfield. 20cm, 47pp; *no. II* 19cm, 96pp. (Anr. ed. 1846 *no. I* 19cm, 48pp., *no. II* 20cm, 96pp., *no. III*. 20cm, 96pp. ($)).
($ @)
820.$ ---. 1847a. *Hazen's composition book no. I & II: designed to accompany The grammatic readers, or any other grammar*. New York: J.S Redfield. 27cm, 24pp. each.
($)
821.$ ---. 1850. *The new speller and definer: with the structures of the language, systematically arranged, for exercises in applying words on the principles of Hazen's Practical grammar*. Philadelphia. 20cm. (Anr. ed. 1851, 312pp. ($); anr. ed. 1860 ($)).
($ @)
822.$ ---. 1852. *The analytic and synthetic English grammar: in which the subject is discussed by parts of speech and by structures: in three parts*.

New York: Cornish, Lamport & Co. 16cm, viii+[9]-108pp. (Anr. ed. 1854, New York: F.J. Huntington/J.S. Redfield, 18/19cm, viii+[9]-312pp. ($ @)).

($ @)

823.$ Hazen, Marshman William (1845-1911). 1899. *Observation, thought and expression, or, seeing, thinking, knowledge, talking and writing.* (Hazen's Language Series). n.p. 19cm.

($)

824. Hazlitt, William (1778-1830). 1810. *A new and improved grammar of the English tongue: for the use of schools. In which the genius of our speech is especially attended to, and the discoveries of Mr Horne Tooke and other modern writers on the formation of language are for the first time incorporated; to which is added, A new guide to the English tongue, in a letter to Mr W.F. Mylius, author of the school dictionary, by Edward Baldwin, Esq.* (pseud. of William Godwin). London: Richard Taylor & Co., for M.J. Godwin. 13x19, xx+205pp. (*A new guide to the English tongue*: 160-205).

($ C L O *Br, Hu, Ma, Sk, Lw*)

[There is a complex relationship between the two grammars: Godwin was trying to elbow Hazlitt's out in favour of his own, inferior one. A spirited move to get away from Latin-based grammar, by basing his arguments on Horne Tooke - but avoiding his errors and inconsistencies; Baldwin's complement is on inflexion and word-formation. Hazlitt undertakes to render "the Genius of our Speech" by attacking the traditional Latin-based model; one way is to incorporate in a form appropriate for school children "the Discoveries of Mr. Horne Tooke and the other Modern Writers on the Formation of the Language". More or less restricted to E and S - he doubts whether O and P belong to grammar but includes short sections to conform with tradition. Very clear and full exposition with few footnotes, remarks and references to Lowth, Tooke, Murray and Booth. The appended "New Guide to the English Tongue" (160-205) is on word-formation; no reason is given why it is here reprinted from the second ed. of Mylius' *New School Dictionary*.]

825. ---. 1829. *English grammar.* In *The Atlas*, 15 March.

(*Mi, Mp*)

[A lively attack on traditional English grammar: "One of those subjects on which the human understanding has played the fool ... The definitions ... seem calculated for no other purpose than to *mystify* and *stultify* the understanding." Why have Horne Tooke's discoveries not been applied?]

826. Heald, A. 1892. *The Queen's English (?) up to date: an exposition of the prevailing grammatical errors of the day, with numerous examples.*

(Published anon., by "Anglophil"). London: Economic Pr. & Publ. Co. xii+190pp. (Anr. ed. 1898, London: The Literary Revision & Translation Office, 18x11.5, xii+192pp.).
(@ L)
[The most important collection of errors of the late 19th century which contains enough systematic exposition to be classified as a grammar. Misuses of all types are carefully explained - information that largely overlaps with the Fowlers' guides. Very conservative and very prescriptive.]

827.$ Heath, Mrs. Nelly Lloyd Knox. 1896-. *Elementary lessons in English. The parts of speech: and how they are inflected*. Indiana/Boston: Ginn & Co. 19cm, v+149pp.
(@)
[Cf. nos. 1043 & 1850.]

828.$ ---. 1896-. *Common school course in English*. (Common School Language Series). Boston/London: Ginn & Co. 18cm.
(@)

829.$ --- & William Dwight Whitney (1827-1894). 1880. *Elementary lessons in English for home and school use*. (Ginn & Heath's Language Series). 2 vols. n.p. 18cm ($ @). (Anr. ed. 1884 (Ginn, Heath & Co.'s Language Series), 19cm ($); anr. ed. 1886, 2 vols., 19cm ($ @); anr. ed. 1887, 2 vols., 18/19cm. ($ @); anr. ed. 1888 (@); anr. ed. 1889, *Part first, How to speak and write correctly*, (Minnesota Text-Book Series), 19cm, 192pp. ($); anr. ed. 1890 (@); anr. ed. 1891 (@); anr. ed. 1892 (@); anr. ed. 1895 (Whitney & Knox Language Series)).
($ @)

830. Heeley, Francis. 1881. *Sentences for analysis for use in schools*. (Chambers's Educational Series). London/Edinburgh: Chambers. 16.5x 10.5, 32pp., 3d.
(L)
[To supplement examples provided in grammars, Heeley selected 191 sentences/passages, with no comment or method or key supplied.]

831.$ Henderson, George E. 1897. *Exercises in English*. (also quoted as *E. in grammar*). Toronto: Educational Publishing Co. 126pp. (Anr. ed. 1899 ($)).
(L $)

832.$ --- & A.B. Cushing. 1897. *Hard places in grammar made easy. With a large number of carefully selected sentences and passages for practice*. Toronto: Educational Publishing Co. 16x11, 109pp, 20c.
(L)

[The syntax of the seven major parts of speech is described, with great attention devoted to the verb. Each section is followed by exercises. The latter part deals with sentence analysis. The book complements Henderson's *Grammar* (no. 831).]

833.$ ---, C.G. Fraser & G.A. Fraser. 1898a. *Junior language lessons for first, second and third classes.* Toronto: Educational Publishing Co. 16x11, 94pp., 15c.
(L)
[Exercises on various parts of grammar and composition only. The authors do not relate to any particular grammar or grammatical system. Advertises no. 833a, *for third and fourth classes.*]

833a.$ ---, --- & ---. 1898b. *Exercises in grammar.* Toronto: Educational Publishing Co. 16x11, 126pp., 15c.
(L)
[Exercises devoted to the eight parts of speech followed by, miscellaneous exercises, and those devoted to sentence analysis (phrases, clauses). Geared to the authors' grammar, and of no independent value.]

834.$ Henderson, H. M. 1828. *Grammar made easy and interesting; or, A practical grammar of the English language, systematically arranged ...* n.p. 21cm, 80pp.
($)

835.$ Henderson, Thomas (Teacher). 1859. *A comprehensive grammar of the English language: containing many original features, especially in the treatment of verbs and the omission of technical terms: in two parts: comprising a complete elementary course.* Philadelphia: J.B. Lippincott & Co. 18/19cm, xxxiii+[35]-124pp.
($)

836.$ Hendrick, J.L. 1843?. *A grammatical manual, or, An outline of English grammar: designed for the use of the students of Onondaga Academy.* n.p. (Anr. ed. 1844 (from 1843 ed.), Syracuse, N.Y.: L.W. Hall & Co. 15/16cm, ix+[11]-105pp. ($ *Br*)).
($ @ *Br*)

837.$ Hendrickson, Clarence Rutherford. 1884. *Grammar made brief by the omission of superfluities. Practical lessons in English grammar: being a complete practical, analytical, and synthetical treatise on the English language for the use of schools.* Chattanooga, Tenn.: The Times Printing Co. 17cm, viii+[9]-109pp.
($)

838. entry deleted

839. Henshall, Samuel (Philologist, 1764-1807). 1807. *Etymological organic reasoner.* n.p.

(*Sk*)
840.$! Hewett, D. 1838. *English grammar*. New York. Folio, 16pp.
(*Br*)
841. Hewitt, Henry Marmaduke. 1887. *A manual of our mother tongue.* (Hughes' Matriculation Manuals). London: Hughes. (^{4}1889, 19cm, xii+843pp. ($); ^{8}1892; ^{10}1894, 2 vols. in 1, 8° (@)).
($ @ C)
[On ^{8}1892: Overwhelmingly complete: includes a history of the language; summary of Anglo-Saxon grammar; lists of authors; behaviour in examinations; papers from public examinations.]
842.$ Heyden, A. V. 1876. *A concise treatise on English epeology designed as a substitute for the old theory of English grammar, digested on an entire different principle, having an entire different (yet truthful) nomenclature from that of the old theory* ... n.p. 19cm, 49pp.
($ @)
843. Hickey, M. 1881-82. *Graduated exercises in English grammar with definitions. Standards 2-6*. Manchester etc.: John Heywood. 16cm. 3 parts. II:16pp., IV:32pp., V:32pp. (Enl. ed. 1884, with added *Standard 5*, Manchester, 16cm).
(@ O L)
[Questions asking students to pick out certain parts of speech, with minimal introductory definitions; very slight.]
844. Higginson, Edward (1807-1880). 1864. *An English grammar, specially intended for classical schools and private students*. London: Longman, Green, Longman, Roberts & Green. 18x10, xii+207pp. (Anr. ed. 1865, 19cm, xii+207pp. ($)).
($ @ L O)
[Conventional, scholarly; rather rambling appendix "On pure English, as understood from the history of the language." Commended by Alford (no. 2230)]
845. Higginson, T.E. 1803. *English grammar, with a praxis perfectly elucidating each chapter, and an appendix for more advanced students. Designed for the use of schools and private education, and calculated to make the subject of grammar more easy and familiar*. Dublin: W. Porter. 18cm, iv+ii+171pp.
($ @ *Br*)
846.$ Hildreth, Ezekiel (1784-1856). 1842. *Logopolis, or, City of words; containing a development of the science, grammar, syntax, logic and rhetoric of the English language*. Pittsburgh: A. Jaynes. 19x10.5, vii+[9]-216pp.
($ L)

[Philosophical treatment which includes a long lecture on logic; discursive, somewhat speculative and not totally convincing; no references to other grammars.]

847. Hiley, Richard. 1831. *Hiley's grammar abridged.* London. 12°. (L). [2]1833 as *An abridgement of Hiley's English grammar: together with appropriate questions and exercises progressively arranged.* London: Longman etc. 14cm. ([3]1834; [4]1835; [4]1841, London: Longman & Co., iii-196pp. (@); [5]1846, 185pp. (@); enl. ed. [6]1853, 8°; [11]1860, 1s9d; new ed. 1878, title has changed to ... *with questions and exercises in parsing and the structure of sentences. Arranged in progressive lessons*, London: Longmans, Green & Co., 15cm, 222pp. (@); many further editions to 1890).

(@ C O *Br, Hu, Lw*)

[Very condensed exposition with plenty of erroneous syntax appended for correction.]

848. ---. 1832. *A grammar of the English language; together with the principles of eloquence and rhetoric.* London: Simpkin & Marshall, pr. in Leeds. xxviii+282pp. (L) (enl. and impr. ed. [2]1835, title has changed to *A treatise on English grammar, style and poetry with preparatory logic; to which is added advice to the student of the understanding*, London: Simpkin & Marshall/Longman, 18cm, xxiv+362pp. ($ @); [3]1840, 18cm, xxiv+269pp. ($ @); rev. ed. [4]1846, title has changed to *English grammar, style, rhetoric, and poetry; to which are added, preparatory logic, and advice to the student, on the improvement of the understanding* ... xxxiii+[1]-271pp. (@); [5]1853, London, 8° (L); [11]1860, 3s6d (L); [21]1876, title has changed to *English grammar, style and poetry: with chapters on style at different periods, and original composition; to which is added advice to the student on the attainment and application of knowledge*, London: Longmans, Green & Co., 18cm, xvi+330pp. (@); many more editions to 1885).

(@ C L O *Br, Hu, Lw*)

[Grammar occupies only the first half of the book; conventional, verbose, but popular for being so comprehensive. The grammar is stodgy, but the book is significant because it is one of the few which keep grammar associated with rhetoric, especially composition, and with literature. The work was popular for this reason. *Athenaeum* praised "the great merits of this Grammar, and its superiority to Murray's". (Advertisement in *Key* to no. 852.). The first edition (1832) is much better than the following ones.]

849. Hiley, Richard. 1835. *English grammar and style.* London: Longman. ([5]1852, London, 12° (L)).

(L)
850. entry deleted
851. entry deleted
852. ---. ³1842. *Questions and exercises adapted to Hiley's English grammar, progressively arranged.* Impr. and adapted to the last ed. of the grammar. London: Longman & Co. 19cm, viii+120pp. (Later on the title was changed to *Questions and exercises adapted to Hiley's English grammar, style, and poetry*; anr. ed. [1846] London, 17.5x11, ix+193pp., 3s; ¹⁰[a1863]; ¹²1867, 2s6d).
Key 1846, London: Longman, pr. in Leeds. 17.5x11, 113pp., 3s. (O). (²1857, rev. by R. W. Hiley (L); rester. ed. ⁷1868 (L); ¹⁸1878 (L)).
(@ L O)
[Carefully constructed specimens, with syntax predominating, and a great deal of style included. "In selecting the instances of false construction, care has been taken to avoid those which are glaringly erroneous, and which would never occur in the conversation of persons of even a tolerable education. ... For many of the examples under *Perspicuity*, I am indebted to the writings of Murray and Crombie" (vii).]

853. ---. 1848. *The child's first English grammar, divided into easy and progressive lessons, to each of which are attached copious questions and exercises.* London: Longman etc. 12°, iv+100pp. (⁷1863 advertised at 1s; ¹⁶1876, London: Longmans, Green & Co., 15cm, 106pp. (@)).
(@ L O)
[Elementary definitions, OESP; the book is seen as a stepping-stone to the author's more comprehensive books.]

854.! ---. [a1867]. *Explanatory English grammar.* (Gleig's School Series). London: Longmans, Green & Co.
[Advertised in Hiley's *Questions and exercises adapted to Hiley's English grammar, style, and poetry* 1867.]

855. entry deleted

856.$ Hill, Charles Applewhite. 1818. *An improved American grammar of the English language for the use or schools.* n.p. 14cm, 82pp.
($ @)

857. Hill, E.D. 1864. *An elementary grammar of the English language.* London: Simpkin, Marshall & Co. / Cheltenham: T.K. Eaton. 16.5x10.5, 49pp.
(@ L O)
[Written for his pupils and intended to be short, simple and "to facilitate the study of Latin and Greek"; the condensation is extreme, but quite intelligently done.]

858. ---. [a1887]. *Outlines of English grammar. For the use of boys preparing for the public schools.* n.p. (Rev. ed. 1887, London: Simpkin Marshall, 8°, 64pp.)
(L O)
[Latinate; much attention to clause analysis.]

859.! Hill, William (of Huddersfield). [1830s?]. *A companion to The rational school grammar and entertaining class book.* n.p.
[Advertised in the 5th edition, n.d. of no. 860.]

860. Hill, William (1806-1881). 1833. *Fifteen lessons, on the analogy and syntax of the English language; for adults who have neglected grammar.* Huddersfield: T.G. Lancashire, for the author / London: Simpkin & Marshall. 19cm, 115pp.
(C L *Hu*, *Sk*)
[Complains about the Latin tradition and suggests five parts of speech (interjection, noun, verb, descriptives [= articles, adjectives, adverbs], connectives and pronouns); these are discussed in fifteen lessons, with many references to Lowth, Blair, Cobbett, Lennie, Murray, Shaw, Wallis, Smetham, Lewis, Priestley, Crombie, Dalton, Russell, W. Allen, Horne Tooke, Gilchrist, Ash, Lyon, etc.]

861.! ---. [a1839]. *The grammatical text book.* 32pp. n.p. (^{2}1839, Leeds).
(*Hu*, *Lw*)
[Repeats his previously expressed view that English grammar is full of "mysterious nonsense" derived from Latin grammar and is badly taught. Five parts of speech (N., Vb., Descriptive, Connective, Pronoun).]

862. Hill, William. [between 1833 and 1839]. *The rational school grammar, and entertaining class book.* Manchester: A. Heywood. (Rev., cor. and amended ed. ^{5}[c1870], Manchester, 14cm, 95pp., written in narrative style (@)).
(@ *Hu*)

863. Hill, William. [between 1833 and 1839]. *Progressive exercises: selected with great care and adapted to the rules and observations respectively contained in his fifteen lessons of the analogy and syntax of the English language.* n.p. (Rev. and cor. ed. ^{3}1842, title has changed to *Progressive exercises: adapted to the rules and observations in his fifteen lessons on the analogy and syntax of the English language, and rational school grammar*, London etc., 15cm, 70pp. ($ @)).
($ @)

864. Hillocks, James I. 1849. *The new writer; or, How to write letters, cards of compliments, etc. (...) to which are prefixed (...) The outlines of English grammar.* Edinburgh: Johnstone & Hunter. 36pp.
(L)

[The very modest letter writer has a minimal grammar, pp. 6-18, in form of Q/A, on orthography and etymology (eight to nine parts of speech); prosody irrelevant, syntax apparently felt to be covered by advice on composition.]

865.$ Hinds, Arthur (b.1856). 1881. *Some topics in English grammar: for the pupil, the teacher, and the general reader.* New York: Baker & Godwin. 18cm, 141pp.
($ @)

866.$ Hindsdale, Burke Aaron (1837-1900). [18-?]. ... *Objects to be sought in teaching English Grammar* ... n.p.: Ann Arbor?. 15cm, 26pp.
(@)

867.$ ---. 1896. *Teaching the language arts, speech, reading, composition.* (International Education Series, v. 34). n.p. 19cm, xxv+205pp. (Anr. ed. 1897, with comments by Mrs. Sarah Tarney-Campbell, for the special use of the Indiana Teachers' Reading Circle, New York: D. Appleton, 20cm, [v]-xxv+213pp. (@); anr. ed. 1898, 20cm, xxv+213pp. (@); anr. ed. 1899, New York: D. Appleton & Co., xxv+213pp. (@)).
($ @)

868. Hinton, R.W. [1886]. *English grammar companion; containing comprehensive parsing and analysis tables.* Manchester: Heywood.
(L)

869. Hoare, Clement (1789-1849). 1829. *Orthographical exercises, with a brief introduction to ... grammar.* Chichester: W. Mason. i+61pp.
(L)
[The grammar takes up the first fifty pages. L. Murray's, and most other grammars, it is claimed, contain too much information.]

870.$ Hodge, H.D. 1848. *Comprehensive grammar or analysis of English language on a new and improved plan.* Concord: Brown. 198pp.
(@)

871.$ ---. 1849. *A practical analysis of the English language: with selections for parsing: designed for the use of schools.* Boston: Fitz & Hobbs. 16cm, 124pp. (Anr. ed. 1849, title has changed to ... *selections for parsing, designed for common and high schools, academies, and other seminaries of learning,* Concord: Brown, 96pp. (@)).
($ @)

872.$ ---. 1852. *Parsing book: containing choice gems of thought and of literature, together with a practical system of analyzing words and sentences.* Boston: M. Cotton. 16cm, 108pp.
($ @)

873. Hodgson, William. M.D. (1745-1851). 1819. *A critical grammar of the French and English languages; with tabular elucidations to aid the English student in the acquirement of the French language, and to give the French scholar a knowledge of the English tongue.* London: John Souter. xxxii+744pp. (^{2}1882; ^{6}1889, vii+221pp.).
(@ L)
[Vocabulary; Accidence; Syntax; Rhetoric; each part consists of quotations with comments on their errors.]

874. Hodgson, William Ballantyne (Professor of Political Economy, University of Edinburgh, 1815-80). 1881. *Errors in the Use of English.* Ed. by Francis A. Teall. Edinburgh: D. Douglas. 20cm, [iii]-v+221pp. (Am. rev. ed. ^{2}1882, New York: D. Appleton & Co. / Edinburgh: D. Douglas, 20cm, vi-246/221pp. (@ G); ^{4}1882, Edinburgh: D. Douglas, 20cm (@); seven Am. rev. 1885, New York: Appleton, 246pp. (@); editions 1885-95.
(@ G L)
[Published posthumously, edited by his widow. Four parts: vocabulary, accidence, syntax, rhetoric, each comprising quotations with comments.]

875.$ ---. 1885. *School edition of Hodgson's Errors in the use of English. A class-book for use in schools, based on Hodgson's Errors in the use of English.* Comp. and ed. by J. Douglas Christie. New York: D. Appleton & Co. 19cm, viii+135pp.
(@)

876.$ Hoenshel, Eli J. (b. 1846). 1895. *English grammar: for common and high schools.* Holton, Kan. 18x13, 205pp. (Anr. ed. 1896, as *Hoenshel's complete English grammar for common and high schools*, Topeka, Kan.: Crane & Co. 20cm, 196pp. (@); anr. ed. 1897, 20cm, 304/320pp. ($)).
($ @)
[The relationship of early and later editions needs further investigation.]

877.$ ---. 1897. *Key and manual for Hoenshel's complete grammar.* Topeka, Kan.: Crane & Co. / New York/Chicago etc.: American Book Co. 19/20cm, 152pp.
($ @)

878.$ ---.1899a. *Hoenshel's advanced grammar.* New York/Cincinnati: American Book Co. 20cm, 314pp. (Anr. ed. 1899, Topeka, Kan.: Crane & Co., 20cm, 196/314pp. ($ @); anr. ed. 1899, 20cm, 320pp. ($)).
($ @)

879.$ ---. 1899b. *Hoenshel's language lessons and elementary grammar.* Topeka, Kan.: Crane & Co. 20cm, 196pp.
($ @)

880.$ Holbrook, Alfred (1816-1909). 1872. *Training lessons in the elements of English grammar.* Cincinnati, etc.: American Book Co. 19/20cm, viii-120/135pp. (Anr. ed. 1872, Cincinnati: G.E. Stevens, 20cm, 120pp. ($)).
($)

881.$ ---. 1873a. *An (A new) English grammar, conformed to present usage; with an objective method of teaching the elements of the English language.* Cincinnati: G.E. Stevens & Co. 19cm, xxx+[1]-204/xxx+197pp. ($). (Anr. ed. [c1873], Cincinnati: Van Antwerp, Bragg & Co., 20cm, xxx+210pp. (@); anr. ed. 1874, Cincinnati, 20cm, xxx+204pp. ($ @ L); anr. ed. 1889 (Eclectic Educational Series), 20cm, 272pp ($)).
($ @ L)

882. Holland, John (Minister, Bank Street Chapel, Bolton, 1766-1826). 1804. *Definitions, maxims, proverbs, and precepts on grammar, etc.* Manchester. (^{2}1804, Bolton, 72pp.).
(L)

[Mainly intended as copies for penmanship.]

883.! ---. 1813. *English grammar.* n.p.
(Mi)

884.$ Holloway, Robert S. 1833. *An easy and lucid guide to a knowledge of English grammar, containing the principles and rules of the language, conformed to the best modern usages ... a philosophic exposition of the derivation and original meaning of words: to which are added, a key to false syntax, and punctuation, and a new parsing key ... especially designed for private learners and schools.* St. Clairsville. 19x11, 187+xiv+[202]-204pp.
($ @)

885.$ Holmes, George Frederick (Professor of history, general literature and rhetoric, University of Virginia, 1820-1897). 1868. *An elementary grammar of the English language.* New York: Richardson & Co. / New Orleans: D.H. Maury etc. 20cm, 238pp. ($ @). (Anr. ed. 1869, New York: Richardson & Co. / University Publishing, 18.5x11.5, i+238pp. (L); anr. ed. 1870, 20cm, 1 p.l., 238pp. ($)).
($ @ L)

[Intended as an adaptation of the best "in the numerous grammars of the English tongue recently published in England", the work became more independent than intended. Holmes says he is endebted to Wallis, Horne Tooke, Taylor, Latham, Marsh, Clark, Alford and Max Müller, and is devoted to historical explanations. OESP, nine parts of speech. Short definitions followed by examples and observations; some 600 questions at the bottom of the pages meant to test the pupil's comprehension. An

"Introduction" (7-36) is followed by the Elementary Grammar proper: a short section on orthography, etymology in three parts (classification of words, 50-83; inflection, 83-154; derivation, 154-63) followed by syntax (164-98) and prosody (199-219, includes punctuation). In style and structure, the book is more conservative than the author admits; competent but dry.]

886.$ ---. 1871. *A grammar of the English language.* New York: University Publ. Co. 20cm, 246pp. (Anr. ed. 1873, 20cm, 264pp. ($ @); anr. ed. 1875 (@); anr. ed. 1878, New York/Baltimore (@)).
($ @)

887.$ ---. [1873?]. *First lessons in English grammar. (Illustrated).* n.p. (Anr. ed. 1877, New York/Baltimore, 18cm, 160pp. ($ @); anr. ed. 1878, New York: University Publ. Co. (@); anr. ed. 1879 (from 1873 ed.) ($); anr. ed. 1891. ($ @)).
($ @)

888. Holyoake, George Jacob (1817-1906). 1844. *Practical grammar; or Composition divested of difficulties: with selected examples from the writings of elegant authors; containing all that is necessary for ordinary purposes, and no more; and intended for those who have little time for study.* London: James Watson. 17cm. (Rev. ed. [5]1847, title has changed to *Practical grammar; or composition divested of difficulties: intended for those who have little time to study,* iii/iv+72pp. (@); anr. ed. 1850 (@); anr. ed. 1852, 5th thousand (@); [8]1870, title has changed to *Practical grammar: ... with graduated exercises,* London: Bookstore, 20cm, 115pp. (@)).
(@ L *Hu, Lw*)
[The author assumes that grammar *is* correct usage. Five parts of speech (N., Descriptive, Pron., Connective, Vb.). For more go to Priestley, Hazlitt, [Justin] Brenan, Simmonite. First used the term 'secularism'.]

889. ---. 1846. *The hand-book of grammar.* London.
(L *Hu, Lw*)
[Comprises questions on his *Practical grammar.*]

890. Anon. 1855. *The home grammar.* London: David Bogue. 17x11cm, 92pp.
(L)
[Intentionally simplified Q/A account, OES, with examples for parsing appended; nine parts of speech with inappropriate space devoted to verbs. Otherwise the style chosen is quite effective: "designed to adapt (grammar) to the comprehension of young children, and to shed light on the path which so many traverse in darkness and in tears".]

891. Anon. n.d. *The home grammar.* Burslem: Warwick Savage. 5pp.
(L O)

[Briefest information on adjectives, adverbs, pronouns and verbs - but including *dost, didst.*]

892. Hope, A. 1806. *A compendious grammar of the English language.* Carlisle: W. Hodgson. 18cm, 163pp. (²1814; cor. and enl. ed. ³1823, title has changed to *A compendious grammar of the English language; with appendices, addenda, and exercises; extracted chiefly, from the works of the most approved writers on the subject, and adapted to the use of schools*, Annan: the author, 184pp., 3s (L)).

(L *Hu, Lw*)

[Concentrating on etymology and syntax, very brief on OP; the function of the appended matter, often difficult to reconcile with the main body, is unclear. The extensive fusion of various sources has produced a badly arranged book of the traditional kind.]

893. Horn, Joseph Stephenson. 1870. *The penny grammar; part I, containing a series of simple lessons and exercises on the analysis of sentences, part II containing a series of simple lessons and exercises in the outlines of English grammar.* Manchester: John Heywood. Part 2: 1872. 16x10, 24pp. each, 1d. (²¹1894, new title: *English grammar, containing a series of simple lessons and exercises on the analysis of sentences*, Part 2, London/Manchester: John Heywood / London: Simpkin, Marshall, J.C. Tacey, 16x9.5, I: *On etymology*, 24pp., II: *On analysis of sentences*, pp. 25-48).

(@ O L)

[Short definitions of parts of speech and syntax, somewhat new terms ('adjective sentence' = 'relative clause' etc.; 'enlargement' = 'predicative noun'; 'extension' = 'adverbial, object or completion'. Very brief and incomplete definitions, with great weight given to parsing and analysis; eight parts of speech. The two booklets were also bound together and sold as the *The Twopenny grammar.*]

894. ---. 1891. *Elementary grammar.* Manchester: Heywood. 48pp. (²¹1892, ⁷⁸1928; ⁷⁹1932).

(L)

[Two sections: parts of speech; analysis of sentences.]

895. Horne, Hubert T.M. [1884]. *Experimentum brevissimum; or, A concise critical view of English grammar, from a mathematical standpoint.* London. 18cm, vi+82pp.

(L O)

[Argues that all spoken forms are relative: "my grammar" is how I use language. The distinctiveness of "my" grammar is defined statistically by its departures from the norm.]

896. Hornsey, John. ²1816. *An abridgment of Hornsey's English grammar. Designed for the use of children from six to ten years of age.* York: Thomas Wilson. 70pp.
(L)
[The 1816 edition is the "second abridged edition", of which no copy is known. Ref. Alston 1, 469. The 1818 edition, at L, is the "second edition enlarged". The latter cannot be a second edition of the parent grammar, which had a second edition in 1798. Very modest book in simple language; nine parts of speech, two cases, mainly Etymology, with false English and Q/As appended.]

897. ---. ⁵1839. *English exercises, orthographical & grammatical.* York. 18°/24°.
(@)

898. Horsfall, William. 1849. *A small help to the study of English grammar.* Halifax: Whitley & Booth. 16x10, iv+68pp.
(L)
[On parts of speech, concentrating on the verb (moods and tenses); solid and unexciting; no explanation is given for the claim that inquirers can "find the knowledge of syntax" on the basis of the restricted data.]

899. ---. ?1852. *Horsfallian system of teaching English grammar with exercises adapted thereto.* New ed., enl. and improved. Halifax, printed in Leeds. 18cm. (new enl. and impr. ed. ³1853, Glasgow: George Gallie, 18cm).
(C L O)
[There is no system. Loose remarks about usage.]

900. Hort, William Jillard. 1812. *Miscellaneous English exercises: consisting of selected pieces of prose and poetry, written in false spelling, false grammar, and without stops, calculated to promote improvement in the orthography of our own language.* Bristol.
(A)

901. ---. 1822a. *An introduction to English grammar: equally adapted to domestic and to school education.* London: Longman etc. 14/15cm, 219pp.
(@ L O *Br*, *Hu*, *Lw*, *Ma*)
[OESP, eight parts of speech, sober but unexciting, with some problematic statements (p.64 on tenses); syntax includes rhetoric; part V on Punctuation. Martin 1824:273: "This little treatise is not *neat* but *elegant*, and not more so than useful. Mr Hort has published a portable library for the purpose of domestic education: if the Grammar may be taken as a pattern, private families will find cause to thank him for his ingenuity and perseverance.]

902. ---. 1822b. *Exercises for the illustration and enforcement of the rules of the English grammar: equally adapted to domestic and to school education.* London: Longman etc. 14.5x8.5, 143pp.
(L O)
["A set of progressive exercises, to the illustration and enforcement of the several rules of the English Grammar, and, at the same time, to excite and sustain the attention of the young student, by selecting, as far as possible, sentences containing sense, connection, and interest." OES and punctuation, with syntax predominating (36-126, largely 'false English') Referring to Hort's *IEG* throughout.]

903. ---. 1822c. *Key to the Exercises for the illustration and enforcement of the rules of the English grammar.* London. viii+136pp.
(L O)
[Texts correcting the 'false English', referring to the *Grammar* and *Exercises* throughout.]

904.$ Hosterman, Charlotte O. 1883. *English grammar simplified, or, lessons for the young in prose and verse.* n.p. 18pp.
($)

905.$ Houston, Samuel (1758-1839). 1817. *The essence of English grammar.* Harrisburg: Lawrence Wartmann. 17cm, 44pp.
($)

906. Hovelacque, Abel. 1877. *The science of language; linguistics, philology, etymology.* Translated by A.H. Keene. London: Chapman & Hall / Philadelphia: J.B. Lippincott & Co. 21cm, xv+340pp.
(@ L)

907.! Howard, E. J. 1864. *A new grammar of the English tongue. Used in the Government Schools Bombay, the Punjaub, and Central India.* London: Longmans.
[Quoted in J. W. F. Rogers, *Grammar and logic* 1883.]

908.$ Howe, D. P. 1870. *Howe's science of language, or, seven-hour system of grammar.* Manchester, N.H.: C.H. Livingston. 19cm, 47/49pp. (Rev. ed.[3]1874, (@); anr. ed. 1874, Boston: Howe, 16° (@)).
($)

909.$ Howe, Samuel L. 1838. *The high school philotaxian grammar: being a concise and lucid guide to a knowledge of the English language: containing a new and comprehensive system of parsing, and a complete order for correcting false syntax; and exhibiting the cases of nouns and pronouns, and the moods and tenses of verbs in a new and systematic arrangement: designed for schools and private learners.* Lancaster, Ohio: Wright & Moeller. 17cm, xii+[13]-176pp. (@). (Anr. ed. 1870, Chicago: J.B. Alden & Co., 20cm, 121pp. (@); anr. ed. 1871, Chicago:

Bassett Bros., 20cm, vi+[7-8]+ix-xiv+[15]-154pp. (@); anr. ed. 1873? (@); ⁴1875, Detroit: Tribune Book & Job Office, 158pp. (@)).
($ @)
[Identical with the English grammar mentioned by Brown for the author in 1838?]

910. Ho Wing-Siu. 1897. *Elementary lessons in English grammar*. Hongkong: Hongkong Printing Press. 16.5x10.5, ii+59pp.
(L)
[OES, with derivation; short and sometimes inadequate definitions. Although produced for local use, there is no indication of TEFL considerations.]

911. Hoyle, W.T. (Head Master, Board School, Cloughfold). [1882] *The sentence grammar. Part I, Standard II and II. Part II, Standard IV. Part III, Standard V, VI and VII*. Rev. ed. (World School Series). Manchester: James B. Ledsham. 16+20+40pp.
(L O)
[Rudimentary definitions and exercises.]

912.! Hoyle, W.T. & J. Berry. [1882]. *(Ledsham's) Handy helps to parsing, analysis and word-building. With tests*. Manchester: Ledsham. 24pp.
(*Mp*)

913.$ Hubbard, Austin Osgood. 1827. *Elements of English grammar: with an appendix, containing exercises in parsing, examples of false orthography, violations of the rules of syntax, exercises in punctuation, and questions for examination: designed for the use of schools, academies, and private learners*. Baltimore: Cushing. 18/19cm, 220pp.
($ @)

914. Hughes, E. [1869]. *Some of the peculiarities of English grammar; being a collection from various sources, of exceptions to rules*. (The Cambrian Educational Course). Cardigan: J.R. James. 15.5x9, 32pp.
(L)
[A very modest booklet of stray remarks on individual points not intended to be coherent or comprehensive. Of no independent value. An attempt to meet the alleged emphasis in public examinations on "exceptions and peculiarities." Gathered from Angus, Latham, Bromby, Cornwell, Sullivan and several others", to be "used as a supplement to the common Grammars in our Elementary Schools".]

915.$ Hull, Joseph Hervey. 1823. *English grammar, by lectures; comprehending the principles and rules of syntactical parsing, systematically; containing exercises in syntax, and a key to the exercises*. Hagers-town, Md.: W.D. Bell. 19cm, 107pp. (@). (Rev. and cor. ed. ²1824, title has changed to ... *containing exercises in syntax, and a key to the exercises*

with a lecture on rhetoric, Steubenville: J. Wilson (@); anr. ed. 1824, title has changed to *English grammar, by lectures, comprehending the principles and rules of syntactical parsing, on a new and highly approved system; intended as text book for students; containing exercises in syntax, rules for parsing by transposition, critical notes, and a lecture on rhetoric*, n.p. 20cm, 108pp. ($); [3]1827, New-Brunswick: Terhune & Letson, 17x10, 48pp. (L *Br*); [4]1828 (from 1827 ed.), Boston, 12mo, 72pp (*Br*); [5]1829, Norwich: J. Dunham (@); [6]1830, Saratoga Springs, N.Y.: G.M. Davison, 18/19cm, 144pp. ($ @); [7]1833, Maysville, 11x19, xxii[23]-144pp. ($ @)).
($ L *Br*)
[Conforms with Murray. Orthography intentionally omitted; ES only. Ten parts of speech, traditional treatment; "false syntax" appended. The lecture form does not go well with some topics, nor with questions or exercises.]

916.$ ---. 1828. *Appendix to lectures on English grammar: containing an additional number of incorrect phrases, or vulgarisms, and a selection of nearly four hundred words, which are frequently pronounced contrary to the best usage.* n.p. 18/19cm, 12pp.
($)

917.$ ---. 1846. *Notes on the structure and philosophy of the English language, designed for mutual or self-instruction: also a text book for review in high schools, academies, and colleges; with a lecture on elocution. By the author of Lectures on the English Language.* New York: Redfield & Savage. 13cm, 43pp.
(@)

918. Hunt, L.H. [1823?]. Master of the Classical and Commercial School, Charles Street, Westminster. *A syntax of the English language; with new and copious examples, from some of our best authors in verse and prose so arranged, that the particular points of each rule may frequently occur in a single extract. For the use of higher classes in schools, as well as for the enquiring amongst other classes.* Saffron Walden: G. Youngman. 18x10, 72pp. (Anr. ed. [1823?] 20cm, 93pp. (@)).
(@ L O *Hu*)
[Without any more general introduction to grammar the author gives 16 syntactical rules followed by examples and rules; style and argument very much 18th-century. Lowth, Ash, Fisher, Lennie, Williams, Murray mentioned as patterns.]

919. entry deleted

920. Hunter, Rev. John (Principal of Uxbridge School, (1849-1917), Vice-President of the Training Institution, Battersea). [a1845]. *Text-book of*

920. Hunter, Rev. John

English grammar: A treatise on the etymology and syntax of the English language: including exercises in parsing, punctuation, and the correction of improper diction; an etymological vocabulary of grammatical terms; and a copious list of the principal works on English grammar. For the use of students in training colleges, and the upper classes in national and other elementary schools. London: Longman etc. (Anr. ed. 1848, 17.5x 10.5, xx+190pp., 2s6d ($); anr. ed. 1855, 18cm, xvi+180pp. ($); new ed. 1859).

($ @ C L O *Lw*)

[Quite a substantial considerate exposition of traditional grammar, with many references to other authors (see bibliography 170-79, quoted as *Hu*), exercises. His pages on the structure of compound sentences are forward-looking and pedagogically important.]

921. ---. 1845. *Exercises in English parsing, progressively arranged and adapted to the author's Text-book of English grammar.* London: Longman etc. 6d. (^{3}1848, 17cm, 44pp. (@); ^{4}1849; ^{6}1851 (O)).

(@ L O)

[Advising to omit the parenthetical parts of definitions, for practical convenience, in quotation, and for memorizing. References to the *Textbook* throughout.]

922. ---. 1853a. *Manual of English grammar, in which the etymology and syntax of the English language are explained and illustrated in a form adapted to the use of pupils in elementary schools.* London: National Society's Depository. 16x10, 64pp. (New ed. 1855, xvi+180pp. (@); anr. ed. 1872, 16cm, 54pp. (@)).

(@ L O *Lw*)

[Quite competent definitions, rules, and illustrations followed by sections of question ("examination"); orderly but unexciting. Parsing appended; there is no reference to orthography and prosody. Cf. the abstract in no. 1881.]

923. entry deleted

924. ---. 1858. *Paraphrasing and analysis of sentences, simplified for the use of schools; and forming a manual of instruction and exercise for normal students, pupil teachers, etc.* London. 18x10.5, iv+68pp., 1s3d.
Key 1860, 18x10, 50pp.

(L)

[Part I, on paraphrasing, is not closely related to II, on the analysis of sentences, in which simple, compound and abridged sentences are defined and analysed in a clear and competent way. The author has to admit that paraphrasing destroys literary qualities; his sentence analysis is standard.]

925. Hunter, William (Rector of Paisley Grammar School). 1835. *The principles of English grammar*. Glasgow.
($ G L E)

926.$ Hurd, Nathan A. 1846. *A new and compendious English grammar: containing definitions in etymology, rules of syntax, and exercises in parsing*. n.p. 10cm, 104+10pp.
($)

927.$ Hurd, Seth T. [1827]. *A grammatical chart, or private instructer of the English language. Presenting at one view all the rudiments of the English grammar*. Boston. 48x61cm. (^{2}1827, Boston (*Br*)).
(@ Br)

928.$ ---. [1847]. *A grammatical corrector; or, Vocabulary of the common errors of speech ... peculiar to the different states of the Union ...* Philadelphia: E.H. Butler & Co. 12°, xi[i]+1+[14]-124pp.
(@)

929. Hutchinson, H. (of Derby). 1877. *Grammar as science. An enquiry into the nature, growth, forces and classification of words as "Parts of speech"*. London/Derby: Simpkin & Marshall. 22cm, 39pp.
(@ L)

930. entry deleted

931. Hutchinson, James (M.A.). [1850]. *The practical English grammar, for the use of schools and private families*. London: Wright, Simpkin & Co. 14cm, 144pp. (^{9}1854; ^{16}1859, 13cm, 144pp.).
(@ E O)
[Dull and old-fashioned; relies on L. Murray. A *Key* was advertised in 1854.]

932. ---. ^{3}1851. *The juvenile grammar*. London. (^{6}1853; ^{9}1854 (Lv); ^{59}1881 title has changed to ... *for the use of schools and private families*, London: Wright & Simpkin, 14cm, vi+[7]-108pp. (@)).
($ Lv O)
[An abbreviation of his *Practical grammar*, no. 931.]

933. Huthersall, John. [a1814]. *A compendious system of practical English grammar; in which nothing is introduced, but what is absolutely necessary, etc*. England. 18mo. (Rev. and enl. ed. ^{4}1814, title has changed to ... *and the exercises of which are so methodical and progressive, that they may with facility be comprehended by pupils at an early age*, London: Charles Law/Longman & Co. 16cm, 132pp. (@)).
(@ Br)

934.$ Hyde, Mary Frances. 1887. *Practical lessons in the use of English: for primary and grammar schools*. (Hyde's Language Series, 1). n.p. 19cm, x+142pp. (Anr. ed. 1887, 19cm, viii+56pp. ($); anr. ed. 1888, 19cm,

934. Hyde, Mary Frances

x+113+26+[115]-116pp. ($); anr. ed. 1889 (@); anr. ed. 1890 (@); anr. ed. 1891, 19cm, x+142pp. ($); anr. ed. 1892, 19cm, x+142pp. ($); anr. ed. 1893, title has changed to *Intermediate grammar. Practical ...*, Indianapolis: Indiana School Book Series, 19cm, v+124pp. (@); anr. ed. 1893, x-142pp. (@); anr. ed. 1894, 18cm, xi+142pp. ($); anr. ed. 1895, xiii+342pp. (@); anr. ed. 1896?; anr. ed. 1897, xiii+342pp. (@); anr. ed. 1898 (@); anr. ed. 1899 (from 1896 ed.), 19cm, vii+275pp. ($); anr. ed. 1899, 19cm, x+142pp. ($)).
($)
[The similarity of titles may have led to some misqualifications of nos. 934. to 938; note the varying numbers of pages.]

935.$ ---. [1887]. *Practical lessons in the use of English for grammar schools: with supplement.* n.p. (Anr. ed. 1888, 20cm, xi+226pp. ($); anr. ed. 1889?; anr. ed. 1890 (from 1887 ed.), 19cm, x+113+26pp. ($); anr. ed. 1890 (from 1888 ed.), 19cm ($); anr. ed. 1891 (from 1888 ed.) (Hyde's Language Series, 2), 19cm, xi+226pp. ($); anr. ed. 1891 (from 1888 ed.), 19cm, xiii+342pp. ($); anr. ed. 1892 (from 1889 ed.), 19cm, xiii+342pp. ($); anr. ed. 1895 (Hyde's Series in English), 19cm, xiii+342pp. ($)).
($)

936.$ ---. 1889. *Supplementary lessons in the use of English for grammar schools.* Boston: D.C. Heath & Co. 19cm, iv+121pp.
($ @)

937.$ ---. 1893a. *Advanced lessons in English for advanced grammar grades, high schools, academies, and ungraded schools.* (Hyde's Language Series). Boston: D.C. Heath & Co. 197pp. (Anr. ed. 1894, Boston: D.C. Heath & Co., 19cm, vii+199pp. ($); anr. ed. 1895, as *Advanced lessons in English. A practical English grammar for grammar schools, ungraded schools, academies, and the lower grades in high schools*, Boston: D.C. Heath & Co., 19cm, vii+199pp.; anr. ed. 1896 (@); anr. ed. 1897 (@)).
($ @)
[The book is probably identical with no. 938.]

938. ---. 1893b. *A practical English grammar, for grammar schools, ungraded schools, academies, and the lower grades in high schools.* n.p. 18x12.5, vii+199pp. ($). (Anr. ed.? 1895, *Adapted to the use of Canadian schools by Dr. F. W. Kelley ... and P. J. Leitch,* Toronto: Copp, Clark Co. viii+269pp. (L); anr. ed. 1896, 19cm, vii+200/viii+251pp. ($ @); anr. ed. 1896 (State Series), viii+269pp. ($); anr. ed. 1898, 19cm, viii+275pp. (@); anr. ed. 1899, vii+201pp. (@)).
($ @ L)

[Sentence analysis is used to determine the functions and thereby define the eight parts of speech, whose properties and forms are then dealt with one by one, with examples, exercises and stylistic analyses of literary texts interspersed. 166-78 have specimens of orders, model letters etc. with 'exercises in composition' following. "The structure and analysis of sentences" (205-32) is again followed by exercises; 254-9 has rules for spelling. The scheme chosen results in duplications and an arrangement which is not easy to follow - a book not fit for systematic teaching.]

939. Anon. 1880. *Illustrated English grammar*. London: George Philip. 24pp.
(*Al*)

940. Anon. [c1845]. *The illustrated English grammar; or, Lindley Murray simplified*. (Contained in: *The Book of Fun*. Cover title: *The comic English grammar*). London: Gilbert. (Facs. repr. London: Routledge/ Thoemmes Press, 1996, in: Reibel 1996, vol.II, *Lindley Murray's Grammar in Caricature: Four Parodies*).
(Reibel 1996)
[cf. Reibel 1996:xif.]

941. Imeson, W.T. 1846. *Language of the English, or the grammarian's textbook* ... London: Simpkin, Marshall & Co., pr. in Ramsgate. 16x10, x+137pp.
(C O L)
[OES, with sections on language history and Latin roots added. Seven parts of speech, short definitions supplemented by tables, "observations for advanced readers". Exercises at end. Despite some innovative traits, quite traditional (syntax = concord and government); Blair, Crombie and Latham quoted.]

942.$! Anon. 1829. *An inductive grammar*. Windsor, Vt. 12mo, 185pp.
(*Br*)
[Cf. no. 615; same book?]

943. Anon. 1822. *The infant's grammar, or a pic-nic party of the parts of speech*. London. (Anr. ed. 1824 (L); anr. ed. [1825], Baltimore: Fielding Lucas, Jr., 17x11 (@); Scolar Press facsimile edition 1977).
(@)

944.$ Ingersoll, Charles M. 1821. *Conversations on English grammar: explaining the principles and rules of the language: illustrated by appropriate exercises: abridged and adapted to the use of schools*. New York: Wiley & Halstead. 19cm, xii+296/xii+377pp. (^{2}1822, xix+296/ xx+290pp. ($ @); anr. ed. 1823?; anr. ed. 1824, xiv+298pp. ($); anr. ed. 1825, xi+[13]-288pp. (@); anr. ed. 1826, 248pp. ($); ^{6}1828, iv+ [13]-264pp. ($ @); ^{7}1828, 249pp. (@); ^{8}1830, 251pp. ($ @); ^{9}1831 (@);

[10]1832 (from 1823 ed.) ($ @); anr. ed. 1834 ($); anr. ed. 1835, Philadelphia ($ L)).
($ @ L *Br*)

945.$ ---. 1822. *Conversations on etymology and syntax: being an abstract of conversations on English grammar: to which exercises in false syntax are annexed: adapted to the use of families and schools.* Philadelphia: Bennett & Walton. 15cm, viii+172pp. (@). (Anr. ed. 1824, Portland, Maine: W. Hyde. 15cm, vi+[8]-188pp.).
($ @)

946.$ ---. 1833. *An introduction to English grammar: exemplifying in easy lessons the general principles and rules of the language: designed especially for young learners.* New York. 19cm, iv+108pp.
($ @)

947.$ Anon. 1832. *Interrogative grammar; in a series of progressive and practical questions: illustrating the principles of the English language, and the syntactical mode of parsing.* Boston: Hilliard, Gray, Little & Wilkins. 18x11.5, vi+70pp. (Rev. and cor. ed. [2]1835, Providence, 72pp.).
(@ L *Br*)
[Simple Q/A style. Concentrating on parts of speech and etymological parsing. Unexciting.]

948. Anon. 1829. *Interrogative system: the tutor's key to Murray's Grammar and Irving's Elements of English composition.* n.p.
(Dt)

949. Anon. 1852. *A introduction to aid in parsing the English language: forming also an elementary grammar ... By an educator.* (by H.B.) London. x+38pp.
(E)

950. Anon. 1854. *Introduction to English grammar.* (Chambers' Educational Course). London/Edinburgh: Chambers. 17x11, iv+52pp., 10d. (Anr. ed. 1858 (L); anr. ed. 1878 (@)).
(@ L O)
[Very brief account of orthography, parts of speech and inflexion and construction of sentences, concentrating on brief definitions and rules (generally adequate), examples and exercises. Unassuming, but quite competent.]

951.$ Anon. 1853. *An introductory grammar, for beginners.* By a common school teacher. Portland, Me.: W. Hyde & Son. 16cm, 69pp. (Anr. ed. 1873 (Laurie's Manuals of Specific Instruction), 32pp.).
(@ L)
[Parts of speech and parsing only.]

952. Anon. 1880. *Introductory little lectures on grammar for little children. By a lady*. Dublin: J. Duffy.
(L)
953.$ Irish, Frank van Buren (1848-1940). 1883. *Introduction to "Grammar and analysis made easy by diagrams": containing a selection of sentences diagrammed by the improved straight-line system: designed for both teachers and pupils*. Ada, Ohio: the author. 22cm, 16pp.
(@)
954.$ ---. 1883. *Grammar and analysis made easy and attractive by diagrams; containing all the difficult sentences of Harvey's grammar diagrammed; also, many difficult sentences from other grammars and Greene's analysis; designed for both teachers and pupils*. (Eclectic Educational Series). New York: American Book Co. 23cm, 118pp. (Anr. ed. 1884, Lima, Ohio: the author, 23cm, 117/118pp. ($); anr. ed. [c1884] (Eclectic Educational Series), Cincinnati/New York: Van Antwerp, Bragg & Co., 23cm, vii+[8]-118pp.).
($ @)
[Supplementary to nos. 804 and 720.]
955. Ireland. Board of National Education. 1838. *An English grammar, for the use of schools*. (Anr. ed. 1842, Dublin: The Direction of the Commissioners of National Education/Council of Public Instruction for Upper Canada, 14cm, 178pp. (@); anr. ed. 1845, Dublin, 178pp. (@); anr. ed. 1846, Dublin, re-pr. at Montreal: Armour & Ramsay (@); anr. ed. 1863, Dublin: A. Thom, 24°, 176pp. (@); anr. ed. 1876, 14cm, 175pp. (@)).
(@ Lw)
[For *Key* cf. no. 1020]
[The book is probably identical with: "Irish National Schools. 1847. *An English grammar*. Dublin." (*Hu*)]
956. Irvine, William Balfour (Headmaster ... Young Ladies, Dundee, and Principal of School for Boys, Dundee). [a1870]. *The parts of speech: an easy grammar for beginners*. n.p. 3d/5d. (^{2}1870, Edinburgh: John Menzies; ^{10}1876; ^{11}1877, Edinburgh, 14cm, 36pp. (@); ^{13}1882, Edinburgh, 36pp. (@); anr. ed. 1883, London: Relfe Bros., 16.5x10.5, 78pp. (@)).
(@ L)
[Words/morphology and parsing only, with exercises.]
957. ---. [1872] ^{2}1875. *An English grammar: being a sequel to the parts of speech*. n.p. (^{2}1875, Edinburgh: John Menzies & James Thin etc., 15.5x9.5, 71pp., 9d).
(L)

[Eight parts of speech discussed in 49 chapters, traditional with much attention given to exercises. Unexciting.]

958.! ---. [a1898]. *Analytical exercise book.* London: Relfe Bros.
[Advertised in 1898.]

959. Irving, Christopher (Holyrood-House Academy, Southampton, d.1856). [1821?]. *A catechism of English grammar; carefully compiled from the best authors: with numerous exercises. For the use of schools.* London: Longman etc., pr. in Romsey, Hampshire. 13.5x18.5, iv+85pp. (New ed. [1870], rev. and enl. by E. Wickes, (Souter's New Series of Catechisms), London: Souter & Law, 14cm, 108pp. (@); ^{12}1876, rev. by Robert James Mann, (Irving's Improved Catechisms), London, 15cm).
(@ L O)
[Forms part of a series of catechisms (on History, Mythology, Botany, Chemistry etc.) some of which were also written by Christopher Irving. OESP, with parsing and punctuation; a few exercises.]

960. Isbister, Alexander Kennedy (Headmaster of Stationer's School, London, 1822-1883). 1865. *Outlines of the English language.* Part 1. (Advertised in three parts, 12mo, 6d each). London: Longmans, Green & Co. 16.5x10.5, 34pp.
(L)
[OE only (the other sections probably treated in parts II and III); traditional account, providing definitions, observations and exercises; alternative solutions discussed in footnotes. Apparently well informed about the state of the art; exposition solid but dry.]

961. ---. 1865-68. *The elements of English grammar and analysis simplified for beginners.* 2 parts. London: Longman, Green, Longman, Roberts & Green. 16cm, Part I:iv+50pp, Part II (title slightly modified): ii+[51]-115pp., 6d/9d each. (New ed. 1875, title has changed to *The elements ... Including the analysis of sentences. Simplified ...*, London: Longman, Green & Co., 17cm, iv+115pp. (@); ^{18}1882 (@)).
(L O)
[The two booklets form a unit; OES, followed by Punctuation, Figurative Language and Prosody, with an appendix on Composition. Compressing too many, and too abstract, arguments within 115pp., contradicting the author's preface with promised "simplicity". Isbister distinguishes his approach from that of L. Murray as giving "an insight into the laws and structure of the speech with which he is already familiar. The title of Part 2 is *The elements of English grammar and composition.*]

962. ---. [1867]. *A first book of grammar, geography and English history.* (Repr. from *First steps in reading and learning*). London: Longmans, Green & Co. 17cm, 42pp.

(O L)

[The thirteen pages devoted to English Grammar permit the author to provide the barest outline of OES only; consists largely of definitions (often unsatisfactory) and a few exercises.]

963. J., H.R. [1882]. *Grammar for the million, based upon Cobbett's Grammar in ten lessons giving plain instructions for acquiring knowledge of English grammar and also intended for those who wish to have a handy book of reference on the subject.* Preface signed by H.R.J. Manchester/London: John Heywood. 16.5x10, 24pp., 4d.

(L)

[Intended to condense Cobbett by omitting diversions and establishing a lighter frame. Nine parts of speech first treated under etymology, and then for their syntactical properties. Generally clear and to the point, an achievement for the small space available.]

964. Jackson, Rev. E.D. 1850. *[Murray's] English grammar abridged, with notes, questions and additional exercises.* Manchester: John Heywood. 126pp., 6d.

(L)

["This edition contains 1. Lindlay Murray's Text. 2. Copious Notes. 3. Exercises in all the Parts of Speech, and rules of Syntax, Prosody, Punctuation, &c. 4. Exercises in English Composition, Questions and Answers in connection with every portion of the Work." (adv. in *Schoolboy*)]

965. Jackson, Robert J. (Headmaster of the Bristol... Institution for the Instruction of Deaf and Dumb Children). 1868. *A grammar without rules, or useful synonyms exemplified.* Bristol. vii+147pp.

(O)

[Grammatical categories are learnt through the study of synonyms varied through different parts of speech.]

966. Jackson, Robert. 1893. *English grammar.* London: Percival. 18x12, xii+280pp.

(L O)

[An extensive treatment of nine parts of speech is followed by sentences and clause analysis. Questions from examination papers. Definitions generally adequate, but dull. Has used Mason, Morris, Adams *et al.*]

967. James, D.M.J. 1898. *Paraphrasing, analysis and correction of sentences.* (Blackwood's Leaving Certificate Handbooks). London: Blackwood. (Anr. ed. 1899).

(L)

968. James, J.H. (Esq. of London). 1847. *The elements of grammar, according to Dr. Becker's system, displayed by the structure of the English*

tongue (with copious examples from the best writers); arranged as a practice for translation into foreign languages. London: Longman etc. 19x10.5, x+156pp.

($ C L O *Hu, Lw*)

[Another exponent of Becker and a significant text historically. Good discussion of modern grammar. A break-away from tradition "by considering language, generally as the organic expression of thought, and all particular forms of speech as expressions of particular relations of thought and notions ... In modern grammar, the *signification* is the basis of the whole system, but not the *form*, as in the older" - concepts leading on to universal grammar.]

969. ---. 1848. *Primary instruction in English grammar, systematically developed according to modern views.* London. 17cm, viii+103pp.

(C L O *Hu, Lw*)

[Shortened from no. 968; James wants to reintroduce logic into a universal language; warns against studying language at too early an age.]

970. James, Rev. Samuel Benjamin (Curate of Winkfield, Berks). [1870]. *(Murby's) Penny grammar for parish schools. For standards I, II & III.* London: Thomas Murby. 16x10.

(@ L)

[This grammar is "for the roughest and youngest minds", "intended to reach even them only through the teacher's *vivâ voce* explanations"; eight parts of speech insufficiently defined followed by examples and exercises; one of the poorest grammars extant. (Advertises Robinson's *Introductory Grammar* 64pp. 3d; *Grammar and Analysis Taught Simultaneously* 128pp. 6d/9d., both untraced, cf. nos. 1531-2).]

971.$ Jamieson, Alexander. 1818a. *A grammar of rhetoric and polite literature; comprehending the principles of language and style, the elements of taste and criticism, with rules for the study of composition and eloquence, illustrated by appropriate examples selected chiefly from the British classics ...* n.p. 306pp. ($). (Anr. ed. 1818, 19cm, xx+373pp. ($ L); first Am. ed. 1820 (from the last London ed.), title has changed to *A grammar of rhetoric and polite literature; from the British classics, for the use of schools, or private instruction*, Newhaven: A.H. Maltby, 18cm, xvi+345pp. ($ @ *Br*); 2nd Am. ed. 1821, Newhaven, 19cm, xviii+[21]-332pp. (@); anr. ed. 1821 ($); anr. ed. 1822 ($); ^{2}1823, London, 19cm, xx+412pp. (@); ^{4}1826, New Haven (British and Continental Rhetoric and Elocution, Reel 5, No. 47), 18/19cm, xviii+[19]-310/306pp. ($ @); anr. ed. 1826 ($); ^{5}1831 ($ @); ^{10}1833 ($ @); ^{15}1835 ($ @); ^{16}1836 ($ @); ^{17}1837 ($ @); anr. ed. 1838 ($); ^{19}1839 ($ @); ^{20}1840 ($ @); ^{21}1841 ($ @); ^{22}1842 ($ @); ^{24}1844 ($); ^{25}1845, New

Haven: Maltby (@); anr. ed. 1847 ($); [27]1848 ($ @); anr. ed. 1849 ($); 35th Am. ed. ster. [184?], New York: Kiggins & Kellog (@); anr. ed. 1850, 19cm, 306pp. ($); [31]1851, New Haven (@); anr. ed. 1852 ($); anr. ed. 1854 ($); anr. ed. 1870?; anr. ed. [187-?], New York: Houghton, Osgood & Co., for A. Mason (@); [[52]187-?], New York: Kiggins, Tooker & Co. (@); anr. ed. 1874 ($); anr. ed. 1879 (from 1870 ed.) ($); [[53]1880], New York: Kiggins, Tooker & Co. (@)).
($ @ Br)
[Intended to follow the study of English grammar. Six books: 1. Language & style; 2. General grammar; 3. Sentences; 4. Figures; 5. Taste; 6. Style.]

972.$ ---. 1818b. *The rhetorical examiner, comprehending questions and exercises on The grammar of rhetoric.* London: Whittaker. 102pp. (Anr. ed. 1821, as *Questions to Jamieson's grammar of rhetoric*, 14/15cm, 93pp. ($); anr. ed. 1831, title has changed to ... *The grammar of rhetoric and polite literature for the use of schools and private students*, in 6 vols., New Haven: Maltby, 18cm, 56pp. (@)).
($ @ C L)
[Q/A form; interesting and searching on grammar, usage and literary judgement]

973.$ ---. 1820. *Questions to Jamieson's grammar of rhetoric.* New Haven: A.H. Maltby & Co. (Anr. ed. 1821 (@)).
(@)

974.$ Jamieson, Peter (d. 1847). 1847. *A rhyming grammar of the English language, in verse: to assist the memory, with questions and answers: with examples of parsing to illustrate the rules: applied/adapted to the different classes of learners.* Milton, Ia.: Philip Smith. 19cm, 206+[1]pp.
($ @)

975.$ Jaudon, Daniel (1767-1826). 1812. *The union grammar, in three parts.* Philadelphia: Tower & Hogan. 14/15cm, xi+[13]-216pp. ($ Br). (Anr. ed. 1815, 15cm, 216pp. ($); [4]1828).
($ @ Br)

976.$ Jenkins, Amaziah. 1835. *Systematick lectures on English grammar, on a new and highly improved plan: containing a systematick order for parsing, extensive examples of false syntax for oral corrections, and a key to the oral exercises.* Rochester, N.Y. 17cm, vii+1+[9]-256pp. (Anr. ed. 1836, Rochester, N.Y.: W. Alling & Co. ($ @)).
($ @ Br)

977. Jennings, M.W. (Assistent Mistress in Queen's College, Barbados). [1898]. *English grammar.* Revised by James George Jennings, Professor

of English Literature, Muir College, Allahabad. London: Longman. 18x12, iv+181pp.

(L O)

[Solid; eight parts of speech; clause analysis; illustrations from English literature. "The sole claim to originality [...] lies in the plan, consistently followed, of illustrating all rules laid down by examples taken from acknowledged classics".]

978. Jenour, Rev. Alfred. 1832. *A treatise on languages, their origin, structure, and connection; and on the best method of learning and teaching them containing an account of the most useful elementary books Latin, Greek, French, Italian, Spanish, and German; as also in Syriac, Arabic, Persian, and Hindoostanee, with particular directions for the study of the Hebrew.* London. 17cm, [vii]-xi+72pp.

(@ G L)

979.$ Jewell, Rev. Frederick Swartz (1821-1903). 1851. *Aids to the study of the English language.* New York: A.S. Barnes & Co. 19cm, 14pp.

($ @)

980.$ ---. 1867. *Grammatical diagrams defended and improved: with directions for their proper construction and application: accompanied by a comprehensive outline of classification, and a complete scheme of examples of practice.* New York: A.S. Barnes & Co. 18cm, vi+[7]-207pp. (Anr. ed. 1877 ($ @); anr. ed. 1869 (@)).

($ @)

981.! Jodrell, Richard Paul. 1820. *Philology of the English language.* London.

(*Ch*)

[cf. Keith Walker. "Johnson's business". *London Review of Books*, Feb., 15, 1980.]

[Quotations illustrating omissions and deficiences in Johnson's grammar.]

982.! Anon. [1882]. *John Heywood's grammatical copy-books. A series of books containing exercises on English grammar, designed for the use of the upper classes of schools.* Manchester: Heywood. F'cap 4to oblong, 2d each.

[Advertised on back cover of Wright, J.C. 1882 - illustrating the 'musts' in the upper classes. Advertised contents: "1. The definitions of the Subject, Words, the Alphabet, Vowels, Consonants, Orthography, and the Nine Parts of Speech 2. Nouns - Common and Proper, their Number, Person, Gender, Case, &c. 3. Verbs - Regular and Irregular, Weak and Strong, Transitive and Intransitive, Active, Passive, and Neuter 4. Mood, Tense, Number and Person 5. Pronouns 6. Adjectives, with their degrees of comparison 7. Adverbs of Time, Place, Number, Manner, Degree, Affirmation, and Negation 8. Parts of a Sentence -

Subject, Predicate, Object &c. 9. Syntactical Rules relating to Nouns, Pronouns, Verbs, Adjectives, Adverbs 10. Cautions and Rules of Syntax 11. Syntactical Rules 12. Specimen of Parsing."]

983.! Johns, Bennett George (Headmaster of the Grammar School, Dulwich College, 1820/21-1900). 1848. *Short and simple grammar lessons.* London.
(*Hu, Lw*)

984. Johnstone, John (1779-1857). 1812. *An English collection: or, Pieces in prose and poetry, selected from the best writers; with a series of introductory lessons calculated for the younger classes of learners. To which is added, a compendium of English grammar.* Dunfermline: John Miller. 17.5x10, xii+[13]-304pp.
(O)
[The anthology is of historical importance but the summary of grammar, though careful along traditional lines, is not.]

985.$ Johonnot, James (1823-1888). 1885. *The sentence and word book, a guide to writing, spelling, and composition by the word and sentence methods.* New York: D. Appleton & Co. 19cm, 184pp.
($)

986. Jones, E. & Thomas Hargreaves. [1877-]. *The home lesson grammar. Standard III. Nouns, verbs, adjectives, and analysis of simple sentences.* (World School Series). Manchester: J.B. Ledsham. 16x10, 20pp.
(O)
[Elementary definitions with exercises. Quotes *Code 1877* on the title page: "The Class Examination will be conducted so as to show the intelligence and not the mere memory of the scholars".]

987. J[ones], E. [1880?]. *Grammar for children.* Fakenham: T.J. Miller. 16x11.5, 29pp.
(L)
[Elementary description of nine parts of speech, followed by 13 rules for syntax; a questionable attempt to make grammar more palatable to children.]

988. Jones, John I. 1884. *A practical and philological text-book on the analysis of sentences, parsing and punctuation.* London: Longman. viii+211pp.
(L)

989. Jones, Rev. Joseph (Perpetual Curate of Repton, 1782-1856). [1852]. *A concise sketch of English grammar, designed for the use of village schools.* London/Derby: Hamilton, Adams & Co. 17cm, i+28pp. (Anr. ed. [1862] (C)).
(C O L)
[Most elementary catechism.]

990.$ Jones, Joshua. 1833. *English grammar, in two parts: the first, a brief analysis of the English language, the second, a practical system of etymology and syntax: with exercises in parsing and corrections.* n.p. 18cm, 171pp.
($)

991.$ ---. 1841. *English grammar: founded upon the natural principles of speech: and adapted to the most common understanding.* Philadelphia. 15cm, 152pp.
($ *Br*)

992. Jowsey, Richard. 1836. *A supplement to Murray's abridgment of English grammar, chiefly selected from Murray's larger grammar, with an exemplification of syntactical parsing.* Sheffield: E.M. Charles. 40pp.
(Sc)

993.$ Judson, Adoniram Jr. (1788-1850). 1808. *The elements of English grammar.* Boston: Cushing & Lincoln. 19x11, v+[6]-56pp.
($ @ L *Br*)
[OESP, with additions. Very elementary, in Q/A form. Ten parts of speech; mostly inadequate definitions.]

994. Anon. [1857]. *The junior school English grammar: adapted to 'The Elements of English Grammar'. With copious exercises in parsing and false syntax; and an appendix.* London: Wyand. 18cm, 82pp. (Anr. ed. 1858).
(C E L O)
[Simplistic account strongly based on Latin.]

995.$! Anon. 1829. *The juvenile English grammar.* Boston: B. Perkins & Co. 18mo, 89pp.
(*Br*)

996.$ Karl, Simon. ²1860. *A primary grammar of the English language.* New York.
(L)

997. Kavanagh, Maurice D. (of University College, London). 1859. *A new English grammar: calculated to perfect students in the knowledge of grammar, parsing, derivation, and the principles of composition.* London: Catholic Publishing & Bookselling Co. 16x10, viii+118pp.
(L O *Lw*)
[The author holds the surprising view that elementary grammars lack systematic arrangement. Short and sometimes unsatisfactory definitions.]

998. Kavanagh, Morgan Peter (d. 1874). 1844. *The discovery of the science of languages: in which are shown, the real nature of the parts of speech; the meanings which all words carry in themselves, as their own defini-*

tions; and the origin of words, letters, figures, etc. 2 vols. London: Longman, Brown, Green & Longmans. 22x13.5, xi+401+viii+358pp.
(L O)
[Philosophical (highly speculative) account; discursive and universal. Parts of speech reduced to one (influenced by Horne Tooke). Some 'etymologies' offered can only be taken as a joke today. There is no relation with the common grammars of the time.]

999. Kelke, William Henry Hastings (b.1839). 1885. *An epitome of English grammar, for the use of students, adapted to the London matriculation course and similar examinations.* London: Kegan Paul, Trench & Co. 18x12, xiii+264pp.
(C L O)
[The grammar includes the results of comparative linguistics and the recent science of phonetics; eight parts of speech rightly connected with syntax rather than accidence; the amount of data and historical explanation make it very awkward to read. "London University Matriculation Papers in English Language" are appended.]

1000.$ Kelley, Hall Jackson (1790-1874). 1820?. *The instructor: designed for the common schools in America: containing the elements of the English language, and lessons in orthography and reading.* n.p. 15cm, 84pp. (Anr. ed. 1821 (from 1820 ed.); [4]1823, Boston: Lincoln & Edmands, 15cm, 84pp (@); [5]1824 (@)).
($ @)

1001. Kellner, Leon (1859-1928). 1892. *Historical outlines of English syntax.* London/New York: Macmillan. 19cm, xxii+336pp.
($ L)

1002.$ Kennedy, Platt. 1801. *The new grammatical spelling book, being an easy introduction to the English language, teaching the different parts of speech, and definitions of all the words contained in the tables of spelling ... also, a synopsis of English grammar ...* n.p. 175pp.
($)

1003.$ Kennicott, E.D. 1835. *The grammatical expositor: consisting of a course of explanatory lectures, in which the principles of orthography, etymology, syntax, and prosody, are correctly illustrated and explained. Containing also, exercises in syntactical parsing, and false syntax.* Rochester: The Gem Office. 128pp.
($)

1004. Kennion, Charlotte. 1842. *The etymology and syntax of Murray's English grammar systematically arranged and containing much additional matter, with copious exercises and directions for parsing.* London: Simpkin. 19cm, xi+156+[1]pp. (New ed. 1873, with supplement).

($ C L O *Br*)
[Work book without any exciting features.]

1005.! Kennion, T. [error for C.?]. [a1847]. *Keystone of grammar laid; or, The governess's assistant in simplifying that science*. n.p.
[Advertised in 1847.]

1006. Kenny, William David. 1858. *An English grammar; adapted to the comprehension of young persons, with syntactical observations for more advanced students, orthographical exercises ... and questions for examination*. London: Routledge, Warne & Routledge. 17cm, viii+119pp. (New ed. 1861 (@)).
(@ C L O *Lw*)
[Traditional account, dry and unoriginal.]

1007. Kenny, William Stopford. 1832. *The grammatical omnibus, or A methodical arrangement of the improprieties frequent in writing and conversation, with corrections*. n.p. (^{8}1853, London: Allman).
(G)

1008.$ Kenyon, William Colgrove (1812-1867). 1849. *Elements of English grammar, analytical and synthetical: arranged in progressive exercise*. n.p. 19cm, viii+328pp. ($). (^{2}1849, Rochester: E. Darrow / New York: Baker & Scribner (@); ^{3}1850, ster. by E.G. Champlin, Rochester: Erastus Darrow / New York: Baker & Scribner / Philadelphia: Hogan & Thompson (@); four more editions recorded up to 1866).
($ @)

1009.$ Kerl, Simon. 1859. *A comprehensive grammar: a treatise on the English language: for the use of schools, colleges, and private students*. Philadelphia: J.B. Lippincott & Co. / Cincinnati: Moore, Wilstach, Keys & Co. 21cm, xx+536pp.
($ @)
[From the advertisement in no. 1011: "designed for the use of High-Schools, Colleges, and Private Students (embracing) the history, etymology, grammar, and structure of the language, with copious illustrations and critical remarks, an essay on composition, an essay on delivery, and a collection of synonyms."]

1010.$ ---. ^{2}1860. *A primary grammar of the English language*. New York: Phinney, Blakeman & Mason. 19.5x12, vi+68pp., 25c.
(@ L)
[Geared to the author's *Comprehensive English grammar* (no. 1011), which can be used for greater detail; a not quite convincing attempt at simplification, concentrating on (nine) parts of speech with a section on analysis appended. OESP, with sections on 'false syntax' and punctua-

tion under prosody. Short definitions of terms are often insufficient; long lists of specimens are given without further differentiation.]

1011.$ ---. 1861. *A comprehensive grammar of the English language: for the use of schools*. New York: Phinney, Blakeman & Mason / Buffalo: Breed, Butler & Co. 20cm, iv+[2]+354pp. ($ @). (Anr. ed. 1862, New York/Cincinnati etc.: American Book Company, 18.5x12, vi+354pp. ($ @); ⁶1863, New York: Blakeman & Mason / Buffalo: Breed, Butler & Co., 19cm, iv+[2]+374pp. (@); four more editions up to 1868, all presumably unchanged).
($ @ L)
[One of the more ambitious American grammars comprising discussions of the nine parts of speech and syntax/parsing in great detail - including rare specimens and subdistinctions in small print. Partly in Q/A form, with illustrations, annotations and exercises (many on parsing) interspersed. Claims to be more comprehensive than other grammars and innovative in the arrangement - but may be too complex to be useful in teaching, for which no. 1010 is to be preferred.]

1012.$ ---. ⁶1863. *An elementary grammar of the English language*. New York: Blakeman & Mason, 19cm, 140pp. (Anr. ed. 1864, New York: Oakley & Mason/Ivison, Phinney, Blakeman & Co., 19cm, 164pp. ($ @); anr. ed. 1866, New York (@); anr. ed. 1868, New York ($ @); anr. ed. 1869, New York: Ivison, Phinney, Blakeman & Co. / Chicago: S.C. Griggs & Co. (@); anr. ed. 1872 ($); anr. ed. 1877 (Kerl's Series of English Grammar) ($)).
($ @)

1013.$ ---. 1865?a. *A common school grammar of the English language*. n.p. (Anr. ed. 1866, New York: Ivison, Blakeman, Taylor & Co., 20x12, iv+350pp. ($ @); anr. ed. 1867, New York, iv+350pp. ($ @); anr. ed. 1868 (from 1865 ed.) ($); anr. ed. 1869 ($); anr. ed. 1870 ($); twelve further editions up to 1892, all from 1870 ed. and New York(/Chicago): Ivison, Blakeman, Taylor, & Co.; repr. Delmar: Scholars' Facsimiles & Reprints 1985 (from 1878 ed.), vi+350pp.).
($ @)
[Though largely dependent on Murray, Kerl also has 'modern' elements such as the 'inductive method' which had become popular from the 1840s on. He claims to have achieved, in particular, a "simple and scientific nature of the general plan", "clearness, brevity, and uniformity of definitions" and an "abundance and appropriateness of the illustrations and exercises" (1878:iv). The structure of the book is slightly unusual as can be seen from the titles of the six parts: "An outline for beginners; words uncombined; words grammatically combined; words logically

combined; words improperly combined; ornament and finish". Nine parts of speech; some false syntax; includes some language history.]

1014.$ ---. 1865b. *First lessons in English grammar.* New York: Ivison, Phinney, Blakeman & Co. 17cm, [4]+168pp. ($). (Anr. ed. 1866, New York: Ivison, Phinney, Blakeman & Co. / Chicago: S.C. Griggs & Co., 17cm, 168pp. ($ @); anr. ed. 1867, New York (@); another eleven editions recorded until 1881; the 1868 ed. was published in Kerl's Language Series, the 1874 ed. in American Educational Series; all editions presumably unchanged and published in New York(/Chicago)).
($ @)

1015.$ ---. 1869. *Elements of composition and rhetoric. Practical, concise and comprehensive.* New York: Ivison, Phinney, Blakeman & Co. 20cm, 408pp. (Anr. ed. 1870 (@); anr. ed. 1871, New York/Chicago (@)).
(@)

1016.$ ---. 1870. *A shorter course in English grammar.* New York/Chicago: Ivison, Blakeman, Taylor & Co. 19cm, 240pp. (Anr. ed. 1871, New York, 19cm, 240pp. ($ @)).
($ @)
[*NUC* states "a revised ed. of the author's *Elementary grammar*", cf. no. 1012.]

1017.$ ---. 1878. *Kerl's language lessons: an elementary text-book of English grammar. Ed. by S.M. Perkins.* New York/Chicago: Ivison, Blakeman, Taylor & Co. 18cm, 191pp. (Anr. ed. 1880, New York/Chicago (@)).
($ @)

1018. Kerlin, Patrick. 1874. *English grammar, simplified for the use of schools, and arranged to suit the result's programme.* Belfast etc.: James Reed. 16cm, iv+63pp., 6d.
(O)
[The author says there are many grammars already but a concise one is needed. Nine parts of speech; conventional.]

1019.$ Kerney, Martin Joseph (1819-1861). 1846. *Kerney's abridgement of Murray's English grammar and exercise, designed to perfect students in the knowledge of grammar, parsing, and the principles of composition. With an appendix, containing rules for writing with perspicuity and accuracy.* n.p. 17cm, 144pp. (Anr. ed. 1848, 15cm, 140pp. ($)).
($)

1020. Anon. 1842. *Key to Exercises in the English grammar.* Dublin. (Anr. ed. 1853, Dublin: Alexander Thom, 36pp. (L); anr. ed. 1858).
(L)
[This belongs to 955. Advertised in 1868 for 1d.]

1021. Anon. 1843. *The key-stone of grammar laid; or, The governess's assistant for simplifying that science.* (By T.C.). London: Hatchard.
(L O)

1022.$ Kiddle, Henry (1824-1891). 1889a. *Brown's language lessons: with graded exercises in analysis, parsing, construction, and composition: an introduction to Goold Brown's series of English grammar.* New York: W. Wood. 20cm, iv+[7]-170pp.
($)

[Quote from preface: "The publication of this little manual is due to demand, on the part of teachers who use Goold Brown's admirable system of English grammar, for an introductory work simpler and more elementary than the *First lines.*"]

1023.$ ---. 1889b. *Three thousand grammar questions. With answers.* Syracuse. 18cm.
(@)

1024. Kigan, John. 1823. *Remarks on the practice of grammarians; with an attempt to discover the principles of a new system of English grammar.* London: Longmans & Co. etc. 18x10, 160pp.
($ A G L O *Hu*, *Lw*)

[Argues for clearer terms and methods; excludes O, P as not relevant; censuring parts of speech classification he suggests division into Substances, Attributes and Actions = Substantive Names, Attributive Names and Active Names, etc. Extensive quotes from Murray and Lowth (to show their inadequacy). One of the most thoughtful criticisms of traditional grammar. Very critically reviewed by Martin 1824:274.]

1025. ---. 1825. *A practical English grammar, agreeably to a new system. Adapted to the use of schools, and private students; containing copious examples of wrong choice of words, under etymology; and wrong arrangement of them under syntax. With a key ... and questions.* Belfast: Simms & McIntyre. 15x9, 140pp.
(A C O)

[The suggestions of 1823 are here put into practice: "This grammar, shows the practice, agreeably to the principles in the treatise" (p. iv) In Etymology, the proposed system cuts right across the traditional classes. Kigan suggests to divide into nouns (substantive, attributive, active, personal) and verbs (definitive, descriptive, ascriptive, affirmative, comparative, relative) - a system which is somewhat abstruse and was not taken up by other grammarians. The structure of the sentence and punctuation are described in more traditional ways. The key on pp. 103-23 is followed by examples of syntactical parsing taken from Murray on pp. 124-8.]

1026. Kilham, Hannah. 1818. *Lessons on language; or, An easy introduction to the nine parts of speech.* London: Darton & Harvey. 23pp.
(Lf)
[A rather desperate attempt to keep it all simple.]

1027.$ King, A. C. (of Terre-Haute, Ia.) & Geo H. Spencer. 1845. *The western grammar of the English language: adapted to the modern system of lecturing, the use of the select and common schools, and the private learner. It being a new arrangement, containing several alterations and improvements, with copious examples, illustrations, and exercises.* Terre-Haute, Ia.: T. Dowling. 18cm, 96pp.
($ @)

1028. King, Rev. George (of Upper Holloway). ?1845. *A succinct and comprehensive grammar of the English language.* n.p.
(L *Lw*)

1029. ---. ^{3}1854. *A new and comprehensive grammar of the English language, arranged in a popular form, with numerous analytical and synthetical illustrations, for the use of schools and private individuals.* Coventry: G.R. & F.W. King. 18°, 81pp.
(L O)
[Thoughtful account of OESP with traditional definitions and some small innovations in terminology; special points, like controversies with other grammarians (normally unnamed) are in footnotes.]

1030. King, Walter William. 1841. *A grammatical chart; or a key to English grammar.* 2 parts. London: Johns, Houlston & Stoneman. 14x8.5, x+76pp. and one folding chart.
(L O *Br*)
[A simplified catechism, seven parts of speech, with illustrations largely taken from the Bible and definitions based on Latin etymologies. Grammar treats "Letters, words, sentences and emphasis". "Who gave us the power to write? - Our kind Creator."]

1031. ---. [a1856]. *Grammar at sight, a chart and key to the English language, including rules for the composition of verse and prose, illustrations of the figures of speech, and a few useful hints on oratory.* n.p. (^{2}1856, London).
(C L)
[Modest, simplified account without independent value.]

1032. Kington-Oliphant, Thomas Laurence. 1886. *The new English.* 2 vols. London/New York: Macmillan & Co. 19cm, [245]-527pp.
(@)

1033.$ Kirkham, Samuel. 1820. *English grammar in familiar lectures.* Harrisburgh, Pa. 12mo, 144-228pp. (Enl. ed. ^{2}1825, Harrisburg: J.S. Wiest-

ling, 144pp. (@); enl. and much impr. ed. ³1826, Cincinatti: Lodge & Fisher, for the author, 18cm, 180pp. (@); ¹²1829; ²⁰1830, New York: M'Elrath & Bangs, 228pp.; ²⁶1831, Cincinnati: Morgan & Sankay, 228pp.; ³⁶1834, Baltimore: Plaskett & Armstrong; repr. Delmar: Scholars' Facsimiles & Reprints, 1989).
(@ *Br, Lw*)

1034.$ ---. 1823. *A compendium of English grammar, accompanied by an appendix in familiar lectures; containing a new systematic mode of parsing; likewise exercises in false syntax and a key to the exercises designed for the use of private learners and schools.* Frederick-town, Md.: J.P. Thomson at the Herald Press, for the author. 18cm, iii-iv+ [7]-84pp. ($ @). (Anr. ed. 1828; ¹¹1829; ²⁶1831; ⁴³1837; anr. ed. 1844; anr. ed. 1857; further editions).
($ @)
[The book was announced in a prospectus (41x29) by W. Newell as: *A compendium of English grammar: designed, not to be studied, but to be spread before the learner in parsing, previous to his having the definitions and rules committed to memory.*]

1035.$ ---. 1824. *English grammar in familiar lectures, accompanied by a compendium; embracing a new systematic order of parsing, a new system of punctuation, exercises in false syntax, and a system of philosophical grammar in notes: to which are added an appendix, and a key to the exercises, designed for the use of schools and private learners.* n.p. 18cm, 144pp. ($). (Anr. ed. 1825 ($); anr. ed. 1827, 18cm, xiv+[15]- 192pp. ($); anr. ed. 1828, 18/19/20cm, 192/216/228pp. ($); anr. ed. 1829 ($); anr. ed. 1830 ($); enl. and impr. ed. ²⁴1831, Rochester, N.Y.: Marshall, Dean & Co. ($ L); anr. ed. 1832, 20cm, 240pp. ($); anr. ed. 1833, 18/19cm, 228pp. ($); anr. ed. 1834 ($); enl. and impr. ²⁷1835, New York (L $); at least twenty further editions, most of them (from 1829 ed.), between 1836 and 1859 ($)).
($ L)
[Preface of ¹⁰1828, much revised, says that the "philosophical notes" are included because "a portion of the community" are "under the influence of a kind of *philosophical manla*". But the notes are not necessary for a practical knowledge of grammar.]

1036. Kirkus, Rev. William (LL.B., of Hackney). 1863. *English grammar: for the use of the junior classes in schools.* (School-books for the Use of Junior Classes; 1). London: Longman, Green, Longman, Roberts & Green. 16x10, iii+66pp.
(L O)

[Simple, conversational style, definitions in bold (to be memorized), eight parts of speech, most attention given to the verb; nine primary and four compound tenses, two pages on syntax at end; not a very successful attempt at reducing grammar to beginners' capacities; mentions Latham's and Mason's grammars: "the last is, for elder pupils, by far the best English Grammar with which I am acquainted."]

1037. Kirwan, George Richard. 1892. *A primer of English grammar, to which are attached some rules for English composition and for scanning Shakespearian blank verse. For use in the Wyggeston Boys' School, Leicester.* London: Longman. 8°, vi+39pp.
(L)
[Almost exclusively definitions of parts of speech and their forms, with parsing lessons; appendix: rules for composition and for scanning blank verse.]

1038.$ Knapp, O.S. 1854. *Grammar without a master, or, key to grammatical conversation.* Boston: Dayton & Wentworth. 18cm, 64pp.
($)

1039.$ Knighton, Frederick (1812-1888). 1852. *Primary grammar, or, an introduction to the American school grammar.* (R.E. Peterson's Cheap Educational Series). Philadelphia: R.E. Peterson & Co. 17x11, vi+[7]-67pp.
($ @ C L O)
[Meant for beginners; rules and definitions "are inductions from given examples". Definitions of nine parts of speech with explanations, examples and exercises are followed by their special properties and a short chapter on syntax; the book ends with parsing exercises and questions.]

1040.! Knowles, James (1759-1840). 1829a. *A philosophical and practical grammar of the English language.* n.p.
(Lw)

1041. ---. 1829b. *Orthoepy and elocution; or, The first part of a philosophical and practical grammar of the English language, for the use of teachers, academies, and public speakers. In which, also, the principles of elocution are fully ... developed.* Glasgow: the author. vii+228+24pp. (The first section (24pp.) of the author's *Examination of Mr Walker's '599 Principles of pronunciation'* is appended. (@)).
(@ L)
[Series of lectures; Knowles feels endebted to Harris, Lowth, Horne Tooke and Sheridan in particular, universal grammar being seen as the prerequisite for a proper understanding of English. Although individual chapters have questions appended, the book does not qualify as a proper grammar.]

1042.$! Knowlton, Joseph. 1818. *English grammar.* Salem, Mass. 18mo, 84pp. (²1832).
(*Br*)
[Possibly identical with *Br*'s further entry: J.K., 1832, *A short but comprehensive grammar: designed for the use of schools.*]

1043.$ Knox, Nelly Loyd. 1887. *Elementary lessons in English, part second: the parts of speech and how to use them.* n.p. 18cm, vii+396pp.
($)
[For the complete set see no. 1850. Also cf. no. 827]

1044.$ Kurken, A. 1853. *A brief grammar of the English language, explained in twenty lessons.* Venice: S. Lazarus Armenian College. 14+366pp.
($ @)

1045. Anon. 1818. *The ladies' grammar: or, An easy and familiar introduction to the English tongue ... By a clergyman.* London: C. Didier. iv+39pp.
(L)

1046. Laisné, M. 1816. *A grammar of the English language, in which the rules are illustrated by examples, selected from the best authors, for the use of schools.* London: the author. 17.5x10, vi+74pp.
(L)
[Laisné, who wrote grammars of Latin, Spanish, Portuguese, French and Italian, carried over their structures. Parts of speech described, with explanations, in a discursive way; definitions, illustrations (from the best authors), but no exercises. Not complete and not very systematic; some mistakes in the author's English.]

1047. ---. 1817a. *The English student's companion; or a series of rules and exercises to facilitate the composing of the English language with ease and elegance, and to illustrate the English grammar.* London: the author. 17.5x10, 120pp., 3s.
(L)
[The book is an expanded version of no. 1046 with many examples and exercises added; it could be considered a second edition.]

1048. ---. 1817b. *The key to the English student's companion intended to serve as exercises to the French classes already advanced, with the help of the comparative view of the English and French languages.* London: the author. 17.5x10, iv+72pp.
(L)
[The three books by Laisné (no. 1046, 1047, 1048) are noteworthy because they are based on the author's earlier manuals written in French - apparently he wished to repeat the success of his books directed at foreign learners. Specimen sentences only, without any guidance as to

what to do with them; the alleged contrastive view is not apparent. Otherwise traditional.]

1049. Lambe, J. 1849. *The Westminster handbook to the study of the science of universal grammar, exemplified in its application to the English language.* London: H. Hurst. 17cm, viii+88pp.

(O L *Lw*)

[More quotations than definitions and exposition; the author's sympathies are with Horne Tooke and against usage, "the miserable doctrine of conventionality" which "has made our language the wilderness it is" (38); mainly devoted to Etymology (17-70), very short on OSP.]

1050. Larkin, Joseph. 1867. *A grammar for the people. Three parts.* Manchester. 24pp., 1d.

(L O)

[Simple exercises on the completion of sentences.]

1051.$ Lash, W.D. 1885. *Practical lessons in English grammar: printed by order of the board of education, for use in the B senior grade of the public schools, of Zanesville, Ohio.* n.p. 22cm, 107pp.

($)

1052. Latham, Robert Gordon (Professor of English in University College, London, 1812-1888). 1841. *The English language.* London. 22x13.5, xxii+418pp., 3s6d/4s6d. ($). (Rev. and enl. ed. ^{2}1848, Pt.I: *General ethnological relations of the English language.* Pt. II: *History and analysis of the English language.* Pt. III: *Sounds, letters, pronunciation, and spelling.* Pt. IV: *Etymology*; Part V: *Syntax*; Part VI: *On the prosody of the English language. Appendix*, London: Taylor & Walton, xviii+581pp. (@ *Wm*); rev. and greatly enl. ed. ^{3}1850, London: Taylor, Walton & Maberly, 22cm, xliii+609pp. (@); rev. and enl. ed. ^{4}1855, London: Walton, 2 vols., Vol. I: *Origins, Dialects.* Vol. II: *Phônêsis. Etymology. Syntax. Prosody*; rev. and enl. ed. ^{5}1862, London: Walton & Maberly. xxx+720pp. (@); anr. ed. 1873 (@)).

($ @ L O *Br*, *Hu*, *Wm*)

[Latham sets out to redefine terms and classifications and to describe the chief principles of "General and Comparative Etymology" (which takes in both OE and "the bearings of Provincial Dialects"). A historical account of English is followed by Pronunciation, stress and orthography; Etymology deals with inflection, derivation and borrowing, in the individual parts of speech. There is a disappointingly short chapter on Syntax (356-79) and another on Prosody (371-84). The fusion of structural and comparative description is not achieved, the 'historical' interest predominating. Discusses modern critical work.]

1053. ---. 1843. *An elementary English grammar for the use of schools*. London: Taylor & Walton. 18x10.5, ix+214pp. (²1847, London: Taylor & Walton, 19cm, xv+219+[1]pp. (@); ⁴1849, London: Taylor, 216pp. (@); ⁵1850; repr. 1851, London: Taylor, Walton & Maberly ($); anr. ed. 1851; rev. ed. 1852 (from 1851 ed.), Cambridge: J. Bartlett, 19cm, xii+236pp. ($); 2nd Am. ed. 1853, Cambridge: J. Bartlett, 18/19cm, xii+250pp./xi+216pp. ($ @); anr. ed. 1854, 18th thous., Cambridge, 19cm, xii+250pp. ($ @); anr. ed. 1855 ($); rev. and enl. ed. 1860, London: Walton & Maberly, 19cm, ix+230pp. (@); anr. ed. 1861 (@); anr. ed. 1866 (@); new and rev. ed. 1875, London, 8°; new ed. 1876 (@)).
($ @ C L O *Br, Hu, Lw*)
[Traditional OESP with Anglo-Saxon sources used in interpretations, preceded by a historical introduction; (on new edition 1860) New edition with history, logic enlarged, and syntax divided; some exercises at end. Latham's descriptive method for the structure of English, combined with elements of universal grammar, gained high praise from contemporaries (e.g. Bromby 1848:iii (209.): Latham "is the modern writer who has undertaken the task of analysing the true principles of the English Language" - even though "the larger work is painfully crammed with matter"); philology added. Though dry, pedantic and largely indiscriminate, the book sold well (editions to 1875) and Latham's academic reputation was high. His historical works are much better. Quirk, in his inaugural lecture for the chair which Latham once held, refers to "the enormous contribution to grammar-writing through which his name became a household word for much of Queen Victoria's reign". Latham was also commended by Hunter (no. 920) ?1848, McLeod (no. 1152) ?1851, Clarke (no. 329), Mason (no. 1180) and Kirkus (no. 1036).]

1054. ---. 1847. *First outlines of logic, applied to grammar and etymology*. London: Taylor, Walton, & Maberly. 34pp., 1s6d.
(@ L *Hu, Lw*)

1055. ---. 1849. *The elements of English grammar, for the use of ladies' schools*. London: Taylor, Walton & Maberly. 16°, 4-100pp., 1s6d.
(@ C L O)
[Very elementary, but burdened with a history of English at the beginning, and intrusions of Old English in the grammatical descriptions.]

1056. ---. 1850. *A grammar of the English language, for the use of commercial schools*. London: Taylor, Walton, & Maberly. 16x10, v+136pp., 1s6d.
(C L O *Lw*)
[A history of English, pronunciation and spelling, inflection, composition and derivation (with parts of speech), syntax (concord and government)

and prosody, all treated in conversational style, but a great amount of detail under pronunciation (drawn from Walker). His longer grammar is largely preferable.]

1057. ---. 1851. *A handbook of the English language, for the use of students in the universities and higher classes of schools*. London: Taylor, Walton, & Maberly. 19cm, xxiv+398pp. (Anr. ed. 1852, New York: D. Appleton & Co. (@); ^{2}1855 ($); ^{4}1855, London: Walton, 2 vols. (@); repr. 1857 ($); ^{3}1858, 19cm, xxiv+440pp. ($); ^{4}1860, London: Walton & Maberly, 20cm, xxiv+442pp. ($ @); anr. ed. 1861 ($); ^{5}1862, 20cm, xxiv+442pp. ($); anr. ed. 1864, New York: D. Appleton, 20cm, [v-xxiv]+398pp. (@); ^{6}1864, London: Walton & Maberly/Longman, Green, Longman, Robert & Green, 19cm, xxiv+442pp. ($ @); anr. ed. 1866, New York: D. Appleton, 20cm, [v-xxiv]+398pp. (@); anr. ed. 1870, xxiv+398pp. ($); ^{8}1873, London: Longmans, Green, xxiv+442pp. ($ @); anr. ed. 1873, xxiv+398pp. ($); ^{8}1875, 20cm, 500pp., 6s. ($); ^{9}1875, London: Longmans & Green, xlv+500pp. (@); anr. ed. 1876, New York: D. Appleton & Co., 21cm, xxiv+398pp. ($ @); ^{9}1878?).
($ @)
[His usual material, with "General ethnological relations" of English, and a section on dialects. Obviously there are parallel editions of 442/398 pages from London and New York; therefore the numbering of editions is somewhat obscure.]

1058. ---. 1856. *Logic in its application to language*. London: Walton & Maberly. 20cm, xvi+282pp.
(@)

1059. --- & Mary Caroline Maberly. 1861. *A smaller English grammar for the use of schools*. London. 17cm, vi+140pp. (^{2}1861; ^{4}1867, London: James Walton (@)).
(@ L O)
[Historical sketch, OESP, punctuation, exercises for examination; somewhat learned with many historical explanations.]

1060. ---. ^{3}1861. *An English grammar for classical schools*. Rev. and enl. ed. London: Walton & Maberly. 8°, vii+133pp., 2s6d.
(L O)
[History, Grammar, Etymology, Syntax treated with a great deal of comparative linguistics and historical explanation, with specimens from older and modern stages of various Germanic languages, modern phonetic terminology (surds and sonants etc.).]

1061. ---. 1876. *Essential rules and principles for the study of English grammar*. London: Longman, Green, & Co. 14x19, viii+119pp.

(L O)

["Limited to Etymology and Syntax [...] the purely grammatical part of our language" - a clear exposition which has profited from the reduction, though still somewhat burdened with exceptions and historical explanations. Much praised by Quirk.]

1062. ---. 1878. *Outlines of general or developmental philology: inflection.* n.p. xvi+190pp.

(L)

[Argues that languages develop and become more "advanced". English now is at the most advanced stage.]

1063. Laurie, James Stuart (1831-1904). [1868]. *English grammar simplified, framed with especial reference to analysis and composition.* Part 1. (Laurie's Sixpenny Manuals of Instructions). London: John Marshall & Frank Laurie. 64pp. (Enl. ed. ⁶1877, as ... *English grammar simplified: with an introduction to analysis. Copious examples and exercises*, London: Central School-Dept., etc. (@)).

(@ L)

[Kinds of words; inflexions and rules of syntax discussed in easy language, with examples and exercises (also for parsing). Mentions as best grammars available: Dr Morell, Mason, Bain, Dalgleish.]

1064. ---. [c1875]. ... *First lessons in grammar. Including a key to English spelling.* (Laurie's Manuals of Specific Instruction). London: John Marshall etc. 16cm, 24pp.

(@)

1065. Laurie, William S. 1869. *The grammar of words. A handbook for elementary classes.* London. 18cm, vi+70pp.

($ L)

[Rules to be memorised; ordinary and dull.]

1066.! Lawson, R. [a1860?]. *English grammar.* n.p.
[Advertised in McLachlan a1863]

1067. Anon. 1833. *The leading principles of English grammar. [With a Persian version by A'zam al-Din Hasan, Balgrami.].* Calcutta: Calcutta School-Book Society. 177pp.

(L)

1068.$ Leavitt, Dudley (Teacher of Meredith Academick School). 1826a. *Complete directions for parsing the English language; or, the rules of grammar made easy: being a new grammatical essay, designed as a supplement to Lindley Murray's grammar; for the use of students as soon as they begin to parse.* Concord, N.H.: J.B. Moore. 13.5x8, vii+[9]-60pp.

($ L)

[Adapted to Murray who is praised (with few minor corrections); p.31 has the title "syntactical parsing explained; or Lindley Murray's Rules of Syntax made easy". (Adequate) directions for parsing are followed by specimens with full explanations; the introduction points out all the necessary subclassifications. Technical and unoriginal, but appropriate as a text book.]

1069. Ledsham, James Boardman. [1879]. *Ledsham's sure guide to English grammar. By a schoolmaster.* (World School Series). 2 parts. Part I: *For Standards II and III.* Manchester: J.B. Ledsham. 8°, 20pp.
(L O)
[Part One: Very brief explanations of parts of speech and parsing.]

1070. ---. 1883. *Ledsham's card for the analysis of sentences, by a schoolmaster.* Manchester: J.B. Ledsham. 4pp.
(O)
[One cardboard card with definitions arranged in nine 'lessons'.]

1071.! ---. n.d. *Ledsham's penny grammar, with copious exercises. For Standards II. III. IV. with special notes for pupil teachers.* Manchester: J.B. Ledsham. 16pp.
[Advertised in no. 1070.]

1072.$ Lee, Mary & Hiram Hadley. 1873. *Hadley's Series. English grammar. An advanced course of lessons in language.* (Hadley's Series). n.p. 20cm, 308pp. (Anr. ed. 1874, Chicago, 19x12, 308pp. ($ L)).
($ L)
[(To supplement Hadley's *Lessons in Language*, no. 762). Inductive method employed - which the students should also learn to use; parsing and analysis are complemented by composing exercises. Starting with the sentence and its structure, the parts of speech are defined by their syntactical functions. Informal style, addressing the reader, with definitions and extensive exercises interspersed. Appendixes on punctuation, figurative language and letter-writing. The authors "expect the book to find little favor with the mechanical, routine teacher, or task-master, who is accustomed to measure his success by the amount of cramming done".]

1073. Leigh, Percival (1813-1889). 1840. *The comic English grammar; a new and facetious introduction to the English tongue, by the author of The comic Latin grammar. Embellished with upwards of fifty characteristic illustrations by J. Leech.* London: Richard Bentley. 19/20cm, 163pp. ($ A). (Anr. ed. 1840, 20cm, [vii]+xii+228pp. ($ @ *Tm*, 25); anr. ed. 1845, New York: Wilson, 144pp. (@); new ed. 1848, London (@); new ed. 1851, London: Richard Bentley (Bentley's Shilling Series), 17cm, vi+154pp. ($ E); anr. ed. 1852 ($); anr. ed. 1856, 16cm; anr. ed. 1860?; new ed. 1863, London, 17cm; new ed. [c1875], London, 18cm;

facs. repr. London: Bracken Books, 1989, xii+228pp. (E); further facs. repr. London: Routledge/Thoemmes Press, 1996 (In: Reibel 1996, vol.II, *Lindley Murray's Grammar in Caricature: Four Parodies*). ($ @ A C E L O *Tm*)
[Witty remarks on style, genteelism, female and American language, mixed with traditional grammar in four sections; of interest for the student of early Victorian humour. "The first, best, most complete, and probably best-known of the parodies of Lindley Murray's *English Grammar*", Reibel (1996:viii).]

1074. ---. [1858]. *Paul Prendergast; or, The comic schoolmaster, comprising a new and facetious introduction to the English language [The comic English grammar]; arithmetic [The comic cocker]; and the classics [The comic Eton grammar. 3 parts]*. London: Ward & Lock. 16x10, iii+154, viii+148, 156pp.
(O)
[An extension of the earlier book with part I retained, and satires on arithmetic and Eton Latin Grammar added.]

1075. Leinstein, Madame. [c1820]. *The rudiments of grammar, in verse; or, A party to the fair*. London: Dean & Munday. (Anr. ed. 1823? ($); anr. ed. 1826? ($); anr. ed. 1828? ($); anr. ed. 1847 ($)).
($ L)
[Amusing but grammatically rudimentary.]

1076. Leitch, Neil (Principal of the Church of Scotland Normal School, Glasgow). [a1860]. *An outline of English grammar*. n.p.: J. Burnett. 3d.
(L)

1077. Lennie, William (Teacher of English, Edinburgh, and Author of the *Child's Ladder*, 1779-1852). 1810. *The principles of English grammar briefly defined, and neatly arranged ... etc*. Edinburgh. (^{2}1812, as *The principles of English grammar, comprising the substance of all the most approved English grammars extant, briefly defined, and neatly arranged; with copious exercises in parsing and syntax*, Edinburgh: Oliver & Boyd, for the author, 14cm, 119+1pp., 1s6d (@); ^{2}1814; ^{3}1815, title as ^{2}1812, Edinburgh: Oliver & Boyd, for the author, 120pp., 1s6d (L); ^{5}1819, 15x9, 142pp. ($); ^{6}1821, with improvements, Edinburgh, iv+178pp. (O A); ^{7}1821; ^{8}1823, Edinburgh: the author, sold by Guthrie & Tait, iv+[5]-178pp. ($ @); ^{9}1824 ($ @); ^{10}1827, Edinburgh, 15cm, iv+[5]-178pp. (@); ^{11}1828 ($ @); anr. ed. 1830 ($); ^{13}1831 ($ @); ^{16}1835 (*Tm*); ^{19}1838, 1s6d; ^{20}1839 ($ @); ^{22}1841 (@); ^{19}1841, St. John: McMillan (@); anr. ed. 1842, St. John (L); anr. ed. 1842, Montreal: Armour & Ramsey (@); anr. ed. 1845 ($); ^{27}1847; ^{24}1848 (@); anr. ed. 1850 ($); anr. ed. 1851 ($); anr. ed. 1852 ($); ^{33}1853, Edinburgh (L); rev. ed. ^{36}1854 ...

with extensive alterations and improvements ..., Edinburgh: Oliver & Boyd (@); anr. ed. 1855, Edinburgh, 15cm, 178pp., on cover: New Ed. Hali., MacKinley (@); [43]1857, Edinburgh (L); [44]1858, Edinburgh, 180pp. ($ L); [48]1859, Edinburgh (L); anr. ed. 1861, Hali.: Muir, 15cm, 178pp. (@); anr. ed. 1862, Montreal: J. Lovell ($ @); anr. ed. 1863, Montreal: J. Lovell (@); new ed. 1863, rev. by P. Austin Nuttall, London; anr. ed. 1863, as *A new English grammar, comprising the substance of Lennie's Principles of English grammar with extensive alterations and improvements, and additional chapters on derivation, analysis and composition, by J. P. Bidlake*, London (L); [58]1864, with alterations, Edinburgh; new and corr. ed. 1864, London; rev. ed. [61]1865, ... *with extensive alterations and improvements* ... (@); anr. ed. 1866, 180pp. ($); [64]1868, with alterations, Edinburgh; [66]1869, Edinburgh: Oliver & Boyd, 179pp. (L); anr. ed.? 1869 ($); new ed. 1870, rev. by P.A. Nuttall, ... *critically revised and amended for the use of schools, and enlarged by a full explanation of the analysis of sentences* ..., London: G. Routledge & Sons, 15cm, viii+136pp (@); [69]1871, Edinburgh (L); [71]1872, ... *with the author's latest improvements, and an appendix in which analysis of sentences is fully treated* ..., Edinburgh: Oliver & Boyd, 216pp. (@); [72]1873 (L); [74]1874, Edinburgh (L); anr. ed. 1874, Halifax: N.S., R.T. Muir & Co. (@); anr. ed. 1876 (@); [80]1878, Edinburgh (L); new ed. 1879, with numerous additions, London: W. Tegg, 180pp. (@); [81]1880, ... *with the author's latest improvements, and an appendix in which analysis of sentences is fully treated* ..., Edinburgh: Oliver & Boyd, iv+220pp. (@); [85]1886 (L); [93]1894 (L)). ($ @ A E L O *Br, Hu, Lw, Tm*)

[Very compressed account of Etymology and Syntax, with a short section on Prosody appended; rules with 'observations' and exercises added. Self-praise claims the book is eminently superior to Murray's which it is hopeful to replace, cf. the quotation from advertisement in [19]1838:179: "The preceding Grammar, owing to the uncommon precision and brevity of the Definitions, Rules, and Notes, is not only better adapted to the capacity of children than the generality of those styled Introductory Grammars, but it is so extensively provided with exercises of every sort, that it will entirely supersede the use of Mr Murray's *Larger* Grammar and *Exercises*; for this is not a mere *Outline*, like his *Abridgement*, which contains only about *seven* pages of exercises on *bad* Grammar. [...] In short, by abridging every subject of minor importance, by omitting discussion on the numberless points about which grammars differ; by rendering the rules and definitions more perspicuous, and at the same time abridging them more than *one-half*; by selecting short sentences on bad grammar [...] the learner will acquire as much knowledge of grammar with this in *six* months, as with all these volumes in *twelve*. Martin 1824:272-73: "Mr Lennie has the honour of having been educated in the same school in which St. Paul distinguished himself: that is, the school of the Pharisees. Mr. Lennie informs us that "a sore head" signifies "the head ache," and amuses us with such phrases as "I dinna ken", and the like; which has reduced an experienced schoolmaster very wittily to remark, that his book is "calculated for the meridian of Edinburgh." There are - mostly favourable - references to this work in Hill (no. 863), Cramp (no. 386), Hunter (no. 920) ²1848, Young (no. 1933) and many others.]

1078. ---. [a1816]. *A key to Lennie's Principles of English grammar, containing an enlarged account (²1816 'an abstract') of the author's method of teaching grammar, intended for ladies, junior teachers, private students, and others.* n.p. (²1816, Edinburgh, 14x8.5, 107pp., 3s6d (L); ⁵1822; ⁶1824; ⁸1831 (@); ¹³1843; new ed. 1850, with some corrections ... *intended for parents who assist their children at home, private students and others*, Edinburgh: Oliver & Boyd, 190pp. ($ @); new, corr. and impr. ed. 1854, Edinburgh: Oliver & Boyd, 190pp. (@); anr. ed. 1860; anr. ed. 1870; anr. ed. 1871; ⁷1894, as *Key to the improved edition of Lennie's Principles of English grammar*, Edinburgh: Oliver & Boyd, 14cm, 235pp. (L); at least three further editions to 1894, then as *Key to the improved edition of Lennie's Principles of English grammar*).
($ @ E L O)
[Advice to teachers on individual points in his grammar, additional exercises and two insightful introductions (to first and second editions) make this *key* much more than a list of solutions.]

1079. ---. [1871]. *Analysis of sentences: being the appendix to Lennie's English grammar adapted for general use.* Edinburgh etc.: Oliver & Boyd. 15cm, 36pp., 3d.
Key Edinburgh: Oliver & Boyd, n.d. 47pp, 6d.
(L O)
[Brief definitions with plenty of examples and exercises; clear but dry. References to Lennie's *Grammar* throughout. A 'teacher's handbook' discussing didactic problems and strategies as well as providing solutions. Sentence analysis often in tabular form.]

1080.$ Leonard, Seth. 1817. *The key to etymology and syntax.* n.p. 32pp.
($)

1081.$ ---. ³1819. *The American grammar to which is added, Elements of reading and oratory: with a short explanation of the seven liberal arts and sciences. Designed for schools and academies, and for the amuse-*

ment of gentlemen and ladies. Rev. and impr. ed. New York: M'Duffer & Farrand. 19cm, x+[11]-144pp.
($ @)

1082. Anon. [a1860]. *Lessons in English grammar for a child*. London: Joseph Masters. 4d.
(L)

1083.$ Lewis, Alonzo (1794-1861). 1822. *Lessons in English grammar: designed to render the study of the English language simple and familiar to young learners*. Boston: Lincoln & Edmands. 15cm, iv+[5]-50pp.
($ @ Br)

1084. Lewis, Edwin Herbert (1866-1938). 1899. *A first manual of composition, designed for use in the highest grammar grade and the lower high-school grades*. London/New York: Macmillan. 19cm, xxvi+236/239pp.
($ @)

1085.$ Lewis, Frances W. 1889. *500 choice selections from prose and poetry: for grammatical exercises and memorizing: with a drill book for review in English grammar and analysis*. Boston: Eastern Educational Bureau. 20cm, 51+107pp.
($ @)

1086. Lewis, Henry. 1866. Assistant English Lecturer in Battersea Training College. *The English language: its grammar and history*. London: Williams & Norgate. 16x10, ii+82pp., 1s6d.
(L O)
[OESP with a few words on the history of English (74-80); the description of the functions of nine parts of speech is followed by syntax (parsing, analysis). Clear and succinct definitions based on logical distinctions, arguments well arranged. Quite a commendable attempt at reduction.]

1087. ---. 1869. *The English language: its grammar and history. Together with a treatise on English composition, and exercises*. London. 17cm (^{3}1872, with examination papers, London (L); ^{4}1873; ^{7}1877, London: Edward Stanford, viii+199pp. (@); ^{9}1881 (@ L)).
(@ L O)
[Alphabet, parts of speech, syntax, an "introduction to the study of the words and the history of the English language" and two pages of prosody; succinct and generally competent definitions (to be memorized) accompanied by well-chosen examples.]

1088. ---. 1871. *English grammar for beginners in a series of easy lessons, intended for the use of junior classes and as an introduction to the author's larger English grammar*. London: Edward Stanford. 16pp., 15x9, 2d. (^{2}a1876; ^{3}1878, 20pp. (@)).

(@ L O)
["Selected only the most important parts of the subject, making all explanations as simple as possible." Parts of speech and their characteristics only are discussed in non-technical language, with examples and exercises. Criticises Murray, both his grammar and the abridgment, for inconsistency caused by a desire to please everyone.]

1089.$ Lewis, John. 1825. *Analytical outlines of the English language; or, A cursory examination of its materials and structure ... in the form of familiar dialogues, intended to accompany grammatical studies.* Richmond: Shepherd & Pollard. 25cm, xii+178pp.
($)

1090.$! ---. 1828. *English grammar.* New York. 18mo, 48pp.
(*Br*)

1091. Lewis, William Greatheed. 1821. *A grammar of the English language; in which the genius of the English tongue is consulted, and all imitations of the Greek and Latin grammars are discarded; adapted to the comprehension of persons desirous of teaching themselves, and intended for the use of schools and young persons. To which is added, a brief view of the discoveries of Mr. Horne Tooke, on the formation of language.* London: T. Dolby. viii+216pp. (^{4}1825, as *A new system of English grammar ...*, London: T. Dolby, 15cm, xi+[1]+204pp. (@)).
(@ L *Br*, *Hu*, *Lw*, *Ma*)
[Traditional OESP pattern, but diverging in the explanations and terms from the predecessors; the rules are to be memorized, but there are extensive notes discussing solutions suggested by other grammarians, notes which are too abstract for the intended learners. Reviewed by Martin 1824:23-25.]

1092.$ Lind, George Dallas (b. 1847). 1899. *200 lessons outlined in U.S. history, geography, English grammar, arithmetic, and physiology.* New York: Hends & Noble. 19cm, 2 p. l., [9]-200pp.
($ @)

1093. Anon. 1809. *Lindley Murray examined; or An address to classical, French, and English teachers; in which several absurdities, contradictions and grammatical errors in Murray are pointed out; and in which is likewise shown the necessity of the "Essentials".* (By a Member of the University of Oxford). Oxford: J. Munday, for the author. 21cm, 66pp.
(@ O *Hu*, *Lw*, *Sk*)

1094. Lindsay, Rev. John (Fellow of Dulwich College). 1842. *English grammar for the use of national and other elementary schools.* London: Rivington. 12°, 88pp., 1s.
(L O *Br*, *Hu*, *Lw*)

[OESP account, partly using new terminology; eight parts of speech.]
1095.$ Little, George. (b. 1791). 1840?. *An exposition of English grammar in conversational or familiar lectures, containing a systematic order for parsing and false syntax corrected and why it is false: also, rules for parsing by transposition, observations on letter writing and comprehensive lectures on rhetoric and elocution designed for those persons who have not had the advantage of this branch of education in early life, and also for the use of schools*. Baltimore: J. Young. (Anr. ed. 1841, 19cm, iv+[5]-219pp. ($)).
($ @)
1096. Livesey, Thomas. [1881]. *How to teach grammar, illustrated in a series of notes of lessons*. London: Moffatt & Paige. 18cm, viii+147pp. (^{5}n.d.).
(@)
[The author expresses obligations to Mason; syntax neglected: concord and government can be taught from the beginning.]
1097.$ Livor, John. 1851. *A new system of English grammar on the oral method: to which is added a key to the exercises*. n.p. 18cm, iv+79pp. (Ster. ed. ^{2}1851, New York: L.W. Schmidt (@)).
($ @)
1098.! Lloyd, Miss E. [1813]. *Grammatical dialogues*. London. (^{2}1814, 1s6d) (*Lw, Ma, Mi, Wa*)
1099. Lloyd, Richard John. 1899. *Northern English. Phonetics, grammar, texts*. (Skizzen lebender Sprachen). Leipzig: B.G. Teubner etc. 17.5x 11.5, vi+127pp.
($ @ C L)
[A synchronic description, largely non-contrastive, of the educated speech of people living between Birmingham and Durham. Chapters on pronunciation and grammar (nine parts of speech) are followed by texts with phonetic transcription.]
1100. Locke, Cyril L.C. (Assistant Master of Clifton College). 1883. *A primer of English parsing and analysis*. New York: Longmans & Green. 16.5x 10, viii+96pp. (@ L). (^{2}1885 (L)).
(@ L)
[For the lower forms in classical schools, also to assist in the acquisition of Latin. Examples taken from poetry "where the order of words is constantly inverted". Acknowledges the assistance derived from Maetzner, Mason, Bain and Adams. Definitions of nine parts of speech followed by discussions of the simple and compound sentence; sober and traditional. Exercises interspersed and at end.]
1101.$! Locke, John. 1827. *Small English grammar*. Cincinnati, Ohio. 18mo.

(*Br, We*)

1102.$ Lockwood, Sara Elizabeth Husted (b. 1854). 1888. *Lessons in English: adapted to the study of American classics: a textbook for high schools and academies.* Boston: Ginn & Co. 19cm, xix+403+10pp. ($ @). (Anr. ed. 1889 ($ @); anr. ed. 1890 ($ @); seven more editions recorded to 1899, Boston: Ginn & Co., all presumably unchanged).
($ @)

1103.$ Long, C.C. [1855]. *Language exercises: grammar and composition.* Part III. Cincinnati: Van Antwerp, Bragg & Co. 20cm, vi+[7]-150pp.
(@)

1104.$ ---. 1882. *Language exercises for primary schools: following the course of study in language adopted by the Cincinnati Pedagogical Association.* Cincinnati?. 20cm, 3 vol. in 1, 43+45+84pp.
($)

1105.$ ---. 1889. *New language exercises: for primary schools.* (Eclectic Educational Series). 2 vols. New York: Van Antwerp, Bragg & Co. 19cm. (Anr. ed. 1890, New York/Cincinnati: American Book Company (@)).
($ @)

1106.$ ---. 1890. *Lessons in English: grammar and composition.* New York/Cincinnati: American Book Company. 19cm, iv+[5]-144pp.
($ @)

1107.$ Long, Harriet. 1873. *Introduction to English grammar: an easy method for beginners.* (First lessons in English Grammar). n.p. 17cm, 55pp. (Anr. ed. 1874 ($)).
($)

1108.$ Longwell. O.H. 1897. *A complete English grammar: based on the inductive method of teaching.* n.p. 20cm, vii+246(346?)+5pp. (^{2}1897, Des Moines, Iowa: O.H. Longwell (@)).
($ @)

1109. Lord, Walter John. 1832. *A new arrangement of the English grammar, adapted to the Junior Class of learners. In which the expressions, definitions and rules by, Lindley Murray, are attempted to be simplified and rendered more easy of acquirement and retention.* Trowbridge: J. Diplock. 16cm, iv+56pp.
(L O)
["In this work, elegance of expression, perhaps the greatest error of Murray's grammar, is sacrificed to a lucid and philosophical arrangement" (iii). The first part contains Etymology only, with two pages on Orthography; a second part was promised. Adequate summary of Murray.]

1110.$ Lothrop, Reuel. 1815. *The English grammar in miniature, designed for the use of children.* n.p. 12cm, 42pp.
($)
1111. Low, Walter Humboldt. 1887. *The English language, its history and structure.* (University Tutorial Series). n.p. 18cm, vi+[2]+224pp. ($ L). (Anr. ed. 1890? ($ L); anr. ed. 1892, London: University Correspondence College Press; ²1893, London: W.B. Clive (@ L); anr. ed. 1896 ($); rev. ed. ⁴1897, London: W.B. Clive (@ L); ⁵1899 (L)).
($ @ L)
[British Library Catalogue adds: "Matriculation Model answers English Language. Being the London Matriculation Papers in English language from June 1886 to January 1891, with answers by W.H.L."]
1112.$ Lowell, Anna Cabot (1811-1874). 1843. *Edward's first lessons in grammar.* Boston: T.H. Webb & Co. 16cm, 108pp.
($ @)
1113. Anon. 1890. *Lower grade English grammar.* (Royal English Classbooks). London: Nelson. 102pp.
(L)
1114. Lowres, Jacob (Certificated Master). ²1851. *A system of English parsing and derivation: with the rudiments of English grammar, including the construction of sentences and a short history of the English language, specially adapted to the tuition of pupil teachers. For the use of schools.* London. 14x9, 156pp. (New ed. 1860, London: Longmans, Green & Co. 14cm, 156pp. (@); anr. ed. 1864).
(@ L *Lw*)
[The author distinguishes between syntax and "construction"; rules of syntax interspersed with examples and exercises make, for all the insightful remarks, a disorderly impression; a short history of the English language and part IV on derivation (122-56) do not really fit with the general plan; much on word formation and roots.]
1115. ---. 1862. *Companion to English grammar; being a guide to analysis of sentences, paraphrasing, higher order of parsing, punctuation, composition or style, figurative language. With numerous exercises for pupils. For the use of schools. Specially adapted to the tuition of pupil-teachers, Queen scholars, and the advanced pupils in academies, seminaries, and boarding schools.* London. 17/18cm. (²1864, London: Longmans, Green, Longman, Roberts & Green, 18cm, viii+176pp. ($ @)).
($ @ L O *Lw*)
[The author says that public examinations now make sentence analysis, parsing and précis very important; some stylistics included.]

116. ---. 1863. *Grammar of English grammars; or Advanced manual of English grammar and language, critically and historically considered ... With numerous exercises. Specially adapted to the tuition of pupil-teachers, Queen scholars, and all persons preparing for government examinations.* London: Longman, Green etc. 17x10, viii+318pp. (New ed. 1876, London: Longmans, Green & Co. (@); anr. ed. 1882, London (@)).
(@ L O)
[The book contains a chronological list of about 250 English grammars from the 16th to the 19th century; the ones listed from between 1800 and 1863 are here quoted as *Lw*.]

117. Lyde, Lionel William (Writer on Geography, 1863-1947). 1893. *Notes on English grammar.* London: Methuen. 8°, viii+60pp.
(@ L O)
[History of English followed by II "Practical", in which "letters, sounds, derivation, parts of speech, inflection" is followed by a brief discussion of nouns, pronouns, adjectives, verbs, infinitives etc. and link-words (prepositions and conjugations) - the briefest of sketches, selective, with historical explanations.]

118. Lyell, James. 1804. *The rudiments of the English tongue; or, A plain and easy introduction to English grammar; wherein the principles of the language are methodically digested, with useful notes and observations, explaining the terms of grammar, and farther improving its rules.* Arbroath: J. Findlay.
(A G)
[The copy in Glasgow Univ. Library is incomplete (iv+24pp.). "English Grammar being in much esteem, may in a short time become, as it really ought to be, the *first language* so [i.e. grammatically] taught." All in Q/A form, much to be memorised.]

119.$ Lyle, John (1769-1825). 1804. *The new American grammar containing the different kinds, relations, and changes of words, syntax, or the right construction of sentences, a table of irregular verbs, an example of grammatical resolution ...* Lexington, Ky.: J. Charles. 15x5, 108pp.
($ @)

120. Lynch, Patrick (Secretary of the Gaelic Society of Dublin). 1805. *A plain, easy and comprehensive grammar of the English tongue, in which the definitions and rules necessary to be committed to memory are composed in familiar verse. With a preliminary essay, containing ... a critical review of the most celebrated English grammars, etc.* [preface dated 1802]. Carrick: John Stacy. 15x9, xvi+122pp., 2s6d.
(L)

[OESP; short rules are translated into rhymed couplets and accompanied by extensive explanations on the same page. 18th-century traditions, with a great deal of classical knowledge added. Ten parts of speech. Noteworthy only for an early use of rhyme which is justified at great length.]

1121.$ Lynde, John. 1818. *A synopsis of the rudiments of English grammar, designed to lead youth with ease and sententious brevity into a competent knowledge of this useful branch of education, by a numeral and literal index to facilitate the progress of the learner in examples of grammatical resolution; so methodically arranged, as to be comprehended by the lowest capacity.* Brookfield, Mass.: E. Merriam & Co. 25x21, 16pp.
(@)

1122.$ ---. 1821. *Key to English grammar: in which the most difficult examples of syntax are illustrated: to abridge the labour of the instructor, and facilitate the progress of the learner.* Woodstock, Vt.: D. Watson. 15cm, 108pp.
($ @)

1123.$ ---. 1894. *An introduction to Murray's English grammar. Designed for the use of schools.* n.p. 17cm, 36pp.
($)

1124. Lyon, Charles Jobson. 1832. *Analysis of the seven parts of speech of the English language, with a view to fix their character, and furnish simple rules for ascertaining them; as also to elucidate and facilitate the method of parsing.* Edinburgh: Oliver & Boyd. 17x10.5, iv+127pp.
(L O Lw)
[Attacks the metaphysical obscurities of traditional grammar, and the overlapping of parts of speech. Pro-Horne-Tooke and very critical of Murray and Cobbett (for political as well as linguistic reasons). Offers a new system of seven parts of speech (noun, pronoun, adjective, preposition, verb, adverb, conjunction), stressing the independence of English of Latin.]

1125.$ Lyons, T.L. 1839. *The English grammar, newly arranged and adapted to the use of schools and private learners.* Lexington, Ky.: Noble & Dunlop. 17cm, vi+[7]-72pp.
(@)

1126.$ ---. 1850?. *A new grammar of the English language: familiarly explained, and adapted to the use of schools and private students.* Cincinnati: H.S. & J. Applegate, 19cm, 196pp. (Anr. ed. 1851 ($) @).
($ @)

1127.$ Lyte, Eliphalet Oram (1842-1913). 1879. *Forms of parsing and analysis, oral and written: with forms of correcting false syntax.* Lancaster, Pa.: Normal Publishing Company. 18cm, 116pp.

($ @)

1128.$ ---. 1883. *Advance pages of an English grammar for the use of schools, based on the inductive method.* Lancaster, Pa.: the author. 18cm, 216pp.
(@)

1129.$ ---. 1886. *Grammar and composition: for common schools.* New York: D. Appleton. 20cm, iv+270pp. (Anr. ed. 1887, New York ($ @); anr. ed. 1888 ($ @); anr. ed. 1889, 20cm, iv+270pp. ($); anr. ed. 1890, 20cm, iv+270pp. ($)).
($ @)

1130.$ ---. 1898a. *Elementary English.* (Lyte's Language Series). New York/Cincinnati: American Book Company. 19cm, 160pp.
($ @)

1131.$ ---. 1898b. *Elements of English grammar and composition.* (Lyte's Language Series). New York/Cincinnati: American Book Company. 19cm, 224pp.
($)

1132.$ ---. 1899. *Advanced grammar and composition.* (Lyte's Language Series). New York/Cincinnati: American Book Company. 19cm, 368pp.
($)

1133. Macaleer, I. 1840. *A general key to English parsing: a new invention.* Belfast.
(L)

1134.$ Macallum, Archibald (1824-1879). 1867. *An eclectic grammar practical and analytical of the English language adapted to the wants of our public schools and seminaries of learning in the dominion of Canada on the basis of Bullions and Morell.* n.p. xvi+171pp.
($)

1135. McArthur, Alexander. 1836. *An outline of English grammar for the use of schools.* (Publ. anon.). Dublin: The Commissioners of National Education, Ireland, sold by R. Groombridge, London. 13cm, 178pp. (Anr. ed. 1838, including *Key*, 19cm, viii+296pp. ($); anr. ed. 1842, n.p.: The Council of Public Instruction for Upper Canada, 14cm (@); anr. ed. 1845 (@); anr. ed. 1846, repr. at Montreal: Armour & Ramsay (@); ?1849; several editions to at least 1876).
(@ L O)

[OESP, nine parts of speech, short rules, with examples, exercises and directions to teachers in small print; longer discussions about tenses (37-8), *have* (39-40) and future (41). Appendices on derivation, punctuation and style. Quite a reliable summary of traditional grammar.]

1136.$ MacCabe, John Alexander (1842-1902). 1873. *An English grammar for the use of schools including copious exercises for parsing, with exam-*

ples, and an explanation of the leading principles of analysis, paraphrasing, and punctuation. Prescribed ... for use in the public schools of Nova Scotia. Halifax: MacKinlay. 17cm, 98pp. (^{2}1874, 17cm, 156pp. (@); anr. ed. 1876 ($ @)).
($ @)

1137.$ ---. 1892. *Hints for language lessons and plans for grammar lessons. A handbook for teachers.* Boston: Ginn & Co. 19cm, 58pp.
(@)

1138.$ M'Chesney, John I. 1822. *An English grammar: compendiously compiled: for the use of schools.* Philadelphia: the author. 18cm, 108pp.
($ @)

1139.$ ---. 1823. *Introductory lectures to John I. M'Chesney's system of English grammar, as delivered to his classes, calculated to enable persons to be their own teachers.* Bridgeton, N.Y.: John Clarke. 21cm, 28pp.
(@)

1139a. McCready, Francis. 1820. *The art of English grammar, in verse, by question and answer: with notes and examples of parsing, to illustrate the rules: adapted to the different classes of learners in academies and schools, as also, for private instruction.* n.p. 18cm, xxii+[19]-249pp.
($)

1140. McCulloch, John Murray. 1834. *A manual of English grammar, philosophical and practical; adapted to the analytical mode of tuition.* Edinburgh: Oliver & Boyd. 14x9, 189pp., 1s6d. (^{2}1835, 1s6d ($); 3rd ed. advertised in 1837; ^{6}1839 (Le); ^{7}1841 (*Br*); ^{9}1845 (*Hu*); ^{13}1853 (E); price in 1855: 1s6d; ^{16}1856 (L); ^{18}1859 (L); anr. ed. 1865, 16cm, 180pp. ($); anr. ed. 1865; ^{24}1873 (L)).
($ A L Le O *Br*, *Hu*, *Lw*)
[Treats grammar as a science and gives full attention to orthography, derivation and arrangement, while reducing prosody. Eight parts of speech (no articles); short rules (to be memorized); some linguistic history; exercises at end of chapters.]

1141.$ M'Dougall, John. 1835. *An introduction to the study of English.* n.p. 17cm, 29+53pp.
($)
[Possibly identical with no. 1141a.?]

1141a.! Anon. n.d. *McDougall's grammar with composition suited to requirements of latest code. Standards VI & VII.* Edinburgh: McDougall's Educational Company Ltd. / London: Hamilton, Adams & Co. 84pp.
(*Wm*)

[Contents: XVII units including reviews of parsing and syntax; analysis; Compound Sentences; historical sources of words; derivational morphology ("Formation"); Latin and Greek roots; Composition; Appendix: Précis writing and Business Terms.]

1142. MacGowan, Rev. James (Teacher of languages, Edinburgh). 1817. *A practical English grammar, in which the syntax is greatly simplified.* Edinburgh. 196pp. (Impr. and considerably enl. ed. ^{3}1825, as *A practical English grammar, with original and appropriate exercises, on scientific principles, by which a key is rendered unnecessary, and the study of grammar is made a perpetual exercise of the intellectual faculties, and an effectual introduction to composition*, London: Sherwood, Jones & Co., 15cm, 248pp. (@); ^{4}1836, with improvements, London: Sherwood, Gilbert & Piper, 15cm, xii+204pp. (@)).

(@ E L *Lw*)

[The treatment is unusual in linking the grammar to the linguistic development of children, e.g. relatives and conjunctions are dealt with later than other parts of speech, interjections are treated first. Probably identical with *Br*'s reference: 1825. *English grammar*. London. 18mo, 218pp.]

1143.$! M'Illigott, James N. 1846. *The young analyzer.* New York. 12mo, 54pp.

(*Br*)

1144. MacIntosh, Daniel (Master of Meadowside Academy, Dundee). 1852. *Elements of English grammar.* Edinburgh: Sutherland & Knox. 16cm, iii-v+[5]-148pp.

(@ C L O *Lw*)

[Modest epitome of little worth.]

1145. Macintyre, William. 1831. *An intellectual grammar of the English language: or, The elements of English grammar.* Glasgow. 12cm. xi+67pp.

(O)

[Admirable and historically important. The "intellectual" method is to teach pupils to think for themselves; they should be exercised not on "detached sentences" but on "a piece of connected composition."]

1146.$ M'Jilton, John Nelson (1805-1875). 1857. *The Maryland primary grammar: designed for beginners in the study of the science.* Baltimore. 15cm, 107pp.

($ @)

1147.$ McNemar, Richard (1770-1839). 1831. *A compendium of English grammar selected from Wells, Kirkham, Murray, Perry, &c.* n.p. [12]pp.

($)

1148.$ Mack, Evered J. 1835. *The self-instructor, and practical English grammar: in a series of inductive lessons and familiar lectures, with an analysis of one thousand sentences parsed in full: whereby a complete knowledge of the science can be attained without the aid of oral instruction from a teacher: designed as a text book for students and private learners.* Springfield, Mass.: the author. 19cm, 180pp. (Anr. ed. 1836 ($)).
($ @ *Br*)
[*Br*: "An egregious plagiarism from G. Brown."]

1149. [Mackenzie, Eneas]. [1856]. *M(urray)'s English grammar, complete. With an appendix, containing exercises in orthography, syntax, parsing and punctuation. Designed for the younger classes of learners. A new edition with copious parsing questions.* (Mackenzie's Educational Books) London: Robert Hardwicke. 14.5x10, 64pp., 2d.
(L)
[The book was published in Mackenzie's Educational Books, 21 elementary works and 23 catechisms being listed on the back cover (here termed Murray's School GRAMMAR). How much of Murray survives in this modest compilation is uncertain.]

1150.! Mackintosh. 1808. *Mackintosh's essay on English grammar.* n.p. 8vo.
(*Sk*)

1151. McLachlan, John (Headmaster of Dr Bell's School, Edinburgh). [a1863]. *A first grammar.* Edinburgh. 14x9, 36pp., 3d. (^{6}1876 (M'Lachlan's Elementary Series), Edinburgh/Glasgow: J. Menzies, 15cm, 36pp. (@)).
(@ L)
["Contains as much grammar as the greater number of Scholars in our Elementary Schools are ever likely to need or acquire". "The Scholars listen, while the Teacher explains. When the main ideas have been well wrought out from their minds, this little Manual will give visible order, form and compactness to their knowledge" (3). Descriptions in very plain language, skilful reduction of grammatical knowledge, but without independent value.]

1152. McLeod, Walter (Head Master of the Model School, Royal Military Asylum, Chelsea, 1815-1875). 1850. *An explanatory English grammar for beginners.* (Gleig's School Series). London. (L). (New ed. 1851, London: Longman, Brown, Green & Longmans, 14.5x9, xii+143pp., 9d. (@); anr. ed. 1868 (Gleig's School Series), London: Longmans, Green & Co., viii+152pp. (@)).
(@ L O *Lw*)
[Treats parts of speech (starting with nouns) before other 'divisions of grammar'; only syntax is given extensive treatment, pp.98-140. Hunter's *Text Book* and Latham's Elementary English Grammar are suggested as

complements. Definitions to be learnt by heart. Thoughtful and discriminating. Among the innovations listed are: definitions of parts of speech to follow their illustrations; composition more important than parsing.]
1153.! ---. [a1866]. *English grammatical definitions.* London: Longman. 1d.
(*Mp*)
[Advertised in 1863.]
1154. ---. 1874. *A handbook of the analysis of sentences; with numerous illustrative examples and a complete series of exercises, for school and home work.* London/Glasgow: W. Collins. 16.5x11, 147pp., 1s6d. (Anr. ed. 1876 (Gm)).
(@ L Gm)
[Written to supply a textbook for the Analysis of Sentences which "may now be regarded as a necessary subject of study in all good primary schools". Three sections are denoted to Analysis, the fourth to Exercises (also to be used for parsing lessons). A necessarily dull elaborate account of various methods of clause analysis.]
1155. MacMillan, Michael (1853-1925) & Dossabhai Byramji Hakim. 1897. *Handbook of English grammar and composition for Indian students.* London: Macmillan & Co. 17x11.5, xii+392pp.
(L O)
[The first chapters, on eight individual parts of speech, contain very solid and detailed advice for all students; only occasional reference is made to Indian learners. Though the text is likely to be compiled from various sources and is slightly conservative it can stand comparison with other good grammars of the time. Book II on Composition contains practical advice and models for essays and letter writing as well as insightful guidance on 'misuse of words', 'awkwardness and ambiguity' etc., written with a view to common learners' mistakes.]
1156. MacMullen, James Alexander (Formerly English master in the High School of the Queen's College, Liverpool). 1860. *A manual of English grammar, with copious exercises and an appendix on derivations.* London: Mair & Son, pr. in Douglas. 14x8.5, iv+155pp. (Reissue in 1862 (L)).
(L C O)
[Naif, even though meant for inexperienced teachers. Very traditional OESP account - Priestley, Lowth, Crombie, Horne Tooke, Beard, Murray quoted as major authorities, "but especially the last, whom writers on the English language in the present day are so fond of decrying and - copying" (iv). Succinct definitions with some useful exercises - but note (vi) that "The structure of the examples may occasionally appear a little

harsh, owing to the ordinary arrangement having been departed from, to exercise the ingenuity of the pupils".]

1157.$ McMunn, John. B. 1853. *McMunn's graphic grammar. A grammar of the English language, designed for the illustration of a series of grammar charts.* New York: Lamport, Blakeman & Law. 19cm, viii+[9]-154pp. (42pp.?).
(@ L)
[Largely composed of exercises in sentence completion; pedestrian.]

1158. Macpherson, Angus. [a1854]. *English education. Being an attempt to place the study and teaching of the English language on a truer and broader basis.* n.p. (^{2}1854, Glasgow: D. Robertson, 38pp. (@)).
(@ Dt L)
[Does not live up to its title; little about grammar; unimaginative.]

1159.! MacQueen, John. 1861. *Easy lessons in English grammar, for home study.* London.
(*Mi*)
[Once in Carlisle Public Library, not now known]

1160. ---. [1869]. *Easy exercises in English.* London: Whitehaven, Crosthwaite & Co. 18x11.5, 42pp.
(L O)
[Exercises only; without introduction, definitions, advice or comment. No grammar mentioned for reference.]

1161. Maetzner, Eduard Adolf Ferdinand (1805-1892). 1874. *An English grammar; methodical, analytical and historical; with a treatise on the orthography, prosody, inflections and syntax of the English tongue, and numerous authorities cited in order of historical development.* 3 vols. Translated from the German by Clair James Grece. London: Murray / Boston: Roberts & Bros. 22x14, I:vii+510, II:iv+494, III:xvi+571pp. (Anr. ed. 1876, London: J. Munat (@)).
($ @ A E L O)
[Maetzner's book was a scholarly grammar of a new type: starting from a system quite new, analysing the language in minutest detail and supporting his conclusions with an enormous amount of historical and comparative evidence: the sheer size of some 1500 densely printed pages illustrates the new start made. Note that the translation is often clumsy or wordy. Maetzner exclusively relies on written sources and does not, in all cases, distinguish clearly enough between synchronic facts and chronological developments (all Shakespearian data are subsumed under ModE), and terms like 'accusative' are freely used.]
Lit: Leitner, Gerhard, in: Leitner 1991:233-56.

1162. Major, Henry, publ. 1876. *Major's New Code (1875) grammar.* 8 parts. Nottingham: Henry Major, etc. 16.5x10, Standard II: 16pp, Standard III: 24pp, Standard IV: 24pp, Standard V: 24pp., Standard VI: 24pp., 1d, complete 6d.
(O)
[Eight parts of speech, simple definitions, repeated in the individual parts, exercises include parsing.]

1163. Manneville, William (Translator of languages, and teacher of the classics and mathematics). 1851. *English grammar simplified. Designed for the use of schools and self-tuition. With an appendix containing a discussion of several points in dispute among grammarians.* London: Simpkin, Marshall & Co. 14x12, xx+168pp.
(L *Lw*)
[The author is well-acquainted with the tradition (Booth, Horne Tooke, Johnson, Lowth, McCulloch and Priestley are quoted; he commends Crombie and Webster, but blames the latter for retaining moods and passive. Manneville holds that "an English Grammar, especially when intended for the use of the unlearned, should be entirely divested of those technicalities which, however appropriate they may be in the Grammars of complex languages and necessary to impart a correct knowledge of them, are totally inapplicable to the study of our simple vernacular idiom" (viii). Seven branches: Orthoepy, Orthography, Accidence, Syntax, Etymology, Punctuation and Prosody. The appendix (145-68) discusses questions where grammarians disagree and matter "too abstruse for beginners, thought improper to encumber the text". Sensible; defends his innovations in terminology (*adnoun, prenoun, prepositive*; widely read.]

1163a. Manson, George. 1846. *The pupil's guide to English etymology, with copious exercises on prefixes and affixes.* Edinburgh. 24°. (^{16}1856 ($)).
($ @ L)

1164. Anon. ^{4}1865. *A manual of English grammar with numerous exercises.* Madras: The Christian Vernacular Education Society for India. 14cm, 130pp. (Anr. ed. [1867], London: Christian Vernacular Education Society for India, 13.5x8.5, iv+[5]-142pp. (L)).
(L)
[The fullest account in the series, comprising discussions of style, punctuation and derivation, probably the source of the Madras primer (cf. no. 692a), which is shortened by omission of explanations, notes and some exercises. Eight parts of speech. Includes many exercises in errors and 'false syntax in standard authors' (104-7).]

⇒ Anon. 1846. *A manual of instruction for the South African College. Literature ...* - see Adamson, James, no. 16

1165. Anon. 1856. *Manual of the analysis of language.* London. viii+24pp.
(L)
[The study of analysis "comparatively new in this country". Logical analysis (i.e. sentences); verbal analysis; all language is reducible to names, predicates and particles.]

1166. Anon. [1869]. *A manual of words curiously derived, for the use of students of the English language. By a teacher.* (Cambrian Educational Course). Cardigan.
(L)

1167. Marcet, Mrs Jane Haldimand (1769-1858). 1835. *Mary's grammar; interspersed with stories and intended for the use of children.* London: Rees, Orme, Brown, Green & Longman. 15x9.5, vi+286pp. ($ @). (^{2}1836; rev. and enl. ed. ^{3}1838; nine further editions until 1875 of which at least two were publ. in New York by D. Appleton, price in 1865: 3s6d; rev. and enl. ed. [1875], London: Longmans, Green & Co., 371pp. (@); rev. and enl. ed. 1875, New York: D. Apppleton, 19cm, iv+[5]-240pp. (@)).
($ @ G L O *Br, Hu, Lw*)
[Narrative form used "to render so dry and abstruse a subject easy and familiar"; "the stories have been introduced with a view of amusing children during the prosecution of so dry a study; but they may occasionally be used with advantage as parsing exercises" (iv). Individual chapters are devoted to a particular part of speech discussed in a conversation between mother and daughter. She is worried by the "metaphysical difficulties" she has had to pass over.]

1168. ---. 1842. *The game of grammar.* (Cards and counters.) London. Price in 1845: 8s.
(L)
["With a Book of Conversions (8vo) showing the Rules of the Game, and affording Examples of the manner of playing at it" (advertisement)]

1169. ---. 1844. *Conversations on language, for children.* London. 8vo, 4s6d.
(L)
[Good of its kind; historical; diffusion of ideas; derivation.]

1170. ---. 1845. *Willy's grammar; interspersed with stories and intended for the use of children.* London. 2s6d. (^{3}1850 (Le); anr. ed. 1853, 2s6d (L); anr. ed. 1861, 14x9, iv+360pp. ($); anr. ed. 1882).
($ L Le O *Hu, Lw*)

[Explicitly patterned on *Mary's grammar*, with "illustrations more suitable to the ideas and habits of boys", the book "has little claim to novelty".]

1171.$ March, Francis Andrew (1825-1911). 1869. *A parser and analyzer for beginners: with diagrams and suggestive pictures.* New York: American Book Co. 17cm, vi+88pp. (Anr. ed. 1869, New York: Harper & Bros, ($ @); anr. ed. 1870 (@); at least seven more editions until 1897, presumably all published in New York by Harper & Bros; anr. ed. 1897 New York/Cincinnati: American Book Company ($ @)).
($ @)

1172.$ Maris, George Lewis (b. 1842). 1880. *The normal English grammar: a manual of analysis and parsing. For the use of schools and teachers.* West Chester, Pa.: F.S. Hickman. 18cm, iv+[5]-112pp. (Anr. ed. 1888, Philadelphia: Eldredge & Brother, 19cm, vi+[7]-119pp. ($ @)).
($ @)

1173. Marles, Henry (Author of the National Air "Sway the Sceptre"). [1858]. *A compendious English grammar in which the elements of the language are simplified and explained. Interspersed with ample progressive exercises in parsing.* London: Jarrold & Sons. 14x9, vi+172pp.
(L)
[OESP, traditional account; the simplification has led to some vagueness; some exercises, but no 'false syntax'. "The utmost care has been taken to introduce exalted sentiments, and moral and religious instruction into a book intended *to live* in the memory".]

1174.$ Marsh, Joseph Walker. 1893. *A brief outline of English grammar.* Forest Grove, Or.: Forest Grove Times Steam Print. 19cm, ix+46pp.
($ @)

1175. Marsh, Thomas (Professor of Languages). 1862. *Grammar of the English language, inculcating its history and development with all the latest improvements; particularly adapted for schools, and those who wish to investigate the mechanism of their mother-tongue with a view to becoming linguists.* London: Simpkin & Marshall, pr. in Jersey. 17/ 19cm, viii+186pp.
(C L O)
[Somewhat pompous style, not always clear, with tables illustrating the results of parsing]

1176. Martin, Thomas (of Birmingham). 1824. *A philological grammar of the English language; in a series of lessons. Containing many original and important observations on the nature and construction of language; on the comparative merits of more than 100 treatises on English grammar; on the various new and popular modes of teaching; on the necessity of*

examining the principles of grammars and grammarians. London: Rivingtons & W.B. Whittaker. 18x10.5, xii+401pp. ("Catalogue of English grammars", p. 265-76).
(@ C L O *Hu, Lw, Sk*)
[The book is one of the most ambitious attempts of its time; the author compared more than a hundred grammars, which are quoted throughout (here listed as *Ma*) and the major works also reviewed (often in caustic form, as Cobbett is for his grammatical system and political persuasions, pp. 5-7 and *passim*). Martin frequently refers to Wallis and has adverse comments about H. Tooke. Stresses derivation. However, his description is greatly flawed by what is also the main attraction: referring to so many sources, Martin fails to provide a coherent system of his own; moreover, he is inadequate in many things typical of his age; e.g. he does not properly distinguish between letters and sounds; his treatment of etymology does not show any impact of comparative philology; Hebrew is claimed to be the original language, which results in a completely distorted speculative history of the English language (263-65) - but he praises Bosworth's *Anglo-Saxon grammar* (399-400). Although very partizan and partly confused the book should be reprinted for the summary of 18th- and early 19th-century grammatical thinking which it comprises in a unique form.]

1177. Martin, William (1801-1867). 1851. *The intellectual expositor and vocabulary; comprising tables of prefixes, affixes, and primitive roots with an extensive list of synonymes, and Latin and French phrases in common use.* n.p. (L) (²n.d.; ³[1865], London, 1s6d (@ L)).
(@ L)

1178. ---. 1852. *The intellectual grammar; comprising orthography, etymology, syntax, and prosody; the principles of articulation, spelling, and pronunciation; with definitions, examples, exercises, illustrations, model lessons, hints to the teacher and pupil, upwards of a thousand interrogations on the text, and numerous explanatory and suggestive notes, with an elementary course of juvenile composition.* London: Simpkin, Marshall & Co. 17.5x10.5, iv+104pp., 1s. (Anr. ed. 1854 ($)).
($ @ L *Lw*)
[Meant "to develop the true principles of Grammar, that the philosophy of language may proceed with the practice" - an aim that is not achieved by somewhat unsatisfactory definitions, strange classifications and an inadequate arrangement. OESP, without any useful innovation. Links grammar with composition; regards the completion of sentences (blanks) as an important new technique.]

1179. ---. 1863. *First English course, based upon the analysis of sentences; comprising the structure and history of the English language with copious exercises.* London: Longman, Green, Longman, Roberts & Green. 17x10, xii+191pp., 2s6d.
(L O)
[Consistent attempt at basing grammar on the analysis of sentences (1-122); "The analysis of sentences ... forms the foundation of grammatical knowledge". Followed by a "History of the language" (123-45) and by various appendixes listing paradigms and roots (147-91).]

1180. Mason, Charles Peter (Fellow of University College, London, 1820-1900). 1858. *English grammar; including the principles of grammatical analysis.* London: Walton & Maberly. 18x11, xii+182pp. (^{2}1861, London, 17cm (L O); ^{14}1861, London, xii+170pp. ($ L); ^{14}1870 (@); rev. eds. $^{15+16}$1871, London (L O); ^{17}1872, 3s; rev. ed. ^{18}1873, London (O); enl. ed. ^{19}1874, London (A O); enl. ed. ^{20}1875, London (O); ^{21}1876, London: Bell & Sons, 19cm, viii+266pp. (@ C); anr. ed. 1877, viii+270pp. ($); ^{22}1879, 3s6d; ^{23}1878 (@); ^{24}1881, vii+268pp. (L); ^{25}1881; new ed. [1881] (W.J. Gage & Co.'s Educational Series), Toronto: W.J. Gage, 20cm, vii+268+xivpp. (@); ^{27}1884, London: Bell & Sons, 18cm, vii+271, 104th th., 3s6d (L O); ^{28}1885 (L O); ^{30}1887 (L O); ^{32}1890 (@); ^{36}1894, London/New York: Bell & Sons (@); ^{37}1896 ($ @); anr. ed. 1897 ($); ^{39}1898, London 18cm (O); ^{40}1901 (177th to 182nd thousand), London/New York: Bell & Sons ($ E L O)).
($ @ A C E L O)
Lit.: Anon. 1874 (on ^{18}1873).
[Very influential, with at least forty editions, frequently enlarged. Uses Becker's system as applied to English by Morell; well ordered, succinct and with usually adequate definitions. The 21st edition partly diverged from Becker, being now based on Mätzner and Koch. The book is a serious attempt at a structural description of English, using parallels from Latin and Old English evidence (only) where helpful to explain PDE structures; quite dense and certainly not a learner's grammar.]

1181. ---. [1861]. *First steps in English grammar for junior classes.* London: Walton & Maberly. 14x9, 88pp., 1s9d. (Rev. and enl. ed. 1876, 24th thousand, London: G. Bell & Sons, 14cm, 94pp. (@); price in 1882: 1s; anr. ed. 1883).
(@ E L)
[A succinct account of the nine parts of speech and of syntax based on his larger grammar, with elementary definitions "together with so much Syntax as is necessary for parsing an ordinary sentence". Plentiful exercises at end (70-88). Quite a successful abridgment.]

1182. ---. 1872a. *First notions of grammar for young learners*. London: Bell & Daldy. 16x10, iii+44pp., 9d. (Anr. ed. 1878, 7th thousand, London: G. Bell, 16cm, 44pp. (@); anr. ed. 1884, iv+120pp.; price in 1882: 8d; ^{6}1885, London: Bell, 120pp. (@); in total at least nineteen editions to 1899).
(@ E L)
[Chatty; confined to parts of speech; uses blanks. "not a complete grammar, even in outline [...] a perfectly simple and familiar style has been adopted" "designed to render the first principles of the science intelligible to young beginners, without perplexing them with the difficult terms and definitions of systematic grammar" (1872b: iii). The author sees this procedure as laying foundations for a systematic grammar at a later stage.]

1183. ---. 1872b. *Outlines of English grammar for the use of junior classes*. London: Bell & Daldy. 16.5x10, vi+126pp. (^{5}1878, London: Bell, (@); ^{6}1879, 1s6d (@); ^{7}1880, London, 17cm, viii+168pp.; ^{10}1883; ^{11}1884, 48th th., London, 2s (@); ^{12}1885; ^{20}1897, London/New York: Bell & Sons, viii+172pp.).
(@ E L O)
["Modified and enlarged edition of the author's *First steps in English grammar* ... reduced to regular form, and presented in orderly sequence" (cf. no. 1181). Mainly ES, with carefully chosen exercises, pp. 76-100, and an appendix on derivation/roots.]

1184. ---. 1879a. *A shorter English grammar with copious and carefully graduated exercises*. London: G. Bell. 18x12, xii+243pp. 3s6d. (^{2}1880, London: Bell & Sons, xii+253pp., 2s; ^{4}1884, 21st th., London: Bell, 3s6d, 18cm, xii+254pp.; ^{5}1886; ^{8}1890; ^{12}1898; ^{13}1899, London/New York: George Bell & Sons, xii+254pp.).
(L O)
[An expansion of his *Outlines* (no. 1183) most of which it incorporates. One of Mason's major grammars which advances through pronunciation/spelling through Etymology (parts of speech) to syntax.]

1185. ---. 1879b. *English grammar exercises*. (Miller & Co.'s Educational Series). n.p. iv+[7]-243pp.
($)

1186. ---. 1879c. *English grammar practice*. (A section of his *Shorter English Grammar*). London: Bell & Sons. 18x12, vi+68pp. (^{2}1884, London, 68pp. (@)).
($ @ E L O)
[Reprint of the exercises appended to *A shorter English grammar* (cf. no. 1184); to be used with any good text book.]

1187. ---. [1881]. *Essential memoranda of English grammar. Compiled ... from Mr. Mason's Shorter grammar [by W. B. A.]*. London: Relfe Bros.
(L)

1188. ---. [1883-84]. *Code standard English grammar*. 4 parts. n.p. Part I for Standard II, 2d. (Anr. ed. 1898, London/New York: George Bell & Sons, 5 parts (L)).
(L)

[Based on *First Notions* (no. 1182), "rewritten and adapted to the requirements of the successive Standards of the New Code for Elementary Schools", as explained: I = Nouns and Verbs, II = remaining parts of speech, III = recapitulation and parsing, IV = Elementary manual for grammatical analysis.]

1189. ---. 1888. *Practice and help in the analysis of sentences*. London: Bell. xii+130pp.
(E L)

[Elaborate and exhaustive treatment of sentence and clause analysis: "Few intellectual exercises are more delightful than the disentanglement of a hard and intricate passage."]

1190. Matheson, John. 1819. *The theory and practice of English grammar; adapted to the new modes of instruction, in which every rule and observation in syntax is elucidated by various examples; also, remarks on punctuation, prosody, rhetoric and composition*. London: Baldwin, Cradock & Joy. ii+138pp. (^{2}1821).
(A L *Br*, *Hu*, *Lw*, *Ma*)

[OES, followed by exercises, punctuation, prosody, rhetoric and composition; very succinct rules, generally competent, with exemplifications; partly in Q/A form.]

1191. Mathews, Edward & Emma. 1853. *Catechism of English grammar*. (Popular Catechisms, 8). London. 15cm. (E L). (Anr. ed. 1874, as *New and revised issue of the popular catechisms, English grammar*, 25th thous., London: Houlston, 16x10, 28pp., 2d. (O)).
(E L O)

[OESP in traditional Q/A style. This is no 7. of eight catechisms produced by the authors.]

1192.$ Mathews, Harriet. 1892. *Outlines of English grammar with continuous selections for practice*. Boston, Mass.: Heath & Co. 18.5x13, xvii+250pp.
($ @ L)

[Literary (patriotic) excerpts used for sentence analysis and the explanation of parts of speech. Definitions, specimens of blackboard work, and lessons to each chapter. Few terms, intended for early primary language teaching; aims at presenting "the truths of the subject in a definite and logical order and by a method in harmony with the psychological principles of teaching". Attempting to be innovative with moderate success: the style is often cramped and the arrangement not easy to follow - in spite of long "suggestions to the teacher" providing detailed school-room strategies.]

1193. entry deleted

1194.! ---. [c1825]. *The miniature English grammar*. London. 96pp.
(*Tm*, 27)
[A revised form of the grammar was included in Maunder's *The treasury of knowledge*, 1830, of which there were many editions to 1869. Cf. no. 1197.]

1195. ---. 1836. *The little linguist or, a complete guide to English philology, comprising a grammar in miniature, with all the rules of syntax; verbal distinctions, etc., and numerous English examples. The whole designed to promote a habit of perspicuity in speaking and writing the language.* London: George Nodes. (*Tm*, 20). (Anr. ed. 1838 (@); later ed. 1846 (*Lw*); anr. ed. 1847 (*Tm*, 37)).
(@ Lw Tm)

1196.! ---. 1839. *The practical English Linguæduct; Part 2, A short and comprehensive grammar*. n.p.
(Hu, Lw)
[An improvement of the original from which was extracted the compendium for Maunder's anonymous *The treasury of knowledge*. Cf. no. 1197.]

1197. Maunder, Samuel (1785-1849). 1830. *Maunder's treasury of knowledge, and library of reference. Contents. - Pt.I: A new and enlarged dictionary of the English language ... preceded by a compendium of English grammar [etc] - Pt.II: A new universal gazetteer ... A compendious classical dictionary ... a chronological analysis of general history, a dictionary of law terms, and various useful addenda ...* [published anonymously]. 2 parts. London. 16x10. (^{2}1830, London: S. Maunder (@); ^{3}1831, New York, 12mo, prefixed grammar: 22pp. ($ @ *Br*); anr. ed. 1833 ($); ^{8}1836 ($ @); ^{12}1840 ($ @); anr. ed. 1843 ($); rev. and enl. ed. ^{17}1847, London: Longman, Brown, Green & Longmans (@); ^{18}1848 (@); anr. ed. 1850, New York, prefixed grammar: 7-32pp. ($ L); anr. ed. 1851 ($); $^{19+20}$1853, 10s ($ @); ^{21}1854; anr. ed. 1855, New York ($ @ L); anr. ed. 1862, 899pp. ($); new ed. 1866, rev. throughout by J. Morris ... and W. Hughes, London: Longmans, Green & Co. (@); new ed. 1873, rev. throughout by B.B. Woodward assisted by John Morris ... and W. Hughes, London: Longmans & Green & Co. (@)).

($ @ L Lw *Br*)
[The prefixed grammar of 20pp. in 1830 (*Br*) is a very succinct description in form of definitions and brief examples; OESP; of no independent value. The other brief grammars by Maunder are likely to be largely identical with this text. Cf. nos. 1194, 1196.]

1198. Mavor, William Fordyce (1758-1837). 1820. *English grammar. Catechism of English grammar, in four parts, with exercises in grammatical resolution and in false syntax and orthography*. London. 18mo, 70pp.
(C *Br*)

1199. ---. [186-]. *Mavor's first book for children, intended as an introduction to a correct knowledge of the English language*. [London]: The Booksellers. 22cm, 16pp.

1200.$ Maxwell, William Henry (Superintendent of Public Instruction, Brooklyn, N.Y., 1852-1920). 1886. *Primary lessons in language and composition*. (Maxwell's English Series). New York: American Book Co. 19cm, 2 v.
($)

1201.$ ---. 1888a. *Advanced lessons in English grammar: for use in higher grammar classes*. New York/Chicago: A.S. Barnes & Co. 20cm, x+151pp. (@). (Anr. ed. 1891 (Maxwell's English Series 3), New York/Cincinnati: American Book Company, 18.5x12.5, 334pp; anr. ed. 1891 ($)).
($ @ O)
[Starts with Part I on "The sentence" (functions, analysis) before continuing with the traditional pattern: OESP, with a history of the English language and a chapter on style added. Otherwise quite traditional for the date of publication, exhausting and often not particularly clear.]

1202.$ ---. 1888b. *Introductory lessons in English grammar: for use in lower grammar grades*. (Maxwell's English Series 3). New York/Cincinnati. 19/20cm, x+151pp.
($)

1203.$ ---. 1894a. *Introductory lessons in English grammar for use in intermediate grades*. (Maxwell's English Series 2). New York/Cincinnati: American Book Company. 19/20cm, iv+172pp.
($)

1204.$ ---. 1894b. *First book in English*. (Maxwell's English Series). New York/Cincinnati: American Book Company. 19cm, iv+172pp.
($)

1205. Mayo, Robert (1784-1864). 1818. *English elements*. n.p. 72pp.
($)

1206. entry deleted

1207. entry deleted
1208. entry deleted
1209.$ Mead, Irene M. 1896. *The English language and its grammar.* New York/Boston: Silver, Burdett & Co. 19cm, 265pp. (Anr. ed. 1899, New York, 19cm, 177pp. ($ @)).
($ @)
1210. Meiklejohn, John Miller Dow (Professor of Education, University of St Andrews, 1830-1902). 1862-66. *An easy English grammar for beginners; being a plain doctrine of words and sentences.* (Herbert Series of Short School Books). 4 parts. Manchester/London. 1s6d each. (1862, I: *Of words and their changes*, London: A. Ireland, iv+58pp.; 1862, II: *Of sentences, words and their growth*, London: Simpkin & Marshall, 60pp.; 1864, III: *Of the verb, syntax and parsing*, London: Simpkin & Marshall, ii+60pp.; 1866, IV: *Of complex sentences, and the history of the language*, London: Simpkin & Marshall, 73pp.).
(L O)
[On part I: Contains what "can be learned by a child of average capacity, in five months"; exercises to be done before the text is read. Discusses the limits of grammatical explanation in "Notice to teachers", I, ii-iii. In very simple language, but quite competently and attractively presented. Definitions followed by exercises, 32-58; (on part II) Analysis of simple sentences; relationships of words; exercises 46-60.; (on part III: exercises 50-60; (on part IV) attractively presented step by step. With exercises on pp.37-62. Even though the distribution of the material in four small volumes is awkward, together they represent a serious attempt at presenting with a radical air grammatical knowledge in an easy and coherent form.]
1211. ---. 1866a. *An easy English grammar in four parts. Being a complete course of etymology, syntax and analysis. With four hundred exercises.* (Herbert Series of School Book). London: Simpkin, Marshall, etc. 4 books in 1 vol. 17cm. (^{5}1877 (Herbert Series of School Books), London: Simpkin, Marshall, 17cm (@); ^{7}1880 (Herbert Series of School Books), London: Simpkin, Marshall, 17cm (@)).
(@)
1212. ---. 1866b. *Primary school grammar, for the use of public and national schools, with two hundred and thirty-one exercises.* London: Simpkin, Marshall etc. 16cm, iv+74+60pp. (Running title: *Easy English Grammar*).
(@)
1213. ---. [1877]. *The book of the English language.* (Stewart's Local Exam. Series). London: W. Stewart. 128pp. (Anr. ed. 1891).

(L)
[Strictly historical-comparative; vocabulary, morphology.]
1214. ---. 1880-c.82?. *The standard English grammar, Books 1-3*. (Chambers's Educational Course). London/Edinburgh: Chambers. 128pp. (*Book III, adapted to Standard IV.* pp.81-128. = 48pages (O)).
(L O)
[The preceding sections (Books I & II) devoted to nouns, verbs, adjectives, adverbs and pronouns are advertised on the back cover. This section (Book III) on joining words, syntax and preparation for parsing completes the course.]
1215. entry deleted
1216. ---. 1886. *A new grammar of the English tongue. With chapters on composition, versification, paraphrasing, and punctuation*. London/Edinburgh: William Blackwood & Sons. 20/21cm. (= Parts 1 & 2 of his *The English language: its grammar, history and literature: with chapters on composition, versification, paraphrasing, and punctuation*. London/Edinburgh: William Blackwood & Sons. 20/21cm, viii+388pp.). (New ed. 1887, Boston/New York: D.C. Heath & Co. ($ @) / London/Edinburgh: William Blackwood & Sons, 20cm, iv+252pp. (L); anr. ed. 1888, London: Blackwood & Sons ($ @); anr. ed. 1889 ($); anr. ed. 1890, Boston: D.C. Heath & Co. ($ @); anr. ed. 1891 ($); anr. ed. 1892 (from 1887 ed.), vi+271-461pp. ($ @); anr. ed. 1893 ($); anr. ed. 1894, ii+[3]-268pp. ($); [12]1895, London: Alfred M. Holden; anr. ed. 1896 (from 1887 ed.) 289pp. ($); [14]1896, enl. with exercises and additional analysis, London: A.M. Holden, iv+268pp. (@); anr. ed. 1897 ($); anr. ed. 1897 (from 1887 ed.), 20cm ($); [10]1898 (H); [18]1898, Boston: D.C. Heath (@); [17]1899, enl. with exercises and additional analysis, Toronto: W.J. Gage & Co., 268pp. (@)). (Also published separately: Part 3: *A short history of the English language*, Part 4: *An outline history of English literature*). 5th ed. = 4s6d.
Key London 1894, 19cm (L O).
($ @ L O)
[The author claims: "The study of English Grammar is becoming every day more historical and necessarily so."]
1217. ---. 1887. *English grammar with chapters on composition, versification, paraphrasing, and punctuation*. n.p. iv+268pp. (Anr. ed. 1889, Boston: D.C. Heath & Co. (@); anr. ed. 1891, 20cm, viii+252pp. ($); anr. ed. 1892 ($); anr. ed. 1894 (@)).
($ @)
1218. ---. 1888. *Exercises and examination papers to accompany Professor Meiklejohn's New Grammar of the English Tongue*. London etc. 19cm.

(O)
1219. ---. 1890. *A short grammar of the English tongue with three hundred and thirty exercises*. (Professor Meiklejohn's Series). London: Simpkin & Marshall. 18x12, iv+176pp., 1s. (Anr. ed. 1891 (W.J. Gage & Co.'s Educational Series) ($); anr. ed. 1895, London: A.M. Holden ($); ^{10}1899 (@); at least 23 editions).
($ @ L O)
[Six parts of speech (adjective, noun, preposition; adverb, verb, conjunction) described and their divisions, changes, and rules explained; Meiklejohn then turns to the 'building-up' and analysis of sentences, and the grammar of rhythmic speech or verse. Stresses the syntagmatic aspect; simple definitions, plenty of exercises. Some fanciful etymologies (p. 98: suffix **m** illustrated by *game* derived from *go*, etc.)]

1220. ---. 1895. *Fifty new lessons in English grammar, being a method of historical parsing*. London: A.M. Holden. 20cm, 102pp., 1s6d.
(@ L)
[An attack on Latinate forms of parsing and on "a new kind of grammatical drill [which] about thirty years ago ... appeared from Germany". "Parsing put the English language into a strait jacket; and then Analysis came and added to it the torture of the boot."]

1221. Meilan, Rev. Mark Anthony (b. ca. 1743). 1803. *An introduction to the English language; with an appendix, containing five hundred violations of grammar, extracted from many of our best writers, and here corrected: to which are added, instances of false figures, and other anomalies of style; with reasonings on them*. 2 vols. London: the author. 18cm, I: xx+216pp., II: iv+132pp.
($ A L *Br*, *Hu*, *Lw*)
[Vol 1 is a traditional grammar (ten parts of speech), the text to be learnt by heart, but accompanied by critical notes. Vol 2 is a collection of errors from "the best writers", with corrections. Rather pedantic, but thoughtful.]

1222. Mendenhall, William (1778-1853). 1813. *The classification of words; or, The English youth's first step in the study of language; but more particularly in the grammar of his own*. Bath: the author. (Anr. ed. 1814, Philadelphia, 19cm, 36pp. ($ *Br*)).
($ G *Br*)
[Sentence structure taught through cumulative additions to a basic phrase. Elementary but sensible.]

1223.$! Merchant, Aaron M. 1824. *Murray's small grammar, enlarged*. New York. 18mo, 216pp.
(*Br*)

1224.$ ---. 1828. *The American school grammar of the English language: simplified and improved: comprising rules and exercises in orthography, syntax and punctuation principally selected from Murray: arranged in natural order and suited to the capacities of learners. Designed for the use of schools and academies in the United States.* New York: J.C. Totten. 15cm, vi+[7]-216pp.
($)

1225.$ Meredith, L.P. 1872. *Every-day errors of speech.* Philadelphia: J.B. Lippincott & Co. (@). (Anr. ed. 1873, Philadelphia: J.B. Lippincott & Co. (@); anr. ed. 1874, Philadelphia: J.B. Lippincott; anr. ed. 1876 (@); anr. ed. 1877, rev. and corr. by Rev. T.H.L. Leary, London: W. Tegg, 144pp. (@); anr. ed. 1877, Philadelphia: Lippincott & Co., 17cm, viii+[9]-96pp.; anr. ed. 1882 (@); anr. ed. 1890 (@)).
(@)

1226.! Merrick, Harriot. 1820. *An easy introduction to English grammar; for children under 8 years.* London.
(*Hu, Lw*)

1227.$ Metcalf, Robert Comfort & Orville T. Bright. 1889. *Language exercises.* (Metcalf's Language Series). New York/Chicago: Ivison, Blakeman & Co. 19cm, vi+223pp. (Anr. ed. 1894-96, New York/Chicago: American Book Company (@)).
($ @)
["A rearrangement of the lessons in Metcalf's and Bright's Language exercises." - Preface.]

1228.$ --- & ---. 1895. *Elementary English.* New York/Cincinnati: American Book Co. 20cm, 200pp.
($ @)

1229.$ Metcalf, Robert Comfort & Thomas Metcalf. 1894. *English grammar for common schools.* New York/Cincinnati: American Book Co. 19/20cm, 288pp.
($ @)

1230. Meyrick, Frederick (Rector of Blickling, Prebendary of Lincoln; (...) for ten years Her Majesty's Inspector of Schools). [1873]. *An English grammar for the use of learners.* London etc.: Cassell, Petter & Galpin. 16x10, viii+154pp., 1s6d.
(L O)
[Letters and syllables, words (nine parts of speech), syntax and construction and analysis of sentences; definitions and observations often burdened with learned remarks and comparisons with Latin: form and function not clearly separated (as in 'case', or in the eight 'tenses', indefinite present, strict present, imperfect, indefinite past or aorist,

definite past or perfect, pluperfect, simple future, future perfect). The author's attempt "to supply the deficiency in regard to Grammars" which he found as a Her Majesty's Inspector of Schools is not convincing.]

1231. Millar, James (English Master, Edinburgh Ladies Institution, Park Place. Rev., of Cumberland). 1855. *Outlines of English grammar; arranged for being taught on the intellectual system.* Edinburgh: Sutherland & Knox. 14x9, 35pp.
(O L)
["The Reasoning Powers, rather than the Memory of the Pupil to be exercised" - rules, then, not to be memorized. Quite well-done minimal grammar, as to definitions and examples; ES only (with parsing).]

1232. Millard, J.B. [1872?]. *John Heywood's grammatical copy books. Being a series of copy books on English grammar, designed for the use of the upper classes of schools.* No. 1-12. Manchester: J. Heywood / London: Simpkin & Marshall & Co. 16x20. (The series includes [1869] *The grammatical copybook, No. 1*; [1870] *Mood, tense, number, and person (Grammatical copy book No. 4)*, [1870] *Adjectives, with their degrees of comparison (Grammatical copybook No. 6)*).
(@ C)

1233. Millard, John (Professor). 1869. *Grammar of elocution.* London. 18cm, xxii+216pp. (Anr. ed. 1882, London: Longmans, Green & Co. ($); ^{3}1884, London (@); ^{5}1889, London/New York: Longmans, Green (@)).
($ @)

1234.! Millen, Ebenezer (George Square Academy, Glasgow). [a1870]. *Exercises on English grammar.* n.p.
[Advertised in 1870.]

1235. Millen, John (Teacher of English, George Square, Glasgow). 1846. *An initiatory grammar of the English language with numerous exercises.* (Glasgow)/Edinburgh: Oliver Boyd. 14cm, 126pp., 1s. (Anr. ed. 1850; anr. ed. 1857).
(L O *Hu*, *Lw*)
[Professes no originality. Emphasises "the formation of one part of speech from another."]

1236.$ Miller, Ferdinand H. 1843. *The ready grammarian: to abridge labor, refresh the memory and prepare classes for thorough instruction: arranged expressly for the benefit of both teachers and students.* Ithaca, N.Y.: Square. 16cm, 24pp. (^{3}1844, Rochester: D. Hoyt, 17cm, 32pp. ($).
($ @ *Br*)
[On cover: The ready grammarian: or, A familiar friend in a new dress]

1237.$ ---. ⁴1845. *The oral grammar, or ready grammarian: to abridge labor, refresh the memory and prepare classes for thorough instruction; arranged expressly for the benefit of both teachers and students.* Dansville, N.Y.: A.R. Know & F.H. Miller. 16cm, vi+[7]-128pp.
($ @)

1238.$ Miller, George Benjamin (1795-1869). 1842. *The Dansville grammar: being an attempt to render the study of grammar more effectual, more easy, and more satisfactory than by the usual method.* Dansville?. 18cm, 70pp.
($)

1239.$ Miller, John Ornsby (1861-1936). 1898. *Analysis, parsing and supplementary reading.* n.p. 72+[1]pp.
($)

1240. Miller, The Misses (of the Preparatory Boarding School, Brighton). 1830. *The Brighton English grammar.* London: Longman, Rees, Orme, Brown & Green. 14.5x9, 63pp.
(G L O *Br*)
[Based on the method of Morgan's *Questions on the Eton Latin grammar*. Nothing unusual except for the opening sentence: "The subject of Grammar is sentences." Simple definitions, with exercises interspersed to check whether the preceding passages have been properly learnt; OESP plus punctuation; nine parts of speech, six tenses.]

1241.$! Miller, Tobias Ham. 1823. *Murray's abridgement with questions.* Portsmouth, N.H. 12mo, 76pp.
(*Br*)

1242. Milligan, George. 1831. *A catechism of English grammar; with select exercises.* Edinburgh: Oliver & Boyd. 18mo, 74pp. (²1839, Edinburgh, 14cm, 72pp. (@)).
(@ L *Br*)
[On cover: Oliver & Boyd's catechism of elementary knowledge. Traditional, in Q/A form, parts of speech and syntax.]

1243.! Anon. 1813. *A miscellaneous selection of ungrammatical sentences from various authors: in order to exercise the ingenuity of young persons in applying the rules of English grammar.* n.p.
(*Tm*)
[89 pages of quotations.]

1244. Mitchell, J. 1859. *A manual of punctuation for self-teaching and for schools. By a practical printer.* (Publ. anon.). Manchester.
(@ C E L)

1245. Moffatt, William (Publisher). [1880]. *Outlines of grammar*. 96pp. ([1887] reissued as *Moffatt's English grammar, analysis and parsing. With exercises*, London: Moffatt & Paige, 18x12, 152pp., 1s6d.).
(L O)
[OESP, with Etymology including the history of English and the provenance of its vocabulary. Short definitions, usually adequate; the style is as nontechnical as can be justified; "faulty expressions" and "exercises" at end.]

1246. Mongan, James Roscoe. 1864a. *The practical English grammar, comprising also an analysis of sentences; composition, etc*. London: Longman, Green, Longman, Roberts & Green. 17x10.5, viii+[9]-292pp., 3s6d. (Ster. ed. 1866, London: Longmans, Green, Reader & Dyer (@)).
(@ G L O)
[Mongan, a very prolific editor of Greek and Latin classical authors, appears to have done his two grammars as a by-product. "Competitive examinations" have, so the author, led to a demand for "a more accurate and scientific Grammar of the English language" (rather than "such defective compilations as those of Lindley Murray"). Mongan has "freely drawn" on the works of Priestley, Lowth, Ash, Harrison, Hazlitt, Murray, Knowles, Rothwell, W. Angus, W. Allen, Grant and Lennie, and explicitly thanks Trench, Latham, Craik, Crombie, Adams, Rogers, Morell, Marsh, Key, Brown, D'Orsey, Fowler, Reid, Connon, Wilson, Hunter, Lowres, Martin and Angus for their advice. ES, Punctuation, P; descriptive aims based on usage. Nine parts of speech; etymology includes inflexion, word-formation and provenance. A clear exposition of traditional knowledge, but stressing the independence of English; short definitions, with observations and footnotes in small print. Appendixes on style, composition and official documents.]

1247. ---. 1864b. *An abridgment of The Practical English grammar*. London. 14x9, xii+[13]-212pp.
(L O)
[A skilful condensation of his larger work which retains its structure and most relevant information.]

1248. Moody, T. (Principal of Charlton Adam Academy, Somerton). [1857]. *A catechism of English grammar, on an entirely new and improved principle*. London: Judd & Glass, pr. in South Petherton. 14x9, 84pp.
(E L O)
["An enlargement of the author's former sketch of English Grammar" (which appears not to be extant); "in form of familiar dialogue to render the study of Grammar interesting and attractive". Sounds, syllables,

words, parsing, syntax discussed in Q/A form in informal terms; with exercises.]

1249. Morell, John Daniel (1816-1891). [1852]. *The analysis of sentences explained and systematised: with an exposition of the fundamental laws of syntax. After the plan of Becker's German grammar.* London: Theobald. 21cm, 75pp. (@). (Anr. ed. 1853, London: Theobald, 20cm, viii+103pp. ($); anr. ed. 1854 ($); ^{9}1858, rev. and furnished with illustrative exercises, London (@); anr. ed. 1876, London: Longmans, Green & Co. (@); anr. ed. 1891, London: R. Theobald, 21cm, 75pp. ($ @)).
($ @ C Dt E L O)
[Interesting sketch of traditional/structuralist methods transcending parsing. Important pedagogically, because the rigidities of sentence analysis derive from it; relevant for anyone studying the influence of Becker.]

1250. ---. [1854]. *The essentials of English grammar: and analysis.* London. First published in two parts: I: 16cm, 18pp., 2d. II: 12cm, 27pp., 3d. (^{2}[1855], London 16cm, 56pp. ($); ^{4}1858; new ed. 1868, London: Longmans, Green & Co., 17cm, iv+[5]-64pp. (@); editions to [c1891]).
(@ E L O)
[Describes three different methods of parsing.]

1251. ---. 1857a. *A grammar of the English language, together with an exposition of the analysis of sentences.* (Constable's Educational Series). Edinburgh: Thomas Constable. 18/20cm, viii+118pp. (Anr. ed. 1860, Edinburgh (@); anr. ed. 1862 (from the last Edinburgh ed.), New York: J.F. Trow / Toronto: Rollo & Adam (@); anr. ed. 1863, Edinburgh; anr. ed. 1864, Edinburgh ($); anr. ed. 1865, London; new ed. 1866, with his *A series of graduated exercises, adapted to Morell's grammar and analysis*, London: Longman, Green & Co., 19cm , 124pp. ($ @); anr. ed. 1873, New York: Wilbour, 61pp. (@); anr. ed. [1873], rev. by A.G. Palmer, as *Morell's grammar simplified*; anr. ed. 1893, rev. by P.A. Barnett, as *The new Morell*, London: Allman & Son, viii+256pp.).
(@ C L O Lw)
Lit.: Anon. 1874 (on ?1870).
[Based on Latin patterns, but with an attempt "to make the treatment of grammar logical". The interrelationship of the editions, and the question whether Barnett's and Palmer's revisions should count as independent entries, need further investigation.]

1252. ---. 1857b. *A series of graduated exercises, adapted to Morell's Grammar and analysis.* (Constable's Educational Series). Edinburgh: T. Constable. 19cm, viii+[9]-63pp. (Anr. ed. 1860, Edinburgh; anr. ed. 1864 ($); new ed. 1875, London: Longmans, Green & Co. (@)).

Key by W.B. Morgan published in 1870. (4s).
($ @ L)

1253. ---. 1866. *A series of graduated exercises, adapted to Morell's grammar and analysis.* New ed. London: Longmans, Green & Co. 19cm, viii+ [9]-63+[1]pp.
(@)
[Same book as no. 1252?]

1254. ---. [c. 1870]. *A complete key to the graduated exercises adapted to Morell's grammar and analysis.* New ed. London: W. Stewart & Co. / Edinburgh: J. Menzies & Co. 19cm, vi+[7]-152pp.
(@)

1255. ---. 1871. *The first step in grammar.* London: Longmans, Green & Co. 17x10.5, 40pp. (Anr. ed. 1875, London: Longmans, Green & Co., 18cm, 40pp. (@)).
(@ L)
[Intentionally naive description leads to various questionable statements; concentrates on the eight parts of speech, followed by one page on syntax and 71 exercises.]

1256.$ Morey, Amos C. 1829. *A system of English grammar: explaining the principles and structure of the English language. For the use of schools.* Albany, N.Y.: G.J. Loomis. 17cm, 106pp. (Anr. ed. 1829, 16cm, iv+[5]-198pp. ($)).
($ Br)

1257.$ Morgan, Jonathan Jr. (1777-1871). 1814. *Elements of English grammar, with a postscript, analysis and appendix.* Hallowell, Me. 12mo, 405pp. (Anr. ed. 1814, Hallowell, Me.: Goodale & Burton, 18cm, [284]pp. ($); rev. and corr. ed. ^{2}1844, Portland, Me.: Thurston, Ilsley & Co., 20cm, vi+[7]-180pp. ($)).
($ @ L Br).
["Praises the 'neglected Webster'". The relationship of the editions has to be investigated: note the widely divergent numbers of pages.]

1258. Morgan, William Browning (Head Master of the Cathedral School, Bristol). 1872. *The learner's companion to Morell's grammar and analysis; comprising the substance of the author's oral instruction on the books; with hints and devices for determining the various kinds of words, phrases, and sentences required to be known for working out the exercises appended to Dr. Morell's treatise.* London: Longmans, Green, & Co. 19cm, 48pp., 6d.
(O L)
[Purely derivative, with references to Morell "to be used conjointly with it". Also by Morgan [c1875]: *The key to Morell's grammar and analysis.*

London: Longman, Green & Co. 12mo, 4s. (L). Same book as no. 1253?]

1259. ---. 1875a. *The code grammar series of the English language. For the pupils of elementary schools.* Pt. 2 and 3. London: W. Stewart. II: 17x11, 23pp., 2d. III: 17x11, 63pp., 4d.
(L)
[On II: "The CGS has been prepared expressly to suit the requirements of the CODE for 1875". The noun (more fully treated in I), verb and adjective are defined, with explanations, examples and exercises; somewhat longwinded in parts. On III: OES, "a complete manual of grammar up to ... parsing", with seventy exercises; attempts at logical definitions. Eight parts of speech; contents and definitions (not always adequate) determined by use in class, the pattern influenced by Morell's *Grammar*.]

1260. ---. 1875b. *The training examiner in grammar and the analysis of sentences. For the use of teachers, pupils, and private students. Supplemented by test papers framed on the models of those set by the university local examiners.* London: Longmans, Green & Co. 17cm, 4d. *Key* (1875), supplemented by a second course "comprising over 900 questions". London: Longman, Green & Co. 17x10.5, 30pp., 1s.
(@ L)
[Questions and exercises to control pupils' progress in grammar, accompanied by *Key*.]

1261.$ Morison, Nathaniel Holmes (1815-1890). 1867. *A school manual: prepared for the use of his pupils.* n.p. 20cm, 188pp.
($)

1262.$! Morley, Charles. 1836. *School grammar.* (With cuts). Hartford, Ct. 12mo, 86pp.
(*Br*)

1263.$ Morris, Isaiah J. 1850. *A new and philosophical grammar of the English language, in which words are classified according to their meaning and use.* La Fayette, Ala., Montgomery: J.H. & T.F. Martin. 15cm, viii+126pp.
(@)

1264.$ ---. 1857a. *Morris's grammar. A philosophical and practical grammar of the English language, dialogically and progressively arranged; in which every word is parsed according to its use.* (Ster. and rev. ed.). New York. 19cm, xx+192pp. (Anr. ed. 1858 ($); anr. ed. 1860 ($); anr. ed. 1868 ($)).
($ L)

1265.$ ---. 1857b. *Scrapbook.* n.p.

($)
1266. Morris, Richard (LL.D., 1833-1894). 1875. *English grammar.* (Literature Primers). London: Macmillan. 15/16cm, viii+115/18pp. (Anr. ed. 1875 ($); anr. ed. 1876 ($); anr. ed. 1878 ($); anr. ed. 1879 ($); anr. ed. 1881 ($); anr. ed. 1886 ($); anr. ed. 1893 (from 1886 ed.) ($); repr. ^{2}1896, London/New York: Macmillan & Co.; ^{3}1897, rev. by Henry Bradley, London).
($ H L O)
[Very elementary presentation under scholarly control.]

1267. --- & Herbert Courthope Bowen. 1878. *English grammar exercises.* (Literature Primers). London: Macmillan & Co. 15x10, 107pp. (Anr. ed. 1880 ($); anr. ed. 1881, viii+118pp. ($); anr. ed. 1890 ($)).
($ @ L O)
[Inductive method advised to make pupils see what they know; eight parts of speech individually discussed as parts of a sentence. Exercises are "intended to be used with Dr. Morris's "English Grammar Primer". Rules and definitions are formulated in a leisurely way and are occasionally accompanied by didactic directions to the teacher; there are extensive exercises. Short chapters on Word-making and Syntax/Parsing at the end.]

1268. Morrison, Thomas (LL.D., Rector of the Free Church Normal School, Glasgow). 1856. *An initiatory English grammar for junior classes.* (Nelson's School Series). London: Nelson. 12°. (Anr. ed. 1872, 17x11, v+72pp. (O)).
(L O)
[Classification of words, subdivision of the parts of speech (eight, no article) and Inflection, with Rules of Syntax appended; condensed from his larger grammar.]

1269. ---. 1872. *An English grammar for the use of schools.* London: Nelson. 17.5x11, viii+150pp. (Anr. ed. 1877 ($); anr. ed. 1878 ($); anr. ed. 1895 ($)).
($ L O)
[Classification, Subdivision of parts of speech, Inflection, Syntax (= Concord, Government, Usage), Analysis of Sentences and Punctuation in a series of lessons; no definitions since "The child is taught to form the Definition from examples given" (appendix with a great deal of help from the teacher). Sentence analysis, he says, was neglected, then made into a kind of drill, now there is a danger that it will be neglected. Nine American eds. to 1888, at least four further editions to 1898.]

1270. ---. 1873. *Advanced English grammar for use in schools and colleges. With numerous exercises, systematically arranged, consisting of extracts*

from standard authors. (Collins' School Series). London/Glasgow: William Collins. 17x11.5, 200pp. (Anr. ed. 1878, London/Glasgow: William Collins. (C O)).
(C O)
["... For use mainly in the Higher classes of the Public and Private Schools, where the elements of Grammar may be supposed to have been acquired". "[...] in no text book [...] so many elegant extracts from standard English writers". OESP, with separate parts for "Analysis of sentences" and "Figures of speech" inserted after "Syntax". Eight parts of speech, traditional account, with clear definitions, tables, and exercises (some on bad English) interspersed. Latinate features include "dative and vocative case" and Syntax = Concord and Government, whereas other parts are separated off as "Analysis of Sentences". Nine Tenses: complete tenses (*I have risen*) vs. incomplete (*I am rising*) - *I have been rising* not mentioned.]

1271. ---. 1882a. *English grammar for standards 2-7.* (British School Series). 6 parts. London etc. 16cm.
(L O)

1272. ---. 1882b. *Complete English grammar for the use of schools.* (British School Series). London/Edinburgh: Gall & Inglis. 16.5x10.5, iv+124pp.
(O)
[Traditional account of OES plus analysis of sentences; brief definitions (generally competent) interspersed with exercises and notes; unexciting.]

1273. Mosse, Mr. 1814. *Enclytica; being outlines of a course of instruction on the principles of universal grammar: as deduced in an analysis of the vernacular tongue.* (publ. anon.; Gale & Curtis, eds.). London: John Booth. 21.5x13, vii+133pp. + tables.
(A $ L O *Br, Hu*)
[The author (identified as 'Mr Mosse' in the B.L. copy) reflects on linguistic categories, drawing in the history of English and other Indo-European languages. The argument is discursive, not well ordered and sometimes marred by errors and speculation.]

1274. Mudie, George (Formerly editor of *The Sun* newspaper). [1841]. *The grammar of the English language truly made easy and amusing, by the invention of three hundred moveable parts of speech. For the use of schools or private families, and of adults whose knowledge of grammar may be defective, who may speedily become self-instructed, with the aid of this work.* (With cards). London: John Cleave. 14x9, xvi+[17]-130pp. +18pp. of 'movable parts'.
(G L)

[Mudie, who taught grammar at the Strand, continued his newly invented system of teaching the alphabet by a new method of grammar, lashing out against earlier authors, protesting against the ill-timed introduction of categories and terms. Rules are not to be mentioned "until the pupils have first learnt the practical *realities* of Grammar." The functions of the nine parts of speech are explained with reference to his sentence-building system in a chatty style; discursive exposition, without use of typographical distinctions, notes or exercises. The book was to be complemented by a *Philosophy of Grammar*, to deal with "Rhetorical and Written Composition" (which may not have been published).]

1275.$ Mugan, Marion Durand. 1891. *A new graded method in English grammar, letter writing and composition. Complete in one volume.* n.p. 19cm, 265pp., grammar on pp. 137-144.
($)

1276.$ --- & A.M. Hootman. 1886. *A graded method for oral instruction in English grammar.* St. Louis: Nixon-Jones. 17cm, iv+[5]-33pp.
(@)

1277.$ --- & ---. [c1889]. *The Metropolitan Business College English training course, consisting of letterwriting, composition, word-analysis, pronunciation, and graded lessons in English grammar.* Chicago: O.M. Powers.
(@)

1278. Mulligan, John (b. 1793). ¹1840?. *Exposition of the grammatical structure of the English language; being an attempt to furnish an improved method of teaching grammar. For the use of schools and colleges.* London: Simpkin, Marshall & Co. (Anr. ed. 1852, New York/London: Appleton & Co., 21/22cm, xiv+574pp. (E); anr. ed.? 1852, Belfast (O); anr. ed. 1853, New York: D. Appleton & Co. ($ @); anr. ed. 1854, Edinburgh, 19/20cm, viii+301pp. ($ O); abridged ed. 1854, New York: Ivison & Phinney, xiv+574pp. (@); anr. ed. 1857, New York: D. Appleton (@); anr. ed. 1860 (@); anr. ed. 1867 (from 1853 ed.) ($); anr. ed. 1868 (@); anr. ed. 1869 (@); anr. ed. 1871 ($); anr. ed. 1884 ($)).
($ @ E O)
[Unbearably prolix: Mulligan spends 156,000 words on "accessory" (subordinate) clauses alone. Emphasis on sentence analysis. Said by Tillearde (1855) to have introduced Becker's work into the USA.]

1279.$ Munro, Robert G. 1821. *Practical exercises in etymological and syntactical parsing: being a supplementary appendix adapted to the Abridgment of Murray's English grammar: containing general directions, examples of parsing in etymology and syntax, and the principal notes attached to the rules of syntax: with correspondent examples of false construction*. n.p. 14cm, viii+[10]-47pp.

($)

1280.$ Munsell, Hezekiah Jr. 1817. *English grammar made easy by the means of a new and improved grammatical chart calculated to assist the understanding of the pupil, and to lighten the labors of the instructor*. Bennington, Vt.: Davius Clark. 5.5x4.5.

($ @)

1281.$ ---. 1851. *A manual of practical English grammar on a new and easy plan: for schools, families and self-instructors*. (Munsell's Press, 2nd Series; vol. 16). Albany: J. Munsell. 19x11, 66pp.

($ L)

[Revised form of a treatise privately circulated; traditional OESP account summarizing the common traditional knowledge, brief rules, notes in small print, and specimens of parsing inserted.]

1282. entry deleted

1283. Murby, Thomas (b.1834). [1881]. *(Murby's) Imperial grammar and analysis. Adapted to the requirements of the Government Code of 1880*. London: Thomas Murby. 17cm, iv+142pp. (Standard III: *To Point out the Verbs, Adjectives, Adverbs, and Personal Pronouns*, pp. 17-32; Standards V and VI, pp. 65-112 = 48pp. (O)).

(L O)

[Parts of a larger scheme. Standard III: short definitions followed by exercises. Standards V & VI on analysis, punctuation, composition and exercises appended complete a course of 142 pages.]

1284.$ Murch, Ephraim M. 1874. *The child's grammar: first lessons in language*. (American Standard School Series). Louisville: J.P. Morton & Co. 18cm, 288pp.

($ @)

1285. Murison, Alexander Falconer (English Master in the Grammar School, Aberdeen, 1847-1934). 1875. *First work in English: grammar and composition taught by a comparative study of equivalent forms*. London: Longmans, Green & Co., pr. in Aberdeen. 16.5x10, xvi+352pp. (^{2}1880, London: Longmans, Green & Co. (@)).

(@ C L O)

[Detailed practical guide, with extensive exercises and examples; idiosyncratic but stimulating in non-technical language. In three parts: seven parts of speech defined and illustrated by substitutions to show how they function in phrase and sentence giving particular attention to many-worded expressions, ellipsis and pleonasm - a work of some originality, praised by Bain. It is more empirical than most texts at this level, but he does not avoid the contemporary obsession with ellipsis.]

1286.$ Murphy, John P. 1890. *Principles of English grammar. Used by the Brothers of the Christian schools.* New York: W.H. Sadler. 19/20cm, x+260pp.
($ @)

1287.$! Anon. 1822. *Murray's abridgement, "with additions".* Newhaven, Ct.: A.H. Malthy & Co. 18mo, 120pp.
(*Br*)

1288.$! Anon. 1821. *Murray's abridgement, with alterations and improvements; by a teacher of youth.* Boston: Lawson Lyon/James Loring. 18mo, 72pp.
(*Br*)

1289. Murray, Gerald. 1847. *The reformed grammar, or Philosophical test of English composition written for the assistance of teachers and satisfaction of learners.* London: the author. 18x10.5, vi+249pp., 4s. (Anr. ed. 1849, abridged by the author).
(@ C L O *Lw*)
[OES (though not so named) followed by punctuation etc. An attempt at a 'philosophical' description, with quotes from Locke, Harris' *Hermes*, Lowth, L. Murray, Horne Tooke etc. and copious annotations criticizing Crombie, Grant etc.; idiosyncratic terminology. Murray is so polemical that his negative views outweigh his attempts at being constructive. His reformed terminology for the parts of speech is almost wholly cosmetic. Not very important, except that any originality is welcome.]

1290.$ Murray, J.E. 1885. *Essential lessons in English composition, analysis, and grammar.* (Murray's Language Series, Book 1). Philadelphia: J.E. Potter & Co. 18cm, vi+[7]-226pp.
($ @)

1291.$ ---. 1886. *Advanced lessons in English: composition, analysis, and grammar.* (Murray's Language Series; 2). Philadelphia: J.E. Potter & Co. 18cm, xii+384pp.
($)

1292.$ Murray, John. 1840. *A new improved abridgment of Lindley Murray's English grammar, having the exercises incorporated: in which errors are corrected, obscurities elucidated, doubtful points settled, controverted opinions adjusted, and questions for examination superadded, with a large portion of new matter, critical and illustrative.* n.p. 15cm, 238pp.
($)

1293. Murray, L. pseud.?. [1814?]. *The young man's best companion, and book of general knowledge, containing English grammar, book-keeping,*

drawing ... general observations on gardening ... a brief sketch of naval and military affairs, an account of the various religious sects ... observations on behaviours and manners, with rules for conversation. Also a choice selection of the most useful and important receipts and the different branches of art and science. (Anr. ed. 1821, London: Thomas Kelly, vii+574pp. (L); anr. ed. 1824; anr. ed. 1828).
(@ L N O)
[The preface is dated 1814, no revision indicated in BL copy of 1821. The Grammar takes up a small section, pp. 1-37, in this encyclopedia; the treatment (traditional OESP) is not adequate even considering the context. The author refers to Murray, Lowth and Grant for further information.]

1294. Murray, Lindley (1745-1826). 1808. *An English grammar, comprehending the principles and rules of the language. Illustrated by appropriate exercises and a key to the exercises. A new edition.* 2 vols. York: Thomas Wilson & Co. 21cm. (O) (Impr. ed. of vol.I ²1809, York, 21cm (L O); ³1816, York, 2 vols., 8° (O); ⁴1819, York; impr. ed. ⁵1824, York, 2 vols., 23cm (O); ⁶1834, London: Longman, Rees, Orme, Brown, Green & Longman/Darton & Hervey / York: Wilson & Sons, 2 vols., 24cm (L); impr. ster. ed. 1833, as *Murray's English exercises: ... Being a counterpart to the English teacher*, ed. by I. Alger, Cincinnati/ Boston (L); ⁸1835; ⁴⁴1836 York (L); ⁴⁵1838 York (L); anr. ed. 1838, rev. by I. Alger, Boston (L)).
(L O *Hu, Lw*)
[This two-volume revision of Murray's most important grammar, comprising the grammar, the exercises on it, and the key to the exercises, is here included for its all-pervading influence, although the original grammar and abridgment were of course first published in 1795/1797 (cf. appendix). The editions need a great deal of sorting out, between the one-volume and two-volume editions, between British and American editions, between Murray's own books and versions bearing (and exploiting) his name; between the full grammar and Murray's abridgment of it; between Murray's abridgment and abridgments made by others.]
Lit: Tieken-Boon (1996); Reibel (1996).

1295.$ Murray, William Wright. 1828. *Murray's improved English grammar and English exercises: revised, and greatly enlarged, with additional notes, selected from the most eminent authors, and a series of new parsing lessons adapted to the rules and notes.* n.p. 15cm, iii+292pp.
($)

1296.$ Musser, W.J. 1892. *Plain English: a practical work on the English language for use in the Washington Business College, Washington, Penn'a.* n.p. 21cm, viii+222+[2]pp.
($)
1297. Muston, Charles. 1813. *Grammatical questions on the English grammar.* London.
(G)
1298. Mylne, Rev. Dr. Andrew (1775?-1856). [1811]. *An epitome of English grammar, with a variety of exercises for the use of schools.* n.p. 15cm, ix+170pp. ($). (^{5}1818, Edinburgh: W. Blackwood, x+170pp; impr. ed. ^{7}1820, Edinburgh: W. Blackwood/Oliver & Boyd, 15cm, x+170pp. (@); ^{11}1832; ^{12}1837; anr. ed. 1854, ... *With important alterations and additions, adapted for the use of American schools*, New York: C.B. Morton, 16cm, 159pp. ($ @)).
($ @ E *Br, Hu, Lw*)
[Mylne admits that he has "not scrupled to borrow freely". Nine parts of speech; appendix on "barbarisms".]
1299.$ Nash, H.A. 1876. *A synthetic(al) grammar of the English language, adapted to the instruction of private students, containing rules and observations well illustrated for assisting the student to write with perspicuity and accuracy.* Charleston, W.Va.: J. Gibbens, Atkinson & Co. 23cm, vi+95pp.
($ @)
1300.$ Nasmith, Mrs. [1856]. *(Mrs Nasmith's) Map of English grammar.* Kingsland, Georgia.
(L O)
1301.$ Nasmith, Mrs.. 1862. *Nasmith's parsing exercise book.* n.p.
(C)
1302. Anon. [1878]. *National English grammar, adapted to the standard of the latest government code.* 4 parts. (Standards II, III, IV, V&VI). London: National Society's Depository. 17cm, together 96pp. (Anr. ed. [1882]).
(L O)
[Simple explanations, with elementary exercises, identifying parts of speech, leading on to parsing complex sentences.]
1303. Needes, Richard. 1812. *Examples of parsing, for children. Intended as an introduction to the parsing of those parts of sentences, etc. given in Mr Murray's small grammar as parsing exercises.* London: Darton, Harvey & Darton. 14x8.5, 23pp.
(L)

[As indicated in the title the booklet is purely derivative; the items are classified, with minimal explanations, but no general syntactical rules are given.]

1304. Needham, S. 1828. *The first footstep to grammar being an easy and familiar explication of the parts of speech; in terms and language suitable for and adapted to the capacities of children of both sexes from the age of five to seven years: accompanied with interesting illustrations and familiar examples. ... to which is prefixed, six introductory conversational lessons.* London: John Chappell. 14x8. x+70pp.
(L)

['Conversational' chapters leading on to a catechism, in which the basics are taught in Q/A form - obviously appropriate for the age group intended but disguising how much system is behind this, and what tradition the author followed.]

1305. Nelson, W.L. 1840. *Rudiments of English grammar.* n.p.: Paton & Ritchie. 6d.
(L)

1306. Nesbit, Anthony (Proprietor of the Classical, Commercial and Scientific Academy, Kennington, 1778-1859). [1817]. *An introduction to English parsing, adapted to Murray's Grammar and exercises.* London. (^{2}1823, York, 15cm, xxxvi+216pp. ($); ^{2}1823, York, 18mo, 213pp. *(Br)*; ^{6}1837, York: Thomas Wilson).
($ L *Br*)

1307. Nesbitt, M.L. 1874. *Grammar-land; or, Grammar in fun for the children of Schoolroomshire.* London: Houlston. 18cm, viii+120. (^{2}1875 ($); ^{3}1877 ($); ^{3}1878, New York: H. Holt (@); anr. ed. 1885 ($); ^{4}1889).
($ BU H Lc *Lw*)

1308.! Nesfield, John Collinson (Late Director of Public Instruction, N.W. Provinces, Oudh, India). 1895. *Idiom, grammar, synthesis: A manual of practical and theoretical English for high school and university students.* 5 parts. London: Macmillan. 352pp.
(*Ke, Mp*)

1309. ---. 1895-1911. *English grammar series. With Key. [Edited] by J. C. Nesfield.* London etc.: Macmillan & Co. 17cm.
(L O)

I *The parts of speech* for the use of elementary classes in European and other English-teaching schools. 1895. 17x11.5, 46pp.

[Definitions of ten parts of speech, with exercises, and "interchanged parts of speech appended; simple non-terminological language aimed at.]

II *Easy parsing and analysis.* 1895. 17x11.5, 95pp.

[Ten parts of speech defined in easy language, with illustrations of etymological parsing. Very traditional.]
III *Key to idiom and grammar* ... 1895. 17x11.5, 112pp.
[Solutions to questions arranged in four sections.]
IV *Idiom, grammar, and synthesis* [not available] *Supplement to Nesfield's idiom, grammar and synthesis.* 1900. 17x11.5, 44pp.
[A mixed complement to preceding volumes. Further volumes (*keys* etc.) were published well into the 20th century, most books co-published in Bombay & Calcutta. Nesfield became the incarnation of correct usage in India.]

1310. ---. 1898a. *English Grammar, past and present.* 3 parts. New York/London: Macmillan. 17x11.5, viii+470pp. (Repr. 1899, 4s6d; anr. ed. 1900, title has changed to ... *With appendices on prosody, synonyms, and other subjects*, viii+470pp. (@)).
($ @ C L O Le)
[Classic traditional grammar, frequently reprinted. Nesfield states his exhaustive experience with English language teaching in India referring to a manual of grammar (untraced) which he compiled in India, but the book is nevertheless cluttered with detail and unexplained terms; definitions often not satisfactory; mixture of historical and synchronic description; arrangement in three parts not convincing. However, this monumental book has exerted a unique influence on ELT: partly because of Nesfield's experience, and partly because it offered to contemporary readers the ideal combination of modern grammar (1-146), idiom and construction (147-220, somewhat of a ratbag) and historical English word-formation. His 'grammar' includes Accidence, Analysis, Syntax and Punctuation, but concentrates on the classification of the eight parts of speech ("The articles are adjectives, and not a separate part of speech. This is proved by their origin" p.159); only ten pages are devoted to syntax (but the use of tenses, word order, and special problems of prepositions and conjuctions, etc. follow in Part II). With all its qualities, it is not quite easy to see how its wordiness, lack of clear structure, mixture of synchronic description and diachronic explanation and often unclear definitions gave the book the immense impact it had.]

1311. ---. 1898b. *Manual of English grammar and composition.* London: Macmillan & Co. 8°, iv+347. (Anr. ed. 1898, 18cm, xxii+423pp. ($ Nc); price in 1899: 2s6d).
Key. London, 1900, 8°.
($ L Nc O)
[The subject matter - wider than in *English Grammar past and present* - is arranged under "Parsing and analysis", "composition" (includes punc-

tuation, word order and structure of sentences), "Enlargement of vocabulary", "Prose and poetry" and "history of the language". Since Nesfield is more succinct here, his exposition of grammar in part I (definition, exemplification, exercises) is more successful than in no. 1310

1312. ---. 1899a. *The uses of the parts of speech as shown by examples.* London: Macmillan. 17x12, 48pp.
(L)
[The booklet concentrates on exercises, with definitions taken from Nesfield's grammars interspersed; not of any independent value.]

1313. ---. 1899b. *English grammar, alternative course. Standard IV (Uses of the parts of speech as shown by examples), Standard V (Modifications of subject, predicate, and object, by words, phrases, and easy sentences), Standard VI (Parsing and easy analysis), Standard VII (Analysis and word-forming by prefixes and suffixes).* London: Macmillan. 17cm, 48pp. each.
(O)
[Apparently from his *English grammar past and present*, rephrased and rearranged, adapted to the individual standards; no introduction. Definitions in italics "should be remembered as well as understood".]

1314. ---. 1900a. *Key and companion to English grammar, past and present.* London: Macmillan. 8°, 142pp.
(C O)
[The book provides answers to questions and gives fuller arguments to points raised in no. 1310., and is therefore not really a 'companion'.]

1315. ---. 1900b. *Outline of English grammar.* (London: Macmillan?). 8°, 168pp., 1s6d.
Key 1902.
(L O)
[A shortened form of his *English grammar past & present*, and without the historical parts.]

1316. Anon. ^{4}1800. *A new abridgment of Murray's English grammar with an appendix containing exercises in orthography, in parsing, in syntax and in punctuation. Designed for the younger classes of learners by Lindley Murray.* 13.5x8, 104pp. (^{16}1803; ^{53}1817, introduction dated Holdgate near York 1797, London: Darton, Harvey & Darton, 14x8.5, 128pp.)
(O)
[The classic form of the author's abridgment dates to 1797 but was reprinted throughout the 19th century, with even more elementary works based on this. OESP, in simple language, meant as a stepping stone to his *English Grammar*; cf. no. 1294.]

1317.$ Anon. 1811. *A new abridgement of Murray's English grammar, with alterations and improvements. By a gentleman of Newhampshire.* Walpole, N.H.: Isaiah Thomas & Co. 13x8, iv+52pp.
(L)
[Etymology and Syntax (with a few pages on punctuation), with Murray's text preserved where the abridgment permitted. Of no independent value - except for the potentials of reduction it illustrates.]

1318. Anon. 1836. *New and enlarged dictionary of the English language, compiled from the best editions of the most eminent authorities, from Johnson to Webster. The pronunciation carefully marked and modelled, with important variations on the plan of Walker. Preceded by a complete English grammar, compiled from Louth, Johnson, L. Murray, Cobbett &c. With additions, corrections, and improvements. Stereotype edition.* London: Isaac, Tuckey & Co., 22x13.5, 1072pp. (Ster. ed. 1856 (@)).
(@ L)
[BL Catalogue comments: "Without the grammar. An earlier issue, entitled *Dictionary*, is entered under Penny Grammar".]

1319.! Anon. [a1877]. *New elementary grammar.* London/Glasgow: Collins. 48pp., 4d.
[Advertised in 1877.]

1320.$ Newcomb, John Burton (b. 1809). ^{2}1879. *What I know about grammar. Intended for the old as well as the young; for the college bred, as well as the common school scholar ... A plain guide to clear and logical composition. To which are added discourses on various other subjects relating to school teachers and education generally.* San Antonio, Texas: Texas Sun Print. 22cm, 81pp.
($)

1321. Newton, Thomas (Headmaster, Gerard Street Board Schools, Derby). [1880]. *(Bemrose's) Standard grammar containing 66 lessons and 160 exercises.* London: Bemrose. 16x10.5, iv+102pp., 8d. (Also published in three parts, 2d each).
(L)
[Eight parts of speech, inflexion of words and analysis of sentences treated in simple style directly addressing his young pupils. Rules (in bold, to be memorized) followed by discursive explanations and exercises interspersed; recapitulations and a balance of technical information and plain language make the book quite successful.]

1322. Niblett, Alfred Newson (Dr., First Assistant-master in the Collegiate School, Sheffield). 1861. *English class handy-book: comprising the outlines of English grammar, parsing, and analysis; aids to juvenile*

composition, ... Compiled by A. N. N. London: Simpkin, Marshall & Co. 16x10, ix+[11]-101pp. (Anr. ed. [1869] (L)).
(L O)
[The 'composition' part is made up of English Grammar, pp. 11-38, and easy rules for writing English themes and essays, pp. 38-45; arithmetic etc. follows. The grammar is very rudimentary and of no independent value.]

1323. Nicholson, W. 1843. *The young man's self-teaching grammar of the English language.* London.
(L Lw)

1324. Nicholson, William (of Halifax). 1864. *The grammar of the English language made easy: with numerous practical exercises in orthography, etymology, syntax and prosody: also, derivation; comprising Anglo-Saxon, or English, Latin, and Greek affixes, and prefixes, and very comprehensive lists ... amounting to nearly 10,000 words.* Halifax: W. Nicholson & Sons, etc. 14/15cm, 288pp. (Anr. ed. [1870], Wakefield: W. Nicholson, vi+[7]-287pp. (@)).
(@ C E L O)
[Somewhat longwinded, very detailed, with many notes and exercises in small print; author thinks his chapter on derivation (a stepping-stone to Latin and French) especially innovative and important.]

1325. Nightingale, Rev. Joseph. 1822. *The lady's grammar; or, An easy and familiar introduction to the English tongue; with select reading exercises, in prose and verse, designed, principally, for the instruction of young ladies, and for the assistance of teachers. To which are added, three hundred questions, adapted to the respective lessons.* (Running title: *The young lady's grammar*). London: Hodgson & Co. 17/18cm, iv+[5]-96pp.
(L O Br, Lw, Ma)
[Based on L. Murray; OESP, nine parts of speech, definitions mostly inadequate, slightly chatty - and highly selective: "Passing over any further observations on that part of etymology which treats of the derivation of words, as too learned, difficult, and doubtful for the young student, we come to the third part of grammar" (37). Pp. 51-85 made up by religious and moral excerpts, 86-96 of questions. Not a worthy complement to Murray. Martin 1824:231: "[...] All that can be said in favour of the work, is its moral design and the plainness of the style [...]".]

1326. Nisbet, Charles & Don Lemon (pseud.). 1891. *Everybody's writing-desk book.* London: Saxon. 14cm, 301pp. (Anr. ed. 1892, ed. and rev. by James Baldwin, New York: Harper & Brothers. 15cm, iv+310pp. (@);

anr. ed. 1893 (@); anr. ed. [1895], London: Saxon & Co., 14cm, 345pp. (@)).
($ @)

1327. Nixon, H. (Private tutor). 1826. *The English parser; being a complete and original system of English parsing, with examples and models.* London: Longman & Co. 18/19cm, iv+164pp.
($ @ L Br)
[An attempt at methodological innovation through pervasively numbered rules, examples, models, exceptions. Uses Goldsmith's *History of England* as text.]

1328.! ---. 1833. *A new and comprehensive English grammar.* London. 12mo.
(Br, Mi)

1329.! Nixon-Smith, E.H. [a1898]. *The elements of English grammar.* London: Relfe Bros.
[Advertised in 1898.]

1330. Norman, Francis Martin (Commander). ³1875. *The teacher's English grammar assistant: A progressive elementary grammar for schools and private tuition; in which parsing, syntax, and analysis are simultaneously taught on a plain and progressive plan; with hints on "letter writing". In four parts.* By the author of the 'Schoolmaster's drill assistant' (F.M. Norman). Rev. ed. London: Bemrose. 17/18cm, [vii]-xv+183pp.
(@ L O)
[Definitions of eight 'sorts of words' followed by the syntax of simple, then of complex sentences, compound and collateral sentences, punctuation and directions at end. Exercises interspersed and at end of chapters. Unassuming clear style, and well-organized; quotes Morell, Mason and Bain (rarely) in matters of dispute.]

1331. Norman, Frederick Byron. 1899. *English grammar with numerous exercises.* Vienna: A. Pichler's Widow & Son. 20x12.5, v+242pp.
(L)
[OESP, with minimal attention given to spelling and large weight devoted to the nine parts of speech (3-135). Descriptive, with some implicit consideration of the TEFL situation, with many examples, exercises and questions. Sober, unexciting and certainly not quite up to ELT developments.]

1332. Anon. 1885. *Notes of grammar lessons.* n.p.
(L)

1333. Anon. 1845. *Notes on English grammar, comprising the leading rules simplified and made plain for the use of juvenile pupils.* London: Simpkin, Marshall, & Co. / Derby: H. Mozley & Sons. 14x8.5, iv+70pp.
(L O)

[Possibly identical with no. 487. In simple language, "auxiliary to works of a larger description", short definitions alternating with study questions; parsing exercises (48-55) and questions "to be answered on the slate" (60-70). Of no independent value. The full title is *Notes ... made plain, for the use of juvenile pupils*. The author is female, and writes from Laurel House Ladies School, Guilsborough, Northampton.]

1334. Anon. n.d. *Notes on grammar, written and compiled from various sources, for the use of pupils of Epworth College, Rhyl*. Manchester: Heywood. 19pp.
(O)
[Elementary definitions and notes, no questions or exercises.]

1335.! Anon. 1827. *The nursery companion to Lowth's English grammar. By a lady*. Hales.
(private collection)

1336.$ Nutting, I.H. 1858. *Analytical grammar of the English language for the use of schools*. Boston: Crosby, Nichols & Co. 19cm, 112pp.
($ @)

1337.$ ---. 1859. *Analytic and synthetic manual of English grammar*. Cambridge: Thurston, Miles & Pritchett.
(@)

1338.$ ---. 1860. *A suggestive grammar of the English language with pictorial exercises: a manual for schools*. Boston: J.M. Whittemore & Co. 18/ 19cm, xv+184pp.
($ @)

1339.$ Nutting, Rufus (1793-1878). ^{2}1823. *A practical grammar of the English language: accompanied with notes critical and explanatory*. Montpelier, Vt.: E.P. Walton. 18cm, 144pp. ($). (^{3}1826 (L *Br*); ^{4}1828 ($ L); ^{5}1829 (from 1826 ed.) ($)).
($ L *Br*)

1340.$ ---. 1840. *Nutting's new grammar. A grammar of the English language in three parts: part 1, introduction to plain parsing, on the inductive plan; part 2, the doctrines and precepts of English grammar, part 3, exercises on part 2: with an appendix, explanatory of many logical and rhetorical terms*. Montpelier, Vt.: E.P. Walton & Sons. 18cm, viii+ 184pp.
($)

1341.$ ---. 1850. *Outline of the three analyses: designed as a help to philological interpretation, adapted to schools and academies*. Hudson, Ohio. 19cm, 118pp. (Anr. ed. 1851, Ingersoll, 19cm, 130pp. ($ @); anr. ed. 1856, Hudson, 118pp. (@)).
($ @)

1342. Anon. 1824. *Observations on grammar, and its arrangement etc. for the use of the grammar school, Leeds*. Leeds: Robinson & Hernaman. 60pp. (²1826, 9cm, 93pp. (@)).
(@ Lp Ls)
1343. entry deleted
1344.! Oliver, Edward. 1807. *A short practical grammar*. London. 12mo, 178pp.
(Br)
1345. Oliver, Samuel. 1825. *A general, critical grammar of the Inglish [sic] language; on a system novel, and extensive: exhibiting investigations of the analogies of language, written, and spoken, discussions on the authorities of grammarians, and a general grammatical criticism of the learned and the modern languages in comparative illustration of the Inglish tongue: to which is prefixt a discourse on the study of languages in polite education*. London: Baldwin, Cradock & Joy, for the author. 22cm, xxxii+377pp. (Anr. ed. 1826).
($ @ A L O *Br, Sk*)
[Idiosyncratic, cantankerous, mostly traditional. Brief estimates of earlier grammarians: Tooke ("Gothick virtu"), Priestley ("scienced reveries"), L. Murray ("inerudite"). Defends nine parts of speech against other systems ranging from two to thirty.]
1346.! Olley, F.B. 1827. *The root of grammar correctly taught in one month, particularly recommended for the nursery, preparatory schools and parents*. London.
[cf. *CBEL*, 3.135]
1347.$ Oram, Elizabeth. 1855. *First lessons in English grammar and composition, with exercises in the elements of pronunciation, words for dictation and subjects for composition*. New York: Paine & Daniel Burgess. 18x11, iv+221pp. (Preface dated, and entered, 1846).
($ @ L *Lw*)
[Mainly an (idiosyncratic) introduction to phonetics, which has short definitions of parts of speech and other grammatical terms interspersed. Hymnic texts supplied for dictation and grammatical analysis. A major part of the book is taken up by long lists of polysyllabic words for which stress is indicated "according to present national and reputable use". Syntax is summarized in 14 rules (194-211). The mixture of the two strands of phonetics/accentuation and grammar is unique - and didactically dubious.]
1348.$ Orne, Martha Russell. 1894. *A manual of analysis and parsing: consisting of simple, compound, and complex sentences. Selected and classi-*

fied by M.R. Orne. *Designed to be used as a supplement to any grammar*. Boston: Lee & Shepard. 19cm, iv+115pp.
($ @)

1349. Oswald, Rev. John (1804-1867). [a1839]. *Outlines of English grammar*. n.p. (Impr. and enl. ed. ⁵1839, Edinburgh: Adam & Charles Black / London: Longman, Orme, Brown, Green & Longmans, 15x9, 54pp., 6d; impr. and enl. ed. ⁶1849; anr. ed. 1850, Edinburgh: Black (L)).
(@ L *Hu, Lw*)
[Short and often inadequate rules, apparently meant for memorizing, large space being taken by verbal paradigms. Unoriginal, old-fashioned and unexciting.]

1350.! Anon. [a1872]. *Our first grammar. An elementary textbook*. (Cassell's Primary Series). London: Cassell, Petter & Galpin. 1s.
[Advertised in 1872.]

1351. Anon. [a1857]. *Outline of English grammar*. London: Sunday School Union.
(Lc)

1352. Anon. 1899. *Outline of English grammar (in English and Maltese) compiled for the use of pupils attending the government elementary school*. n.p. 126pp. ($).
($)

1353.$ Anon. 1856. *An outline of the general principles of grammar, with a brief exposition of the chief idiomatic peculiarities of the English language. Edited and enlarged by J. Graeff Barton*. New York: Harper & Bros. 156pp.
(L)
[Probably the enlarged edition of no. 114.]

1354. Anon. [a1860]. *Outlines of English grammar*. London: J.A. Wilson.
(L)

1355.$ Anon. 1853. *Outlines of English grammar. On the basis of the Anglo-Saxon... By a literary association*. (American System of Education). New York. 18/20cm, 160pp.
($ O)

1356. Anon. [1883]. *The Oxford and Cambridge examiner. English grammar, parsing, and analysis, comprising the Oxford and Cambridge examination papers from 1858 to the present day*. London: Allman & Son. 127pp.
Key 1884. London: Allman & Son. 17.5x11.5, 173pp.
(L O)
[Though not a grammar, the up to 1,000 questions permit interesting insights into what levels of grammatical knowledge were expected in

junior and senior examinations, in classification, correct grammar, parsing, analysis and the history of English. The *Key* is purely complementary to the *Questions*.]

1357. Packwood, Josiah (of Rugeley). 1816. *Introductory English exercises arranged under the rules of syntax in Murray's abridgment, intended more effectually to impress on the mind of the pupil, the leading principles of grammar to qualify him for the study of the larger grammar and exercises, and the science of language in general.* Rugeley: J. Leonard. 14.5x9, viii+76pp.

(L)

[Complementary to Murray, the slim book concentrates on exercises of false English to be corrected, with rules and questions interspersed; the categories used are very Latinate, and the whole is of dubious didactic value.]

1358. Palmer, A.G. [1869]. *A catechism of Morell's grammar.* London.

(L O)

1359. ---. [1873]. *Morell's grammar simplified, especially adapted for the use of young pupils.* Published with the sanction of Dr. J.D. Morell. London: Thomas Joseph Allman. 13.5x9, iv+[5]-80pp.

(L)

[Drastic reduction in simple language, but with some facts of language history included; descriptively adequate, but with misleading statements resulting from the simplification.]

1360. Palmer, Charlotte. 1811. *Roots of knowledge; or, Foundational lessons on English grammar: occasionally interspersed with letters on various subjects. Designed for the use of young ladies from sixteen to twenty years of age.* London. 36pp., but apparently to be continued in fortnightly 'numbers'.

(G)

["The work is erratic and disturbed, with little reference to English grammar".]

1361.$ Palmer, Mary (School teacher). 1803. *A concise system of English grammar, selected and abridged for the use of schools.* By Mary Palmer, teacher of a grammar school in New-York. New York: T. & J. Swords. 18cm, 48pp.

($ *Br*)

1362. Pape, Daniel (Vicar of Penns, Staffs). 1806. *A compendious English grammar.* London: Thomas Ostell. viii+166pp.

(L St *Lw*, *Ma*)

[An expansion (from 48 to 166 pages) of his *A key to English grammar*, 1790. OESP, with grammatical exercises and false grammar, syntax and punctuation (72-100); key appended as pp. 143-66. Bridging the 18th and 19th century, traditional, not very well ordered and unexciting. Martin 1824:271: "The key was first printed in 1790. Mr. PAPE's Grammar is at least equal to either of its immediate predecessors, though now offered for sale at three shilling per dozen. *A fact!*"]

1363. Park, Abraham (Head Master, Albion Schools, Ashton-under-Lyne). [1875]. *The new code standard examination primer of English grammar arranged for standards II and III, and combining suggestions for simple methods of instruction, so as to enable pupils to be prepared by junior pupil teachers for a successful examination in this branch of study.* Rev. ed. London: Thomas Murby. 16cm, 31pp.
(L O)
[Explanations of parts of speech, with identifying exercises; no special method apparent.]

1364. ---. [1876]. *The young scholar's English grammar.* Part 1 and 2. (Marshall's School Series). London: John Marshall. (Enl. ed. n.d., as *An elementary English grammar and analysis*, London: John Marshall, 16x10, 63pp.).
(L)
[Short unassuming definitions, with exercises interspersed, meant for school use. Unexciting.]

1365.$ Park, J.G. 1894. *A practical and complete English grammar.* (Park's Language Course). Ada, Ohio. 19/21cm, vi+256/274pp. (Anr. ed. 1898, as *A complete and practical English analysis*, Ada, Ohio (Park's Language Course), 19cm, iv+193pp. ($ @)).
($ @)

1366.$ ---. 1898. *Language lessons: including composition and inductive grammar.* (Park's Language Course). New York/Cincinnati, etc.: American Book Company. 19cm, 144pp.
($ @)

1367.$ Parker, Richard Green (Principal of the Johnson Grammar School, Boston, 1798-1869) & Charles Fox (A.M. Principal of the Boylston Grammar School, Boston). 1834-40. *Progressive exercises in English grammar.* 3 parts. Boston: Crocker & Brewster / New York: Leavitt, Lord & Co. I:1834, *Containing the principles of analysis, or English parsing.* 19x10.5, 96pp. (^{2}1835, Boston: Crocker & Brewster / New York: Leavitt, Lord & Co. 18cm (@); anr. ed. 1837; ^{6}1838, Boston (@); ^{7}1839 (@); ^{8}1841, 122pp. (L); ^{10}1843; anr. ed. 1837: two vols. in one, 18cm (@)); II:1835, *Containing the principles of the synthesis or construction of the English language*, Boston, Mass., 19cm, 60pp. (^{3}1835, 122pp. (@ L); ^{4}1839). III:1840, *Containing the rules of ortho-*

graphy and punctuation, the principles of etymology, and the prosody of the English language. Boston, Mass. 20cm, 122pp. (116pp.+ long list of works consulted). (@ L). (Anr. ed. 1849, 122pp.).
($ @ L *Br, Hu, Lw*)
[The authors purposely start with analysis, while etymology and more difficult syntax (strong emphasis on ellipsis) are dealt with later; they neglected "elegances of diction" and avoided a colloquial style. The second part rejects syntax rules which are purely rhetorical; many exercises on errors to be corrected by "the principles of synthesis". The third part is rather a ragbag of versification, rhetoric, logic, composition. The three parts combined are intended as a comprehensive grammar, "progressively adapted to the wants of teachers and pupils of every grade". Generally clear definitions, exercises include faulty English to be corrected, and extensive footnotes.]

1368.$ Parker, William Henry (Principal of Ringgold Grammar School, Philadelphia). 1865?. *A grammar of the English language, based upon the analysis of the English sentence, with copious examples and exercises in parsing and the correction of false syntax, and an appendix, containing critical and explanatory notes, and lists of peculiar and exceptional forms: for the use of schools and academies, and those who write.* n.p. (Anr. ed. 1866 (from 1865 ed.), Philadelphia: Eldridge & Brothers, 18.5x11, 312/384pp. ($); anr. ed. 1867, Philadelphia (L); anr. ed. 1869 (from 1865 ed.), 384pp. ($)).
($ @ L)
[The ambitious grammar introduces a number of innovations such as the consistent distinction between spoken and written language, or the stimulating combination of etymology and syntax (e.g. to treat 'case' and 'transitivity' together). Analysis precedes synthesis before the parts of grammar are treated. However, the book is cluttered with so much detail that much of the force is lost (even more detail provided in notes, pp. 313-84).]

1369.$ ---. 1866. *Introductory lessons in the grammar of the English language, based upon an analysis of the English sentence.* Philadelphia: Eldredge & Bros. 17cm, 119pp.
($ @)

1370.$ Parkhurst, John Luke (1789-1850). 1820. *A systematic introduction to English grammar.* Concord, N.H. 18mo, 104pp. (Anr. ed. 1821, 12cm, 94+[2]pp. ($); enl. and impr. ed. ²1824, Concord, N.H.: J.W. Shepard, 13/15cm, 102pp. ($ @)).
($ @ L *Br*)

[Sensible attempt to simplify and sharpen teaching methods; no grammatical significance.]

1371.$ ---. 1838. *English grammar for beginners, on the inductive method of instruction.* Andover, Mass./New York: Gould & Newman, 15cm, xvi+[17]-180pp.
($ *Br, Hu, Lw*)

1372. Parminter, George Henry. 1856. *Materials for a grammar of the modern English language. Being an attempt to fuse in one system the grammatical principles of the English and ancient classical languages for the better elucidation of the classical structure of English literature.* Cambridge: Macmillan & Co. 17/18cm, x+219pp., 3s6d.
($ C L O)
[Traditional unexciting account.]

1373. Anon. n.d. *The parser's companion.* Gloucester: T.B. Bird. 16x9.5, 16pp., 1d.
(L)
["This Abstract is intended for use in connection with a larger Text Book, or with thorough Oral Teaching". Minimal information on parts of speech, with tables for verb forms, to enable students to parse.]

1374.$ Parshall, Nelson C. 1878. *Graded exercises in analysis, synthesis, and false syntax, with an exemplified outline of the classification of sentences and causes, and a table of diacritical marks, with questions.* Rochester/New York: the author. 18cm, 166pp. (Anr. ed. 1880 ($)).
($ @)

1375. Anon. n.d. *The parsing of the English verb, with copious exercises and abundant pattern parsing.* (The "Guide" Series). Birmingham: Davis & Moughton. 24pp.
(O)
[Specific problems of English verb forms discussed, including *-ing* and irregular verbs; for class II.]

1376.$! Parsons, Samuel H. 1836. *English grammar.* Philadelphia. 18mo, 107pp.
(*Br*)

1377.! Anon. 1822. *The path of learning strewed with roses.* London: John Marshall.
(*Mi*)
["Published by John Marshall in imitation of no. 1378)."]

1378. Anon. 1820. *The paths of learning strewed with flowers: or English grammar illustrated.* London: John Harris. 17cm, 16pp. (Anr. ed. 1826, [Hartford], 30cm (@)).
(@ L O)

[A delightful and famous work for nurseries. "The purpose of this little work is to obviate the reluctance Children evince to the irksome and insipid task of learning the Names and meaning of the component Parts of Grammar..." Ten parts of speech with a short definition and hand-coloured illustration each.]

1379.$ Patrick, James Newton. 1891. *Essentials of English for schools, academies and institutes.* St. Louis, Mo. 19cm, 224pp.
($ @)

1380.$ ---. 1892. *Lessons in English for intermediate grades.* (St. Louis?). 160pp.
($)

1381.$ ---. 1896. *Higher English for high schools and academies.* St. Louis, Mo.: Beckford & Co. 19cm, vi+[7]-192pp.
($ @)

1382.$ ---. [c1897]. *Lessons in grammar for school reviews and teachers' institutes.* St. Louis, Mo.: Beckford Co. 19cm, vi+[7]-144pp. (Anr. ed. [1898], Mound City Publ. Co., vi+[7]-232pp. (@)).
(@)

1383.$ ---. 1898a. *Lessons in grammar: for schools and teacher's institutes.* (Lippincott's Language Series). n.p. 19/20cm, 232pp.
($)

1384.$ ---. 1898b. *Lessons in language.* (Lippincott's Language Series). n.p. 19/20cm, 224pp. (Anr. ed. 1898, 200pp. ($)).
($)

1385.$ Patterson, Calvin (1847-1902). 1882. *Elements of grammar and composition: including analysis and synthesis, and a complete system of diagrams.* (Patterson's Language Series, Book 1). n.p. 19cm, vii+238pp. (Anr. ed. 1882, vii+224pp. ($); anr. ed. 1883, as *Elements of grammar: with practical exercises in the correct use of language: containing also analysis and synthesis of sentences, and a complete system of diagrams* ($); anr. ed. 1884 ($); anr. ed. 1886 ($)).
($)

1386.$ ---. 1887. *Advanced grammar and elements of rhetoric.* (Patterson's Language Series, Book 2). n.p. 19cm, x+399pp.
($)

1387. entry deleted

1388. Payne, George. LL.D. 1843. *Elements of language and general grammar.* London: John Gladding. xiv+236pp. (Anr. ed. 1845 ($)).
($ *Lw*)

[Assumes mastery of such a book as "Murray's Grammar"; illustrated from British writers only; uses Tooke, Harris, Crombie, Monboddo, Dewar.]

1389.$ Peabody, Nathaniel. 1830. *First lessons in grammar on the plan of Pestalozzi.* (Publ. anon.). Boston. 17.5x11, v+[7]-60pp.
($ L *Br*)
[Discursive didactic advice to teachers in intelligible, not technical language, with suggestions to teachers at the beginning and questions for examination at end. An interesting attempt to develop an empirical approach, starting from a literary text.]

1390. Peacock, Thomas Love. 1814. *Sir Hornbook; or, Childe Launcelot's expedition. A grammatico-allegorical ballad.* London. (^{2}1815, 13/14cm, 29+[2]pp. ($); $^{3+5}$1815 (O); anr. ed. 1843, 17cm, 28+3+[5]pp. ($); at least five further editions between 1815 and 1855).
($)
[cf. *NCBEL*, 3.701]

1391. Pearson, William, C.M. 1865. *The self-help grammar of the English language; intended for reading, dictation, parsing, composition and home-work in the second and third classes in an elementary school.* London etc.: Hamilton etc. 14cm, 43pp.
(L O)
[OESP, very simple definitions; Pearson stresses syllable-based spelling, and prides himself for omitting *thou*; simple parsing exercises; some remarks on difficulties of dialect speakers (Yorkshire).]

1392. Anon. 1840. *A peep at grammar for children, with questions and exercises. By a private teacher.* London: Darton & Clark. 14x9, 36pp., 6d.
(L O)
[Discursive, no rules, or clear structure. Advertised on back cover: "Preparing for Publication, (Price one Shilling) *A second peep at grammar*, for those that have made good use of the first. With Questions and Answers." - ever published?]

1393. Peile, John. 1877. *A primer of philology.* n.p. 164pp. (^{2}1877; ^{4}1880).
(L)

1394.$ Peirce, Oliver Beale (b. 1808). 1836? *Grammatical instructor, or, common school grammar: designed and adapted to facilitate the progress of the student, and, to impart, to the unaided private learner, a practical knowledge of the principles of the English language.* n.p. (Anr. ed. 1837 (from 1836 ed.), 19cm, 371pp. ($)).
($)

1395.$ ---. 1839. *The grammar of the English language.* New York: Robinson & Franklin. 18x11, 384pp. (Anr. ed. 1843, 20cm, 404pp. ($)).

($ L *Br*)
[Leisurely, clear exposition in Q/A form, with stress laid on understanding. Some use of non-traditional terms, as in the ten parts of speech: Names, Substitutes, Asserters, Adnames, Modifiers, Relatives, Connectives, Interrogatives, Repliers, and Exclamations. Plentiful examples; lessons (for parsing, correction, etc.) at the end of chapters. Apart from the terminology and too much detail in places quite an achievement; cf. the author's long justification of his methods in the appendix, pp. 309-77.]

1396.$ ---. 1840. *Peirce's abridgement of the grammar of the English language*. Boston/New York/Watertown: Weeks, Jordan & Co. 15x9, x+[11]-144pp. (Anr. ed. 1843 ($)).
($ L)
[Considerate exposition of the science of language: "Never allow your pupils to commit to memory what they do not understand. Never teach, as *truth*, anything, however trifling it may seem, which Reason's utmost force and brilliancy, can ever afterwards *un*teach. " OESP; succinct and clear; references to "the large grammar", no. 1395.]

1397.$ Peissner, Elias. 1853. *A comparative English-German grammar based on the affinity of the two languages*. n.p. 19cm, xii+246+lxxiiipp. ($)

1398. Pemberton, Robert. 1851. *The natural method of teaching the elements of grammar, for the nursery and infant schools*. London. 17cm, viii+120+3pp., 2s6d.
($ C L O)
[Reduces grammar rules to sets of cards; thoroughly traditional, method questionable.]

1399. Pengelley, Edward. 1840. *The elements of English grammar illustrating its four divisions; with an appendix, or exercises on its various rules*. London: Simpkin, Marshall & Co. / Plymouth: Jenkin Thomas. 14.5x 9.5, iv+[5]-108pp, 1s6d.
(E L *Br*, *Lw*)
[OESP; simplified definitions, often misleading. Nine parts of speech, with extensive treatment of verbs. Parsing, false syntax and punctuation at end. Traditional and unoriginal (P. calls himself 'the compiler').].

1400. Anon. [c1830]. *A penny grammar and dictionary, etc. Pt 1-11.* (Containing the *Complete English grammar* and the *Dictionary of the English tongue*, A-Cubation). (Penny National Library Series). London: Fred. Lawrence. (Reissue 1836, as *A new and enlarged dictionary of the English language ... Preceded by a complete English grammar ...* Ster. ed., London: Isaac, Tuckey & Co., 1027pp.).

(L)

1401.$ Perley, Daniel. 1834. *A grammar of the English language.* Andover, Mass.: Gould & Newman. 14.5x9, iv+[5]-80pp.
($ L *Br*).
[OESP, eight parts of speech plus particles; derivation succinctly described; syntax summarized in forty rules, followed by parsing. Appendix of vulgarisms. Traditional and unexciting.]

1402.! Phillips, John. 1847. *The popular class room grammar; for the grammatical class of the People's Institute, Rochdale.* Rochdale.
(*Hu, Lw*)

1403. Phillips, Sir Richard (1767-1840). [a1809]. *A practical grammar of the English language, accompanied by numerous exercises and adapted throughout to the use of schools.* By the Rev. David Blair. n.p. (^{4}1809, London: Richard Phillips, 12mo, ix+168pp.; ^{5}1811, London: Richard Phillips, ix+168pp (L); ^{7}1815, 15cm, xii+167pp. ($); anr. ed. 1816; ^{10}1819, London: G. Sydney ($ @); ^{10}1820; ^{12}1824, London: G. & W.B. Whittaker, vii+[8]-203pp. (@); ^{15}1826, 2s6d; ^{18}1842).
($ @ G L *Br, Hu, Lw, Ma, Sk*)
["Phillips wrote, compiled, or took credit for, textbooks under a variety of names: S. Barrow; David Blair, J. Goldsmith; Mary or Margaret Pelham; C.C. Clarke; James Adair". Martin 1824:273: "This, also, is an excellent Grammar; indeed, it is one of the best".]

1404. ---. 1811. *The universal preceptor, or, General grammar of arts, sciences, and useful knowledge: for the use of schools.* n.p. (L). (^{2}1811 (H); ^{4}1812 (Lu); ^{7}1814 (Lc N); ^{8}1816 (L); anr. ed. ^{12}1820; ^{15}1823; anr. ed. ^{23}1830, London: Sir Richard Phillips & Co., 15cm, iv+323pp. (Li); ^{65}1835; ^{69}1837; ^{72}1841; ^{75}1846; anr. ed. 1855; ^{79}1858).
(H L Lc Lu Li N)
[The work is typical of a book devoted to the teaching of useful knowledge - with only eight of its 292 pages covering grammar.]

1405. ---. [1824]a. *Five hundred questions and exercises on Murray's English Grammar, and abridgment; also, on Irving's Elements of English composition. Calculated to perfect students in the knowledge of grammar and composition.* By James Adair. London: Geo. & W.B. Whittaker. 14x8.5, vi+[8]-72pp, 1s (*Key* separately 9d). (Anr. ed. 1826, London: Phillips & Co. 72pp. (L)).
(L)
["Teaching of Interrogatories ... is now generally recognized, admired, and adopted ... These questions call upon the thinking powers of the student ..." Based on "Mr. Murray's excellent books... the Abridgement and the Grammar in chief". 312 questions (on 7-39) geared to sections

in the two Murray books, some involving discussions in the size of minor papers. Purely complementary, no independent explanations offered. Questions 313-500 on English composition are on Irving's handbook, followed by a "glossary of terms used in Grammar and rhetoric" (59-72). The 80 titles advertised by Whittaker form a kind of a series described with the words: "It is unnecessary to expatiate on the high pretensions of the above Books to universal preference for their respective purposes. Every intelligent Preceptor must be sensible of the practical character of the several works". They include Allan's *English Grammar* 2s6d, Blair's *English Grammar* 2s6d, Adair (as above) and Irving's *Composition* 7s6d, and various small handbooks called *Grammar of ... Geography, History, Natural Philosophy, Classical Literature, Astronomy, Sacred history, Medicine, Health* and *Longevity*.]

1406. ---. 1824b. *The first French and English grammar: containing everything essential and nothing superfluous.* n.p. 15cm, xi+[1]+130+28+8pp. ($)

1407.! ---. [a1830]. *Little English grammar.* (Publ. under pseud. James Adair]. London: Poole & Edwards. 1s.
[Advertised by Poole & Edwards in 1830.]

1408. ---. 1832. *The secretary's companion, containing a synopsis of English grammar ... directions for superscription, commencement and conclusion of letters to persons of every rank.* (Publ. under pseud. Rev. David Blair). Glasgow: Atkinson & Co. 98pp.
(L)

1409. Pickering, William. 1847. *General principles of grammar.* (Small Books on Great Subjects, edited by a few well wishers to ...). n.p. 17cm, 118pp.
($)

1410.$ Picket, Albert (1771-1850). 1805. *Sequel to The union spelling book comprising a collection of all the most difficult and irregular words in the English language: with an introduction to reading ...: to which is added, the abridgment of L. Murray's English grammar.* n.p. 168pp.
($)

1411.$ ---. 1808. *The juvenile expositor, or, Sequel to the common spelling book: containing an collection of the most useful words in the English language, clearly explained, and adapted to the comprehension of young persons, being an introduction to Walker's dictionary, with a course of reading lessons in prose and verse, selected from the best writers; designed to assist youth in acquiring, with ease, the theory of speech and to facilitate their improvement in knowledge, and in the use and meaning of words. To which is added, the abridgment of L. Murray's English*

grammar ... *with an additional appendix, containing a practical and methodical course of parsing lessons, interspersed with notes and explanatory observations.* n.p. 17/18cm, xxi+[22]-347+[3]pp. ($). (²1806, New York; anr. ed. 1810 (Modern and Useful School-Books, No. 4) ($); anr. ed. 1813 (American School Class-Book, No. 4), n.p. 18cm, 361+[3]pp. ($); anr. ed. 1816, as *The juvenile expositor, or, American school class-book, no. 4. Improved and enlarged, embracing radical and derivative orthography, with concise and appropriate definitions: designed to aid youth in acquiring the art of reading fluently and understandingly: together with a grammar, in which the principles of the English language are methodically digested in plain and easy rules: illustrated by examples, explaining the terms of grammar and improving its use*, 17cm, 394/395pp.; impr. and enl. ed. 1818 ..., ... *a grammar in which the principles of the English language are methodically digested* ..., 381pp. ($); impr. and enl. ed. 1819 ($); anr. ed. 1820 ($); anr. ed. 1821 ($); anr. ed. 1823 ($); anr. ed. 1829 ($); anr. ed. 1831).
($)

412.$ ---. 1812. *The juvenile instructor, or, Natural grammar and reader comprising a plain and easy analysis of the English language.* (American School Class-Book; No. 2). New York. 200pp. ($). (Anr. ed. 1815, as *The juvenile instructor, containing a new method of analytical and synthetical parsing of the English language, by means of a vinculum or chain; with miscellaneous exemplifications, in prose and poetry: adapted to the capacities of learners, who have made some progress in spelling and reading; designed to succeed the Juvenile and other spelling books, and as an introduction to the Juvenile Mentor and Expositor*, New York, 18cm, iv+[5]-198+[2]pp. ($); anr. ed. 1818, 12mo in 6s, iv+[5]-202+[2]pp. ($); anr. ed. 1820, 214pp. ($); anr. ed. 1830, as *The juvenile instructor: being a natural grammar and reader* ($); anr. ed. 1827, iv+[5]-214+[2]pp. ($)).
($)
[Conventional and rather naif. Grammar is seen as teaching "to connect ideas with words, and the different parts of speech with each other." Probably identical with: Picket, A. 1834. *The new juvenile instructor; containing a practical analysis of words, with definitional readings: and the elements of composition and English grammar.* (American School Class-Books, No. 2). n.p. 19cm, 214+[2]pp. ($)]

413.$! ---. 1823a. *Analytical school grammar.* New York. 18mo, 252pp. (²1824).
(*Br*)

1414.$ ---. 1823b. *Picket's grammar of the English language: comprising its principles and rules: adapted to the business of instruction in primary schools.* n.p. 16cm, 234pp. (Anr. ed. 1824, 16cm, 252pp. ($)).
($)

1415.$ ---. 1829?. *The essentials of English grammar: being the second part of The juvenile spelling book: containing obvious definitions and rules for speaking and writing correctly.* (American School Class-Books). n.p. (Anr. ed. 1830 (from 1829 ed.), 15cm, 234pp. ($)).
($)

1416.$ ---. 1837. *The principles of English grammar.* (Picket's Class Book, No. 5). n.p. 17cm, 213pp.
($)

1417.$ --- & John W. Picket (1771-1850). 1847. *The analyzer and expositor: containing exercises in English etymology, definition, and reading.* Cincinnati. 19cm, 192pp.
($)
[This is a revised edition of *The juvenile expositor* (cf. no. 1411). Analysis (*fixture*, what is its root?) Synthesis (*fix*, what derivatives may be made?).]

1418. Pimm, I.R. 1829. *The introduction to the teaching of children the different parts of speech by the use of marked works and engraved counters.* London: W.R. Newman. 12pp.
(C L O)
[Two books of text, one marked with parts of speech, one not; accompanied by counters similarly marked. Obscure.]

1419. Pinder, William (Master of Foxdale Mines' National School). 1856. *First steps in English grammar, for little children.* London: Simpkin & Marshall / Douglas: J. Mylrea. 14x8.5, 34pp., 3d.
(L O)
[OES; nine parts of speech, with extensive treatment of conjugation; the briefest of definitions, with minimal examples, apparently to be memorized; no notes or discussion; syntax summarized in 23 rules.]

1420.$ Pinneo, Timothy Stone (1804-1893). [1849]. *Pinneo's primary grammar of the English language for beginners.* (Eclectic Educational Series). Cincinnati: Winthrop B. Smith & Co. 15x9, vi+[7]-110pp. ($ L). (Anr. ed. 1854, 17cm, 160pp. ($); anr. ed. 1882 (from 1854 ed.) ($)).
($ L).
[Very elementary, talking down to beginners in simple language and endless questions extracted from preceding paragraphs; a great number of parsing exercises. Continually reference is made to the author's larger grammar.]

1421.$ ---. 1850. *Pinneo's analytical grammar of the English language: designed for schools.* (Eclectic Educational Series). Cincinnati. 19cm, 240pp. ($). (Anr. ed. 1850, 216pp. ($); anr. ed. 1859, 240pp. ($); anr. ed. 1859 (from 1850 ed.) ($); anr. ed. 1868 (from 1859 ed.), 19cm, 214pp. ($)).
($)

1422.$ ---. 1852. *Pinneo's English teacher: in which is taught the structure of sentences by analysis and synthesis: including exercises in English grammar.* (Eclectic Educational Series). Cincinnati. 19/20cm, 240pp.
($)

1423.$ ---. 1867. *Pinneo's exercises in false syntax: for the correction of errors in the grammatical construction of sentences: designed to aid in the study of the author's grammars of the English language.* (Eclectic Educational Series). Cincinnati. 19/20cm, 104pp.
($)

1424. Pinnock, George. 1854. *First steps to English grammar.* London: Allman. 62pp. (Anr. ed. 1878).
(L)

⇒ Pinnock, William. (1782-1843). [a1820]. (series editor) - see Anon. [12]1820, no. 296.

1425. Pinnock, William. (1782-1843). [20]1828. *The principles of English grammar: to which are added, for the exercise of the learner, some easy parsing lessons, as an exemplification of the rules of parsing. By a friend to youth.* (Pinnock's Catechism). London: George Byron Whittaker. 13.5x8, 72pp.
(O)
[Skilful reduction of grammatical knowledge in Q/A form adapted to less educated readers, with great stress laid on parsing; mainly ES.]

1426. ---. 1829. *A comprehensive grammar of the English language, with exercises written in a familiar style; accompanied with questions for examination, and notes critical and explanatory. Intended for the use of schools, and for private tuition.* London: Poole & Edwards. 17cm, 318pp. (Anr. ed. 1830, 18cm, xvi+318pp. ($); [3]1835; [4]1838).
($ L C O Br, Hu, Lw)
[Provides a lengthy synthesis of previous grammars; includes rhetoric. Derivative but not contemptible.]

1427.! ---. 1830. *English grammar made easy, for the use of young children.* London: W. Sell. (New ed. 1839, London).
(Hu, Lw)
[Advertised in his *First steps* ... 1831.]

1428.! ---. [a1831]. *(Pinnock's) Improved edition of Murray's Abridged English grammar, with numerous exercises, questions for examination, and explanatory notes.* London: W. Sell.
(*Mc, Mi*)

1429. ---. ?1854-60. *English grammar.* (First Steps to Knowledge Series). London: Allman. (Anr. ed. 1878).
(L)

1430. Pinnock, William Henry (1813-1885). 1837. *An elementary English grammar, upon an entirely new principle, especially adapted, by its simplicity and numerous exercises, for the junior classes in schools, for private tuition or for self-instruction.* London: Effingham Wilson. 14.5x9, iv+152pp.
(L)

[The new principle (which is never spelt out) seems to be only that the pupil should be helped to understand the textbook he is studying. After finishing the exercises he should learn the text by heart. Simple and frequently misleading definitions, with questions and exercises interspersed; allegedly OESP, but mainly etymology dealt with. Of no grammatical significance.]

1431. Anon. [1871]. *A plain practical English grammar, on an original plan; being a collection of short definitions, designed to be commited to memory, with examples and exercises by two schoolmasters.* Manchester: John Heywood / London: Simpkin, Marshall & Co. 15x9, 87pp., 9d.
(O)

[Grammar and analysis only treated; eight parts of speech. Short definitions to reduce the information to "exercises and memory work" - "all that most boys can be made to assimilate and employ in their school life". The authors claim "the merits of clearness, efficiency, novelty, and unparallelled cheapness." Unoriginal and unexciting.]

1432. Anon. 1812. *The plainest and most necessary principles of English grammar ... calculated for the instruction of young children: and printed for the use of Bridport Grammar School.* Dorchester. 114pp.
(L)

[Ninety-nine pages of text in Q/A form, about half of which is to be learnt by heart. Nine parts of speech; "constructive" and "radical" etymology.]

1433. Anon. 1835. *A pocket dictionary of English and Tamil. To which is prefixed a short English grammar.* Madras?: Church Mission Press for W.E. xviii+240pp.
(L)

1434. Anon. 1858. *Points in English grammar*. In: *London Quarterly Review*. 10:358-81.
(*Ke*)
1435. Poix-Tyrel, J. de. 1861. *Grammar of household words adapted to the separate or simultaneous study of English and French*. London: Longman, Green, Longman & Roberts. 18x10.5, xvi+179+xxviipp. (O). (^{2}1863, as *Grammar of household words in four languages, adapted to the separate or simultaneous study of English, German, French, and Italian*, London, 12x18 (O)).
(O)
[The work is based on the author's four-language grammar, split up into pairs of languages, after it had been suggested that this "would form an invaluable school book if published in separate parts". The parallel arrangement has led the author to stress the similarities of linguistic categories rather than unique features and has sometimes led to inadequate formulations (p.28-9: "In English nouns are partly inflected and declined with prepositions ~ In French nouns are not inflected, but declined with the definite article", etc.)]
1436.$ Pond, Enoch. [1826]. *Murray's system of English grammar, improved, and adapted to the present mode of instruction in this branch of science*. Worcester: Dorr & Howland. 66pp. (^{3}1830; ^{18}1834, Worcester, Mass.: Lazell (*Dw*); ^{6}1835, Worcester, Mass., 12mo, 228pp. (L *Br*)).
(L *Br*)
[An extreme abridgment of Murray, reduced to what is necessary "to parse English with propriety". Nine parts of speech explained, followed by questions and illustrations, parsing exercises and improprieties to be corrected, with an appendix on punctuation. *Br*: "Also under the same title, *A petty grammar with cuts*: New ed. 1835, Worcester. 18mo, 71pp."]
1437.! Anon. 1827. *Popular errors in English grammar, particularly in pronunciation, familiarly pointed out*.
(*Mi*)
[cf. NBL 1946]
1438.$ Powell, William Bramwell (1836-1904). 1882. *How to talk, or, Primary lessons in the English language*. (Powell's Language Series, pt. 2). n.p. 19cm, 208pp.
($)
1439.$ ---. 1882. *How to write, or, Secondary lessons in the English language*. (Powell's Language Series, pt. 3). n.p. 19cm, 239pp.
($)

1440.$ ---. 1899. *A rational grammar of the English language.* n.p. 19cm, 320pp.
($)
1441.$ Powers, Daniel. 1845. *A grammar on an entirely new system.* West Brookfield, Mass. 18cm, 188pp.
($ L *Br*)
["The new system is to rely on reading and not on parsing".]
1442.! Anon. [a1867]. *A practical grammar of the English language, including analysis of sentences.* Glasgow: Collins. 144pp., 9d.
[Advertised in 1867.]
1443.! Praeger, Sophia Rosamund. 1900. *The child's picture grammar.* n.p.: Allen.
(*Mp*)
1444.! [Preston, Thomas]. [1880]. *A dictionary of daily blunders, containing a collection of mistakes often made in speaking and writing.* London: Whittaker. 127pp.
(*Tm*, 49)
1445. Price, David. 1850. *An elementary English grammar. Containing also punctuation, the notes under rules in syntax, and lessons in parsing: to the latter of which are prefixed, specimens illustrative of that exercise, and false syntax to be corrected. The rules and definitions taken mostly from Murray. To all which is adapted a new system of questions.* n.p. 16cm, 108pp.
($)
1446. Anon. n.d. *Primer of English, consisting of English grammar, analysis, and wordbuilding, with special attention to correct writing and speaking, by a graduate and principal of a primary teaching centre, written as simply as possible for evening schools, preparatory classes in P.T. centres and the higher classes in elementary schools.* Blackburn: R. Denham. 72pp.
(L)
[Mainly morphology, with some syntax; clear rules with exemplification; exercises on parsing and remarks on errors in speaking and writing.]
1447. Anon. 1836. *The principles of English grammar.* Published by the Jaffna Book Society. Jaffna: American Mission Press. 14cm, 52pp. (Anr. ed. 1840 (@)).
(@)
1448. Anon. 1851. *Principles of English grammar and idiomatic sentences, in English and Maráthí.* Bombay: American Mission Press. xi+284pp.
(L)

1449. Anon. [c1860]. *The principles of English grammar; or, No. viii of a new series of school-books*. (Ster. impr. ed.). Edinburgh: Scottish Schoolbook Association. 14cm.
(O)

1450. Anon. 1838c. *The principles of English grammar, in raised letters, for the use of the blind*. (Books for the Blind). Glasgow: Institution Press. 21x25, 100pp. (unpaginated), 5s.
(L O)
[Traditional OESP account, certainly not original, but copied from an established grammar; includes a great deal of 'false syntax' underneath the numbered rules. Punctuation at end.]

1451. Anon. ⁴1841. *The principles of English grammar; with the rules of syntax exemplified; drawn up for the Scottish School-Book Association (No. VIII. of a New Series of School-Books)*. Edinburgh: William Whyte for Scottish School Book Association. 126pp. (Ster. ed. 1847; anr. ed. 1852; anr. ed. 1861, Glasgow).
(L O Hu, Lw)
[Clear, but unexciting; ES, with a few pages on style, prosody and Scotticisms at end; plenty of notes and exercises interspersed. A sequel to *The young child's grammar*.]

1452. Anon. [1893]. *The private tutor, or a Book for the million. [Lesson in English grammar for Bengali students.]* Calcutta: Milan Press. 132pp.
(L)

1453. Proctor, F.J. 1882. *A first grammar*. London: Hamilton, Adams & Co. / Portsmouth: H. Lewis. 18x12, 24pp., 2d.
(L)
[Minimal information on nine parts of speech and eight rules of syntax on p.24; one of the most barren books of its type.]

1454. Anon. 1834. *Progressive exercises; or easy steps to the knowledge of grammar. By the author of Flora's offering to the young*. London.
(G L)

1455. Pucket, E.B. 1853. *Principles of English grammar*. n.p.
($)

1456.$ Pue, Hugh A. (1812-1867). 1841. *A grammar of the English language in a series of letters, addressed to every American youth*. Philadelphia. 15cm, 149pp.
($ Br)

1457. Pullen, P.H. 1820. *The mother's book; or, grammar of English parsing: exemplifying Pestalozzi's plan of awakening the understanding of children in language, drawing, geometry, geography, and numbers*. London: Black. 19cm, xii+1-20, 48-275. (Anr. ed. 1822, xxviii+321pp. ($)).

($ L *Br, Hu, Lw, Ma*)
[The reference to Pestalozzi is true only for the short introduction relating to language *inter alia*; part II is a traditional grammar without innovative features, including syntax, parsing, composition and style. Reviewed by Martin 1824:155-60.]

1458. Pulling, E. (Head Master, New Barnet Schools, London). [1887-89]. *English grammar for the standards. Standard I-V.* Dublin etc.: Alexander Thom & Co. 17cm, Standard II: 16pp., Standard III: 32pp., Standard IV: 48pp., Standard V: 48pp. (Standard II-V (O)). Also includes Standards VI and VII.
(L O)
[The series treats noun & verb; pronoun, adjective and adverb and other parts of speech, sentence formation; uses of parts of speech, parsing examples and grammatical questions set by H.M. Inspectors; analysis and word-building; analysis of complex sentences, government and composition, with numerous exercises. No regard is taken to teaching in Ireland. Also available in one book, for Pupil Teachers.]

1459. Anon. 1892. *The pupil's English grammar: being an introduction to the study of English grammar based on the analysis of sentences.* London: Blackie. 16x10.5, 207pp.
(L O)
[Explained in a leisurely style, with easy definitions; the concentration on analysis (no orthography, vocabulary, or prosody are included) permits the author to avoid too compressed exposition. He acknowledges "his indebtedness to Canon Daniel's lecture and Grammar".]

1460. Anon. n.d. *The Pupils' own grammar. For all the standards.* (Derby Series). Derby: The Central Educational Company, Ltd. etc. 48pp.
(O)
[OESP, minimal definitions; exercises mainly on classification, analysis and parsing; rules for composition and word-formation at the end.]

1461.! Anon. [a1848]. *The pupil teacher's English grammar and etymology. With an introduction upon the best mode of conducting classes in this subject.* London: Simpkin & Marshall.
[Advertised in 1848.]

1462.$ Putnam, John March. 1825. *English grammar.* (Murray's Modified). Concord, N.H. 18mo, 162pp. (Anr. ed. 1825, 18cm, viii+142pp. ($); anr. ed. 1828, as *English grammar, with an improved syntax. Part I. Comprehending at one view what is necessary to be committed to memory. Part II. Containing a recapitulation, with various illustrations and critical remarks. Designed for the use of schools*, 15cm, ix+180pp. ($);

ster. ed. 1831, Concord, N.H.: Hoag & Atwood, 14.5x8.5, 162+[2]pp. (140pp., Samuel Beede's *Questions*, appended) ($ L)).
($ @ L *Br*)
[OESP, nine parts of speech. Traditional compilation from various sources (unnamed); definitions and rules followed by illustrations and discussions; parsing exercises (145-52). Samuel Beede's *Questions*, designed to assist the pupil in acquiring a knowledge of English grammar, particularly adapted to Putnam's Grammar (12pp.) are bound, and advertised, with the grammar and cannot be considered an independent publication. For study questions also cf. no. 140.]

1463.$ ---. 1848. *A comprehensive grammar, or, Analysis of the English language, on a new and improved plan: designed for common and high schools, and other seminaries of learning.* n.p. 18cm, 198pp. (Anr. ed. 1849 ($)).
($)

1464.$! Putnam, Samuel. ?1828. *Putnam's Murray.* (Impr. ster. ed.) *An abridgement of Murray's English grammar. Containing also punctuation, the notes under rules in syntax and lessons in parsing. ... To ... which is adapted, a new system of questions.* From the second Portsmouth ed., enl. and impr. Dover, N.G. 18mo, 108pp.
(*Br*)

1465. Putsey, W. (Master of the Grammar School, Pickering, Yorks). 1821. *A practical English grammar, for the use of schools, containing rules arranged under their proper heads, for acquiring a competent knowledge of the English language; with an appendix containing a great variety of exercises in orthography, syntax, parsing, and punctuation. Accompanied also by a grammatical retrospect, or questions for a thorough examination of the pupil in every department of grammar.* London: Longman, Hurst, Rees, Orme & Brown, etc. 14.5x8.5, viii+189pp., 2s. (²1829, 18mo, 211pp.).
(A C L *Br*)
[An intermediate version between Murray's *Abridgment* and *Grammar* to supply information "necessary to be attained by young gentlemen intended for commercial pursuits". OESP, succinct, dry definitions, largely derivative. A large appendix (101-79) comprises exercises in orthography, parsing, syntax and punctuation. A *key* was envisaged, but apparently never published.]

1466.$ Quackenbos, George Payn. (Principal of "The Collegiate School", 1826-1881). 1862. *An English grammar.* New York: Appleton. 18x11.5, 288pp. (Anr. ed. 1863 ($); anr. ed. 1864 ($); at least seven further editions between 1865 and 1888 ($)).

($ L)

[Prompted by his revision of Weld (no. 1822) to write a grammar of his own. OESP; nine parts of speech. Very detailed arguments, notes in small print, exercises inserted, further questions printed as footnotes; generally clear, but somewhat overloaded. Some 'false syntax'.]

1467.$ ---. 1851. *First lessons in composition: in which the principles of the art are developed in connection with the principles of grammar; embracing full directions on the subject of punctuation, with copious exercises.* n.p. 18/19cm, 182pp. ($). (Anr. ed. 1852 ($); anr. ed. 1853 ($); anr. ed. 1856 ($); thirteen editions recorded between 1858 and 1886 ($)).
($)

1468.$ ---. 1864. *First book in English grammar.* n.p. 17cm, 120pp. (Anr. ed. 1868, 17cm, 120pp. ($); anr. ed. 1871 ($); anr. ed. 1874 ($); anr. ed. 1883 ($)).
($)

1469.$ ---. 1876. *Illustrated lessons in our language, or, How to speak and write correctly: designed to teach English grammar, without its technicalities.* n.p. (Anr. ed. 1877, 18cm, 180pp.; anr. ed. 1878, as *Illustrated lessons on language* ... ($); anr. ed. 1880 (from 1876 ed.), (Minnesota Textbook Series), 192pp. ($)).
($)

1470.! Quentin, D.St. 1812. *The rudiments of general grammar, applicable to all languages [but applied to English only].* n.p.
(*Ma*)

[Reviewed in Martin 1824:160-1.]

1471. Querini, S.E. 1884. *First lessons in English grammar.* London: Wyman & Sons. 16x10, 31pp. (in large print).
(L O)

[(Eight) parts of speech in rudimentary definitions, with questions.]

1472.$ Anon. 1839. *Question on grammar used in Union Female Academy.* Danville, Va: Union Female Academy. 16cm, 22pp.
($)

1473. R., J.W. 1839. *An epitome of English grammar; calculated to facilitate the study of the English language, with questions for examination at the end of each division; and an appendix, containing exercises in parsing: designed for the younger classes of learners.* London: Jonathan Wacey. 15cm, 118pp.
(L O)

[OESP, nine parts of speech, traditional (diluted Latin base). Rules to be memorized "not allowing the omission of a letter"; questions at end of chapters.]

1474. Rae, George. 1844. *First lessons in English grammar.* Edinburgh: Oliver & Boyd / London: Simpkin, Marshall & Co. 6d.
(L *Lw*)
1475.! Rae, Hugh Rose. [a1882]. *An explanatory English grammar.* n.p.
[Inferred from no. 1476.]
1476. ---. [1882]. *How to analyse: being Part 2 of An Explanatory English grammar.* London. 15cm, 45pp.
(L O)
[Sentence analysis ("particular") and clause analysis ("general").]
1477. Ramsay, Samuel. 1892. *The English language and English grammar. An historical study of the sources, development, and analogies of the language and of the principles governing its usages* ... London/New York: G. P. Putnam & Sons. 24/25cm, iv+571pp., $2.
($ E L O)
[The second part, pp. 217-551, treats the parts of speech and syntax in a discursive way; all relevant topics are discussed, but not in form of rules and exceptions. Moderately historical.]
1478. Ramsay, Rev. Walter Marlo (Incumbent of St. Ninian's, Castle-Douglas). 1875. *A treatise on the analysis of sentences.* London: Whittaker. 18x12, 56pp. (^{2}1877; ^{3}1885, Manchester).
(L)
[Various types of sentences, clauses and phrases defined, with exercises appended to each chapter; the methods geared to practical analysis. Unexciting; acknowledges Morell, Mason, Dalgleish and others.]
1479. Ramsey, E.M. (Late Assistant Mistress at the Wimbledon High School for Girls) & C.L. 1895-96. *Steps to English parsing and analysis.* 2 vols. (Parallel Grammar Series). London: Swan Sonnenschein & Co. 18cm, vii+80pp.
(O)
[Exercises only, mainly classification of words, changes of construction - not a proper grammar.]
1480.$ Rand, Asa. 1832. *Teacher's manual for instructing in English grammar. Re-published from the Education Reporter, with amendments and additions.* Boston: Richardson, Lord & Holbrook. 14x9, iv+[5]-90pp.
(L *Br*)
[Discusses strategies available to teachers to introduce etymology and syntax to beginners, dealing with the relevant categories and terms in a chatty way, pointing to the general unintelligibility of grammar definitions and discussing alternatives. An early though not quite convincing attempt at teaching grammar "on the inductive plan".]

1481.$ Raub, Albert Newton (1840-1904). 1880a. *Lessons in English: A practical course of language lessons and elementary grammar.* n.p. 18cm, 160/176pp. (Anr. ed. 1880, 19cm, 256pp. ($), anr. ed. 1894, 176pp. ($)).
($)

1482.$ ---. 1880b. *A practical English grammar: for the use of schools and private students.* n.p. 20cm, 256pp. (Anr. ed. 1894).
($)

1483.$ ---. 1885. *Grammatical analysis by diagrams.* n.p. 19cm, 48pp.
($)

1484.$ ---. 1889. *Hints and helps on English grammar. A discussion of difficulties found in hard sentences. For the use of private students and teachers of English grammar.* n.p. 19cm, 302pp.
($)

1485.$ ---. 1897. *Helps in the use of good English: a hand-book for all who desire to speak or write correct English.* n.p. 20cm, 260pp.
($)

1486.! Raw, George (Formerly second master of the Grammar School, Kirkby Lonsdale). [a1893]. *The parser's companion ... containing the definitions and derivations of the eight parts of speech, together with a full scheme for parsing each of them.* (Anr. ed. 1893, fifth thousand, Manchester).
(*Mp*)
[Nothing of interest.]

1487.! Rawlinson, William Wyndham. 1815. *Practical English grammar.* London.
(*Ma, Mi*)
[Reviewed by Martin 1824:36-38.]

1488.$ Ray, J.S. 1858. *A practical English grammar, in which words are parsed as they are used by our best writers and speakers.* n.p. 103pp.
($)

1489.$ Reed, Alonzo. (d. 1899). 1876. *Graded lessons in English: an elementary English grammar consisting of one hundred practical lessons, carefully graded and adapted to the classroom.* n.p. 17/18cm, 143pp. (Anr. ed. 1878, 164pp. ($); anr. ed. 1879 ($); anr. ed. 1883 (from 1878 ed.) ($); anr. ed. 1884 ($); anr. ed. 1885 ($); anr. ed. 1886 ($); anr. ed. 1889; anr. ed. 1890, 200pp. ($); anr. ed. 1891 ($); anr. ed. 1894 ($); anr. ed. 1895 ($); anr. ed. 1896, 164pp. ($)).
($)
["consisting of one hundred practical lessons carefully graded and adapted to the class room". *Graded* and *Higher* Lessons "completely cover the ground of grammar and composition from the time the scholar

usually begins the study until it is finished in the High School and Academy" (advertisement, 1886).]

1490.$ ---. 1879. *Elementary English grammar: consisting of one hundred practical lessons, carefully graded and adapted to the class-room.* (Graded Lessons in English). n.p. 17/18cm, 164pp. (Anr. ed. 1883, 215pp. ($); anr. ed. 1889, 200pp. ($); anr. ed. 1896, 215pp. ($)). ($)
[Probably the same book as no. 1489.]

1491.$ ---. 1888. *A one-book course in English: in which the pupil is led by a series of observation lessons to discover and apply the principles that underlie the construction of the sentence, and that control the use of grammatical forms: a complete text-book on grammar and composition: for schools whose curriculum will not allow time for the authors' two-book course.* n.p. 17cm, 328pp. (Anr. ed. 1891 ($); anr. ed. 1895 ($)). ($)

1492.$ ---. 1889. *Key containing diagrams of the sentences given for analysis: in Reed and Kellogg's Graded lessons in English and Higher lessons in English.* n.p. 19cm, 6+131pp. (Anr. ed. 1891, 19cm, 6+128pp. ($)). ($)

1493.$ ---. 1891. *Introductory language work: a simple, varied, and pleasing, but methodical, series of exercises in English to precede the study of technical grammar.* n.p. 17cm, 253pp. (Anr. ed. 1898 ($)). ($)

1494.$ ---. 1892. *Word lessons for intermediate and grammar grades* ... n.p. 20cm, 188pp.
($)

1495.$ --- & Brainerd Kellogg. 1877?. *Higher lessons in English: a work on English grammar and composition, in which the science of the language is made tributary to the art of expression. A course of practical lessons carefully graded, and adapted to everyday use in the schoolroom.* n.p. (Anr. ed. 1878, 17/18cm, 264/280pp. ($); anr. ed. 1879, 282pp. ($); anr. ed. 1880 ($); anr. ed. 1882 ($); anr. ed. 1883 ($); anr. ed. 1884 ($); anr. ed. 1885 ($); rev. ed. ?1886, New York: Clark & Maynard; anr. ed. 1887 ($); anr. ed. 1889 ($); anr. ed. 1890 ($); anr. ed. 1891 ($); anr. ed. 1892, 316+63pp. ($); anr. ed. 1893, 328pp. ($); anr. ed. 1894, 316pp. ($); anr. ed. 1895, 316pp. ($); anr. ed. 1896, x+386+63pp. ($); anr. ed. 1897, x+386+76/x+386pp. ($); anr. ed. 1889, 316pp. ($); anr. ed. 1893 ($); repr. 1987, Delmar: Scholars' Facsimiles & Reprints).
($)

[This, and the *Graded Lessons*, make a complete grammar course; how popular the work was can be seen from the number of editions published. "Introductory hints" provided for pupils to prepare them for definitions (in bold) - the inductive method is consistently used to make pupils understand rather than learn by rote. Stresses the value of "practice by varied and exhaustive drill in composition", starting with the sentence. Eight parts of speech. Analysis and parsing visualized through simple diagrams (possibly stimulated by Harvey no. 804.). Advice on style at end (284-316).]

1496.$! Reed, Caleb. 1821. *English grammar*. Boston. 18mo, 36pp.
(*Br, We*)

1497.! Rees. n.d. chapter on "Grammar" in Rees's *Encyclopaedia*.
(*Ma*)
[Reviewed in Martin 1824:396-7.]

1498. Reid, Alexander (Rector of the Circus-Place School, Edinburgh, 1802-1860). 1837. *Rudiments of English grammar*. Edinburgh: Oliver & Boyd. 48pp., 6d. (^{2}1839, London, 18mo, 46pp.; ^{4}1843, Edinburgh; ^{11}1854; ^{14}1861 (*Wm*); rev. ed. ^{21}1872, with exercises and a new chapter, Edinburgh, 15cm; ^{23}1874; 23 editions recorded to 1874).
(L O *Br, Hu, Lw, Wm*)
[For use in Elementary classes, rules "expressed so briefly so as to admit of being readily committed to memory (...) all explanations left to the Teacher". The relationship with books of similar titles mentioned by early grammar writers is not clear: *Lw*: *Rudiments ...*, 1837, no place; *Br*: *Engl. Gram.*, ^{2}1839. London. 18mo, 46pp.; *Hu*: *Rudimentaries...*, ^{4}1839. Edinburgh. There is also a book called *Rudiments of English composition; designed as a practical introduction to correctness and perspicuity in writing, and to the study of criticism: with copious exercises. For the use of schools*. Edinburgh: Oliver & Boyd / London: Simpkin, Marshall, & Co., ^{14}1861. Part I: Spelling, Punctuation, Use of Words, Structure of Sentences, Arrangement of Sentences; Part II: Style, Figurative Language; Part III: Original Composition. 134pp. (*Wm*)].

1499. Reid, Hugo (Principal, People's College, Nottingham). 1850. *Outlines of English grammar, with a series of instructive extracts, for lessons in reading and grammatical exercises*. Nottingham: W. Taylor. 136pp.
(N)
[Combines a grammar, Latinate, with a reader. The only Shakespeare extract is from *Titus Andronicus*!]

1500. Reid, John (1764/5-1830). 1829. *An outline of English grammar; with explanatory notes and orthographical exercises. For the use of schools*. Glasgow. 12mo, iv+68pp. (Anr. ed. 1830, Glasgow ($)).

($ Gm *Br*)
[Very odd. Q/A form, with exercises in false English. Uses Perry's phonetic system to show pronunciation. Gives second person pronouns six cases. A little on history of language.]

1501. $ Reinhart, Jacob Albert. 1890. *Grammar for the use of teachers and those preparing to teach. Complete with answers.* (Analytical Question Series, No. 3). New York/Chicago: E.L. Kellogg & Co. 17cm, 104pp. ($ @)

1502. $ Anon. 1843. *Report of the executive committee on the subject of English grammar.* New York/Boston: American Society for the Diffusion of Useful Knowledge. 22cm, 24pp. ($).

1503. Revis, B., pseud.. 1856. *English grammar in metre, for memories short; to pleasant pass-time, and availing pass-port.* London: Mozley. 14cm, 26pp.
(L O)
[In poor verse, with longer prose passages for definitions interspersed.]

1504. Reynolds, Fred. W. 1899. *Notes and exercises on paragraph structure and punctuation.* n.p. 19cm, 63pp.
($)

1505. Reynolds, George. 1813. *The Madras school grammar; or, The new system reduced to questions and answers. ... chiefly arranged from the Rev. Dr. Bell's instructions ...* London: Philanthropic Society. iv+32pp.
(L)
[Elementary catechism for Madras schools.]

1506. Reynolds, I.L. 1876. *The history and grammar of the English language: adapted to the use of pupil teachers and normal schools.* New ed. London: Simpkin & Marshall. 18x11.5, v+175pp.
(C O)
[Bromby's well-known grammar of 1848, out of print after twenty-five editions, was revised by ILR to make it "more suitable for the new generation of Elementary Teachers", omitting some of the History, and adding a chapter on Analysis. OES were published independently before and are here continued with Analysis. A close comparison with Bromby would be necessary to test the reviser's claims.]

1507. Rice, M. 1835, *An initiatory step to English composition, or grammatical analysis facilitated by means of an expository theory: accompanied by suitable exercises ...* London: Nathaniel Hailes. 19cm, x+167pp.
($ L *Lw*)
[Some general discussion of language and of the parts of speech. Three methods of sentence analysis. More thoughtful than many.]

1508. Richardson, J.L. (of Brompton Board Schools). [1885]. *'English' practice in analysis, parsing, word formation, composition, and paraphrasing.* London: George Philip. iv+82pp.
(H)

1509. ---. 1886. *Watson's graduated exercises in parsing for standards III and IV.* 2 parts. London: Simpkin, Marshall & Co., etc.
(O)
[Minimal definitions; mainly sentences for parsing; "arranged with an eye to speedy, accurate work, and ready reference to points requiring frequent revisal".]

1510. Riches, Arthur. 1883. *A public examination grammar.* London: Relfe Bros. 18x12, vi+196pp. (^{5}[a1898]).
(L)
[Q/A form in examination style, arranged according to the nine parts of speech, with 'various' questions appended (including some historical/etymological matter and a section on syntax). Places weight on using actual examination questions from university locals, and acknowledges his debt to Angus, Latham, Adams, Bain, Mason and Morell.]

1511. Rickard, Truman (1814-1861). 1847?. *Class book of prose and poetry: consisting of selections from the best English and American authors: designed as exercises in parsing: for the use of common schools and academies.* n.p. (Anr. ed. 1850 (from 1847 ed.), 16cm, 120pp. ($)).
($)

1512. Ricker, George Hodgson. 1887a. *Elements of English: an introduction to English grammar: for the use of schools.* n.p. 19cm, 100pp.
($).

1513. Ricord, Frederick William (1819-1897). 1853?. *The youth's grammar, or, Easy lessons in etymology.* n.p. (Anr. ed. 1855 (from 1853 ed.), 18cm, 118pp. ($); anr. ed. 1856 ($)).
($)

1514. Ridpath, John Clark (1840-1900). 1880?. *An inductive grammar of the English language: for the use of common and graded schools.* (Inductive Series). n.p. (Anr. ed. 1881 (from 1880 ed.) 19cm, vi+327pp. ($)).
($)

1515.$ Rigdon, Jonathan (Professor, Central Normal College, 1858-1933). 1886?. *Language and grammar for the grades.* n.p. 20cm, 241pp.
($)

1516.$ ---. 1890. *Grammar of the English sentence, and introduction to composition.* Danville, Ind.: Indiana Publ. Co. 19.5x12.5, iii+281pp., 85c. (Anr. ed. 1891 ($)).
($ L)

[Starting from the sentence and defining the functions and properties of eight parts of speech with great care. Exercises for parsing and analysis throughout, introducing (202-) complex diagrams illustrating sentence structure; composition at end.]

1517.$! ---. [a1890]. *Analysis of the English sentence with diagrams.* n.p. 75c. [Inferred from no. 1516.]

1518.$ ---. 1896a. *English grammar for the common school.* n.p. 19cm, 266pp.
($)

1519.$ ---. 1896b. *English grammar for beginners with language.* n.p. 20cm, 266pp.
($)

1520. Ritchie, Francis. 1886. *English grammar and analysis.* London: Rivington. 16cm, 211pp./xi+215pp.
(L O)

[Etymology - eight parts of speech - and syntax/analysis only; tense/aspect arranged under tense (making nine options); quite detailed, but not optimally organized.]

1521.$ Robbins, Manasseh. 1826. *Rudimental lessons in etymology and syntax: in which these two parts of grammar are exhibited in parallel columns: carefully adapted to the capacity of young learners.* Providence, R.I. 19cm, 69/70pp.
($ *Br*)

1522. Robertson, John (LL.D., of Upton Park School, late lecturer at the Glasgow Church of Scotland Training College). [1873?]. *Daily exercises in English and French grammar.* London. 16x10, 106pp.
(O)

[The book consists of 432 questions to English grammar spread over 54 days (= nine weeks, Sundays are days of rest) and another 296 for 48 days on French grammar. There are no explanations whatsoever, but "An Answer Book may be had on application to the publisher". Note that the distinction between 'John' and 'P.' Robertson is not quite clear.]

1523. ---. [1878?]. *The analysis of sentences.* London: Thomas Murby. 16pp. 1d. (Anr. ed. [1888], London: Thomas Murby).
(L)

[Definitions and exercises only, of no independent value.]

1524. ---. [1879a]. *English analysis papers.* n.p.
(L)

1525. ---. [1879b]. *English parsing papers.* n.p.
(L)

1526. ---. [1879c]. *Summary of English grammar.* London: Thomas Murby. 16cm, 16pp.
(L O)
[Eight parts of speech only discussed; no OSP; short definitions with specimens enumerated.]

1527. ---. [1888]. *Grammatical analysis; with numerous exercises.* London: Thomas Murby. 16x10, 32pp., 2d.
(L)
[Short definitions, explanations and directions to analysis with plentiful exercises. Of no independent value.]

1528. Robertson, P. (Lecturer at the Glasgow Training College). [1868]. *(Murby's) Introductory English grammar.* London: Thomas Murby. 16cm, 62pp., 3d. (^{2}1868).
(L O)
[Abridged from *Murby's grammar and analysis*; eight parts of speech defined, with a sprinkling of syntax. Mentions six Divisions of grammar at end: Orthography, Pronunciation, Classification, Inflection, Syntax, Composition (7. Etymology) - of which only classification and inflection are here treated.]

1529. ---. [1869]. *(Murby's) English grammar and analysis, taught simultaneously with numerous exercises.* London: Thomas Murby. 16cm, 124pp., 6d/9d. (L). (Anr. ed. 1874 (New Brunswick School Series), 124pp. ($); new ed. 1880, 128pp. (L); new and enl. ed. [1882], London, 16cm; new and enl. ed. [1888], London, 160pp.(L)).
($ L O)
[Minimal definitions geared to the parsing exercises interspersed, with great weight given to the verb, and leading up to complex and compound sentences.]

1530.$! Robinson, John. 1830. *English grammar.* Maysville. 12mo, 95pp.
(*Br*)

1531.! ---. [a1870a]. *Introductory Grammar.* n.p. 64pp., 3d.
[Advertised in no. 970.]

1532.! ---. [a1870b]. *Grammar and analysis taught simultaneously.* n.p.
[Advertised in no. 970.]

1533. Rogers, Henry (Professor of the English Language and Literature, University College, London, President of Lancashire Independent College, 1807-66). 1838. *A general introduction to a course of lectures on English grammar and composition.* London: William Ball. 14.5x8.5, v+131pp.
(L O)

[Two introductory lectures on English grammar and composition "in the widest sense." Adult in tone, scholarly, adopts H. Tooke's parts of speech.]

1534. Roome, Thomas. 1812. *A companion to English grammar, or familiar exercises, adapted to the capacities of children, and designed as an introduction to the study of the English language.* Nottingham. iv + 54pp.
(N)

1535. Rose, A.S. & (S. E.) Lang (Inspectors of Schools, Manitoba). 1899. *An introduction to English grammar with special reference to the logical study of the sentence.* Toronto: The Copp, Clark Company. 18x12, ix + 173pp.
($ L)
[Said to be "a preparation for the more advanced study of English grammar", but making some demands on the reader by way of logical analysis and philosophical interpretation. Exercises (99-173) to identify 'thought forms and predications'. Decidedly non-mainstream.]

1536.! Ross, James. 1819. *Grammatical studies on the Latin and English languages.* n.p.
(*Mp*)

1537. Ross, John (Rector of the Grammar School, Selkirk). 1805. *A compendium of English grammar, with a few exercises in geography.* Hawick: the author. 24pp., 4d.
(E)
[Derivative; slight.]

1538.! Ross, William (Vicar of St Anne's, Alderney). 1842. *An elementary etymological manual of the English language for the use of schools. To which is prefixed, practical observations on the teaching of etymology.* 38pp. n.p. (Anr. ed. 1854, London: Longman).
(L *Mp*)
[Sensible approach to roots and word formation. Deplores practice of learning the dictionary by heart.]

1539. Ross, William Stewart. [1870]. *A practical textbook of grammatical analysis.* Edinburgh.
(C L O)
[Praises contemporary emphasis on sentence analysis: "excelled by no branch of study" in exercising "thinking and discriminating powers."]

1540. Anon. [1887]. *The royal grammar books. A new series to suit the present code.* 3 parts: *Grammar exercises for standards III - IV. Arranged for use with the "Royal Readers" and the "Royal Star Readers".* London: Thomas Nelson. 12 + 24pp.
(O)

[Minimal or no definitions, various types of exercises.]

1541.! Anon. n.d. *The rudiments of grammar, familiarly explained, in verse.* London: Dean & Munday.
[Advertised by Dean & Munday in Mrs Kentish's *The two friends* n.d.; with 13 coloured engravings.]

1542. Anon. 1853. *The rugged path made smooth; or, Grammar illustrated in scriptural truths.* By a lady. London: Wertheim. 150pp.
(C E L O)
[Grammar is confused with literacy; pietistic chat between mother and children.]

1543. Rusher, John Goldby. [1829]. *The English spelling book improved: containing, in a progressive series, a variety of tables of spelling, instructive lessons, and entertaining stories, adapted to the capacity of the youth. To which are added, a correct set of improved arithmetical tables (...), a concise English grammar, chronological tables, etc.* Banbury. 18x11, viii+[9]-164pp. (^{2}1830, Banbury; anr. ed. 1853 ($); anr. ed. [1874?], Banbury).
($ O)
["A concise grammar" takes up only pp. 142-7, providing minimal guidance on parts of speech and punctuation; while not of independent value, the book illustrates the educational context in which grammar teaching was placed for beginners.]

1544. Rushton, William (M.A. of University College, London, Professor of History & English Literature, Queen's College, Cork). 1869. *Rules and cautions in English grammar, founded on the analysis of sentences.* London: Longmans, Green & Co. 18x11, xix+316pp. (^{2}1870, xix+341pp.).
($ L O)
[The principles for analysis of sentences are followed by rules and cautions of the individual parts of speech, in which the author discusses problems and exceptions, quoting from the best grammarians, listed on p.ii); treats relation between grammar and logic, especially in the use of the copula; ambitious and not very clear. Elaborate sentence and clause analysis.]

1545. Russell, John (Prebendary of Canterbury, late Headmaster of Charterhouse, 1787-1863). 1833. *English grammar.* London: Christian Knowledge Society. 15cm, 167pp. (Anr. ed 1835; ^{9}1840 (L); ^{10}1842; ^{11}1851, 168pp.).
($ L *Br*, *Hu*, *Lw*)
[Designed as twenty-six "instructions" to William, who can answer questions pertly. Philosophical tone; biblical exhortation.]

1546. Russell, John. [1870]. *Murby's handbook of English etymology, with exercises and suggestions for teachers.* London: Thomas Murby. 46pp.
(C L O)

1547.$! Russell, William (1798-1873). 1819. *An abridgment of Murray's grammar.* Hartford. 18mo, 142pp.
(*Br*)

1548.$ ---. 1823a. *A grammar of composition: including a practical review of the principles of rhetoric, a series of exercises in rhetorical analysis, and six introductory courses of composition.* Newhaven. 19cm, 150pp.
($ *Br*)

1549.$ ---. 1823b. *Suggestions on education; relating particularly to the method of instruction commonly adopted in geography, history, grammar, logic, and the classics.* n.p. 22cm, [3], 4-32pp.
($)

1550.$ ---. 1856a. *Exercises on words. Designed as a course of practice on the rudiments of grammar and rhetoric.* Boston: Whittemore, Niles & Hall. 19cm, 225pp. ($).
($)

1551.$ ---. 1856b. *(Ins)titutes: or, An easy introduction to Dr. Lowth's English grammar, of grammar and rhetoric.* n.p. 19cm, vi+[7]-225pp.
($)

1552.! S., J. [1820]. *A compilation of the elements of English grammar, with a concise view of the principles of rhetoric; and rules of punctuation for the use of the scholars at Poplar House Academy.* London: Plummer & Brewis. 92pp.
(private ownership)

1553.! Sabine, H. 1802. *English grammar.* n.p.
(Allibone 1852)

1554. Sabine, John. 1807. *A guide to elocution, divided into six parts.* n.p.
(O *Lw*)

1555. Sadler, Percy. 1853. *The stepping stone to English grammar: calculated to enable children to acquire, by easy and agreeable means, a correct manner of expressing their ideas.* London: Longman, Green & Longmans. 14x9, 72pp., 1s. (New ed. 1867, 1s).
(E L O)
[For children aged six, upwards, applicable to all languages. Three general classes of words (N, V, Particle). Uses an adaption of Abbé Gaultier's grammatical game.]

1556. St. Quentin, Dominique de. 1812. *The first rudiment(arie)s of general grammar, applicable to all languages. Comprised in twelve elementary lessons. Particularly calculated for the instruction of children, and*

1556. St. Quentin, Dominique de

adapted to the Abbé Gaultier's method of teaching (with analytical tables). London: Longman, Hurst, Rees, Orme & Brown. 17cm, xix+163pp., 6s. With board and counters.
($ Br, Hu, Lw)

1557.$ Salamonski, Theodore J. 1885. *Grammar at a glance; a chart that defines, explains and illustrates the fundamental principles of English grammar.* St. Louis, Mo.: The Pioneer Publishing. 17cm, [5]pp. (Anr. ed. 1885, St. Louis, Mo./Hartford, Conn.: T. Salamonski (@)).
($ @)

1558. Salmon, David (H.?). 1876. *Exercises in English grammar and composition.* London: Moffatt & Paige. 18cm, 87pp. (Anr. ed. [1882]).
(L O)
["Not based on any particular grammar", with most of the sentences drawn "from classic writings"; the exercises are arranged under 'parts of speech, analysis, composition': "pick out and classify", etc.]

1559. ---. 1888. *A school grammar.* London/New York: Longman, Green & Co. 19cm, vii+264pp. (Anr. ed. 1891, as *Longman's school grammar with preface by Edgar A. Allen,* New York: Longman, Green & Co. ($ @); anr. ed. 1893 ($); anr. ed. 1896 ($); anr. ed. 1897 ($); anr. ed. 1899, [v]-vii+264pp. ($); anr. ed. 1900 (@)).
($ @ L)
[Eight parts of speech; standard material includes history and derivation.]

1560. ---. 1889. *Junior school grammar.* London/New York: Longman, Green & Co. iv+124pp. (Anr. ed. 1892, London (@); anr. ed. 1896, New York (@)).
(@ L)
[Also advertised in Jennings 1898 "school books specially prepared for India and Burma" as (...) *for India*; co-author A.J. Cooper Oakley, Madras (a revision?). *NUC* claims that the book has iv+305pp.]

1561. ---. 1892. *Longman's school composition.* n.p.: Longman. 19cm, 305pp.
($)

1562. ---. 1899. *Longman's briefer grammar.* n.p.: Longman. 19cm, iv+124pp.
($)

1563. Sampson, Theophilus. 1874. *Progressive lessons in English. Being an English conversational grammar for the use of Chinese students.* Hong Kong: Kelly & Walsh. 21x13.5, iv+204+iv pp. (^{7}1898).
(L)
[The book is interesting as an early attempt to depart from traditional English grammar which proved to be useless for the teaching of Chinese;

Sampson relies on many illustrative examples, but refrains from giving a comprehensive grammatical description.]

1564.$ Sanborn, Dyer Hook (Principal of the Woodman Sandborton Academy, 1799-1871). 1836. *An analytical grammar of the English language, embracing the inductive and productive methods of teaching ...: in five parts: being a complete system of grammar, and an appendix containing much new matter not found in other grammars* ... Concord, N.H./ Boston: March, Capen & Lyon. 19cm, v+[7]-299pp. (^{2}1840, 289pp. ($); ^{3}1840 (@); ^{4}1842, vi+[7]-288pp. ($ @); ^{6}1844 ($); impr. ed. ^{8}1846 (from 1836 ed.) ($ @); ^{13}1848 ($ @)).
($ @ L *Br*)
[Approves of exercises in false syntax; rhetoric and grammar should be taught together.]

1565.$ ---. 1846. *Sanborn's normal school grammar: being an abridgment of The analytical grammar the English language*. Concord, N.H.: G.P. Lyon. 18/19cm, iv+[5]-143pp. (^{4}1848 (@); anr. ed. 1850 ($); anr. ed. 1852 (@); anr. ed. 1855 (@); anr. ed. 1861 (from 1856 ed.) ($)).
($ @)

1566.$ Sanders, Charles Walton (1805-1889) & J.C. 1847. *The young grammarian. For the use of beginners in the study of English grammar*. Rochester, N.Y: 18cm, 120pp.
($ *Br*)

1567.$ Saul, S.S. 1877. *The English language: suggestions for its correct and fluent use without technical grammar*. San Leandro: B.F. Sterett, for the author. 15cm, 52pp.
($ @)

1568. Sayce, Archibald Henry. 1880. *Introduction to the science of language*. 2 vols. London: Kegan Paul & Co. (^{2}1883 (@); ^{3}1890 (@); anr. ed. 1900 (@)).
(@)

1569.$ Scheib, Heinrich (1808-1897). 1849. *The thought and its expression. A grammar after the system introduced into the best schools of Germany*. Baltimore: J.F. Zetzner. 17cm, xii+144pp. ($ @). (Anr. ed. 1873, ... *Prepared from the most approved authorities on the subject*, 18cm, xii+164pp. ($)).
($ @)

1570.$ Schellhous, E.J. 1869. *Manual of English grammar, designed for public and private instruction*. n.p. 78pp.
($)

1571. Schlieder, Leopoldina. 1855. *The principles of English grammar*. Dessau: Neubuerger. 20.5x12, vi+82pp.

(L)

[A compilation made during the author's stay in Britain, drawn from the best English grammars and much condensed. OESP, short definitions, with rules and observations interspersed. Unoriginal - the alleged usefulness for German learners is not apparent.]

1572. Anon. 1863. *The schoolboy's short English grammar, on an original plan; being a collection of short definitions, designed to be committed to memory, with examples and exercises.* Manchester: John Heywood / London: Simpkin, Marshall & Co. 16x10, 48pp., 2d/4d. (Later edited as Anon. 1871. *A plain, practical English grammar, on an original plan, being a collection of short definitions ... with examples and exercises. By two Schoolmasters.* Manchester: John Heywood / London: Simpkin, Marshall & Co., 16x10, 87pp. (L)).

(E L O)

["On an original plan; being a collection of short definitions, designed to be committed to memory, with examples and exercises", advertised in Yaks 1871. (On Anon. 1871): Treats grammar and analysis only, seven parts of speech plus interjection. Elementary, no long explanations (to be left to the teacher); claims the merits of clearness, efficiency, novelty and unparallelled cheapness.]

1573. Anon. 1832. *The schoolmaster at home. Errors in speaking and writing corrected (etc.).* n.p. (O). (Anr. ed. 1835 ($); anr. ed. 1855 ($ L); anr. ed. 1857, New York; anr. ed. 1866).

($ L O)

1574. Scotson, James (Head Master of Peter Street Schools, Manchester). [1876]. *An English grammar and analysis, with copious exercises. For elementary schools. Expressly arranged to assist pupil teachers in giving lessons ...* Manchester/Frome/London: Ledsham. 16.5x10.5, iv+68pp.

(L O)

[Discursive and simple style, with explicit advice for pupil teachers on how to proceed, making the book a blend of a grammar and reflexions on how to teach. Parts of speech analysis, inflexions, with many exercises, not always optimally arranged. Scotson's books were mostly published anonymously; cf. no. 1575]

1575. ---. [1876]. *(Ledsham's) Grammar for standards II, III, and IV, expressly arranged to assist pupil teachers in giving lessons.* Manchester: J.B. Ledsham. 16pp.

(L O)

[Eight parts of speech briefly discussed, with exercises; parsing added at end. The author wants "to make lessons not merely a matter of memory but of thought (...) compelling the student to depend on function, not on form or order.]

1576.! ---. [1877]. *Ledsham's grammatical test cards. Standard III. Thirty-six different cards*. n.p. 1s.
[Advertised in no. 986.]

1577. Scott, A. (Writer on Grammar). 1820. *Grammar of the English language; being the precursor of a series of grammars constructed on a simple and economical plan, and constituting a general system of education*. London: John Joseph Stockdale. 18cm, xii+[13]-262pp.
(@ L *Hu*, *Lw*)

1578.$ Scott, Allen M. 1861. *A new southern grammar of the English language designed for the use of schools and private learners*. Memphis. 19cm, 96pp.
($ @)

1579. Scott, Walter (Master of the Grammar School, Bourn). [1855]. *The parts of speech: an introduction to English grammar, in verse; with questions and remarks appended to each part of speech, together with numerous examples in parsing*. London: Jarrold & Sons, pr. in Norwich. 14x9, vi+62pp., 9d.
(L)
[Mediocre verses are accompanied by explanatory footnotes and questions to check whether the contents are understood. The author's laudable aim of making grammar more attractive cannot have been very successful. Mainly on parts of speech, but with extensive parsing lessons.]

1580. entry deleted.

1581. Searle, Rev. Thomas. 1822. *An English grammar in verse, with examples selected from scripture*. Chipping Norton: the author. 15/16cm, viii+114pp.
(@ C L O *Br*, *Lw*)
[Traditional OESP grammar; the verse is quite metrical and competent in most places. Nine parts of speech. Intended as an introduction to Lindley Murray. Written in verse because "the study of the English language is generally irksome". He claims, incorrectly, that his use of the verse form is unique.]

1582.$ Seath, John (Inspector of High Schools for Ontario, 1844-1919). 1887. *The high school English grammar based on Whitney's Essentials of English grammar*. Toronto: Canada Publishing Co. 19x12.5, 405pp. ($).
(^{2}1899, Toronto: Canada Publishing Co., 416pp. ($ @ L)).
($ @ L)

[On ²1899: Sentence-based account; classes of sentences, words and their components, followed by the syntax of parts of speech; a historical outline, affixes, exercises at end. Very careful reasoning leading up to definitions; seven parts of speech (three independent: N, Pron, V; two modifiers: Adj, Adv; two connectives: Prep, Conj; plus Interjection). Detailed and informative, but not for use in schools. The first edition of 1886 was based on Whitney, Maetzner and Lounsbury, to which 1899 a number of sources were added (e.g. Kellner and Sweet's *New English Grammar.*]

1583. Anon. 1803. *The secretary, and complete letter writer; containing a collection of letters upon most occasions and situations in life. To which is added, an essay on letter writing, by S. Johnson, and an introduction to English grammar.* Birmingham: Knott & Lloyd, also sold by L.B. Seeley & Vernor & Hood, London. 19cm, 5 p.l., lxxii + 168pp.
(@ L O)
[The grammar is found on pp. i-lxxi. OES, ten parts of speech; 18th-century style; preterimperfect tense etc.]

1584. Anon. 1822. *A self-guide to the knowledge of the English language in English and Bengalee, containing words of one to seven syllables with their pronounciation and meaning. To which is added a short English grammar chiefly intended for natives of all capacity.* Calcutta: Bengalee Press. 19.5x12, 152pp.
(L)
[Pp.120-136 contain a very brief English grammar with Bengali translation. OE, nine parts of speech, elementary, and noteworthy only for the early combination with an Indian language.]

1585. Anon. 1807. *The self-instructor, or young man's best companion; being an introduction to all the various branches of useful knowledge: containing writing, grammar, arithmetic, astronomy, geography, chronology, and miscellaneous articles.* ... Liverpool: pr. Nuttall, Fisher & Dixon. 21x13, iv + 596pp. (Anr. ed. 1813; anr. ed. 1815; anr. ed. [1837?], London: H. Fisher, Son & Co., 23cm, 3 p.l., 593 + [3]pp. (@)).
(@ L)
[Only a tiny portion, pp. 1-23, is devoted to grammar (letters, sounds, words, punctuations and various mixed information on parts of speech) without apparent order or any independent value.]

1586. Serjeant, W.T. [1890]. *Ledsham's grammatical questions. Four parts (for standard III, IV, V, VI.* Manchester: James B. Ledsham. 12 pages each.
(O)
[Questions and exercises for repetition, no key.]

1587. Sewell, Elizabeth Missing (1815-1906). 1872. *Grammar made easy.* London: Longmans, Green & Co. 16.5x10.5, x+115pp.
(@ L)
[Conversational tone, in Q/A form; ES, eight parts of speech, with remarks on polyfunctional elements (96-102); parsing exercises at end. Summaries at end of chapters to be committed to memory. Traditional and unexciting.]

1588. Sharpley, Charles Gregory (Master of an academy, St Thomas's St., Birmingham). 1803. *Instructions in the first principles of grammar and arithmetic, in the form of dialogue.* Birmingham: the author. 58pp.
(L O)
[Dialogue form; very poor.]

1589. Shatford, W. (Schoolmaster, Kettering). 1834. *An English grammar, adapted to the younger classes of learners.* London: William Edwards. 14x8.5, ii+104pp., 15d.
(L Br)
[Modest, traditional OESP account, with examples for practice following short rules (obviously to be memorized); key at end, pp. 98-104.]

1590.$ Anon. 1895. *Sheldon's advanced language lessons: grammar and composition.* (Sheldon's Language Series). New York: Sheldon & Co. 20cm, 376pp. (Anr. ed. 1899 (from 1895 ed.), New York: Butler, Sheldon & Co. (@)).
($ @)

1591. Shelley, Edward. ²1848. *The people's grammar; or English grammar without difficulties for 'the million'.* Huddersfield: Bond & Hardy. ([³1850], Huddersfield: Bond & Hardy, 24pp.). 12cm, ii+26pp.
(L O)
[Stressing the want of such a brief "manual in Infant Schools, the Nursery, and Day Schools, and especially in Night Schools and Mechanics Institutions" and aiming at "simplicity, clearness and PRICE ... useful, especially to the mechanic and hard-working youth, in their solitary struggles for the acquirement of knowledge". Very rudimentary and unexciting.]

1592.$ Shepherd, Henry Elliot (1844-1929). 1881. *An elementary grammar of the English language.* Baltimore: J.B. Piet. 19cm, iv+128pp.
($)

1593.$ ---. 1883. *A grammar of the English language.* (Language Series). Baltimore: J.B. Piet. 19cm, 144pp.
($)

1594.$! Sherman, John (1772-1828). 1826a. *American grammar.* Trenton Falls, N.Y. 12mo, 323pp.

(*Br*)

1595. ---. 1826b. *The philosophy of language illustrated; an entirely new system of grammar: wholly divested of scholastic rubbish, of traditionary falsehood and absurdity, and reduced to principles of fact and common sense: according to the real nature, genius, and idiom of the English tongue: designed for colleges, academies, and district schools in the United States.* Trenton Falls, N.Y.: Dawby & Maynard. 19cm, vi+ 324pp.
($ @)
[A highly personal cry for innovation: "I thank God that I live in a country whose forefathers were driven to a wilderness, because they were *innovators*." Orthography, etymology and prosody are no part of grammar; the nine parts of speech (with new names) are "a matter of absolute fact." Uses Horne Tooke.]

1596. Shewan, James Smith (of the Girl's High School, Aberdeen, and the High School, Arbroath). 1890. *Exercises in the correction of grammatical errors.* Aberdeen: Walker. 17.5x11.5, 39pp., 6d.
(L)
[Short remarks on concord, government and word order introduce 550 specimens originally collected for the University Local Examinations. "The correcting of faulty expressions may not seem the direct route to English Composition but no better method can be found of giving alertness to pupils."]

1596a. Anon. (?). 1871. *A short abstract of the history and science of the English language.* Bridlington: pr. W. Taylor. 17x10.5, 33pp.
(L)
[OESP, an unsatisfactory mix of generalizations and speculation (on the Japhetic origin of languages), concentrates on (eight) parts of speech, with a few rules for syntax, and with exercises appended.]

1597. Anon. 1800. *Short and easy rules for attaining a knowledge of English grammar. To which are added a few letters for the formation of juvenile correspondence.* (Library for Youth). London: John Wallis. 24°, 64pp. (Anr. ed. 1801; editions to 1813).
(C L Lc N O)
[Grammar: pp. 1-32. A miniature book, with elementary rules. Minimal definitions of ten parts of speech; note on p. 33: "Thus much we have introduced for our grammatical department. More copious information may be obtained by consulting the little works of the ingenious and philanthropic LADY FENN; we mean the little grammars and lessons which she has with so much care compiled for the instruction of the

rising generation"; pp. 33-64 are taken up by specimen letters [juvenile correspondence].]

1598. Anon. n.d. *A short and rational analysis of the parts of speech for the use of young scholars.* n.p.
(G)

1599.$ Anon. 1818. *A short but comprehensive grammar. Designed for the use of schools, by a teacher of youth.* Salem: pr. T.C. Cushing. 14x8, 42pp.
($ L)
[Simple grammar, OESP, in Q/A form. Some chapters have introductory rhymes; a few footnotes. Unassuming and unoriginal.]

1600.$ Siglar, Henry Ward (1833-1918). 1874. *Progressive English exercises in analysis, composition and spelling by the use of symbols.* New York: H. Holt & Co. 19cm, xvi+176pp.
($ @)

1601.$ ---. 1876. *A practical English grammar based on progressive exercises in analysis, composition, and spelling by the use of symbols.* New York: H. Holt & Co. 19cm, xvi+176pp.
(@)

1602.$ Sill, John Mahelon Berry (Teacher of the English language in the Michigan State Normal School, 1831-1901). 1856. *Synthesis of the English sentence, or, an elementary grammar on the synthetic method.* (Anr. ed. 1857, New York: Ivison & Phinney / Chicago: S.C. Griggs, 18cm, vii+[9]-173pp. (@); anr. ed. 1859 ($); anr. ed. 1860, 123pp. ($); enl. impr. ed. 1863, New York/Chicago: Ivison, Phinney & Co., 18.5x 11.5, x+[11]-231pp. ($ @ L); anr. ed. 1871 ($)).
($ @ L)
["For beginners, on a synthetic plan", based on Welch. Analysis of Sentence and Phrase yields structures and constituents which leads to parts of speech and their properties. Considerate exposition, with plenty of notes, questions, exercises and advice to the teacher interspersed. Many specimens for parsing at end.]

1603.$ ---. 1880. *Practical lessons in English: made brief by the omission of non-essentials.* New York/Chicago: A.S. Barnes & Co. 18/19cm, iv+202pp.
($)

1604.$ Silvestre de Sacy, Antoine Isaak, Baron. (1758-1838). 1834. *Principles of general grammar, adapted to the capacity of youth, and proper to serve as an introduction to the study of languages.* Translated by D. Fosdick, Jr. First Am., from the Fifth French edition. (First published in French in 1799, this is the first edition in English). Andover, Mass.: Flagg, Gould & Newman. 19cm, xii+[13]-156pp. (2nd Am. ed. 1837,

Andover, N.Y.: Gould & Newman, 19cm, xii+[13]-156pp. (@); 3rd Am. ed. [184-?] (from the 5th French ed.), New York (@)).
(@)
(*Tm*)

1605. Simmonite, William Joseph (of Sheffield). 1841. *The practical self-teaching grammar of the English language: comprising orthography, etymology, syntax, and prosody, with copious exercises and practical illustrations. Also, style, rhetoric, and a complete system of composition: with a key to the promiscuous syntactical exercises. For the use of schools, local preachers, and young men.* Sheffield/London: Whittaker. 18x10, xii+228pp.
(L O S *Br*, *Hu*, *Lw*)
[Very detailed and conscientious account, criticizing both Murray and Cobbett, stressing utility, explicitness and intelligibility, praising Hiley. OESP, nine parts of speech with detailed notes, illustrations, exercises, questions for examinations - much of this reflecting and summarizing 18th-century traditions.]

1606. ---. 1843. *Simmonite's juvenile grammar of the English language. Being an abridgement of The practical self-teaching grammar, comprising orthography, etymology, syntax, and prosody, with exercises and illustrations; also an introductory system of composition, for the use of schools.* Sheffield: J.H. Greaves / London: Simpkin, Marshall & Co. 13/14cm, 108pp.
(L O S *Hu*)
[Based on no. 1605. Definitions and rules to be committed to memory, "abbreviated to accommodate the juvenile capacity (...) The *Exercises* to the Rules are copious". Otherwise the OESP structure is retained.]

1607.! Simson, Robert. 1832 (Master of Colebrooks House Academy, Islington). *English grammar simplified.* n.p.
(*Lw*)

1608. ---. 1838 *The parent's guide to a liberal and comprehensive education; containing a copious selection of questions affording the means of minute examination on the works of creation, English grammar, history, geography [etc.].* London: James Duncan. 18x10, iv+[5]-150pp.
(L)
[The "grammar", pp. 26-36, does not deserve the name: a few introductory reflections are followed by specimens of parsing and questions relating to an unnamed grammar - possibly the author's earlier work.]

1609.! Sinclair, James. [a1812]. *Grammatical exercises.* n.p.
[Inferred from no. 1610.]

1610. ---. 1812. *A key to the grammatical exercises.* Edinburgh. 81pp.

(E G L)

1611. Singleton, James Edward (of Kendal). [1882]. *Notes on lessons on English grammar for the use of teachers in elementary schools.* (Jarrold's Pupil Teachers' Series). London: Jarrold & Sons. 18/19cm. 156pp.
($ L O)
[Exceptionally explicit instructions for teachers on how to present knowledge on classification of words, inflexions, parsing, analysis and formation of words, breaking up the lessons into four to nine methodological steps, with illustrations by way of guidelines to the teacher in imperative form.]

1612. Sinnett, John Taylor (English Tutor to Armand Carrels, the Junius of France). 1847. *The plain and easy English grammar for the industrious classes.* London: John Dicks. 20x13.5, ii + 84pp. (@). (Anr. ed. 1848, London: John Dicks, 6d.; anr. ed. 1853).
(@ L Lw)
[The book is remarkable for its style, meant for less-educated readers, and critical attitude - it is rightly dedicated to Charles Knight. Intelligible definitions, partly Q/A form, exercises to be corrected, with remarks on composition and oratory appended. Blames poor writing on the "feverish haste" with which "periodical compositions" are written for the press.]

1613. Anon. 1820. *Sketch of etymology, syntax, punctuation, and prosody: founded on the genius of the English language ... by an American gentleman.* n.p. 18cm, 156pp.
($)

1614. Skillern, Richard Solloway. (Master of Crypt Grammar School, Glocester). 1802. *A new system of English grammar; or English so illustrated, as to facilitate the acquisition of other languages, whether ancient or modern. With an appendix, containing a complete system of parsing.* Gloucester: Walker. 18/19cm, vii + 190pp. (^{2}1808, with additions, xvi + 184pp. (@)).
(@ L O Br, Hu, Lw)
[18th-century style; Skillern added "a table of those Vulgarisms and Solecisms, which too often fall from the lips even of the polite (...). This indirect mode of information will have its weight on those, who are rather to be convinced by the representation of an absurdity, than led by the direct dogma of rules." Preparatory to the learning of other languages, OESP, nine parts of speech, simple rules, no exercises. Appendix contains Grammatical Figures and Punctuation.]

1615. Slater, Eliza (Mrs. John). 1830. *One hundred and ten aphorisms in general and English grammar, with illustrations and authorities, intended chiefly to revive the memory of rules learned in youth, calculated also for the higher classes in schools.* London: Suttaby, Fox & Suttaby, etc. 17cm, xi+79pp.

(L O)

[The aphorisms are rules on etymology, orthography, punctuation and composition, with exemplifications in the second half (29-79); clear but prescriptive.]

1616.! Anon. [a1845]. *A slight sketch of English grammar.* Derby: T. Richardson.

[Advertised by T. Richardson, Derby, c.1845]

1617. Smart, Benjamin Humphrey (1786?-1872). 1811. *The rudiments of English grammar elucidated, or a guide to parsing: containing a view of grammatical distinctions upon rational principles calculated for learners of different classes accompanied by directions and tables for parsing ...* London: J. Richardson. 18cm, v+148pp.

($ @ Lw, Sk)

["The arrangement corresponds with that of Mr. Murray's grammar."]

1618. ---. 1812. *A grammar of English sounds, or the first step in elocution.* London: Richardson. lii+150pp.

(L)

[An abbreviation of his *Practical grammar of English pronunciation* (not traced). Smart's long introduction restates his theory; the rest is in Q/A form.]

1619. ---. 1831. *An outline of semantology; or, An essay towards establishing a new theory of grammar, logic and rhetoric.* London: John Richardson. 23cm, 252pp.

(@ L)

Lit.: Bartine 1989:131-140.

[Wide-ranging and very interesting modern reconstruction of the trivium. In grammar "no definition ... should be brought forward, till absolutely required by the examples."]

1620. ---. 1841a. *The accidence and principles of English grammar: with the manual of exercises, and key.* London: Longman, Orme *et al.* 18x10.5, x+liii+280pp. (^{2}1847 ($)).

($ @ L O Lw, Sk)

[Smart's central idea, throughout, is the interrelation of grammar, rhetoric and logic: "Back to the trivium". The 1841 *Accidence* really needs to be accompanied by *Grammar on its true basis ... auxiliary to the accidence & principles,* 1847 (192pp.) and by *An introduction to grammar on its true basis,* 1858 (40pp.). Argues for a retention of old terms, but interpretation from philosophy (Locke, Hume, Kant, Horne Tooke, Hearn, Mill, Whewell) added. OESP, nine parts of speech; E includes the history of English, derivation and inflexion, S = Concord and government, and "Principles of grammatical construction extended and modified by logic" and "Interference of rhetoric with logic and grammar" - the most original sections. The *Accidence* was also printed separately, 1s.]

1621. ---. 1841b. *Alphabetical index to the accidence, principles, and manual.* n.p. 18cm, 192pp.
($)

1622. ---. 1847. *Grammar on its true basis. A manual of grammar, containing examination questions, exercises in orthography, etymology, syntax, prosody... auxiliary to the Accidence and principles of English grammar, with a key.* 2 vols. London: Longman etc. 16.5x10.5, 192+82pp. (Anr. ed. 1850 (Smart's Course of English), London: Longman, Brown, Green & Longmans, 19cm, 280pp. ($ @)).
($ @ C L *Br, Hu*)
[Exercises, questions, and examples only, referring to the other parts of Smart's set; the index, too, covers the three books (151-90). The grammar-on-its-true-basis set which forms Smart's *Theoretical and practical English grammar* consists of *The accidence*, *The principles*, *The manual* and the *Key*. They were sold separately (at 1s, 3s6d, 2s6d, 1s) or in various combinations bound together. There are Manuals of Rhetoric and of Logic to accompany the set.]

1623. ---. 1848. *Manual of rhetoric: with exercises for the improvement of style or diction, subjects for narratives, familiar letters, school orations, etc: being one of two sequels to "Grammar on its true basis".* London. 19cm, viii+98pp.
($ L)
[The book is relevant because all Smart's work, in logic, rhetoric and grammar, hangs together. A sound treatment within the traditional categories.]

1624. ---. 1849. *A manual of logic: being one of the sequels to grammar on its true basis.* London: Longman, Brown, Green & Longmans, xii+[11]-268pp.
(L)
[Smart claims a measure of originality for the work, which could be considered (now) as much psychological as logical. "Paged as a continuation of "Grammar on its true basis" - BL catalogue.]

1625. ---. 1858. *An introduction to grammar on its true basis, with relation to logic and rhetoric; submitted to teachers as well as learners.* London. 17cm, 40pp.
(@ C L)

[He hopes that he has shown how "language represents thought".]
1626. Smith, Charles John (Vicar of Erith, 1804?-1872). 1846. *A manual of English grammar; adapted to the use of classical and the upper classes in Parochial Schools.* London: W.J. Cleaver. 17cm, iv+84pp.
(@ C L O *Hu*, *Lw*)
[Traditional account with some interesting 'criticism' attached, closely following Crombie's *The etymology and syntax of the English grammar*.]
1627.$ Smith, E. 1833. *Philosophical grammar of the English language: in connection with the laws of matter and of thought, deduced from the English language alone ... to which is added a hieroglyphical key composed of letters, figures and algebraical signs.* York, Pa.: Glossbrenner & May. 19cm, 94pp. (Amended, enl. and impr. ed. ^{2}1835, Pittsburgh: L. Loomis, 19cm, xi+[1]+204pp. ($)).
($ @)
1628.$ Smith, Edward B. (A.M.). 1883. *English grammar, a class-book of methods.* South Carrollton, Ky. 16cm, 80pp.
(@)
1629.$ ---. [1889]. *Exercises in English grammar; prepared for use in the Central Normal College of Great Bend, Kansas.* Great Bend, Kan.: Barton County Democrat. 17cm, 45+[1]pp.
(@)
1630.$ ---. 1894. *Etymology and syntax: an English grammar for use in normal schools, high schools, and academies.* Chicago: A. Flanagan. 17/21cm, 228pp.
($ @)
1631.$ Smith, Eli. 1812. *American grammar of the principles of language and the elements of geography. First course of English studies.* Philadelphia: D. Heatt, for the author. 14cm, 108pp.
($ @ *Br*)
1632. Smith, Harriet (Private Teacher in Leicester and Bristol, Writer of English). 1848. *English Grammar simplified.* Bath: Binns & Goodwin. 14cm, 31pp.
(L O *Hu*, *Lw*)
[Minimal catechism, Etymology only.]
1633. Smith, Henry Dunn. 1872. *English grammar simplified, with numerous exercises.* London/New York: T. Nelson. 17cm, vi+96pp. (^{2}1880, London/New York: T. Nelson, 17cm, vi+[7]-96pp. (@)).
(@ L O)
["... By a process of induction. ... From the observation of certain well-known examples taken from ordinary discourse, the Pupil is in each instance gradually led up to the general principle or rule involved". Eight

parts of speech, two tenses (plus compound tenses). Not very clear in method and arrangement.]

1634. Smith, James Hamblin (Late lecturer at St. Peter's College, Cambridge, 1829-1901). 1876. *The rudiments of English grammar and composition.* London. 17cm. (²1882, London: Rivingtons, 16cm, xvi+204pp. (L O)). (L O)
[The simple sentence (with parts of speech classified), the compound sentence, the verb, rules of construction, the complex sentence, analysis of sentences, special rules of construction, composition and derivation of words; punctuation discussed in an innovative, but not entirely convincing sequence and coherence. Illustrations largely from Shakespeare, Milton, Pope and the Authorised Version - disregarding obvious diachronic problems.]

1635. Smith, John (Schoolmaster, of Norwich). ²1816. *A grammar of the English language containing rules and exercises, so arranged and constructed, as to render the work a key to itself, upon improved principles, as defined in the preface.* Norwich: Bacon, Kinnebrook & Co., for the author. 17cm, xvi+204pp. (³1820, Norwich: Burks & Kinnebrook, xiv+216pp., with separate *Key to the false exercises, under the syntax rules, in the third edition of a grammar of the English language,* Norwich: Burks & Kinnebrook, 80pp. (A)).
(A C L O *Br, Sk*)
[OESP, ten parts of speech; Latinate bias and dubious definitions of 'tense' and 'case', and of four conjugations, otherwise clear and well-ordered; with short rules, plenty of notes and word lists, in simple and somewhat longwinded language, and with exercises interspersed. Some misleading statements - such as *do* as a 'sign' of the present tense (58) and in terms of tenses (preterimperfect, 69). With an appendix on punctuation and propriety in reading and speaking and on "False syntax" (181-216).]

1636. ---. [c1820]. *A key to the false exercises, under the syntax rules, in the third edition of A grammar of the English language ... containing also general specimens of parsing. With an appendix.* Norwich. 17x10, 80pp. (A L)
[The greater part is supplementary to the grammar; a short section on prosody is appended (75-80). Explains, and suggests a formula for, syntactical parsing.]

1637. ---. [1825?]. *Exercises in false English; distinctive, instructive, and entertaining.* Norwich: Burks & Kinnebrook. 16°, 108pp.
(L)

[The book is mostly in faulty spelling; rules for writing and composing letters, factual information and anecdotes/jokes are mixed with exercises/questions in normal orthography.]

1638. Smith, Lucy Toulmin. 1886. *A manual of the English grammar and language, for self-help.* London/New York: Ward, Lock & Co. 18cm, vi+163pp.
(L O)
[Etymology (= classification, inflexion and accidence, derivation; eight parts of speech), Orthography and Syntax; very detailed, but not always clear; a great amount of historical explanation. "Reprinted from the *Universal instructor*".]

1639. ---. 1824. *A practical guide to the composition and application of the English language; or a compendious system of English grammar, literary criticism, and practical logic, illustrated by appropriate definitions, rules, and exercises.* Edinburgh/London. 19cm, xii+436pp.
($ G L *Br*, *Lw*, *Sk*)
[Argues that grammar is not enough to produce a good style; therefore literary criticism is needed; but logic is needed to provide critical approach to criticism.]

1640. Smith, Peter (A.M., Philologist). 1826. *An analytical system of English grammar; Arranged upon a new and an improved plan, and illustrated by appropriate rules, examples and exercises, which are so explained as to render every part of the grammar intelligible to the learner. Adapted to the use of public schools and private seminaries.* Edinburgh: Oliver & Boyd. 15cm, 176pp.
(A L O)
["An abridgment of the grammatical part of his *A practical guide.*" OESP; diligent attempt at precision, with many illustrations, exercises and footnotes - a somewhat dense and overdetailed traditional account.]

1641.$ Smith, Roswell Chamberlain (1797-1875). 1829. *Intellectual and practical grammar: in a series of inductive questions, connected with exercises in composition.* 2 vols. Providence: the author. 18cm, xii+276pp. (Anr. ed. 1830, Boston: Perkins & Martin (@); anr. ed. 1831, 2v. in 1 ($); anr. ed. 1832 (from 1831 ed.), 19cm, 123+82pp. ($); anr. ed. 1833, Raleigh (@)).
($ @)

1642.$! ---. 1830. *English grammar on the inductive system.* Boston. 12mo, 205pp. (²1831).
(*Br*)

1643.$ ---. 1831. *English grammar on the productive system: a method of instruction recently adopted in Germany and Switzerland, in the place of*

the inductive system. Designed for schools and academies. Boston: Richardson, Lord & Holbrook / New York: Collins & Hannay. 19/20cm, 204pp. ($ @). (Anr. ed. 1832, 192pp. ($); anr. ed. 1832 (from 1831 ed.), 2 vols. in 1 ($); anr. ed. 1833 (from 1832 ed.) (Smith's New Grammar), ($); anr. ed. 1834 ($); anr. ed. 1835 ($); at least eight further editions (based on 1832 ed. and apparently unchanged) between 1836 and 1843 and eighteen further repr. to 1860; anr. ed. 1863, 200pp. ($); anr. ed. 1864, 216pp. ($), repr. Delmar: Scholars' Facsimiles & Reprints, 1983; five editions 1865-1873, 192pp.; at least four further editions between 1877 and 1886, all 208pp. ($)).
($ @ *Br*)
[*Br*: "A sham.". One of the most popular grammar books of the mid-century, largely following Murray in method and terminology. However, the preface describes the productive system (children originate as well as receive ideas) and its origins in Pestalozzi; the book is therefore also important for the history of language acquisition. In Q/A form, 696 numbered paragraphs plus syntax. No innovation in the grammatical material: sentence-building is strangely combined with exercises in false syntax.]

1644. $ ---. 1834. *Introduction to Smith's productive grammar. The little grammar; containing the elementary principles of the English language, adapted to the capacity of the youngest learner. Designed as an introduction to the improved edition of the productive grammar.* Cincinnati: Truman, Smith & Co.
(@)

1645. $ ---. 1865. *Louisiana English grammar.* Published by order of His Excellency, Henry W. Allen, Governor of Louisiana. Shreveport, La.: The Office of Southwestern. 20cm, 100pp.
($ @)
["Compiled from the 'New English grammar' of Roswell C. Smith".]

1646. Smith, T.P. 1859. *Catechism of English grammar for the use of schools and general students.* London: Ward & Lock. 16cm, 32pp., 6d.
(L O)
[Q/A form "in the most intelligible and comprehensive form, by expunging all superfluous words and phrases, so as to meet the abilities of the youngest pupil, or freshen the memory of the most accomplished scholar".]

1647.! Smith, Thomas. 1832. *Smith's edition of L. Murray's grammar.* London. 18mo, 128pp.
(*Br*)
[*Br*: "Very petty authorship."]

1648. Smith, Rev. William Brownrigg (Headmaster of the City of London Freemen's Orphan School). 1860. *Abridgment of Murray's English grammar, with an appendix. Designed for the younger classes of learners. A new edition by the Rev W. B. Smith.* London: T. Nelson & Sons / William Tegg. 14.5x9 / 14x8.5, xxxiii+204/126/126pp.
(L)
[Largely a reprint of Murray. Smith amended some definitions of parts of speech and introduced a few additions to "make it a fitter introduction to the larger grammars now used by more advanced students". A detailed study would be necessary to see where Smith emended and why he did so.]

1649. ---. 1863. *The universal letter writer; or, the art of polite correspondence. To which are added, the complete petitioner, forms of law, &c. Also, an abridgement of Murray's English grammar. By the Rev. W.B. Smith entirely reedited.* n.p. 12x7.5, 256pp., grammar = pp. 13-46].
(L)
[The summary of Cobbett, rudimentary as it is, brings out the structures competently, a successful summary to serve in a letter writer. The four pages of Murray (how much of this is really by him?) do not make up a rudimentary grammar - too short even for the auxiliary purpose in the book.]

1650. Smith, Sir William (Editor of the Classical and Latin Dictionaries, 1813-1893) & Theophilus Dwight Hall (Fellow of University College, London) 1873. *A school manual of English grammar, with copious exercises.* London: John Murray. 18/19cm, xiv+240pp. ($). (^{4}1877, Tor. Campbell, 19cm, xxi+248pp. (@); ^{5}1877 (Dr. Wm. Smith's English Course) ($ @); rev. ed. ^{9}1886 ($ @); anr. ed. 1899, xxi+254pp. ($)).
Key 1887.
($ @ L O)
Lit.: Anon. 1874.
[Stresses systematic treatment of syntax, exemplified by the best authors, to illustrate existing English grammars, with Analysis of Sentences, Punctuation and Prosody added; not well arranged, and complicated by the intrusion of historical explanations throughout; much less innovative than claimed.]

1651. --- & ---. 1887. *Key to the school manual of English grammar.* London: John Murray. 74pp.
(L O)
[Exclusively answers to questions in *Manual*; "This key is entrusted confidentially to ... being intended for Schoolmasters, Tutors, and Instructors only".]

1652.$ Smithdeal, Grace H. 1892. *Smithdeal's practical grammar, speller and letter-writer. For use in business colleges, academies, public and private schools.* n.p. (Anr. ed. 1894, Richmond, Va.: Taylor & Taylor/B.F. Johnson, 20cm, 214/224pp. ($ @); anr. ed. 1895, [Richmond] ($ @); anr. ed. 1896, Richmond, Va.: B.F. Johnson Publishing Co. (@)).
($ @)

1653.$ Smythe, Charles Winslow (1829-1856). 1861. *Smythe's primary grammar. Our own primary grammar: for the use of beginners.* Greensborough, N.C.: Sterling & Campbell / Richmond, Va.: W.H. White / Charleston, S.C.: M'Carter & Dawson. 18cm, 72pp. (Anr. ed. 1862, Greensborough, N.C.: Sterling, Campbell & Albright ($ @); ³1863, Greensborough, N.C.: Sterling, Campbell & Albright / Richmond, Va.: W.H. White ($ @)).
($ @)

1654.$ ---. 1862. *Our own school grammar: designed for our schools and academies, as a sequel to the Primary grammar.* Greensborough/Richmond: Charleston. 19cm, 208pp.
($ @)

1655.$ ---. 1863. *Our own elementary grammar: intermediate between the primary and high school grammars, and especially adapted to the wants of the common schools.* Greensborough, N.C.: Sterling, Campbell & Albright / Richmond, Va.: W.H. White. 18cm, 148pp.
($ @)

1656.! Snaith, W.A. & Major, Henry. 1872. *English grammar in three parts.* Manchester: Heywood. 32pp., 2d each.
(*Mp*)
[Eight parts of speech; Saxon, Latin & Greek derivation.]

1657.$ Snyder, W. 1834b?. *Grammatical poineer, of, Rational instructor: analytical grammar, containing the principles of the English language, arranged in progressive order, and illustrated by appropriate examples.* [Winchester, Va.]: E.W. Robinson. 19cm, xvi+164pp.
($ @ Br)

1658. Somervell, R. (Assistant master, Harrow School). 1891. *The structure of sentences: an aid to translation and composition.* London: Percival. xii+50pp., 1s6d. (Anr. ed. 1895; anr. ed. 1900).
(L)
[Simple exposition of sentence and clause; aimed especially at those going on to translate from other languages.]

1659. Sonnenburg, Rudolf. 1870. *Abstract of English grammar with questions.* (Formed on the plan of *Grammatik der englischen Sprache*). Berlin: Julius Springer. (Rev. and enl. ed. ³1880, ... *and based on, and partly*

compiled from Adams, Angus, Allen and Cornwell, Latham, Morris, Murray, Smart, Webster and others, Berlin: Julius Springer, 22.5x14, 89pp. (Table of contents gives 293pp. - for the German ed.?) (@)).
(@ L)
[History, etymology (nine parts of speech) and "the principal rules of Syntax" and prosody, traditional, with some contrasts with German equivalents throughout, and 276 questions at end.]

1660. Sonnenschein, Eduard Adolf. *et al.* (Professor of Classics in the Mason College, Birmingham, Editor of Parallel Grammar Series, 1851-1929). 1889. *An English grammar for schools, based on the principles and requirements of the Grammatical Society*. (Parallel Grammar Series). 2 parts. Part 1: *Parts of speech*, by J. Hall, Head Master of the Hulme Grammar School. Manchester, & EAS, and *Accidence* (by EAS). 18.5x13, 64pp. Part 2: *Analysis and Syntax*, by A. J. Cooper, Head Mistress of the Edgebaston High School, & EAS. London: Swan Sonnenschein & Co. 18.5x13, viii+24pp. (Ster. ed. 1890; anr. ed. 1891 (@)).
(@ L)
[The author claims in the preface that the "work of the Grammatical Society has been turned to account. Brief statements of usage, based inductively upon preceding examples, have been substituted for the customary definitions. The pupil's attention is thus called to what each part of speech *does*, rather than to what it *is*. The learner is also relieved of the burden of unnecessary sub-classifications". He says he is "indebted to the works of Koch (revised by Zupitza), Maetzner, Mason and Vietor", and that "the main results of modern phonetics in a simple and intelligible form" have been included. After all this, the grammar is disappointing: incomplete, incoherent and misleading in, e.g., its equation of tenses in six European languages; quotations from OE do not really help either, nor do other historical explanations.]
Lit: Leitner, Gerhard, in: Leitner 1991:57-80

1661.$ Sornberger, Samuel John (1849-1925). 1884. *Normal language lessons*. (School Bulletin Publications). Syracuse, N.Y.: C.W. Bardeen. 18cm, iv+[7]-81pp. (@). (Rev. ed. ²1888, Syracuse ($ @)).
($ @)

1662.$ Southworth, Gordon Augustus (1838-1915). 1887. *Our language: its use and structure taught by practice and example*. Boston/New York: Leach, Shewell & Sanborn. 19cm, iv+108+286pp.
($ @)

1663.$ ---. 1887. *Elements of composition and grammar.* n.p. (Anr. ed. 1889, iv+300+iv pp. ($); anr. ed. 1899 (from 1887 ed.), Boston/New York: Leach, Shewell & Sanborn, 20cm, vi+326+iv pp. (@)).
($ @)

1664.$ ---. 1891. *First lessons in language.* Boston/New York: Leach, Shewell & Sanborn. 20cm, iv+156pp. (Anr. ed. 1899, Boston: T.R. Shewell & Co. (@)).
($ @)
[Co-author Goddard? Inferred from no. 1665.]

1665.$ ---. [c1892]. *A course of language study in outline, to accompany Southwark & Goddards's "First lessons in language" and "Elements of composition and grammar". With comments on special forms of language teaching.* Boston/New York: Leach, Shewell & Sanborn. 18cm, 28pp. (Anr. ed. 1893, Boston/New York (@)).
(@)

1666.$ Spalding, Charles. 1825. *The rudiments of English grammar, illustrated by parsing lessons: containing also a table of questions, on the parts of speech, arranged in systematic order, designed to facilitate the pupil's progress, and initiate him in the principles of etymology; together with twenty-four syntactical rules, ellipsis, and a few observations on the uses of what and its.* Onondaga, N.Y.: L.H. Redfield, for the author. 18cm, 24pp.
(@ Br)

1667.$ Spear, Matthew P. 1845. *The teacher's manual of English grammar: consisting of three parts in one volume: Part I. contains the principles of analysis, or parsing: Part II. contains observations upon orthography, etymology, and syntax: Part III. contains the principles of the synthesis, or the idiom of the English language.* Boston: W.D. Ticknor & Co. 19cm, 116pp.
($ @ Br)

1668. Speers, Adam. 1879. *An introduction to English grammar, including the analysis of sentences: with exercises.* (Sullivans' Series of School Books). Dublin: Sullivan Bros / London: Longmans/Simpkin, Marshall & Co. / Melbourne/Sydney/Adelaide: G. Robertson. 16cm, 138pp. (^{2}1880, Dublin: Sullivan, 17cm, 144pp. (@)).
(@ L O)
["*Essentials* ... brought before the minds of the young. The language used throughout being of the simplest possible kind ... Prosody, Derivation, and Punctuation, are not dealt with at all". Graded: pp. 5-39 first course, pp. 40-93 second course, pp. 94-end "sufficient for the require-

ments of the highest classes". OES, with parsing exercises, structure and various definitions not quite convincing.]

1669. Spencer, Alexander (Schoolmaster at Fordoun). 1831. *A selection of moral lessons, natural history, bible lessons, and poetry. Also an appendix containing a short English grammar.* Montrose: Smith & Co. 17.5x 10.5, x+146pp.
(L)
[The "Compendium of English Grammar", pp. 135-42, is too short and defective to have any independent value.]

1670. Spencer, George H. 1849. *Spencer's grammar and lectures, being entirely a new arrangement, containing a great variety of new examples in false exercises, and parsing lessons: each designed to convey some useful information; geographical, historical, or some good maxim ...* n.p. 20cm, iv+[5]-162pp.
($)

1671.$ Spencer, George (d. 1856). ²1849. *An English grammar, on synthetical principles: illustrated by exercises for grammatical analysis, with numerous examples of false syntax: adapted to all classes of learners.* Terre-Haute, Ind.: D.S. Danaldson. 20cm, iv+[5]-162pp. (Anr. ed. 1850?; anr. ed. 1851, 178pp. ($); anr. ed. 1852 ($); anr. ed. 1853 ($); anr. ed. 1854 ($)).
($)

1672.$ Spencer, John T. (d. 1863). 1866. *English grammar simplified and adapted to all classes of learners: for the use of schools and academies.* Ed. by S.A. Hayden. Rev. ster. ed. New Orleans: S.A. Hayden. 19cm, vi+[7]-208pp.
($ @)

1673. Stafford, J.E. [1877]. *Stafford's grammar: an easy catechism for little children.* Manchester: John Heywood. 16cm, 16pp. (in large print).
(@ O)
["Intended *solely* for the use of *little* children - those poor wee mites of seven or eight who sigh dolefully and declare they 'never can learn this lesson, it is so hard'"; the shortest exposition, in Q/A form, imaginable; eight parts of speech treated.]

1674. Anon. 1874-. *The standard English grammar.* 4 parts. (Holborn Series). London.
(L)

1675. Anon. 1873. *Standard lesson series in grammar.* Manchester: Heywood.
(L)

1676.$ Staniford, Daniel (Author of the Art of Reading, Member of the Society of Associated Instructors of Youth in the town of Boston and its

vicinity). 1813. *The elements of English grammar; designed for the use of schools*. Boston: West & Richardson. 14.5x8, vi+[7]-86pp. ($ @). (^{2}1815, Boston: West & Richardson, 14cm, iv+[5]-108pp. (@); ^{3}1821, Boston, Mass.: T. Wells (L)).
($ @ L)
[Brief definitions and rules, but extensive verbal paradigms; OESP and directions for parsing; very short advice on punctuation and prosody at end.]

1677. Stanton, W.R. (Grammarian). 1881a. *Arithmetical tables and definitions of terms in English grammar and analysis*. Wisbech: Leach & Son. 13.5x9.5, 32pp.
(L)
["Definitions in English Grammar" (9-32) consist of lists of rules and definitions with some exemplification, but space did not permit to give more than the barest information.]

1678.$ Starck, Eduard Leon. 1887. *Grammar and language: a philosophical study. An attempt at the introduction of logic into grammar*. Boston: W.B. Clarke & Carruth. 20cm, xiv+185pp.
($ @)

1679.$ Stearns, George. 1843. *The last grammar: an automathic system of English grammar: in which many old errors are superseded by newly-discovered truths*. Boston: Reid & Rand. 28cm, 17pp.
($ @ Br)

1680. Steedman, John. [1883]. *The grammar help*. 96pp. London: Simpkin & Co., pr. in Nottingham. Standards II & III: 48pp., 3d; IV & V: 96pp, 4d.; VI & VII, 44pp. (=97-140), 3p.; all 16.5x10.5.
(L)
[Graduated courses of exercises with some advice to teachers. The set covers parts of speech, some derivation, and sentence analysis adapted to the requirements of the Code; exercises greatly predominate - obviously the booklets were made for use in class.]

1681. Steel, G. (Lecturer on Science and Method under the School Board for London). 1894. *An English grammar and analysis for students and young teachers*. London: Longmans, Green & Co. 18cm, vi+300pp.
(L O)
[A thoughtful rewriting of grammar as a scientific description with good definitions, though not easy to comprehend for the normal student. Refers to Earle, Skeat, Angus and Morris. Parts of speech defined and classified; the sentence, syntax and composition, vocabulary and a short history of English.]

1682. Steele, Robert (Secretary of the Protestant Evangelical Mission). [1858]. *An Abridgment of the Comprehensive English grammar.* Bolton: T. Abbatt. 18x10, 29pp.
(L)
[The full form was probably never published; the author says that he "had in view the publication of a larger work on the subject, when Mr. Morell's Analysis appeared (a work of distinguished merit, and from which much has been extracted, on account of its simplicity and common sense)". The present book on etymology and syntax (sentence analysis) is poor, providing traditional definitions, often inadequate, with examples and a few exercises.]

1683. Steill, Benjamin. 1844. *Pictorial grammar for children.* London: Benjamin Steill.
(C E L O *Hu*)
[Insignificant for style and content.]

1684.! ---. 1845. *Outline of English grammar.* (Steill's Royal Pictorial Toy-Books). London: Benjamin Steill.
($ *Hu, Lw*)

1685. Stephen, Henry Lushington. 1863. *A grammar of the English language.* n.p.
(Dt)
[According to *NSTC* a version of Cobbett?]

1686.! Anon. [a1884]. *The stepping stone to English grammar.* London: Longman.
[Advertised by Longman, 1884 at 1s.]

1687.! Sternhold, Thomas. 1820. *Essentials of English grammar, done into metre.* n.p.
(*Lw*)

1688. Stewart, William. n.d. *Stewart's first English grammar.* (Stewart's Educational Series). London: W. Stewart & Co. 16x10.5, 32pp.
(O)
[Minimal information (but extensive verbal paradigms) provided; OESP, etymology only treated in unsatisfactory definitions, simple exercises and lists of illustrations.]

1689. Stewart, William (Teacher of English, Geography, and History, Perth; Author of *Orthoepic primer*). 1849. *A grammar of the English language.* Edinburgh: T. & T. Clark. 14.5x9, iv+144pp.
(A L *Lw*)
[Latinate, dull, solid, with rules and exercises. Short definitions, extensive parsing, errors to be corrected - not very systematically arranged.]

1690. Stoker, Jane (Teacher of English language, Stockwell Training College). 1882. *Textbook of analysis and composition.* London: W. Stewart. 103pp.
(L O)
[A mixture of stodgy and sensible advice within a conventional framework.]

1691. Stormonth, James (Head Master, Burgh School of Canongate). 1861. *The school grammar. Combined throughout with aids to English composition: being an attempt to exhibit the structure of the English language on a proper basis, and to render the acquisitions of its rules and principles easy and natural.* Edinburgh: Adam & Charles Black. 16cm, viii+160pp.
(L O)
[On words, sentences, spelling, punctuation, composition and poetry; eight parts of speech; short, not always satisfactory definitions, with many simple exercises inserted.]

1692.$ Strang, Hugh Innes (1841-1919). ^{3}1884. *Exercises in false syntax, and other forms of bad English.* Toronto: The Copp, Clark Company. 16cm, vii+92pp.
(@)

1693.$ ---. 1886. *The public school grammar and elements of composition with numerous exercises.* n.p. 190pp. (Anr. ed. 1899, 190pp. ($)).
($)

1694.$ ---. 1888. *Exercises in English: selected and classified for criticism or correction.* Boston: D.C. Heath & Co. 19cm, viii+92pp. (Anr. ed. [c1892], 146pp. (@); rev. ed. 1893, with additions by G.R. Carpenter, xiv+146pp. (@); rev. ed. 1894, with additions by G.R.C., 12°, xiv+146pp. (@); rev. ed. ^{23}1897, with add. by G.R.C. (@)).
($ @)

1695.$ ---. 1894. *Key to Strang's Exercises in English, by G.R. Carpenter.* Boston: D.C. Heath & Co. 19cm, 26pp.
(@)

1696.$ ---. 1895. *Grammatical analysis explained and illustrated with a large number of carefully selected sentences and passages for practice for the use of teachers, and of candidates preparing for entrance, public school leaving, and primary examinations.* 2 parts. Toronto: The Copp, Clark Company. 55pp.
($ @)

1697. Strong, James. 1854. "English grammar". *Methodist Quarterly Review* 14:368-92.
(*Ke*)

1698. Stronge, S. English (Inspector of Schools) & Alexander Richard Eagar (First Senior Moderator, and sometime professor of English Language at Alexandra College, Dublin). 1892. *An English grammar, with analysis and prosody, for the use of teachers and the higher classes in schools.* London: Sampson Low, Marston & Co. 18cm, xxi+239pp.
(L O)
[Generally sound treatment of OESP, with analysis and parsing included; the authors claim many improvements to other grammars, of which the reduction of the verb paradigm is one. Many explanations draw on OE.]

1699. Style, E.C. [1883]. *Sure steps in English grammar. Adapted to the Revised Code.* 3 parts. London: Allman & Son. 16cm, 3x32=96pp.
(L O)
[Simple, and not satisfactory definitions combined with easy exercises.]

1700. Sullivan, Robert Joseph (Inspector of Schools, 1800-1868). ^{2}1843. *An attempt to simplify English grammar; with observations on the method of teaching it.* Dublin. (^{3}1844, Dublin, 14cm, 71pp. ($ @); rev. and corr. ed. ^{4}1847, Dublin: W. Curry, Jr., vi+[7]-179pp. (@); rev. and corr. ed. ^{5}1847, Dublin (@); price in 1848: 1s; ^{12}1849; rev. and impr. ed. $^{15+17}$1852, Dublin (@); rev. and impr. ed. ^{24}1855; rev. and impr. ed. ^{25}1855, Dublin: Marcus & John Sullivan / London: Longman, Brown, Green & Longman, viii+[9]-180pp. (@); anr. ed. 1857 ($); enl. and impr. ed. ^{44}1861, Dublin; ^{57}1864; anr. ed. 1866, 15cm, viii+216pp. ($); ^{85}1869; ^{109}1873).
($ @ C G L O *Hu, Lw*)
Lit.: McAlester 1961.
[Though apparently quite popular, not convincing in arrangement and clearness of definitions; many footnotes, minor rules in small print and questions interspersed. Frequently referred to, e.g. by Hunter (no. 920) ^{2}1848, Dawnay (no.435) and Mathews (no. 1191) $^?$1874.]

1701. Sullivan, Robert. (1800-68). [a1868? 1876]. *First English grammar, abridged from R. Sullivan's English grammar.* Dublin: Sullivan. 13cm, iv+[5]-72pp. (^{2}1876, Dublin: Sullivan, 13/14cm (@ L O)).
(@ L O)
[Elementary instruction in form of rules and simple exercises.]

1702.$ ---. [1879]. *An English grammar for the use of schools and academies. According to Dr. Sullivan's "Attempt to simplify English grammar", with revisions and addenda. By a practical teacher.* New York: Benzinger Bros. 12°, iv+[7]-83pp.
(@)

1703. ---. 1885. *A summary of English grammar.* (A posthumous compilation). n.p.

($)
1704. Anon. 1885. *Summary of English grammar. Compiled for the use of the Notting Hill High School.* London: Rivington. 17.5x11, 144pp. (²1887, 150pp.; ³1890, 150pp.).
($ L O)
[Traditional account. Accidence, SEP, with Etymology in its modern understanding. Prescriptive and somewhat Latinate, with some historical information, but clear and well arranged.]

1705. Anon. [1898]. *A summary of English grammar, with aids to difficult parsing.* Edinburgh?: McDougall's Educational Co. 41pp.
(L)

1706. Sumner, E.C. [1887]. *The little folks grammar, Lady Holles's School.* London: George Philip, etc. 16x10, 24pp., 3d.
(L)
[OES, intentionally simplified to a degree that definitions become misleading; punctuation, sentence analysis and parsing at end. Definitions to be learnt by rote.]

1707. Sutcliffe, Joseph. 1815. *A grammar of the English language. To which is added, a series of classical examples of the structure of sentences, and three important systems of the time of verbs.* London: T. Cadell & W. Davis. 18cm, 238pp. (²1821, re-composed and made into a new work as *A grammar of the English language, illustrated with etymologies, commentaries, criticisms, and classical examples*, Bristol/London: Baldwin, Cradock & Joy, 18x11. xii+262pp., 4s, bound together with *The English Cratylus* 1825 (C O)).
($ C L O Br, Hu, Lw, Ma)
[Comprehensive, diligent and generally clear account of '18th-century' traditional grammar, with some historical explanations, OESP, ten parts of speech, including discussions of Lowth, Priestley, Murray, Blair etc. and Latin grammar to provide, in a slightly longwinded method, the established knowledge of the time; sometimes rhapsodic, strongly rationalistic. Appendices on tense, analytical etymology, advice to youth, etc.]

1708. Sweet, Henry (formerly President of the Philological Society, M.A., 1845-1912). 1890. *A primer of spoken English.* (Clarendon Press Series). Oxford: Clarendon, 18cm, xii+97pp. ($). (³1900, Oxford: Clarendon; anr. ed. 1895 ($)).
($ L O)

1709. ---. 1892-98. *A new English grammar, logical and historical.* (Clarendon Press Series). 2 vols. (Part I: Introduction, Phonology, and Accidence;

Part II: Syntax). Oxford: Clarendon Press. 18/19cm (Part I: xxiv + 499pp.). (Anr. ed. Part I: 1900, Oxford: Clarendon Press, 20cm ($ E)).
($ @ A C E L Nc O)
[Part One is the classic account combining descriptive and historical grammar (not always in a persuasive fusion), with careful reasoning about methods.]

1710. ---. 1892. *A short historical English grammar.* (Clarendon Press Series). Oxford: Clarendon Press. 17/18cm, xii + 264pp.
($ @ A C E L O)
[Abridgment of the historical portions of the *New English grammar*, no. 1709., omitting syntax; of little value for 19th-century English.]

1711. ---. 1892. *A primer of historical English grammar.* (Clarendon Press Series). Oxford: Clarendon Press. 17cm, viii + 112pp. ($). (Anr. ed. 1893 (O)).
($ L O)

1712.$ Swett, Josiah (Teacher of Moral Science and English Literature, and Lecturer on History, in the New-England Seminary, Windsor, Vt.). 1843. *Swett's grammar: An English grammar: comprehending the principles and rules of the language, illustrated by appropriate exercises: on the basis of Murray. ... Improved edition.* Windsor, Vt.: J. Swett. 19x11, v + 1 + [7]-180pp. ($). (Impr. ed. 1844, Claremont, N.H.: Claremont Manufacturing Co., viii + [9]-192pp. ($ @ L)).
($ @ L)
[The first edition appears to have been 1843, with improvements after one year of teaching which lead to the revision of 1844. Swett rewrote and abridged Murray, revising verb classification, parts of syntax and versification; study questions and key rejected as not helpful. The new edition has changes mainly in 'Etymology'; OESP, as in Murray; short definitions/rules, with notes in smaller print interspersed. Swett said about Murray: "As Murray made no scruples in copying from the works of others; so modern compilers have made no scruples in copying from his work. The language of his grammar seems, indeed, to have been regarded, and not without reason, as common property, and all have used it, altered or amended it, as if it were their own."]

1713.$ ---. 1846. *Swett's Primary school grammar. First lessons in English grammar, comprising a summary of the principles and rules of the language.* Claremont: The Claremont Manufacturing Co. 18cm, viii + [9]-120pp.
($ @)

1714.$ Swinton, William (1833-1892). 1872. *A progressive grammar of the English tongue, based on the results of modern philology.* New York:

Harper & Brothers. 18/19cm, xi+207pp. ($). (Rev. ed. ?1874, New York: Harper & Brothers, 19cm, xi+207pp. ($ @); at least five further editions, between 1875 and 1880, all apparently unchanged, often reprinted ($ @)).
($ @)

1715.$ ---. 1873?. *Language lessons: an introductory grammar and composition for intermediate and grammar grades.* (Harper's Language Series). New York: Harper & Brothers. (Anr. ed. 1874 (from 1873 ed.), New York, 17/18cm, viii+176pp. ($ @); anr. ed. 1875, New York, viii+256pp. (@); anr. ed. 1876, viii+177pp. ($); anr. ed. 1877 ($); anr. ed. 1878 ($); six other editions recorded between 1879 and 1898 (@)).
($ @)

1716.$ ---. 1874a. *Language primer: beginners' lessons in speaking and writing English.* (Harper's Language Series). New York: American Book Company. 19cm, vi+102pp. (Anr. ed. 1874, New York: Harper & Brothers (@); anr. ed. 1879, New York (@); anr. ed. 1883 ($ @); three further editions recorded until 1887, all New York: Harper & Brothers (@)).
($ @)

1717.$ ---. 1874b. *School composition: being advanced language-lessons for grammar schools.* (Harper's Language Series). New York: Harper & Brothers. 18cm, vi+151+8pp. ($ @). (Anr. ed. 1874, 17cm, vi+119pp. ($); anr. ed. 1875, vi+151+7pp. ($ @); anr. ed. 1876, New York ($ @); at least two more editions until 1882 (@)).
($ @)

1718.$ ---. 1874?. *A school manual of English composition: for advanced grammar grades, and for high schools, academies, etc.* (Harper's Language Series). (Anr. ed. 1877, 18/19cm, iv+113pp. ($); anr. ed. [c1877], New York: American Book Co. (@); anr. ed. 1878, New York: Harper & Brothers ($ @); anr. ed. 1881 ($); anr. ed. 1884 ($); anr. ed. 1886 ($); anr. ed. 1888 ($); at least seven further editions between 1879 and 1890 (@)).
($ @)

1719.$ ---. 1877. *(Campbell's) new language lessons: an elementary grammar and composition.* (Harper's Language Series). New York/Cincinnati: American Book Company. 18cm, vii+192pp. ($ @). (Anr. ed. 1878, Toronto: Canada Publishing Co., vii+84pp. (@); at least thirteen further editions between 1878 and 1890, all apparently unchanged ($ @)).
($ @)

1720.$ ---. 1877. *Grammar containing the etymology and syntax of the English language: For advanced grammar grades, and for high schools, acade-*

mies, etc.. (Harper's Language Series). New York: American Book Company. 18/19cm, viii+256pp. ($ @). (Anr. ed. 1877, New York: Harper & Brothers (@); anr. ed. 1878, 113pp. ($); anr. ed. 1878, New York: Harper & Brothers, viii+256pp. ($ @); anr. ed. 1879, New York ($); anr. ed. 1885, viii+256+iv+113pp. ($); anr. ed. 1885, viii+256pp. ($); anr. ed. 1886, viii+256pp. ($); anr. ed. 1887, viii+256pp. ($); anr. ed. 1888, viii+256pp. ($); anr. ed. 1890, viii+256+113pp. ($)).
($ @)
[The 256 and 113 pages obviously refer to two parts which were sometimes bound together.]

1721.$ ---. 1878. *New English grammar in three parts etymology, syntax, & analysis.* (Miller & Co.'s Educational Series). n.p. 234pp.
($)

1722.$ ---. 1898. *Talking with the pencil: Primary lessons in English.* New York/Cincinnati: American Book Co. 19cm, 128pp.
($ @)

1723. Sydenham, Rev. George (Head Master of the Hall Court Grammar School, Cannock). 1868. *Sydenham's English grammar and analysis, to which is appended a series of questions taken from the Oxford and Cambridge local examinations, College of Preceptors, &c., specially prepared for candidates for examination.* Stafford: R. & W. Wright. 16x10, iv+54pp. (²1871, iv+69pp.).
(C E L O)
[For local use, not to "supersede the more complete works of a Mason or Morell"; OES, including word-formation and analysis of sentences; Latin roots, figures of speech and examination questions; unsatisfactory, short definitions with exemplifications and notes in small print. Basic and unexciting.]

1724. Sykes, George Frederick H. 1878. *Grammar through analysis, a natural introduction to the elementary laws of English grammar.* London: Daldy, Isbister & Co. 16/17cm, ix+147pp.
(@ L O)
["Written in a conversational style", analytical method used (preceding synthesis); few technical terms introduced. "I do not consider any of the definitions here attempted accurate enough to be committed to memory;" ... examples taken almost entirely from *Robinson Crusoe*; endebted to Mason. Inductive method leading to rules, exercises and summaries.]

1725.$ Anon. 1894. *Syllabus of language work and suggestions to teachers concerning lessons in speaking, reading, writing, spelling, and grammar:*

for the use of Indian day schools and reservation boarding schools. n.p. 23cm, 42pp.
($)

1726.$ Tabb, John Banister (1845-1909). 1897. *Bone rules; or, Skeleton of English grammar.* New York/Cincinnati: Benzinger Bros. 17cm, 109pp.
($ @)

1727.$ Talbot, William K. 1830. *A definition grammar, critical and practical, on a plan entirely new* ... n.p. 14cm, 16pp.
($)

1728. Tancock, Rev. Osborne William (Assistant Master of Sherborne School). 1872. *An English grammar and reading book for lower forms in classical schools.* (Clarendon Press Series). Oxford: Clarendon. 16cm, vi+332pp. (of which pp. 32-105 are on "Grammar"), 1s6d.
(L O)
[Rules with examples slightly marred by classical terms (accusative, aorist) and OE matter; syntax restricted to agreement/concord; system similar to other books of Tancock's.]

1729. ---. 1877. *An elementary English grammar and exercise book.* (Clarendon Press Series). Oxford: Clarendon. 16/17cm, ii+92pp. (^{2}1881, Oxford).
(@ L O)
[Four (seven) parts of speech: nouns, pronouns, verbs, particles (= adverb, preposition, conjunction, interjection - uninflected); includes remarks on derivation, analysis and parsing, and exercises at end. Incomplete; definitions sometimes questionable.]

1730.$ Tarbell, Horace Sumner (1838-1904). 1890?. *Lessons in language; first book.* n.p. (Anr. ed. 1892, Boston: Ginn & Co. ($ @); anr. ed. 1893 (from 1890 ed.), Boston: Ginn & Co., 19cm, 214pp. ($ @); anr. ed. 1894, Boston: Ginn & Co., 19cm (@); at least four more editions until 1899 (@)).
($ @)

1731.$ ---. 1892. *A teachers' manual of lessons in language.* Boston: Ginn & Co. 19cm, 111pp. (Anr. ed. 1895 (@)).
(@)

1732.$ Tarbell, Horace Sumner & Martha Tarbell (1838-1904). 1899. *Lessons in language and grammar.* Boston: Ginn & Company. 19cm. (Anr. ed. 1900 (@)).
($ @)

1733. Taylor, John. 1821. *A grammar of the English language.* Bolton.
(A C L)

1734. Taylor, Joseph (Head Master of the Academy, Dronfield). 1804. *A system of English grammar, upon a plan entirely new; intended as a means of facilitating the progress both of public and private education.* London: Montgomery, Hartshead & Hurst / Sheffield: J. Montgomery. 18x10.5, xvi+295pp.
(A G L S Sc)
[Aims at "practical utility, rather than affected novelty" but spoils this by lengthy and Latin-based definitions (p. 21 gives paradigms with six cases in singular and plural; verb paradigms taking up pp. 72-203 etc.).]

1735. Taylor, T.S. (Undergraduate of London). [1878]. *First principles of English grammar.* London: Relfe Bros. 16cm, 94pp., 1s. (^{2}1880, vi+[7]-94pp. (@); ^{3}1824 (@); anr. ed. 1885 (@); anr. ed. 1889 ($)).
($ @ L O)
[Slightly chatty and not very precise; endebted to Earle's *Philology of the English Tongue* and Latham's *English Grammar*.]

1736.$ Teeters, James M. 1836. *The inductive, analytical, and synthetic system of English grammar: in which the philosophy and idiom of the language are adopted, without regard to the structure of other languages; in a series of lectures; embracing a concise methodical order of parsing, with appropriate exercises; a complete system of punctuation; and a short treatise on composition; accompanied by a large synoptical chart; in three parts.* Canton, Ohio: Dunbar & Gotshall. 18/19cm, xi+[13]-204pp.
($ @)

1737. Anon. [1880]. *Test cards in grammar and analysis, based on the Elementary English grammar and analysis of sentences.* (Blackie's Comprehensive School Series). London: Blackie & Son.
(L)

1738. Texier de La Pommeraye, Arnaud. 1822. *Abridgement of a French and English grammar.* Philadelphia. 22cm, 272pp.
($ @)

1739. Thackwray, Mrs. (Beckford House School, Walworth). 1809. *A grammatical catechism.* n.p. (Anr. ed. ^{2}1813, London: W. Darton, Jr., 96pp. (N)).
(N *Ma*)
[Young ladies dislike grammar because it is not an accomplishment; Q/A form will make it more interesting. Based on L. Murray, but in second ed. a new section on philology added. Reviewed by Martin 1824:225-7: "Arranged in the form of question and answers, but it is not of the conversational kind. The first part contains the outlines of MURRAY, carefully compiled [...] the plan of repeating questions and answers by

rote is still objectionable, though applied to "Catechisms" of every species. The second part [...] consists of derivations [...] the analysis of the several properties of each part of speech [...] The work [...] is highly creditable to the writer, and consequently deserves recommendation".]

1740.$ Thomas, Enoch. 1838. *A practical grammar of the English language, for the use of common schools and private learners.* Winchester, Va.: J.W. Hollis. 17cm, 108pp.
($ @)

1741. Thomas, Henry (of Brighton, Tasmania). [1841]. *The elements of English grammar.* Hobart Town. 15.5x10, vii+[8]-35pp., 1s6d.
(L)
[The book is remarkable for a modest colonial compilation, mainly based on Grant, Lennie and Murray; the "larger Grammar with more extensive exercises" (promised on p.vii) appears not to have been published. Very short definitions and rules with little exemplification.]

1742. Thompson, J. (Delph Grammar School). 1831. *Notes of syntax, adapted to Murray's English exercises. Designed for the younger classes of learners.* London: Whittaker, Treacher & Co. 15x8.5, iv+28pp.
(E L)
[Purely auxiliary, rules with illustrations taken from Murray and referring to his exercises, to prepare a student for the larger grammar.]

1743. Thompson, J.B. 1858. *A concise grammar of the English language, for the use of beginners.* London: Simpkin, Marshall & Co. 16cm, 64pp.
(L O)
[Complains about grammar terms - but uses them; definitions and classifications often muddled. ES only.]

1744. Thomson, Ebenezer (Teacher of Latin and Greek). 1813. *Elements of English and Latin grammar.* Air (Ayr): Wilson & Paul. 11.5x7.5, viii+100pp.
(O)
[An odd attempt at describing the two languages together (which leads to very Latinate categories in English) *and* "to furnish the juvenile student with a simple and inviting outline of the science of Universal Grammar" (iii).]

1745. Thring, Rev. Edward (Headmaster of Uppingham, Fellow of King's College, Cambridge, 1821-1887). 1851. *The elements of grammar taught in English; with questions.* Cambridge: Macmillan & Co. 14x9, iv+124pp. (^{2}1854, Cambridge: Macmillan & Co., vii+136pp. (@); ^{3}1860, Cambridge ($ A); new ed. 1872, London: Macmillan ($ @); new ed. 1880, London: Cassell & Co., 16cm, 253pp.; at least two further edi-

tions before the new ed. 1885, Uppingham: J. Hawthorn, 16cm, 248pp.).
($ @ C L O *Lw*)
[Very modest account for teachers and learners, with questions; very similar to no. 1746.: relationship needs to be checked.]

1746. ---. 1852. *The child's grammar: being the substance of "The elements of grammar taught in English"; adapted for the use of junior classes.* London: George Bell / Cambridge: Macmillan & Co. etc. 14x8.5, iv+86pp. (New ed. 1866, London/Cambridge: Macmillan & Co. (@)).
(@ E L O)
[A successful attempt at reducing his *Elements of grammar*; skilful argumentation leading up to definitions, with questions at foot of page immediately checking the understanding. Somewhat independent of the common diction.]

1747. ---. 1868a. *On the principles of grammar.* (Clarendon Press Series). Oxford: Clarendon. 18cm, viii+368pp., 4s.
($ L)
[Conventional clause analysis is replaced by an analysis of moods, illustrated by about 4000 quotations from Shakespeare, Wordsworth and Tennyson, filling nearly three-quarters of the book.]

1748. ---. 1868b. *Exercises in grammatical analysis.* (Clarendon Press Series). Oxford: Clarendon. 18cm, 224pp.
(C E L O)

1749.! ---. n.d. *Grammatical analysis.* Oxford: Clarendon.
[Advertised in Earle, *The philology of the English tongue.* 1871.]

1750. Thring, Llewellyn Charles W. 1893. *Some elements of English grammar. Specially compiled for use in preparatory schools and junior forms of grammar schools.* [Title from 2nd ed.]. (^{2}[1898], London: Relfe Bros., 18x11.5, i+101pp.).
(L O)
[Pedantic preparation for Latin, following the phraseology of the Latin primer. Somewhat incoherent mixture of definitions, examples and 'observations', with longer exercises interspersed. Inept sentence analysis.]

1751.! Tickell, Sidney Spencer Claude. [1899]. *Newmann's parsing and analysis scheme.* London: O. Newmann.
(*Mp*)
[A ludicrous piece of ignorant over-elaboration. Pseudo-complexities which the author cannot clarify. Offers a postal service for the analysis of difficult clauses.]

1752. Ticken, William (Writing Master). 1806. *A practical English grammar for the use of students preparing for the Royal Military College.* London: Lackington, Allen & Co. 12mo, 147pp., 2s6d.
($ @ *Br*)

1753. Tidmarsh, Rev. William (Principal of Putney School, S.W.). 1873. *English grammar.* Pt.1. Wandsworth: E. Carter. 17.5x11.5, ii+37pp., 2s6d.
(O)
[OE, all data provided in tabular form, which leaves no room for proper definitions and discussion; thus, a dubious attempt "to simplify the study of Grammar for my own pupils", unlikely to have fulfilled the author's expectations that "it will afford me much pleasure to find it in use in other schools".]

1754. ---. 1882. *A practical English grammar for schools and colleges and for students preparing for examinations with exercises.* London: Rivingtons. 16x10, viii+200pp., 2s6d.
(@ L O)
[An admittedly unoriginal account of orthography, syntax with inflection, analysis and parsing, with the origin of English and derivation added; eight parts of speech (determined by their use in a sentence). Brief definitions with examples; some footnotes for details. Unnecessary innovation in the classification of verbs as 'facient', 'copulative' and 'attributive', with subclasses. Almost all examples taken from the Authorized Version of the Bible and from *The Merchant of Venice.*]

1755.$ Tillotson, D.C. 1897. *Studies in the English language ... Being an elementary English grammar.* Parsons, Kan: The Foley Railway Printing Co. 19cm.
($)

1756. Timson, John R. (Head Master, Board Schools, Royston, Barnsley). [1900]. *First grammar reader, containing elementary lessons in the principles of grammar.* London: John Marshall / Leeds: E.J. Arnold. 18.5x12, viii+166pp.
(L)
[Grammar (=synthesis & analysis) is the science of the correct use of language. Starting from a communication model and leading on to the functions of parts of speech and their properties - a modern approach which dispenses with much of the rigor of the old.]

1757. Tobitt, R. 1825. *Grammatical institutes, or the principles and rules of English grammar. Abridged and versified for the use of schools and young persons.* London: John Souter. 12mo, xi+72pp.
($ *Br*)

1758.$ Todd, Lewis C. 1826. *An abridgement of English grammar; or a plain development of etymology and syntax: designed principally for the use of common schools in the United States.* Fredonia, N.Y.: Oliver Spafford. 17cm, vii+[9]-126pp. (Enl. and impr. ed. ²1827 (@)).
(@ Br)

1759.$ Tower, Benjamin Franklin (1811-1896). 1850. *Gradual lessons in grammar; or, Guide to the construction of the English language, by the analysis and composition of sentences.* New York: Cady & Burgess / Boston: W.J. Reynolds & Co.
(@)

1760.$ Tower, David Bates (1808-1868). 1846. *Gradual lessons in grammar; or, Guide to the construction of the English language, by the analysis and composition of sentences.* (Tower's Series of School Books). Boston: Crosby, Nichols & Co. (Anr. ed. 1846, Boston: Sanborn, Carter, Bazin & Co., 20cm, 288pp. (@); anr. ed. 1847 (from 1846 ed.), Boston: W.J. Reynolds & Co. / New York: Cady & Burgess, 17cm, 180pp. ($ @); anr. ed. 1848, New York: Cady & Burgess (@); anr. ed. 1850 (@); anr. ed. 1852 (@); anr. ed. 1854 (@); anr. ed. 1855, New York, 18x11, 288pp. ($ L); anr. ed. 1856 ($); at least three further editions until 1864 (@)).
($ @ L)
[Starting with simple sentences, a plan "somewhat analogous to that pursued in the best German schools, though greatly modified"; no new terms introduced. Specimen sentences analysed, with a great deal of repetition, and questions and exercises interspersed.]

1761.$ --- & Benjamin F. Tweed (1808-1868). 1848. *Sequel to gradual lessons in grammar.* Boston: Sanborn, Carters, Bazin & Co. 17cm, 288pp. (Anr. ed. 1850, New York (@)).
($ @)

1762.$ --- & ---. 1853? *Tower's elements. First lessons in language; or Elements of English grammar.* Boston: Crosby, Nichols & Co., 16/18cm, 140pp. ($ @). (Anr. ed. 1853, New York: D. Burgess, 125pp. ($ @); anr. ed. 1854, New York: D. Burgess, 16.5x10, 125pp. ($ @ L); anr. ed. 1855 ($); at least thirteen further editions between 1856 and 1873 ($, @)).
($ @ L)
[The attempt "to make grammar an intellectual exercise" has resulted in a lively Q/A exposition which, however, largely lacks logical structure. The first section on Language (8-73) is devoted mainly to etymology, but is badly organized. Analysis, or Parsing follows (74-95), continued into Rules (of syntax, 95-100). Various collections of examples follow.]

1763.$ --- & ---. 1855. *A grammar of composition; or, Gradual exercises in writing the English language.* New York: D. Burgess & Co. / Philadelphia: J.B. Lippincott & Co., 18x11, 228pp. ($ @). (Anr. ed. 1856, New York ($ L); anr. ed. 1856; New York: D. Burgess & Co. / Philadelphia: J.B. Lippincott & Co. (@); anr. ed. 1859, Boston: Crosby, Nichols & Co. (@); anr. ed. 1877 ($)).
($ @ L)
[The stress laid on practice determined the great number of exercises; starting from the sentence, and consideration of composition, made the authors lose the rigid coherence of the traditional pattern, splitting up their arguments into many unconnected chapters.]

1764.$ ---. 1859. *Tower's common school grammar: with models of clausal, phrasal, and verbal analysis and parsing; gradually developing the construction of the English sentence.* Boston: Crosby, Nichols & Co. 19cm, viii+243pp. ($ @). (Anr. ed. 1859, viii+[9]-232pp. ($); anr. ed. 1860, Boston, viii+243pp. ($ @); anr. ed. 1860, Macon, Ga.: J.W. Burke (@); anr. ed. 1861 ($); anr. ed. 1862 (@); anr. ed. 1865 (@); anr. ed. 1867 ($); anr. ed. 1870 (@)).
($ @)

1765.$ Townsend, Julius L. 1890. *Townsend's exercises in grammatical analysis, synthesis and syntax: adapted to progressive instruction in the science of grammar.* Rochester, N.Y.: Scrantom, Wetmore & Co. 19cm, 114pp.
($ @)

1766. Anon. [c1855]. *The toy grammar; or, Learning without labour.* (Dean's Sixpenny Coloured Toy Books). London: Dean.
(Lv)

1767. Trays, Henry. 1855. *An English grammar for the use of schools and private study.* London: Houlston & Stoneman, pr. in Plymouth. 18cm, 85pp., 1s6d.
(C L O)
[Very short, with plenty of parsing exercises.]

1768. Trenow, F.J.C. (of Dorchester Academy). [47][1819]. *The pupil's assistant, consisting of grammatical questions, with an example to each rule, of the exercises in false syntax, corrected and parsed at length, with observations; taken from the abridgment of Murray's English grammar.* Dorchester: J. Criswick. 64pp.
(L)
[A very modest book consisting of grammatical questions and corrections of ill-formed sentences.]

1769. Trotter, Rev. Alexander M. 1878. *A manual of English grammar and analysis of sentences.* (Collins School Series). London/Glasgow: Collins. 16x10, 152pp. (Anr. ed. [c1900], 176pp.).
(L O)
[Accidence, Syntax and Analysis of Sentences (with a brief section of Orthography preceding) treated with very brief definitions and an abundance of exercises; dry and factual.]

1770.$ Tucker, Benjamin. ^{4}1812. *A short introduction to English grammar comprehending only what is immediately necessary to be committed to memory. To which is added, a praxis of grammatical resolution.* Philadelphia. 18mo, 36pp.
(@ Br)

1771. Tuckey, Mary Ann. 1829. *Assisting questions on English grammar, with answers; comprising an explanation of etymology, and the rules of syntax.* London: Boosey & Sons. 17x10.5, vi+106pp.
(L O)
[Intended as a companion volume to L. Murray, improved by the influence of Crombie. Traditional OESP account in Q/A form; unexciting.]

1772. Turner, Rev. C. Brandon. 1840. *A new English grammar, in which the principles of that science are fully explained, and adapted to the comprehension of young persons, containing a series of exercises for parsing, for oral correction, and for writing; with questions for examination.* (An edition of English use by Selection and Adaptation from Goold Brown's *Institutes*). London: Scott, Webster & Greary. 16cm, iii+238pp. (^{6}1858; anr. ed. 1859, 1s6d).
(L O Br, Hu, Lw)
["A much revised ed. of Goold Brown's *The institutes of English grammar* [...]. Turner's book was usually treated [...] as a new work." Quite successful in simplifying (Murray's) grammar: clear though simple definitions, with examples, and with questions at the bottom of the pages; extensive parsing exercises. Ten parts of speech, six tenses - the traditional pattern. False syntax immediately corrected. Slightly too many notes and observations make the structure opaque in places.]

1773. Turner, James Arnold (Assistant Master in Haileybury College) & Archibald Rhys Smith Hallidie (Formerly Junior Student of Christ Church, Oxford). 1893a. *Exercises in English grammar and analysis.* London: Rivington, Percival & Co. 18.5x12, 122pp. (Anr. ed. 1894, London, 18cm).
(L O)

[125 exercises "primarily intended for use with English Grammar by the same authors, references to the sections in which are inserted throughout". Conventional.]

1774. --- & ---. 1893b. *A primary English grammar*. London: Rivington, Percival & Co. 17cm, xi+138pp., 2s. (^{2}1894, as *A primary English grammar and exercises*, London, 18/19cm, xii+166pp. (@); ^{3}1899).
(@ L O)
[Concentrating on parts of speech and the construction and analysis of sentences, "treated on the lines of Latin Grammar, and the terminology of that Grammar has been adopted wherever practicable", with historical explanations often distorting the evidence ('dative case').]

1775. --- & ---. 1894. *English grammar. Adapted to the use of those preparing for local and other examinations*. London: Rivington, Percival & Co. 18cm, xii+148pp., 2s6d. (^{2}1895, with a preface by the Hon. and Rev. E. Lyttleton ($)).
($ L O)
[Identical with no. 1774. (^{2}1894) except for short appendices on parsing and on punctuation, and an index added at the end.]

1776. Turner, John (of Brighton, Rock House Academy). 1843. *The intellectual English grammar, on a new and comprehensive plan*. Brighton: the author, sold by J. Tyler etc. 14cm, 107pp.
(O *Lw*)
[OESP, nine parts of speech, six tenses; introductory, traditional, unexciting. Many pages of text for parsing.]

1777.! Anon. 1851. *Tutor's English grammar*. (Contained in the first volume of the 'Family Tutor'.) London: Houlston & Stoneman.
(*Lw*)

1778.$ Tweed, Benjamin Franklin (1811-1896). 1886. *Grammar for common schools*. Boston: Lee & Shepherd. 18cm, v+113pp. (Anr. ed. 1888, Boston (@); anr. ed. 1889, Boston, v+127pp. (@); anr. ed. 1890 (@); anr. ed. 1892 (@)).
($ @)

1779.$ Twitchell, Mark. 1825. *The American instructer: being a system of English grammar, on a new and improved plan: designed for the use of families and schools: to which is annexed an explanation of the most difficult sentences in Pope's Essay on Man*. Portland, Me.: Todd & Smith. 15cm, iv+[5]-106pp.
($ @ Br)

1780. Anon. 1835. *Universal grammar illustrated: with observations upon the construction of the English language*. London: Whittaker. 17.5x11, vii+[9]-171pp.

(L)
[Eight parts of speech discussed and increased by the 'particle' (grammaticalized words and prefixes) and the 'plusortal' (deictic adverb?). Universalist categories apparently influenced by Latin, often speculative and muddled - possibly in some respects a late follower of Horne Tooke; good reflections mixed with trivial and absurd remarks and unnecessary subcategorization.]

1781. Unwin, William Jordan (Principal of Homerton College, 1811-1877). [1862]. *English grammar.* [Bound together with:] *Exercises on English grammar.* (Training School Manuals). London: Ward. 16cm, 76pp. & iv+32pp. (Anr. ed. 1870).
(L O)
[OES, eight parts of speech, with punctuation added. Unnecessarily complicated language makes understanding difficult, as in (p.68): "§122. Concessory sentences are those in which the accessory expresses a concession *admitted* by the speaker, and, notwithstanding which, the assertion is made, and made *absolutely*, not *conditionally*."]

1782. Anon. 1858. *The useful English grammar, in which the studies [sic] of the English language is made attractive and easy.* London: Houlston & Wright. 48pp.
(L O)

1783. Valentine, Easton Smith (Second English Master in the High School of Dundee). [1890]. *An atlas of English grammar, to be used along with all grammars.* (Professor Meiklejohn's Series). London: Holden/Simpkin, Marshall, etc. 19x25, 18 folios. (^{2}1890, 21 folios).
($ H L O)
[Grammatical knowledge reduced to 18 graphs which illustrate categories, classifications and correlations, with minimal verbal definitions.]

1784.$ Vasey, George G. 1860. *Grammar made easy, and adapted to the capacity of children in which English accidence and etymological parsing are rendered simple and attractive.* (Lovell's Series of School Books). n.p. 96pp. (Anr. ed. 1866 ($)).
($)

1785.$ Vernon, N. 1847. *An essay on the origin and structure of language. With a concise system of English grammar, illustrated, by examples and explanatory notes. Peculiarly adapted to youth and foreigners.* Frederick-city, Md.: D. Schley & T. Haller. 19cm, 119pp.
($ @)

1786. Verron, Albert. 1876. *The construction or arrangement of words and sentences in the present English language.* 3 parts. Münster: Coppenrath. 4°.

($ @)
1787. Vickers, John (Schoolmaster of the Grammar School, Blakesley, Towcester). [1866]. *A new course of practical grammar; or, Plain straight road to good English. Being an attempt to teach simply and thoroughly, English spelling, inflection, and composition in one volume, and with an improved system of exercises, adapted both for schools and for self-instruction.* London: F. Pitman. 16.5x10, viii+215pp., 2s6d.
(L O)
[Spelling (with pronunciation), Sentence-making (includes parts of speech) and Composition are considered the three pillars for the teaching of a Practical Grammar, "more as an *art* than as a *science.*" Mentions 41 distinct sounds (='phonemes', p.1) and gives some attention to dialect pronunciation. Exercises greatly exceed short definitions; the success of the book must have greatly depended on the teacher.]

1788.$ Vickroy, Thomas Rhys (President of Lebanon Valley College, b. 1833). 1868. *The principles of English grammar: with comprehensive outlines, and a concise and progressive system of analysis and parsing: for schools and colleges.* Philadelphia: J.A. Bancroft & Co. / Chicago: E. Speakman. 19x12, 214pp.
($ @ L)
[Considerate approach "to rescue English Grammar from [an] empirical state and reduce it to a *Science.*" "Grammar treats the *formal* element and investigates the principles, relations and forms of words combined into a sentence." Language is established by convention. Three parts of speech: ideative (= N, Pron, Adj, V, Adv), connective (= Prep, Conj) and particle (= Interj, Expletives, Correlatives, Intensives); new terms in other parts, too ('morphepology' dealing with words and their forms). Detailed expositions, with remarks, notes, exercises inserted. In spite of its idiosyncracies worth closer analysis.]

1789.$ ---. 1870a. *An introduction to the study of English grammar, for beginners.* St. Louis: Hendricks & Chittenden. 20cm, 96pp.
($)

1790.$ ---. 1870b. *A treatise on the grammar of the English language, containing a complete system of analysis and parsing, progressively arranged.* St. Louis: Hendricks & Chittenden. 19cm, xxxvi+[13]-240pp.
($ @)

1791.$ ---. 1875-80. *A first [to fourth] circle in English grammar for the fourth [to the seventh and eighth] years or grades.* St. Louis: G.I. Jones & Co. 19cm. (Anr. ed. 1875-80, St. Louis: The Polytechnic Publishing Company, 18cm, 60pp. (@)).
($ @)

1792.$ ---. 1891. *Complete course in language and grammar: for higher grades.* (Columbian Educational Series). St. Louis: Great Western School Book Co., 19cm, 304pp. (@). (Anr. ed. 1892, St. Louis: Columbian Book Co. ($ @); rev. ed. n.d., Chicago/New York: The Werner Company (@)).
($ @)

1793.$ ---. 1891. *Elements of language and grammar: for middle grades.* (Vickroy's Educational Series). St. Louis, Mo.: Great Western School Book Company. 19cm, 136pp. (Anr. ed. 1892, St. Louis: Columbian Book Co. ($ @)).
($)

1794.$ ---. 1895. *Columbian language lessons.* (Columbian Educational Series). Chicago/New York: The Werner Company. 19cm, 192pp.
($ @)

1795. Vos, J. G. R. 1860. *English grammar for the use of the Cadets of the Royal Naval College at Willemsoord.* Nieuwediep: J.C. de Buisonjé. 19x12, iv+223pp. (Enl. ed. ²1872).
(L)
[An introductory History is followed by Orthography (7-46), Grammar (47-200) and Style (201-13). Diffuse and characterized by endless enumerations of rules and examples; hardly any attention given to Dutch learners; negligible in every respect.]

1796.$ Vose, James Edward. 1880. *Handbook of grammar and analysis.* Ashburnham, Mass.: the author. 17cm, 183pp.
($ @)

1797. Anon. 1826. *Vulgarities of speech corrected, with elegant expressions for provincial and vulgar English, Scots, and Irish.* 12mo. n.p. (Anr. ed. 1830).
(L *Sk*)
[Although not arranged as a grammar book, the treatment of incorrect language covers all levels of English grammar with great insight and sociolinguistic precision.]

1798.$ Waggener, Leslie. 1890. *Definitions and exercises in the analysis of the sentence.* Austin, Tex.: Hutchings Printing House. 22cm, 2 p. l., 61pp.
($ @)

1799.$ Waldo, John (1762-1826). 1811. *Rudiments of English grammar, designed for the instruction of the youth of different ages of capacities.* Georgetown, S.C.: Francis M. Baxter. 21cm, 238pp. ($). (Anr. ed. 1813, Philadelphia, 12mo. (*Br*); rev. and corr. ed. ²1818, Georgetown, S.C.: the author, pr. in Philadelphia, 19cm, 239pp. ($ @)).
($ @ *Br*)

1800.$ ---. 1814. *An abridgement of Waldo's Rudiments of English grammar to which is added, critical notes from Dr. Priestley's grammar, and from Dr. Campbell's Philosophy of rhetoric. Designed for the use of young pupils.* Philadelphia: the author. 124pp.
($ @)

1801.$ Walker, H.D. 1869. *Elements of grammar. The first book of English grammar: prepared as a text-book for public schools, and for the primary classes of high school and academies.* n.p. 18cm, xiv+[15]-261pp.
($)

1802. Walker, John (Author of the Critical Pronouncing Dictionary, Elements of Elocution, 1732-1807). 1805. *Outlines of English grammar; calculated for the use of both sexes at school: in which the practical rules of the language are clearly and distinctly laid down, and the speculative difficulties as much as possible avoided.* London: Johnston, for the author. 18x10, xii+118pp. (Anr. ed. 1810).
($ @ A L *Br, Hu, Lw, Ma*)
[Conservative in categories and terminology. There has been "a multitude of grammars" since Lowth's but one is needed for the middle stage of education. Praises Knowles, Crombie, L. Murray, Shaw of Rochdale.]

1803. Walker, William. 1877. *Abridgment of Murray's English grammar, with an appendix ... A new edition with ... additions ... by W. Walker.* London, Otley: Walker.
(L)

1804. Walkey, Charles Collyns (Head Master of Pierrepont's Foundation Grammar School in Lucton). 1868. *Guide to English parsing: intended both for commercial and grammar schools.* Leominster: S. Partridge. 14.5x11, vi+59pp.
(C L O)
[Parts of speech defined and directions for parsing provided, esp. the resolution of propositions and sentences. A core grammar (34-47) is inserted "for boys who use no English grammar". 30 passages for parsing at end. Obviously more adequate for teachers than pupils; the author wants to lay some foundations also for the teaching of Latin.]

1805. Wall, George (Teacher). 1810-12. *The Hibernian preceptor, comprising the elements of ... spelling, ... a series of reading lessons. ... Also an introduction to English grammar, etc.* 2 vols. I: Parsontown 1810; II: Dublin 1812. (Anr. ed. 1820-21, Dublin. (L)).
(L)
[The grammar is old-fashioned, rather naif, but with a cranky individuality.]

1806.$ Wallbank, Nellie B. 1897. *Outlines and exercises in English grammar.* Chicago: A. Flanagan. 18/20cm, 129pp.
($)

1807.$ Ware, Jonathan (1767-1838). 1814. *A new introduction to English grammar composed on the principles of the English language, exclusively.* Windsor, Vt.: Jesse Cochran, for the author. 16/17cm, 48pp.
($ @ Br)
[*NUC*: "The work ... challenges the honor of being the first English grammar, composed on the principle of the English language, exclusively." - Preface. The author calls nouns "names", verbs "words", adjectives and adverbs "assistants". "Exercises in orthography, grammar, and punctuation"]

1808. Warren, Elizabeth. 1850. *Aunt Jane's grammar. Question and answer, for the use of schools and families.* London: Charles Adeney. 14x9, iv+[5]-84pp.
(C L O)
[Elementary Q/A style - which presupposes the knowledge of a great number of terms. OESP, the rules of syntax largely copied from Murray. Didactically not a convincing solution. Refers to grammars by Hunt (*Syntax*, no. 918), Murray, Rev. Robert Simson and Alex. Reid (*Rudiments*, no. 1498).]

1809.$ Waterman, Jesse. 1811. *A plain, comprehensive, practical English grammar in two parts: compiled on a plan entirely new: calculated to facilitate the study of this important branch of education, whereby a knowledge of the science may be obtained in much less time, and with less labour, than by the ordinary modes of teaching.* Philadelphia: Brown. 15cm, xxiii+190+[1]pp. (Impr. ed. ^{3}1827, *To which is annexed a key, comprising a brief and plain mode of correcting false syntax*, Philadelphia: the author. xiii+[15]-215pp. ($)).
($)

1810.$ Waters, Robert. 1883. *How to get on in the world, as demonstrated by the life and language of W. Cobbett, to which is added Cobbett's English grammar with notes.* 2 parts. New York: J.W. Pratt. 20cm, xiv+285+xiv+272pp.
($ L)
[The first half of the book is a thorough biography of Cobbett; bound together, with a new preface and pagination, with Cobbett's *Grammar* (Dedication dated Nov. 25th, 1820). The "Notes by Robert Waters" mentioned on the title page seem to be restricted to his "preface" (iii-x); Cobbett's text was apparently not tampered with.]

1811. Watkins, Charles R.W. 1872-74. *English grammar. Adapted for schools*. London: John B. Bateman. 15cm, 171pp.

(L O)

[Divides grammar into Logothesia (OE) and Philogogy (SP). Semi-educated; teems with newly coined (and useless) terms; lists of core vocabulary according to etymology; nine parts of speech. Encumbered by progressions, speculative elements, quasi-historical explanations, and needless terminological verbiage.]

1812. Watson, William (of Preston). [1886]. *(Watson's) English, containing grammar and poetry for standards II-VI*. Preston: W. Watson, etc. 16cm, 46pp. (L). (Anr. ed. [1888] (O); enl. ed. Standard III [1894] (O)).

(L O)

[Simple definitions followed by exercises; three poems paraphrased and annotated.]

1813.$ Weaver, Abram. 1832. *The common sense grammar, illustrated by diagrams, in which every word is parsed according to its use and office*. Georgetown, Tex. 16cm, viii+[7]-112p.

($ @)

1814.$ Webber, Samuel (President of Harvard College, Mass., 1797-1880). 1832. *An introduction to English grammar on an analytical plan, adapted to the use of students in colleges and the higher classes in schools and academies*. Cambridge, Mass.: Hillard & Brown / Boston: Carter & Hendee. 18.5x11, viii+116pp.

($ L *Br*)

[Rearrangement on the basis of Lowth and Murray by using induction (rather than 'synthesis'); "not designed for the elementary instruction of *young* beginners". (An abridged form was envisaged but not published), OES, with an appendix on *shall/will*. Eight parts of speech, with verbs treated in great detail; a clear section on syntax. Considerate reflexions often result in an involved style, but the presentation is generally successful.]

1815.$ Webster, George H. 1884. *A presentation of the grammar of New English, beginning with the age of Elizabeth*. Pittsburgh: Herald Printing Co. 19.5x13, xv+160pp.

($ O)

[Intelligent and innovative definitions in the Introduction are followed by sections on meaning, change of function, order, and syntax; the ambitious attempt seems to contain some unusual features worthy of closer investigation.]

1816.$ Webster, Noah (1758-1843). 1807. *A philosophical and practical grammar*. Newhaven, Ct.: O. Steele & Co., for Brisban & Brannan,

New York, 18/19cm, 250pp. (²1822, New Haven: Howe & Spalding, 223pp. (@)).
($ @ Br)

1817.$ ---. 1828. *A philosophical and practical grammar of the English language*. (Prefixed to his *Dictionary*). New York: Converse. unpag. (Anr. ed. 1831-32, London, 2 vols., 27cm (A); anr. ed. 1858, 29cm ($); various reprints).
($ L *Hu*, *Lw*)
[In his Advertisement, Webster claims that most of the improvements in the 1808 revised edition of Murray were cribbed from his (1807). Corrects "prominent errors of English grammars", such as "the admission of the article", wrong classification, imperfect description of the verb system and of syntax, and "false rules of construction". OES, formulated in clear and succinct rules; a short section on punctuation at end.]

1818.$ ---. 1831. *An improved grammar of the English language*. Newhaven, Ct.: H. Howe. 18/19cm, 180pp. (Anr. ed. 1833, Newhaven: Durrie & Peck, 192pp. ($ @); anr. ed. 1836, Cincinnati: Corey & Webster, ($ @); anr. ed. 1839, New Haven: S. Babcock ($ @); new ed. 1842 ($ @); anr. ed. 1843 ($)).
($ @ Br, *Hu*, *Lw*)
[An improved version of no. 1817.]

1819. Weedon, Thomas. 1848. *A practical grammar of the English language*. London: H.G. Collins. 16cm, v+116pp.
(@ C L O *Hu*, *Lw*)
[Modest, small 'teach-yourself' grammar, with useful discussions of syntactic and stylistic errors found in respectable writing at end.]

1820.$ Weineck, Oscar. 1893. *A common sense guide to English for foreigners*. New York: F.W. Christern, Dyrsen & Pfeiffer. 19cm, xii+265pp.
($ @)

1821.$ Welch, Adonijah Strong (Principal of Michigan State Normal School, 1821-1889). 1854? *Analysis of the English sentence, designed for advanced classes in English grammar*. n.p. (Anr. ed. 1855 New York: A.S. Barnes & Co., 18x12, 264pp. ($ @ L); ²1856 (National Series of Standard School Books), 269pp. ($); anr. ed. 1860 ($); impr. ed. 1862, New York: A.S. Barnes & Co., 267pp. ($ @); anr. ed. 1863, vi+116pp. ($)).
($ @ L)
[The book is a complement to Clark's *New English Grammar*; Welch hopes to contribute to a systematic analysis, "as a means of mental development". Referring to Milligan, Green and Clark, he discusses synthesis and analysis (13-21), then grammatical elements (22-34), to

give full attention to the functional classes of subject, object, complement, verb, adjunct, infinitive constructions etc.; examples for exercise and review at end. A sober, competent description.]

1822.$ Weld, Allen Hayden (1812-1882). [1845?]. *Weld's English grammar: illustrated by exercises in composition, analyzing and parsing.* (Anr. ed. 1846?; anr. ed. 1847, 19cm, 228pp. ($); [7]1847, Portland, Me.: Sanborn & Carter (@); [12]1847, Portland, Me.: Sanborn & Carter (@); anr. ed. 1847 (from 1846 ed.), as *English grammar ...* ($); anr. ed. 1848 ($); [20]1848 (@); anr. ed. 1849, 16cm, 84pp. ($ @); anr. ed. 1849, 231/234pp. ($ @); anr. ed. 1850 (from 1849 ed.), 234pp. ($); anr. ed. 1852, as *Weld's New English grammar. Weld's English grammar: illustrated by exercises in composition, analyzing and parsing*, 231pp. ($); anr. ed. 1853, 234pp. ($); anr. ed. 1854 ($); anr. ed. 1856 ($ @); anr. ed. 1857, 228pp. ($); anr. ed. 1858 (@)).
($ @)
[The book may be identical with: Weld, A.H. 1846. *The principles of English grammar: illustrated by exercises for composition, analyzing and parsing.* (Weld's Exercises in Grammar and Composition). Portland, Me.: Sanborn & Carter. 19cm, 216pp.]

1823.$ ---. [1847?]. *Parsing book, containing rules of syntax, and models for analyzing and transposing. Together with selections of prose and poetry, from writers of standard authority.* Auburn: Wanzer & Gillan. ([2]1847, Portland, Me.: Sanborn & Carter (@); [7]1847 (@); [15]1848 (@); anr. ed. 1853, 17cm, 111pp. ($ @); [50]1853 (@); at least four further editions between 1854 and 1860 (@)).
($ @)

1824.$ ---. 1848. *Weld's abridgment. An English grammar, illustrated by exercises in composition, analysing, and parsing. Abridged from 20th ed.* Portland, Mo.: Sanborn & Carter. 19cm, 144pp.
(@)

1825.$ ---. 1859. *Weld's progressive English grammar: illustrated with exercises in analysis, parsing and composition. Adapted to schools and academies of every grade.* Portland, Me.: Bailey & Noyer. 20cm, vi+[7]-238pp. ($ @). (Anr. ed. 1860, Boston: Brown, Taggard & Chase ($ @); anr. ed. 1863, 282pp.($); anr. ed. 1864, vi+282pp. ($)).
($ @)

1826.$! ---. a1876. *Weld and Quackenbos' new English grammar.* n.p.: Norton.
[Inferred from nos. 1827. and 1466.]

1827.$ ---. 1876. *Revised progressive parsing book: arranged for Norton's Weld and Quackenbos' New English grammar, and adapted to all*

1827. Weld, Allen Hayden

English grammars: containing selections of prose and poetry, from the best American and English authors: for analysis and parsing: also, a brief course of syntax. Portland, Me.: Bailey & Noyer. 17cm, 144pp.
($ @)

1828.$ Wells, William Harvey (Instructor in Phillips Academy, Andover, Mass., 1812-1885). 1846a. *A grammar of the English language; for the use of schools.* Boston: Jewett & Co. / Andover, Mass.: Allen, Morrill & Wardwell. 18x11, viii+[9]-220pp. (Anr. ed. 1846, New York: M.H. Newman / Andover: Allen, Morrill & Wardwell, viii+214pp. ($ @); anr. ed. 1846, viii+204pp. ($); anr. ed. 1847, 19th thousand, Cincinnati: W.H. Moore & Co. / Detroit: A.M. Farren, 19cm, viii+[9]-214pp. ($ @); anr. ed. 1847, 32nd thousand, Portland, Me.: Sanborn & Carter / Andover: Allen, Morrill & Wardwell, x+[11]-212pp. ($); anr. ed. 1847, New York: Huntington & Savage (@); anr. ed. 1848, 220pp. ($); at least ten further editions between 1849 and 1866, all presumably unchanged ($); repr. Delmar: Scholars' Facsimiles & Reprints, 1984).
($ @ *Hu, Lw*)
[Based on the author's collection of 300-400 treatises on grammar (of which 138 are named on pp. v-viii) and teaching successive classes of teachers. An introductory model of "oral instruction" (1-22) is followed by OESP; short definitions, eight parts of speech, some exercises and plenty of footnotes (testifying to the extensive reading) - quite ambitious, but traditional.]

1829.$ ---. 1846b. *Oral instruction in English grammar.* Boston: Allen, Morrill & Wardwell. 21cm, 12pp.
($ @)

1830.$ ---. 1848. *The elements of English grammar.* Andover: W.H. Wardwell. 17cm, 144pp. (Anr. ed. 1849, 16cm, 144pp. ($); [90]1860, Chicago: S.C. Griggs & Co. / New York: Ivison, Phinney & Co. (@)).
($ @)

1831.$ ---. 1880. *A shorter course in English grammar and composition.* New York/Chicago: Ivison, Blakeman, Taylor & Co. 19cm, 189pp. ($ @). (Anr. ed. 1881 ($)).
($ @)

1832.$ Welsh, Alfred Hix (1850-1889). 1884. *Essentials of English for schools, colleges, and private study,* ... Chicago: S.C. Griggs & Co. 20cm, 2 p. l., [vii]+xvi+314pp. ([3-5]1884, Chicago: J.C. Buckbee & Co. (@); [6]1884, New York: Silver & Burdett (@); [7]1899, New York: Silver & Burdett, xvi+306pp. ($ @)).
($ @)

1833.$ ---. 1887. *Lessons in English grammar.* Chicago: J.C. Buckbee & Co. 19cm, 237pp. ($ @). (Anr. ed. 1888, vii+[2]+237pp. ($)).
($ @)
1834.$ ---. 1888. *First lessons in English.* (Welsh's Language Series). Chicago: J.C. Buckbee & Co. 19cm, viii+205pp.
($ @)
1835.$ ---. 1892a. *The elements of language and grammar: a practical course for use in intermediate, ungraded, and grammar schools: based upon Welsh's "First lessons in English".* (The Normal Course in English). Boston/New York: Silver, Burdett & Co. 19cm, 224pp. (@). (Anr. ed. 1893, Boston/New York (@); anr. ed. 1894, New York ($ @); anr. ed. 1896, New York ($ @)).
($ @)
1836.$ ---. 1892b. *Studies in English grammar: a comprehensive course for grammar schools, high schools and academies. Based upon Welsh's "Lessons in English grammar".* Edited by J.M. Greenbaum. (The Normal Course in English). Boston/New York: Silver, Burdett & Co. 19cm, 240pp. (Anr. ed. 1893 ($ @); anr. ed. 1896 ($ @)).
($ @)
1837.$ Welsh, Judson Perry. 1889. *A practical English grammar: with lessons in composition and letter-writing.* Philadelphia: C. Sower Company. 19/20cm, viii+272pp.
($ @)
1838.$ ---.1896. *First lessons in English grammar and composition.* Philadelphia: C. Sower Company. 19cm, 133pp.
($)
1839. West, Alfred Slater (Trinity College Cambridge, Fellow of University College London, 1846-1932). 1893. *The elements of English grammar.* (Pitt Press Series). Cambridge: University Press. 16/17cm, ix+288pp. (^{2}1894 (@); anr. ed. 1895 (@); anr. ed. 1896 ($); anr. ed. 1897 (@); enl. ed. 1898, 18cm, ix+304pp. ($)).
($ @ H L O)
[Historical survey followed by a treatment of sounds/letters, parts of speech, Analysis, Parsing and Syntax. Discursive, with good definitions, but somewhat incoherent; comparative and historical arguments included. Questions at end of chapters.]
1840. ---. $^?$1895. *English grammar for beginners.* (Pitt Press Series). Cambridge: University Press. 16cm, 120pp., 2s6d. (Anr. ed. 1895, 19cm, ix+256pp. ($); ^{2}1895, viii+120pp; anr. ed. 1897, Toronto: Copp, Clark & Co., 166pp; reissue of the 1895 ed. in 1899, Cambridge).
($ @ L O)

[A sensible treatment of conventional material for pupils of sixteen; intentionally slight historical treatment; the difference in number of pages needs further investigation.]

1841. Wetherell, John. 1882. *Exercises on Morris's grammar (of the English language)*. (Literature primers, ed. by J.R. Green). London: Macmillan. 15cm, [7]-126pp. (Anr. ed. 1891, London: Macmillan (@)).
(@ L)

1842.$ Wheeler, William Henry (1854-1936). 1898. *Wheeler's graded studies in English: first lessons in grammar and composition*. Chicago: W.H. Wheeler & Co. 19/20cm, 192pp.
($ @)

1843. White, Frederick Averne. 1882. *English grammar*. London: Kegan Paul & Co. 16/17cm, xiv+229. (^{2}1883, as *An unconventional English grammar*, London: W. Swan Sonnenschein (L O)).
(L O)
["Careful to winnow out the meal from the chaff of language; to teach English as it is, not as it was ... to raise the study to the dignity of a science". An introduction (history, grammatology, etymology, orthography) is followed by Accidence, Syntax (synthesis, analysis, prosody, punctuation) and Semeiology. Some proliferation of categories (seven moods), but normally carefully reasoned. No exercises or notes.]

1844. White, John (Teacher, etc. Edinburgh, 1813?-1857). 1850. *A system of English grammar; with numerous exercises progressively arranged. For the use of schools and private students*. Edinburgh: Oliver & Boyd. 16cm, 1s6d. (Anr. ed. 1863, 17cm, 177pp. ($); ^{115}1874).
($ C E L O Lw)
[Traditional account, with many exercises (corrections of faulty sentences); no specific interest.]

1845. Anon. [1895]. *The Whitehall English grammar and repetition. Standard II*. (By T. W. Good.). (Gill's School Series). London.
(L)

1846. Whitehead, Laura. [1892]. *The home grammar: or, Helps and rules for spelling, parsing, punctuation and analysis for young boys and girls preparing for school*. London: Burns & Oates. 16.5x10.5, viii+190pp.
(L)
[Despite the author's intention to use "language too childish for use in schools" she makes some demands as regard terms and contents; not well ordered and didactically unconvincing.]

1847.$ Whiting, Joseph (1800-1845). 1844?. *The principles of English grammar: adapted to the use of common schools*. n.p. (Anr. ed. 1845 (from

1844 ed.), Detroit: A. McFarran / New York: M.H. Newman, 19cm, iv+[5]-60pp. ($ @ Br)).
($ @ Br)
1848.$ Whitney, Samuel Worcester (1822-1905). 1875. *Elements of English grammar*. New York: J.W. Schermerhorn & Co. 17cm, 160pp. (Anr. ed. 1876 (@); anr. ed. 1877, New York: Steiger (@)).
($ @)
1849.$ Whitney, William Dwight (1827-1894). Philologist. 1877. *Essentials of English grammar for the use of schools*. London: Henry S. King / Boston: Ginn & Heath. 18/20cm, xi+260+16pp. (Anr. ed. 1880, Boston, xi+260pp. ($ @); anr. ed. 1883 ($ @); at least fourteen further editions between 1882 and 1898, all Boston: Ginn & Heath, xi+260+[16]pp. ($ @); repr. Delmar: Scholars' Facsimiles & Reprints, 1988).
($ @ C L O)
[Largely descriptive, detailed exposition, with many examples and exercises. Whitney acknowledges his debt to Maetzner; in his diagrams illustrating sentence structure he is close to Harvey and Reed & Kellogg. Considering the fact that Whitney was Professor of Sanskrit and Comparative Philology there is remarkably little historical argumentation.]
Lit: Wächtler, Kurt, in: Leitner 1991:39-56.
1850.$ ---. 1879. *Elementary lessons in English: for home and school use. Part I*. (Minnesota Text-book Series). St. Paul, Minn.: D.D. Merrill. 18/19cm, vi+192pp. (Anr. ed. 1880 (Ginn & Heath's Language Series), Boston: Ginn & Heath, 18/19cm, vi+192pp. ($ @); anr. ed. 1881 (@); anr. ed. 1882 ($ @); anr. ed. 1883 (W.J. Gage & Co.'s Language Series), Boston: Ginn & Heath, ix+200pp. ($ @); at least two more editions until\1885 (@); anr. ed. 1886 ($ @); anr. ed. 1888 ($)). Part I co-authored by Nelly Lloyd Knox (The Whitney and Knox Language Series).
($ @)
[For part II see Knox 1887, no. 1043. Also cf. no. 827.]
1851.$ ---. 1892. *An English grammar for higher grades in grammar schools. Adapted from "Essentials of English grammar"*. n.p. 19cm, v+253pp. (Anr. ed. 1892 (*With new arrangement and additional exercises suitable for younger pupils*), (Whitney & Lockwood's English Grammar), Boston: Ginn & Co., 19cm, v+264pp. ($ @); anr. ed. 1893, Boston, v+253pp. ($); anr. ed. 1894, Boston (@); anr. ed. 1896, Boston ($ @); anr. ed. 1897, Boston, v+264pp. ($ @); anr. ed. 1898, Boston ($ @); anr. ed. 1899, Boston (@)).
($ @)

1852. Whitworth, T. (Professor of the Greek, Latin, and English classics in London). 1819. *A complete parsing grammar; or, A practical key to the grammatical construction of the English language. For the use of families, private teachers, public academies, and senior as well as junior students.* London: the author. 18cm, xvi+216pp.
(@ L *Br, Hu, Lw*)
[Verbose and uninteresting.]

1853. Whyte, R. 1848. *A popular English grammar.* (In John Boag's *A popular English dictionary, exhibiting the pronunciation, etymology, and explanation of every word usually employed in science, literature, and art.* Ed. by the Rev. John Boag. Edinburgh: A. Fullarton & Co. 1850 (@)).
(@ C L O)
[The grammar in Vol. 1, pp. 5-32 is selectively derivative; it begins with the sentence and demands that logic, rhetoric, grammar and "philosophical Inquiry" should form a science of language.]

1854.! Wickes, Edward Walter. ²1841. *English grammar.* London. 18mo, 196pp.
(*Br*)

1855. Wicks, John Harris (Master of the Boarding School, Englefield House, Egham). 1817. *The remembrancer, containing a selection of questions in ... arithmetic and English grammar, etc.* London: pr. in Egham.
(L)
[The book is intended for revision, in all subjects; questions on English grammar pp. 55-63. Insignificant.]

1856.$! Wilbur, Josiah. 1815. *English grammar.* Bellows Falls, N.H. 12mo, 132pp. (²1822).
(*Br*)

1857.$ ---. 1821. *The grammatical key: which by questions and answers represents the method of learning the parts of speech by characters that stand to represent them: with rules and parsing lessons calculated in conjunction with an atlas for parsing: which will facilitate the intricate study of English grammar by an ocular demonstration.* n.p. 17cm, 108pp. (²1822, Bellows Fall, Vt.: Blake, Cutler & Co., for the author, 17cm, 132pp. ($ @)).
($ @)

1858.$ --- & William Livingston. 1814. *The grammatical alphabet including the method of learning the parts of speech by certain spaces or characters which stands as their representative, with rules and parsing lessons calculated, in conjunction with the grammar chart, to elucidate the*

intricate study of English grammar. (With a chart). Hartford: B. & J. Russell. 14cm, 36pp. ($). (^{2}1815, Albany: C. Southwick (@)).
($ @ Br)

1859.$ Wilcox, A.F. 1828. *A catechetical and practical grammar of the English language: for the use of schools.* Newhaven, Ct.: Wadsworth. 14cm, vi+110pp.
($ @ Br)

1860. Wilkins, James. 1818. *Grammatical questions, with notes, adapted to Lindley Murray's Abridgment of English grammar. With an appendix; containing observations on the sounds of letters; rules for spelling and dividing words into syllables; exercises; and directions for scanning and reading English verse.* Stamford: John Drakard. 14x8.5, 87pp.
(L)
["This humble attempt to improve the rising generation in the rudiments of their mother tongue" (3) consists of questions (9-41) and an appendix on "the sounds of letters" and "reading poetry". Not a full grammar.]

1861.$ Willard, Samuel (1776-1859). 1810. *An abstract of English grammar; or the principles of etymology and syntax, deduced from the philosophy and established usages of the language, and studiously accommodated to the understandings of all.* Greenfield, Mass.: A. Phelps. 15cm, 54pp. (@). (Anr. ed. 1816, Greenfield, Mass.: A. Phelps ($ @ Br)).
($ @ Br)

1862.! Williams, David. [a1813]. *Grammatical questions: or English grammar taught rationally, not by rote.* London.
(*Hu*)
[Advertised by Sherwood, Gilbert & Piper in 1813.]

1863. Williams, David (Author of "The Preceptor's Assistant", Master of a school). 1818. *The catechism of English grammar: containing the principles of the language, and rules and directions for speaking and writing it with propriety and accuracy. With a variety of exercises... To which is subjoined, a copious list of solecisms, or vulgar and erroneous modes of expression.* London. 86pp., 1s6d.
(C G L)
[Q/A form; six parts of grammar: OESP, Orthoepy, Etymology/Derivation. Uses *adnoun* for adjective.]

1864. Williams, Henry Wilkinson. (Wesleyan Minister). 1836. *A treatise on English composition; including a general view of the grammar of the English language.* London: Thomas Tegg & Son. 18cm, 76pp. (Rev. ed. ^{2}1843, London).
(C E L O)

[Discursive treatment of "the intimate connexion of Etymology and Syntax with English Composition"; most topics of grammar mentioned, but not in form of rules, which makes the underlying system less apparent, especially since the style is allusive and tentative.]

1865. Williams, Mrs. Honoria. 1821. *Conversations on English grammar, in a series of familiar and entertaining dialogues between a mother and her daughters... with a number of appropriate questions following each conversation. Adapted to the use of establishments for young ladies, as well as to private tuition, and to preparatory schools for young gentlemen.* London. 18cm, xxiii+213pp. ($). (^{2}1825, ... *with considerable additions and improvements*, London: G.B. Whittaker, 18cm, xxiv+223pp. (@); ^{3}1826; ^{4}1830).

($ @ L Br, Hu, Lw, Ma)

[Narrative form tries to make it interesting but overelaborate rules and definitions are to be memorised. Martin 1824:129: "(...) combines instruction with such amusement as cannot fail to attract the attention of the junior classes in female schools (...) perhaps it is the only book of the kind that deserves to be recommended."]

1866. Williams, John (of Lancaster). 1870. *The parser's manual: embracing classified examples in nearly every variety of English construction: designed for schools and for the use of private students.* n.p. 20cm, 264pp. (Anr. ed. 1871 ($)).

($)

1867.$ Williams, Louis Lafayette (1841-1919). 1888. *Practical English grammar and business correspondence: for use in business colleges, normal and high schools, and advanced classes in public schools.* Rochester, N.Y.: E.R. Andrews. 26cm, 89pp. (Anr. ed. 1889, 68+[2]+74pp. (@); anr. ed. 1890, 26cm, 68+74pp. ($)).

($ @)

1868.$ ---. 1894. *New practical English grammar.* n.p. 24cm, 100pp. (Anr. ed. 1895, ... *for use in business colleges, academies, normal and high schools, and advanced classes in public schools*, Rochester, N.Y.: E.R. Andrews, 25cm, 96pp. (@)).

($ @)

1869.$! Williams, R.O. 1897. *Some questions of good English examined in controversies with Dr. Fitzedward Hall.* New York.

(Dk)

1870.! Williams, T. 1883. *The grammatical errors of the educated.* London.

(Ch)

1871. Williams, Sir Thomas Marchant (Master of the Bangor Practising School, 1845-1914). 1870. *Grammatical cards. (Texts and progressive)*. Manchester: John Heywood. 24 cards, 1s.
(L)
["These cards have been drawn up mainly with the view of affording to those Teachers of Elementary Schools who take grammar as their 'extra subject', the means of testing as well as of aiding the progress of their Pupils in the subject. It is hoped, too, that all Teachers of both Private and Public Elementary Schools, who may be engaged in instructing Young Pupils in the Elements of English Grammar, will find these Exercises of very great service to them." (publisher's advertisement in Yates 1871, no. 1923.)]

1872.$ Williams, William. 1887. *Composition and practical English with exercises adapted for use in high schools and colleges. Authorized by the Minister of education*. Toronto: Canada Pub. Co. [2]+238pp.
($ @)

1873. Williams, William C(harles). 1851. *A plain English grammar, for the use of the North-London Collegiate School, High Street, Camden Town*. London: Francis & John Rivington. 13cm, 48pp.
(L O)
["Meant only as an outline or skeleton of English Grammar, the details are to be filled in by oral explanation and illustration". Minimal definitions of ES and punctuation rules. The author is a delayed member of the select group of grammarians who can find a pluperfect infinitive in English.]

1874.$ Williams, William George (1822-1902). 1887. *Outlines of English grammar*. Oclaware, Ohio/Cincinnati: Aldine Printing Works. 16cm, 119pp. (Anr. ed. 1887, 18/19cm, iii+122pp. ($)).
($ @)

1875. Williamson, C.W. 1896. *Practical lessons in the use of English: for intermediate and grammar schools*. n.p. 20cm, 142pp.
($)

1876. Wills, Herbert. n.d. *Ledsham's world series standard grammars No. 1 - for standards II and III*. Manchester: Ledsham. 4pp.
(O)
[Cardboard cards with definitions of OE.]

1877. Wilmshurst, Miss. 1833. *The first part of the progressive parsing lessons; or, an introduction to Murray's grammar*. Maldon: P.H. Youngman. 102pp, with 6pp. list of books and materials used in the seminary.
(O)

["Probably first issued before 1833: the preface says that a new ed. of Part 2 is being prepared."]

1878.! Wilmshurst, Misses. [p1834]. *The child's first [to] fifth English grammar lessons.* (6p each). n.p.
(*Mp*)

1879. Wilson, Rev. Alexander (Master of the National Society's Central School, 1813?-1898). [a1842]. *Outlines of English grammar, compiled for the use of national and other schools.* London: J.G.F. & J. Rivington. 13cm, 18pp. (2nd thousand 1842). (New ed. 1845, price 1s4d a dozen; anr. ed. 1848, London: Society for Promoting Christian Knowledge, 14cm, 24pp. (@); rev. ed. [c1870]), London: National Society's Depository (@)).
(@ L O *Hu*, *Lw*)
["Published under the direction of the Committee of general literature and education, appointed by the Society for Promoting Christian Knowledge". Minimal OES, with O and S having one page each.]

1880. ---. 1853. *Abstract of the 'Manual of English grammar'* [of J. Hunter] *for the use of pupils in elementary schools.* London: National Society. 14x8.5, 24pp., 1s4d a dozen. (New ed. [1862] as *Abstract of English grammar*, 24pp.).
(L O)
[OES, very rudimentary: syntax summarized in ten 'rules' on p.23 without examples. Very brief definitions, generally quite competent; extensive lists of conjugations.]

1881. ---. 1862. *Abstract of English grammar.* London. 13cm, 24pp. (First published as *Abstract of the 'Manual of English grammar'* [of J. Hunter] *for the use of pupils in elementary schools* in 1853; new ed. n.d., London: The National Society's Depository, 24pp.).
(O)
[OESP, nine parts of speech; though rudimentary, clear definitions aimed at; for beginners - "when sufficient progress has been made, recourse should be had to [Hunter's] Manual", no. 922.]

1882.! Wilson, J. ^{3}1803. *English grammar.* Congleton. 18mo, 184pp.
(*Br*)

1883.$ Wilson, Jacob (1831-1914). 1858. *Rough notes on the errors of grammar, and the nature of language. An original work.* Canajoharie, N.Y.: L.S. Backus. 23cm, 128+7pp. (Anr. ed. 1860 (@)).
($ @)

1884.$ ---. [a1870]. *A practical grammar of the English language, plain, pointed and complete.* Rev. ed. Rochester, N.Y.: E. Darrow. 19cm, 128pp.

(@)
1885.$ Wilson, James F. 1874. *An introduction to verbal analysis; with tables of significant elements, and an alphabet of examples*. Cambridge, Mass.: The Riverside Press. 19cm, 13/14pp.
($ @)
1886.$ Wilson, James Patriot (1769-1830). 1817. *An essay on grammar: principles of which are exemplified and appended in an English grammar*. Philadelphia: W. Fry. 8vo, 281pp. (Anr. ed. 1817, 21cm, xv+230+li pp.).
($ @ Br, Sk)
1887.$ Wilson, John Dawson. 1889. *English grammar made practical. One hundred lessons in grammar and composition, with illustrated specimens of actual work by pupils*. (School Bulletin Publication). Syracuse, N.Y. 18cm, v+1+[9]-112pp.
($)
1888.$ ---. 1891. *Elementary English prepared with reference to the Regent's examination in the state of New York*. Syracuse, N.Y.: C.W. Bardeen.
(@)
1889.! Wilson, M. n.d. *First step to English grammar*. n.p.: the author. 1s.
(*So*) [Same as no. 1892.?]
1890.! ---. n.d. *The grammatical primer*. n.p.: the author. 1s.
(*So*) [Same as no. 1893.?]
1891.$ Wilson, Mary E. & Elizabeth P. Sargent. 1889. *Lessons in language*. (California State Series of School Text-books ed. by W.H.V. Raymond). Sacramento, Calif.: State Printing Office. 19cm, 158pp.
($ @)
1892. Wilson, Mathew (Principal of the Glasgow Model Schools, Eight Years Head Master of the Glasgow Normal Seminary). [a1855]. *First step to English grammar, being an easy introduction to the grammatical primer*. New ed. (Series of Books for the Use of Schools, No. VIII). Edinburgh: J. Menzies. 13cm, 56pp.
(@)
1893. ---. [pref. 1855]. *The grammatical primer, being an easy introduction to the principles of English grammar, arranged on a plan adapted for use in large schools*. Ster. ed. [3]. Edinburgh: J. Menzies.
(@)
1894. ---. 1855. *A complete English grammar, for the use of advanced classes in large schools and pupil teachers*. London. 2s. (Ster. ed. ^{2}1855 (Wilson's School Series), Edinburgh: J. Menzies, 17cm, vi+[7]-278pp. (@); ^{3}1860?, London: R. Griffin (@); ^{5}1872 (Laurie's Kensington Series), London: Thomas Laurie (@); anr. ed. [1884]).

(@ O *Lw*)

[Historical introduction of 30 pages followed by OESP; eight parts of speech. Traditional account, with plenty of questions and exercises (and notes in smaller print) inserted. A great amount of false syntax from best authors.]

1895. ---. [pref. 1856]. ... *Key to the grammatical primer containing the exercises in that work cor. and explained, and developing the mode of teaching English grammar, as practised by the author.* (Wilson's School Series). London: R. Griffin. 14cm, 154pp.

(@)

1896. Wilson, Richard (of Grantham grammar school). 1845. *Interrogative English grammar.* Grantham: T. Bushby, for the author. 15cm, 44pp. in large print.

(L O)

[Very short catechism, OESP, with Prosody = pronunciation; nine parts of speech; punctuation at end.]

1897. Wilson, T. [a1860]. *First catechism of English grammar.* London: Darton. 9d.

(L)

1898.$ Wisely, John Benjamin. 1896. *A new English grammar.* Terre Haute, Ind.: The Inland Publishing Company. (@). (Anr. ed 1898 (from 1886 ed.), 20cm, 227pp. ($)).

($ @)

1899.$ ---. 1896. *Studies in the science of English grammar.* Terre Haute, Ind.: The Inland Publishing Company. 20cm, 318pp.

($ @)

1900. Wiseman, Thomas John. 1846. *A school grammar of the English language.* (Publ. anon. by "the Brothers of the Christian Schools of Ireland"). Dublin: William Powell. 8°, 132pp. (^{7}1860, Dublin: J.F. Fowler, 142pp.)

(O)

[Very wide-ranging, for a small book; good composition. OESP, nine classes; succinct definitions, mostly competent; footnotes for details and exceptions. In syntax, rules with examples are followed by exercises; notably free of Biblical quotes. - "... in strict accordance with their peculiar system of instruction, which combines the truths of religion with the principles of science, and the inculcation of sound morality with the development and training of the mental faculties" (advertisement for the Elementary Works Series).]

1901.! Wood, Helen. 1827. *The grammatical reading class-book, or Easy introduction to English grammar, in entertaining conversations between a lady and her daughters: in which the parts of speech are familiarly explained, and the rules of grammar introduced and illustrated in a pleasing manner ... Intended for the use of schools and families.* London. 207pp. (^{3}1828; ^{6}1841; ^{7}1844; ^{10}1865).

(*Br, Hu, Lw*)

[Not a proper grammar but a reading book with grammatical tasks suggesting that pupils read each lesson seven times.]

1902.! Wood, John. 1839. *First element(arie)s of English grammar; by the compiler of the Edinburgh Sessional School-Books.* Edinburgh.

(*Hu, Lw*)

1903. [Wood, John] (of Northwich). [1879]. *Wood's lessons in English grammar. Standards II-VI.* 3 parts. Manchester: Heywood. 16x9.5. Standard IV: 32pp., 2d each).

(O)

[Standard IV is the second part of a work issued in three sections for standards II-III, IV and V-VI; the first is devoted to Noun, Verb, Adjective; the second to all the parts of speech and examples of parsing; the third to lessons on analysis, all accompanied by exercises - not a convincing method and style.]

1904.$ Woodbridge, William (1755-1838). 1800. *A plain and concise grammar of the English language; containing large exercises of parsing and incorrect English.* Middleton, Conn.: Tertius Dunning. 12°, 60pp.

(@)

1905.$ ---. 1801. *A key to the English language, or a spelling, parsing, derivative, and defining dictionary; selected from the most approved authors.* Middletown, Conn.: T. & J.B. Dunning. 13cm, iv+174pp.

(@)

1906. Woods, Mary A. (Late Headmistress of the Clifton High School). 1890. *English examples and exercises. Part 1: Outline lessons and exercises in English accidence.* London: Swan Sonnenschein & Co. (Parallel Grammar Series). 58pp.

(L O)

[Part 2 *Analysis* by Alice J. Cooper]

1907.$! Woodworth, A. 1823. *Grammar demonstrated.* Auburn, N.Y. 12mo, 72pp.

(*Br*)

1908. Woollaston, M.W., ed. 1835. *Principles of English grammar, for the use of the natives of India. With a translation into Sanscrit, by Madhusudama Tarkalankára.* Calcutta. 17/19cm.

(@ O)

1909.$ Worcester, Samuel. (1793-1844). 1831. *A first book of English grammar.* Boston: Crocker & Brewster / New York: J. Leavitt. 15cm, 36pp.
($ @ Br)

1910.$ Worrell, Adolphus Spalding. (b. 1831). 1861. *The principles of English grammar.* Nashville, Tenn.: Graves, Marks & Co./Southwestern Publishing House. 19cm, 159pp.
($ @)

1911. Worthington, R.N. (Head Certificated Master of the Liverpool School Board South Corporation Schools). 1874. *English grammar. A text book for the use of pupils and the assistance of teachers.* London: Daldy & Isbister. 16x9.5, vi+72pp.
(L O)
[Brief definitions and explanations of nine parts of speech followed by rules of syntax and analysis of sentences, with many examples and exercises; Latin affixes, model essays and French words at end. Generally sober and trustworthy, but not new.]

1912. Wright, J.C. (of St. James's-School). [1842]. *The elements of the English grammar ... simplified by ... for the use of juvenile pupils.* Lynn: John Thew. 16x10, 28pp.
(O)
[Q/A form of the simplest kind, dealing with parts of speech and parsing, starting: "Q. What did God ordain the human voice to utter?" Well-meant, but very deficient, accompanied by a poetic preface and farewell address.]

1913. Wright, John Charles (of Eastborne, b. 1852). 1882. *English grammar and the analysis of sentences. Together with lessons in composition; paraphrasing, etc.* Manchester: Heywood. 16.5x10.5, 176pp., 1s6d.
(L O)
[Descriptions of nine parts of speech (1-93) followed by sentence structure (syntax, parsing) and a brief chapter on comparative philology; in intentionally simple language, progressing to greater complexity and with some 502 exercises inserted. The methods are carefully geared to the code of 1882. Inadequate definitions, leaving much room to the teacher. Also bound separately as *English grammar for standard II* (24pp., 1d), III (24pp., 1d), IV (32pp., 2d), IV (32pp., 2d), V (32pp., 2d), IV (32pp., 2d), IV (32pp., 2d) and VII (32pp., 2d).]

1914.$ Wright, Joseph W. 1838. *A philosophical grammar of the English language: adapted equally to the use of schools or private study: in which are contained, in numerous instances, theoretical and practical refutations of the most prevailing systems in modern use.* New York:

Spinney (Spinning?) & Hodges / London: Whittaker & Co. 19cm, 251/ 252pp.
($ @ Br)
1915.$ ---. 1840?. *Extracts from Wright's practical grammar of the English language.* 4 parts. n.p. 24cm.
($)
1916.$ ---. 1842. *An abridgment of Wright's practical grammar of the English language. Prepared from the 4th duodecimo ed.* New York: R. Barnard & Co. 17cm, 126pp.
(@)
1917.$ ---. [4]1842. *A practical grammar of the English language: adapted to the use of all classes of learners: in which are contained, in numerous instances, theoretical and practical refutations of the most prevailing systems of grammar in modern use.* New York: Richard Barnard & Co. Rev. and enl. ed. 18x10.5, [12pp. of recommendations]+276pp.
($ L)
[OESP, traditional account close to Murray, who is frequently quoted, but in a highly involved style which affects the clarity. Somewhat turgid definitions followed by remarks in small print, in which semi-learned long discussions of particulars are found.]
1918. Wrightson, William Garmonsway (1836-1900). 1882. *Examination of the functional elements of an English sentence: together with a new system of analytic marks.* London. 19cm, xv+163+61pp.
($)
[Strong historical element. Describes an over-elaborate system of sentence and clause analysis, using varieties of underlining. Innovative but impractical.]
1919.$ Wylie, Andrew (1789-1851). 1820. *A new and improved English grammar: intended for the use of colleges, schools, and private students.* Pittsburgh: Eichbaum & Johnston. 15cm, 124pp.
($ @)
1920.$ Yaeger, George (Principal of the Livingstone Grammar School of Philadelphia). 1855. *Class book of parsing, containing a complete collection of parsing models and a new and original system of grammatical notation.* n.p.
(L)
[The system proposed is notational only - and is unlikely to have been found worth learning, even though the author promises that much time can be saved. The book does not provide any new insight into *grammatical* analysis.]

1921. Yardley, Robert. 1808. *An appendix to Lindley Murray's grammar; or, An etymological vocabulary, designed for the use of the junior classes.* Manchester: Nanfan & Davis. 52pp.
(L)
[Ten parts of speech; lists of words grouped by endings.]

1922. Yates, Matthew Thompson. (Wesleyan School, Bodley, Leeds). [a1871]. *Primary language lessons, or Grammar made easy by 200 graded exercises in prose and rhyme including script work, reproduction work, suggestions for dictation, the rules of grammar in rhyme, 100 subjects for composition, and picture aids to composition.* Manchester: John Heywood. 1d. (Ref. in *Young student's English grammar*). (Anr. ed. 1895, Cleveland, Ohio: J.R. Holcomb & Co., 18cm, 47pp. (@)).
(@ L)

1923. ---. [1871]. *Grammar made easy, in rhyme.* Manchester: John Heywood, etc. 16x9, 15pp., 1d.
(L)
[Minimal definitions of eight parts of speech followed by abominable verses and exercises (also rhymed); possibly the worst of its kind.]

1924. Yates, W.V. 1873. (Windermere Grammar School) *The civil service English grammar: being notes on the history and grammar of the English language. For the use of civil service candidates, the higher classes in public schools; and students in training colleges.* London: Lockwood. 16x10, vii+118pp., 1s6d. (Rev. ed. ^{2}1884, London, viii+128pp.).
(@ L O)
[In five parts: history of English, etymology (inflexion), derivation, syntax and analysis of sentences: although Yates quotes OESP as the divisions of English grammar (p.13), he does not stick to this frame. Generally clear definitions, conventional.]

1925. Yonge, Charles Duke. 1879. *A short English grammar for the use of schools.* London: Longmans, Green & Co. 18cm, vii+150pp.
(C L O)
[Loosely structured series of chapters with no claim of being comprehensive; influenced by Max Müller.]

1926.$ York, Brantley (1805-1891). 1854. *An illustrative and constructive grammar of the English language accompanied by several original diagrams ... also, an extensive glossary of the derivation of the principal scientific terms used in this work.* Salisbury, N.C.: J.J. Brunner. 22/24cm, xi+[13]-112pp. (Anr. ed. 1860, xx+[21]-231/xx+228pp. ($)).
($ @)

1927. $ ---. 1860. *An analytical, illustrative, and constructive grammar of the English language accompanied by several original diagrams, exhibiting an occular [sic] illustration of some of the most difficult principles of the science of language; also, an extensive glossary of the derivation of the principal scientific terms used in this work, in two parts, for the use of every one who might want to use it.* n.p. 24cm, 231pp. (^{3}1862, ... *for the use of every one who may wish to adopt it*, Raleigh, N.C.: W.L. Brantley, 21/22cm, xx+[21]-219pp. ($ @)).
($ @)
1928. $ ---. 1860. *Introduction to the illustrative and constructive grammar; or, A grammar for beginners.* Raleigh, N.C.: W.L. Pomeroy.
(@)
1929. $ ---. ^{3}1864. *York's English grammar revised and adapted to southern schools.* Raleigh, N.C.: Branson, Farrar & Co. 20cm, ix+120pp. (^{3}1865 (@)).
($ @)
1930. $ ---. ^{4}1879. *An analytical, synthetical, and illustrated grammar of the English language: accompanied by several original diagrams exhibiting an occular illustration of some of the most difficult principles of the science of language; also, an extensive glossary of the derivation of the principal scientific terms used in this work, in two parts, for the use of high schools and colleges.* Raleigh, N.C.: L. Branson. 22cm, 295pp. (Anr. ed. 1881 (@)). [Apparently a new ed. of no. 1927.]
($ @)
1931. $ ---. 1880. *Introduction to the analytical, synthetical and illustrated grammar: or, A grammar for common schools and beginners, illustrated by several original diagrams, embracing analysis and construction of sentences in familiar lessons, with models, copious exercises and directions. In two parts.* Rev. ed. Raleigh, N.C.: L. Branson. 21cm, viii+130pp. (^{3}1885 (@)). [A new ed. of no. 1928?]
($ @)
1932. Anon. 1846. *The young child's grammar.* (Easy Introduction to *The principles of English grammar*). Edinburgh: Scottish School book Association. 36pp., 3d.
(L *Hu*, *Lw*)
[Parts of speech and syntax combined. Exercises in false syntax.]
1933. Young, Henry (Second Master, Guildford Grammar School). 1832. *The youth's memoriter and English exercise book, in two parts; containing a rational grammar of the English language, in which cases, moods, compound tenses, and the numbers and persons of our verbs have been rejected. ... a verbal analysis, or a method of acquiring the significations*

of words by a knowledge of their component parts or elements; and orthographical exercises, upon a plan entirely new ... comprising in one volume all that is necessary for an English scholar to commit to memory, and all the exercises usually put into his hands. London: Whittaker, Treacher & Co. xxiv+225pp.
(L)
[Includes etymology, syntax, punctuation, prosody, exercises in composition, verbal analysis, foreign words, arithmetical tables, and advice on spelling: slightly chaotic.]

1934. Anon. 1847. *The young lady's new grammar; or, a summary of the various rules of English grammar familiarly explained with numerous exercises in etymological and syntactical parsing. By a lady.* (L.B.). London: James Madden. 17cm, iii+104pp.
(C L O Lw)
[Simplified, with easy examples, OESP, nine parts of speech, six tenses; many parsing exercises. Despite the title, not noticeably different from other grammars.]

1935. Anon. [1871a]. *The young student's English grammar for schools. Including the formation and derivation of words, the analysis of sentences and numerous exercises.* (By the author of *The youth's English grammar*). (Class-book of English grammar). Manchester: Heywood. 16.5x10, 1s6d.
(E L O)
[OES (Prosody not felt to be part of grammar); unexciting definitions with plentiful exercises; no corrections of bad grammar inserted. Probably written by the same author as no. 1936.]

1936. Anon. [1871b]. *The youth's English grammar, for the use in junior classes; an introduction to 'The young student's English grammar'.* Manchester: John Heywood. 17cm, 56pp., 8d.
(L O)
[Sentence analysis, as subject, adjunct, predicate, adjunct; object is called the "completion".]

Appendix: Titles not included in the main list

Work on catalogues and computerized printouts of these yielded a great number of books which, although listed as 19th-century grammars, do not classify for my bibliography. They are here printed in various groups because they may be of interest to researchers investigating related topics - also, the dividing line between grammars and other handbooks/ school books is not always quite clear: a few of the books here listed may have a claim to be 'upgraded' into the grammar list (as others, on inspection, will prove *not* to be a proper grammar and in consequence will be downgraded to one of the reject groups). Since I have not made a systematic search for any of the reject categories the evidence here found can at best be supplementary to special bibliographies devoted to any of the sections. No attempt has been made in this section at full bibliographical description and documentation of library holdings.

0. *18th century works*

Some grammars are here included because they testify to the survival of earlier grammars in the 19th century.

1937. Adam, Alexander. (1741-1809). 1772. *The principles of Latin and English grammar: designed to facilitate the study of both languages, by connecting them together.* Edinburgh: pr. for A. Kincaid & W. Creech; T. Caddell, London. 8vo, 16cm, vii+217pp. new rev. ed. 1846. Edinburgh: Bell & Bradfute. xv+324pp. (L)). (^{4}1793 Edinburgh, as *The rudiments of Latin and English grammar*; anr. ed. 1803, 17cm, x+302pp.; anr. ed. 1846 rev. by W.Pyper, Edinburgh; at least 16 eds. up to 1846). ($ A E L O)

1938. Alexander, Caleb. (1755-1828). 1792. *A grammatical system of the English language; comprehending a plain and familiar scheme of teaching young gentlemen and ladies the art of speaking and writing correctly their native tongue: with an appendix.* Boston: Samuel Hall. (^{2}1793, Boston: I. Thomas & E.T. Andrews; ^{6}1801, 17/18cm, iv+96pp. ($); ^{7}1803, corrected by the author. Boston: I. Thomas & E.T. Andrews. anr. ed. 1822, 84pp. ($); at least 15 eds. up to 1822).
($ L *Ke, Mi*) [Alston, I:87]

1939. Arnold, Theodor. 1718. *A new English grammar, or A short but clear and sure direction for the true pronunciation, accentuation and compleat acquisition of the English tongue. (Neue englische Grammatica, oder Kurzgefaßte, jedoch deutliche und sichere Anweisung).* Hanover: Nicholas Förstner. 606pp. (L) [Alston, II:80]

1940. Ash, John. (1724?-1779). 1775. *The new and complete dictionary of the English language. (...). To which is prefixed, a compendious grammar.* 2vols. 8vo. London: Edward & Charles Dilly. [Alston, V: 53]

1941. ---. (1724?-1779). [^{1}1763]. 1784. *Grammatical institutes: or, an easy introduction to Dr. Lowth's English Grammar: designed for the use of schools, and to lead young gentlemen and ladies into the knowledge of the first principles of the English language.* New ed. corrected and enlarged. For Charles Dilly. First published in 1760 as *Grammatical institutes: or grammar, adapted to the genius of the English language* [in fact pre-dating Lowth's Grammar]. 174pp. (+[vi] pages of advertisement). anr. ed. 1823, 12cm, 168pp. ($); at least 13 eds. up to 1823).
($ A L) [Facs. EL 9; Alston, I:32]

1942. ---. (1724?-1779). 1804. *Attempt to illustrate some of the differences between Elizabethan English grammar, designed for the use of schools.* n.p. 18cm, 76pp. ($)

1943. ---. 1807. *Compendium of Ash's Grammatical Institutes, or , An easy Introduction to Dr Lowth's English Grammar with considerable alterations, and a concise syntax, adapted to the use of schools.* 15cm, 72pp. [Shortened version of 1941.]

($ *Sk*) [Alston, I:38]

1944. Barrie, Alexander. [9]1800. *An epitome of English grammar.* Edinburgh: George Caw. 15cm, 54pp. (@) [Alston, I:107]

1945. Beattie, James. (ca. 1785?) 1838. *The grammarian; or, The English writer and speaker's assistant, comprising shall and will made easy to foreigners, with instances of the misuse on the part of natives of England. Also Scotticisms; designed to correct improprieties of speech and writing.* London: Smith, Elder & Co. 8.5x14.5, 84pp.

(L)

1946.$ Bingham, Caleb. (1757-1817). [3]1789. *The young lady's accidence, or, a short and easy introduction to English grammar: designed principally to the use of young learners, more especially those of the fair sex, though proper for either.* Boston: Greenleaf & Freeman, pr. by I. Thomas & Co. (@). ([4]1790 Boston: pr. by I. Thomas & E.T. Andrews, 24°, 57pp. (@); [20]1815 (from 1805 ed.), 14cm, 60pp. ($ *Br*)). ($ @ *Br*) [Alston, I:77]

1947. Bowen, Rev. T. 1799. *The rudiments of English grammar; intended for the use of the Rev. T. Bowen's Academy, at Walsall.* Walsall. (Anr. ed. 1806, Walsall: pr. F. Milward. 14.5x9.5, iv+62pp. (O)). (O) [Alston, I:105]

1948. Burn, John. [[1]1766]. *Practical grammar of the English language.* Glasgow: pr. by Archibald M'Lean, Junior. 16cm, iv+[1]-203pp.; [2]1772, xxiv+240pp.; [3]1778; [4]1786 (@); [8]1802 Glasgow (G L); [9]1805 Glasgow (G); [10]1810 Glasgow).

(@ A G L) [Alston, I:51]

1949.$ Burr, Jonathan. (1757-1842). 1797. *A compendium of English grammar for the use of schools, and private instructers. To which are annexed, exercises, corresponding to the grammar.* Boston: pr. by Samuel Hall. 15cm, 72pp. (@ L). ([2]1804, rev. and corr. ed., Boston: pr. by Munroe & Francis, for Hall & Hiller (@); [3]1818 ($)).

(@ $ L) [Alston, I:99]

[The work may be identical with Burr, Jonathan. [3]1818. *A compendium of English syntax, with concise exercises corresponding to the same, designed as an appendix to Murray's larger grammar and exercises. For the use of Beacon-street School.* Boston: pr. by James Loring. 15cm, 36pp. (@)]

1950. Carter, John. (Teacher of the English Language). 1773. *A practical English grammar, with exercises of bad spelling and bad English, etc.* Leeds: John Binns. 180pp.

(L) [Alston, I:59]

1951. Anon. 1770?. *The complete letter-writer, containing familiar letters on the most common occasions in life. Also a variety of elegant letters for the direction and embellishment of stile, on business, duty ... and other subjects to which are prefixed a plain and compendious grammar of the English language...* anr. ed. 1824 Derby: Henry Mozley, 215pp. (L); at least 3 eds. up to 1824). (L) [Alston, III:65]

1952. Cooke, Rev. Thomas, A.B. ?1818 [[1]1770? [1]1773?]. *The universal letter-writer; or, New art of polite correspondence... With a plain and easy grammar of the English language.* Derby: Henry Mozley. 17cm, 215pp (Grammar: 11-17). (later eds. Derby 1825, 17cm.; anr. ed. 1845 new title *The universal letter-writer; or, New art of polite correspondence. Also a new grammar of the English language*, Halifax: William Milner, 12cm, 256pp.; anr. ed. 1848 London: Thomas Allman, Otley: William Walker; new impr. ed., largely repr. from the original ed. 1860 *Cooke's universal letter writer; or the art of polite correspondence. To which are added The complete petitioner, forms of law, &c. Also an abridgment of Cobbett's English*

grammar; anr. ed. entirely re-edited as *The universal letter writer. ... Also, an abridgement of Murray's English Grammar*. By Rev. W. B. Smith 1863; several eds. up to 1863). (L O) [Alston, III:67]
[The few pages, of uncertain source, do not deserve the name 'grammar'; they are not even geared to the main body of the book; contents and style derive from the 18th centry. The book had numerous reeditions, always claiming to be 'considerably improved', 'entirely re-edited', etc.]

1953. Davies, Charles. (Master of Swansea Free Grammar School). 1753. *Busby's English introduction to the Latin tongue examined, by way of question and answer: with the memorial verses expressing the declensions, terminations and genders of nouns; and the memorial verses for forming the verbs, construed, etc.* Cirencester: printed by Samuel Rudder. vi+118pp. (L)

1954. Devis, Ellin. (died ca. 1784). 1775. *The accidence; or, first rudiments of English grammar: designed for the use of young ladies.* London: the author, 140pp. ($) ([11]1803 London: C. Law. 140pp. (L *Ke*); [18]1827 London: Geo. B. Whittaker. iv+140pp. (L)). ($ L *Ke*) [Alston, I:60]

1955. Dilworth, Thomas. (died 1780). [1]1751. 1802. *A new guide to the English tongue: in five parts, containing, (...)* n.p. 18cm, 144pp. anr. ed. 1802, 141pp. ($); (...) 1879 (from 1861 ed.?) *New guide to the English language: to which are now first added, Murray's English grammar, (...).* 18cm, 142pp. ($); at least 17 eds. up to 1879).
($) [Facs. EL 4; Alston, IV:67]

1956. Entick, John. (1703?-1773). 1765. *Entick's New Spelling Dictionary: (...) To which is prefixed a comprehensive grammar of the English tongue ...* By W. Crakelt [Rector of Nursted and Ifield in Kent]. (Anr. ed. 1795, n.p.; 1800, London: J. Mawman. xxxvi+492pp. (L); anr. ed. 1807 (called from then on) *Entick's New Spelling Dictionary: teaching to write and pronounce the English tongue with ease and propriety: (...) ... To this work is prefixed an abridgment of English grammar.* 14cm, 400pp. ($); anr. ed. 1812, 11x14, 494pp. ($); at least 11 eds. up to 1812).
($ L) [Alston, V:46-50]

1957. Anon. 1778. *Exempla minora: or New English examples, to be rendered into Latin; adapted to the rules of the Latin grammar... A new edition revised.* (The reviser's advertisement signed: T. M., i.e. Thomas Morell). Eton: printed by J. Pote. 187pp. (L)

1958. Fenn, Lady Eleanor. (1743-1813). [[1]1785?]. 1803. *The child's grammar: corresponding with parsing lessons; and forming part of a series for teaching.* [Mrs. Lovechild]. n.p. (Anr. ed. 1807 London, 14cm, 29+vi+ii+64pp.; [4]1847; [47]1855).
(L *Hu*) [cf. Alston I:104]

1959.! ---. [[1]1798]. 1803. *Parsing lessons for elder pupils, resolved into their elements: for the assistance of parents and teachers.* [Mrs. Lovechild]. n.p. 14cm, xii+127pp. ([2]1803; [4]1811; *Gentleman's Magazine* 68.ii. (Oct.1798) p.879). [Alston, I:104]

1960. ---. [[1]1798]. *Parsing lessons for young children.* n.p. ([8]1832 London: John Harris, 14cm, xi+122pp. (@ L)). (L) [Alston, I:104]

1961. ---. 1790. *The Mother's Grammar.* [Mrs. Lovechild]. (Continuation of *The child's grammar*). n.p. 95pp. (Anr. ed. 1798 (L); [20]1838 (Moon)).
(N *Br, Hu*) [Alston, I:104]

1962. Fenning, Daniel. 1771. *A new grammar of the English language.* ([2]1773, corr. and impr., London: S. Crowder. viii+180pp.). (L) [Facs. EL 19; Alston, I:55]

1963. Fernandez, Felipe. [2]1800. *A new practical grammar of the Spanish language: in five parts ... The whole in Spanish and English, calculated to render the study of the Spanish language, easy, comprehensive, and entertaining. To which is prefixed an*

English grammar, for the use of Spaniards. London. 8°. (³1805. rev. ed. London, 20cm; new ed., considerably altered by George Heaven, ed. London 1828, 18cm; at least 7 eds. up to 1828). (L O)

1964. Fisher, Anne. (1719?-1778). 1762. *The new English tutor, or, modern preceptor: consisting of orthography, or the art of speaking and reading ... : also, a practical abstract of English grammar.* n.p. (¹⁸1821). ($) [Alston, IV:104]

1965. ---. 1792. *Fisher's grammar improved, or, An English grammar in which Fisher's plan is preserved: and the work made more perfect, by various amendments in orthography and prosody, from Walker, Sheridan, and others, and in etymology and syntax, principally from Lowth.* Congleton: J. Dean / Gainsborough: Mozley. (³¹1800 Newcastle; ³⁵1811 Newcastle). ($) [Alston, I:29]

1966. ---. ¹⁸1779. *A practical new grammar, with exercises of bad English: or an easy guide to speaking and writing the English language properly and correctly.* (impr. enl. ed.). Newcastle: Tho. Slack. xii+180pp. ([1780] new corr. impr. ed. Leeds: John Binns. xii+180pp. (L); ²⁸1795 enl. impr. ed. Newcastle: S. Hodgons. xii+180pp. (L)). (L) [Alston, I:25-28]

1967. Gentleman, Robert. 1788. *The young English scholar's complete pocket companion. In six parts. Selected from the best writers. I. A compendious English grammar. (...) By R. Gentleman.* Kidderminster: printed and sold by G. Gower. (...) 18cm, [4],185,[3]pp. (L) [Alston, III:87]

1968. Anon. 1711. *A grammar of the English tongue, with notes, giving the grounds and reasons of grammar in general.* Edited by J. Brightland. London: for the editor. iv+180pp. (²1712 London: for the editor. ii+264pp. (L)).
(L) [Facs. EL 25; Alston, I:13]

1969. Greenwood, Edward J. (Surmaster of St. Paul's School). 1711. *An essay towards a practical English grammar.* London: R. Tookey. (²1722 London: J. Clarke. 315pp.; ³1729 London; ⁵1753 London). (L) [Alston, I:15]

1970. Harrison, Ralph. (1748-1810). 1777. Rev. ²1784. *Institutes of English grammar. Containing: I. The different kinds, relations, and changes of words. II. Syntax, or the right construction of sentences. (...).* Manchester: Charles Wheeler. (⁹1805 enl. ed.).
(L) [Facs. EL 3; Alston, I:62]

1971. ---. 1787. *Rudiments of English grammar containing, I. the different kinds of relations and changes of words, II. syntax, or the right construction of sentences, with an appendix comprehending a table of verbs regularly inflected: remarks on some grammatical figures, a praxis on the grammar, rules of punctuation, and examples of true and false construction.* (Anr. ed. 1801, n.p. 14/16cm, 120pp. ($); 1812, 15cm, 108pp. ($); at least 9 eds. up to 1812). ($) [Alston, I:62]

1972.! Hoole, [Charles]. 1797. *Hoole's terminations and examples to the several declensions of nouns and conjugations of verbs; also, Lily's rules for the genders of nouns (...).* Dublin: John Gough.

1973. Hornsey, John. 1793. *A short grammar of the English language, in two parts: simplified to the capacities of children. And a great variety of entertaining and useful exercises upon a plan entirely new (...).* Newcastle: for the author. (³1802).
[Alston, V, I:89]

1974. Hutchins, John. (1747-1833). 1791. *An abstract of the first principles of English grammar. Compiled for the use of his own school.* Philadelphia: pr. by Thomas Dobson. 14cm, 180pp. (Anr. ed. 1810, Philadelphia: pr. by J. Bioren, title has changed to *An abstract of the first principles of English grammar*, 18cm, iii-vi+[7]-207pp. (@); at least 3 eds. up to 1810).
(@) [Alston, I:86, who gives Joseph as first name.]

1975. Ireland, J. 1784. *Beauties in prose and verse: or, the new, pleasing and entertaining collection, selected from the most eminent English authors. To which is added a practical English grammar. By the Rev. J. Ireland.* Newcastle: printed by T. Angus. xi+292pp. (L) [Alston, III:83]
1976. Johnson, Samuel. (1709-1784) [3]1764. *The compleat art of writing letters, adapted to all classes and conditions of life. (...) To which is prefixed, a short but useful grammar of the English language. (...) By Mr. Johnson.* London: printed for R. Baldwin and T. Lowndes. 18cm. xi+222pp. (L) [Alston: III:62]
1977. ---. 1805. *The synonymous, etymological and pronouncing English dictionary; in which the words are deduced from their originals ... To which is prefixed an English grammar. By W. Perry.* 4 Vs. London. 23cm, xl+[845]pp. (Many revised editions in the 19th century; at least 17 eds. up to 1844). ($ L) [Alston, V:30-41]
1978. Kitson, Roger. 1789. *A short introduction to English grammar.* Norwich: Stevenson & Matchett. 12mo. (L). (Anr. ed. 1807 (*Br*)). (L *Br*) [Alston, I:103]
1979.$ Livingston, William. (1723-1790). ?1817. *An English grammar calculated in conjunction with the syntactical atlas, to render the study of grammar easy and pleasing to the scholar.* Middlebury: Francis Burnap. 84pp. plus one sheet. ($ @)
1980. Lowth, Robert. (Successively, Bishop of St. David of Oxford, and of London. 1710-1787). 1762. *A short introduction to English grammar with critical notes.* London: A. Millar, R. & J. Dodsley xv+186pp. (At least 12 eds. up to 1811).
(L) [Facs. EL 18; Alston, I:42; Reibel 1995]
1981. Murray, Lindley. (1745-1826). 1795. *English grammar, adapted to the different classes of learners, with an appendix, containing rules, and observations for assisting the note advanced students to write with perspicuity and accuracy promoting perspicuity in speaking and writing.* York: Wilson & Spence. 16.5x10, 292pp., 3s6d (L). ([2]1796 York; [3]1797 York; 1st American ed. 1800 Boston: Joseph Nancrede 288pp. (L); [6]1800 corr. ed. York. (O); [7]1801 impr. ed. York (L); [8]1802 with considerable improvements, York (L); [9]1804 York 336pp. (L); [10]1805 York 328pp. (L); [12]1805 impr. ed. London: Longman & Co. 336pp. (L); [13]1806 impr. ed. York (L); [14]1806 impr. ed. York (L); [15]1806 impr. ed. York: T. Wilson and R. Spence; [16]1807 impr. ed. York (L); [20]1810 York (L); anr. ed. 1812 Middlebury, Ve.: Swift (L); anr. ed. from the 18th Engl. ed., enl. by the author 1812 Hallowell (Maine): Goodale & N. Cheever (L); [23]1812 York (L); [24]1813 York (L); [28]1816 York (L); [29]1817 York, 17cm (O); [32]1819 London: Longman & Co. 346pp. (L); anr. ed. 1819 from the stereo. ed. containing the author's last improvements, Hanover (U.S.): J. Hinds (L); anr. ed. 1821 from the improved stereo. ed. Bellows Falls (L); anr. ed. 1821 from the last English ed. Exeter (U.S.) (L); [34]1821 York, 12° (O); [36]1822 London / York, 348pp. (L); [38]1824 London / York (L); [39]1825 London / York (L); [40]1826 York; anr. ed 1826 York (L); anr. ed. 1826 Bridgeport (L); [42]1828 London: Longman, Rees, Orme, Brown, Green & Longman, Harvey & Darton; York: Wilson & Sons, 348pp. (L); [44]1830 York (L); anr. ed. 1831 Calcutta: School-Book Society xii+322pp. (L); [46]1832 York (L); anr. ed. 1834 Windsor, Vt.: Ide & Goddard, New York printed (L); [47]1834 London / York (L); [1845] ... *observations, for assisting the more advanced students to write with perspicuity and accuracy.* London: Thomas Allman, 336pp. (L); [54]1846 London: Longman & Co., 348pp. (L); anr. ed. 1854, 16cm, 264pp. ($)). ($ L O *Mi*) [Facs. EL 106; Alston, I:92-6; Reibel 1996]
- see also Davis, John 1830b.
[There were intermittent, unnumbered, editions in Belfast and Dublin. One of many complications is that the York and London editions appeared in different numbering

sequences. Michael knows of 36 adaptions of Murray by named authors, British and American, most in several editions.]

1982. ---. 1797a. *Abridgement of Murray's English grammar; with an appendix, containing an exemplification of the parts of speech, and exercise in syntax. Designed for the younger Class of Learners.* 1s. York. (^{2}1798 cor. enl. ed. London: Darton & Harvey, 118pp. (L); ^{3}1799 York; ^{4}1800 London/York, 12° (O); ^{5}1801, London; ^{8}1803 London; ^{11}1804 impr. London (L); ^{27}1809 London (L); ^{7}1810 Dublin: John Gough, 124pp. (L); ^{125}1812 London, etc.: Longman, Hurst, Rees, Orme, & Brown, etc. 228pp.; other edn. published by Harvey & Darton, etc, London; Wilson & Son, New York; 1812 new corr. ed. from the 30th English ed. New York, 13cm; ^{47}1815 from the 30th English ed. London, 13cm; ^{53}1817 London: Darton, Harvey & Co. 128pp. (L); ^{54}1817 London (L); 1823 15th Boston ed. with alterations and improvements by a teacher of the youth, Boston: J. Loring, 72pp. (L); anr. ed. 1819, 6to, 15cm, 107pp. ($); 1836 new ed. London (L); 1836 new ed. from the 30th English ed. Banbury, 13cm; 1837 *An abridgement of Murray's English grammar, in question and answer, with explanatory notes, by John Ellis.* London (1839 London; 58th thousand 1853 pr. London: Webb, Millington & Co.; Leeds printed, 144pp.) (L); 1840 new ed. with an appendix containing exercises ... for the younger classes of learners, London: W. Harris, 126pp. (L); 1840 new edn. Merthyr Tydfil: H. W. White, 15cm. 126pp.; 1841 impr. with an enl. appendix by J. Harvey, London: Simpkin, Marshall & Co, Ipswich pr. 125pp.; $^?$1844 Nottingham (L); new ed. 1845 Lisbon: Rolland (L); new edn. [1854] Derby: John and Charles Mozley. 15cm, 126pp.; ^{33}1864; ^{101}1877 London, Otley: Walker (L)). - see also Davis, John. [a.1864] and Ellis, John 1837 and Giles, J. A. 1839 and Harvey, J. 1841. and Walker, W. 1877 and Smith, W.B. 1860 [title in advert: *A key to the English Exercises; calculated to enable private learners, to become their own instructers in grammar and composition*, 4th ed. 2s] ($ O L) [Alston, I:99; Reibel 1996] [Its record soon becomes hugely complicated, with a 117th edition in York (1834) and a 133rd in London, (1864). There are also numerous unnumbered editions. American editions and versions of the abridgment are numerous and varied. Alston in 1956 noted 166 American issues, without looking for them.]

1983. ---. 1797b. *English exercises, adapted to the grammar lately published by L. Murray. Consisting of exemplifications of the parts of speech; instances of false orthography; violations of the rules of syntax; defects in punctuation; and violations of the rules respecting perspicuity and accuracy. Designed for the benefit of private learners, as well as the use of schools.* York: Wilson, Spence & Mawman. 187pp. (^{3}1798 corr. ed. York (L); ^{4}1799 corr. ed. London (L); ^{4}1800 2s (O); ^{4}1801; ^{5}1801 corr. ed. with a key, York. 17cm. (L O); ^{6}1802 York (L); ^{7}1803 impr. ed. York (L); ^{9}1805 London: Longman & Co. 216pp. (L); ^{10}1806; ^{12}1815 impr. ed. Dublin: W. Porter etc. 180pp. (L); ^{14}1810 York, 16cm; ^{17}1812 York, 16cm (O); ^{20}1815 York (L); ^{22}1816 York (L); ^{24}1818 York (L); ^{25}1814 York, 17cm. (O); ^{25}1819 York / London, i+227pp. (*Tm* 25); ^{27}1820 York; 1821 1st Portland from the 9th Boston and 20th English ed. Portland (L); ^{30}1823 York, 17cm. (O); ^{32}1824 York (L); ^{34}1825 York (L); ^{35}1826 London, 227pp. (L); ^{37}1828 York (L); ^{38}1829 London / York (L); ^{39}1830 London (L); [1830] anr. rev. impr. ed. London (L); anr. ed. 1830 enl. by J. Davis Belfast; ^{42}1833 London / York (L); ^{44}1836 York, 17cm. (O); ^{50}1846 London; ^{52}1850 London, 17cm (O); $^?$1863 London). (L O, *Tm*) - see also Davis, John 1830a.

(L O) [Alston, III:94; Reibel 1996]

1984. ---. 1797c. *Key to the exercises adapted to Murray's English grammar... By the author of the exercises.* [York]. ($^?$1801 York, 18cm (O); ^{8}1805 improved ed. Lon-

0. 18th century works

don: Longman & Co. 168pp. (L); ^{9}1806 impr.: York (L); ^{10}1808 impr. York (L); anr. ed. 1811 (12th?) from the 10th London ed., with corrections and improvements by the author: New York (L); ^{15}1818: York (L); anr. ed. 1819: New York (L); ^{16}1822: York (L); ^{18}1827: York (L); $^?$1830: Belfast, enl. by J. Davis (L); ^{23}1837 York; anr. ed. 1839: Derby (L)). - see also Davis, John 1830c.(L O) [Reibel 1996]

1985. Mauger, Claude. ^{20}1705. *Claudius Mauger's French grammar with additions. (...) To which are subjoined a vocabulary, and a most exact new grammar of the English tongue. Exactly corrected and enlarged by the author.* London: printed for R. Wellington, and are to be sold by Tho. Guy. 18cm, 432pp. (L)

1986. Mecan, Benjamin. [1752-1756]. *An English grammar, wrote in a plain familiar manner, adapted to the youth of both sexes. To which are added, some general rules in orthography,- stops or points,- emphasis,- and composition.* St. John's in Antigua. n.d. 9x17. (@)

1987. Mercy, Blanch. 1799. *A short introduction to English grammar.* 2 parts. London: the authoress. (L) [Alston, I:106]

1988. Anon. 1763. *A new dictionary and grammar of the English language. Containing, the various senses in which every word is used (...).* London: printed for J. Cooke. 18cm, [446]pp. (L) [Alston, V:45]

1989. Peirce, John. 1782. *The new American spelling-book, improved: in three parts, containing (...) III. A plain and easy introduction to English grammar, particularly adapted to the capacities of the youth.* (^{6}1804, Philadelphia. 17cm, 200pp.; anr. ed. 1808, iv+200pp. ($)). ($ Br) [Alston, IV:118]

1990. Perry, William. (Lecturer in the Academy at Edinburgh). 1775. *The royal standard dictionary (...) to which is prefixed, a comprehensive grammar of the English language...* n.p. (Anr. ed. 1801, 14 x 13, 586pp. ($); anr. ed. 1801, 14cm, [4]+596pp. ($); anr. ed. 1804, 429pp. ($)). ($) [Alston V:53]

1991. ---. 1776. *The only sure guide to the English tongue, or, New pronouncing, spelling book to which is added, a grammar of the English language, (...)* n.p. (Anr. ed. 1801, 17cm, 180pp. ($); anr. ed. 1803 ($)). [cf. Perry 1795] ($) [Alston, IV:111]

1992.! ---. 1795. *Grammar in dictionary.* n.p. (Anr. ed. 1801 Edinburgh, 12mo. (*Br*)).
(*Br*)

1993. Priestley, Joseph. (1733-1804). 1762. *English grammar; Lectures on the theory of language and universal grammar; and on oratory and criticism.* Also in: 1833. *Works* collected and edited by J.T. Rutt. London 26cm, xii+526pp.
($ A) [1762, Facs. EL 126; Alston, I:40]

1994. Scott, William. (1750-1804). Teacher of Elocution and Geography in Edinburgh. 1777. *Principles of English grammar.* Edinburgh: Elliott. (Anr. ed. 1809 as *A concise system of English grammar.* Edinburgh: William Whyte. 15x9, iv+[5]-136pp.). (Ep L Mi) [Alston, I:64]

1995. Sheridan, Thomas. M.A. (Teacher of Elocution). 1781. *A rhetorical grammar of the English language. Calculated solely for the purposes of teaching propriety of pronunciation, and justness of delivery, in that tongue, by the organs of speech.* Dublin: for Messrs. Price, W. and H. Whitestone, etc. 18cm, 238pp.
(L) [Facs. EL 146; Alston, VI:101]

1996.$ Staniford, Daniel. (Author of the Art of Reading; Member of the Society of Associated Instructors of Youth in the town of Boston and its vicinity). 1797. *Short but comprehensive grammar rendered simple and easy by familiar questions and answers: adapted to the capacity of youth: and designed for the use of schools and private families: to which is added an appendix, comprehending a list of vulgarisms and grammatical improprieties used in common conversation.* Boston: the author. 16cm, iv+1+[6]-84pp. (@). (Anr. ed. 1807 Boston. 17cm, 96pp. ($ *Br*); anr. ed. 1810, iv+94pp. ($); anr. ed. 1815 (*Br*)). ($ @ *Br*) [Alston, I:102]

1997. Story, Joshua. 1778. *An introduction to English grammar, to which is annexed a treatise on rhetorick.* (^{3}1783; with additions, Newcastle upon Tyne: printed by T. Angus, for T. Longman; ^{5}1792). x+180pp. (L) [Alston, I:67]

1998. Ussher, George Nelville. 1785. *The elements of English grammar: methodically arranged for the assistance of young persons (...).* 1/6. (Anr. ed. 1786 Glocester: pr. R. Raikes. 17x10, 1s6d.; ^{6}1806 London). ($ O) [Alston, I:79]

1999. Walker, John. 1785. *A Rhetorical Grammar in which the common improprieties in reading and speaking are detected.* (^{3}1801; ^{4}1807; ^{6}1816, London: G. Wilkie, Cadell & Davies, et al., 373pp.; 1. American ed.: Boston: J.T. Buckingham. 1814, 356pp.) [Facs. EL 266; Alston, VI:82]

2000. Watt, Thomas. 1704. *Grammar made easy. Containing Despauter's grammar reformed, and rendered plain and obvious to the capacity of youth. Together with a new method of teaching Latin by the English particles. To which is added a critical syntax.* (^{4}1730, carefully corrected. Edinburgh: J. Paton & W. Brown. 17cm, 74,21,6[3]pp.; anr. ed. 1763 (@); anr. ed. 1772 (@); anr. ed. 1774 (@)). (@) [Facs. EL 340]

2001. Webster, Noah. (1758-1843). 1784. *A grammatical institute of the English language: comprising, an easy, concise, and systematical method of education. Designed for the use of English schools in America. In three parts. Part second. A plain and comprehensive grammar grounded on the true principles and idioms of the language.* Hartford: Hudson & Goodwin, for the author. anr. ed. 1806, 112pp. ($). ($) [Facs. EL 89,90; Alston, I:72]

2002. ---. 1789. *Dissertations on the English language.* Boston: for the author, 19x11, xvi+[17]-410pp. (*Hu, Sk*) [Facs. EL 54; Alston, III:89]

2003. ---. 1790. *Rudiments of English Grammar: being an abridgement of the philosophical and practical grammar of the English language compiled at the desire of the Committee of the grammar school in Hartford. Published according to statute.* Hartford: pr. Elisha Babcock. 32°, 80pp. (@). (...) anr. ed. 1831, 15cm, 87pp. ($). [At least 3 eds. up to 1831] ($ @ *Br*) [Alston, I:86]

2004.! ---. ^{6}1800. *A plain and comprehensive grammar.* Hartford, Ct. 12mo, 131pp. (*Br*)

2005.$ Wilson, Samuel, of Kentucky. 1797. *The Kentucky English grammar, or, New grammatical institute containing a comprehensive system of English grammar, in which the whole structure and essential principles of that most copious language, according to the most approved modern standards, are concisely, yet completely exhibited, and explained in a manner intelligible to the weakest capacities.* n.p. (@). (Anr. ed. 1802; anr. ed. 1806, 16cm, ix+[11]-97pp.; anr. ed. 1812, 108pp. ($)). ($ @) [Alston, I:103]

2006. Wright, Thomas. (Schoolmaster). [c.1795]. *An English grammar.* Great Yarmouth?. 69pp. (L) [Alston, I:108]

1. Books on Anglo-Saxon & language history

Grammars tend to include a section on language history from at last 1850 onwards; the subsequent list has entries which are exclusively historical-comparative.

2007.$ Bernard, Emil Alexander Wilhelm. (born 1850). 1874. *Grammatical treatise on the language of William Langland, preceded by a sketch of his life and his poem Piers the Plowman....* n.p. 22cm, 94pp. ($)

2008. Bosworth, Joseph. 1823. *The elements of Anglo-Saxon grammar, with copious notes, illustrating the structure of the Saxon and the formation of the English language: and a grammatical praxis with a literal English version. To which are prefixed, remarks on the history and use of the Anglo-Saxon, and an introduction, on the origin and progress of alphabetic writing.* London: Harding, Mavor, & Lepard. 8vo., [iv]+xlvii+[i]+332pp. (A L)

2009. ---. 1826. *A compendious grammar of the primitive English or Anglo-Saxon language ... Being chiefly a selection of what is most valuable in the Elements of Anglo-Saxon Grammar, with some additional observations.* London. 22cm, xii+84pp. (A L O)

2010.$ Bright, James Wilson. (1852-1926). 1894. *An outline of Anglo-Saxon grammar.* n.p. 19cm, lxxix pp. ($)

2011.! Campbell, David. 1876. *Outlines of the history of the English language.* Edinburgh: Laurie's Kensington Series. vi+65pp. (Mp)

2012.! Chambers, Robert. 1835. *History of the English language and literature.* Edinburgh: W. & R. Chambers. viii+278+6+8pp. (^{2}1836; ^{4}1837; anr. ed. 1837 Hartford, Conn. ... to which is added a history of American contributions to the English language and literature, by Rev. Royal Robbins; ^{7}1838). (Mp)

2013. Champneys, Arthur Charles. 1893. *History of English. A sketch of the origin and development of the English language, with examples, down to the present day.* London: Percival. 20cm, xiv+414pp. (L)

2014. Clark, Thomas. (Headmaster of the Propriety School, Taunton). 1862. *The Student's handbook of comparative grammar. Applied to the Sanskrit, Zend, Greek, Latin, Gothic, Anglo-Saxon, and English languages.* London: Longman & Co. xii+335pp. (A L M)

2015. Clarke, Benjamin. 1849. *Language. An essay on the source and constitution of the English language, with a review of the origin, construction and progress of oral and written communication among the ancients.* London(?). 116pp. (Reissued 1853).(L)

2016. Cook, Albert Stanburrough. 1894. *A first book in Old English. Grammar, reader, notes and vocabulary.* Boston: Ginn & Co. xii+314pp. (^{3}1906 London (A)). (A L)

2017.! Craik, George Lillie. 1851. *Outlines of the history of the English language for the use of junior classes in colleges and the higher classes in schools.* London: Chapman & Hall. vii+176pp. (^{3}1859, ^{5}1864).

2018. Dalgleish, Walter Scott. (1834-1897). Vice-Principal of Dreghorn College. 1895. *Higher Grade English. History of the language; analysis; style; prosody.* (Royal English Class-Books). London: T. Nelson & Sons. 18x12, vi+150pp. (@ L) [Intended to cover the language requirements in various examinations; obligations expressed to Max Müller, Earle, Skeat, Sweet, Abbott and R. Morris. "Grammar treated in its historical development (69-84). The book complements Dalgleish's *Outlines*, no. 405.]

2019.! Dickinson, W.J. 1880. *Short history of the English language with Saxon, Latin and Greek prefixes, and hints on composition.* Hughes. 32pp.

2020.! D'Oull, James. 1877. *Questions on Archbishop Trench's "English Past and Present".* Dublin.

2021.! Earle, John. (Rector of Swanswick, and some time Professor of Anglo-Saxon in the University of Oxford. 1824-1903). 1860. *A sketch of the history of the English language.* Bath: T.D. Taylor.

2022. ---. 1871. *The philology of the English tongue.* Oxford. v+599pp., 16,5x11. (L) (^{2}1873, rev. and enl., 18cm, viii+679pp. ($ N^c); anr. ed. 1879, viii+700pp. ($); 4th ed. rev. and rewritten in parts, 1887). ($ L Nc)

[Written by one of the foremost Anglo-Saxonists of his time, the book contains a history of English (1-98), in which all structures are explained by their diachronic development. Roughly OESP, the categorization includes quite a few ideas, partly suggested by the historical approach, and partly by new grammatical thinking. (Earle refers to Thring). Expository prose combining analysis and explanation; no attempt at formulating rules and imposing a very strict framework.]

2023.! ---. 1876. *A Word for the Mother Tongue. An Inaugural Lecture.* Oxford.

2024.$ ---. 1884. *Book for the beginner in Anglo-Saxon; comprising a short grammar some selections from the gospels & a parsing glossary.* (Clarendon Press Series). n.p. 112pp. ($)

2025.! Edwards, John. 1850. *A history of the English language.* Gleig's School Series. (Anr. ed. 1858; 1859).

2026.! Anon. [a1887]. *English language: sources, growth, history, literature.* London: Moffatt & Paige.

2027.$ Govett, Robert. (born 1813). 1869. *English derived from Hebrew: with glances at Greek and Latin.* 22cm, 135pp. ($)

2028.! Hadley, James. 1880. *A brief history of the English language.* Belfast. (Anr. ed. 1890 rev. by G.L. Kittredge).

2029. Helfenstein, Jacob. 1870. *A comparative grammar of the Teutonic languages, being at the same time a historical grammar of the English language; and comprising Gothic, Anglo-Saxon, Early English, Modern English, Icelandic (Old Norse), Danish, Swedish, Old High German, Middle High German, Modern German, Old Saxon, Old Frisian, Dutch.* London: Macmillan & Co. Oxford printed. 22x14, xviii+[2]+525pp. ($ A B L O)

2030. Henry, Victor. (1850-1907). 1894. *A short comparative grammar of English and German, traced back to their common origin and contrasted with the classical languages. Précis de grammaire comparée de l'anglais et de l'allemand.* Translated from French. London: Sonnenschein & Co. 18/20cm, xxviii+394pp. ($ A L O)

2031. Ingram, James. (Translator). 1823. *The Saxon Chronicle, with an English translation, and notes ... to which are added chronological, topographical, and glossarial indices, a short grammar of the Anglo-Saxon language.* London. (A)

2032. Isberg, Carl. (1840-1911). 1872. *Grammatical studies of Chaucer's language.* n.p. 22cm, 38+[2]pp. ($)

2033.! Keane, Augustus Henry. 1860. *Handbook of the history of the English language for the use of schools and colleges.* (Anr. ed. 1875, London: Longman).

2034.$ Kellogg, Brainerd. 1893. *The English language: a brief history of its grammatical changes and its vocabulary: with exercises on synonyms, prefixes and suffixes, word-analysis and word-building: a text-book for high schools and colleges.* n.p. 17cm, v+220pp. ($)

2035.! Key, T. Hewitt. 1874. *Language: its origin and development.* London: George Bell and Sons. 8vo., xv+547pp.

2036.!$ Kington-Oliphant, Thomas Laurence. 1873. *The sources of Standard English.* London.

2037. Klipstein, Louis F. 1849?. *A grammar of the Anglo-Saxon language.* n.p. (Anr. ed. 1858, 19cm, 276pp. ($)). ($)

2038. Lange, Franz K.W. [1882]. *Colloquial German grammar, with special reference to the Anglo-Saxon element in the English language.* London. 19cm. (O)

2039. Latham, Robert Gordon. (1812-1888). 1849. *History and etymology of the English language.* London: Taylor, Walton, and Maberly. iv+96pp. Part I: History of the English Language; Part II: Sounds, Letters, and Accent; part III: Inflection; Part VI:

English Affinities to Other Languages. Appendix: (Extracts from Anglo-Norman, "Semi-Saxon", Dutch, Frisian, Modern German, Old High German. (^{2}1854 London, 16° (@)). (@)
2040. ---. 1862. *Elements of Comparative Philology*. London. (L)
2041.! March, Francis Andrew. (1825-1911). 1870a. *A Comparative grammar of the Anglo-Saxon language*. London. (Dk)
2042.$ March, Francis Andrew. (1825-1911). 1870b. *Introduction to Anglo-Saxon: an Anglo-Saxon reader with philological notes, a brief grammar, and a vocabulary*. n.p. (...) anr. ed. 1892, 24cm, viii+166pp. ($); at least 4 eds. up to 1892). ($)
2043. Marsh, George Perkins. (1801-1882). 1859. *Lectures on the English language*. First series. New York and London. (Anr. ed. 1860 New York: Charles Scribner, 22cm, viii+697pp.) (@)
[One of the most influential 19th-century books on English language history, very frequently reprinted in the US and Britain, 1861-1887.]
2044.!$ ---. 1862. *The Origin and History of the English Language*. London.
2045. Morris, Richard. LL. D. (1833-1894). ed. 1872. *Historical outlines of English accidence, comprising chapters on the history and development of the language, and on word-formation*. London. 18cm, xv+378pp. (...) (Rev. ed. 1895 by L. Kellner with the assistance of H. Bradley. London; New York: Macmillan. 18cm, xiii+463pp.; anr. ed. 1912; at least 13 eds. up to 1912). ($ Nc)
2046. ---. 1874. *Elementary lessons in historical English grammar, containing accidence and word formation*. London. 15cm. (Anr. ed. 1875, 16cm, xii+254pp. ($); new ed. 1897 rev. by Henry Bradley, London: Macmillan & Co., 16cm, v+256pp.; anr. ed. 1900; at least 13 eds. up to 1900). ($ L O)
2047.! Nesfield, John Collinson. 1898. *Historical English and derivation*. London: Macmillan. iv+284pp.
2048.! Anon. 1882. *Outlines of the history of the English language*. Edinburgh: Chambers. 96pp.
2049.! Page, Thomas. [1881]. *Sources and growth of the English language*. London: Moffatt & Paige. 72pp., 9d.
2050. Payne, Joseph. (Professor at the College of Preceptors. 1808-1876). [1867/68]. *Studies in English prose: consisting of specimens of the language in its earliest, succeeding, and latest stages, with notes explanatory and critical. Together with a sketch of the history of the English language, and a concise Anglo-Saxon grammar*. London. (Anr. ed. 1872, 18cm, 436pp. ($); ^{2}1881 London: Crosby Lockwood & Co. xliv+435pp). ($ L)
2051.! Robins, Royal. 1837. *History of the English language and literature. To which is added, a history of American contributions*. Edinburgh: Chambers.
2052. Shute, Samuel Moore. (1829-1902). 1867. *A manual of Anglo-Saxon for beginners; comprising a grammar, reader, and glossary, with explanatory notes*. n.p. 19cm, xxi+195pp. ($)
2053. Sievers, Eduard. 1885. *An Old English grammar, translated and edited by A.S. Cook*. Boston, Mass: Ginn, Heath & Co. 18cm, xvi+235. (L O)
2054.! Skeat, Walter William. (1835-1912). 1861. *Origin and progress of the English language*. London: Bell & Daldy. 40pp.
2055.$ ---. 1868. *A Moeso-Gothic glossary: with an introduction, an outline of Moeso-Gothic grammar, and a list of Anglo-Saxon and old and modern English words etymologically connected with Moeso-Gothic*. n.p. 24cm, xxii+340pp. ($)

2054.! Skeat, Walter William. (1835-1912). 1861. *Origin and progress of the English language.* London: Bell & Daldy. 40pp.
2055.$ ---. 1868. *A Moeso-Gothic glossary: with an introduction, an outline of Moeso-Gothic grammar, and a list of Anglo-Saxon and old and modern English words etymologically connected with Moeso-Gothic.* n.p. 24cm, xxii+340pp. ($)
2056.$ Smith, Charles Alphonso. (1864-1924). 1896. *An Old English grammar and exercise book with inflections, syntax, selections for reading, and glossary.* Boston. 18/19cm, vi+129pp. (New ed. rev. and enl. 1898, Boston: Allyn & Bacon, viii+193pp. (L)). ($ O)
2057.! Smith, George. 1848. *The origin and progress of language.* London: Religious Tract Society. (*Mp*)
2058.$ Sturzen-Becker, Vilhelm Teodor Patrick. (1841-1910). 1868. *Some notes on the leading grammatical characteristics of the principal early English dialects.* n.p. 20cm, 81pp. ($)
2059.$ Sweet, Henry, ed. (1845-1912). 1884. *Ancren Riwle. First Middle English primer, extr. from the Ancren Riwle and Ormulum, with grammar and glossary by H. Sweet.* Oxford: Clarendon. (Anr. ed. 1899; at least 6 eds. up to 1899). ($ L O)
2060. ---. 1886. *Second Middle English primer, extracts from Chaucer, with grammar and glossary by H. Sweet.* Oxford: Clarendon. 16/17cm, vi+112pp. (Anr. ed. ²1899). ($ A L O)
2061. ---. 1893. *An Anglo-Saxon Primer: with grammar, notes, and glossary.* (Clarendon Press Series). n.p. 18cm, ix+116pp. ($)
2062. Thomson, Ebenezer. 1853. *On the archaic mode of expressing numbers in English, Saxon, Friesic, etc.: Being an essay towards the settling of the case, Grimm v. Self, Kemble, Vernon, and others.* n.p. 24cm, [1-3] 4-16pp. ($)
2063.! Thorpe, Benjamin. 1830. *A grammar of the Anglo-Saxon tongue, with a praxis.* Transl. from the Danish grammar of Erasmus Rask. Copenhagen: S.L. Moller.
2064.! Toller, Thomas Northcote. 1900. *Outlines of the history of the English language.* Cambridge Series for Schools. xiv+284pp.
2065. Vernon, Edward Johnston. (1814?-1848). 1865. *Guide to the Anglo-Saxon tongue; a grammar after Erasmus Rask.* n.p. 196pp. ($)
2066.! Vesey, F. 1841. *Decline of the English language: the cause and probable consequences.* London. (*Dk*)
2067. Wood, James, of the University of Edinburgh and New College. 1857. *Outlines of English and Anglo-Saxon grammar.* Edinburgh: Sutherland & Knox. 16cm, 96pp. (L O)
2068.! Wright, John Charles. (born 1852). [1881]. *The sources and growth of the English language, with a short sketch of English literature.* Lowth: J.H. Houghton. 72pp.
2069. Wyatt, Alfred John. 1897. *An elementary Old English grammar, early West Saxon.* Cambridge: University Press. 18cm. (L O)

2. Treatises on languages (incl. educational and philosophical reflexions)

2070. Abbott, Edwin Abbott. (1838-1926). Head Master of the Philological School, London. 1872. "On teaching the English language". In: *Lectures on education* vol.I. London: College of Preceptors. (L)
2071.$ Adams, John Q. (President of the USA. 1767-1848). 1810. *Lectures on rhetoric and oratory delivered to the classes of senior and junior sophistors in Harvard University.* 2 vols. Cambridge, N.E.: Hilliard & Metcalf. 21cm. (@ L *Br*)

2. Treatises on languages (incl. educational and philosophical reflexions) 369

2072.$ Allen, Edward Archibald. (1843-). 1887. *The subjunctive in English*. n.p. 8pp. (Anr. ed. 1892 Columbia, Missouri: E.W. Stephens (repr. from *Education* 1887 (@)). ($ @)

2073.$ Balch, William Stevens. (1806-1887). 1838. *Lectures on language, as particularly connected with English grammar. Designed for the use of teachers and advanced learners*. Providence: B. Cranston & Co. 18x11, xii+252pp. ($ @ L Br)

2074. Barclay, John, of Calcoats. 1826. *A sequel to The Diversions of Purley*. London: Smith, Elder & Co. 164pp. (L)

2075. Bengough, Samuel Edmund. [1870]. *A practical guide to the English language*. For the author. (L)

2076. Byrne, James. 1885. *General principles of the structure of language*. 2 vols. London: Trübner. (^{2}1892). (L)

2077. Crombie, Alexander. (1762-1840). 1817. *A few cursory observations, in reply to the strictures of the Reverend Mr. Gilchrist in his Rational Grammar, etc*. London: R. Hunter. 8vo, 70pp. (A L Sk)

2078.! Dawson, Benjamin, B.A. 1806a. *Philologia Anglicana*. Ipswich.

2079.! ---. 1806b. *Prolepsis Philologiae Anglicanae*. Ipswich.

2080. Anon. ^{4}1819. *The decoy; or, an agreeable method of teaching children the elementary parts of English grammar by conversations and familiar examples*. London: Darton, Harvey, & Darton. 71pp. (L)

2081. Ellis, Alexander John. (1814-1890). 1878. *On orthography in relation to etymology and literature*. (A lecture delivered before the College of Preceptors, 14 Nov. 1877). Repr., with additions from the *Educational Times* of Dec. 1877. London: C.F. Hodgson. 21cm, 30pp. (@)

2082.$ Emerson, George Barell. (1797-1881). 1871. *The study of Latin and of English grammar. Remarks of George B. Emerson, at a meeting of the Boston Social Science Association, (...), held February 21, 1867*. Boston: W.F. Brown & Co. 19/23cm, 14pp. ($ @)

2083.$ Erckmann, Ludwig. 1875. *Infinitive and gerund as a means of abbreviating substantive sentences in the English language. Inaugural-dissertation*. Rostock/ Lüneburg: von Stern. 21cm, 35pp. ($ @)

2084. Farrar, Rev. Frederic William. 1865. *Chapters on Language*. London. (L)

2085. Fearn, John. 1824 & 1827. *Anti-Tooke: an analysis of the principles and structures of language, exemplified in the English tongue*. 2 vols. London. (L Hu, Lw)

2086.$ Finch, Ralph K. [1844]. *Report on the method of teaching English grammar and on text books to the Superintendent of Common Schools in the State of New York*. New York. 18.5x11.5, 12pp. (L)

2087. Gilchrist, James. (1783-1835). 1814. *Reason the true arbiter of language; custom a tyrant; or, Intellect set free from arbitrary authority, in which are shown the absurdities of grammar and rhetoric, their tendency to enslave the mind; the close connection between mental and political bondage; the injustice and impolicy of despotic authority*. London: pr. for J. Johnson & Co. 23cm, vii+114pp. (@)

2088. ---. 1815. *The labyrinth demolished; or, the pioneer of rational philosophy*. London: pr. R. & A. Taylor for R. Hunter. 20cm, 47pp. (@ Br)

2089. ---. 1816. *Philosophic etymology, or rational grammar*. London. (L Hu, Lw)

2090. Hall, F. 1880. *Doctor Indoctus: strictures on Professor John Nichol, of Glasgow, with reference to his "English Composition"*. Repr. for the author, with additions and emendations from the London "Statesman". London: Ballantyne & Hanson. 16°, 17cm, 63pp. (@ L)

2091. ---. 1881. *A Letter to the Editor of the New York Nation, relative to certain slanders of the New York Evening Post.* London. 17cm, 27pp. (@)
2092.! ---. 1872. *Recent exemplifications of false philology.* New York: Scribner, Armstrong & Co. 21cm, 124pp. (*Dk*)
2093. ---. 1873. *Modern English.* London/New York: Scribner, Armstrong & Co. 18cm, xv+[1]-394pp. (@) (Anr. ed. 1878 New York: Scribner, 394pp. (@)). (@)
2094. Hime, Maurice Charles. 1887. *Home education: or, Irish versus English grammar schools for Irish boys.* London: Simpkin, Marshall & Co. etc. 8°, 19cm, 330pp.
(@ O)
2095. Holyoake, George Jacob. 1848. *A bill for the better security of grammar. December 1848. Parliamentary grammar class. City of London Mechanics' Institute.* London. 19pp. (L)
2096. Jespersen, Otto. (1860-1943). 1894. *Progress in language: with special reference to English.* London: Sonnenschein and Co. n.p. 19cm, xii p., 1l., 370pp. ($)
2097.! Johnson, Alexander Bryan. 1836. *A treatise on language, or the relation which words bear to things.* New York. (*Lw, Ch*)
2098. Latham, Robert Gordon. (1812-1888). 1834. *An address to the authors of England and America, on the necessity and practability and of permanently remodelling their alphabet and orthography ...* Cambridge: J. & J.J. Deighton. 50pp. (@)
2099.! ---. 1878. *Outlines of general and developmental philology: inflection.* xvi+190pp.
(*Mp*)
2100. Laurie, Simon Somerville. (1829-1909). 1890. *Lectures on language and linguistic method in the school, delivered in the University of Cambridge, Easter term, 1889.* Cambridge: University Press; New York: Macmillan & Co. 18.5x12.5, viii+147pp. (L). (³1899 Edinburgh: Oliver & Boyd. 12°, ix+[1]+200pp. (L)). (@ L)
2101.! Littleton, Nicholas. 1854. *Lexicon of the thoughts in the English language.* London.
(*Ch*)
2102. Moody, Rev. George. 1842. *On the importance of language as a leading branch of elementary instruction; being a paper read at one of the ordinary meetings ... as an introduction to the language class.* London: J. Martin [for] The Parochial & National Schoolmasters Mutual Improvement Society of London. 16°, 36pp. ($ @)
2103. Moon, G. Washington. 1881. *The King's English, etc.* London: Hatchards. (L)
2104.! Mueller, Right Hon. Friedrich Max. 1891. *The science of language founded on lectures... 1861 and 1863.* London.
2105. Odell, Jonathan. 1805. *An essay on the elements, accents, and prosody of the English language.* London: John Budd. (*Tm*, 39). (Anr. ed. 1806, London: Lackington, Allen & Co. 18.5x10.5, vii+205pp., 3s6d. (L *Br*, *Sk*)). (L *Br*, *Sk*)
[Discusses Nares', Sheridan's and Walker's descriptions of sounds, with a chapter on prosody.]
2106. Outis, Gaspar (pseud). 1868. *Remarks on some errors in grammar and syntax; as also in the pronunciation and meaning of certain words together with plain rules, touching the use of adverbs, adjectives, and compound nouns.* London: David Nutt. 21x13.5, 20pp. (@ L)
2107. Parker, Richard Greene. 1839. *Lecture on the teaching of English grammar.* Boston: American Institute of Instruction. (L)
2108. Anon. 1841. *Report of the Subcommittee on English grammar: presented to the annual meeting of the Friends' Educational Society.* London: Harvey & Darton, York printed. 22pp. (L)
2109. Robinson, John. 1800. *Art of teaching the English language by imitation.* 12mo.(*Sk*)

3. Treatments of individual levels

2110. Rogers, J.W.F. 1883. *Grammar and logic in the nineteenth century as seen in a syntactical analysis of the English language.* London: Trübner, pr. in Melbourne. 19x12, xvi+211. (^{2}1892. London: Simpkin, Marshall & Co. xvii+211pp.). (L O)

2111.! Salmon, Nicholas. 1806. *Archai; or, The Evenings of Southill. (In the manner of H. Tooke.).* London: the author. 22cm, 171pp. (Hu)

2112. Skeat, Walter William. (1835-1912). 1888. "English grammars". *Notes and Queries.* Series 7, 6. pp.120-2, 243-4, 302-3. Repr. in Skeat's *Student's Pastime*, 1896: 241-51. (Mi)

2113. Strettell, A.B. 1849. "On the English language and grammar". In: *Introductory lectures delivered at Queen's College, London.* London: W. Parker, 154-81. (L)

2114. Sutcliffe, Joseph. ^{2}1825. *The English Cratylus; or essays on language, grammar, and composition.* London: Baldwin, Craddock & Joy. 18.5x11, 35pp. (L O Hu)

2115. Tilleard, James. (Corresponding Secretary of the United Association of Schoolmasters). 1855. *A lecture on the method of teaching grammar. Delivered before the United Association of Schoolmasters, at the first annual meeting.* London: Longman, Brown, Green & Longmans. 21cm, 16pp. (@ C Dt L O)

2116.$ Vail, Wiliam P. 1829. *Letter, 1829 December 7, Stoudsburg, Pa., to Noah Webster, New Haven, Ct..* n.p. ($)

2117.! Whitney, William Dwight. (1827-1894). Philologist. 1867. *Language and the study of language: twelve lectures on the Principles of linguistic science.* $^?$1868, New York: Charles Scribner. 8vo, [ii]+vi+505pp.

2118.$ Wilson, John, of Washington, D.C. 1814. *A volume for all libraries: peculiarly adapted to the votaries of correct literature, and beneficial to every class of learners: being a system of philological entertainments, comprising altogether an extensive ground work for immense improvements in the English language.* n.p. 14cm, xiv+1+[16]-140pp. ($)

2119.! X. 1819. *A critical examination of Cobbett's English grammar in a letter to a friend: shewing the errors and inconsistencies contained in that work, and the absurdity of the author's proposed changes in the established grammatical terms and usages of the English language.* London: W. Wright. 16x10, 64pp. (Ma)

3. Treatments of individual levels (spelling, pronunciation, punctuation, morphology, derivation)

2120. Allen, Alexander. (1814-1842). 1851. *An English school grammar: with very copious exercises, and a systematic view of the formation and derivation of works, comprising Anglo-Saxon, Latin, Greek lists, which explain the etymology of above seven thousand words.* n.p. 15cm, 162pp. (Anr. ed. 1854, 15cm, 162pp. ($); anr. ed. 1864, 15cm, 162pp. ($); anr. ed. 1866 ($); anr. ed. 1868, 15cm, 71pp. ($); anr. ed. 1873, 15cm, 162pp. ($)). ($)

2121. Anon. 1800. *The book of nouns, or things which may be seen.* London: Darton & Harvey. (...) anr. ed. 1804 Philadelphia: publ. by Jacob Johnson (a miniature book, 5.2x4.4, with 63 engravings) (@); at least 3 eds. up to 1804).
(@) [cf. Rosenbach (1933: No.290)]

2122. Anon. 1844. *The child's first noun book.* London: Seeley, Burnside & Seeley. 13.5x10, unpaginated, 1s. (L)
[A very first speller with illustrations.]

2123.! Addison, Charles James. 1826. *A complete system of punctuation.* viii+103pp.

2124.! Barnes, Daniel H. 1828. *The red book, or Bearcroft's "Practical Orthography" revised and enlarged.* New York. 12mo, 347pp. (Br)

2125. Batchelor, Thomas. 1809. *An orthoepical analysis of the English language.* London. 8°, viii+164pp. (Facs. ed. 1974, Arne Zettersten, Lund: C.W.K. Gleerup). (L)
2126.! Best, Kershaw Thorpe. [a1887]. *An etymological manual ... Nine thousand derivatives from Latin and Greek.* Rev. ed. xiii+173pp. (Mp)
2127.! Black, R. Harrison. [a1825]. *The student's manual: or, an appendage to the English dictionaries. Being an etymological and explanatory vocabulary of words derived from the Greek. In two parts.* 2nd enl. ed. 1825?. London: Longman. vi+100pp. (Many eds. to 1874). (Mp)
2128. Boltwood, Henry Leonidas. (1831-1906). 1871. *English grammar and how to teach it: designed as a textbook for common schools, and for the primary, intermediate, and grammar departments of graded schools.* n.p. 19cm, 209pp. ($)
2129.! Blackley, William Lewery. 1869. *Word gossip: a series of familiar essays on words and their peculiarities.* London: Longman. viii+234pp.
2130.! Bolles, William. 1831. *A Spelling-Book.* Ster. ed., N. London. 12mo, 180pp. (Br)
2131.$ Bradley, Joshua. 1815. *A brief, practical system of punctuation to which are added, rules respecting the use of capitals.* n.p. 22pp. ($)
2132. Brodie, James. 1840. *The alphabet explained; or, science of articulate sounds, viewed in connection with the origin and history of nations.* Edinburgh. 17.5x10.5, viii+[9]-264pp. (L)
2133.! Brown, Thomas Richard. 1838. *A treatise on the English terminations of words [etc.].* Oundle: Richard Todd.
2134. Burton, John Richard. (Headmaster of the Junior Department in the Beds. Middle-Class Public School). [1870]. *Roots and derivations.* London: Educational Trading Co. 19x12.5, 18pp. (L)
2135. Campbell, Hugh Fraser. 1883. *English word study. A series of exercises in English etymology. To which are appended exercises in analysis and composition.* viii+110pp. (Mp)
2136. Coles, James (Schoolmaster) & Tomlin, John Hewitt. 1882. *New code etymology.* (Cole's and Tomlin's School Series). Leeds & London. 32pp. (L)
2137. Anon. [1884]. *Common blunders in speaking, and how to avoid them, etc.* London: Ward Lock. (Preface signed F.Y.). 114pp. (L)
2138. Anon. [1867]. *A compendium of etymology.* Sheffield: Pawson & Brailsford. (L O)
2139. Curtis, John Charles. (Principal of the Training College, Borough Road, London). 1871. *A manual of English etymology.* London: Simpkin, Marshall. 16x10, ii+46pp. (L)
2140. Davidson, John Best. [a1864]. *Punctuation made easy. For schools and self-instruction.* London. (10th thousand, 1864) (L)
2141.! Day, William. ^{2}1847. *Punctuation reduced to a system.* n.p. (^{3}1847; ^{6}1853; ^{7}1862).
2142. Anon. [1885]. *Discriminate... A manual for guidance in the use of correct words and phrases.* (by: Critic [pseud.]). London: Griffith etc. 16°, 80pp. (L)
2143. Douglas, James, Ph.D. (Teacher of English, Queen Street Academy, Edinburgh). 1872. *English etymology; a textbook of derivatives.* Edinburgh: Oliver & Boyd. 168pp. (L E). (^{2}1874 (L)). (L E)
2144. Draper, William. 1822. *The child's friend: being an entirely new, and systematic arrangement of all the sounds, combinations of characters, and exceptions in the English language.* London: pr. for the author, by H. Teape. 18cm, 167pp. 3s6d.
($ L)
2145.! Easthope, Sir John. 1835. *The literal interpreter, or pupil's guide to the meaning of English words derivative and compound.* Jedburgh.

2146. Anon. 1854. *An elementary guide to the etymology of the English language.* London: Charles Bean. ii+30pp. (L)
2147. Anon. [1857]. *Etymological exercises for elementary classes.* London: Constable. ([1870] 4d/6d. (L)). (L)
2148. Fanny, Elizabeth. 1856. *Etymology made easy; being a familiar conversation on the derivation and meaning of some words in common use.* J. Nisbet. 124pp. (L)
2149. Faulder, J. [1853]. *An explanation of the rational alphabet and its uses.* (L)
2150.! Ferris, O. Allen. 1862. *Elementary lessons in English etymology ... Part 1: Separate words.* London: Simpkin Marshall.
2151. Francillon, F. 1842. (Solicitor). *An essay on punctuation, with incidental remarks on composition.* London: Whittaker. 17cm, viii+96pp. (@ G L)
2152.!$ Gould, E.S. 1867. *Good English; or popular errors in language.* New York. *(Dk)*
2153.! Graham, John. 1856. *The English word-book. A manual exhibiting the sources, structure, and affinities of English words.* 2 parts.
2154.! Graham, William. 1829. *Exercises on the derivation of the English language ... intended for the use of the higher classes in English schools.* Cupar: R. Tullis. xii+184pp.
2155.! ---. 1836. *Exercises on Etymology.* Edinburgh. *(Mc)*
2156.!$ Gunn, Charles Hains. 1859. *Exercises on a selection of English synonyms.* (By Elizabeth Whatley). iv+64pp.
2157.$ Gunther, J. H. A. 1899. *A manual of English pronunciation for the use of Dutch students.* n.p. 25cm, 343pp. ($)
2158.! Harrison, J. 1823. *The etymological enchiridion, or practical analyzer, shewing the etymon ... of all the words in the English tongue which are derived from the Latin ... [etc.] ... languages.* Preston: the author. *(Mp)*
2159. Hartley, Charles. 1897. *Everyone's handbook of common blunders in speaking and writing, corrected and explained, etc.* London: Drane. 190pp. (L)
2160. Hazen, Marshman William. (1845-1911). 1884. *Hazen's complete spelling-book: for all grades of public and private schools: containing three parts: adapted to primary, intermediate, grammar and high school.* n.p. 19cm, viii+46+50+90pp.($). (Anr. ed. 1891, viii+46+50+90pp.($)). ($)
2161.$ Henderson, Nathaniel P. 1865. *Henderson's test words in English orthography: with full definitions, also, a list of modern geographical names, with their pronunciation: for the use of grammar schools and academies.* n.p. 16cm, 80pp. ($). (Anr. ed. 1894, 17cm, 103pp. ($); at least 4 eds. up to 1894). ($)
2162. Hodgkin, John. (Calligraphist. 1766-1845). [4]1811. *An introduction to writing, ... To which are added, some sketches of English, Latin, French, and Italian grammar.* London. (L)
2163.$ Hull, Joseph Hervey. 1818. *A guide to the English language: containing the powers of the English alphabet, an extensive vocabulary, with the signification of each word, a numerous list of derivative words, with the part of speech annexed to each, ...* n.p. 20cm, 167pp. ($)
2164.$ ---. 1819. *A guide to the English language, containing the powers of the English alphabetian extensive vocabulary, with the signification of each word; a numerous list of derivative words, with the part of speech annexed to each, &c. In two parts.* Rev. impression. Utica: W. Williams. 2pts in one vol. 17cm. (Anr. ed. 1821; at least 5 eds. up to 1821). (@)
2165. Hunter, Rev. John (Principal of Uxbridge School, Vice-President of the Training Institution, Battersea. 1849-1917). 1853. *Manual of English derivation, containing*

the most useful Greek, Latin and other roots of English words ... Adapted to the use of pupils in elementary schools. London: National Society's Depository. 17.5x10, ii+61pp., 9d. *Abstract*, by Rev. A. Wilson. 1s4d. (C L O)
[The book has Latin, Greek, and French words alphabetically lemmatized, followed by English words based on them.]

2166.$ Hyde, Mary Frances. 1891. *Derivation of words, with exercises on prefixes, suffixes, and stems. An appendix to Practical lessons in the use of English for grammar schools*. Boston: D.C. Heath & Co. 18cm, 62pp. ($ @)

2167.$ Kellogg, Brainerd. 1892. *Word-building with roots, or stems, and prefixes and suffixes*. n.p. 17cm, 63pp. ($)

2168. Laurie, James Stuart. [a1877]. *First steps in etymology*. 56pp. (New ed. [1877]).(L)

2169.! McCulloch, John Murray. n.d. *Curiosities of English etymology*. Greenock: W. Hutchinson. 45pp.

2170.! Manson, George. 1846. *The pupil's guide to English etymology ... [etc.]*. Edinburgh. 132pp. (^{16}1856).

2171. Martin, James. (Formerly Normal Master, Battersea Training College). [1877]. *The scholar's handbook of English etymology*. London: G. Philip. 40pp. (L)

2172. Mason, Charles Peter. (Fellow of University College, London. 1820-1900). 1883. *Word building in English*. (Reprinted from the author's *Shorter English grammar*). London: Bell & Sons. 18x11. 31pp. 3p. (E L)

2173. Mathews, M. 1888. *Epophania: systematic classification and notation of the elements of English speech*. Bristol: J.W. Arrowsmith / London: Simpkin & Marshall. 18x11.5, vii+45pp. (@ L)
[The author attempts to provide a systematic account of the system of phonetics, mainly of English. Not a grammar - not even structured like the phonetic section in one.]

2174.! Mulkey, William. 1834. *An abridgment of Walker's rules on the sounds of the letters*. Boston. 18mo, 124pp. (Br)

2175. Anon. [1851]. *Normal chart of the elementary sounds of the English language*. (L)

2176.! Oswald, John. [a1835]. *An etymological manual of the English language*. ^{4}1835, Edinburgh: Black. (^{8}1842, ^{10}1843, ^{12}1846).

2177.! ---. [a1840]. *An abridgment of the etymological manual*. ^{2}1840, Edinburgh. (Mp)

2178.! ---. [a1850]. *The etymological primer ... of the English language. Part 2*. (^{6}1850, Edinburgh: Black. 72pp.).

2178a. Paul, Arthur. (Lecturer in English, King's College, London). 1897. *Functional analysis of English*. n.p. 48pp. (L O)
[Not a textbook; it is a workbook comprising identical printed pages ruled in columns for sentence analysis.]

2179.! Perry, William. 1805. *The synonymous, etymological, and pronouncing dictionary... To which is prefixed an English grammar*. London: John Walker.

2180.! Pierce, John. 1782. *The new American spelling book ... containing, Part 3, [an English grammar]*. n.p. (^{6}1800; anr. ed. 1808 Philadelphia; at least 8 eds. up to 1808] (Mp)

2181.$ Pike, Samuel. (1717-1773). 1816. *An Hebrew and English lexicon. To which is added, a compendious grammar*. 22cm, viii+192pp. ($)

2182.! Pinnock, William. 1811. *Exercises to the Elements of Punctuation, accompanied with notes critical and explanatory*. Alton. (^{2}[1812?] Newbury). (Mp)

2183. Anon. [a1836]. *Prefixes and affixes of the English language, with examples. To be committed to memory. Extracted chiefly from Mr M'Culloch's Manual of English Grammar.* Edinburgh. (New ed. [c1850], Edinburgh, 14cm.). (O)
2184.$ Prest, J.A. 1831. *The monitorial primer: on new and improved principles, consisting of monosyllables, roots of words, etc. arranged according to the vowel sounds, in the order of grammar, natural history, etc: being an introduction to the Juvenile lexicon.* n.p. 17cm, 48pp. ($)
2185. Ritchie, Francis. 1887. *Exercises in English word formation and derivation.* London: Sonnenschein. 18.5x12, 55pp. (^{3}1897). (L)
2186.! Rousseau, S. 1813. *Rules for punctuation; or, an attempt to facilitate the pointing of a written composition, on the principles of grammar and reason.* Longman. xxiv+236pp.
2187.$ Ruter, Martin. 1829. *The new American spelling book; and juvenile preceptor; adapted to Walker's principles of English orthography and pronunciation. For the use of schools in the United States.* n.p. 17cm, 13-144pp. ($)
2188.$ Sever, F.P. 1897. *The progressive speller: a complete spelling book: arranged for advanced primary, intermediate, and grammar grades.* n.p. 19cm, 166pp. ($)
2189.$ Shaftesbury, Edmund. (1852-1926). 1893. *One hundred lessons in punctuation: a system of fixed rules involving the construction of sentences, the arrangement of thoughts, natural grammar and natural rhetoric.* n.p. 20.5cm, 114pp. ($)
2190.! Skeat, Walter William. (1835-1912). 1887. *Principles of English etymology. First series: the native element.* Oxford. (Mp)
2191.! ---. 1892a. *Primer of English etymology.* Oxford. viii+112pp. (2nd rev. ed. 1895, ^{4}1904, ^{5}1910, ^{6}1928). (Mp)
2192.! ---. 1892b. *Principles of English etymology. Second series: The foreign element.* Oxford. (Mp)
2193.! Smallfield, George. 1838. *Principles on punctuation.* n.p. 70pp. (Mp)
2194. Smart, Benjamin Humphrey. (1786?-1872). 1810. *A practical grammar of English pronunciation, on plain and recognized principles,* ... London: John Richardson; J. Johnson and Co. 20cm, xix+397pp. ($ L)
2195.$ Smith, William W. 1858. *The grammar school speller: containing rules for spelling with numerous examples to illustrate the application of each rule: together with a large collection of the most difficult words in the English language ...: for intermediate classes.* n.p. 19cm, 168pp. ($)
2196.! Stackhouse, Thomas. 1800. *A new essay on punctuation: being an attempt to reduce the practice of pointing to the government of distinct and explicit rules.* n.p. vii+92pp. (^{3}1814). (Mp)
2197.! Sullivan, Robert. (Inspector of Schools). 1831. *A manual of etymology; or a vocabulary of English words derived from the Latin language, principally through the medium of the French; with notes.* Dublin: John Cumming. (Anr. ed. 1860 as ... or first steps to a knowledge of the English language.* Dublin, 144pp.)
2198.! Ussher, Mark N. 1816. *Synonymous terms in the English language explained.* Dublin. (Mp)
2199.$ Westlake, James Willis. (1830-1912). 1874. *Three thousand practice words: with an appendix containing rules for spelling, rules for capitals, etc..* n.p. 17cm, 75pp.($)
2200.! Whately, Elizabeth. 1851. *A selection of English synonyms.* xvi+142pp. (^{2}1852, ^{4}1858, ^{9}1889).
2201.! White, R.G. 1871. *Words and their uses, past and present. A study of the English language.* New York. (Dk)

2202.! ---. 1880. *Every-day English. A sequel to "Words and their uses"*. Boston. (*Dk*)
2203.! Wilson, John. 1844. *A treatise of grammatical punctuation; designed for ... academies and schools*. Manchester. xii+120pp. (^{2}1850 as *A treatise on English punctuation*. Boston, Mass.).
2204.! [Wood, John]. 1833. *Etymological guide to the English language; being a collection, alphabetically arranged, of the principal roots, affixes, and prefixes, with their derivatives and compounds*. Edinburgh: John Wardlow. x+145pp. (^{6}1857). (*Mp*)
2205.! Yoxall, Sir James Henry & Gregory, B. [1891]. *The word-builder and speller. A handbook of spelling and spellings*. London: Edward Arnold.

4. Books on logic, rhetoric, elocution, style and composition

2206.! Barber, Jonathan. 1830. *A grammar of elocution*. Newhaven. 12mo. (*Br*)
2207. Barry, Michael Joseph. (1817-1899). 1899. *A grammmar of eloquence: for the use of colleges, schools, and private students*. n.p. 17cm, vii+575pp. ($)
2208. Beard, John Relly. [1860]. *An easy introduction to the art of letter writing, comprising ... instructions in English grammar and composition*. London: Simpkin, Marshall & Co. / Manchester: John Heywood. 18x12, xvi+114pp. (L)
[A letter writer only, "written to enable the least instructed to acquire the Art of Corresponding in correct grammatical English"; "This is a book of models" - no attempt at even a minimal grammar.]
2209. Breen, Henry Hegart. 1857. *Modern English literature: its blemishes and defects*. London: Longman. xvi+307pp. (L)
2210.! Carey, John. 1809. *Practical English prosody*. London. 12mo, 220pp. (new ed. 1816). (*Br*)
2211. Chapman, Rev. James. (Teacher of the science and practice of elocution). 1821. *The original rhythmical grammar of the English language: or, the art of reading and speaking, on the principles of the music of speech*. Edinburgh: James Robertson. 18.5x10.5, xvii+348pp. (L *Sk*)
2212. Anon. 1883. *English as she is wrote, showing curious ways in which the English language may be made to convey ideas and obscure them. A companion to* English as she is spoke. New York: D. Appleton & Co. 14x12, [5]-96pp. (Anr. ed. [1884] Routledge, 96pp.; anr. ed. [188-?], 17cm, viii+[9]-63pp. (@)). (@ L)
2213. Haslam, Thomas J. 1892. *Good English for beginners*. Dublin: Eason / Belfast / London. 17.5x12, viii+246pp. (L)
[The book is exclusively devoted to literary composition, taught through passages selected from the best authors.]
2214.$ Hill, Adams Sherman. (1833-1910). 1878. *The principles of rhetoric and their application*. [@ has *The principles of rhetoric with an appendix comprising general rules for punctuation*] New York. 18/20cm, vi+296pp.; (Anr. ed. 1895 New York: American Book Co. (@); anr. ed. 1879 New York: Harper & Brothers (@); at least 18 more eds up to 1898 (@)). ($ @)
2215.$ ---. 1892. *The foundation of rhetoric*. New York: Harper & Brothers. 20cm, 337pp. (...) anr. ed. 1897 New York: Harper (@). [at least 7 eds. up to 1897] ($ @)
2216.$ Hincks, Thomas Dix. (1767-1857). 1807. *A short prosody, for the use of schools*. n.p. 18cm, 48pp. ($)
2217. Hutchinson, H., of Derby. 1884. *Thought-symbolisms and grammatic illusions; being a treatise on the nature, purpose, and material of speech, and a demonstration of the unreality, the useless complexity, and the evil effects, of orthodox grammatical rules in*

general. London: Kegan Paul/Trench & Co. vii+243pp. (Anr. ed. 1884, 19x12, vii+248pp. ($)). ($ @ L)
[This treatise is mainly on general linguistics, exploring the logical foundations of grammatical categories; while a few English grammars are quoted from (Latham, Mason, Morell, Hamblin Smith), the book itself is not a grammar.]

2218. Irving, David. (1778-1860). 1801. *Elements of English composition. Containing practical instructions for writing the English language with perspicuity and elegance; and designed in the progress of education, to succeed to the study of English grammar, and of the Latin and Greek classics*. London. anr. ed. 1803, 18cm, xi+238pp. ($); anr. ed. 1820; anr. ed. 1821 as *The elements of English composition: serving as a sequel to the study of grammar*, 20cm, vi+318pp. ($); [at least 11 eds. up to 1841]. ($ L, *Sk, Mi*)

2219. Jamieson, Alexander. 1819. *A grammar of logic and intellectual philosophy in didactic principles; For the use of schools and private instruction*. London: for G. & W.B. Whittaker. 18x10.5, xx+358pp. (O)

2220. Jones, Stephen. (1763-1827). 1796. *Sheridan improved; a general pronouncing and explanatory dictionary of the English language. To which is prefixed a prosodial grammar, (...)* n.p. ³1798 rev. and very considerably enl. London: pr. for Vernor & Hood, 22cm (@). anr. ed. 1853 (@). [at least 23 eds. up to 1853] ($ @)

2221. Littleton, Nicholas. 1855. *Advanced reading teacher for teachers and tyros*. London: W. Kent & Co. 11.5x15, 16pp. (not.paginated)

2222.$ Litch, Samuel. 1813. *A concise treatise of rhetoric extracted from the writings of Dr. Blair, Usher, &c., for the use of common schools and private persons*. n.p. 13cm, 119pp. ($)

2223. Mavor, William Fordyce. (1758-1837). 1801. *The new speaker, or English classbook. To which are prefixed, a short system of rhetoric and an essay on enunciation or delivery, chiefly abstracted from Blair's lectures*. London: J. Wallis. 18cm. (Anr. ed. 1803 London (@); ⁴1811 London (@)). (@)

2224. Merington, Margaret Hamilton. [a1892]. *An English primer*. (³1892, London: Taylor & Francis. x+57pp. 1s). (L)

2225. Nichol, John. (Professor of English Literature and Language, University of Glasgow. 1833-94). 1878. *English composition*. London: Macmillan. (later ed. 1925; anr. ed. 1879, 16cm, [5]-128pp. (@); ²1879, New York: American Book Co. (@); anr. ed. 1880 New York (@); anr. ed. 1882 New York: D. Appleton (@)). (@ L)

2226. Pinnock, William A. (1782-1843). 1813. *The universal explanatory English reader, calculated to assist both teacher and pupil: consisting of selections in prose and poetry, on interesting and improving subjects*. n.p. 19cm, 410pp. ($)

2227. Scott, William. (Teacher of Elocution. 1750-1804). ⁸1800. *Lessons in elocution; or, a selection of pieces in prose and verse for the improvement of youth in reading and speaking. With an appendix containing concise lessons on a new plan, and principles of English grammar*. (8th American ed.). Worcester, Mass.: I. Thomas. 17cm, 436pp. (@). (¹⁵1801; ¹⁷1804, Edinburgh: Mundell & Son, for J. Fairbairn, 396pp. (L); ²1813, Edinburgh: Oliver & Boyd / London: Sherwood, Neely, Jones & C. Law / Dublin: John Cumming, viii+387pp. (@); forty-six American editions to 1850; anr. ed. 1850, *Enlarged by new selections, mostly from American literature*, by James D. Johnson, A.M., Philadelphia: Thomas, Cowperthwaite & Co., 19cm, xii+[13]-368pp. (@); a great number of other editions in *NUC*). (@ L)

2228. Shaha, Brojonath. 1897. *The stylography of the English language*. n.p. 19cm, xx+xx+284+xlvipp. ($)

2229.$ Shute, Katharine Hamer. (born 1862). 1898?. *The land of song.* Selected by K.H.S. Ed. by Larkin Dunton. 3 vols. New York, Boston: Silver, Burdett & Company. 19cm. (Anr. ed. 1899 (from 1898 ed.), 19cm. ($)). ($ @)

5. Advice on good English

2230. Alford, H. (Dean of Canterbury). 1864. *The Queen's English: stray notes on speaking and spelling.* London. (^{2}1866, London as *A plea for the Queen's English*; ^{3}1870). (L)
2231. Brewer, Ebenezer Cobham. 1877. *Errors of speech and spelling.* 2 vols. London: William Tegg. (C L)
2232.$ Compton, Alfred George. 1898. *Some common errors of speech. Suggestions for the avoiding of certain classes of errors; together with examples of bad and good usage.* New York & London: Putnam. 19cm, ix+74pp. (@ L)
2233. Duncan, George P. [i.e. Charles Platt]. [187-]. *How to talk correctly: a pocket manual to promote polite and accurate conversation, writing and reading ... with more than 500 errors in speaking and writing corrected [etc.].* Wakefield: William Nicholson. 125+3pp. (Anr. ed. [1922]). (H)
2234.$ Ellis, Edward Sylvester. (1840-1916). 1894. *Common errors in writing and speaking; what they are and how to avoid them. With a practical treatise on pronunciation and punctuation.* New York: Woolfall. 16cm, 124pp. (Anr. ed. 1895, New York: Hinds, Noble & Eldredge, 8vo, 16cm, 128pp. (@)). ($ @)
2235. Jackson, George. (Accountant). ^{3}1830. *Popular errors in English grammar, particularly in pronunciation, familiarly pointed out: for the use of those persons who want either opportunity or inclination to study this science.* (3rd ed. enl. and greatly improved). London: Effingham Wilson. 14x9, 27pp., 1s. ($ @ L)
2236. Moon, G. Washington. (1823-1909). 1864. *The Dean's English: a criticism on the Dean of Canterbury's essays on the Queen's English.* London. At least twelve eds. to 1878. (first published 1863 as *A Defense of the Queen's English. In reply to "A Plea for the Queen's English"*, by the Dean of Canterbury.) (Dk)
2237.! ---. 1868. *The Bad English of Lindley Murray and other writers on the English language: a series of criticisms.* London. xix+246pp. (^{4}1871 as *Bad English exposed: a series of criticisms on the errors and inconsistencies of Lindley Murray*; at least 9 eds. up to 1869).
[Companion volume to *The Dean's English*, on the English of certain Americans: Murray, Marsh and Gould, concerning adjectives, adverbs, articles, conjunctions, miscellaneous, nouns, prepositions, pronouns, punctuation, sentences, slang, verbs and individual words - criticizing the people who *should* know.]
2238.! ---. 1875. *Common errors in speaking and writing. A paper read before the Royal Society of Literature.* London: Hatchard.
2239.! ---. 1882. *The revisers' English. A series of criticisms, showing the revisers' violations of the laws of the language.* London.
2240.! ---. 1886. *Ecclesiastical English. A series of criticisms showing the Old Testament revisers' violations of the laws of the language, etc. (Being Part II of "The Revisers' English").* London.
2241.! ---. 1892. *Learned men's English: the grammarians. A series of criticisms on the English of Dean Alford, Lindley Murray, and other writers on the language. Being the twelfth edition of "The Dean's English," and "Bad English Exposed".* George Routledge & Sons. 8vo. xxiv+215+[i]+xv+[i]+227pp.

2242. Morison, Nathaniel Holmes. (1815-1890). 1856. *Punctuation and improprieties of speech.* n.p. 19cm, iv+[5]-76pp. ($)
2243.! Revis, B. [pseud.]. 1857. *Right words abused by words wrong or misused. A contribution to philology.*
2244. Routledge, Edmund. [a1866]. *Every-day blunders in speaking.* 16x10.5, 64pp. 6d. ²1866. (L)
2245. Savage, W.H. 1833. *Vulgarisms and improprieties of the English language.* London: pr. by T.S. Porter. (L)
2246. Smith, Charles William. (Professor of Elocution). [a1855]. *Common blunders made in speaking and writing, corrected on the authority of the best grammarians.* n.p. (L). (²1855 (L); ³1855 (L); anr. ed. 1856 (L); new ed. [185?] London: Groombridge & Sons, 14x10.5, 16pp. (@)). (@ L)

6. Bilingual grammars and books meant for foreign learners

2247. Ahn, Johann Franz. (1796-1865). 1876. *Ahn's American interpreter. Ahn's amerikanischer Dolmetscher für Deutsche, zum Erlernen der englischen Sprache ohne Lehrer. Anleitung zur Aussprache des Englischen, kurzgefaßte Grammatik nebst leichten Beispielen, Gesprächen, Wörtersammlungen ....* n.p. 19cm, vii+192pp. (Anr. ed. 1883, 19cm, xlvi+240pp. ($)). ($)
2248. Allen, Alexander and James Cornwell (Ph.D.). 1895. *Chinese and English grammar for beginners: being an introduction to Allen and Cornwell's English School Grammar.* Translated by Kwok Chan Sang. Hongkong. 254pp. (L)
2249. Ambrose, Emma O. 1883. *Elementary grammar. English and Karen.* Toungoo. 66pp. (L)
2250. Augerean, Yaroutiun. 1817. *Grammar, English and Armenian.* Venice: Armenian Academy. 17cm, 181pp. (²1819, ?1832, later ed. by P. Aucher and Lord Byron 1873, 17cm.)). (L O)
2251. Ayre, A. [1882]. *A German grammar for English students.* (Stewart's educational series). London. 8°, 158pp. (L O)
2252. Babad, P. 1820. *A Portuguese and English Grammar, compiled from those of Lobato, Durham, Sane and Vieyra. By a Professor of the Spanish and Portuguese languages in St. Mary's College.* Baltimore: F. Lucas jun. 18cm. viii+[13]-229pp. (L)
2253.$ Baker, Shirley W. 1897. *An English and Tongan vocabulary, also a Tongan and English vocabulary, in which the pupil is led by a series of observation lessons, with a list of idiomatic phrases; and Tongan grammar.* Four Parts. Auckland, N.Z.: pr. by Wilsons & Horton. 23cm, 1, 133, 211, 42pp. ($)
2254. Ballantyne, James Robert. 1847. *Elements of English grammar, in Sanskrit and English.* (signed J.R.B.). Mirzapore (India). 17cm. (O)
2255.$ Baretti, Guiseppe Marco Antonio. (1719-1789). 1750. *A dictionary of the English and Italian languages. (...) To which is added an Italian and English grammar.* 2 parts. London. (@). (Anr. ed. 1807, 21cm ($); anr. ed. 1824, 24cm ($); anr. ed. 1839, 23cm ($)). ($ @)
2256.$ Batchelor, John. (1854-1944). 1889. *An Ainu English Japanese dictionary. And grammar ....* n.p. 24cm, 287pp. ($)
2257. Bossut, Charles. (1730-1814). 1847. *French and English exercises with syntactical rules and corresponding examples: supplementary to the First French grammar, and other easy works of the same author.* n.p. xii+176pp. ($)
2258. Buzacott, Aaron, the Elder. (1800-1864). 1854. *Te akataka reo Rarotonga; or, Rarotongan and English grammar.* Rarotonga. 16cm [interleaved]. (L O)

2259. Cradock, L. 1857. *An English Grammar in Hindoostani, for the use of Mohammedans.* Madras: L. C. Graves. (L)
2260.! Cobbett, William. ²1839. *Englische Sprachlehre: mit steter Hinweisung auf die deutsche Sprache und mit Erläuterung der Vorbegriffe aus der allgemeinen Sprachlehre; Für Deutsche bearbeitet...* Jakob Heinr. Kaltschmidt [Übers.]. Leipzig. (Göttingen).
2261. D., W. H. M. 1822. *A manual of an English and Russian grammar.* St. Petersburg: N. Gretsch. ii+151pp. (L)
2262. D'Orsey, Alexander James Donald. 1859. *A practical grammar of Portuguese and English, in the form of progressive exercises, so planned as to exhibit a complete comparison of the idiomatic peculiarities of both languages.* By Alex. J. D. D'Orsey ... assisted by ... Marcelliano R. de Mendonca. London: Rolandi; Lisboa: Bertrand. 20cm, 241pp. (L)
2263. ---. 1860. *A practical grammar of Portuguese and English, exhibiting in a series of exercises in double translation, the idiomatic structure of both languages ... adapted to Ollendorf's system.* By Alex. J. D. D'Orsey ... assisted by ... Marcelliano R. de Mendonca. London. (³1868 London). (L)
2264. Droz, P. 1842. *A French and English grammar, with copious and easy exercises purposely written for the use of schools and private teaching.* 2 vols. London: Longman & Co. 17.5x10.5, iv+246pp. (L O)
2265. Du Toit, Stephanus Jacobus. 1897. *Fergelijkende Taalkunde fan Afrikaans en Engels. Comparative grammar of English and Cape Dutch.* Paarl: D. F. Du Toit en Co. v+32pp. (L)
2266. Eaton, Mrs. 1830. *A comparative grammar of the English, French and Italian languages; arranged upon a new concise and perspicuous system; with conversations and exercises adapted for the use both of the teacher and the pupil.* London: Holdsworth & Ball. 20cm, 2 p.l. [iii]-x+364pp. (@)
2267. Evans, K. F. Miss. 1880. *Elementary Anglo vernacular grammar (for instruction in English through the vernacular), English and Burmese.* Rangoon: C. Bennett. 21cm, 100pp. ($ L)
2268.$ Evans, Thomas. (1766-1833). 1816. *An English and Welsh vocabulary, or, an easy guide to the ancient British language.* n.p. 22cm, 66pp. ($)
2269. Fuchs, Paul. (Professor). 1867. *Dr. H. G. Ollendorff's new method to learn a language in six months. An English grammar for Russians.* Adapted by P. F. Frankfurt a.M. (L)
2270. Gerard, J. F. (Fellow of the Colleges of Treves and Luxembourg ...). ²1831, considerably improved and enlarged. *New and entertaining dialogues in French and English, on an improved interlinear system. Combining the useful with the agreeable. To which is subjoined a French and English analytical grammar with anecdotes and select pieces from the best French prose writers.* London: J. Souter. 19x11, viii+208pp. (@ L)
2271. Giral del Pino, Hipólito San José. ⁷1800. *A new Spanish grammar; or, The elements of the Spanish language. To which is added an English grammar for the use of Spaniards.* New ed., rev. by Raymundo del Pueyo. (1809 new edn. carefully rev. and impr. by Raymundo Del Pueyo. London: F. Wingrave. 22cm, 232,216pp. (L); new ed. carefully rev. and impr. by Raymundo del Pueyo. London: F. Wingrave. 232, 192pp.(L)). London: F. Wingrave. 8°, 232, 216pp.). (L O)
2272. Guichet, J. 1860. *An Italian and English grammar.* New edition, enlarged and corrected by A. Tommasi. London: C. H. Law. 264pp. (L)

6. Bilingual grammars and books meant for foreign learners

2273. Harrison, I. Henry & R. Sorokhtin. 1861. *Practical course of the English language, with grammar adapted to the exercises by ...* Engl. and Russ. St. Petersburg: A. Jakovson. 3 parts, 22.5x15, 161pp. (L)
2274. Hedley, J.H. 1838. *The English and German dialogist, with a synopsis of the grammar and idiom of both languages.* London. 15cm. (O)
2275. Hoga, Stanislas. 1840. *A grammar of the English language, for the use of Hebrews. By S. H.*. London: A. Macintosh. (L)
2276. Holtrop, John. ³1804. *A complete English Grammar ... to which are added: a vocabulary, ... a collection of letters ... and other writings ... Revised and corrected by B. C. Sowden. Eng. & Dutch.* Dort & Amsterdam: for A. Blussé and W. Holtrop. 17x10.5, xiii+739pp. (L)
2277. Hough, G.H. 1825. *An English and Burman vocabulary, preceded by a concise grammar in which the Burman definitions and words are accompanied with a pronunciation in the English character designed to extend the colloquial use of the Burman language.* Serampore (India). 13x17. (Anr. ed. 1825, 14x19, ii+424pp. ($)). ($ O)
2278. Howard, Edward Irving. 1877. *A collection of words & phrases, with the grammar, pronunciation, derivation and English and Marathi meanings of words, and English and Marathi explanations of phrases occurring in [E. I. H.'s English] Departmental Third Book, New Issue.* Bombay: Asiatic Printing Press. 118pp. (L)
2279. Huebotter, Wilhelm. 1869. *Schlüssel zur englischen Sprache; ... nebst einem Anhange über die prosodische Aussprache der gehobenen und gebundenen Rede aus Murray's English Grammar.* Altona, Leipzig [printed]. (L)
2280. Kapp, Ernst. (Professor of Düsseldorf). 1851. *Die Heimfahrt des Odysseus. Versehen mit einer kurzen Grammatik (in English) und einem Wörterverzeichnis von P. H. The return of Ulysses with a short Grammar and a vocabulary by P. H.* London. (L)
2281.! Kenny, William Stopford. (1788-1867). n.d. *Grammatical exercises upon the French language compared with the English.* n.p.
2282.! Laisne, C. 1817. *A comparative view of the English and French languages, intended to establish an easy and methodical plan for the acquirement of both.* (Mp)
2283. Lobscheid, William. 1864. *Chinese English Grammar.* 2 parts. Hong Kong. (L)
2284. London, Henry. 1838. *The elements of English conversation and English grammar. ... Die Elemente der englischen Unterhaltung, etc. Eng. and German.* Breslau. (L)
2285. Lu Ching-kó. 1894. *A translated English grammar* [i.e. an English grammar in English and Chinese]. Hongkong: Man Yü Tong. 105pp. (L)
2286. ---. ²1896. *An English grammar for Chinese students, with concurrent explanation in Chinese.* By Luk King Fo. Hongkong. vi+141pp. (³1898 rev. enl. ed.). (L)
2287. Meadows, F.S. 1869. *Meadow's Italian and English dictionary in two parts: I: Italian-English; II: English-Italian. ... with a concise grammar.* (²1876, rev., corr., and enl. by J.Jazdowski. London: William Tegg). (B)
2288. Mehrvanji Hormasji Meheta & Navaroji Rustamji Lad. 1840. *The English and Goojratee scholar's assistant; comprising a vocabulary, English and Goojratee, together with the rudimental principles of English grammar, accompanied by a literal Goojratee translation ....* Bombay: Courier Press, iv+56pp. (L)
2289. Midosi, Luiz Francisco. 1832. *A new grammar of the Portuguese and English and English and Portuguese languages.* 2 parts. London. 21cm (A). (²1840 London: J. Warcy, 21cm, viii+248pp. ($)). ($ @ A L O)
2290. Moesch, Ferdinand. 1852. *The principles of English grammar, etc. (Die Grundzüge der englischen Sprachlehre, etc). Eng. and Germ. Pt. 1.* Schweinfurt. (L)

2291. Moody, Clement, ed. 1838. *The new Eton grammar, in which that popular introduction to the Latin tongue is rendered into English; with additional matter.* London. 18cm. (O)
2292. ---, ed. 1840. *The new Eton grammar; or The Eton Greek grammar in English, with notes.* London. 17cm. (O)
2293. Morrison, Robert, D.D. 1823. *A grammar of the English language. For the use of the Anglo-Chinese College.* Macao: The Honourable India Company's Press. 97pp. (L)
2294. Muhammad Ibrahim, Mirza. 1841. *A grammar of the Persian language. To which are subjoined several dialogues, with an alphabetical list of the English and Persian terms of grammar; and an appendix on the use of Arabic words.* London. (L)
2295. Narabhairama, Munshi. 1869. *The student's companion in the acquisition of a practical knowledge of English and Gújaráti, grammar and idioms.* Ahmedabad. (L)
2296. Nicholas, Innocent. 1851. *A vocabulary of English and Tamil words; to which are added ... familiar dialogues, the English grammar and a few letters.* Madras: Prabhacarah Press. 192pp. (L)
2297. O'Conway, Matthias James. 1810. *Hispano-Anglo grammar: containing the definitions, structure, inflections, reference, arrangement, concord, government and combination of various classes of words ....* n.p. ($)
2298. Olivier, William John. 1826. *Choice reading-pieces for Dutch young learners of the English language, to which are added: easy pieces of poetry ... a compendious analytic view of English grammar ... selected and arranged by William John Olivier.* Delft: the Widow of John Allart. viii+214pp. (L)
2299. Ollendorff, Heinrich Godefrey (Gottfried). (1803-1865). 1848. *New grammar for Germans to learn the English language. Ollendorf's neue Methode die englische Sprache zu lernen. Für den deutschen ... Unterricht eingerichtet von P. Gands, etc..* n.p. 12mo., 599pp. ($). (Anr. ed. 1857, New York. (L)). ($ L)
2300. Pearson, John Dorking. 1820. *A grammar of the English language; for the use of natives of Bengal.* Calcutta. (L)
2301. Pellissier, Eugéne. 1891-92. *French and English passages for unseen translation and composition with examination papers in grammar. Junior [middle and senior] course.* 3 vols. London: Percival & Co. (*Junior course* ^{2}1892). (L)
2302.! Picard, George. ^{1}1790. *A grammatical dictionary; containing, in alphabetical order, rules for translating English into French, according to the grammar and genius of that language. With examples and explanatory notes, whereby the difficulties of translation are removed.* Southampton: T. Baker. 12mo, iv+152pp. (Anr ed. 1820).
2303. Pinnock, William. (1782-1843). 1845. *Pinnock's catechism of English grammar, with many additions from Lennie's and other grammars, interpaged with a Canarese translation.* Bangalore: Wesleyan Mission Press. 163pp. (L)
2304. Planquais, Thomas. 1807. *A new Spanish and English grammar.* London. 21cm. (^{2}1813 augmented with a second alphabet, and notes bearing to a sure pronunciation. London: pr. for the author. xii+494pp. (L)). (A L O)
2305. Ravizzotti, Gaetano. [1801]. *A short and easy introduction to the English and Italian grammar.* Romsey. 12°. (L O)
2306. Rykaczewski, E. 1849. *A complete dictionary, English and Polish and Polish and English ... to which is prefixed a grammar of the English language (in Polish).* By E. Rykaczewski. Edited by A. E. Chodzko. 2 parts, Berlin. (Anr. ed. 1851). (L)
2307. Schippers, Benedict J. 1812. *Rudiments of the German language with an appendix containing the pronunciation of the English letters.* n.p. 36+8pp. ($)

6. *Bilingual grammars and books meant for foreign learners* 383

2308. Shakespear, John. (Writer on Hindustani). 1845. *An introduction to the Hindustani language. Comprising a grammar and a vocabulary, English and Hindustani, also short sentences and dialogues, short stories in Persian and Nagari characters ..., Hindustani composition ... and military words of command, Nagari and English.* London. (L)
2309. Slater, John Huddlestone. 1856. *A concise grammar of the English language, adapted to the use of Dutch students.* Utrecht. (L)
2310. Socin, Albert. (1844-1899). 1895. *Arabic grammar; paradigms, literature, exercises and glossary.* n.p. 159pp. ($)
2311. Sonnenburg, Rudolf. (born 1828). ^{4}1875. *Grammatik der englischen Sprache nebst methodischem Uebungsbuch. Für den Gebrauch in Schulen, wie auch für den Selbstunterricht.* Berlin: J. Springer. 22cm, x+[3]+332pp. (@)
2312. Starkey, Samuel Cross. 1849. *A dictionary, English and Puniabee, outlines of grammar, also dialogues, with notes,* by Captain Starkey, assisted by Bussawa Sing, Jemedar. Calcutta. 24cm, 286+xxxvi+116pp. ($ L)
2313. Tourrier, John. 1830. *A treatise on Jacotot's method of teaching languages, adapted to the French: containing the first two books of Telemachus (by Fénelon) in French and English, a comprehensive grammar, and a grammatical analysis.* London. (L)
2314. Urcullu, Jose de. (died 1852). 1852. *The Californian text-book: containing a grammar of the Spanish language in English: of the English in Spanish conversational dialogues in both languages, and a full description of California.* n.p. 15.5/16cm. viii+258pp. ($)
2315. Vergani, Angelo. a1820. *An Italian and English grammar; from Vergani's Italian and French Grammar. Exemplified in twenty lessons; with exercises. By M. Piranesi. A new edition, corrected. In English and Italian, with notes. By J. Guichet. Also a key adapted to the French and Italian, as well as to the English and Italian grammar.* new ed. London. viii+214pp. (A). (New ed. enl. and rev. by A. Tommasi, London [1864], 264pp.; at least 4 eds. up to 1864). (A L)
2316. Vergani, Angelo, P. Piranesi & P. Guicheney. 1820. *A key to the Italian and French grammar by Vergani and Peranesi, and to the Italian and English grammar by M.P. Guicheney.* London. (A)
2317. Verney, A. 1827. *An easy French and English grammar.* London. (L)
2318. Victor, Henry. (1850-1907). *A short comparative grammar of English and German: as traced back to their common origin and contrasted with the classical languages,* tr. [from the French] by the author. London, New York: S. Sonnenschein & Co.; Macmillan & Co. 20cm, xxviii+394pp. (E)
2319. Yates, Edward. (1829-1864). 1857. *The elements of the science of grammar, illustrated by a comparison of the structure of the English and Turkish languages* by E.Y. assisted by Mahmood and Hussein and by Hiry Bey. London: W.H. Allen & Co. 18cm. (@ O)
2320. Wade, Rev. Jonathan. 1861. *Karen vernacular grammar, with English interspersed for the benefit of foreign students. In four parts. Embracing terminology [sic], etymology, syntax and style, etc.* Maulmain. (L)

7. *Dialect*
2321. Barnes, William. (1801-1886). Dorsetshire poet. 1863. *A grammar and glossary of the Dorset dialect, with the history, outspreading, and bearings of south-western English.* (Trans., Philol. Soc. series). Berlin: Asher. 103pp. 8s. (Anr. ed. 1864 London, etc. 22cm.). ($ @ O)

2322. ---. 1886. *A glossary of the Dorset dialect with a grammar of its word shapening and wording*. Dorchester: M. & E. Case; London: Trübner & Co. vii+124pp. ($ @)
2323. Peacock, Robert Backhouse. 1863. *On some leading characteristics of the dialects spoken in the six northern counties of England (or ancient Northumbria): and on the variations in their grammar from that of standard English: with their probable etymological sources*. n.p. 22cm, 35pp. (O $)
2324. Pegge, Samuel, Sen. 1803. *Anecdotes of the English language... Dialect of London*. London. (^{2}1814 (L); ^{3}1844). (L)
2325. Robinson, C. Clough. 1876. *A glossary of words pertaining to the dialect of mid-Yorkshire; with others peculiar to lower Nidderdale. To which is prefixed an outline grammar of the mid-Yorkshire dialect*. (English Dialect Society: Publications no. 14; Series C. Original Glossaries, 5). n.p. 162pp. ($)
2326.!$ Wright, Joseph. (1855-1930). 1898-1905. *The English dialect dictionary, being the complete vocabulary of all dialect words still in use, or known to have been in use during the last two hundred years: founded on the publication of the English dialect society and on a large amount of material never before printed*. 6 vols. London. 29cm.

8. Minimal grammars in dictionaries and encyclopedic works

2327.$ Boag, John. (1775-1863). $^?$1850. *The imperial lexicon of the English language: exhibiting the pronunciation, etymology, and explanation of every word usually employed in science, literature, and art*. 2 vol. n.p. 25cm. (Anr. ed. 1859). ($)
2328.! Bolles, William. 1845. *An explanatory and phonographic pronouncing dictionary of the English language*. Ster. d., New London. Royal octavo, 944pp. (Br)
2329.! Boyce, Edward Jacob. 1878. *Etymological glossary*. n.p.
2330.$ Elwell, William Odell. 1861. *A new and complete dictionary of the English and German languages, for general use, containing a concise grammar of either language, dialogue with reference to grammatical forms and rules on pronunciation*. 2 parts. n.p. xvi+398; xvi+420pp. ($)
2331. Fenby, Thomas. 1853. *A copious dictionary of English synonymes, classified and explained; with a brief outline of English grammar; a selection of Latin and French quotations, with corresponding English translations; a list of French and English abbreviations,....* London: Whittaker & Co.; Liverpool printed. 16x10, xvi+224pp. (Anr. ed. ^{3}1878 enl. and impr. ed. Liverpool: Edward Howell, 17cm, xi+268pp.). ($ L)
2332. Kaltschmidt, Jacob Heinrich. (1800-1873). 1837. *A new and complete dictionary of the English and the German languages; with two sketches of Grammar, English and German. ... Neues vollständiges Wörterbuch der Englischen und Deutschen Sprache. Stereotypausgabe*. 2 parts. Leipzig. (^{2}1855 Leipzig, ^{3}1870). ($ L)
2333. La Voye, Marin J. George de. 1842. *A new English and French lexicon ... preceded by a short French synopsis of English grammar. Nouveau lexique anglais francais, etc.*. London: A.H. Baily and Co. (L)
2334.$ Nuttall, P. Austin. 1890. *Nuttall's Dictionary, of the English language based on the principles and labors of Webster and other eminent lexicographers and authorities of America and Europe ... To which is added a dictionary of synonyms and a comprehensive grammar of the universal language, Volapuk. And a supplement of new words and definitions most of which can be found in no other dictionary*. n.p. 22cm, [ii]-ix+[4]+914pp. (Anr. ed. 1895, 21cm, 922pp. ($)). ($)

9. Introductions to other studies 385

2335.$ Scott, William. (Teacher of Elocution. 1750-1804). 1810. *A new spelling, pronouncing, and explanatory dictionary of the English language: ... to which is prefixed, an introductory essay, in three parts. 1. Elements of English pronunciation.* ... n.p. 16cm, 492pp. (Anr. ed. 1815, 2p. 1., 1x, 441pp, 14x14 ($)). ($)

2336. Smith, William Brownrigg. (Headmaster of the City of London Freemen's Orphan School). 1863. *The universal letter writer; or, The art of polite correspondence. To which are added, The complete petitioner, Forms of Law, &c. Also, an abridgement of Murray's English grammar. By the Rev. W.B. Smith. entirely reedited.* 16°, 256pp., 12x7.5. [grammar = pp.13-46]. (L)

2337.$ Walker, John. (1732-1807). 1867. *Walker's pronouncing dictionary (...) to which are prefixed treatises on the construction, derivation, grammar and pronunciation of the language.* n.p. xxiv+264pp. ($)

9. Introductions to other studies

2338. Cassell, John. 1855. *The child's educator; or, familiar lessons on natural history.* 12 parts. London. vi+594pp. (L)

Indices

A Index of names

A1 *Revisions of earlier grammars listed under the editors' names and keys etc. adapted to individual grammars*

Ash, John 361
Bingham, William 705
Brown, Goold 1022, 1772
Bullions, Peter 1134
Cobbett, William 198, 388, 757, 963, 1810
Crombie, Alexander 552, 1626
Greene, Harris Ray 954
Harvey, Reuben 954
Hunter, John 1880, 1881
Lennie, William 160, 193
Lowth, Robert 775, 1551
Morell, John Daniel 100, 1134, 1258, 1358-59
Murray, Lindley 8, 22, 26-28, 65, 72, 153, 230, 303, 375, 429-30, 533, 552, 588, 597, 623, 625, 638, 650, 689, 711, 712, 745, 747, 750, 758, 760, 802, 915, 931, 948, 964, 992, 1004, 1019, 1068, 1109, 1123, 1149, 1223-24, 1241, 1292, 1303, 1306, 1316-17, 1325, 1335, 1357, 1405, 1410, 1428, 1436, 1445, 1462, 1464, 1547, 1581, 1647-49, 1712, 1742, 1768, 1803, 1921
Priestley, Joseph 744
Putnam, John March 140
Sullivan, Robert 526
Waldo, John 1800
Welch, Adonijah Strong 1602
Whitney, William Dwight 1582

A2 *Second authors (revisers, translators, and pseudonyms)*
The index lists all the co-authors mentioned as well as revisors of grammars not mentioned in the alphabetical list.

A., W.B. 1187
'Adair, James' 1405
Alcock, Ethel Maria 422
Alcock, Joseph Crosby 419-23
Allen, Edgar A. 1559
Armstrong, Thomas 59, 60
'Ayres, Alfred' 339
'Blair, David' 1408
Babbitt, E.H. 292
Baldwin, Edward 663
Baldwin, James 1326
Barnett, P.A. 1251
Barton, I. Graeff 1353
Bingham, William 705
Bittle, Leonard F. 242
Boag, John 1853
Bradley, Henry 1266
Bright, Orville T. 1227
Brook, Charles 657?
Brown, J.H. 641
Carpenter, G.R. 1694-95
Christie, J. Douglas 875
Coar, Thomas 169
Cobbin, Ingham 158
Cooper, Alice J. 766, 1660
Cornwell, James 30, 31
'Crowquill, Alfred' 607-8
Eagar, Alexander Richard 1698
Emerson, Anna M. 413
Federheld, Fritz 576
Fosdick, D. Jun. 1604
Fox, Charles 1367
Grece, Clair James 1161
Greenbaum, J.M. 730, 1836
Hall, Joseph 1660
Hall, Fitzedward 1869
Hall, Theophilus Dwight 1650
Hallidie, Archibald R.S. 1773
Hardwick, J. 537
Hazlitt, William 663
Heycock, Charles 260
Hughes, W. 1197
Jennings, James George 977
Keene, A.H. 906

Index of other grammars mentioned 387

Kelley, F.W. 938
Kellogg, Brainerd 1495
Knox, Nelly Lloyd 1850
Leitch, P.J. 938
Lemon, Don 1326
Lovechild, Mrs. 569, 570-71
Maberly, Mary Caroline 1059
Mann, Robert James 959
March, F.A. 618-19
Markham, R.D. 589
Mathews, Emma 1191
McElroy, John G.R. 3
Metcalf, Thomas 1229
Moore, William 5
Morgan, W.B. 1252
Morris, John 1197
Murray, Lindley 26-27
Mylius, W.F. 663
Oakley, A.J. Cooper 1560

Palmer, A.G. 1251
Picket, John W. 1417
Pitman, Isaak 366
Pribble, Evalin 683
Schwegler, Lydia M. 683
Sharpe, T.T. 636-37
Shaw, Alexander 332
Smith, B.W. 1648-49
Sonnenschein, Edward Adolf 766
Tarbell, Martha 1732
Tarney-Campbell, Sarah 867
Teall, Francis A. 874
Tomlin, John Hewitt 349-50
Tweed, Benjamin F. 1761
Wilson, Emma J., 683
Whitney, William Dwight 829
Woods, Mary A. 374
Woodward, B.B. 1197

A3 *Mentions of other grammars (mainly as sources)*

Abbott, Edwin A. 411
Adams, Charles 46, 80, 314, 403, 411, 449, 644, 966, 1246, 1510, 1659
Adams (Latin) 101
Adelung, Johann Christoph 385
Alford, Henry 473, 885
Alger, Israel Jr. 722
Allen, Alexander & James Cornwell 473, 1659
Allen, William 860, 1246
Andrews & Stoddard (Latin) 773
Angus, Joseph 80, 160, 208, 261, 314, 473, 914, 1246, 1510, 1659, 1681
Arnold, T.K. 80, 435, 473
Ash, John 786, 860, 920, 1246
Bain, Alexander 208, 314, 345, 403, 1063, 1285, 1330, 1510
Balch, William Stevens 666
Beard, John Relly 473, 1156
Beattie, James 49
Becker, Karl Ferdinand 299, 387, 388, 394, 395, 444, 968, 1180, 1249, 1278
Bedford, Frederick William 473
Bingham, William 612
Blair, David [= Richard Phillips] 49, 801, 860, 941
Booth, David 824, 1163
Bosworth, Joseph 1176
Bradley, Henry 801
Breen, Henry H. 80
Brenan, Justin 888
Bromby, Charles Henry 473, 914
Brown, Goold 74, 375, 545, 562, 1148
Brown, James 666, 1246
Butler, Noble 632
Campbell, David 49
Clark, Stephen Watkins 885, 1821
Cobbett, William 473, 860, 1124, 1176, 1318, 1605, 1649
Connel, Robert 261
Connon, Charles Walker 80, 260, 473, 1246
Cornwell, James 914
Craik, George Lillie 46, 1246
Crombie, Alexander 80, 196, 260, 261, 386, 616, 695, 760, 801, 852, 860, 941, 1156, 1163, 1246, 1289, 1388, 1802
Currie, James 473
Dalgleish, Walter Scott 473, 1063, 1478
Dalton, John 196, 860

Daniel, Canon 1459
Daniel, Evan 314
Dasent, Charles Underwood 46
Dewar 1388
D'Orsey, Alexander James Donald 80, 799, 1246
Earle, John 83, 1681, 1735
Ety, E. 80
Fenn, Lady Eleanor 1597
Ferris, O. Allen 80
Fiedler 411
Findlater, Andrew 83
Fisher, Anne 920
Fowler, H.W. 1246
Gaultier, Abbé 596, 1555-56
Gilchrist, James 613, 616, 860
Goodenow, Smith B. 666
Grant, John 261, 1246, 1289, 1293, 1741
Green, Matthias 394-95
Hallam 355
Harris, James 260, 386, 390, 669, 801, 1041, 1289, 1388
Harrison, Mathew 80, 1246
Hazlitt, William 888, 1246
Hiley, Richard 261, 1605
Hornsey, John 660
Hunt, L.H. 1808
Hunter, John 1152, 1246
Irving, Christopher 1405
Johnson, Samuel 981, 1163, 1318
Kames, Lord, Henry Home 49
Keane 160
Kellner, Leon 1582
Kett 196
Kirkham, Samuel 1147
Knowles, James 1246, 1802
Koch, Friedrich 1180, 1660
Kritz 299
Kühner 299
Latham, Robert Gordon 46, 80, 83, 209, 345, 355, 411, 435, 473, 885, 914, 941, 1036, 1152, 1246, 1510, 1659, 1735
Lennie, William 83, 261, 328, 369, 386, 473, 747, 840, 920, 1246, 1741
Lewis, Alonzo 473, 860
Lounsbury, Thomas R. 1582
Lowres, Jacob 1246

Lowth, Robert 361, 386, 390, 752, 801, 824, 860, 1024, 1041, 1156, 1163, 1289, 1293, 1318, 1814
Lyon, Charles Jobson 860
McCulloch, John Murray 345, 386, 602, 1163
Maetzner, Eduard A.F. 411, 1180, 1582, 1660
Mansel 83
Marsh, George Perkins 46, 314, 885, 1246
Martin, Thomas 1246
Mason, Charles Peter 80, 160, 314, 394-95, 411, 449, 644, 966, 1036, 1063, 1096, 1330, 1478, 1510, 1660, 1723-24
Meiklejohn, John Miller Dow 314
Milligan, George 1821
Monboddo, James 1388
Morell, John Daniel 46, 80, 160, 394-95, 403, 473, 1063, 1246, 1259, 1330, 1478, 1510, 1723
Morgan (Latin) 1240
Morris, Isaiah J. 208, 314, 411, 449, 644, 966, 1659, 1681
Müller, Friedrich Max 885, 1925
Murray, Lindley 87, 260-61, 304, 328, 386, 390, 428, 473, 529, 565, 616, 649-50, 660, 666, 668, 722, 752, 773, 786, 799, 824, 852, 860, 869, 920, 1024-25, 1077, 1093, 1124, 1147, 1156, 1246, 1289, 1293, 1318, 1345, 1388, 1605, 1659, 1741, 1802, 1808, 1814, 1917
Peirce, Oliver B. 666
Perley, Daniel 722
Perry, William 1147
Pestalozzi, Johann Heinrich 1389, 1457
Pickbourne 49
Priestley, Joseph 49, 390, 760, 860, 888, 1163, 1246, 1345, 1800
Reid, Alexander 1246, 1808
Rogers, Henry 46, 1246
Rothwell 860
Russell, John 860
Sachs 411
Shaw 860
Shaw of Rochdale 1802
Sheridan, Thomas 597, 1041

Index of British places of publication outside London 389

Simson, Robert 1808
Simmonite, William Joseph 888
Skeat, Walter 1681
Smart, Benjamin Humphrey 799, 1659
Smetham 860
Smith, William 83, 473
Stoddart, Sir John 83
Sullivan, Robert Joseph 160, 435, 473, 914, 920, 1191
Sweet, Henry 1582
Taylor, Joseph 885
Tooke, Horne 196, 329, 355, 368, 386, 406, 613, 616, 647, 824-25, 860, 885, 998, 1041, 1049, 1091, 1124, 1156, 1163, 1176, 1289, 1345, 1533, 1595, 1620, 1780
Trench, Richard Chenevix 46, 314, 473, 1246
Trusler, John 49
Turner, Brandon 80
Valpy 196, 801
Viëtor, Wilhelm 1660
Walker, John 260, 799, 1041, 1056
Wall 260
Wallis, John 860, 885, 1176
Webster, Noah 261, 756, 773, 1163, 1257, 1659
Wells, William Harvey 1147
Welsh, Alfred Hix 730
Whitney, William Dwight 1582
Williams 918
Wilson, Alexander 1246

A4 *Judgements quoted from earlier grammarians*

Lyon, Charles Jobson 336
Martin, Thomas 36, 260, 296, 310, 336, 388, 390, 416, 550, 564, 647, 695, 748, 901, 1024, 1077, 1091, 1470, 1497, 1865

B Index of places of publication (publishers for London)
B1 *Provincial (outside London / the U.S.)*

Aberdeen 775, 1596
Annan 892
Arbroath 1118
Ayr 1744
Banbury 196, 1543
Bath 1222, 1632
Belfast 85, 428-29, 430, 490, 1018, 1025, 1133
Bicester 686
Birmingham 550, 583, 1375, 1583, 1588
Blackburn 1446
Bolton ²882, 1682, 1733
Bridlington 208
Brighton 1776
Bristol 900, 965, 1193, 1707
Burslem 890
Cambridge 1337, 1372, 1745
Canada 1134
Canterbury 141-43
Cardigan 914, 1166
Carlisle 892
Carrick, Ir. 1120
Chelmsford 630
Cheltenham 210, 287
Chester 783
Chichester 760, 869
Chipping Norton 1581
Congleton 1882
Coventry 1029
Derby 365, 1460, 1616
Devonport 698
Dorchester 1432, 1768
Dublin 489, 779, 803, 845, 952, 955, 1020, 1135
Dunfermline 984, 1458, 1668, 1700-1, 1900
Edinburgh 42, 59, 60, 106-7, 109, 134, 182, 345, 353-54, 370-71, 392-93, 402-5, 407, 415, 448, 459, 462, 463-65, 480, 515, 602, 631, 692, 777, 864, 874, 956-57, 1077-79, 1140, 1142, 1144, 1151, 1208, 1231, 1235,

1242, 1251-52, 1282, 1298, 1349,
1449, 1451, 1474, 1498, 1539, 1610-
40, 1689, 1691, 1705? 1844, 1853,
1892-93, 1902, 1932
Exeter 560
Fakenham 987
Glasgow 39, 47, 49, 50-53, 91, 368,
411, 493-95, 925, 1041, 1076?,
1145, 1158, 1408, 1442, 1450, 1500
Gloucester 1373, 1614
Grantham 782, 1895
Hales 1335
Halifax 898-99, 1324, 1591
Hawick
Hertford 475
Huddersfield 478, 511, 694, 1591
Hull 66, 126
Leeds 170, 349, 678, 1342
Lincoln 288
Liverpool 654, 656, 691, 1585
London: see **B2**
Lynn 1912
Maldon 304, 1877
Manchester 133, 190, 269, 419, 633-34,
675, 843, 862, 868, 882, 893-94,
911-12, 963-64, 982, 986, 1050,
1069-71, 1232, 1244, 1334, 1486,
1574-76, 1586, 1656, 1673, 1675,
1871, 1876, 1903, 1913, 1921-23,
1935-36

Montrose 1669
Newcastle 206
Norwich 1635-37
Nottingham 1499, 1534
Oxford 1093, 1708-11, 1728-29, 1747-49
Ormskirk 552
Parsontown, Ir. 1805
Plymouth 1399
Preston 1812
Redditch 543
Rochdale 1402
Rochester 121
Romsey 755
Rugeley 1357
Saffron Walden 918
Sheffield 122, 469, 604, 817, 992, 1605-6
Spalding 660
St Albans 312
Stafford 1723
Stamford 1860
Stoke Newington 536
Taunton 129
Trowbridge 1109
Wandsworth 1753
Wisbech 327-28, 1677
Workington 45
Wymondham 295
York 169, 635, 896-97

B2 *London (by publishers)*

Since publishing was so concentrated in London, it was not advisable to index London as a place of publication, but list publishers instead. Note that only first editions/first publishers are normally indexed. All data have been checked against Philip A.H. Brown, *London Publishers and Printers c. 1800-1870* (1982, London: British Library). Note, however, that many entries are incomplete, places or publishers not being mentioned in catalogues and bibliographies. Moreover, publishing houses tended to fuse and split; in consequence, the listing of the first name as I have done here can be misleading. Finally, publishing houses used to move to London, or to have one branch in London, and as the 19th century advanced, more and more books were published jointly by several publishers (such as London/Manchester/Edinburgh/Dublin, or London/New York etc.). Asterisks refer to publishers whose existence was not to be confirmed with the help of Brown (1982).

*Adams, Hamilton 733
*Adeney, Charles 1808
Allman 100, 112, 160, 162-63, 420-23,
   745-47, 1007, 1356, 1359, 1424,
   1429, 1699
*Arding, W. 689

*Arnold, Edward 181
Baldwin & Cradock 256, 416, 748, 1190, 1345
Ball, William 1533
Bateman, John B. 1811
*Bean, Charles 813
Bell (& Daldy) 12-13, 15, 154, 1182-84, 1186, 1188-89, 1746
Bemrose 1321, 1330
Bentley, Richard 1073
*Beverley 603
Black, Alexander 1457
Black etc. 43
Blackie 17, 283-85, 359, 493, 1459, 1737
Blackwood 173, 496, 519?, 967, 1215-16
Boosey 1771
Booth, J. 1273
Budd, J. 1343
Burns, J. 530
Burns etc. 1846
Cadell & Davis 1707
Cassell etc. 130, 417, 1230, 1350
Catholic Publ. 997
Chambers 58, 468, 516, 830, 950, 1214
Chapman & Hall 455, 906
*Chappell, J. 1304
Chapple, C. 538
*Christian Knowledge Society 1545
*Christian Vernacular ESI 692b, 1164
Cleave, John 1274
Cleaver, W.J. 1626
*Constable, Archibald 89, 293, 521?
Collins 459-602, 1154, 1270, 1319, 1769, 1819
Cooke, Charles? 338
Cooke, Nathaniel 504
Cornish, J. 644
Cradock 442, 751-52
Crosby, B. 246
Daldy & Isbister 1724, 1911
Darling etc. 157
Darton & Clark 1392
Darton (& Harvey) 29, 529, 553, 587, 608*-9*, 649, 650*, 763, 1026, 1303, 1316, 1739, 1897
Dean, Thomas etc. 379, 380, 1075, 1541, 1766

Dicks, J. 1612
*Didier, C. 1045
Dolby T. 336, 1091
Duncan, J. 1608
Economic Pr. 826
*Educational Trading 636
*Educational Training 313
Edwards, W. 1589
Evans, J. & C. 699
Fisher, H. 1585
Gale etc. 185
*Gall & Inglis 286?, 1272
Gilbert 940
*Gill, George 498, 520, 657, 1845
Gladding, John 1388
*Gordon, Robert 61
Griffin, R. 486
Griffith (& Farran) 355, 369, 409, 410, 753
Groombridge 479, 514, 799
Hailes, N. 1507
Hall, Arthur 260
Hamilton etc. 787, 989, 1208, 1391, 1453
Hardwicke, Robert 1149
Harris, J. 570, 572, 1378
Hatchard 1021
*Hempster, John 658
*Heywood, John 757, 893
Hodgson 1325
Hodson, James S. 278
*Holden, A.M. 1220, 1783
Houlston (etc.) 330, 1191, 1307, 1767, 1777, 1782
Hughes, Joseph 124?, 129, 449-52, 841
Hunter, R. 648
*Hurst, H. 1049
*Ireland, A. 1210
*Isaac etc. 1318, 1400
Isbister, William 524, 585
*Japp, Marshall 517, 527
Jaques, C. 436
Jarrold 561, 605, 1173, 1579, 1611
Johnson, J. 390
*Johns etc. 1030
Johnston 1802
Judd & Glass 177, 1248
Kegan Paul 99
Kelly, Thomas 1293

*King, Henry S. 1849
Knight, C. 186
*Knights, S. 607
Lackington 1752
*Laurie, T. 281-82
Law, Charles 933
Law, Charles H. 671
Lockwood 1924
Longman(s) etc. 25, 68, ²80, 82-83, 90, 96-97, 247, 287, 332, 415, 433, 435, 593, 662, 672, 676-77, 754, 760, 789, 844, 847, 850-55, 901-2, 907, 920-21, 933, 959-62, 968, 977, 988, 998, 1024, 1036-37, 1061, 1114-16, 1152-53, 1167, 1179, 1233, 1240, 1246, 1250, 1253, 1255, 1258, 1260, 1285, 1327, 1349, 1435, 1465, 1538, 1544, 1555-56, 1559-62, 1587, 1620, 1622, 1624, 1668, 1681, 1686, 1925
Macmillan 2, 673, 1001, 1032, 1084, 1155, 1266-67, 1308-14, 1841
Madden, James 70
*Mair 1156
Mallett, Joseph 461
Marshall, John 458, 1063-64, 1364, 1377, 1756
Marshall Japp 517
*Martin, G. 18
*Martin, James 5, 501
Masters, Joseph 298, 1082
*Methuen 1117
*Millington 137
*Moffatt & Paige 555, 1096, 1245, 1558
*Montgomery etc. 1734
Mozley 1503
Murby, Thomas 970, 1283, 1363, 1523, 1526-29, 1546
Murray, J. 768, 1161, 1650-51
*National Society's Depository 408, 922-23, 1302, 1880-81
*Nelson 138, 204, 532, 611, 1113, 1269, 1540, 1648
*Newman, W.R. 1418
*Newmann, O. 1751
*Nodes, George 1195
*Normal Correspondence College 445
Ostell, Thomas 1362
Parker, John W. 481?
*Paul, Kegan 99, 191, 930, 999, 1568, 1843
*Percival 966, 1658
*Philanthropic Society 1505
*Philip, George 201-2, 637, 565, 939, 1508, 1706
Phillips, Richard 1403-4
Pickering, W. 381, 653
Piper etc. 108
Pitman, F. 366, 528, 1787
Plummer & Brewis 1552
Poole & Edwards 1407, 1426
Relfe etc. 54, 250, 294, 386, 440, 548, 737, 788, 814, 958, 1187, 1329, 1510, 1735, 1750
Religious Tract Society 46
Richardson 406, 1617-19
Rivington(s) 63-64, 272, 966, 1094, 1176, 1520, 1634, 1704, 1754, 1773-75, 1873, 1879
Rodwell, John 684, 780
Roulston & Stoneman 295
Routledge 1006
*Sampson etc. 702, 1698
*Saxon 1326
Seeley etc. 3, 6, 305
*Sell, W. 1427-28
Shaw, J.F. 590
Sherwood 695-96, 1142
Simpkin etc. 7, 30-31, 38, 42, 59, 131, 208-9, 211, 270, 310, 349, 350, 352, 394-97, 404-5, 418, 427, 434, 448, 472, 491, 507, 540-42, 547, 549, 575, 582, 599, 606, 610, 633, 740, 778, 802, 848-49, 857-58, 860, 929, 931, 941, 1004, 1163, 1175, 1178, 1193, 1211-12, 1219, 1232, 1278, 1322, 1333, 1399, 1419, 1431, 1474, 1461, 1506, 1509, 1572, 1574, 1606, 1668, 1680, 1743, 1783
Smith, J.R. 98
Souter, J. 180, 765, 873, 1757
*SPCK 391, 534
Stevens 136
Stanford, Edward 591, 652, 1087-88
Steill, B. 1683-84
Stewart, W. 393, 473, 581, 1213, 1254, 1259, 1688, 1690
Stock, Elliot 447
Stockdale, J.J. 1577

*Sunday School Union 1351
Suttaby etc. 1615
*Swan Sonnenschein, W. 373-74, 592, 766, 1479, 1660, 1906
Taylor, R. (etc.) 824, 1052-57
Tegg 1864
Theobald 1249
Thomas, Joseph 693
Trübner 279
*University Corr. Coll. A. 1111
Varty & Owen 659
Wacey, Jonathan 1473
Wallis, John 183-84, 1597
Walton (& Maberly) 1058-60, 1180-81
Ward (& Lock) 685, 1074, 1638, 1646, 1781

Watson 888
*Watt 574
*Weak, John 329
Webb etc. 503
Wertheim 1542
Westley, F. etc. 340, 342
*Whitehaven & Crosthwaite 1160
Whittaker (etc.) 36, 198, 387, 784, 786, 972, 1405, 1425, 1444, 1478, 1605, 1742, 1780, 1865, 1914, 1933
Williams & Norgate 1086
Wilson, Effingham, 798, 1430
*Woodbridge 533
Wright etc. 931-32
*Wyand 994
Wyman 1471

B3 *The United States*
(Only the first place will normally be indexed)

Ada, O. 953, 1365
Albany, N.Y. 21, 103, 220, 400-1, 512, 1256, 1281
Andover, Mass. 1371, 1401, 1604
Ann Arbor 866?
Ashburnham, Mass. 1796
Auburn, N.Y. 1823, 1907
Austin, Tex. 1798
Baltimore 225-26, 622, 639, 913, 1095, 1146, 1569, 1592-93
Battle Creek, Mich. 144-48, 150
Bennington, Vt. 1280
Boston 4, 8, 20, 22, 26-28, 87, 101, 104, 115-16, 120, 171, 175, 200, 218-19, 232, 297, 334-35, 344, 346, 378, 467, 476, 488, 566, 586, 612-17, 625-26, 664-66, 669, 670, 682, 688, 708, 713, 729, 730, 733, 742-43, 758, 776, 808, 827-28, 872, 927, 936-37, 947, 993, 995, 1000, 1038, 1083, 1085, 1102, 1112, 1137, 1192, 1288, 1336, 1338, 1348, 1367, 1389, 1396, 1480, 1496, 1550, 1642-43, 1662-65, 1667, 1676, 1678-79, 1694-95, 1730-32, 1760-62, 1764, 1778, 1828-29, 1835-36, 1851, 1909
Brattleborough 728
Bridgeton, N.Y. 1139

Brookfield, Mass. 1121
Brooklyn, Conn. 123, 203
Cambridge, Mass 253-54, 1337, 1814, 1885
Canajoharie, N.Y. 1883
Canton, Ohio 1736
Charleston, W.Va. 1299
Chattanooga, Tenn. 837
Chicago 187, 255, 683, 762, 771-72, 815-16, 1072, 1277, 1630, 1794, 1806, 1830, 1832-34, 1842
Cincinnati, Ohio 128, 271, 446, 805-7, 880-81, 1101, 1103-4?, 1126, 1130-32, 1417, 1420-23, 1694
Claremont, N.H. 1712-13
Cleveland, Ohio 348, 812
Columbus, Ohio 770
Concord, N.H. 140, 870-71, 1068, 1370, 1462, 1564-65
Danville, Ind. 1516
Danville, Va. 1472
Dan(s)ville 1237-38?
Des Moines, Iowa 1108
Dover, N.G. 1464
East Millstone, N.J. 567
Erie, Pa. 687
Forest Grove, Or. 1174
Frankfort, Ky. 153

Frederickciy, Md. 1785
Frederick-town 1034
Fredonia, N.Y. 1758
Gardiner, Me. 723-25
Georgetown, S.C. 1799
Georgetown, Tex. 1813
Great Bendd, Kan. 1629
Greensborough, N.C. 1653-55
Hagers-town, Md. 915
Hallowell, Me. 303, 1257
Harrisburg, Pa. 905, 1033
Hartford, Conn. 139, 597, 601, 1262, 1547, 1858
Haverhill, Mass. 722
Hudson, Ohio 1341
Indianapolis 492
Ithaca, N.Y. 438-39, 1236
Keene, N.H. 667
Kingsland, Ga. 1300
La Fayette, Ala. 1263
Lancaster, Pa. 909, 1127-28
Leicester, Mass. 11
Leominster, Mass. 9
Lexington, Ky. 1119, 1125
Louisville 152, 178, 273, 275-76, 632, 1284
Macon, Ga. 399
Maysville 1530
Memphis 1578
Middleton, Conn. 466, 1904-5
Milton, Ia. 974
Montgomery, Ala. 117
Montpellier, Vt. 10, 1339-40
Newbury? 37
Newhaven, Ct. 302, 643, 971, 973, 1287, 1548, 1816, 1818, 1859
New Orleans 1672
New York 34, 72, 76-77, 81, 84, 88, 92-93, 95, 102, 110-11, 114, 118, 158, 176, 192, 213-17, 257-58, 261-68, 289-90, 299, 306, 309, 316-26, 336, 347, 367, 382, 413, 437, 437, 441, 497, 526, 563, 584, 598, 618-19, 624, 646, 703, 708, 736, 739, 773, 785, 804, 818-20, 822, 840, 865, 867, 875, 878, 885, 886, 887, 917, 944, 946, 954, 979-80, 985, 996, 1010-17, 1022, 1081, 1090, 1092, 1097, .1100, 1105-6, 1129, 1143, 1157, 1171, 1200-4, 1209, 1223-24, 1227-29, 1264, 1286, 1294, 1347, 1353, 1355, 1361, 1366, 1395, 1411-13, 1466, 1495, 1501-2, 1573, 1590, 1600-3, 1702, 1714-20, 1722, 1726, 1759, 1763, 1810, 1817, 1820-21, 1831, 1848, 1869, 1914, 1916-17
Norwich, Ct. 545
Oclaware, O. 1874
Onondaga, N.Y. 1666
Oshkosh, Wis. 205
Parsons, Kan 1755
Philadelphia 40, 62, 78-79, 94, 168, 174, 193, 223, 227-31, 233-42, 244, 259, 277, 291, 300, 357, 375-76, 431-32, 578, 595, 620, 627, 641, 704, 714, 715-21, 793-95, 797, 821, 835, 928, 945, 975, 991, 1009, 1039, 1138, 1225, 1290-91, 1368-69, 1376, 1456, 1631, 1738, 1770, 1788, 1800, 1809, 1837-38, 1886
Pittsburgh 274, 383, 846, 1815, 1919
Plainfield, Ct. 398
Plymouth, Mass. 629
Portland, Me. 668, 710-11, 726, 951, 1779, 1822, 1824-25, 1827
Portsmouth, N.H. 1241
Providence, R.I. 19, 23, 44, 172, 315, 562, 640, 1521, 1641
Raleigh, N.C. 199, 1927-31
Reading, Pa. 251
Richmond, Va. 1089, 1652
Rochester, N.Y. 661, 774, 1003, 1008, 1374, 1566, 1765, 1867-68, 1884
Rockville, Conn. 781
Sacramento, Cal. 1891
Salem, Mass. 164, 568, 1042, 1599
Salisbury, N.C. 1926
San Antonio, Tex.
San Francisco 761
San Loandro 1567
Savannah, Ga. 600
Shreveport, La. 1645
Southbridge, Mass. 565
South Carrollton, Ky. 1628
South Hanover, Ind. 505
Springfield, Mass. 301, 767, 1148
St. Clairsville 884
St. Louis, Mo. 1276, 1379-82. 1557,

Index of 'Colonial' places of publication   395

1789-93
St. Paul, Minn. 1850
Syracuse, N.Y. 32, 544, 836, 1023, 1661, 1887-88
Terre-Haute, Ind. 1027, 1671, 1898-99
Topeka, Mass. 876, 877, 879
Trenton Falls, N.Y. 1594-95
Trinity College, N.C. 56
Troy, N.Y. 221, 506, 588
Utica 69, 74-75, 105, 113
Walpole, N.H. 1317
Washington 222, 224, 361

Watertown, N.Y. 456
Wellsborough, Pa. 508
West Brookfield, Mass. 1441
West Chester, Pa. 1172
West Unity, O. 454
Whitesboro, N.Y. 73
Wilmington, Del. 412
Winchester, Va. 1657, 1740
Windsor, Vt. 86, 197, 1712, 1807
Woodstock, Vt. 1122
Worcester, Mass. 706-7, 1436, 1580
York, Pa. 1627

B4 *Colonial*

Bangalore 502
Bombay 372, 1448
Calcutta 500?, 1067, 1452, 1584, 1908
Canada 414
Cape Town 16, 331
Dacca 642
Halifax, N.S. Canada 195, 212, 248, 525, 1136
Hobart 1741
Hong Kong 910

Jaffna 1447
Madras 692a, 1164
Malta 559, 577, 1352, 1433?
Melbourne 182a, 444
Montreal 594
New Brunswick 810-11?
Ontario 41, 425
Sydney 681
Toronto 207, 426, 831-33a, 938, 1692, 1696, 1719, 1872
Wellington 188-89

B5 *The European Continent*

Augsburg 74
Berlin 1659
Cologne 119
Dessau 1571
Göttingen 245
Leipzig 1099

Munich 546
Münster 1786
Nieuwediep 1795
Slagelse 628
Venice 1044
Vienna 1331

In the LIBRARY AND INFORMATION SOURCES IN LINGUISTICS (LISL) series (Series Editor: E.F. Konrad Koerner) the following titles have been published thus far:

1. ANTTILA, Raimo & Warren A. BREWER: *Analogy: A basic bibliography.* 1977.
2. SABOURIN, Conrad: *Adverbs and Comparatives: An analytical bibliography.* 1977
3. TRANSLATION THEORY: *A comprehensive bibliography.*
4. VERSCHUEREN, Jef: *Pragmatics: An annotated bibliography.* 1978.
5. LAVER, John: *Voice Quality: A classified research bibliography.* 1979.
6. McKAY, John C.: *A Guide to Romance Reference Grammars: The modern standard languages.* 1979.
7. CANNON, Garland: *Sir William Jones. A bibliography of primary and secondary sources.* 1979.
8. GUIMIER, Claude: *Prepositions: an analytical bibliography.* 1981.
9. LEOPOLD, Joan: *The Letter Liveth: The Life, Work and Library of August Friedrich Pott (1802-87).* 1983.
10. KOERNER, Konrad: *Bibliographie Saussurienne, 1876-1976.*
11. KOERNER, Konrad & Matsuji TAJIMA (comps): *Noam Chomsky: A personal bibliography, 1951-1986.* 1986.
12. SPILLNER, Bernd: *Error Analysis. A comprehensive bibliography.* 1991.
13. TAJIMA, Matsuji (comp.): *Old and Middle English Language Studies. A classified bibliography 1923-1985.* 1988.
14. DECHERT, Hans W., Monika BRÜGGEMEIER & Dietmar FÜTTERER (comps): *Transfer and Interference in Language. A Selected Bibliography.* 1984.
15. McKAY, John C.: *A Guide to Germanic Reference Grammars. The modern standard languages.* 1984.
16. ESCHBACH, Achim & Viktoria ESCHBACH-SZABÓ (comps): *Bibliography of Semiotics, 1975-1985.* 1986.
17. NOPPEN, Jean-Pierre van et al. (comps): *Metaphor: A bibliography of post-1970 publications.* 1985.
18. BEARD, Robert & Bogdan SZYMANEK (comps): *Bibliography of Morphology, 1960-1985.* 1988.
19. TROIKE, Rudolph C. (comp.): *Bibliography of Bibliographies of the Languages of the World. Volume I: General and Indo-European languages of Europe.* 1990.
20. NOPPEN, J.P. van, and Edith HOLS (comps): *Metaphor II. An classified bibliography of publications from 1985 to 1990.* 1990.
21. OSTLER, Rosemarie: *Theoretical Syntax 1980-1990. An annotated and classified bibliography.* 1992.
22. NEVIS, Joel, Brian D. JOSEPH, Dieter WANNER and Arnold M. ZWICKY: *Clitics. A comprehensive bibliography 1892-1991.* 1994.
23. FERNÁNDEZ, Mauro: *Diglossia. A comprehensive bibliography, 1960-1990, and supplements. With an introduction by W.F.Mackey.* 1993.
24. KESS, Joseph F. and Tadao MIYAMOTO: *Japanese Psycholinguistics. A classified and annotated research bibliograhy.* 1994.
25. KÖHLER, Reinhard: *Bibliography of Quantitative Linguistics.* 1995.
26. GÖRLACH, Manfred: An Annotated Bibliography of 19th-Century Grammars of English. 1998.